www.wadsworth.com

P9-BJO-220

www.wadsworth.com is the World Wide Web site for Wadsworth and is your direct source to dozens of online resources.

At www.wadsworth.com you can find out about supplements, demonstration software, and student resources. You can also send email to many of our authors and preview new publications and exciting new technologies.

www.wadsworth.com
Changing the way the world learns®

Corwin & Peltason's
UNDERSTANDING THE
CONSTITUTION

SIXTEENTH EDITION

Corwin & Peltason's
UNDERSTANDING THE
CONSTITUTION

SIXTEENTH EDITION

SUE DAVIS
University of Delaware

J. W. PELTASON
University of California

THOMSON
——★——™
WADSWORTH

Australia • Canada • Mexico • Singapore • Spain
United Kingdom • United States

Executive Editor: David Tatom
Assistant Editor: Amy McGaughey
Editorial Assistant: Reena Thomas
Technology Project Manager:
  Melinda Newfarmer
Marketing Manager: Janise Fry
Marketing Assistant: Mary Ho
Advertising Project Manager:
  Nathaniel Bergson-Michelson

Project Manager, Editorial Production:
  Paula Berman
Print/Media Buyer: Rebecca Cross
Permissions Editor: Sommy Ko
Production Service: Carlisle Communications
Cover Designer: Sue Hart
Cover Image: Steve Cole/Getty Images
Text and Cover Printer: Webcom
Compositor: Carlisle Communications

Printed in Canada
1 2 3 4 5 6 7 07 06 05 04 03

For more information about our products, contact us at:
Thomson Learning Academic Resource Center
1-800-423-0563

For permission to use material from this text, contact us by:
Phone: 1-800-730-2214 **Fax:** 1-800-730-2215
Web: http://www.thomsonrights.com

Library of Congress Control Number: 2003107465

ISBN 0-534-61407-8

Wadsworth/Thomson Learning
10 Davis Drive
Belmont, CA 94002-3098
USA

Asia
Thomson Learning
5 Shenton Way #01-01
UIC Building
Singapore 068808

Australia/New Zealand
Thomson Learning
102 Dodds Street
Southbank, Victoria 3006
Australia

Canada
Nelson
1120 Birchmount Road
Toronto, Ontario M1K 5G4
Canada

Europe/Middle East/Africa
Thomson Learning
High Holborn House
50/51 Bedford Row
London WC1R 4LR
United Kingdom

Latin America
Thomson Learning
Seneca, 53
Colonia Polanco
11560 Mexico D.F.
Mexico

Spain/Portugal
Paraninfo
Calle/Magallanes, 25
28015 Madrid, Spain

For my friend T.S. Eliot
who has kept me company many late nights
dozing on top of the computer monitor.

PREFACE

Corwin and Peltason's *Understanding the Constitution* has undergone a variety of major changes since the First Edition was published in 1949. Those changes reflect the developments in the United States that have transformed the Constitution. In 1949 the states had not yet approved the Twenty-second Amendment, which limits the president to two terms in office. The poll tax would not be constitutionally proscribed by the Twenty-fourth Amendment for another fifteen years, and it would be an additional seven years before the Twenty-sixth Amendment recognized the right to vote for eighteen-year-olds. The Constitution has six more amendments today than it did in 1949, but its transformation goes far beyond the addition of formal amendments. In 1949 the Court had not yet declared segregation to be inherently unequal and Justice Felix Frankfurter's opinion permitting states to prohibit women from obtaining a license to tend bar was still "good law." In 1949 the Supreme Court had just begun to invalidate the schemes that the southern states devised to avoid complying with the constitutional proscription on racial discrimination in voting and only about 3 percent of African Americans of voting age in the South voted. The Court had not yet entered "the political thicket" of legislative reapportionment, and state and congressional districts reflected the demographics of a rural, small-town American that no longer existed. Nor had the Court yet held that most of the provisions in the Bill of Rights restrict the states through the due process clause of the Fourteenth Amendment. As the Supreme Court's interpretation of the Constitution has changed, the document that permitted legal segregation and discrimination against women, allowed individuals accused of crimes to be tried without a lawyer or a jury, and did not recognize a constitutionally protected right to privacy now reflects—in some ways at least—the values of equality and human dignity.

The Sixteenth Edition includes the major developments in Constitutional law since the publication of the Fifteenth Edition in 2000, including the contested presidential election of 2000 and the Supreme Court's role in its resolution, the impact of the events of September 11, 2001 on civil liberties, and the Court's increasing preference for limiting the powers of the federal government vis-à-vis the states. The most recent constitutional developments in the areas of freedom of expression, the religious clauses of the First Amendment, the rights of individuals accused or convicted of crimes, race and legislative districting, affirmative action, the right to privacy, and the issue of discrimination on the basis of sexual orientation are also included.

The Sixteenth Edition includes the Supreme Court's decisions through June 2003. Although it would be impossible to cover every relevant case, my hope is that the new edition reflects the most recent and most important developments in constitutional law. The Sixteenth Edition also has been written with the intent to incorporate as much as possible recent scholarship in constitutional law and judicial decision making. I have also introduced questions at the end of each chapter and included a list of key terms, as well as a list of suggestions for further reading.

I hope that this edition of *Understanding the Constitution* will convey to readers that the endeavor to understand the Constitution is an ongoing, constantly evolving process. Jack Peltason captured the overarching purpose of the book in the Preface to the Fourteenth Edition:

> It is not enough, however, to celebrate the Constitution. We should also—or at least a considerable number of us should—**cerebrate** about it. We need to understand that, important as it is to see the forest, the forest is made up of trees, and unless someone tends them, there will be no forest to be seen. That is one of the purposes of this volume—to go beyond generalities and discover the major constitutional issues of our times.

ACKNOWLEDGMENTS

I have been fortunate to have the support of a large number of colleagues, friends, and mentors over the years. First, I would like to thank Jack W. Peltason for inviting me to join him as coauthor of *Understanding the Constitution* beginning with the Fifteenth Edition. Although the subsequent editions have been based on Jack Peltason's and the late Edward S. Corwin's earlier work, the responsibility for revisions is mine. Jack Peltason's comment in his Preface to the Eighth Edition in 1979 applies here as well: "It is more than the usual cliché, . . . for me to acknowledge that whatever is its merit is attributable to the teacher; the errors to his student."

Second, I wish to single out just a few of my teachers and mentors who have contributed in crucial ways to my own understanding of the Constitution. Walter F. Murphy provided support and intellectual guidance at the beginning of my career when it was very much needed. As a graduate student at the University of California, Santa Barbara, I was fortunate in having the chance to study with C. Herman Pritchett, who was a wonderful teacher and an extraordinary human being. Gordan E. Baker, another professor with whom I had the pleasure to study at UCSB, taught me about the ideas of the Progressive era, and it was from his work that I first learned about reapportionment. As an undergraduate at Western Washington State College in 1972 I took a course in constitutional law from Dick Payne and he initiated my endeavor to understand the Constitution.

Third, I would like to express my gratitude to several scholars of my own generation whose work I have found particularly helpful in revising *Understanding the Constitution*. Lee Epstein and Thomas G. Walker's two-volume *Constitutional Law for a Changing America* sets the standard in casebooks for clarity and accessibility to undergraduates. I frequently turned to their work for guidance in making a technical point more readily understandable. This book benefited tremendously from Epstein and Walker's work. I also found Craig R. Ducat's *Constitutional Interpretation* immensely valuable, and I have borrowed several of his tables. Additionally, I owe a great deal to the political scientists who have developed the new historical institutionalism in the field of law and courts including but not limited to Rogers M. Smith, Howard Gillman, Cornell Clayton, and Ronald Kahn.

For the Sixteenth Addition, my colleague James K. Oliver provided knowledgeable and insightful comments about the International Law dimensions of

Bush Administration's policy toward Iraq in the winter of 2003, for which I am grateful. Additionally, my student James Catella, who wrote his senior thesis on the Supreme Court's decision in *Bush v Gore*, provided crucial assistance with the details of the litigation surrounding the disputed presidential election of 2000 as well as with sifting through the scholarly commentary on the Court's decision.

On a personal note, the friends and colleagues in Delaware I would like to thank for their consistent support and understanding include Sue Cherrin, Jeff Davidson, Fredy Rodriguez, Graciela Cabana, Gerry Moll, Emma Bricker, Jessica Shadian, Alice Ba, Candace Archer, Henry Reynolds, Dan Green, Deborah Compton, Susan Rash, Cindy Schmidt-Cruz, Fatima Correa, Leslie Knight, Miriam Willis, Margo Perkins, Marge Purcell, Jean Dunn, Jean Pfeffer, Carmen Nelson, and Phyllis Lord. Additionally, my friends in the Yucatán, including Elia María Negron, María de Lourdes Can Tun, Juan Aben Ali Rivero Muñoz, Cinthia Rivero Muñoz, Pilar Diaz Rubio, Enrique Cardenas, María Rosario Gonzalez Cicero, Graciela Rodriguez, Greg Anderson, and James Callaghan, have allowed me to share their lives in a way that I deeply appreciate.

Finally, I wish to thank the editors and staff at Wadsworth, Thomson Learning, including David Tatom, Amy McGaughey, and Janise Fry, and Cindy Miller at Carlisle Communications for their patience and support. It has been a pleasure to work with them. I also am indebted to the external reviewers of the Fifteenth Edition who provided helpful suggestions for the revisions: Philip A. Dynia, Loyola University New Orleans; Carolyn P. Johnson, University of Kansas; Laurence F. Jones, Angelo State University; Mark Carl Rom, Georgetown University; George Zilbergeld, Montclair State Universtiy.

SUE DAVIS

CHELEM, YUCATÁN, MEXICO

JULY 2003

CONTENTS

PART THREE

THE AMENDMENTS

PART FOUR

THE DOCUMENTS

HISTORY AND CONTEXT

CONSTITUTIONAL BACKGROUNDS

We begin the enterprise of *Understanding the Constitution* by examining some of the historical background of the charter for American government and symbol of national values that has become the world's oldest written constitution. The history of the United States Constitution can be traced to 1215 when King John signed the Magna Carta, and thereby initiated the notion of constitutional limitations on governmental authority.[1] Because "the history of the American Constitution is a history of ideas,"[2] we begin our introduction to the Constitution by examining the political thought of the revolutionary era. The goal of our brief discussion is to provide some useful insights into the underlying themes and values of the Declaration of Independence as well as the Constitution. We then summarize the developments that led to the drafting of the Declaration and the fight for American independence. Next, we examine the major features of the nation's first written charter, the Articles of Confederation, and consider the conditions that led to the Constitutional Convention in 1787. Finally, we outline the major events in the drafting of the Constitution and the circumstances surrounding its ratification.[3]

THE POLITICAL IDEAS OF THE REVOLUTIONARY ERA

Although the colonists relied heavily on British political thinkers, they were constantly developing their own political traditions, drawing on varied philosophical sources. The political thought of the English philosopher John Locke (1632–1704) had a major influence on the ideas that emerged in the colonies during the revolutionary period. The principle at the heart of Locke's theory was that government was artificial rather than natural—the power of government derived from the people, not from God. He presented his views of human nature and the origins of government by depicting men in a hypothetical

---

[1]Daniel A. Farber and Suzanna Sherry, *A History of the American Constitution* (St. Paul, MN: West Publishing Co., 1990), 3.

[2]*Ibid.*, 7.

[3]The following sections of this chapter are based on Sue Davis, *American Political Thought: Four Hundred Years of Ideas and Ideologies* (Englewood Cliffs, NJ: Prentice Hall, 1996), Chapter 3: The Political Ideas of the Revolutionary Era, The Declaration of Independence and the American Revolution, The Revolutionary State Constitutions and the Articles of Confederation, The Constitutional Convention, and The Ratification Process (The Antifederalists and The Federalists' Defense: The Political Theory of the Constitution).

prepolitical state of nature uncontaminated by the influences of society. In Locke's state of nature, everyone was free and equal. But inconveniences arising from the lack of an impartial authority to resolve disputes—each man had to be judge in his own case—marred the state of nature, rendering natural rights to life, liberty, and property insecure. People therefore left the state of nature to secure protection of those rights. In Locke's scenario, the process of moving from the state of nature to government involved two contracts. In the first, individuals agreed to enter society. Locke suggested that once people made the decision to create a social order they could never return to the state of nature.

In the second contract, they agreed to establish government and to operate by the principle of majority rule. The government was not a party to the contract that established its authority; rather, the government had a fiduciary or trustee relationship to the people. Thus, the people retained the power to remove or alter the government if it violated the trust—that is, if it failed to protect the natural rights of individuals. If the people resorted to revolution to defend their rights, they abolished only the second contract. The first, the contract of society, remained in place. Thus, for Locke, the decision to abolish a particular government would not entail a rebellion against the social order and a return to the state of nature. Locke's political theory contained the major ingredients of modern liberalism: government's authority is based on a contract among individuals who possess certain natural rights including life, liberty, and property. Indeed, in Locke's view, government was a necessary evil whose function was limited to protecting the rights of individuals.

Carl L. Becker's *The Declaration of Independence*, first published in 1922, asserted that "[m]ost Americans had absorbed Locke's works as a kind of political gospel; and the Declaration in its form, in its phraseology, follows closely certain sentences in Locke's second treatise on government."[4] Becker noted that the Declaration, indeed, the political theory and practice of the American Revolution was thoroughly grounded in the language of natural rights. Locke's ideas, he argued, were so commonplace in the colonies that the men who declared independence from England simply adapted those ideas to meet the emergency created by the British government's determination to raise revenue through taxation at the expense of the colonists. The colonists were merely exercising their natural rights in framing a government to suit their needs in America, initially voluntarily retaining a union with the people of Great Britain and only withdrawing when the King violated the rights of the colonists. From such a perspective, the colonists who fought for independence were primarily motivated by a concern for their rights—particularly their property rights—which were threatened by the British government's determination to tax the colonies. Resistance was justified because the government had failed to protect the natural rights of individuals to life, liberty, and property.

The beginning of the second paragraph of the Declaration reflects the political philosophy of Locke's **liberalism** with its proclamation of the self-evident

---

[4]Carl L. Becker, *The Declaration of Independence: A Study in the History of Political Ideas* (New York: Vintage Books, 1958), 140.

truths of equality and inalienable rights and its claim that governments are instituted to secure those rights, "deriving their just powers from the consent of
the governed; that whenever any form of government becomes destructive of
these ends, it is the right of the people to alter or to abolish it, and to institute
new government, laying its foundation on such principles, and organizing its
powers in such form, as to them shall seem most likely to effect their safety and
happiness."[5]

Although a concern with securing the natural rights of individuals is evident
in the language of the Declaration of Independence, Locke's liberalism was not
the only political theory that influenced the colonists during the revolutionary period. The ideas and values of **republicanism** were also important to eighteenth-
century Americans. Liberalism and republicanism actually overlapped. Both
emphasized liberty and assumed that the economic independence that came with
property ownership provided an essential foundation of political freedom.[6] Yet
the two political theories diverged in important ways. While Locke's liberty revolved around personal autonomy, the republican conception of liberty was tied
to active involvement in public life. Republicanism held that human beings were
naturally social and able to develop fully only in association with others—only
in the context of a community rather than in isolation. Consequently, republicanism assigned the community an important role that liberalism rejected. While
liberalism focused on the rights of individuals—natural rights that government
must protect—republicanism posited that human fulfillment could be achieved
by setting aside self-interest to pursue the common good. Thus, obligations rather
than rights and the common good rather than individual self-interest were the
central concerns of republicanism. Republican freedom was invariably linked to
the common rights of the entire community. The primary purpose of government
was, accordingly, the creation of an environment conducive to the achievement of
the shared goals of that community.

Another defining characteristic of republicanism was a suspicion of power.
In the early sixteenth century, Florentine statesman and political philosopher
Niccolo Machiavelli (1469–1527) pointed out that governments tend to become corrupt, to degenerate into tyranny, and to deprive citizens of their liberty. The only force capable of reversing that trend was a body of virtuous
citizens who, through vigorous participation in public affairs, revitalize the political life of their community and rid it of corruption. Civic virtue, a concern
with and willingness to pursue the public good in contrast to preoccupation
with self-interest, was, according to republicanism, essential to the preservation
of liberty. With its focus on the opposition between power and liberty, and corruption and virtue, republicanism prescribed active participation in public life
and the transcendence of self-interest for the good of the community. It also envisioned a society whose members were tied together by common interests.

In contrast, liberalism perceived society as a collection of individuals engaged in the pursuit of private interests. While republicanism embodied the notion that self-realization is possible only through active participation in public

---

[5]*The Declaration of Independence.*
[6]Eric Foner, *The Story of American Freedom* (New York: W.W. Norton, 1998), 8–9.

life, liberalism—with its emphasis on the individual, natural rights, and diversity of interests—placed one's choice of activity beyond the judgment of others: it was simply a matter of private preference. Although the idea that people should strive to be virtuous citizens in order to protect the rights of their community had a definite democratic element, republicanism had an inegalitarian dimension as well. Running through republican thought was the notion that civic virtue was only attainable by those who owned property. It was, after all, property ownership that gave people the economic independence that made it possible for them to transcend self-interest.

Scholars who have examined the political literature of the years preceding the American Revolution have found it to be dominated by the theme of power—its nature, its dangers, and the conviction that "what turned power into a malignant force, was not its nature so much as the nature of man—his susceptibility to corruption and his lust for self-aggrandizement."[7] Thus, the idea that the protection of liberty against power lay in a balanced government and a constitution that effectively limited power through the distribution of functions among the different components of society was central to revolutionary thought.[8] Before 1763, the colonists viewed the laws and institutions of England as the embodiment of "the most perfect combination of human powers in society which finite wisdom has yet contrived and reduced to practice for the preservation of liberty and the production of happiness."[9] During the ten years after the Stamp Act, however, the colonists began to see an active conspiracy to destroy not only their liberty but also the liberty of the entire British Empire by destroying the English Constitution and all the rights and privileges that it protected. From a republican perspective, taxation without the consent of the colonists was particularly dangerous because it gave additional power to British officials and thereby threatened the liberty of the colonists. Additionally, measures to constrain colonial courts by limiting the tenure of judges to the discretion of the crown, and the extension of the jurisdiction of vice-admiralty courts composed not of juries but of single judges appointed by the royal governors to enforce the new parliamentary legislation, destroyed the essential balance of powers by stripping the judiciary of all independence. Moreover, such actions "denied Americans a crucial measure of the protection of the British constitution."[10] The decision to station British troops in Boston in the fall of 1768 further signaled the destruction of the principles of the English Constitution. Any doubt that might have remained among the colonists that they were the victims of a deliberate assault on their liberty was eliminated by the Boston Massacre in 1770 and the subsequent acquittal of the soldiers indicted for the murder of the youths who attacked them with snowballs. While the colonists were convinced that the British government's policies

---

[7]Bernard Bailyn, *The Ideological Origins of the American Revolution: An Interpretation* (Cambridge, MA: Belnap Press of Harvard University Press, 1967), 59.
[8]The term *constitution* as commonly used among the colonists at the beginning of the revolutionary period did not refer to a written document of even an unwritten design of government, but rather an arrangement of governmental institutions, laws, and customs, and the principles and goals that animated them. *Ibid.*, 68.
[9]Charles Francis Adams, ed., *The Works of John Adams*, Volume III, 477, as quoted in Bailyn, *The Ideological Origins of the American Revolution*, 67.
[10]Bailyn, 109.

constituted a threat to their individual inalienable rights, they also condemned those policies, which they perceived as indicative of the corruption of the King's ministers that was spreading through the British government to the colonies, as a threat to the liberty of the people throughout Europe. The remedy for the corruption was American independence. In his famous pamphlet, *Common Sense*, Tom Paine exhorted Americans to declare their complete independence from England and argued that the British government was in constant conflict with the most important principle of government: frequent elections and the exchange between the people and their representatives. He noted that, "as this frequent interchange will establish a common interest with every part of the community, they will mutually and naturally support each other, and on this . . . *depends the strength of government, and the happiness of the governed.*"[11]

Republican ideas are also evident in the Declaration of Independence. For example, the second paragraph concluded with a condemnation of the King who had inflicted "repeated injuries and usurpations, all having in direct object the establishment of an absolute tyranny" over the colonies.[12] One of the Declaration's specific charges against the King asserted that he had abolished the "free system of English laws . . . establishing therein an arbitrary government, and enlarging its boundaries, so as to render it at once an example and fit instrument for introducing the same absolute rule into these colonies."[13] Thus, a republican concern with preserving balanced government against the threat of corruption and tyranny combined with a liberal mandate for government to protect the inalienable rights of individuals to justify the colonists' break with England.

A third tradition, **ascriptivism** was also apparent in the political thought of the revolutionary era although it has not often been acknowledged. As Rogers M. Smith has written, "From the revolutionary era on, many American leaders deliberately promoted the popular notion that Americans had a distinctive character, born of their freedom-loving Anglo-Saxon ancestors and heightened by the favorable conditions of the new world. This character made them the last hope to preserve human freedom once the English had become corrupt—it also set them above blacks and truly Native Americans."[14] The presence of ascriptivism alongside liberalism and republicanism goes a long way to explain the Declaration's most glaring contradiction. While the Declaration proclaimed that it was "self-evident, that all men are created equal and endowed by their Creator with certain inalienable Rights, that among these are life, liberty, and the pursuit of happiness," the institution of chattel slavery in the colonies placed such ideals far beyond the realm of possibility for nearly half a million black slaves. Additionally, the principles of liberalism and republicanism did not extend to women who had no voice in the drafting of the Declaration of Independence or in any of the decisions of the state or national governments dur-

---

[11] *Common Sense, the Rights of Man, and Other Essential Writings of Thomas Paine* (New York: Penguin Books, 1984), 26.
[12] The Declaration of Independence.
[13] *Ibid.*
[14] Rogers M. Smith, "The 'American Creed' and American Identity: The Limits of Liberal Citizenship in the United States." *Western Political Quarterly* 41 (1988): 225–251, 233.

ing the revolutionary era. Moreover, the principles of the English common law precluded the possibility of a legal or economic existence for a woman independent of that of her father or husband. Liberalism's personal autonomy and republicanism's civic virtue were, in short, reserved for free property-owning white males.

THE DECLARATION OF INDEPENDENCE AND THE AMERICAN REVOLUTION

The First **Continental Congress** convened in Philadelphia in September 1774. In October, the delegates issued a compromise resolution denying Parliament's authority to legislate for the colonists because they were unrepresented but declaring that the colonies would voluntarily submit to regulation of trade. The Second Continental Congress assembled in May 1775 after the war began at Lexington and Concord in April. The Continental Congress became the de facto government that conducted the war, raising an army, sending and receiving diplomatic agents, and entering into treaties with foreign countries.[15] On May 15, 1776, the Congress adopted a resolution sponsored by John Adams, advising the various colonies to assume complete powers of government within themselves. On June 7, Richard Henry Lee, following the instructions of his Virginia constituents, moved a resolution "to declare the United Colonies are, and of right ought to be, free and independent states . . . and that all political connection between them and the state of Britain is, and ought to be, totally dissolved."[16] While Congress debated the resolution but failed to reach agreement, a frustrated John Adams wrote to a friend, "We are in the midst of a Revolution, the most complete, unexpected, and remarkable of any in the history of nations."[17] Congress did, however, appoint a committee to frame a declaration in conformity with the Virginia resolution. The members of the committee were Thomas Jefferson, John Adams, Benjamin Franklin, Roger Sherman, and Robert R. Livingston, with the thirty-three-year-old Jefferson designated as chair and drafter. On July 2, Congress adopted the Virginia resolution and two days later it adopted the **Declaration of Independence,** for the first time using the term *United States of America*.[18] With full recognition of the gravity of their acts, the men who signed the Declaration pledged their lives, their fortunes, and their sacred honor.

Congress directed that copies be sent to the assemblies or conventions of the various states, and to the army. When the Declaration was read at a public meeting on the common in New York, the crowd pulled down a statue of George III. In Boston, after a reading of the Declaration at the State House, the King's Arms were pulled down from over the State House door and burned.

---

[15]C. Herman Pritchett, *Constitutional Law of the Federal System* (Englewood Cliffs, NJ: Prentice Hall, 1984), 4.
[16]As quoted in Page Smith, *A New Age Now Begins: A People's History of the American Revolution* (New York: McGraw-Hill, 1976), Vol. I, 692.
[17]As quoted in *ibid.*, 693.
[18]Previous practice had been to refer to the *United Colonies*.

THE REVOLUTIONARY STATE CONSTITUTIONS AND THE ARTICLES OF CONFEDERATION

Between 1776 and 1778, eleven states drafted new constitutions.[19] By 1780, all the former colonies had formed new state governments based on written constitutions. These constitutions incorporated some of the principles of the Revolution by, for example, reducing or abolishing property qualifications for suffrage, requiring annual elections, limiting terms of office, and adding bills of rights. Virginia's Constitution began with a bill of rights that stated, "[A]ll power is vested in, and consequently derived from, the people; that magistrates are their trustees and servants, and at all times amenable to them."[20]

To prevent the power of government from encroaching on liberty, the revolutionary state constitutions took away most of the traditional powers of the executive and gave them to the legislature. Pennsylvania abolished the office of governor, replacing it with a council of twelve members elected by the people. The legislatures represented the people, the constitution-makers reasoned, whereas the executive, like the British king, was particularly susceptible to corruption. The revolutionary state constitutions were intended to remedy the failures of British rule by limiting the powers of government—particularly that of the executive—and locating that power in the people thereby protecting their liberty. In the context of the eighteenth century, the revolutionary constitutions were bold democratic experiments. By today's standards, however, they were seriously lacking in their commitment to democratic principles: the exclusion of women and blacks was nearly universal.[21]

Because the Continental Congress was created in haste as a kind of provisional government, its members quickly began to take steps to establish a more solid legal basis for the central government. In 1776, before it adopted the Declaration of Independence, Congress appointed a committee to draft a constitution and, in 1777, drafted a document and submitted it to the states. By March 1781, all the states had accepted the document and thereby legally established the **Articles of Confederation.**

The thirteen articles that comprised the first United States constitution did not materially alter the structure or powers of the government that had been operating since 1775. The Articles established a league of friendship, a "perpetual Union" of states. They established a unicameral Congress with each state having one vote. Delegates were chosen by their state legislatures, paid by their states, and subject to recall. Each state could send no fewer than two and no more than seven delegates, and no one could serve as a delegate for more than three years in six. The Articles of Confederation resembled the revolutionary state constitutions in their emphasis on legislative power at the expense of the executive. Indeed, under the Articles, there was no real executive—the

---

[19]Farber and Sherry, 15.

[20]As quoted in Edmund S. Morgan, *The Birth of the Republic, 1763–1789* (Chicago, IL: University of Chicago Press, 1956), 91.

[21]Mark Tushnet, "The Constitution from a Progressive Point of View," in Jules Lobel, ed. *A Less Than Perfect Union: Alternative Perspectives on the U.S. Constitution* (New York: Monthly Review Press, 1988), 41.

"president" was merely the presiding officer of Congress. Congress performed executive functions initially through committees and later created departments. There was no separate judiciary.

Under the provisions of Article 1, Congress had the authority to conduct foreign relations, to determine war and peace, to requisition the states for men and money, to coin and borrow money, and to regulate Indian affairs. Although a simple majority of seven states was needed for minor matters, a larger majority, nine states, was required in specified important matters, including engaging in war, making treaties, and coining and borrowing money. Provisions that were designed to reduce friction among the states required each state to give full faith and credit to the judicial proceedings of the others and made Congress a court of last resort for territorial disputes among states.

Article 2 provided that "each State retains its sovereignty, freedom and independence, and every power, jurisdiction, and right, which is not by this confederation expressly delegated to the United States, in Congress assembled." Article 3 went on to declare that the Confederation represented a firm league of friendship among states. The Articles of Confederation, thus, resembled more of a treaty among sovereign states rather than a single government. The powers of commercial regulation and taxation remained with the states. Because Congress lacked the power to regulate foreign or interstate commerce, commercial treaties with foreign countries had little value. Amending the Articles required the consent of all the states. Some of the most notable features of the Articles—the absence of an executive, the withholding of important powers from Congress, and the provisions rendering Congress unable to act independently of the states—placed the Articles squarely within the revolutionary tradition but soon came to be viewed as fatal flaws.

A number of problems that became increasingly apparent by the end of the war led to some state constitutional reforms and culminated in a movement for a new constitution for the central government. Politics in the states was chaotic, based primarily on local, narrow interests. By the mid-1780s, for example, state legislatures were printing paper money and passing various acts on behalf of debtors. States commonly engaged in commercial discrimination against each other. The Northern port states, New York and Pennsylvania in particular, imposed import duties on foreign goods, creating a financial benefit for themselves, but putting a burden on consumers in the states where the goods ended up. Southern states tried to gain an advantage in exporting their goods. Attempting to make up for the lack of their own shipping industry for transporting crops to foreign markets, they encouraged British shipping by taxing exports lightly or not at all. Some states imposed higher tariffs on goods imported from other states than on domestic goods. States with ports and navigable rivers charged ships from other states higher navigation fees than were charged to local ships. A nationwide recession in 1785–1786 resulted from the combination of a high national debt, increasing trade deficits, and economic infighting among the states.[22]

---

[22]Farber and Sherry, 25.

All the state legislatures went beyond the authority granted by their constitutions by assuming executive and judicial duties, such as directing military operations and setting aside decisions of courts. Executive power had been curbed because it was dangerous to liberty, but now it seemed that legislative power was just as hazardous. State constitutions were revised, beginning with New York in 1777, Massachusetts in 1780, and New Hampshire in 1784, to strengthen the executives, senates, and judiciaries. The changes reduced the lower houses in size and restricted their authority. The problems continued despite state constitutional reform. In the fall of 1786, nearly two thousand farmers in western Massachusetts, led by Daniel Shays, rose in armed rebellion and closed the courts in three counties, preventing creditors from collecting debts. The state militia defeated the rebellion but in early 1787 the voters elected sympathizers of Shays, who proceeded to enact debtor relief legislation.

Debtors in New Hampshire, Connecticut, Rhode Island, New Jersey, Maryland, Virginia, and South Carolina also rioted. According to the official interpretation, such events, particularly Shays's Rebellion, were uprisings of the poor against the rich, designed to take control of the government and to annihilate all debts. Thus, in Massachusetts men of property drew together and began to call for a strong government that could suppress such threats to property. Ebenezer Wales wrote, "I believe that the Tumults here, in this State will Alarm the other States; and by that Means Congress will Soon have Suffict Powers For the Benefitt of the Whole."[23]

The central government under the Articles of Confederation lacked the strength to counteract the problems that plagued the country. Leaders in Congress, including James Madison, Alexander Hamilton, and Robert Morris, who tried to make the most of Congress's powers under the Articles of Confederation, had only limited success and even that evaporated when the war ended. Morris, a wealthy merchant from Philadelphia, as Superintendent of Finance, hoped to enable Congress to raise adequate revenues without depending on the states so that the Confederation could pay its debts and increase the attractiveness of its bonds. He managed to get Congress to authorize the first National Bank in 1781 and tried but failed to secure an amendment to the Articles giving the Confederation the power to levy a 5 percent duty on imports.

By the end of the war, Congress seemed to be paralyzed. It often lacked a quorum. The provision prohibiting delegates from serving more than three years in six effectively precluded the emergence of any strong leaders. Congress had no power to compel the states to comply with congressional resolutions or to supply their allotted requisitions. Neither was it able to regulate trade effectively nor to conduct diplomacy. The major European nations remained closed to trade and Congress had no authority to retaliate with trade regulations. Britain ignored its obligations under the peace treaty to evacuate the posts of the Northwest. The states, likewise, violated the agreement to restore the property of the loyalists that had been confiscated during the war. Spain refused to recognize American claims to the territory between the Ohio River and Florida

---

[23]As quoted in Jackson Turner Main, *The Antifederalists: Critics of the Constitution, 1781–1788* (Chapel Hill, NC: University of North Carolina Press, 1961), 64.

and, in 1784, closed the Mississippi to American trade. Seven of the nine states required for ratification agreed to a treaty that would have opened Spain to American trade on the condition that America renounce all claims to navigate the Mississippi for twenty-five or thirty years.

The Articles of Confederation had serious shortcomings. Nevertheless, the Confederation years were not a complete disaster. Under the Articles, the government successfully concluded the war and negotiated the Treaty of Paris of 1783, which formally gave the United States the status of a nation. It also established a system for the development of western lands and refined the practices of interstate cooperation, which gave Americans experience in handling national problems.

THE CONSTITUTIONAL CONVENTION

The weaknesses of the central government under the Articles of Confederation and the abuses of "the vile State governments"[24] seemed to many political leaders to threaten the very existence of the new nation. Those leaders agreed that reform was needed and focused their efforts on strengthening the central government. Creditors and commercial interests, among the first to become dissatisfied with the central government's lack of power, were joined by other groups. Southerners, for example, wanted to gain additional representation for their growing population. Most prominently, many people who were wealthy felt that their property was threatened by what they saw as majoritarian tyranny in the states.

In January 1786, the Virginia legislature called for an interstate convention to "consider how far a uniform system in their commercial regulations may be necessary for their common interest and permanent harmony."[25] In September, delegates from five states convened in Annapolis. After three days, they concluded that more reforms were needed than they were authorized to make and called for another convention to "take into consideration the situation of the United States, to devise such further provisions as shall appear to them necessary to render the constitution of the Federal Government adequate to the exigencies of the Union; and to report such an Act for that purpose to the United States in Congress assembled."[26] In February 1787, Congress authorized a convention to meet in Philadelphia in May, stipulating that the delegates should meet "for the sole and express purpose of revising the Articles of Confederation."

Even before Congress authorized the Convention, several of the state legislatures began to choose delegates. Seventy-four men were appointed to be delegates and fifty-five delegates representing twelve states (Rhode Island, whose leaders opposed reform, refused to participate) attended, and thirty-nine took a leading part in the deliberations. Most of the delegates were not only well educated but also experienced in politics. Thirty-nine had served in Congress, eight had

---

[24]As quoted in Gordon S. Wood, *The Creation of the American Republic, 1776–1787* (New York: W.W. Norton, 1969), 467.
[25]As quoted in Farber and Sherry, 25.
[26]As quoted in *ibid.*, 26.

worked in the state constitutional conventions, seven had been state governors, and thirty-four were lawyers. Twenty-seven were farmers (nine of those were also lawyers). At least nineteen of the farmers were slaveholders and at least eleven of the nonfarmers held slaves.[27] There were also merchants, manufacturers, and bankers but no small farmers or city mechanics. The rural areas were very much underrepresented. Despite their considerable experience, most of the delegates were young. The youngest was only twenty-six, six were under thirty-one, and only twelve were over fifty-four. All of the delegates were white and male. Several leaders of the Revolution were conspicuous in their absence from the Convention. Patrick Henry was chosen as a delegate but refused to attend, remarking, "I smelt a rat." Neither Samuel Adams nor John Hancock was selected as a delegate. Tom Paine had returned to England. Thomas Jefferson and John Adams were abroad, representing the United States in a diplomatic capacity.

Several delegates stand out because of either their prominence or the influential roles they played at the Convention. George Washington and Benjamin Franklin brought their considerable prestige to the Convention. Washington, who as commander in chief of the Continental Army had led the colonies to victory against the British, had come to be a symbol of liberty around the world. Although he intended to retire from public life when he resigned his commission in 1783 and to spend his time on his farm in the Virginia countryside, he finally agreed to attend the Convention largely because his presence would lend the meeting legitimacy. It was generally believed that without Washington the Convention was unlikely to succeed. Selected unanimously to preside over the Convention, he seldom participated in the debate. Still, his influence and endorsement were considered to be essential to the final adoption of the Constitution.[28] After Washington, Benjamin Franklin was the most influential American of his time, but at eighty-one (he was the oldest delegate) was unable to take an active part in debate. Still, he played the role of peacemaker, diffusing tension and preventing bitterness at critical moments with his sagacious and humorous remarks. Edmund Randolph, then thirty-four, was governor of Virginia and a member of one of Virginia's most prominent families. Although he declined to sign the Constitution, he later advocated its ratification. Another Pennsylvania delegate, James Wilson, read most of Franklin's speeches to the Convention. Wilson, a Scottish-born and Scottish-trained lawyer, had signed the Declaration of Independence and subsequently had become a delegate to the Continental Congress. As a member of the Committee on Detail, he wrote the second draft of the Constitution, which received the approval of the other four members of that committee. Gouverneur Morris, the third Pennsylvania delegate, was an eloquent speaker and addressed the Convention more often than any other member. A member of the Committee of Style that had the task of rewriting the provisions of the document "to give it order, clarity, and elegance,"[29] he was responsible for drafting the final version of the Constitution.

---

[27]Forrest McDonald, *Novus Ordo Seclorum: The Intellectual Origins of the Constitution* (Lawrence, KS: University Press of Kansas, 1985), 220.
[28]C. Herman Pritchett, *Constitutional Law of the Federal System*, 9.
[29]Christopher Collier and James Lincoln Collier, *Decision in Philadelphia: The Constitutional Convention of 1787* (New York: Random House, 1986), 253.

The role that James Madison played in the events that led to the Convention, the framing of the Constitution, and its ratification earned him the honorary title of "Father of the Constitution." He served in the Virginia House of Delegates and in the Continental Congress. He led the movement for the Convention, introducing the resolutions in the Virginia Assembly calling for the appointment of delegates to Philadelphia. Madison brought his considerable knowledge of political history and his own political theory to the Convention. In fact, the two manuscripts he prepared in 1786 and 1787 lend credence to the claim that of all the delegates the thirty-six-year-old Madison was the best prepared.[30] In one of those manuscripts, he outlined the failures of the Articles of Confederation and suggested some general remedies. His analysis provided the basis for the case he would make at the Convention for a strong national government. As the chief architect of the Virginia Plan and subsequently one of its most enthusiastic defenders, he played a major role in setting the agenda of the Convention to design a new constitution rather than simply to revise the Articles of Confederation. Additionally, the daily notes of the proceedings that Madison kept so diligently provide the fullest and most accurate record we have of the Convention.

Alexander Hamilton was another prominent delegate although he played a limited role at the Convention. He remained silent during the early days but eventually rose to speak and spent several hours advocating a powerful centralized government, with a life-tenured senate and executive. He proposed that the states be reduced to administrative units with governors appointed by the national government. Hamilton went so far as to suggest that it would be useful economically to extinguish the states. The other delegates largely ignored his remarks. He was the sole delegate from New York for the last two months of the Convention and declined to take responsibility for casting his state's vote on whether to submit the Constitution to the states.

The rules governing the Convention's procedures mandated that the sessions be kept secret. The delegates agreed not to divulge information concerning the proceedings for fifty years. The mandate for secrecy was so effective that at one point Philadelphians speculated that the delegates were negotiating with the second son of George II as a possible monarch for the United States. Even Congress had no information about the substance of the proceedings.[31] The Convention Journal recorded only motions and votes and was not published until 1819. James Madison's more complete notes of the Convention were not published until 1840. Aside from strict secrecy, the delegates established flexible procedural rules including rules regarding reconsideration of issues, a decision to proceed as a committee of the whole and thereby to relax rules of parliamentary procedure, and the practice of assigning difficult questions to smaller committees. They also agreed that each state would have a single vote. A majority of each state delegation determined that vote.

---

[30]The two manuscripts were, "Notes on Ancient and Modern Confederacies," which he wrote in the spring of 1786, and "Vices of the Political System," which he outlined in the spring of 1787. Richard K. Matthews, *If Men Were Angels: James Madison and the Heartless Empire of Reason* (Lawrence, KS: University Press of Kansas, 1995), 52.

[31]Farber and Sherry, 27.

The delegates agreed that the situation was urgent—they had to devise an acceptable, workable scheme of national government or the union would dissolve. They also agreed on the basic outline of the new government. The federal government needed the power to act independently of the state governments. It needed the power to levy and collect taxes, to make laws, and to enforce them through its own administrative agencies. Additionally, most of the delegates agreed that the central government under the new constitution should be divided into separate and independent departments.

On the third day of the Convention, Edmund Randolph presented a series of fifteen resolutions that James Madison had drafted. Those resolutions, known as the **Virginia Plan,** with some important changes, eventually became the United States Constitution. Strongly nationalist in character, the Virginia Plan provided for a two-house national legislature with the broad authority to legislate "in all cases to which the states are incompetent" and "to negative all laws passed by the several states, contravening in the opinion of the National Legislature, the articles of Union." The lower house was to be popularly elected and representation in both houses was to be proportional based on either population or amount of taxation. A national executive was to be appointed by the legislature. The Virginia Plan also included a national judiciary and provided that the executive and members of the judiciary should combine to form a Council of Revision with veto power over both state and national legislatures. Ratification of the new document was to be by popularly elected conventions in the states rather than by state legislatures.

During the next two weeks as the Convention debated the Virginia Plan, the delegates from the smaller states continued to object to the proposal to create an independent national government to replace the confederated alliance of the thirteen states. William Paterson of New Jersey took the lead in opposing the Virginia Plan first by asking for more time to consider it and then by presenting an alternative scheme designed by delegates from Connecticut, New York, and Delaware as well as New Jersey. The **New Jersey Plan** essentially amended the Articles of Confederation by enlarging the powers of Congress and maintaining the sovereignty of the states. It called for a national government with the power to levy taxes and to regulate interstate commerce. An executive was to be appointed by and removable by Congress. A Supreme Court with the authority to review decisions of state courts was to be appointed by the executive. The New Jersey Plan proposed a one-house legislature in which each state would have one vote. Generally, delegates who were committed nationalists and from the larger states supported the Virginia Plan, whereas the smaller states and delegates who later became Antifederalists favored the New Jersey Plan.

The vote of the Committee of the Whole on June 19 against the New Jersey Plan gave the nationalists a victory as the Convention resumed discussion of the Virginia Plan. Still, it would take three more months to work out the details of the new Constitution. One of the most serious disagreements arose over representation in the national government. The nationalists advocated proportional representation for both houses based on population so that legislative representation would be based directly on the people and not on the states.

Such a method was particularly attractive to delegates from the large states. The proponents of the New Jersey Plan preferred to retain the method of allotting one vote to each state, but when the convention rejected that proposal, they fought for equal representation for states in the upper house of the legislature and the Convention became deadlocked. A committee composed of one delegate from each state—the Committee of Eleven—managed to break the impasse with the **Great Compromise.** The key element of that compromise was a proposal for a two-house legislature consisting of an upper house in which the states would be represented equally and a lower house in which representation would be based on population, with each slave counting as three-fifths of a person. The compromise resolving the dispute over representation in the Senate is regarded as the turning point of the Convention. If delegates from the large states had not accepted the arrangement, the Convention might have fallen apart and "the last best hope for preserving the Union might have evaporated as well."[32]

Although the nationalists made a major concession by agreeing to equal representation of the states in the Senate, the final version of the Constitution retained the basic features of the Virginia Plan with two important exceptions. In contrast to the Virginia Plan's grant to Congress of the broad and amorphous power to legislate "in all cases in which the states are incompetent" and to veto state laws, the Constitution in Article I, Section 8, lists the powers of Congress and in Article I, Section 10, forbids the states from exercising the powers that caused problems in the 1780s, including coining money and enacting laws to relieve debtors of the obligations of their contracts. The Virginia Plan provided that the president be elected by the national legislature but the Constitution provided instead for local elections of "electors" equal in number to the representatives and senators from each state who would cast ballots for the president.

The other major compromise over representation concerned slavery. Delegates from the southern states sought to include slaves as part of their population for purposes of representation in order to increase the power of the South in Congress. Delegates from the North opposed such a measure. They compromised, agreeing to provide that "all other persons" would be counted as three-fifths of "free persons."[33] Another compromise also concerned slavery. Delegates from the Deep South threatened to reject the Constitution if it did not include a provision explicitly denying Congress the power to tax or prohibit the importation "of such persons as the several States shall think proper to admit."[34] The delegates settled on a statement that Congress would not have the power to prohibit the slave trade until 1808.[35] Additionally, the delegates agreed to include a fugitive slave clause.[36] The abolitionist William Lloyd Garrison had these compromises in mind in 1843 when he denounced the Constitution as a corrupt bargain between North and South, " 'a covenant with death

---

[32]Jack N. Rakove, *Original Meanings: Politics and Ideas in the Making of the Constitution* (New York: Alfred A. Knopf, 1996), 58.
[33]*The United States Constitution*, Article I, Section 2.
[34]Max Farrand, ed., *The Records of the Federal Convention of 1787* (4 Vols., New Haven, CT: Yale University Press, 1937), Vol. II, 183.
[35]*The United States Constitution*, Article I, Section 9.
[36]*The United States Constitution*, Article IV, Section 2.

TABLE 1-1   The Articles of Confederation and the Constitution

Articles of Confederation (1781)	The Constitution (1787)
No executive branch	Independent president with extensive powers
No federal judiciary	A Supreme Court and inferior federal courts
Unanimous consent of states required to amend	Simpler amending process requiring consent of ¾ of states
All states have an equal vote	States have equal votes in Senate; proportional vote according to population in House of Representatives
States superior to central government in federal scheme	National government superior to states
Sovereignty located in the states	Sovereignty located in the people
Congress lacked power to	Congress had power to
• regulate interstate and foreign commerce	• regulate interstate and foreign commerce
• raise taxes	• raise taxes
• control currency	• control currency
• enforce its laws	• enforce its laws
• enforce treaty provisions	• enforce treaty provisions
No provisions for checks and balances or separation of powers	Clear system of checks and balances through separation of powers

Source: From *The March of Liberty* by Melvin I. Urofsky, copyright © 1988 by Melvin I. Urofsky. Used by permission of Alfred A. Knopf, a division of Random House.

and an agreement with hell'—involving both parties in atrocious criminality; [that] should be immediately annulled."[37]

To maximize the chances that the new Constitution would be ratified, the delegates retained the Virginia Plan's provision requiring submission to state conventions elected for that purpose rather than to the state legislatures. They also provided that the Constitution would take effect upon ratification by nine of the thirteen states (Table 1-1).

On September 15, all the state delegations voted to approve the Constitution. On September 17, the convention met for the last time. After someone read the Constitution, James Wilson read a speech that Benjamin Franklin had prepared. Franklin's comments, designed to convince those delegates who still had reservations to sign the Constitution, urged "every member of the Convention who may still have objections to it . . . [to] doubt a little of his own infallibility and to make manifest our unanimity, put his name to this instrument."[38] When Wilson finished, Franklin moved that all the delegates

---

[37]As quoted in William M. Merrill, *Against Wind and Tide: A Biography of William Lloyd Garrison* (Cambridge, MA: Harvard University Press, 1963), 205.
[38]As quoted in Clinton Rossiter, *1787: The Grand Convention* (New York: Macmillan, 1966), 235.

sign as witnesses to the fact of "the unanimous consent of the States present."[39] Alexander Hamilton also appealed for unanimity, noting that "no man's ideas were more remote from the plan than his own were known to be," but that he could not hesitate "between anarchy and confusion on one side and the chance of good . . . on the other."[40] Of the forty-two delegates who were present on that final day, only three did not give their approval to the Constitution.[41] The Convention ended, and, as George Washington wrote in his diary, the "members adjourned to the City Tavern, dined together and took a cordial leave of each other."[42]

THE RATIFICATION PROCESS

The Antifederalists

The ratification controversy has most often been examined from the perspective of the **Federalists**, who quickly organized and adopted that name, and emerged victorious in their defense of the new Constitution. The perspective of the opponents of the Constitution—the **Antifederalists**—nevertheless, contributes to an understanding of the principles of the document. In contrast to the Federalists, who mounted a concerted campaign for ratification, the Antifederalists were not an organized group but included a wide variety of individuals throughout the country who opposed ratification and presented their arguments at state conventions and in pamphlets, letters, and newspaper articles in 1787 and 1788 when the Constitution was before the states.

Although the Antifederalists conceded that the Articles of Confederation needed to be revised, they denied that there was a crisis that called for a new Constitution. In their view, the credit of the United States was not in danger nor were property rights threatened. There was no danger from any foreign power, nor did a serious economic crisis exist. They were convinced that the depression would soon lift and the states would be able to pay their debts; taxes would be paid and the country would be prosperous and secure. One Antifederalist, who wrote under the pseudonym of John DeWitt, asserted that the people were living "under a government of our own choice, constructed by ourselves, upon unequivocal principles, and [it] requires but to be well administered to make us as happy under it as generally falls to the lot of humanity."[43] Amendment of the Articles to enlarge the powers to Congress giving it control over commerce and authority to levy taxes in states that did not comply with the requisitions would have been sufficient for many of the Antifederalists.

---

[39]*Ibid.*, 235–236. The motion was Gouverneur Morris's idea but it seemed that it would have a better chance of success if it came from Franklin. See also, Max Farrand, *The Framing of the Constitution of the United States* (New Haven, CT: Yale University Press, 1913), 192.

[40]As quoted in Lance Banning, "The Constitutional Convention," in Leonard W. Levy and Dennis J. Mahoney, eds. *The Framing and Ratification of the Constitution* (New York: Macmillan Publishing Co., 1987), 112–131, 131.

[41]The three who refused to sign were Elbridge Gerry, George Mason, and Edmund Randolph.

[42]Farrand, *The Framing of the Constitution*, 194–195.

[43]As quoted in Main, 180.

They considered it imperative to continue with a confederation of sovereign states based on the principle of local self-government. Although they disagreed concerning many of the details, they were united in their basic assessment of the new Constitution: it created a central government that was too strong. It did not establish a federal government, as the Federalists maintained, but a national government that would consolidate the previously independent states into one overarching authority.

The Antifederalists examined every provision of the Constitution to demonstrate that it granted excessive power to the national government, tended toward aristocracy, and would destroy liberty. For example, contending that the Constitution gave the executive excessive power, the Antifederalists in New York proposed a council to help in appointments, and argued that the president should not have authority over the armed forces or the power to grant pardons without the consent of Congress. The executive, moreover, should be limited to a single term of eight years.[44] There was considerable concern among Antifederalists that the Senate and the President would unite, combine their powers, and that the more democratic House of Representatives would be unable to protect the liberty of the people.

The Constitution also granted too much power to Congress according to the Antifederalists. Indeed, they worried that the provisions in Article I, Section 8, bestowing on Congress the authority to provide for the "general welfare" and "to make laws that shall be necessary and proper" would provide the legislative branch with unlimited power. Moreover, Congress's power to tax (also in Article I, Section 8) and the supremacy clause (in Article VI) would destroy the states. The opponents of the Constitution were firmly convinced that a bill of rights was essential and were particularly adamant that protections for freedom of religion, the right to trial by jury, and freedom of the press be included.

"Observations On the New Constitution, and on the Federal and State Conventions. By A Columbian Patriot," a pamphlet that was distributed in New York in the spring of 1788, listed eighteen objections to the Constitution. The author, Mercy Otis Warren, a playwright, poet, and historian of the Revolutionary War, concluded her comments in a tone of resignation: if the people did not decide that the Constitution should "be thrown out with indignation," if they instead, "generally give their voice for a voluntary dereliction of their privileges, let every individual who chooses the active scenes of life, strive to support the peace and unanimity of his country, though every other blessing may expire."[45]

The Antifederalists' criticisms of the Constitution grew out of some fundamental ideas about politics—ideas that were firmly grounded in the political thought of the Revolution. As did many other Americans during the revolutionary era, the Antifederalists were convinced that a republic could only exist in a small territory with a homogeneous population. Because the public good

---

[44]Main, 142.
[45]"Observations On the New Constitution, and on the Federal and State Conventions. By A Columbian Patriot," in Herbert J. Storing, ed. *The Complete Anti-Federalist* (Chicago, IL: University of Chicago Press, 1981), Vol. 4, 286.

would be lost amidst all the conflicting interests, republican government was inconceivable in a larger area where the people did not share concerns or customs. Moreover, the government would be too far removed from the people to truly represent them. Only in a small republic would elected officials be genuinely responsible to the people. Likewise only in a small republic would the people feel connected to their government and voluntarily attach themselves to it. Thus, local self-government was essential to liberty, and for the Antifederalists that meant state government.

The Antifederalists viewed the movement that culminated in the writing of the Constitution and the campaign for ratification as the work of a few aristocrats who had betrayed the principles of the Revolution. The new Constitution reversed the achievements of the Revolution by transferring power from the people to a central government that to many of the Antifederalists—who feared power as much as most Americans did at the outset of the Revolution—was as dangerous as the British monarchy. The strong central government that the Constitution established would inevitably become tyrannical because it would be impossible for it to consider the interests of all the people in the country. The people elected to office in the new national government would be from the wealthiest portion of society, would have no connection with ordinary people, and could never share their concerns or look after their interests. The Antifederalists rejected the idea that a few individuals of high status—the natural aristocracy—could represent the common people:

> [O]nly ordinary men, men not distinguished by the characteristics of aristocratic wealth and taste, men "in middling circumstances" untempted by the attractions of a cosmopolitan world and thus "more temperate, of better morals, and less ambitious, than the great," could be trusted to speak for the great body of the people, for those who were coming more and more to be referred to as "the middling and lower classes of people."[46]

The Antifederalists defended the values of republicanism by condemning the Constitution. The proposition that "the state was a cohesive organic entity with a single homogeneous interest"[47] ran through their opposition to the proposed national government. For them, the ideal was a small community held together by an independent, virtuous citizenry united in its concerns and willing to transcend individual interests for the public good. The Constitution seemed to be constructed on the liberal assumption that society comprised many different interests and that most people, overwhelmingly concerned with the private side of life, completely lacked anything that resembled civic virtue. Paradoxically, the Antifederalists questioned the foundations of republicanism. By denying the ability of an elite to represent the common people, they also challenged the idea of a community united in a common interest. If all the members of a community were connected, the elite would share the interests of the common people, and therefore, representation by a few, who possessed wealth and talent, would

---

[46]Wood, 491.
[47]Ibid., 499.

not pose any threat to the common good. Thus, while the Antifederalists seemed to cling to the values of republicanism, at the same time they conceded that America "was not an organic hierarchy composed of ranks and degrees indissolubly linked one to another; rather it was a heterogeneous mixture of 'many different classes or orders of people.'"[48]

The Antifederalists sought to protect the values of republicanism against what they perceived as an attack by the Federalists. Their opposition to the Constitution was also based on democratic ideas and principles of equality. They were convinced that to protect liberty, the people must be allowed to participate directly in governing. Many of the Antifederalists were small farmers, people who must have felt that they would be disadvantaged by the proposed Constitution. It is undeniable that their own position in eighteenth-century America influenced their thought. Still, their arguments, particularly when contrasted with those of their opponents, clearly reflect democratic values.

The Federalists' Defense: The Political Theory of the Constitution

By the end of June 1788, ten states had ratified the new document. Only New York, Rhode Island, and North Carolina had not acted. Although only nine states were required for the Constitution to take effect, New York's approval was viewed as crucial to the success of the new government. Determined to secure ratification in New York, Alexander Hamilton recruited James Madison and John Jay to help him write the essays that eventually became *The Federalist.* The eighty-five essays published in four of the five New York City newspapers in the winter of 1787–1788 comprised a major propaganda effort to convince New Yorkers to ratify the Constitution. Although the effort failed—the New York Convention initially voted against ratification by a margin of two-to-one[49]—*The Federalist* has generally been considered the greatest work in American political philosophy. The essays praised the idea of a federal government, condemned the Articles of Confederation, and analyzed and defended virtually every aspect of the Constitution. In *Federalist 39*, for example, James Madison argued that the Constitution provided for a republican form of government, "which derives its power directly or indirectly from the great body of the people."[50] He went on to examine several aspects of the new document in an effort to demonstrate that it would create a federal rather than a national government.

Madison's *Federalist 10* and *51* reveal the extent to which the proponents of the Constitution believed that the future of republican government depended on removing power from the direct control of the people. In *Federalist 10*, Madison defended, against objections of the Antifederalists, the expansion of a single republican government to cover a large area with a diverse population,

---

[48]*Ibid.*, 491.
[49]After Hamilton spread a rumor that New York City would secede from the state and join the Union if New York did not ratify the Constitution, the convention changed its position. Thus, ratification in New York was due primarily to Hamilton's political activities rather than his literary efforts.
[50]James Madison, *Federalist 39*, in *The Federalist Papers by Alexander Hamilton, James Madison, and John Jay* (New York: Bantam Books, 1982), 190.

demonstrating not only that it was possible but that it was necessary to protect liberty. Conflicting interests are inevitable; they are "sown in the nature of man,"[51] Madison contended. Different interests arise out of distinctions in wealth, property, occupations, religion, and politics. Factions, which posed the most serious threat to republican governments, were inevitable, but government could be designed so that their effects could be controlled. Madison explained that a faction is most dangerous when it is composed of a majority and is, consequently, able to achieve its goals at the expense of others. For example, if they are sufficiently numerous, debtors might be able to convince the legislature to cancel all debts and thereby destroy the property rights of their creditors. That would be likely to occur in what Madison referred to as a democracy, "a society consisting of small number of citizens, who assemble and administer the government in person."[52] But in a larger society with more people, and consequently a wider variety of interests, it would be nearly impossible for any group to unite around a single interest and achieve a majority. Thus, to enlarge the size of the state would render the rights of the people more secure. For Madison, the solution to the problem of factions lay in representative government, a system in which a large number of citizens elect a small number of representatives. Those representatives would "refine and enlarge the public views" and would have the wisdom to "discern the true interest of their country," the "public voice, pronounced by the representatives of the people, will be more consonant to the public good than if pronounced by the people themselves."[53]

In *Federalist 51,* Madison applied the same principle to government as he did to society in *Federalist 10* to demonstrate that large government need not be viewed as a threat to liberty. In fact, if designed carefully, a powerful central government would act as a safeguard to liberty by controlling the passions of the people and by controlling itself. With the separation of powers augmented by checks and balances, the Constitution guaranteed that governmental power would always be limited. The Constitution, as Madison explained in both *Federalist 10* and *51,* compensated for the flaws in human nature that led people to be selfish and shortsighted. Through the clashing and checking of the multitude of different interests in both society and government, both individual rights and the public good would find protection.

The ideas expressed in *The Federalist* and the arguments against ratification advanced by the Antifederalists are essential to understanding the Constitution. More than that is needed, however. It is important to approach the document from the perspective of politics and society in the 1780s. Accordingly, it is helpful to know as much as possible about life in America in the late eighteenth century, including the events leading up to the Constitutional Convention, the characteristics of the Federalists and the Antifederalists, as well as their values, goals, and ideals.

Using a wide variety of sources, twentieth-century scholars have reached different conclusions about the ideological underpinnings of the Constitution.

---

[51]James Madison, *Federalist 10,* in *ibid.,* 44.
[52]*Ibid.,* 46.
[53]*Ibid.,* 46–47.

In the early years of the twentieth century, Progressive historians argued that the Framers designed the Constitution with their own financial interests in mind. Charles Beard found that most of the delegates had invested in public securities of the United States and thus stood to benefit by strengthening public credit.[54] Although the Constitution provided the basis for economic growth that was clearly in the interest of the Framers and others, the "Beard thesis" has been criticized extensively.[55] Nevertheless, other scholars have confirmed that the division between Federalists and Antifederalists followed lines of class. Men of wealth were more likely to support the Constitution.[56] There were exceptions, nonetheless. In Virginia, large planters were Antifederalists, and in Delaware there was virtually no opposition to the Constitution. Also, people who lived in towns, regardless of their class, united in support of the Constitution. Historian Jackson Turner Main argued that the division between Federalists and Antifederalists is best explained with reference to commercial interests. Those who had such interests—merchants and other people who lived in towns, farmers who depended on the major cities, and farmers who produced a surplus for export—were Federalists. The Federalists included most of the public and private creditors, large landowners, lawyers, judges, manufacturers, shipowners, higher ranking civil and military officials, and college graduates. Those without commercial concerns lived away from the path of commerce and were less well-to-do because they produced only enough for their own needs. It was such people who composed the rank and file of the Antifederalists.[57]

The Framers have also been portrayed as simply pragmatic politicians who worked hard, bargaining and compromising to produce a document that would be acceptable to the people back home. Although the Framers were, from this perspective, superbly skilled in the art of democratic politics, their inspiration came from their experience as professional politicians.[58] The economic interpretation and the emphasis on the Framers as pragmatic politicians minimize the importance of political ideas in the Constitution.

From still another perspective, the Constitution was a political device designed to control the social forces that the Revolution had released; nevertheless, political ideas were central to it. The Constitution reflected new ways of understanding the political world. Gordon S. Wood, a historian whose work has revealed the importance of republican ideas in the revolutionary era, has explained some important ideological aspects of the Constitution. First, the Constitution was meant to restore and to prolong the traditional kind of elitist influence in politics that had been undermined since the Revolution. It was an aristocratic document designed to check the democratic tendencies of the period. One of the effects of the Revolution was to bring many new men into the

---

[54]Charles Beard, *An Economic Interpretation of the Constitution of the United States* (New York: Macmillan Co., 1913).

[55]See, for example, Robert E. Brown, *Charles Beard and the Constitution* (Princeton, NJ: Princeton University Press, 1956); Forrest McDonald, *We the People: The Economic Origins of the Constitution* (Chicago, IL: University of Chicago Press, 1958).

[56]Main, 261–266.

[57]*Ibid.*, 274–280.

[58]John P. Roche, "The Founding Fathers: A Reform Caucus in Action," *American Political Science Review* 55 (1961): 799–816.

world of politics and business. To the established political elite, these new people were the wrong sort, individuals who lacked the traditional requisites for leadership: the attributes of social superiority, including education, experience, connections, and wealth.[59] Indeed, it was these new people who dominated state politics and who were, therefore, most often blamed for the confusion and instability that threatened the future of the country. The Revolution seemed to have allowed government to fall "into the Hands of those whose ability or situation in Life does not entitle them to it."[60] The revolutionary leaders had replaced the artificial aristocracy of England based on a hereditary nobility with the notion of a natural aristocracy of talent and virtue. The new participants took the revolutionary maxim that all men are created equal seriously. But the established social and political leaders considered such men to be their inferiors and unfit for politics. They considered it essential to ensure that the proper amount of inequality and natural distinctions be recognized. The Federalists believed that the increased social mobility resulted in disorder; to regain the order necessary for the health of the republic, the equality of the Revolution had to be renounced in favor of the traditional hierarchy.

Second, according to Wood, the Federalists structured the Constitution so that it would severely constrain popular participation, justifying it with the claim that they had discovered a positive method of protecting liberty. The problems that plagued the states demonstrated that the government was not always the source of threats to liberty. Indeed, as Madison explained in *Federalist 10,* selfish, shortsighted people who organized around their own narrow interests with no regard for the rights of others or for the common good posed the most serious danger. While democracy did not offer a solution, a republican government over a large continent and a large population of diverse groups and interests did because with such an arrangement it would be virtually impossible for any one group to gain control of the government. The best way to eliminate the democratic localism that plagued politics in the 1780s, the Federalists believed, was to enlarge the arena of politics, expanding the electorate and reducing the number and changing the character of those elected to legislative office. Thus, the Federalists saw themselves as saving the Revolution from its excesses. They not only had to reject the new equality, but also found it necessary to limit democracy for the sake of protecting liberty.

Third, Wood demonstrated that the Constitution reflected a shift in emphasis away from republicanism and toward liberalism. The belief—prevalent during the revolutionary era—that government tends to accumulate power at the expense of liberty, made less sense in the 1780s when popular despotism rather than powerful government seemed to be the problem. People could accept the prospects of a powerful central government because they had come to fear the power of people with different interests and different demands more than they feared the power of government. Society was no longer viewed as an organic homogeneous community threatened by corrupt government but had come to be viewed as a collection of individuals with conflicting interests who

---

[59]Wood, 475–483.
[60]As quoted in Wood, 477.

needed government to protect their rights. Old words and concepts took on new meanings. Liberty, for example, lost its republican connotation—its association with the right of the people to share in the government—and took on a liberal meaning: the protection of individual rights. The idea of civic virtue lost much of its importance because the new prevailing assumption was that most people were concerned with individual, private happiness. As Wood noted, "America would remain free not because of any quality in its citizens of spartan self-sacrifice to some nebulous public good, but in the last analysis because of the concern each individual would have in his own self-interest and personal freedom."[61] In short, government came to be grounded in liberal self-interest and consent rather than republican public virtue.

Viewed from Wood's perspective, the Constitution marked the decline of republican principles and values in American political culture in favor of liberalism. The idea of community was discarded in favor of individualism as society came to be viewed as a variety of clashing interests rather than an organic body. From the Federalists' perspective, the communities of the late eighteenth century failed to protect the most important aspect of liberty: individual rights. The Constitution also renounced the equality and the democracy of the revolutionary era and accepted the idea that, although government derives its power from the people, it must be protected from those people. Only a few were suited to rule because most people were overwhelmingly concerned with personal—not public—interests.

The Final Outcome

As the delegates at the Philadelphia Convention specified, the Constitution was ratified by statewide conventions whose members were chosen mainly by town meetings in New England and by countywide elections elsewhere. A total of approximately 1,750 men were chosen for those conventions.[62] By July 1788, eleven states had given their approval to the new Constitution. North Carolina finally voted to ratify in 1789 and Rhode Island finally assented in 1790 (see Table 1-2). The largest and most powerful states, Virginia and New York, ratified by very slim margins. The Constitution received the fastest endorsement in smaller states that were less capable of maintaining an independent existence—Delaware, New Jersey, Connecticut, and Maryland—or that needed strong central government for purposes of protection as Georgia did with its fear of Indian attacks.[63] There was more disagreement in Pennsylvania, South Carolina, New Hampshire, and Massachusetts. In the states where the outcome was uncertain, the Federalists won crucial votes by promising to add amendments incorporating Antifederalist demands for a bill of rights. The Federalists' success is most often attributed to their superior organization, the largely proratification press, as well as the promise of amendments. In some states, convention delegates were elected not for their position on ratification

---

[61]Wood, 612.
[62]Michael Allen Gillespie and Michael Lienesch, eds. *Ratifying the Constitution* (Lawrence, KS: University Press of Kansas, 1989), ix.
[63]Alfred H. Kelly, Winfred A. Harbison, and Herman Belz, *The American Constitution: Its Origins and Development* (New York: W.W. Norton, 1991), 114.

TABLE 1-2   The Ratification Process

State	Date of Action	Decision	Margin
Delaware	December 7, 1787	ratified	30–0
Pennsylvania	December 12, 1787	ratified	46–23
New Jersey	December 18, 1787	ratified	38–0
Georgia	December 31, 1787	ratified	26–0
Connecticut	January 9, 1788	ratified	128–40
Massachusetts	February 6, 1788	ratified with amendments	187–168
Maryland	April 26, 1788	ratified	63–11
South Carolina	May 23, 1788	ratified with amendments	149–73
New Hampshire	June 21, 1788	ratified with amendments	57–47
Virginia	June 25, 1788	ratified with amendments	89–79
New York	July 26, 1788	ratified with amendments	30–27
North Carolina	August 2, 1788	rejected	184–841
	November 21, 1789	ratified with amendments	94–77
Rhode Island	May 29, 1790	ratified with amendments	34–32

Source: Daniel Farber and Suzanna Sherry, *A History of the American Constitution* (St. Paul, MN: West Publishing Co., 1990), 216.

but rather because they were well known and respected. Such individuals tended to be involved in national politics, exposed to influences beyond the local sphere, and consequently leaned toward the Federalist position.[64] The Antifederalists accepted defeat and thus helped assure a peaceful transition from the Articles of Confederation to the Constitution. Patrick Henry, for example, who voted against ratification in Virginia, graciously conceded,

> If I shall be in the minority, I shall have those painful sensations which arise from a conviction of *being overpowered in a good cause.* Yet I will be a peaceable citizen. My head, my hand, and my heart, shall be at liberty to retrieve the loss of liberty, and remove the defects of that system in a constitutional way. I wish not to go to violence, but will wait with hopes that the spirit which predominated in the revolution is not yet gone, nor the cause of those who are attached to the revolution yet lost. I shall there patiently wait in expectation of seeing that government changed, so as to be compatible with the safety, liberty, and happiness, of the people.[65]

On October 10, 1788, the Continental Congress adjourned permanently after adopting an ordinance establishing the seat of the new government in New York and arranging for the election of the president and the convening of the new Congress on March 4, 1789.[66]

---

[64]Farber and Sherry, 216.
[65]Virginia Ratifying Convention, June 25, 1788, as quoted in *ibid.,* 217.
[66]Melvin Urofsky, *A March of Liberty: A Constitutional History of the United States* (New York: Alfred A. Knopf, 1988), 100–101.

QUESTIONS

1. What was the purpose of the Philadelphia Convention's mandate of secrecy?

   How might the Constitution have turned out differently if the proceedings had been open to the public?

2. The resolution of the dispute over representation in the Senate is generally considered to have been crucial to the success of the Convention. The other major compromise, however, which allowed the southern states to count three-fifths of their slaves for purposes of representation in the House of Representatives, may have "doomed [the Framers'] deepest aspirations for a more perfect Union to the horror of civil war."[67] Do you think the delegates from the northern states should have acted decisively against slavery? Is it possible to justify the compromise over slavery from a practical or moral perspective?

3. Did the Philadelphia Convention have the authority to propose a new Constitution?

   Recall that the Continental Congress adopted the suggestion of the Annapolis Convention and authorized a convention to meet in Philadelphia "for the sole and express purpose of revising the Articles of Confederation" to render that document "adequate to the exigencies of government and the preservation of the Union." During the debates over ratification, Antifederalists frequently alleged that because the Convention had the authority only to consider alterations to the Articles of Confederation it had acted illegally by making a new constitution. How would you respond to this charge? Further, given that the Articles required unanimous state consent for constitutional amendments, how could the Philadelphia Convention justify its decision to require ratification by only nine states? Readers may find it useful to examine *Federalist 40* in which Madison answered both charges.

4. One of the reasons the Philadelphia Convention specified that the states should call ratifying conventions was that the delegates feared the state legislatures, reluctant to give up any of their powers, would be unlikely to support the new Constitution. What other legal or strategic reasons might the Constitution's proponents have had for submitting the document to state conventions? Would the state legislatures have had the authority to ratify the Constitution? What was the significance of obtaining approval of the *people* rather than the *states?*

5. Consider Madison's analysis of the problems of faction in *Federalist 10*. Is it possible that the Philadelphia Convention was a factional assembly? If so, how could it be justified?[68]

---

[67]Rakove, 58.
[68]Bruce Ackerman raised this question in *We the People: Foundations* (Cambridge, MA: Belknap Press of Harvard University Press, 1991), 172.

KEY TERMS

Liberalism	Virginia Plan
Republicanism	New Jersey Plan
Ascriptivism	Great Compromise
Continental Congress	Federalists
Declaration of Independence	Antifederalists
Articles of Confederation	*The Federalist*

SUGGESTIONS FOR FURTHER READING

Belz, Herman, Ronald Hoffman, and Peter J. Albert, eds. *To Form a More Perfect Union: The Critical Ideas of the Constitution*. Charlottesville, VA: University Press of Virginia, 1992.

Berkin, Carol. *A Brilliant Solution: Inventing the American Constitution*. New York: Harcourt, 2002.

Collier, Christopher, and James Lincoln Collier. *Decision in Philadelphia: The Constitutional Convention of 1787*. New York: Random House.

Farber, Daniel A., and Suzanna Sherry. *A History of the American Constitution*. St. Paul, MN: West Publishing Co., 1990, Chapters 1–7.

Foner, Eric. *The Story of American Freedom*. New York: W.W. Norton, 1998.

Gillespie, Michael Allen, and Michael Lienesch, eds. *Ratifying the Constitution*. Lawrence, KS: University Press of Kansas, 1989.

Hamilton, Alexander, James Madison, and John Jay. *The Federalist Papers*. New York: Bantam Books, 1982.

Kammen, Michael, ed. *The Origins of the American Constitution: A Documentary History*. New York: Penguin Books, 1986.

Kelly, Alfred H., Winfred A. Harbison, and Herman Belz. *The American Constitution: Its Origins and Development*. New York: W.W. Norton, 1991.

Levy, Leonard W. *Essays on the Making of the Constitution*, 2d ed. New York: Oxford University Press, 1987.

Levy, Leonard W., and Dennis J. Mahoney, eds. *The Framing and Ratification of the Constitution*. New York: Macmillan Publishing Co., 1987.

Main, Jackson Turner. *The Antifederalists: Critics of the Constitution, 1781–1788*. Chapel Hill, NC: University of North Carolina Press, 1961.

Matthews, Richard K. *If Men Were Angels: James Madison and the Heartless Empire of Reason*. Lawrence, KS: University Press of Kansas, 1995.

Morgan, Edmund S. *The Birth of the Republic, 1763–1789*. Chicago, IL: University of Chicago Press, 1956.

Rakove, Jack N. *Original Meanings: Politics and Ideas in the Making of the Constitution*. New York: Alfred A. Knopf, 1996.

Rossiter, Clinton. *1787: The Grand Convention*. New York: Macmillan Publishing Co., 1966.

Smith, Rogers M. "Beyond Tocqueville, Myrdal, and Hartz: The Multiple Traditions in America." *American Political Science Review* 87 (1993): 549–566.

Storing, Herbert J. *What the Anti-Federalists Were For: The Political Thought of the Opponents of the Constitution*. Chicago, IL: University of Chicago Press, 1981.

Wood, Gordon S. *The Creation of the American Republic, 1776–1787*. New York: W.W. Norton, 1969.

2

THE CONSTITUTION, AMERICAN POLITICS, AND THE DEVELOPMENT OF AMERICAN CONSTITUTIONAL LAW

BASIC FEATURES OF THE ORIGINAL CONSTITUTION

The Constitution provided a framework for government and established a fundamental law under which the new government would be conducted. Although we discussed the political theory of the Constitution in the preceding chapter, a couple of points are worth reiterating here. The major principles of the Constitution reflect two major objectives. First, the Framers sought to create a central government that would be powerful enough to maintain order but sufficiently limited so that it would not pose a threat to liberty. James Madison observed in *Federalist 51* that the "great difficulty" in designing a government was to "first enable the government to control the governed; and in the next place oblige it to control itself."[1] Second, although they wanted to preserve self-government, the Framers also considered it essential to remove power from the direct control of the people. In *Federalist 10,* Madison warned of the dangers of **"faction"**—a group of people, majority or minority, who attempt to gain control of the government to advance their particular interests at the expense of the rest of the population. Madison believed that the wide variation between individuals in their interests and abilities made factions inevitable, but argued that the "mischiefs of faction" could be cured by controlling their effects.[2]

The system of **separation of powers** and **checks and balances** was the mechanism that would oblige the government to control itself. The first three articles of the Constitution provided for three separate departments of government: legislative, executive, and judicial. Each branch had its own function, personnel, method of selection, and constituency. The Constitution distributed the powers of each department, moreover, so that each branch would check the powers of the other two. For example, Congress enacts the laws, but the presi-

---

[1]Alexander Hamilton, James Madison, and John Jay, *The Federalist Papers* (New York: The New American Library, 1961), 322.
[2]*Ibid.,* 77–84.

dent has the authority to veto those laws; the president is commander in chief of the armed forces, but Congress provides authorization and funding for those forces; the courts interpret the laws, but the president with the advice and consent of the Senate selects the judges. The separation of powers and checks and balances would thus ensure that "Ambition [would] be made to counteract ambition."[3]

Another device for limiting power that was built into the Constitution was federalism —the division of power between the national government and the states. The Constitution established a federal government, enumerating certain powers of the national government and leaving other powers to the states, ensuring that they would retain a distinct role in the constitutional system. The source of power of both the states and the national government is the Constitution. Thus, each level of government has its own power independent of the other.

Representative government—what Madison referred to as a republican form of government—would control the effects of faction. The voters would not participate directly in the making of policy but would elect representatives who would "refine and enlarge the public views," and would have the wisdom to "discern the true interest of their country."[4] In short, wise representatives would filter the passions of ordinary people and mediate between their conflicting interests. Although the Constitution provided for the election of members of the House of Representatives, neither the president nor the Senate was elected directly by the people. Article II provided that Electors chosen by each state would select the president, and Article I specified that the Senators would be chosen by their state legislatures. Moreover, the Constitution did not specify qualifications for voting but left that decision to the states.

The Constitution has been in force for nearly 220 years, longer than any other written national constitution in the world. It has changed dramatically over the course of the years, however. Amendments are one major source of change—we consider the Bill of Rights in Chapters 7 and 8 and the other seventeen amendments in subsequent chapters. Supreme Court decisions in which the justices have found new meanings in constitutional provisions that diverge sharply from previous interpretations have also resulted in major constitutional change. In the late nineteenth and early twentieth centuries, for example, the Court maintained that the equal protection clause of the Fourteenth Amendment did not prohibit state-imposed racial segregation. Beginning in 1954, however, the Court found that "equal protection of the laws" forbade racial segregation in education and other public facilities. Constitutional change by judicial interpretation has always taken place in conjunction with important political developments. For example, the Supreme Court interpreted the president's powers as commander in chief more generously as the United States emerged as a global power. Likewise, the Court began to approve an active and powerful central government against the background of a rapidly transforming economic system in the second third of the twentieth century.

---

[3]*Ibid.*, 322.
[4]*Ibid.*, 82.

CONSTITUTIONAL INTERPRETATION[5]

Difficulties

As noted in Chapter 1, the document that the delegates produced at the Philadelphia Convention was the result of a number of compromises. Thus, although some provisions are precise and their meaning is readily apparent—elections for the House of Representatives take place every two years and presidential candidates must be at least thirty-five years old, for example—many are far from clear. Article I, Section 8 gives Congress the power "To regulate Commerce with foreign Nations, and among the several States, and with the Indian Tribes." The phrase, "among the several states" has been the source of recurring debate over the extent of Congress's power to regulate business and industry as well as a variety of other activities. Many of the Constitution's amendments seem especially vague. The Fourth Amendment prohibits "unreasonable searches and seizures" but fails to provide a definition of "unreasonable." The Eighth Amendment's ban on "cruel and unusual punishments" is even more confusing. What is meant by "cruel"? Is an "unusual" punishment one that is not generally practiced? Does the meaning of the clause change over time according to shifting practices and evolving perceptions of what constitutes cruelty? Does the provision allow punishments that are either cruel *or* unusual but not both cruel *and* unusual?

The fact that the Framers of the Constitution and its amendments found it necessary to compromise among themselves is only one of several reasons that so many provisions are amenable to different interpretations. Another is that conveying complex ideas with absolute precision is immensely difficult. Moreover, the English language has changed over time. Finally, not only because they could not agree but also because they were not always certain of exactly what they wished to establish, the Framers sometimes adopted general language, leaving the working out of details to future generations.[6]

Difficulties in determining the meaning of particular constitutional provisions multiply when one moves to the structure of the Constitution as a whole and considers the relationship between its various provisions. For example, at the end of a list of specific powers granted to Congress, the final clause in Article I, Section 8 authorizes Congress "To make all Laws which shall be necessary and proper for carrying into Execution the foregoing Powers, and all other Powers vested by this Constitution in the Government of the United States, or in any Department or Officer thereof." Although the "necessary and proper" clause suggests that Congress has implied powers beyond the specifics of those that are enumerated, the Tenth Amendment suggests that Congress's power may be more restricted by specifying that "The powers not delegated to the United States by the Constitution, nor prohibited by it to the States, are reserved to the States respectively, or to the people."

---

[5]We rely heavily throughout this section on Walter F. Murphy, James E. Fleming, Sotirios A. Barber, *American Constitutional Interpretation*, 2d ed. (Westbury, NY: Foundation Press, 1995).
[6]*Ibid.*, 8–9.

Another major problem in discerning the meaning of the Constitution and its specific provisions is identified by the question, "What is the Constitution?" Is it simply the text of the document produced in 1787 and its twenty-seven amendments? Or does the Constitution also include traditions, practices, previous interpretations, and political theories? The Supreme Court has commonly turned to tradition in trying to apply the due process clause of the Fourteenth Amendment. Thus, Justice John Marshall Harlan argued in 1961:

> Due process has not been reduced to any formula; its content cannot be determined by reference to any code. The best that can be said is that through the course of this Court's decisions it has represented the balance which our Nation, built upon postulates of respect for the liberty of the individual, has struck between that liberty and the demands of organized society. . . . The balance of which I speak is the balance struck by this country, having regard to what history teaches are the traditions from which it broke. That tradition is a living thing.[7]

Justice William J. Brennan noted that certain interests and practices are at the core of the meaning of liberty in the due process clause, including "freedom from physical restraint, marriage, childbearing, childrearing. . . . Our solicitude for these interests is partly the result of the fact that the Due Process Clause would seem an empty promise if it did not protect them, and partly the result of the historical and traditional importance of these interests in our society."[8]

Determining the meaning of the Constitution is, in sum, no mere mechanical act of discovering objective definitions of terms or phrases. It is instead a complex, creative, and normative endeavor that invariably involves the identification of fundamental political principles and values. Additionally, the search for constitutional meaning most often involves contested issues—there is seldom only one clear correct answer. As Murphy, Fleming, and Barber observed, "When all the problems of language . . . combine with the difficulties of distinguishing what is history and tradition from what is mere myth, there will be ample room for reasonable men and women to differ."[9] As we consider several different approaches to interpreting the Constitution, keep in mind how the approaches are always linked to perceptions of what the Constitution is.

Approaches to Constitutional Interpretation

The different approaches to interpreting the Constitution can be organized around two fundamental questions about the Constitution. First, what is the Constitution? Is it completely encompassed in the text of the document or does it include more, such as previous interpretations, political philosophy, perhaps the entire political system? Is the Constitution a set of rules—a blueprint for government to follow—or is it more—a vision of what the United States should be? The second question involves the political theory on which the Constitution—indeed the entire political system—rests, what does the

---

[7]Dissenting in *Poe v Ullman*, 367 US 497 (1961), as quoted in *ibid.*, 111.
[8]Dissenting in *Michael H. v Gerald D.*, 491 US 110 (1989), as quoted in *ibid.*, 164–165.
[9]*Ibid.*, 15.

TABLE 2-1   Approaches to Constitutional Interpretation

The Organizing Questions

What Is the Constitution?

Only Its Text or More?

A Set of Rules or a Statement of Goals and Values?

Does the Constitution Protect Democracy or Constitutionalism?

Text & Set of Rules, Democracy	*More than Text, Goals & Values, Constitutionalism*
Textualism: meaning of the words	**Doctrinalism:** previous interpretations
—clause bound—specific clauses	**Developmentalism:** doctrinalism plus wider array of historical events
—textual structuralism—whole document	**Philosophic Approach:** reasoned analysis of ideas and concepts
—purposive textualism—purpose of provisions	**Systemic Structuralism:** unity of the constitutional system
Originalism: intent or understanding of framers	**Systemic Purposive Approach:** goals and values of constitutional system
	—doctrine of the clear mistake
	—reinforcing representative democracy
	—protecting fundamental rights
	—aspirational

Source: Adapted from Walter F. Murphy, James E. Fleming, and Sotirios A. Barber, *American Constitutional Interpretation*, 2nd ed. (Westbury, NY: Foundation Press, 1995).

Constitution protect? Does it protect democracy, namely majority rule? Alternatively, does it impose limits on what majorities may do? That is, does it protect constitutionalism rather than democracy? Table 2-1 organizes the approaches to interpretation around these two questions.

Textualism

At the most basic level, a textualist interprets the Constitution by reading its words and phrases and determining their meaning. The most common variety of textualism is clause-bound textualism, which focuses on specific clauses, generally treating them as independent of each other.[10]

---

[10]Textual structuralism places more emphasis on determining the meaning of a particular clause in relation to other provisions and the context of the whole document. Interpreting the establishment clause from the perspective of textual structuralism would require an interpreter to consider not only the words of that particular provision but also those of the adjoining free exercise clause, possibly the equal protection clause of the Fourteenth Amendment, and the prohibition in Article VI on religious tests for federal officials. Purposive textualism, which may be used in conjunction with either of the other two approaches, considers what the goal of either an isolated clause or the text as a whole attempts to achieve and interprets accordingly. Both textual structuralism and purposive textualism rely heavily on the interpreters' understanding of structure and purpose—understandings that vary dramatically. Consequently, both are vulnerable to the charge that they allow the interpreter too much discretion to inject his or her own values into the meaning of the Constitution.

Originalism

Advocates of originalism argue that the meaning of the Constitution and its amendments was fixed at the moment of adoption. Thus, the meaning of the document is static rather than evolving. Originalists might focus on the intent of the Framers of a particular provision or on the Framers' understanding of the meaning of a provision. Because it requires the interpreter to rely on the original meaning of the Constitution and its amendments, originalism has the purported advantage of limiting the interpreters' discretion. There are several problems with originalism, however. The records of the debates in Philadelphia and those at the ratifying conventions fail to reveal any common intentions or understandings over the meaning of specific provisions. Because the Framers differed over constitutional meanings, originalists must choose among various Framers and between Framers and ratifiers, and they must provide justifications for their choices. Further, they need to establish that later interpreters should be bound by original understandings or intentions. A particularly troubling question for originalists is whether the Framers of the original Constitution intended their intentions or understandings to provide the authoritative guide to future interpreters.[11] Finally, opponents of originalism contend that rigid adherence to original intent or understanding—assuming they can be discovered—renders the Constitution incapable of adapting to a changing world. As Table 2-1 indicates, textualism and originalism are approaches to constitutional interpretation that are consistent with the notion that the Constitution protects democracy. Thus, both approaches limit the circumstances in which the judiciary is justified in invalidating policies that have been approved by majoritarian processes. The other approaches, in contrast, focus on the idea that the Constitution restricts the power of the majority to infringe on certain basic rights of individuals.

Doctrinalism

In contrast to originalism, doctrinalism revolves around the idea that the Constitution is developing rather than static. Doctrinalists rely on past interpretations in their search for the meaning of constitutional provisions. Although doctrinalism allows the Constitution to adapt to current problems and to cope with new issues that could not have been foreseen by the Framers, textualists charge that it diverts attention from the Constitution itself to what others have said about it. Additionally, doctrinalism leaves a great deal of discretion to interpreters who typically have a range of previous interpretations from which to choose.

Constitutional Development

Interpreters who believe that the Constitution is evolving rather than static use a developmental approach or developmentalism to ascertain the meaning of constitutional provisions. Developmentalism resembles doctrinalism but

---

[11]See H. Jefferson Powell, "The Original Understanding of Original Intent." *Harvard Law Review* 98 (1984–1985): 885–948.

expands the sources beyond previous interpretations to include informal practices, usages, and even political culture. Chief Justice Earl Warren's argument that the key to the Eighth Amendment's meaning lies in "evolving standards of decency that mark the progress of a maturing society" is a well-known example of developmentalism.[12] Because the developmental approach looks to historical events, it shares the problems that originalism has in trying to understand the past. In contrast to originalism, however, developmentalism encourages constitutional change.

Philosophic Approach

Proponents of a philosophic approach argue that the meaning of the words and phrases of the Constitution cannot be interpreted without examining underlying assumptions and concepts. They argue that interpreters do not have a choice between a philosophic and a nonphilosophic approach; rather, they must choose between pursuing philosophic methods responsibly or irresponsibly. Thus, interpreters should put their choices on the table rather than purport to rely on the text or the intent of the Framers. The main problem with a philosophic approach is that interpreters have such a wide variety of philosophic teachings to choose from—including natural rights, legal positivism, pragmatism, and democratic theory—that their interpretations may be largely a matter of which theory they find most appealing.

Structuralist Approaches

Interpreters who believe that the Constitution includes more than its text—that in fact the Constitution encompasses the entire political system, the text, traditions, practices, and interpretations—are likely to find **systemic structuralism** useful. When Justice William O. Douglas located the right to privacy in "the totality of the constitutional scheme under which we live,"[13] he was using systemic structuralism. Examples of such an approach are most often found in cases involving federalism and the distribution of powers among the three branches of the national government. Both are subjects about which the text alone does not provide sufficient information.[14]

The objectives of the Constitution can also be placed at the center of the task of interpreting the document. With such an approach, known as **purposive structuralism,** an interpreter gleans the meaning of constitutional provisions from the purpose of the Constitution. Thus, part of the task of interpretation becomes that of discovering the Constitution's goals, and different interpreters have different understandings of what those goals are. Thus, there are several varieties of purposive structuralism (see Table 2-1). The approach known as "Protecting fundamental rights" requires judges to take an active role in protecting rights such as the right to privacy, equality, or the rights of private property. The per-

---

[12]Plurality opinion in *Trop v Dulles*, 356 US 86 (1958), as quoted in Murphy, Fleming, and Barber, 396.
[13]*Ibid.*, 400.
[14]Murphy, Fleming, and Barber also identify another version, transcendent structuralism, which interpreters find useful if they believe that the Constitution includes political theories as well as the other components, 400.

sistent disagreement among interpreters over which rights qualify as fundamental points to the central problem with this approach. An aspirational approach, another variety of purposive structuralism, asks what kind of society the Constitution wants the United States to strive to be. Accordingly, it seeks to discern constitutional meaning from the nation's ideals. Justice Brennan's condemnation of the death penalty as inconsistent with the Eighth Amendment's prohibition on cruel or unusual punishments illustrates the aspirational approach. He contended that the punishment of death violates the principle that "the State, even as it punishes, must treat its citizens in a manner consistent with their intrinsic worth as human beings—a punishment must not be so severe as to be degrading to human dignity."[15] Brennan captured the essence of the aspirational view of the Constitution in a lecture he delivered in 1985:

> [T]he Constitution embodies the aspiration to social justice, brotherhood, and human dignity that brought this nation into being. The Declaration of Independence, the Constitution, and the Bill of Rights solemnly committed the United States to be a country where the dignity and rights of all persons were equal before all authority. In all candor we must concede that part of this egalitarianism in America has been more pretension than realized fact. But we are an aspiring people, a people with faith in progress. Our amended Constitution is the lodestar for our aspirations.[16]

When the Court considers challenges to public policies on the grounds that they violate a particular constitutional provision, the justices frequently clash over interpretive approaches. Consequently, a basic understanding of the competing approaches to constitutional interpretation will be useful when we begin to examine the Constitution's specific provisions in Chapter 3. Additionally, it is important to be aware that not only do some of the interpretive approaches overlap but also interpreters commonly use more than one approach to resolve constitutional questions. Supreme Court justices—even those who explicitly advocate a particular approach—often shift approaches depending on the issue and the constitutional provision. For example, Chief Justice Rehnquist who is a proponent of textualism and originalism has moved to a purposive structural analysis in cases involving federalism in order to protect the role of the states vis-à-vis the national government.[17] Justices also sometimes combine different approaches in one opinion. Consequently, it is more useful to look for elements of the different approaches in judicial opinions than to attempt to identify the justices as practitioners of a single approach.

Who Are the Interpreters?

In our discussion of approaches to constitutional interpretation we used the term *interpreters* rather than *judges* to convey the idea that judges are not the only authoritative interpreters of the Constitution. As we consider each part of

---

[15]*Gregg v Georgia*, 428 US 153 (1976), 229 (dissenting opinion).
[16]William J. Brennan, Jr., "The Constitution of the United States: Contemporary Ratification." Lecture delivered at Georgetown University, October 12, 1985, in Murphy, Fleming, and Barber, 236–242, 236.
[17]See, for example, *National League of Cities v Usery*, 426 US 833 (1976) (majority opinion) and *Garcia v San Antonio Metropolitan Transit Authority*, 469 US 528 (1985) (dissenting opinion).

the Constitution in the following chapters, we focus primarily on the ways that the Supreme Court has resolved disputes regarding the meaning of constitutional provisions. Nevertheless, it is important to keep in mind that other institutions also interpret the Constitution. When it enacts legislation, for example, Congress must construe the extent of its power under the Constitution to determine whether it has the authority to act. Congress might consider whether it is enacting a law that falls within the realm of the necessary and proper clause or it might need to determine whether it is acting within the terms of the Fourteenth Amendment's authorization to Congress to enact "appropriate legislation" for carrying out the other provisions of the Amendment.[18] Additionally, the president interprets the Constitution when recommending legislation to Congress; more directly, Article II specifies that the president must take an oath to "preserve, protect, and defend" the Constitution. The president has to determine the meaning of the Constitution to fulfill that oath. Indeed, every public official takes an oath to support the Constitution and so may be said to be an interpreter. Ordinary citizens at times engage in constitutional interpretation when they choose between candidates for public office or engage in other political activities.

Judicial Review

Article III specifies that the judicial power shall extend to "all cases, in law and equity, arising under this Constitution." Judges, like all other public officials, take an oath to support the Constitution. Thus, the authority of federal judges to interpret the Constitution is not in doubt. What the text of the Constitution did not make clear, however, was the proper role of the judiciary in relation to other governmental institutions. **Judicial review**—the power of the courts to determine that acts of other governmental institutions are null and void on the grounds that they violate the Constitution—is not mentioned in the text of the document. In *Federalist 78*, however, Alexander Hamilton explained the need for constitutional limits on the lawmaking power, suggesting a rationale for judicial review:

> No legislative act, . . . contrary to the Constitution, can be valid. To deny this would be to affirm that the deputy is greater than his principal; that the servant is above his master; that the representatives of the people are superior to the people themselves; that men acting by virtue of powers may do not only what their powers do not authorize, but what they forbid.[19]

The Supreme Court explicitly asserted the power of judicial review in 1803 in *Marbury v Madison*.[20] In his opinion for the Court, Chief Justice John Marshall made an objective case for the logical necessity of judicial review. Thus,

---

[18]The Thirteenth, Fifteenth, Nineteenth, Twenty-fourth, and Twenty-sixth Amendments have similar authorizing provisions.
[19]*The Federalist Papers*, 467.
[20]5 US (1 Cranch) 137 (1803).

Marbury v Madison provides an excellent illustration of constitutional interpretation. The case also is indicative of the way that judicial decision making takes place in dynamic interaction with the other institutions of government.

In 1800, John Adams lost his bid for reelection to the presidency to Thomas Jefferson; the Federalists also lost control of Congress. Between the election and Jefferson's inauguration on March 4, 1801, Federalists took several steps to maintain their influence in the judiciary. In January, Adams nominated his Secretary of State, John Marshall, to be Chief Justice. The "lame duck" Congress passed the Judiciary Act of 1801 creating a number of new judgeships in the lower federal courts. The 1801 Act also reduced the number of justices on the Supreme Court from six to five so that if a justice retired during Jefferson's term the Republican president would not be able to choose a replacement. Pursuant to legislation authorizing forty-two new justices of the peace for Washington, D.C., President Adams made his "midnight appointments" filling the new positions with loyal Federalists. All the commissions were signed and sealed but the Secretary of State failed to deliver some of them, and when Jefferson assumed office, he gave instructions forbidding their delivery. Several men whose commissions were not delivered—including William Marbury—brought suit in the Supreme Court asking for a writ of mandamus compelling the Secretary of State to deliver their commissions.

The justices granted Marbury's motion for a ruling on whether the executive branch was obligated to deliver the commissions. Marbury claimed that Section 13 of the Judiciary Act of 1789 conferred authority on the Supreme Court to hear his case in its original jurisdiction—that is, he argued that his case did not need to begin in a lower federal court and make its way to the Supreme Court on appeal. The specific provision in Section 13 on which he relied gave the Supreme Court the power to issue writs of mandamus "in cases warranted by the principles and usages of law."[21]

By February 1803 when the Court heard arguments in *Marbury v Madison*, the Republicans had taken several steps against the judiciary. Congress repealed the 1801 Judiciary Act thereby eliminating the new positions that Adams had filled. Fearing that the Court might find the repeal unconstitutional, Congress passed the Amendatory Act, which had the effect of prohibiting the Court from convening for fourteen months prior to February 1803. Additionally, President Jefferson asked the House of Representatives to begin impeachment proceedings against a Federalist judge, John Pickering. Thus, the threat of impeachment hung over the Federalist judges who remained on the courts after the repeal of the 1801 Judiciary Act. Moreover, passage of the Amendatory Act suggested that if the Supreme Court did not bow to the will of the Republicans, Congress would simply prevent the justices from convening.

Given those developments, if Marshall issued the writ of mandamus, Jefferson was likely to ignore it. He could also initiate impeachment proceedings against the Chief Justice. In short, the Supreme Court was hardly politically situated to order the president to deliver Marbury's commission. On the other hand, for Marshall to allow Jefferson to withhold the commission would create

---

[21]A writ of mandamus is a court order directing an officer to carry out a specified duty.

the impression that the Court condoned Jefferson's refusal to deliver the commissions. Such a decision would also expose the Court as a weak, ineffectual branch of government, unable to hold its own with the more powerful executive and legislative branches.

Marshall found a resolution to the Court's dilemma that at once condemned as illegal Jefferson's refusal to issue the commissions, asserted the power of the Supreme Court to issue an order to an executive official, declined to do so on the grounds that the Supreme Court was not the appropriate tribunal to provide Marbury with a remedy, and declared an act of Congress to be invalid. The Court lacked the power to issue a writ of mandamus in cases like Marbury's, Marshall declared. He held that Section 13 of the Judiciary Act of 1789, which apparently granted the Court such power, was, in fact, unconstitutional. Article III, Section 2 of the Constitution defined the Supreme Court's original jurisdiction, limiting it to cases "affecting Ambassadors, other public Ministers and Consuls, and those in which a State shall be Party." Marshall reasoned that Congress could not add to the Court's original jurisdiction as it had tried to do in Section 13 when it authorized the Court to issue writs of mandamus "in cases warranted by the principles and usages of law." Jefferson and most members of his party were adamantly opposed to judicial review, but part of the brilliance of Marshall's opinion in *Marbury* lay in the way he distracted Republicans' attention from the enormity of what the Court had done. Jefferson certainly could not quarrel with Marshall's refusal to issue the writ. Moreover, as the Judiciary Act of 1789 had been passed by Federalists, Republicans were not particularly upset to see a portion of it invalidated. Marshall's concession to the Republicans may be viewed as a short-term concession made in return for a broader and longer-term gain of enhancing the power of the judiciary by establishing the power of judicial review.

Marshall's argument for judicial review began with the question of whether an act repugnant to the Constitution can be law. His answer rested on general principles of constitutional government. A written constitution, he explained, forms "the fundamental and paramount law of the nation, and consequently, the theory of every such government must be, that an act of the legislature, repugnant to the constitution, is void."[22] If not, then ordinary legislation could change the Constitution and the Constitution would thereby not be superior to ordinary law.

Marshall still needed to explain why the Supreme Court rather than some other governmental institution had the responsibility to maintain the primacy of the Constitution by determining when legislation should be invalidated. The explanation that he provided was based on logical inference from the constitutional provisions pertaining to judicial power. Declaring that "It is emphatically the province and duty of the Judicial Department to say what the law is,"[23] he made an uncontroversial claim that the judiciary's task of applying the law to specific cases involved determining which law applies, and, if there is a con-

---

[22]5 US (1 Cranch) 137 (1803), 177.
[23]*Ibid.*, 177.

flict, choosing between them. He claimed that the power of judicial review followed logically:

> So, if a law be in opposition to the Constitution, if both the law and the Constitution apply to a particular case, so that the Court must either decide that case conformably to the law, disregarding the Constitution, or conformably to the Constitution, disregarding the law, the Court must determine which of these conflicting rules governs the case. This is of the very essence of judicial duty.[24]

In effect, Marshall used an analogy between deciding which law applies to a case—something that courts unquestionably had the authority to do—and deciding between a law and the Constitution to prove that courts had a duty to exercise the power of judicial review. The problem with such reasoning is that his conclusion that it is the Court's duty to decide on matters of constitutionality depends on the assumption that questions pertaining to the constitutionality of legislation are just as proper subjects of judicial inquiry as questions of statutory interpretation. Thus, the proof of Marshall's argument was dependent on an assumption of exactly what he sought to prove.[25]

The Chief Justice also relied on the language of Article III, which provides that the judicial power of the United States extends to all cases arising under the Constitution. In deciding such cases, he observed, courts must look into the Constitution—that is, they must interpret it and, in so doing, decide whether legislation is consistent with it. If judges must "close their eyes on the Constitution and only see the law," the Constitution would be meaningless. Additionally, Marshall pointed out that judges take an oath to support the Constitution. They cannot fulfill that oath without the power to invalidate laws that are unconstitutional. If judges are obligated to apply laws that are unconstitutional, they will end up violating the Constitution themselves.

The weaknesses in the logic of Marshall's argument suggest that he might have made a stronger case by employing a more purposive or prudential structural approach. How would the constitutional system work without judicial review? What are the advantages of judicial review over legislative supremacy? He could have built his argument around the notion that judicial review was a practical necessity—it would promote the success of the new nation, and thus the success of the Constitution itself. While his multiple references to the connection between judicial review and written constitutions suggest that "practical necessity" was an element of Marshall's argument, he chose to locate judicial review in specific constitutional provisions. He may have done so to make his decision more palatable to the Republican Administration and the Republican Congress. As Dean Alfange noted, "[A]ny argument by the Supreme Court that the welfare of the polity would be best promoted by granting the judiciary power to check legislative depredations on the Constitution would not, in all likelihood, have been accorded a terribly gracious political reception."[26]

---

[24]*Ibid.*, 178.
[25]Dean Alfange Jr., "*Marbury v Madison* and Original Understandings of Judicial Review: In Defense of Traditional Wisdom." *The Supreme Court Review* (1994): 329–446, 436.
[26]*Ibid.*, 438.

It is because of judicial review that the study of constitutional law is over-whelmingly focused on the analysis of decisions of the Supreme Court. The Court is commonly considered to be the ultimate interpreter of the Constitution. According to the doctrine of judicial supremacy, officials of other governmental institutions are obligated to follow the decisions of the Court—the Court is the final authority in matters of constitutional interpretation. In actual practice, however, Congress, the president, and the states interact with the judiciary in several ways to resolve constitutional questions. First, by a two-thirds vote of both houses Congress may propose and three-quarters of the states may ratify a constitutional amendment to overcome a decision of the Supreme Court. Constitutional amendments have reversed Supreme Court decisions on four occasions. The Eleventh Amendment overcame the Court's ruling in *Chisholm v Georgia*[27] that a plaintiff from another state could sue a state in federal court. The Fourteenth Amendment negated *Dred Scott v Sandford*'s holding that the Constitution did not allow African Americans to be citizens of the United States.[28] The Sixteenth Amendment authorized Congress to enact an income tax, a power that the Court had denied in *Pollock v Farmers' Loan and Trust*.[29] The Twenty-sixth Amendment gave eighteen-year-olds the right to vote in response to the Court's ruling in *Oregon v Mitchell* that the states could withhold the franchise from those under twenty-one.[30]

Second, Congress may enact legislation to overcome a Supreme Court decision with which it disagrees. For example, after the Court invalidated the Texas flag desecration law in *Texas v Johnson*,[31] Congress enacted the Flag Protection Act of 1989. Congress may also enact legislation in response to the Supreme Court's approach to a particular constitutional issue. In the Religious Freedom Restoration Act of 1993, for example, Congress challenged the Court's approach to cases involving the free exercise clause of the First Amendment.

Third, Congress may minimize the impact of a Supreme Court decision with which it disagrees. A series of provisions known as the Hyde Amendment, for example, prohibited funding for abortion after the Court held that a woman's right to choose to terminate a pregnancy was protected by a constitutional right to privacy.[32] Finally, Congress might rely on the provision in Article III, Section 2, which specifies that the Supreme Court shall have appellate jurisdiction with such exceptions and under such regulations as Congress shall make, to eliminate the Court's authority to hear certain types of cases. In 1868, Congress enacted a law removing the Court's appellate jurisdiction in cases involving petitions for federal habeas corpus in an effort to prevent the justices from curtailing the authority of military tribunals over civilians in the South pursuant to Reconstruction legislation. In the twentieth century, Congress proposed, although it did not enact, legislation curbing the Court's appellate jurisdiction in controversial areas such as school prayer, abortion, school busing, and criminal confessions.

---

[27] 2 US (2 Dall) 419 (1793).
[28] 60 US (19 How) 393 (1857).
[29] 157 US 429 (1895).
[30] 400 US 112 (1970). In *Oregon v Mitchell*, the Court held that the states could deny the vote to people under twenty-one in state but not federal elections.
[31] 491 US 397 (1989).
[32] *Roe v Wade*, 410 US 113 (1973).

Although constitutional dialogues take place between the Court and other institutions of government, reversal of a major Supreme Court decision or line of decisions is extremely difficult. Only four constitutional amendments have been added to the Constitution to reverse a Supreme Court decision. The Supreme Court invalidated both the Flag Protection Act of 1989[33] and the Religious Freedom Restoration Act of 1993.[34] Although Congress's efforts to prohibit public funding for abortions were successful, other attempts by Congress and some presidents to overturn the Supreme Court's decisions holding the abortion choice to be a fundamental right have not been enacted into law. The constitutionality of "court curbing" is uncertain. The Court acquiesced to Congress's withdrawal of its appellate jurisdiction to hear habeas corpus appeals by dismissing *Ex Parte McCardle*.[35] But that was an extraordinary case that arose in the context of one of the most serious crises in American history. If Congress were to attempt to remove some of the appellate jurisdiction of the early twenty-first-century Supreme Court in an effort to reverse a controversial decision or line of decisions, the justices might well strike down that legislation.

One of the major criticisms of judicial review that has continued to persist through the years—known as the **countermajoritarian difficulty**—holds that there is an inherent tension between judicial review and democratic government. The argument is that because the Court contravenes majority will when it invalidates a policy enacted by elected officials, it should exercise that power only on the rarest of occasions when a challenged policy is incontrovertibly in violation of the Constitution. Critics of judicial review who espouse such a view emphasize the democratic character of the American political system. If one stresses constitutionalism instead, however, judicial review can be seen as consistent with—indeed, necessary to—maintaining limits on majority rule in order to protect the fundamental rights and values that the Constitution guarantees.

The critics of judicial review can also be answered on their own democratic terms. For example, Robert Dahl argued that lawmaking majorities have generally had their way; the Court has rarely been successful in blocking the will of such a majority on an important policy issue.[36] Additionally, the Court has most often exercised its power to declare both state and national policies unconstitutional when the dominant forces in the elected branches are unable or unwilling to settle some dispute. Elected officials, under such circumstances, "encourage or tacitly support judicial policymaking both as a means of avoiding political responsibility for making tough decisions and as a means of pursuing controversial policy goals that they cannot publicly advance through open legislative and electoral politics."[37] Concern about the countermajoritarian difficulty seems misplaced if the real controversy is generally not

---

[33] *United States v Eichman*, 496 US 310 (1990).

[34] *City of Boerne v Flores*, 521 US 507 (1997).

[35] 7 Wall. 506 (1869); but see *Ex Parte Yerger*, 8 Wall. 85 (1869) in which the Court held that it did have jurisdiction to hear a habeas corpus appeal.

[36] Robert Dahl, "Decision-Making in a Democracy: The Supreme Court as a National Policy-Maker." *Journal of Public Law* 6 (1957): 179–295. By lawmaking majority, Dahl meant a majority of those voting in the House and Senate plus the president.

[37] Mark A. Graber, "The Nonmajoritarian Difficulty: Legislative Deference to the Judiciary." *Studies in American Political Development* 7 (1993): 35–73, 36.

between the Court and the elected branches but between different members of the dominant national coalition or between lawmaking majorities of different institutions. Thus, one can argue that the Court promotes democracy rather than contravenes it insofar as the justices resolve conflicts when elected officials do not.

THE CONSTITUTION AND AMERICAN POLITICS

The Major Eras of American Constitutional Law

It is useful to begin to consider the connections between the Supreme Court and the rest of the American political system by organizing the history of the Supreme Court and the Constitution into five eras (see Table 2-2). The issues that have dominated the Court's agenda and the way the justices have dealt with those issues have varied with each era. It is also helpful to examine some of the individuals who have served on the Court and the goals of the presidents who appointed them.

TABLE 2-2 Major Eras of Constitutional Law

Years	Issues	Resolution
1803–1835	Judicial power	Judicial review
	Nature of the Union	
	Property rights	National supremacy
1836–1864	Nature of the Union	
	Property rights	Dual federalism
		Protection of slavery
1865–1936	Economic rights	Dual federalism
	Governmental intervention in the economy	Substantive due process
1937–1968	Individual rights and equality	Incorporation of the Bill of Rights
		Equal protection clause for racial equality
		Voting rights
1969–2003	More individual rights and equality	No resolution—Fragmentation
	Limits on some precedents of the Warren Court	Decreased role for the judiciary
	More protection for property rights	
	Limits on powers of federal government vis à vis the states	

1803–1835

Once John Marshall had asserted the power of judicial review in *Marbury v Madison*, he worked to fortify the power of the judiciary. During Marshall's tenure as Chief Justice, the Court not only secured its position as a coequal branch of the national government, but also expanded the powers of the national government in relation to the states. In 1816, the Court asserted its power to review decisions of state courts.[38] Then in 1819 in *McCulloch v Maryland*, Marshall declared that the "necessary and proper clause" grants Congress implied powers in addition to those expressly listed in Article I, Section 8.[39] Holding that Congress had the power to incorporate a bank and that a state could not tax that bank, Marshall took the opportunity to promote the doctrine of national supremacy by declaring that the Constitution emanated from the people—it was an agreement between the people—rather than a contract between the states. Thus, the powers of the national government were not limited to those expressly delegated to it by the Constitution. In 1824, interpreting the commerce clause for the first time in *Gibbons v Ogden*, the justices construed the power to regulate commerce *among* the states as a broad grant of authority. Commerce, the Court held, included all commercial activity, not just buying and selling. Moreover, commerce among the states did not stop at a state boundary but included commerce within states so long as it was not completely internal to a state with no effect on other states.[40] Additionally, the Marshall Court used the contract clause to prohibit the states from abridging property rights.[41]

1836–1864

After Marshall's death, President Andrew Jackson chose Roger Brooke Taney to be Chief Justice. Under Taney, the Court continued to fortify judicial power and to work out the relationship between the national government and the states. Although the Taney Court did not reverse the major decisions of the Marshall Court, it nevertheless moved away from the doctrine of national supremacy toward **dual federalism**, which holds that the national and state governments are equal and each is supreme within its own sphere. In the midst of mounting sectional conflict in the 1850s, the justices made concessions to the states, holding, for example, in *Cooley v Board of Wardens* that states may not regulate commerce when the subjects are national. But when the subject is local in character and appropriate for diverse plans of regulation, the state may regulate until Congress chooses to take over the subject.[42] In 1857 in *Dred Scott v Sandford*, the Court entered the controversy over slavery, taking the side of the slaveholders when it ruled that Congress could not prohibit slavery in the territories and that the Constitution prohibited black people from becoming citizens.[43]

---

[38]*Martin v Hunter's Lessee*, 1 Wheat. 304 (1816).
[39]*McCulloch v Maryland*, 4 Wheat. 316 (1819).
[40]*Gibbons v Ogden*, 9 Wheat. 1 (1824).
[41]*Dartmouth College v Woodward*, 4 Wheat. 518 (1819).
[42]*Cooley v Board of Wardens*, 12 How. 229 (1852).
[43]*Dred Scott v Sandford*, 19 How. 393 (1857).

1865–1936

The Civil War resolved the issue of federalism in favor of national supremacy. The Court, however, interpreted the Civil War amendments narrowly, holding, for example, that the Fourteenth Amendment had not changed the distribution of power between the federal government and the states[44] and that it did not give Congress the power to prohibit racial discrimination in public accommodations.[45] In 1896, the justices held that the Fourteenth Amendment did not prohibit official segregation so long as facilities were available for both races—the "separate but equal" doctrine.[46]

After the Civil War, the issues with which the Court was concerned revolved around expanding capitalism and the relationship between business and government. The justices began to focus on protecting the business community against government. Thus, at the same time the Court was ruling that the Civil War amendments did virtually nothing to protect former slaves from racial discrimination, the justices held that corporations were persons within the meaning of Fourteenth Amendment.[47]

At the turn of the twentieth century, the Court adopted the doctrine of **substantive due process** according to which the liberty protected by the due process clause of the Fourteenth Amendment included liberty of contract. Thus, the due process clause became a vehicle for prohibiting the states from regulating business—for example, with maximum hours, minimum wages, regulation of prices—in any way that might be construed as an interference with the right to contract.[48] The justices also protected business from government regulation by reviving the doctrine of dual federalism, finding limits on the power of Congress under the commerce clause. In 1895 in *United States v E.C. Knight,* the Court held that Congress could not regulate manufacturing—it could regulate only interstate commerce itself and that which directly affects interstate commerce.[49] The justices also invalidated Congress's effort to stop employers from using child labor. The Federal Child Labor Act, enacted in 1916, prohibited the shipment of factory products of child labor in interstate commerce. When the law was challenged, the Court held that Congress could only exclude goods from traveling in interstate commerce if their transportation had "harmful results." Otherwise, Congress had no authority to regulate a "purely local matter."[50] The justices also invalidated a 10 percent tax on the profits of industries that employed children, holding that Congress could not use its power to tax for regulatory purposes.[51]

The Court's determination to defend the doctrine of laissez faire against the encroachment of the growing regulatory state by invalidating both state and federal legislation did not end until 1937. Indeed, the Court invalidated many

---

[44]*Slaughterhouse Cases*, 16 Wall. 36 (1873).
[45]*Civil Rights Cases*, 100 US 3 (1883).
[46]*Plessy v Ferguson*, 163 US 537 (1896).
[47]*Santa Clara County v Southern Pacific R.R.*, 118 US 394 (1886).
[48]For example, *Lochner v New York*, 198 US 45 (1905). Substantive due process is explained further in Chapter 10.
[49]*United States v E.C. Knight*, 156 US 1 (1895).
[50]*Hammer v Dagenhart*, 247 US 251 (1918).
[51]*Bailey v Drexel Furniture Co.*, 259 US 20 (1922).

of the early New Deal programs that President Franklin Delano Roosevelt initiated to ease the financial problems of the Depression in the early 1930s. The Court justified its decisions on the grounds that Congress was attempting to regulate intrastate commerce or that it had delegated authority to the president to make policy without sufficient standards.[52] In striking down legislation, the justices were usually divided five to four. George Sutherland, James McReynolds, Pierce Butler, and Willis Van Devanter—the "Four Horsemen"—voted to invalidate, whereas Harlan F. Stone, Benjamin Cardozo, and Louis Brandeis voted to uphold the economic programs. Chief Justice Charles Evans Hughes and Owen Roberts were the "swing votes" with Roberts typically casting the crucial fifth vote to invalidate the New Deal legislation.

1937–1968

President Roosevelt was reelected to a second term in 1936 by a large margin, and the Democrats captured about 80 percent of the seats in Congress. In February 1937, Roosevelt announced his plan to reorganize the federal judiciary—a plan that included a proposal to create one new position on the Supreme Court for every justice who had reached the age of seventy. The maximum number of new seats was to be six, bringing the potential number of justices to fifteen. Six justices were older than seventy when Roosevelt announced his plan. Thus, if enacted, the plan would allow him to appoint six justices, who with the support of just two additional members of the Court, would provide a majority to uphold New Deal programs. Despite Roosevelt's popularity, what was obviously a plan to pack the Court with New Deal supporters was not received favorably. Although the American people clearly wanted the New Deal, they did not appreciate Roosevelt's transparently result-oriented attempt to tamper with the structure of the judiciary. While Congress was deliberating the "court packing plan," Justice Roberts voted to uphold a law that did not differ substantially from one he had voted to strike down only nine months before.[53] Just two weeks later, the Court again by a vote of five to four upheld the National Labor Relations Act—a major piece of New Deal legislation.[54] Although Roberts's crucial vote was termed the "switch in time that saved nine," he had actually shifted his vote two months before Roosevelt announced his plan to enlarge the Court. The Court's decision was not announced until later, however. By 1943, Roosevelt had appointed a total of nine justices to the Court—all were supporters of the New Deal.[55]

The judicial revolution of 1937 marked the beginning of a new constitutional era. The Court repudiated its earlier restrictive readings of Congress's power to regulate commerce and its taxing power in favor of generous interpretations of

---

[52]For example, *Schecter Poultry Corp. v United States*, 295 US 495 (1935); *Carter v Carter Coal Company*, 298 US 238 (1936).

[53]The Court invalidated the New York minimum wage law that applied to women's wages in *Morehead v New York ex rel. Tipaldo*, 298 US 587 (1936). It upheld a Washington state minimum wage law in *West Coast Hotel v Parrish*, 300 US 379 (1937).

[54]*National Labor Relations Board v Jones & Laughlin Steel Corporation*, 301 US 1 (1937).

[55]The nine appointments included the elevation of Stone to Chief Justice when Chief Justice Hughes retired and Roosevelt's replacement of one of his appointees—James Byrnes—with another—Wiley Rutledge.

federal power. Congress could regulate virtually any commercial activity and could tax and spend for the general welfare even if the tax controlled local affairs.[56] The justices also stopped using the due process clause of the Fourteenth Amendment as a substantive limit on economic legislation. In general, the Court turned away from its previous focus on economic rights and turned its attention to legislation that infringed on individual rights. The Court began to examine restrictions on speech more carefully, to pay more attention to state criminal procedures, and to question racial segregation.[57] In 1938, in *United States v Carolene Products* Justice Stone announced that the Court would not hold "regulatory legislation affecting ordinary commercial transactions" unconstitutional unless it was entirely lacking "some rational basis within the knowledge and experience of the legislators." He indicated the Court's new interest in individual rights in Footnote Four of his opinion where he wrote that the "presumption of constitutionality" would not apply in the following situations: (1) Where legislation that is challenged is within a specific prohibition of the Constitution, such as those in the Bill of Rights; (2) where legislation restricts "those political processes which can ordinarily be expected to bring about repeal of undesirable legislation"; (3) where legislation is based on "prejudice against discrete and insular minorities."[58] Economic rights would not disappear from the Court's agenda but instead would take new forms.[59] Issues revolving around individual rights and equality, however, would dominate the Court for the rest of the century.

During the tenure of Chief Justice Earl Warren (1953–1969), the Court continued the judicial revolution of 1937, further expanding the powers of the federal government in relation to the states in a series of controversial decisions protecting the rights of individuals. In 1954, the justices overruled the "separate but equal" doctrine and held that officially segregated schools violated the equal protection clause of the Fourteenth Amendment.[60] During the 1960s, the Court revolutionized the criminal justice system by holding that nearly all the provisions in the Bill of Rights pertaining to the rights of the criminally accused apply to the states as well as the federal government by way of the due process clause of the Fourteenth Amendment.[61] The Warren Court also relied on the Fourteenth Amendment to give force to the principle of equal representation in a series of decisions holding that state legislatures' failure to redraw their legislative districts to reflect twentieth-century population shifts from rural areas and small towns to urban centers violated the equal protection clause.[62] The

---

[56]Robert G. McCloskey, *The American Supreme Court*, 2d ed. Revised by Sanford Levinson (Chicago, IL: University of Chicago Press, 1994, orig. 1960).

[57]See *Herndon v Lowry*, 301 US 242 (1937) (speech); *Palko v Connecticut*, 302 US 319 (1937) (criminal procedure); *Missouri ex. rel. Gaines v Canada*, 305 US 237 (1938) (segregation).

[58]*United States v Carolene Products*, 304 US 144 (1938), footnote 4.

[59]See Martin Shapiro, "The Supreme Court's 'Return' to Economic Regulation," in *Studies in American Political Development*, Karen Oren and Stephen Skowronek, eds. (New Haven, CT: Yale University Press, 1986), 91–141.

[60]*Brown v Board of Education*, 347 US 483 (1954).

[61]For example, *Mapp v Ohio*, 367 US 643 (1961); *Gideon v Wainwright*, 372 US 355 (1963).

[62]For example, *Reynolds v Sims*, 377 US 533 (1964). The Court also held that malapportioned congressional districts violated Article I, Section 2, of the Constitution in *Wesberry v Sanders*, 376 US 1 (1964). The Court also upheld Congress's broad authority to prevent racial discrimination in voting under the enforcement provision of the Fifteenth Amendment. For example, *South Carolina v Katzenbach*, 383 US 301 (1966).

Warren Court expanded freedom of expression and buttressed the wall of separation between church and state. Finally, the Warren Court handed down a series of decisions substantially expanding access to the federal courts for a wider range of litigants and thereby made it possible for the Court to address a broader range of issues than it had previously.[63]

When the seventy-seven-year-old Chief Justice announced his intention to retire in June 1968, he believed that he was allowing sufficient time for President Lyndon Johnson to choose his successor.[64] Johnson's attempt to elevate Associate Justice Abe Fortas to Chief Justice failed, however. Initially some Republicans argued that a lame-duck president should not select the Chief Justice.[65]

Opposition to Fortas's appointment grew when it became known that the Justice had advised the president extensively on major policy matters—including Vietnam—while serving on the Court. Finally, a report surfaced that Fortas had accepted a lecture fee of $15,000 from a fund that his law partner had obtained from five prominent businessmen. Although the Judiciary Committee approved Fortas's appointment, southern Democrats joined Republicans to filibuster on the floor of the Senate. It soon became clear that there were not enough votes to invoke cloture, and Fortas asked the president to withdraw his nomination.

Warren agreed with President-elect Richard Nixon that he would remain on the Court through its next term. In May 1969, the Nixon Justice Department produced documentation that Fortas had agreed to accept a $20,000-a-year lifetime consulting fee from financier Louis Wolfson, who was then under indictment for securities fraud.[66] Fortas then resigned from the Court.

1969–2003

The upshot of the battle over Fortas's nomination and his subsequent resignation was that President Nixon had two positions to fill during his first year in office. During his campaign for the presidency, he had attacked the Warren Court, blaming its criminal justice decisions for rising crime rates. He promised that if he had the opportunity, he would appoint "strict constructionists" who would "interpret the constitution strictly and fairly and objectively," unlike some "who have gone too far in assuming unto themselves a mandate which is not there, and that is, to put their social and economic ideas into their decisions."[67] Nixon chose Warren Burger and Harry Blackmun to replace Earl

---

[63]For example, *Baker v Carr*, 369 US 186 (1962); *Flast v Cohen*, 392 US 83 (1968).
[64]Bruce Allen Murphy, *Fortas: The Rise and Ruin of a Supreme Court Justice* (New York: William Morrow, 1988), 268–269. Murphy notes that with Robert Kennedy's assassination, Warren believed that his longtime political enemy Richard Nixon had an inside track in the election. Warren considered it unacceptable for Nixon to appoint any members of the Supreme Court.
[65]Lyndon Johnson announced on March 31, 1968, that he would not seek reelection.
[66]*Life* magazine initially published a story revealing that Fortas had accepted a $20,000 fee from Wolfson only once. Attorney General John Mitchell subsequently met privately with Earl Warren and provided documents subpoenaed from Wolfson's foundation revealing the contract for the yearly fee for the rest of Fortas's life. Additionally, the contract provided that on Fortas's death the yearly fee would be paid to his wife. *Ibid.*, 562–563. Ed Cray, *Chief Justice: A Biography of Earl Warren* (New York: Simon and Schuster, 1997), 509.
[67]As quoted in James F. Simon, *In His Own Image: The Supreme Court in Richard Nixon's America* (New York: David McKay, 1973), 8.

Warren and Abe Fortas. In 1972, Lewis Powell and William H. Rehnquist assumed the seats vacated by the retirements of Hugo Black and John Marshall Harlan. The predictions of journalists and scholars that the Burger Court would effect a constitutional counterrevolution failed to materialize even after Nixon's successor, Gerald Ford, replaced staunch defender of individual rights William O. Douglas with John Paul Stevens in 1975.

There was some indication of a shift in power away from the federal government back to the states.[68] The Burger Court backtracked somewhat on the rights of criminal defendants.[69] Still, there were no outright reversals of major doctrines. In the area of the rights of the criminally accused, for example, the *Miranda* rule[70] established by the Warren Court that a suspect in police custody must be advised of his or her rights remained in effect although the Burger Court narrowed the rule and carved out some exceptions to it.[71] In 1972, a five-member majority held that the procedures then governing the death penalty violated the Eighth Amendment.[72] Although the justices subsequently allowed the states to reinstate capital punishment with procedural safeguards to prevent it from being imposed arbitrarily, they ruled that the death penalty for any crime other than murder was unconstitutional.[73] In the area of racial equality, the Burger Court approved busing as a tool for remedying the effects of state-sanctioned segregation in the public schools.[74] Additionally, during the Burger years the Court began to construe the equal protection clause as a prohibition on sex discrimination.[75] In 1973, in *Roe v Wade* the Court held that the constitutional right to privacy includes a woman's decision to terminate a pregnancy.[76]

Ronald Reagan had an ambitious agenda for transforming the Court into a body that would reverse all the doctrines of the Warren and Burger Courts but not interfere with the Administration's conservative policies. He was determined to fill vacancies with justices who were committed to a more state-centered federalism and who would vote to overrule *Roe v Wade*, thereby allowing the states to prohibit abortion. Additionally, Reagan wanted justices who would overrule the one-person-one-vote standard of the reapportionment decisions, as well as decisions prohibiting prayer in public schools, approving affirmative action, allowing busing to achieve a racial balance in the public schools, limiting police interrogation of suspects, and prohibiting the use of illegally seized evidence in criminal proceedings. Reagan wanted justices who would also relax prohibitions on discrimination against women, reduce access to the federal courts, allow more public funding for religious schools, and be less sympathetic

---

[68]For example, *National League of Cities v Usery*, 426 US 833 (1976) (protection for the states in the federal system).

[69]For example, *United States v Leon*, 468 US 897 (1984) (good faith exception to the exclusionary rule).

[70]*Miranda v Arizona*, 384 US 436 (1966).

[71]The Court created a "public safety" exception to *Miranda*, for example, in *New York v Quarles*, 467 US 649 (1984). Reasonable people disagree on the impact of the Burger Court on the rights of the accused. Our examination of specific cases in Chapter 4 provides information on which readers may rely to draw their own conclusions.

[72]*Furman v Georgia*, 408 US 238 (1972).

[73]*Coker v Georgia*, 433 US 583 (1977).

[74]*Swann v Charlotte-Mecklenburg Board of Education*, 402 US 1 (1971).

[75]See, for example, *Frontiero v Richardson*, 411 US 677 (1973) and *Craig v Boren*, 429 US 190 (1976).

[76]*Roe v Wade*, 410 US 113 (1973).

to free speech and the press.[77] Reagan's first opportunity to shape the Court came in 1981 with the retirement of Potter Stewart. He chose Sandra Day O'Connor whose views regarding federalism and abortion appeared to be consistent with his own.

When Chief Justice Burger announced his retirement in the spring of 1986 President Ronald Reagan elevated William H. Rehnquist, the Burger Court's most conservative member, to the position of Chief Justice and filled Rehnquist's seat with Antonin Scalia, a conservative member of the Court of Appeals for the District of Columbia. At that point, the constitutional counterrevolution that Reagan sought appeared likely and the prospects increased with the retirement of Lewis Powell in 1987. To replace Powell, the president chose Robert Bork, a judge on the Court of Appeals for the District of Columbia whose views made him an ideal Reagan appointee. But after an acrimonious battle, the Democratic Senate voted against his confirmation. Reagan's second nomination for Powell's position—Douglas H. Ginsburg—failed as well. Ginsburg's nomination was withdrawn after he admitted smoking marijuana when he was a Harvard law professor in the 1970s. The Senate confirmed the president's third choice, Anthony Kennedy. The reversal of all the major Warren Court decisions and many of those of the Burger Court seemed inevitable as Byron White was expected to provide the decisive fifth vote for a Reagan-Rehnquist majority.

Despite the predictions, the major precedents of the Warren and Burger Courts continued to remain in effect even after President George Bush replaced the two most committed liberals on the Court—William J. Brennan and Thurgood Marshall—with David Souter and Clarence Thomas. In 1992, a majority of the justices reaffirmed the principle that a woman has a constitutionally protected right to choose to have an abortion.[78] President Bill Clinton's two appointees, Ruth Bader Ginsburg and Stephen G. Breyer, helped to make the six-member majority to invalidate Colorado's antigay amendment in 1996,[79] and in 2000 Justice Breyer wrote for a five-member majority to strike down Nebraska's ban on a particular abortion procedure known as dilation and extraction.[80] On the other hand, the Rehnquist Court has disapproved affirmative action and has revived the takings clause of the Fifth Amendment to strike down state regulations that allegedly infringe on the rights of property owners. Additionally, the justices have adopted an "accommodationist" view of the First Amendment's establishment clause in contrast to the Warren and Burger Courts' more separationist approach, allowing considerably more state involvement in religion. In 2002, for example, the justices, by a vote of five to four, upheld a school voucher plan that allowed the use of public funds for religious school tuition.[81]

The Reagan and Bush appointees have remained committed to a state-centered federalism although their position has not consistently prevailed. Indeed, the

---

[77]Herman Schwartz, *Packing the Courts: The Conservative Campaign to Rewrite the Constitution* (New York: Charlers Scribner's Sons, 1988), 6.
[78]*Planned Parenthood of Southeastern Pennsylvania v Casey*, 505 US 833 (1992).
[79]*Romer v Evans* 516 US 620 (1996).
[80]*Stenberg v Carhart*, ____ US ____ (2000).
[81]*Zelmans v Simmons-Harris*, ____ US ____ (2002).

Burger and Rehnquist Courts revived the debate that last raged in the 1930s concerning the distribution of power between the national government and the states. Rehnquist revived the Tenth Amendment, arguing that the Court must protect the ability of the states to function within the federal system and that all the powers not delegated to Congress are reserved to the states.[82] The Reagan and Bush justices have, moreover, resurrected the controversy that John Marshall resolved in 1819.[83] In answer to the question of whether the Constitution was an agreement among the people or a compact among the states, Marshall proclaimed that the people and not the states were the parties to the Constitution. Therefore, the states did not have the authority to limit the powers of the national government. Justice Thomas indicated the extent to which the Reagan and Bush justices disagree with Marshall's conception of federalism when he contended, "The ultimate source of the Constitution's authority is the consent of the people of each individual State, not the consent of the undifferentiated people of the nation as a whole."[84] Several recent decisions illustrate the Rehnquist Court's proclivity to limit federal power. In 1995, when the Court invalidated a federal law forbidding the possession of firearms in and around schools by a vote of five to four, it held for the first time in sixty years that Congress had exceeded its authority to regulate interstate commerce.[85] Two years later the same five-member majority held that a federal provision requiring local law enforcement officers to conduct background checks on proposed handgun purchasers offended the principle of state sovereignty by compelling state officers to execute federal laws.[86] The Court has continued the trend of shifting power away from the national government back to the states, holding for example in 2000 that the federal statute providing a civil remedy for victims of gender-motivated crimes of violence was beyond Congress's authority.[87]

Although the Court has not decided uniformly against the exercise of federal power in all its major cases involving the nation-state relationship, the fact that the justices have engaged in a lengthy debate on the nature of the federal system[88] suggests that the Court at the beginning of the twenty-first century may be embarking on a new era in which the major emphasis will be placed on moving to a more state-centered federalism akin to the dual federalism of the late nineteenth and early twentieth centuries.

During the Burger and Rehnquist years, the Court's increasing fragmentation was evidenced by the lower number of opinions for the majority and the higher number of plurality opinions and concurring and dissenting opinions.[89] These de-

---

[82]*National League of Cities v Usery*, 426 US 833 (1976); but see, *Garcia v San Antonio Metropolitan Transit Authority*, 469 US 528 (1985).
[83]*McCulloch v Maryland*, 4 Wheat. 316 (1819).
[84]*U.S. Term Limits v Thornton*, 514 U.S. 779 (1995). Dissenting opinion in which Rehnquist, O'Connor, and Scalia joined.
[85]*United States v Lopez*, 514 US 544 (1995).
[86]*Printz v United States*, 521 US 98 (1997).
[87]*United States v Morrison*, 529 US 598 (2000).
[88]See, for example, *U.S. Term Limits v Thornton*, 514 US 779 (1995).
[89]David M. O'Brien, "Institutional Norms and Supreme Court Opinions: On Reconsidering the Rise of Individual Opinions," in Cornell W. Clayton and Howard Gillman, eds. *Supreme Court Decision Making: New Institutionalist Approaches* (Chicago, IL: University of Chicago Press, 1999), 91–113, 94, 97, 99. O'Brien documents the increase in the total number of opinions as well as a rise in the proportion of dissenting opinions on the Burger and Rehnquist Courts.

velopments were part of a trend that began many years earlier and are not attributable solely to the leadership skills—or lack thereof—of individual chief justices but rather a result of changing institutional norms that began with the Roosevelt Court. Once it was important for the justices to reach agreement on a majority opinion—it lent legitimacy to a controversial decision and contributed to the prestige of the Court. As the norm of consensus declined, much less importance was placed on reaching agreement on a majority opinion.[90] By the 1990s, it appeared that the Chief Justice was doing little to build consensus on the Court. Indeed, a norm of individual expression—"individual opinions and a mere tally of votes"—replaced the norm of consensus.[91] One result is that the Court's decisions, "appear more fragmented, uncertain, less stable, and less predictable."[92]

Under Chief Justice Rehnquist, the Court has significantly reduced the number of cases that it hears each year. The Burger Court heard from 150 to 180 cases each year whereas the Rehnquist Court has been deciding fewer than 100 even though the number of requests to review decisions of lower federal and state courts—petitions for certiorari—has reached more than 8,000 annually.[93] In the 1998 term, the Court decided only 75 cases, less than half of the 175 decided in the 1984 term and the lowest number since the 1953 term. The sharp decline in the number of cases the Court accepts for review is frequently explained as an indication of Rehnquist's success in attempting to reduce the role of the Court in the resolution of constitutional questions and to let conservative decisions of the lower federal and state courts stand.[94]

The trends in constitutional law that we have summarized here suggest several noteworthy aspects of the history of the Supreme Court. First, the Court has invariably built upon the decisions of the previous era. Although it may reverse some earlier decisions and modify others, the norm of *stare decisis*—literally, let the decision stand—has prevailed over the years. Stare decisis is the legal principle according to which the Court decides a case by searching for a similar case decided previously and applies the rule—the precedent—established in that case. The process of matching previous cases to the present case leaves ample room for different conclusions about which of the previous cases provides the best match for the one currently before the Court. Further, justices often disagree about the meaning or reach of the precedent. Still, the tradition of following precedent has a stabilizing effect on the Court. The justices do not overrule precedent unless they have a substantial justification for doing so. The longer a precedent remains in force the more difficult it is for the Court to overrule it, in part because it has become part of the law that governs people's lives.

Second, although legal factors such as stare decisis and the meaning of constitutional provisions are important elements of constitutional decision making, extra-legal elements including the ideological views of the justices are also important.

---

[90]*Ibid.*

[91]*Ibid.*, 111.

[92]*Ibid.*

[93]*Ibid.*

[94]Sue Davis, "The Chief Justice and Judicial Decision Making: The Institutional Basis for Leadership on the Supreme Court," in Cornell W. Clayton and Howard Gillman, eds. *Supreme Court Decision Making: New Institutionalist Approaches* (Chicago, IL: University of Chicago Press, 1999), 135–154, 146.

TABLE 2-3   Appointments to the Supreme Court—Presidents Nixon through Clinton

Richard Nixon (1969–1974)
  Warren Burger (1969–1986)
  Harry Blackmun (1970–1994)
  William H. Rehnquist (1972–1986 Associate Justice)
  Lewis Powell (1972–1987)
Gerald Ford (1974–1977)
  John Paul Stevens (1975–)
Jimmy Carter (1977–1981)
  None
Ronald Reagan (1981–1989)
  Sandra Day O'Connor (1981–)
  William H. Rehnquist (Chief Justice, 1986–)
  Antonin Scalia (1986–)
  Anthony Kennedy (1988–)
George Bush (1989–1993)
  David Souter (1990–)
  Clarence Thomas (1991–)
William Jefferson Clinton (1993–2000)
  Ruth Bader Ginsburg (1993–)
  Stephen G. Breyer (1994–)

Third, the ways in which the dominant issues for the Court have changed over the years and the different ways that the justices have approached constitutional questions involve more than either legal principles or justices' ideologies. The development of constitutional law has invariably been intertwined with broader developments in American politics and the political process.

We turn to the interactive relationship between the Supreme Court and the American political system in the next section.

Electoral Politics and the Supreme Court: Critical Realignments and Dealignment

The political parties and voter preferences have changed during the course of America's history in a way that is usefully explained with reference to successive party systems and realigning—or critical—elections. The term *party system* refers to the division of the electorate into two political groups on the basis of attitudes and beliefs about a set of public issues. A **realignment** is a change in the basic party attachments of the voters that results in a new structure of party conflict and thus

TABLE 2-4   Voting Alignments on the Supreme Court

The Hughes Court, 1931–1935 Terms

Liberals	Center	Conservatives
Benjamin Cardozo	Charles Evans Hughes	Willis Van Devanter
Louis Brandeis	Owen Roberts	George Sutherland
Harlan F. Stone		James McReynolds
		Pierce Butler

The Stone Court, 1944 Term

Liberals	Center	Conservatives
William O. Douglas	Stanley Reed	Harlan F. Stone
Hugo Black	Robert Jackson	Felix Frankfurter
John Rutledge		Owen Roberts
Francis Murphy		

The Warren Court, 1958–1962 Terms

Liberals	Moderates	Conservatives
Hugo Black	Potter Stewart	John Marshall Harlan
Earl Warren		Felix Frankfurter
William J. Brennan		Charles Whittaker
William O. Douglas		Tom Clark

The Burger Court, 1981–1986 Terms

Liberals	Conservatives
Thurgood Marshall	William H. Rehnquist
William J. Brennan	Warren Burger
John Paul Stevens	Sandra Day O'Connor
Harry Blackmun	Lewis Powell
	Byron White

The Rehnquist Court, 1996 Term

Liberals	Moderates	Conservatives
John Paul Stevens	Sandra Day O'Connor	Antonin Scalia
Ruth Bader Ginsburg	Anthony Kennedy	William H. Rehnquist
Stephen G. Breyer	David Souter	Clarence Thomas

Note: The term *liberal* signifies a voting pattern that is in favor of the individual against government in civil liberties cases after 1936. Before 1936, the group of justices who voted to uphold New Deal legislation and other economic regulations are designated as liberal.

in a new party system. The process of realignment begins when a particularly important and divisive—or critical—issue disturbs the prevailing line of partisan cleavage between the parties. The issue is not new but becomes critical under the pressure of triggering events that cause it to become a major concern for a large number of voters. The issue cuts across the old line dividing the parties, dividing the electorate along a new line.

The issue becomes so important that it overrides all the considerations that form the basis of a significant number of voters' attachment to the existing parties and they form two hostile blocs within each party. If a bloc of voters who have not been polarized can gain control and resolve the issue, a realignment may be averted. But if the issue remains unresolved and public concern continues to grow, the polar forces will increase and three groups will fight for control—the two polar blocs and the centrists. Once one of the polar groups gains control of its party it forces the party to take a polar position on the issue. Alternatively, one or more minor third parties may emerge to take the polar position on one or both sides. In either case, the voters who have made up the polar blocs identify with the parties accordingly. A large number of voters shift their party allegiance, the old rationale for the division of voters between the parties is replaced by a new one, and a new party system emerges around the crosscutting issue. One or both parties are changed dramatically.

As voters shift their allegiance from one party to the other, the victorious party gains the presidency and a majority in Congress and maintains control for a period of years.[95]

There have been five realigning elections in American history. In the first, the Republicans emerged victorious over the incumbent Federalists in 1800.[96]

The Republicans maintained control of the government in succeeding elections, and the Federalists never recovered as an organized political force. The first party system had faded by 1820 when James Monroe ran for reelection as a Democratic-Republican without an opposing candidate from the Federalist Party. In the election of 1824 no candidate received a majority of electoral votes and the House of Representatives chose the president, with the delegation from each state casting one vote. The House chose John Quincy Adams even though Andrew Jackson had received a plurality of electoral and popular votes. The House Speaker, Henry Clay, presided over the polling of the state delegations, and Adams subsequently chose him as secretary of state. The second realigning election—Jackson's victory over Adams—followed in 1828. Jackson's supporters emphasized the "corrupt bargain" of 1825 that had put Adams in the White House. Jackson and his supporters called themselves Democrats, whereas Adams's party became known as the National Republicans. Jackson's successful bid for reelection in 1832 resulted in the demise of the National Republicans and the rise of the Whig Party, which consisted of opponents of Jack-

---

[95]James L. Sundquist, *Dynamics of the Party System: Alignment and Realignment of Political Parties in the United States* (Washington, DC: Brookings Institution, 1973), 5–38. See also, Walter Dean Burnham, *Critical Elections and the Mainsprings of American Politics* (New York: W.W. Norton. 1970).
[96]The election of 1800 is not considered to mark the beginning of a new party system because the parties were in such an early stage of development. Some scholars do not even consider 1800 a realigning election.

son's economic policies, particularly his war on the Bank of the United States.[97] For the next twenty-five years Democrats were victorious in presidential elections with the exceptions of 1840 and 1848. The Whigs controlled both houses of Congress only once.

The controversy over slavery was the crosscutting issue that resulted in the birth of the Republican Party in 1854, the disintegration of the Whigs, and the third realignment with the election of Republican candidate Abraham Lincoln in 1860. The Republicans took the position that Congress had the authority and the duty to prohibit slavery in the territories whereas the Democrats pledged to abide by the laws protecting slavery. After the Civil War, the third party system gradually became obsolete with the changes brought by urbanization and industrialization in the late nineteenth century. By the 1870s, the Republicans had abandoned Reconstruction, leaving the fate of the former slaves to southern Democrats. Republicans frequently prevailed in national elections by very narrow margins, and on substantive issues the parties took similar positions. Indeed, "for twenty years, the contests between Democrats and Republicans had been little more than sham battles that decided no consequential issues (except the tariff) but ordained mainly who would gain and allocate the spoils of office."[98]

Just as neither party would address the issue of slavery before 1850, neither the Democrats nor the Republicans in the 1880s would respond to the demands of western farmers or the growing number of urban workers. A new party—the People's Party—also known as the Populists, elected governors, members of Congress, and state legislators in the Midwest and the South in 1890. The Populists' platform of 1892—the year of the party's first national convention—spoke primarily to the needs of farmers. The platform included currency expansion through free coinage of silver, a graduated income tax, and government ownership of railroads and telegraph lines. The Populists also tried to appeal to a broader constituency by including the direct election of United States senators and other democratic reforms. Additionally, calls for a shorter working day and for immigration restriction represented attempts to address the concerns of urban workers.

Currency became the dominant—and crosscutting—issue around which the parties distinguished themselves in the election of 1896. The free coinage of silver would increase the amount of circulating money and thereby benefit farmers who were economically strapped by low prices resulting from tight control of the currency. The Democrats adopted the free silver position and absorbed the Populists. Both the Democrats and the Populists nominated William Jennings Bryan for president, and the Republicans nominated William McKinley and held fast to their hard-money policies, which kept the dollar's worth linked to the gold standard. The Republicans won the presidency and both houses of Congress in what was to be the beginning of a period of Republican dominance that lasted until the late 1920s.

---

[97]Donald Grier Stephenson, Jr., *Campaigns and the Court: The U.S. Supreme Court in Presidential Elections* (New York: Columbia University Press, 1999), 56.
[98]Sundquist, 140.

If the Populists had not been absorbed by the Democrats and had managed to capture a substantial number of workers, they might have replaced the Democrats and prevailed over the Republicans. The fourth party system would then have been one that consisted of an alliance between western farmers and urban workers and immigrants against the Republican Party of eastern business interests. As it was, the Democrats lost voters in the Northeast and Midwest to the Republicans. Urban workers found the Republicans—who supported a tariff to protect American industry and jobs from foreign competition—preferable to the Democrats for economic reasons. Thus, urban workers helped the Republicans carry the industrial Northeast and Midwest. Although most of the third party system was one in which the parties were closely balanced, a Republican majority marked the fourth party system.

The fifth and final realignment was the product of the Great Depression, which began with the crash of the stock market in October 1929. The country and the parties moved to opposing poles over the issue of governmental intervention in the economy. President Herbert Hoover placed the Republican Party squarely on the side of nonintervention, insisting in 1930:

> Economic depression cannot be cured by legislative action or executive pronouncement. Economic wounds must be healed by the action of the cells of the economic body—the producers and consumers themselves. Recovery can be expedited and its effects mitigated by cooperative action. . . .
> The best contribution of government lies in encouragement of this voluntary cooperation in the community.[99]

The Democratic Party did not move to the opposite pole immediately. Indeed, with unemployment at 24 percent in 1932 although the Democratic Party was pretty much an unknown quantity almost one-third of the Republican strength of 1928 was lost to Roosevelt or to minor-party candidates.[100] The Democrats captured not only the presidency but also both houses of Congress by large margins. In 1933 and 1934, the Democratic Party moved decisively to the opposite pole from the Republicans as Roosevelt proposed and Congress enacted legislation concerned with relief and recovery. The midterm elections of 1934 gave the Democrats a majority of 216 in the House and 44 in the Senate.[101]

As it moved into its second stage, the New Deal included policies that created permanent systems of income support, expanded government regulation, and strengthened government and supported organized labor to counteract the power of business. Thus, the National Labor Relations Act guaranteed collective bargaining in most large industries and the Social Security Act instituted a system of income maintenance for the disabled, the unemployed, and the elderly.

The Fair Labor Standards Act contained provisions for minimum wages and maximum hours. In the campaign of 1936, Republicans compared the New Deal to socialism and even to fascism, charging that its economic policies

---

[99]*The Memoirs of Herbert Hoover*, Vol. 3, The Great Depression, 1929–1941 (Macmillan, 1952), 429–430, as quoted in *ibid.*, 185.
[100]Sundquist, 195.
[101]Stephenson, 139.

TABLE 2-5   Party Systems

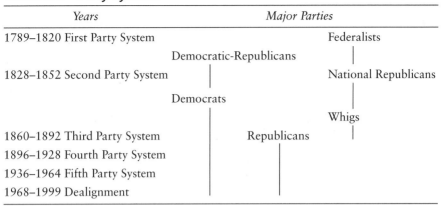

Years	Major Parties

1789–1820 First Party System — Federalists

Democratic-Republicans

1828–1852 Second Party System — National Republicans

Democrats

Whigs

1860–1892 Third Party System — Republicans

1896–1928 Fourth Party System

1936–1964 Fifth Party System

1968–1999 Dealignment

Source: Adapted from Donald Grier Stephenson, Jr., *Campaigns and the Court: The U.S. Supreme Court in Presidential Elections* (New York: Columbia University Press, 1999), 6.

threatened the foundations of the country's free economic system and political tradition. The voters, nevertheless, gave the Democrats their most stunning victory. Roosevelt received 60.8 percent of the popular vote, exceeding any percentage received by a presidential candidate in the history of American presidential politics. Democrats in the House of Representatives added twenty-one seats and in Senate they gained sixteen new seats.[102] The 1936 election marked the climax of the realignment and the beginning of the fifth party system, a period of Democratic dominance that persisted with few exceptions, until 1969 (see Table 2-5).

The connection between the Supreme Court and partisan change has invariably been reflected in the Court's pronouncements in cases involving cross-cutting issues during realigning periods. Several scholars have observed that at the time of a realignment, and for a short time after, the Court lags behind the new party system. That is, "the Court, by virtue of the life tenure of the justices, will be out of step with the political times" as the majority of the justices reflects the preferences of the old electoral coalition and thwarts the will of the new majority on major constitutional questions.[103] But as the administration has the opportunity to fill vacancies on the Court with individuals whose views are more congenial to its own policies, the Court's decisions grow more consistent with the preferences of the new lawmaking majority.[104] The majority that invalidated New Deal legislation after the realigning election 1936, for example, was a holdover from earlier days when the dominant forces in American politics were committed to a policy of laissez faire. As Roosevelt had the

---

[102]*Ibid.,* 140–141.

[103]Richard Funston, "The Supreme Court and Critical Elections." *American Political Science Review* 69 (1975): 795–811, 796.

[104]See, for example, *ibid.,* David Adamany, "Legitimacy, Realigning Elections, and the Supreme Court." *Wisconsin Law Review* 1973 (1973): 790–846.

TABLE 2-6   *Dred Scott v Sandford** Division on the Court over Critical (Realigning) Issue of Slavery

Constitutionality of Missouri Compromise: May Congress Prohibit Slavery in the Territories?

No	Yes
John A. Campbell, Democrat, Alabama (Pierce)**	Samuel Nelson, Democrat, New York (Tyler)
John Catron, Democrat, Tennessee (Jackson)	Benjamin Curtis, Whig, Massachusetts (Fillmore)
Peter V. Daniel, Democrat, Virginia (Van Buren)	John McLean, Democrat, then Republican, Ohio (Jackson)
Robert C. Grier, Democrat, Pennsylvania (Polk)	Roger B. Taney, Democrat, Maryland (Jackson)
James M. Wayne, Democrat, Georgia (Jackson)	

*19 How. 393 (1857).
**Appointing President.
Source: Adapted from William Lasser, "The Supreme Court in Periods of Critical Realignment," *Journal of Politics* 47 (1985): 1174–1187.

opportunity to replace retiring justices with his own choices, the Court resumed the role of legitimizing the policies of the dominant national political coalition.

The lines of division among the justices are not quite so simple, however. William Lasser pointed out that as the issues around which a realignment converges cut across the old line of party cleavage and split the two major parties into competing factions, there is no old dominant coalition position on the issue—both parties are divided. Without a position on which to unite, the justices can be expected to divide over the issue in a way that is unrelated to old partisan loyalties.[105] Thus, as Table 2-6 shows, the justices were divided six to three over the crosscutting issue of slavery in the *Dred Scott* case. The alignment of the justices was based on neither party affiliation nor appointing president.

Lasser argued that during realignment periods the Court has behaved in much the same way as the political parties. The justices split into two groups on the critical issue with the moderates voting to uphold Congress's power to act and a polar group taking the position that Congress is prohibited from acting. In the period preceding the realignment the majority takes the moderate position but subsequently moves to the polar position and strikes down one or more laws related to the critical issue as it did in *Dred Scott* when it invalidated the Missouri Compromise. By declaring the Missouri Compromise unconstitutional, the Court made it clear that any future federal legislation banning slav-

---

[105]William Lasser, "The Supreme Court in Periods of Critical Realignment." *Journal of Politics* 47 (1985): 1174–1187, 1177.

ery in the territories would be unconstitutional and thereby in effect, took a position condemning the Republican Party's platform that promised to ban slavery in all the federal territories. Similarly, in 1895 a majority of the Court invalidated the income tax, which was supported by a number of moderate Republicans and Democrats. Likewise, in 1935 and 1936, the Court struck down the early New Deal legislation that was supported by moderates of both parties and in so doing indicated that it would find more far-reaching New Deal legislation to be unconstitutional. Thus, the Court, in effect, declared the platforms of the progressive extremists and the moderate centrists unconstitutional, and endorsed the platform of the conservative extremists. In so doing, the "Court . . . acted as a catalyst for the polarization of the party system around the critical issue, and helped to set the agenda for the upcoming critical election."[106]

The Court's decisions in *Dred Scott*, the income tax case, and early anti–New Deal cases came about when one or more justices moved from the Court's center to its conservative pole. In each case, the capture of the Court by its polar wing occurred at a key point in the realignment period and had a major political impact. *Dred Scott* followed a presidential election in which the northern and southern wings of the Democratic Party had papered over their differences on the critical issue of slavery in the territories with "popular sovereignty." But then by declaring the southern position to be consistent with the Constitution, the Court made it nearly impossible for the Democratic Party to maintain its unity. The justices handed down their decision in the income tax case just as the free silver issue took hold of the Democratic Party and as conservatives were working to capture the Republican Party. The anti–New Deal decisions came at the same time that opposition to Roosevelt peaked and he was trying to decide whether to follow the suggestions of his moderate or more progressive advisers.

In each case, the Court legitimated the extremist conservative position and delegitimated the moderate position, thereby suggesting that compromise positions would be invalidated and making it easier for conservative extremists to capture one of the major parties and reject all attempts at compromise. After all, conservative extremists reasoned, the Supreme Court had confirmed their views, rendering those views not only politically desirable but also constitutionally required. In all three periods, the Court helped to shape the agenda for the next presidential election—the realigning elections of 1860, 1896, and 1936 (see Table 2-7).[107]

The historical regularity of realigning elections suggests that a sixth realignment should have occurred in the 1960s. Despite the prominence of issues that were potentially crosscutting—policies regarding the war in Vietnam and the persistence of racial inequality along with poverty—there was no realignment. Instead, the **dealignment** that began in the 1960s was evidenced by a rise in independent voting and ticket splitting as party identification declined. Divided government has replaced a dominant governing coalition in

---

[106]*Ibid.*, 1180–1181.
[107]*Ibid.*, 1182.

TABLE 2-7   Realigning Elections and the Supreme Court

Polarizing Decision	Realigning Election	Issue
Dred Scott v Sandford (1857)	1860	Slavery
Pollock v Farmers' Loan and Trust (1895)	1896	Currency
Schechter v United States (1935)	1936	Governmental Intervention in the Economy

Source: Adapted from William Lasser, "The Supreme Court in Periods of Critical Realignment." Journal of Politics 47 (1985): 1174–1187.

national politics, as the president's party has most often not had a majority in Congress.[108] Some scholars have noted the effects that dealignment has had on the Supreme Court whereas others have examined the ways in which the Court's decisions have promoted dealignment.[109] Cornell Clayton has pointed out, for example, that the Court is far more independent of the elected branches under conditions of divided government in part because while either Congress or the executive may oppose the Court it is unlikely that they will combine forces to do so. Additionally, dealignment has had a major impact on the selection process. With divided government, the president cannot rely on the Senate to confirm a Supreme Court nominee, particularly a controversial one. Moreover, the Court has formed alliances with interest groups in part as a result of the decline of the importance of political parties. Those interest groups have played an increasingly prominent role in the selection process by mobilizing and opposing nominees who threaten the judiciary's independence.[110] The battle over Ronald Reagan's nomination of Robert Bork provides an apt illustration. More than three hundred interest groups publicly took stands on Bork's nomination. The political mobilization that ensued helped to turn public opinion against his confirmation. A conservative ideologue as well as a critic of the Court's alliance with interest groups, Bork failed to win confirmation. In contrast, Anthony Kennedy, a political moderate with a reputation as a careful and pragmatic jurist, who distanced his legal positions from Bork's, was easily confirmed. Even with a Democratic majority in the Senate in 1993 and 1994 President Bill Clinton passed over prominent liberals to avoid conflict and chose politically moderate Ruth Bader Ginsburg and Stephen Breyer.

The appointment of more politically centrist justices to the Court is one consequence of dealignment that helps to explain why neither the Burger Court nor its successor under Chief Justice Rehnquist has produced the much-predicted

[108]The only exceptions were in 1977–1980 and 1993–1994 when there was a Democratic majority in Congress and a Democrat in the White House.
[109]See, for example, Cornell Clayton, "Law, Politics and the Rehnquist Court: Structural Influences on Supreme Court Decision Making," in Howard Gillman and Cornell Clayton, The Supreme Court and American Politics: New Institutionalist Perspectives (Lawrence, KS: University Press of Kansas, 1999) (effect of dealignment on the Court); John B. Gates, "The Supreme Court and Partisan Change: Controvening, Provoking, and Diffusing Partisan Conflict," in Howard Gillman and Cornell Clayton, The Supreme Court and American Politics: New Institutionalist Perspectives (Court's role in promoting dealignment).
[110]Clayton, "Law, Politics and the Rehnquist Court."

constitutional counterrevolution described earlier. The Court's increasing independence from the other branches, made possible by divided government and by its alliances with powerful political forces outside government, has also seriously limited the chances that—even when a president is successful in getting his most ideologically ideal choices confirmed—the Court will follow the president's agenda.[111] Nevertheless, as the 2003 term drew to a close and rumors of the retirements of Chief Justice Rehnquist and Sandra Day O'Connor spread through the legal community, civil libertarians grew increasingly concerned while conservatives prepared to celebrate a genuine constitutional counterrevolution in which a majority would reverse the precedent of the previous forty years.

JURISPRUDENCE

Another reason that a constitutional counterrevolution has not materialized lies in the changing ideas about law and the role of judges. We discuss some of those ideas in this section. Our primary concern here is to explore some of the ways that the major developments in legal philosophy or **jurisprudence** in the twentieth century have influenced constitutional law. In our earlier discussion of different approaches to constitutional interpretation, we explained how a particular understanding of what the Constitution is—a constitutional theory—shapes the way one goes about interpreting it. Thus, it should already be possible to see how constitutional theory has influenced the development of constitutional law.

Legal philosophy revolves around the question, "What is law?" That question invariably prompts inquiries into the proper function of judges in discovering or making the law, often articulated as, "What is the proper role of judges and courts in the American legal/political system?" Conceptions of law and judicial role have changed considerably over the years. Moreover, there have been and continue to be major disagreements among the justices of the Supreme Court as well as contemporary legal theorists on these issues.

Legal Formalism is the label commonly applied to the dominant jurisprudence from the end of the Civil War until the 1930s. The law, according to the formalist conception, was an abstract entity, a body of immutable principles. It was the task of judges to discover and apply those principles by engaging in a careful inquiry to discern legal truths. Because formalism envisioned the process of judging as an objective—and attainable—search for the correct rules and principles to apply in a given case, it justified an active role for appellate judges. According to the formalist conception, justices on the Supreme Court engaged in the rigorous but always objective task of sifting through previous decisions to find the one that matched the case before them and decided that case accordingly. Formalism conceived that process of reasoning by analogy or applying

---

[111]On the implications of alliances between the Court and interest groups, see Mark Silverstein and Benjamin Ginsberg, "The Supreme Court and the New Politics of Judicial Power," *Political Science Quarterly* 102 (1987): 371–388.

precedent as the means by which judges discovered the correct resolution to a legal dispute. The formalist description of legal reasoning was accepted not only as a prescription of what judges should do, but also as a description of what they actually did. In short, legal formalism taught that judges discovered the law through a logical, "scientific" process.

By the end of the nineteenth century, formalism had come to seem implausible to a growing number of legal scholars and other observers of the Supreme Court. The Court's determination to invalidate Congress's and the states' attempts to regulate business and industry increasingly appeared to be anything but an objective application of immutable legal principles. Indeed, it appeared that the justices were reading their own political ideologies into the Constitution. Oliver Wendell Holmes, Jr., joined the "revolt against formalism" by emphasizing law's dependence on political and social forces.[112] Holmes defined law as predictions "of what the courts will do in fact, and nothing more pretentious."[113] One of Holmes's most well-known statements captures the spirit of the movement that later came to be known as **Legal Realism:**

> The life of the law has not been logic: it has been experience. The felt necessities of the time, the prevalent moral and political theories, intuitions of public policy, avowed or unconscious, even the prejudices which judges share with their fellow-men, have had a good deal more to do than the syllogism in determining the rules by which men should be governed. The law embodies the story of a nation's development through many centuries, and it cannot be dealt with as if it contained only the axioms and corollaries of a book of mathematics.[114]

In the 1920s and 1930s, Legal Realism was a major intellectual movement that thoroughly undermined formalism. The realists emphasized that judges did not simply find the law but created it. Legal realists like Karl Llewellyn and Jerome Frank emphasized that legal rules and principles were artificial and uncertain and that deference to precedent was a facade behind which judges hid their conservative biases. The realists maintained that there was always a connection between a judicial decision and a judge's values. Frank, for example, observed "[L]aw may vary with the personality of the judge who happens to pass upon any given case."[115] The realists insisted, moreover, that the law could only be understood in connection with its political, economic, social, and historical context. It was not a body of abstract principles but a working social tool that judges must fashion by balancing competing values. In short, for the realists, courts were political institutions and judges were political actors whose decisions were exercises of political power.

---

[112]Morton White, *Social Thought in America: The Revolt Against Formalism* (New York: Oxford University Press, 1975, orig. 1957). White describes that revolt against formalism in law as part of a broader intellectual movement that marked a profound change in American philosophy, economics, sociology, and history.

[113]Oliver Wendell Holmes, Jr., "The Path of the Law," *Harvard Law Review* 10 (1897), reprinted in George C. Christie, *Jurisprudence: Test and Readings on the Philosophy of Law* (St. Paul, MN: West Publishing Co., 1973), 648–663, 651.

[114]Oliver Wendell Holmes, Jr. *The Common Law* (Boston: Little, Brown, 1881), 1.

[115]As quoted in Kermit L. Hall, *The Magic Mirror: Law in American History* (New York: Oxford University Press, 1989), 270.

The breakdown of formalism and the rise of Legal Realism encouraged a proliferation of constitutional theories both on and off the Court.[116] The dominance of liberal legalism after World War II also contributed to the multiplication of constitutional theories. Liberal legalism combined the social reformist impulse of progressivism, the ideas of Legal Realism, and the regulatory responsibility of the state associated with the New Deal and promised that the administrative-legal process and judicial power would produce social justice.[117] Liberal legalism is not so much a legal philosophy as a general favorable outlook about the ability of courts to effect social reform. From its inception, however, liberal legalism was divided and uncertain. As O'Brien pointed out, the Roosevelt Court divided into two groups, one of which contended that the Court should adopt an activist role—by invalidating policies of elected officials to protect individual rights—while the other insisted that the Court should maintain a more restrained position.[118]

Scholarly commentary now reflects a variety of mainstream jurisprudential perspectives as well as radical critiques including critical legal studies, feminist legal theory, and critical race theory. Such theories embrace different conceptions of law and the appropriate role of judges in the American political process, but they have all, nevertheless, built on Legal Realism's identification of the close connection between law and politics. The competing approaches to constitutional interpretation discussed earlier in this chapter ran through the decision making of the Supreme Court in the late 1990s. Some scholars have argued that the expanding number of constitutional theories has been a major factor in the increasing fragmentation and contentiousness among the justices of the Rehnquist Court.[119] Thus, the multiple legal theories that Legal Realism helped to engender is an additional factor that along with electoral dealignment helps to account for the continuing absence of a constitutional counterrevolution despite the ideological proclivities of a majority of the Court.

Legal Realism also reinvigorated the debate about judicial review. Indeed, one of the major themes of the Realist critique of the Court's invalidation of economic regulations was that the judiciary—unelected and unaccountable to the people—represents a threat to the democratic process. Realism thus challenged the Court's legitimacy as a policymaking institution. Much of legal theory since World War II has been devoted to meeting that challenge by reconciling judicial review with majority rule. Some of the arguments we have considered, including Robert Dahl's assertion that the Court is never far out of line with the dominant lawmaking majority and the "countermajoritarian difficulty," arose as responses to the Realists' critique. It will become increasingly apparent as we examine specific provisions of the Constitution that the question "Under what conditions is judicial review legitimate?" continues to be a major concern in constitutional law for the justices, the analysts of the Court's decisions, and the public.

---

[116]Clayton, "Law, Politics and the Rehnquist Court."

[117]Hall, *The Magic Mirror,* 284–285.

[118]O'Brien, "Institutional Norms and Supreme Court Opinions," 102.

[119]See, for example, *ibid.,* and O'Brien, "Institutional Norms and Supreme Court Opinions." See also, Lawrence M. Friedman, *A History of American Law* (New York: Simon and Schuster, 1973), 592.

CONCLUSION

This chapter began with a description of the most prominent features of the Constitution in its original, unamended form. We then discussed the difficulties and the various approaches to constitutional interpretation. An awareness of the differences between those approaches will be useful when we examine Supreme Court decisions in which the justices have been called upon to discern the meaning of specific constitutional provisions. Next, we examined the Court's initial assertion in *Marbury v Madison* of the power of judicial review. The historical context of that case and John Marshall's somewhat problematic attempt to locate the judiciary's authority to invalidate federal laws in the text of the Constitution suggest that the decision is best understood in political as much as legal terms.

We began to explore the connections between the Supreme Court and the American political process by dividing the history of the Court into five eras. Our description of the five eras provided a quick overview of the way the Court's central concerns have shifted over the years and how changes in personnel have affected its decisions. To provide a more complete picture of the relationship between the development of constitutional law and electoral politics we turned next to the subject of "The Supreme Court and Realignment" to explore the role that the Court has played in realigning or critical elections since the first such election in 1800. The Court has been affected by such elections in terms of appointments and pressure from the elected branches. The Court's decisions have also had an influence on realigning elections. When they have decided cases involving critical issues, the justices have played a role in the development of the agendas of the political parties in such a way as to encourage realignment.

Finally, our brief consideration of jurisprudence indicated the profound effect that the demise of formalism and the rise of Legal Realism had on Supreme Court decision making. Indeed, the proliferation of legal theories and approaches to constitutional interpretation that grew out of Realism and liberal legalism along with dealignment goes a long way to explain the persistence of the constitutional doctrine developed by the Warren Court despite almost twenty-five years of Republican appointments to the Court.

QUESTIONS

1. Refer to Table 2-1 in conjunction with the preceding discussion to make your own preliminary assessment of the competing approaches to constitutional interpretation. What are the advantages of textualism and originalism from a democratic (as opposed to a constitutionalist) perspective? What are the advantages of the various versions of doctrinalism, developmentalism, and structuralism from the perspective of constitutionalism?

2. Can you think of any stronger justification for judicial review than the one that John Marshall articulated in *Marbury v Madison*? If so, how might Marshall's use of such an argument have changed the course of American constitutional law?

3. If the Legal Realists and their successors are correct that judges' decisions are not shaped by their discovery of immutable legal principles but by their own values, how might the exercise of judicial review be justified?

4. Which of the following factors do you think have the greatest impact on the decisions of the Supreme Court—the principles of the Constitution, precedent, the ideologies of the justices, the political party in power, the relationship between Congress and the president, the justices' perception of their proper role, the economy?

5. What impact do you think the election of President George W. Bush will have on the decisions of the Supreme Court? Is there any chance that the Court has embarked on or will soon embark on a sixth era of constitutional law?

KEY TERMS

Faction
Separation of powers
Checks and balances
Representative government
Textualism
Originalism
Doctrinalism
Developmentalism
Philosophic approach
Systemic structuralism

Purposive structuralism
Judicial review
Countermajoritarian difficulty
Dual federalism
Substantive due process
Realignment
Dealignment
Jurisprudence
Legal Formalism
Legal Realism

SUGGESTIONS FOR FURTHER READING

Alfange, Dean, Jr. "*Marbury v Madison* and Original Understandings of Judicial Review: In Defense of Traditional Wisdom." *The Supreme Court Review* (1994): 329–437.

Clayton, Cornell W., and Howard Gillman, eds. *Supreme Court Decision Making: New Institutionalist Approaches.* Chicago, IL: University of Chicago Press, 1999.

Crenshaw, Kimberle, Neil Gotanda, Gary Peller, and Kendall Thomas, eds. *Critical Race Theory: The Key Writings That Formed the Movement.* New York: New Press, 1995.

Dahl, Robert A. *How Democratic Is the American Constitution?* New Haven, CT: Yale University Press, 2001.

Fisher, William W. III, Morton J. Horwitz, and Thomas A. Reed, eds. *American Legal Realism.* New York: Oxford University Press, 1993.

Graber, Mark A. "The Nonmajoritarian Difficulty: Legislative Deference to the Judiciary." *Studies in American Political Development* 7 (1993): 35–73.

Griffin, Stephen M., and Robert C. L. Moffat. *Radical Critiques of the Law.* Lawrence, KS: University Press of Kansas, 1997.

Griffin, Stephen M. *American Constitutionalism: From Theory to Politics.* Princeton, NJ: Princeton University Press, 1996.

Knight, Jack, and Lee Epstein. "On the Struggle for Judicial Supremacy." *Law and Society Review* 30 (1996): 87–120.

Lasser, William. *The Limits of Judicial Power: The Supreme Court in American Politics.* Chapel Hill, NC: University of North Carolina Press, 1988.

Lasser, William. "The Supreme Court in Periods of Critical Realignment." *Journal of Politics* 47 (1985): 1174–1187.

McCloskey, Robert G. *The American Supreme Court,* 2d ed. Revised by Sanford Levinson. Chicago, IL: University of Chicago Press, 1994, orig. 1960.

Moore, Wayne D. *Constitutional Rights and Powers of the People.* Princeton, NJ: Princeton University Press, 1996.

Noonan, John T. *Narrowing the Nation's Power: The Supreme Court Sides with the States.* Berkeley, CA: University of California Press, 2002.

Savage, David G. *Turning Right: The Making of the Rehnquist Supreme Court.* New York: John Wiley & Sons, 1992.

Stephenson, Donald Grier, Jr. *Campaigns and the Court: The United States Supreme Court in Presidential Elections.* New York: Columbia University Press, 1999.

Sunstein, Cass R. *One Case at a Time: Judicial Minimalism on the Supreme Court.* Cambridge, MA: Harvard University Press, 1999.

Whittington, Keith E. *Constitutional Interpretation: Textual Meaning, Original Intent, and Judicial Review.* Lawrence, KS: University Press of Kansas, 1999.

PART TWO

THE CONSTITUTION OF 1787

3

THE PREAMBLE AND ARTICLE I: THE LEGISLATIVE BRANCH

In this chapter we begin our examination of the provisions of the original Constitution. Although the prologue to the Constitution, the Preamble, neither grants powers to the national government nor limits governmental authority, it is important as a statement of the Framers' goals. Article I, with which most of this chapter is concerned, is the first of three articles that establish the powers of the three branches of the national government.

THE PREAMBLE

> We the People of the United States, in Order to form a more perfect Union, establish Justice, insure domestic Tranquility, provide for the common defense, promote the general Welfare, and secure the Blessings of Liberty to ourselves and our Posterity, do ordain and establish this Constitution for the United States of America.

After the delegates to the Philadelphia Convention agreed on the general principles of the new constitution, they elected the Committee on Detail to write a "constitution conformable to the Resolutions passed by the Convention."[1] Although the Convention had not recommended it, the Committee drafted the Preamble and it remained in the final draft of the document.

The terms of the Preamble may appear to be little more than sweeping generalities. Nevertheless, the language is significant. By proclaiming that the purpose of the Constitution was to "form a more perfect Union," the authors implied that the new document would succeed where the Articles of Confederation had failed. Thus, they simultaneously drew attention to the flaws of the Articles and to the positive qualities of the new document. Additionally, the Constitution's goal of securing the "Blessings of Liberty" evoked the principles of the Declaration of Independence. The Constitution, the Preamble thus suggested, would guarantee the protection of the inalienable rights to life, liberty, and the pursuit of happiness. The opening words of the Preamble, "We the Peo-

---

[1]As quoted in Leonard W. Levy, *Original Intent and the Framers' Constitution* (New York: Macmillan Publishing Co., 1988), 149.

ple of the United States," also underlined that the overarching principle of the Constitution was that government is based on the consent of the governed.

In short, the Preamble linked the Constitution to at least some of the ideals of the American Revolution. "We the People" also implied that the people rather than the states were the parties to the Constitution—an issue that would become a source of never-ending controversy concerning the relationship between the national government and the states. Finally, the Preamble pointed to the future, giving the Constitution a definite aspirational tone. The hope that the Constitution would establish justice, insure domestic tranquility, promote the general welfare, and secure the blessings of liberty "to ourselves and *our Posterity*," expressed a series of long-term goals, a commitment to a far-off constitutionally ideal state of affairs.[2]

ARTICLE I: THE LEGISLATURE

Background

As noted in Chapter 1, there were serious disagreements among the delegates to the Constitutional Convention over the legislative branch. The proponents of the New Jersey Plan preferred a legislature with strictly limited powers and, more generally, a federal government that would leave the states essentially supreme. The advocates of the Virginia Plan aspired to a more powerful central government with expansive authority residing in a national legislature. After the delegates rejected the New Jersey Plan, major conflicts continued to threaten the project of framing a new constitution.

As we learned in Chapter 1, the disagreement over representation in the two houses of the new Congress and the method of choosing members was resolved by the Great Compromise. Representation in the House of Representatives would be proportional based on population and states would be equally represented in the Senate. The people would elect members of the House whereas the state legislatures would choose senators. A second issue concerned the extent of Congress's powers. Most of the delegates agreed that Congress's lack of power under the Articles of Confederation had been the source of serious problems that threatened the continued existence of the new nation. The issues that proved to be the most controversial, thus, revolved around how much power Congress would have. Specifically, should Congress have the power to veto state laws? And would Congress's enumerated powers imply the existence of any additional powers? The Virginia Plan not only gave broad and vague powers to Congress—to "legislate in all cases to which the separate States are incompetent," for example—but also provided that it would have the authority to veto state laws. Although the Convention eventually rejected the latter proposal, it failed to make the description of Congress's powers more specific. The Committee on Detail added the provisions containing the explicit enumeration of the powers of Congress and the Convention approved what

---

[2]Sotirios A. Barber, *On What the Constitution Means* (Baltimore, MD: Johns Hopkins University Press, 1984), 34.

became Article I, Section 8. Additionally, the Convention could not agree on impeachment procedures and left them to the Committee on Detail.

Section 1

All legislative Powers herein granted shall be vested in a Congress of the United States,

The delegates to the Constitutional Convention seemed to assume that the legislature, which had been the only branch of government under the Articles of Confederation, would continue to be the guiding force in the new government. Nevertheless, the words "herein granted" and "vested" make it clear that Congress's powers were limited. Additionally, "vested" suggests that only Congress may exercise certain powers. Thus, the legislature may not delegate those powers to other branches of the government. By designating that "all legislative powers" belong to Congress, Section 1 began to outline the doctrine of the separation of powers, a major theme that runs through the Constitution.

Section 1

[continued] which shall consist of a Senate and House of Representatives.

Bicameralism is another important principle that the Framers included in the Constitution. Although the Convention deadlocked over the issues of representation, the delegates—with the exception of Ben Franklin, who preferred a unicameral system—agreed that there should be two chambers. The Framers envisioned bicameralism serving much the same function as the separation of powers. Requiring the agreement of both houses would make Congress more careful and reduce the likelihood that it would enact unwise legislation. Bicameralism would also promote balanced government insofar as the two houses would check each other's power. With two houses, moreover, the government would represent the interests of different parts of society. The House would reflect the attitudes of the popular or democratic elements, and the Senate would reflect the views of the aristocratic elements.

Section 2

1. The House of Representatives shall be composed of Members chosen every second Year by the People of the several States, and the Electors in each State shall have the Qualifications requisite for Electors of the most numerous Branch of the State Legislature.

Most of the delegates to the Philadelphia Convention agreed that members of the House should have short terms of office. Although some favored annual terms, believing that "where annual terms end, tyranny begins," others, including James Madison, favored a three-year term. They compromised on a two-year term. The delegates also argued over whether to set property qualifications for voters. Because the qualifications for voting varied widely among the states, it would have been extremely difficult to reach agreement over a uniform national standard. The second part of Article I, Section 2 (1), avoided such a problem by providing that **qualifications for voters** in congressional elections would be the same as those for state legislative elections. Thus, property qualifications were not directly legitimized by the Constitution; nevertheless, the states were left free to include property as a qualification for voting.

The states began to eliminate property qualifications during the 1820s, and subsequent constitutional amendments removed the states' authority to withhold the franchise from adults. Additionally, in 1884 the Court established federal power to protect the right to vote in national elections when it declared that the right to vote in such elections is derived from the Constitution although the states determine qualifications for voting.[3] Article I, Section 2, should be read in conjunction with Article I, Section 4.

The Supreme Court gave force to the mandate that representatives be chosen "by the People" in 1963 when it ruled that states must design their congressional districts so that they are as equal as possible in terms of population. Admonishing that "as nearly as is practicable, one man's vote in a congressional election is to be worth as much as another's," the justices proclaimed the principle of one-person-one-vote.[4]

Section 2

2. No person shall be a Representative who shall not have attained to the Age of twenty five Years, and been seven Years a Citizen of the United States, and who shall not, when elected, be an Inhabitant of that State in which he shall be chosen.

The **age, citizenship, and residency requirements** aroused little disagreement at the Philadelphia Convention. James Wilson argued against a minimum age, noting several men who had "rendered [significant services] in high stations to the public before the age of 25." George Mason rejoined, "It had been said that Congress had proved a good school for our young men . . . [but] they should bear the expense of their own education."[5] Individuals who lack the required age or duration of citizenship at the time of their election may nevertheless be admitted to the House as soon as they become qualified—the same rule applies to the Senate.

The Supreme Court has held that Congress may not require qualifications in addition to age, citizenship, and residency.[6] In 1995, a majority of the justices ruled that Article I, Section 2, also forbids the states from altering the constitutional qualifications for membership in Congress by imposing **term limits.** In so holding, the Court invalidated legal provisions that had been enacted in twenty-three states limiting the number of terms that members of Congress were eligible to serve. Writing for a five-member majority, Justice John Paul Stevens explained, "Permitting individual States to formulate diverse qualifications for their congressional representatives would result in a patchwork that would be inconsistent with the Framers' vision of a uniform national Legislature representing the people of the United States."[7] Justice Clarence Thomas, who wrote for the dissenters,

---

[3]*Ex parte Yarbrough,* 110 US 651 (1884).
[4]*Wesberry v Sanders,* 376 US 1, 7–8 (1964).
[5]As quoted in Daniel Farber and Suzanna Sherry, *A History of the American Constitution* (St. Paul, MN: West Publishing Co., 1990), 142.
[6]*Powell v McCormack,* 395 US 486 (1969).
[7]*U.S. Term Limits Inc. v Thornton,* 514 US 779 (1995).

took the position that nothing in the Constitution "deprives the people of each State of the power to prescribe eligibility requirements for the candidates who seek to represent them in Congress. The Constitution is simply silent on this question. And where the Constitution is silent, it raises no bar to action by the States or the people." His contention that the "source of the Constitution's authority is the consent of the people of each individual State, not the consent of the undifferentiated people of the Nation as a whole"[8] raised a number of important issues concerning the federal-state relationship. Although the question of whether it was the states or the people who agreed to the Constitution was generally considered to have been settled in the 1930s on the side of "the people" and expansive federal power, as our discussion of several other constitutional provisions including some in Article I will show, Thomas's position is consistent with that of several of his colleagues on the Court who revived the debate in the 1970s.

Section 2

3. Representatives and direct Taxes shall be apportioned among the several States which may be included within this Union, according to their respective Numbers, which shall be determined by adding to the whole Number of free Persons, including those bound to Service for a Term of Years, and excluding Indians not taxed, three fifths of all other Persons.[9]

As noted in Chapter 1, the Virginia Plan designated that the states would be represented in both houses of Congress according to population. The delegates from the smaller states and those who favored a more state-centered system of government opposed such an arrangement and in the New Jersey Plan proposed a unicameral legislature in which the states would be represented equally. After the Convention rejected the New Jersey Plan, the delegates remained divided over representation. As a result of the Great Compromise, the number of representatives from each state would be based on the number of people residing there. Congress has enacted legislation providing guidelines for determining the number of representatives to which each state shall be entitled. The Supreme Court has given Congress considerable discretion to choose methods of apportioning representatives. The justices have made it clear that although the **one-person-one-vote** standard requires state legislatures to draw congressional districts as equally as possible in terms of population, Congress may deviate from the ideal of equal representation in apportioning representatives.[10]

Direct taxes were also to be apportioned according to the number of people residing in each state. Although the Constitutional Convention did not provide a definition, direct taxes were taken to mean taxes imposed on land and capitation or head taxes. To apportion direct taxes, Congress would have to devise a formula for determining the appropriate amount of total tax for each state based on its population; it could not simply tax individuals according to the amount of land they owned. In 1796, the Supreme Court limited direct taxes to property

---

[8]*Ibid.*
[9]Changed by the Fourteenth Amendment.
[10]*Department of Commerce v Montana*, 503 US 442 (1992).

taxes and determined that a duty on carriages was an indirect tax.[11] In 1869, the justices ruled that a tax on currency issued by state banks was an indirect tax.[12] In 1895, the Court designated a tax on income a direct tax, prompting Congress to propose and the states to ratify the Sixteenth Amendment.[13]

In the Great Compromise, the delegates also agreed that three-fifths of the slaves—designated as "other persons"—in each state would be counted for purposes of representation. The **three-fifths clause** resolved the conflict between the delegates from the southern states who wanted to count all of their slaves and accordingly increase their power in Congress and the northern delegates who demanded that slaves not be counted at all. Because the clause exemplifies the dynamics of the constitutional conflict over slavery, it is particularly important to the project of *understanding the Constitution*. Legally, however, the clause is obsolete. It was effectively nullified by the Fourteenth Amendment.

The phrase "excluding Indians not taxed" is one of only two provisions in the work of the Philadelphia Convention mentioning the native peoples of North America.[14] The phrase is repeated in the Fourteenth Amendment. Native Americans were not taxed and not counted in apportioning seats in the House of Representatives. The Framers gave indigenous people a distinct constitutional status, treating them as neither citizens nor slaves. Although the Framers viewed them as independent peoples whose tribes were independent nations, by the early nineteenth century the federal government had begun claiming their land and forcibly removing them from it.[15] The constitutional status of Native Americans remains unique. They are under the jurisdiction of the federal government and are free from state interference. The Supreme Court has held that states may not tax commercial activities undertaken on reservations or tax the land itself.[16] Additionally states may not collect taxes from the income earned by Native Americans working and living on reservations.[17]

Section 2

3. [Continued] The actual Enumeration shall be made within three Years after the first Meeting of the Congress of the United States, and within every subsequent Term of ten Years, in such Manner as they shall by Law direct. The Number of Representatives shall not exceed one for every thirty thousand, but each state shall have at Least one Representative; and until such enumeration shall be made, the State of New Hampshire shall be entitled to choose three; Massachusetts eight; Rhode Island and Providence Plantations one; Connecticut five; New York six; New Jersey four; Pennsylvania eight; Delaware one; Maryland six; Virginia ten; North Carolina five; South Carolina five; and Georgia three.

---

[11]*Hylton v United States*, 3 US (3 Dall.) 171 (1796).
[12]*Veasie v Fenno*, 75 US 533 (1869).
[13]*Pollack v Farmers' Loan and Trust*, 157 US 429 (1895) and 158 US 601 (1895).
[14]See Article I, Section 8 (3).
[15]On the constitutional position of Native Americans generally, see John R. Wunder, *'Retained by the People': A History of American Indians and the Bill of Rights* (New York: Oxford University Press, 1997).
[16]*Mescaler Apache Tribe v Jones*, 411 US 145 (1973). But see *Chickasaw Nation v United States* ____ US ____ (2001) in which the Court interpreted an ambiguous provision in the federal law not to exempt tribes from paying gambling-related taxes. The Court did not address any constitutional issues, however.
[17]*Oklahoma Tax Commission v Chickasaw Nation*, 515 US 450 (1995).

The Constitutional Convention provided initial figures for representation that would be subject to alteration after an enumeration or census to be held every ten years. Population growth has rendered the restriction on the number of representatives per person irrelevant. By the 2000 census, the population was 281,421,906. Following the rule that the number of members of the House may reach but must not exceed one for every thirty thousand people would result in a House of Representative composed of 9,381 members.[18] Congress enacted legislation in 1929 limiting the number of representatives to 435.

Congress created the Bureau of the Census, an agency of the Department of Commerce, in 1902. Article I, Section 2 (3), requires a census specifically to determine the number of representatives that each state shall be entitled to send to the House. Nevertheless, Congress also uses statistics from the census to distribute federal money and benefits.

Although the census has always undercounted members of certain racial and ethnic groups, the Supreme Court did not address the question of whether such undercounting violates Article I, Section 2 (3), until 1996. After conducting a major study, the Census Bureau developed a statistical method to adjust the actual census count to reflect more accurately the number of racial and ethnic minorities in the population. The Director of the Census Bureau endorsed the new method for the 1990 census, but the Secretary of Commerce decided that the census would be taken using the traditional method. The City of New York challenged the Secretary's decision, alleging that the decision not to use the new procedure unconstitutionally diluted the political representation of identifiable racial and ethnic groups. Rejecting the challenge, a unanimous Supreme Court reasoned that the Secretary's determination that the census would be best conducted without the statistical adjustment was reasonable and therefore "well within the constitutional bounds of discretion over the conduct of the census provided to the Federal Government."[19]

In 1998, the Census Bureau announced a plan to use statistical sampling in the 2000 census to correct the anticipated undercount of some four million people, including a disproportionate number of members of minority groups living in low-income areas. The Republican majority of the House of Representatives and a group brought together by the conservative Southeastern Legal Foundation challenged the Census Bureau's plan, arguing that it violated the Census Act and the provision in Article I, Section 2 (3), of the Constitution that mandates an "actual enumeration."[20] In 1999, a five-member majority of the Court held that the Census Act prohibits sampling for purposes of apportionment. The Court allowed that sampling might be used to draw district lines within states and to distribute federal funds, however. Although it was unnecessary for the justices to address the constitutional issue—and Sandra Day O'Connor, who wrote the opinion for the majority, refrained from doing so—the four other justices who voted with the majority suggested that sampling would not constitute an "actual enumeration" and thus would be unconstitu-

---

[18]281,421,906 divided by 30,000.
[19]*Wisconsin v City of New York*, 517 US 1 (1996).
[20]The Court decided the two cases, *Clinton v Glavin* and *United States Department of Commerce v United States House of Representatives* together.

tional even if the federal law permitted it. The four dissenters maintained that sampling did not violate either the Census Act or the Constitution.[21]

The Court's decision regarding sampling had a distinct partisan dimension. The racial and ethnic minorities and residents of urban areas whom the census misses tend to be Democratic voters. Consequently, any change in the **apportionment** of House seats that resulted from a census utilizing sampling would favor Democrats. **Redistricting**—conducted by the states—could also be affected as all fifty states have laws or constitutional provisions requiring their legislatures to use federal census figures in drawing district lines. The 1999 case, *Department of Commerce v United States House of Representatives,* involved a dispute between the Democratic Administration and the Republican House of Representatives. Although methods of counting the population are important and the problem of undercounting racial and ethnic minorities is serious, the significance of the case lies primarily in the fact that the Court was willing to become involved in a battle between the legislature and the executive—all of the justices agreed that the case was appropriate for judicial resolution. Moreover, the division of the Court along ideological lines suggested that the justices were not only amenable to becoming involved in a dispute between the two political branches, but also were inclined to take sides.[22]

In 2002 the Court upheld the Census Bureau's use of an alternative to sampling against a challenge that it violated the federal statute and the Constitutional requirement of "an actual enumeration." In the 2000 census the Census Bureau used "hot-deck imputation," a method of filling in gaps in information about the number of people residing in a housing unit by inferring that a unit is similar in population characteristics to its closest neighbor of the same type, to increase the total population count by about 0.4 percent. However, the percentage was spread unevenly across the country, and it made a difference in the apportionment of congressional representatives—North Carolina, for example, received an additional representative, whereas Utah received one less than if the Bureau had not filled in the gaps by adding additional people. Although the justices found it unnecessary to "decide the precise methodological limits foreseen by the Census Clause," they found that imputation was inference in contrast to sampling and was consistent with long-accepted methods of determining the number of missing persons, including asking heads of households, neighbors, landlords, and others about the number of inhabitants in a particular dwelling.[23]

Section 2

4. When vacancies happen in the Representation from any State, the Executive Authority thereof shall issue Writs of Election to fill such Vacancies.

5. The House of Representatives shall chuse their speaker and other Officers;

Article I, Section 2 (4), specifies that vacancies be filled by a special election called by the governor of the state in which the vacancy occurs. When the

---

[21] *United States Department of Commerce v United States House of Representatives,* 525 US 316 (1999).
[22] The majority was comprised of O'Connor, Rehnquist, Scalia, Kennedy, and Thomas. The dissenters were Stevens, Souter, Ginsburg, and Breyer.
[23] *Utah v Evans,* _____ US _____ (2002).

next election has been less than a year away, governors have often declined to call a special election.

In practice, the party that has a majority in the House selects the Speaker. The rules and practices of the House determine the duties and powers of the Speaker and the other officers. The Constitution does not specify that the speaker must be a member of the House, but the Framers assumed that the examples of the British House of Commons and of the state legislatures would be followed.

Section 2

5. [continued] shall have the sole Power of Impeachment.

An important but usually neglected component of the Constitution, the **impeachment power** provides Congress with the legal means for removing federal officials who abuse their office or engage in criminal activity. The constitutional impeachment power cannot be understood without considering the political context in which it has developed. Although impeachment has been used as a political tool for short-term partisan purposes, it should also be viewed in broader terms as a constitutional device that has helped to define the division of powers among the three branches of government.[24]

Article I, Section 2 (5), which we discuss here, is the first of six provisions that explain the impeachment power. We encourage readers to examine all of the following provisions in conjunction with Article I, Section 2 (5):

- Article I, Section 3 (6): procedures for trial in the Senate.
- Article I, Section 3 (7): penalties for impeachment.
- Article II, Section 2 (1): president may not grant pardons.
- Article II, Section 4: who may be impeached and grounds for impeachment.[25]

Article I, Section 2 (5), gives the House of Representatives the power to bring a formal accusation against a public official—a procedure that is analogous to a grand jury indictment in a criminal case. A vote by a majority of the House for impeachment represents its judgment that the charges are serious enough and are supported by sufficient evidence to justify moving to the next step in the process—a trial in the Senate as provided in Article I, Section 3 (6).

Since 1797 when it used the impeachment power for the first time the House has impeached sixteen federal officials, including eleven lower federal court judges, an associate justice of the Supreme Court, a cabinet member, two presidents, and a senator (see Table 3-1).[26]

---

[24]For a convincing presentation of such a view of impeachment, see Keith E. Whittington, *Constitutional Construction: Divided Powers and Constitutional Meaning* (Cambridge, MA: Harvard University Press, 1999), Chapters 2 and 4.

[25]The sixth provision, Article III, Section 2 (3), provides for trial by jury in the state where the crime was committed except in cases of impeachment.

[26]Some accounts include U.S. District Judge Mark Delahay, who resigned in 1873 before the House had formally approved articles of impeachment against him. See, for example, Ruth Marcus and Juliet Eilperin, "House's Challenge: Define 'Impeachable,'" *Washington Post*, September 8, 1998, A1.

TABLE 3-1   Impeachments of Federal Officials

Year	Official	Outcome
1799	William Blount, Senator, Tennessee	Dismissed, lack of jurisdiction
1804	John Pickering, Judge, U.S. District Court, New Hampshire	Removed from office
1805	Samuel Chase, Associate Justice, Supreme Court	Acquitted
1831	James H. Peck, Judge, U.S. District Court, Missouri	Acquitted
1862	West H. Humphreys, Judge, U.S. District Court, Tennessee	Removed from office
1868	Andrew Johnson, President of the United States	Acquitted
1876	William W. Belknap, Secretary of War	Acquitted
1905	Charles Swayne, Judge, U.S. District Court, Florida	Acquitted
1913	Robert W. Archbald, Judge, U.S. Commerce Court	Removed from office
1926	George W. English, Judge, U.S. District Court, Illinois	Resigned, Proceedings dismissed
1933	Harold Louderback, Judge, U.S. District Court, California	Acquitted
1936	Halsted L. Ritter, Judge, U.S. District Court, Florida	Removed from office
1986	Harry E. Claiborne, Judge, U.S. District Court, Nevada	Removed from office
1989	Alcee L. Hastings, Judge, U.S. District Court, Florida	Removed from office
1989	Walter L. Nixon, Judge, U.S. District Court, Mississippi	Removed from office
1998	William Jefferson Clinton, President of the United States	Acquitted (1999)

The well-known impeachments in the nineteenth century were those of Associate Justice Samuel Chase in 1805 and President Andrew Johnson in 1868. The impeachment of Chase was politically motivated, driven by fundamental differences between the Federalists and Jeffersonian Republicans over the role of the federal judiciary in the constitutional system. President Johnson's impeachment grew out of a bitter partisan struggle between a president who was a Southern Democrat and a Republican-controlled Congress over the implementation of Reconstruction following the Civil War. In broader terms, however, those early impeachments helped to define the federal judiciary and the powers of the president in relation to Congress.

In the twentieth century, political conflict has not always been at the center of efforts by the House to impeach federal officials. Five impeachment investigations were initiated by the House between 1936 and 1997 but only one of those—and investigation of Associate Justice William O. Douglas—was driven by partisan motivations and in that investigation the House Judiciary Committee concluded that there were no grounds for impeaching him. In the 1980s three federal judges were impeached by the House and subsequently convicted and removed from office by the Senate. That none of those proceedings were dominated by partisan concerns is evidenced by the fact that in each case, when the House began impeachment proceedings the judge had already been tried for a felony. Two of the three judges had been convicted and were serving prison terms when they were impeached.[27] Moreover, the votes to impeach the three judges were overwhelming in both the Judiciary Committee and the House.[28]

Political opposition to the president was clearly a factor in the initiation of an impeachment inquiry into the alleged misconduct of Richard M. Nixon that stemmed from a tangle of events known as the Watergate affair. Nevertheless, as evidence mounted that he had abused the power of his office in such a fundamental way as to constitute a threat to our system of government, partisan motivations quickly dissipated. In July 1974 after the Supreme Court rejected President Nixon's claim of executive privilege and ordered him to release tapes of his conversations in the White House,[29] the House Judiciary Committee adopted three articles of impeachment against him. The first accused him of obstructing justice by using the powers of his office to cover up the burglary of the Headquarters of the Democratic National Committee at the Watergate Complex in June 1972. The second article alleged that he had engaged in conduct violating the constitutional rights of citizens by authorizing illegal wiretapping, misusing the CIA, maintaining a secret investigative unit within the office of the president that was financed in part with money derived from campaign contributions, and interfering with the FBI. The third article contended that he had

---

[27]The judges were Harry E. Claiborne (for filing false income tax returns, 1986), Alcee L. Hastings (for accepting bribes, 1989), and Walter L. Nixon (for making false statements to a grand jury investigating allegations that he accepted an illegal gratuity in exchange for influencing a state criminal prosecution, 1989). Claiborne and Nixon were convicted in federal court; Hastings was acquitted.

[28]The Committee approved the articles of impeachment against Nixon and Claiborne unanimously; there was only one dissenting vote against the articles of impeachment for Hastings. In the full House there were no votes against the impeachment of Nixon and Claiborne and only three against Hastings' impeachment.

[29]*United States v Nixon*, 418 US 683 (1974).

violated his oath to execute the office of the presidency by refusing to comply with the Judiciary Committee's subpoenas for papers.

In early August 1974, Nixon released three tapes, which came to be known as the "smoking gun," indicating that he had ordered a cover-up of the Watergate burglary and was aware of the involvement of White House officials and his reelection campaign in the burglary. The eleven Republicans on the Judiciary Committee who had voted against the articles of impeachment indicated that they would change their votes when the full House voted. It appeared to be virtually inevitable that President Nixon would be impeached by the House, convicted in the Senate, and removed from office. Four days later, Richard Nixon became the first president to resign from office. The Judiciary Committee proceeded to prepare a report in which it explained its recommendation to impeach the president. The House accepted the report by a vote of 412–3, thereby taking official notice of the Committee's recommendations without adopting the articles of impeachment.

On December 19, 1998, the House of Representatives impeached President William Jefferson Clinton. The circumstances surrounding the first impeachment of a president since 1868 raised a number of questions about the "sole Power of Impeachment." President Clinton was plagued by allegations of criminal wrongdoing from virtually the beginning of his first term in office. Indeed, in 1993—the first year of his presidency—federal regulators, looking at the failed Madison Guaranty Savings and Loan, became suspicious that Clinton and his wife, Hillary Rodham Clinton, had engaged in illegal behavior during the 1980s. A special counsel was appointed in January 1994 to investigate the Clintons' involvement in the Whitewater real estate venture and their activities with regard to Madison Guaranty. In August, Kenneth W. Starr assumed the position of independent counsel.[30] Initially, the special counsel's mandate was to investigate a complicated series of questions about the Clintons' finances and their real estate and business dealings in the 1980s. Starr's investigation quickly expanded, however, to include the suicide of Vincent Foster, White House deputy counsel, and charges that Webster Hubbell, the associate attorney general, had overbilled the law firm where he and Hillary Clinton worked in the 1980s. There were also questions about the location of billing records for work that Hillary Clinton had done for Madison Guaranty—the subpoenaed records were apparently lost but subsequently turned up in the White House. The investigation was also extended to include allegations that the White House improperly received FBI files on Bush and Reagan Administration employees and that associates of the president had arranged payments to Webster Hubbell to secure his silence on Whitewater matters.

Although Starr secured three convictions and twelve plea bargains over a period of three and a half years, he was unable to find any evidence that the

---

[30]The law providing for an independent counsel had lapsed in early 1994 because of Republican opposition. Thus, Attorney General Janet Reno used her own authority to appoint Robert B. Fiske to serve as special prosecutor. When Congress renewed the Independent Counsel Act (Ethics in Government Act, 28 USCA Sections 49, 591–99 (1988) Modified by the Independent Counsel Reauthorization Act of 1994) Reno, acting in accord with the law, asked a special three-judge panel to appoint Fiske as independent counsel but the judges rejected her request and named Ken Starr.

president had engaged in any wrongdoing. In January 1998, however, Starr expanded his investigation to include the president's alleged relationship with former White House intern, Monica Lewinsky. Seeking to garner evidence that Clinton had lied about his relationship with Lewinsky in his deposition in the Paula Jones sexual harassment lawsuit[31] and that he suborned perjury and obstructed justice by urging Lewinsky to lie when she was deposed in that case, Starr subpoenaed a number of witnesses to testify before the grand jury including the president's closest advisers, his secretary, secret service agents, Monica Lewinsky, and the president himself. Testifying under a grant of transactional immunity, Lewinsky revealed that she had sexual contact with the president on a number of occasions. After his testimony before the grand jury, in which he maintained that he had not had sex with Lewinsky, President Clinton delivered a nationally televised address and admitted having an inappropriate relationship with Lewinsky and misleading people about it. He adopted a position that he was to maintain throughout the impeachment process and that would provide grounds for his defense but would also alienate wavering Republicans. He maintained that he had provided answers that were legally accurate and had thus not committed perjury either in the deposition in the Jones lawsuit or in his testimony before the grand jury. He claimed that the sexual contact he had engaged in with Monica Lewinsky did not constitute "sexual relations" according to the legal definition used in the Jones lawsuit.[32]

Pursuant to the Independent Counsel Act, Ken Starr delivered his official report to the House alleging that he had "substantial and credible information" constituting grounds for impeachment. The House Judiciary Committee, by a vote along party lines, set the impeachment process in motion by recommending that Congress open a formal investigation into possible grounds for the impeachment of the president. Thirty-one Democrats then joined all of the Republicans in the House to authorize an impeachment inquiry. The House Judiciary Committee then held hearings that included testimony by Ken Starr, who advanced eleven grounds for impeachment, and a defense of the president presented by the White House. The thrust of the defense was that the president's conduct concerning Lewinsky was indefensible but not impeachable. Witnesses argued that despite Clinton's evasiveness he had not committed perjury. Moreover, they argued, his behavior concerned a private matter and thus was not comparable to Richard Nixon's wide-ranging abuse of power. Even before the White House finished presenting its case, however, Republicans released draft articles of impeachment.

On December 11 and 12, the Judiciary Committee, voting along party lines, defeated a compromise proposal to censure President Clinton and approved four

---

[31]Paula Jones, a former Arkansas state employee, brought a sexual harassment suit against President Clinton in 1994. She accused him of "sexually harassing and assaulting" her in 1991, then defaming her with denial. She accepted a settlement of $850,000 in November 1998.

[32]The legal definition was as follows: "contact with the genitalia, anus, groin, breast, inner thigh or buttocks of any person with an intent to arouse or gratify the sexual desire of any person." A person upon whom oral sex was performed would, according to that definition, not have had sexual relations. Lewinsky testified that she had not only had oral sex with the president but that he had touched her in at least one of the places listed in the definition. Thus, the issue of whether he had committed perjury descended to the level of whether and where the president touched Monica Lewinsky.

articles of impeachment against him. The first article accused the president of providing "perjurious, false and misleading testimony" to the grand jury. The second article accused him of lying in his deposition in the Paula Jones lawsuit about his relationship with Lewinsky. The third accused Clinton of obstruction of justice by encouraging Lewinsky to lie about their relationship in her affidavit in the Paula Jones lawsuit, trying to arrange employment for her in order to secure her silence, and coaching Oval Office secretary Betty Currie to testify that he and Lewinsky never were alone together. The fourth article alleged that Clinton abused his office by lying to Congress in ten of his responses to the eighty-one questions sent to him by the House Judiciary Committee.

The House was scheduled to reconvene on December 17 to consider the articles of impeachment. Although public opinion polls indicated that a majority of Americans believed that the president should not be removed from office, support for Clinton among two dozen Republicans, whose votes would be crucial to prevent approval of the articles of impeachment by the House, was declining. On December 16, President Clinton ordered a series of air strikes against Iraq for its systematic refusals to allow the United Nations to conduct inspections for weapons. After its defeat in the Persian Gulf War in 1991, Iraq agreed to destroy its arsenal as a condition of the cease-fire but repeatedly refused to cooperate with inspectors. On several occasions, including one in the middle of November, the United States had been on the verge of launching an attack but called it off at the last minute. Although some Republicans questioned the president's motives and the timing of the attack, the House postponed a vote on impeachment to consider a resolution of support for the military action.

The House began debate on the articles of impeachment on December 18 over the objections of the Democrats who maintained that it was inappropriate to consider impeaching the president while American troops were engaged in military action against Iraq. Twelve hours of bitter and acrimonious speeches followed. Charging that the process was unfair, Democrats condemned the Republican majority's refusal to allow the House to vote on the alternative proposal to censure the president, pointed to opinion polls indicating that a majority of Americans continued to support the president, and admonished that impeachment would overturn the votes of some fifty million Americans. As to the merits of the articles of impeachment, Democrats argued that, assuming the president committed perjury, lying about a consensual sexual affair does not constitute an impeachable offense. Impeachment, they contended, should not be used as a partisan weapon to destroy political enemies. It should be reserved for serious misconduct involving the president's duties and performance in office. As one member of Congress chided, "Impeachment was designed to rid this nation of traitors and tyrants, not attempts to cover up extramarital affairs."[33] Democrats warned that impeaching President Clinton would distort and degrade the constitutional mechanism for impeachment and lower the standard for its future use and that preserving the rule of law against the threat of a partisan coup d'état demanded the defeat of the articles of impeachment.

---

[33]"Excerpts from Dec. 18 Impeachment Debate," *Washington Post.com Special Report: Clinton Accused,* December 18, 1998. The statement was made by John Conyers (D-Michigan).

At the same time, Republicans proclaimed that respect for the rule of law mandated impeachment. Perjury and obstruction of justice are public acts that cannot be reconciled with the office of the president, argued Chair of the Judiciary Committee, Henry Hyde. Because the president betrayed the trust of the people, Republicans maintained, Clinton was incapacitated from carrying out the duties of his office. At the conclusion of the debate, the Democrats once again tried and failed to bring censure to a vote.

On December 19, 1998, the House of Representatives by a vote of 228 to 206[34] adopted the first article of impeachment. The House also passed the third article, which accused the president of obstruction of justice. A majority rejected the second article, charging that Clinton lied in his deposition in the Jones lawsuit. Ironically, the House thereby essentially eliminated the underlying offense on which the charges stemming from Clinton's grand jury testimony were based. The fourth article also failed to win a majority. A delegation of House Republicans then formally delivered the articles of impeachment to the secretary of the Senate.

Perhaps the most important constitutional question that emerged from the impeachment of President Clinton was, what constitutes an impeachable offense? Should impeachment be reserved for serious official misconduct that endangers our system of government as many Democrats argued? Do the partisan votes in the Judiciary Committee and on the floor of the House suggest that the Republican majority misused the power of impeachment? We discuss these issues with reference to earlier cases of impeachment under Article II, Section 4. Several other constitutional questions arose in the context of the impeachment of 1998. For example, is the Senate obligated to conduct a trial once it receives the articles of impeachment from the House? May the Senate choose to censure the president rather than conduct a trial or after the trial has begun? Would censure constitute a bill of attainder forbidden by Article I, Section 9 (3), of the Constitution? Was the vote for impeachment by the 105th Congress valid for the 106th Congress, which began in January 1999? Or, would the 106th Congress be required to vote again on the articles of impeachment for the Senate to be able to consider them?

Our understanding of the impeachment power is based on experience rather than judicial doctrine. On the grounds that the language of the Constitution commits matters of impeachment to the legislative branch and that courts are not capable of developing and managing standards for impeachment, the Supreme Court has held that impeachment controversies are not subject to judicial review.[35] Thus, the decisions of the House and Senate are final.

Section 3

1. The Senate of the United States shall be composed of two senators from each state, [chosen by the Legislature thereof][36] for six Years; and each Senator shall have one Vote.

---

[34]Five Republicans voted against and five Democrats voted in favor of the first article.
[35]*Nixon v United States*, 506 US 224 (1993).
[36]The section in brackets was superseded by the Seventeenth Amendment.

Although Section 2 of Article I is concerned with the House of Representatives, Section 3 moves to the Senate. As we have noted, the delegates to the Constitutional Convention from the larger states and those inclined to a more powerful central government, who favored representation in both houses based on population, agreed to a compromise whereby representation in the Senate would be based on equality between the states. Regardless of the size of its population, each state has two senators, each of whom has a single vote.

Although the Constitutional Convention had little trouble agreeing on two-year terms for members of the House, there was more controversy over the length of terms in the Senate. After delegates proposed terms that ranged from three years to life, they agreed on seven years. Then after Hugh Williamson of North Carolina, who was a former professor of mathematics, suggested that six years was more convenient for purposes of rotation than seven, they voted against seven years. James Madison argued for a term of nine years so that the Senate "might have an oppt. of acquiring a competent knowledge of public interests."[37] After only three states agreed with Madison, the Convention settled on six years.

Section 3

2. Immediately after they shall be assembled in Consequence of the first Election, they shall be divided as equally as may be into three Classes. The Seats of the Senators of the first Class shall be vacated at the Expiration of the second Year, of the second Class at the Expiration of the fourth Year, and of the third Class at the Expiration of the sixth Year, so that one third may be chosen every second Year;

Despite their differences over the appropriate length of terms for the Senate, the delegates agreed on the principle of rotation—the terms of office of one-third of the senators should expire at a time. The fact that the Senate, unlike the House, is a continuing body has some significant implications. The Supreme Court, for example, has pointed out that, although a Senate subpoena issued five years earlier is still clearly valid, a subpoena issued by the House at the same time may not be valid because "the House is not a continuing body" and the subpoena thus comes from a prior Congress.[38] The continuing nature of the Senate has also generally been taken to mean that its rules remain in effect from one Congress to the next. Thus, the rule that an extraordinary majority is required to terminate debate cannot be set aside by a new Congress except in accord with the rules of the Senate in the previous Congress.

Section 3

2. [continued] and if Vacancies happen by Resignation, or otherwise, during the Recess of the Legislature of any State, the Executive thereof may make temporary Appointments until the next Meeting of the Legislature, which shall then fill such Vacancies.

---

[37] As quoted in Farber and Sherry, 143.
[38] *Eastland v United States Servicemen's Fund*, 421 US 491 (1975).

Article I, Section 3 (2), authorized state governors to fill vacancies that occurred when the state legislature was not in session. The Seventeenth Amendment, which provides for the direct election of senators, modified this provision. Governors may still appoint replacements to serve temporarily until either a special election or the next general election.

Section 3

3. No Person shall be a Senator who shall not have attained to the Age of thirty Years, and been nine Years a Citizen of the United States, and who shall not, when elected, be an Inhabitant of that State for which he shall be chosen.

Like the longer terms, the slightly stricter age, citizenship, and residency requirements for the Senate reflect the Constitutional Convention's determination that the upper house should be a more stable and wise body than the House of Representatives.

Section 3

4. The Vice President of the United States shall be President of the Senate, but shall have no Vote, unless they be equally divided.

The vice president's prerogative to preside over the Senate and to vote in order to break a tie reflects the Framers' scheme of supplementing the principle of the separation of powers with checks and balances by allowing a member of the executive branch to exercise limited legislative functions.

Section 3

5. The Senate shall choose their other Officers, and also a President pro tempore, in the Absence of the Vice President, or when he shall exercise the Office of President of the United States.

Most vice presidents have not spent much time presiding over the Senate so the task of presiding has fallen to the president pro tempore who is chosen by the party holding a majority in the Senate.

Section 3

6. The Senate shall have the sole Power to try all Impeachments. When sitting for that Purpose, they shall be on Oath or Affirmation.

The Senate's role in the impeachment process begins when it receives articles of impeachment from the House. The House designates "managers" who act as prosecutors in the Senate trial. Although the House managers have sometimes been chosen by election of a majority of the House, since the 1980s the Chair of the House Judiciary Committee in consultation with the House leadership has chosen the managers. Judiciary Committee Chair Henry Hyde chose the thirteen House managers—including himself—for President Clinton's trial.

Pursuant to its "Power to try all Impeachments" the Senate has developed twenty-six rules for conducting impeachment proceedings.[39] Those rules, which have changed only slightly since Andrew Johnson's trial in 1868, guided the Senate in the trial of President Clinton. The rules provide that the Senate can compel the attendance of witnesses and enforce its orders. The senators serve as jurors and each is sworn in individually before deliberations begin. The presiding officer rules on questions of evidence. Rule XVII provides for the cross-examination of witnesses and Rule XIX allows the parties to object to the questions. The senators are not allowed to speak during the trial but may question a witness by passing a note to the presiding officer, who then poses the question. During the trial, the proceedings are open but the deliberations take place in closed session. In Clinton's trial, an effort to suspend the rules and open deliberations failed to obtain the necessary two-thirds vote.[40] It is only during the closed deliberations that senators are allowed to debate and even then Rule XXIV limits the duration of their comments to fifteen minutes for each senator.

After they have completed their deliberations, the senators meet in open session to vote on the guilt or innocence of the accused. As provided by Article I, Section 3 (6), a vote of two-thirds or more on any article of impeachment results in conviction and automatic removal from office. The Senate may also vote to disqualify the convicted official from holding office in the future. It is important to remember that the Senate may change any of its rules pertaining to impeachment procedures with the exception of the rules that reiterate the constitutional requirements set forth in Article I, Section 3 (6).

Despite the detailed rules, Senate trials are not strictly legal proceedings. Indeed, there are major differences between Senate impeachment proceedings and criminal trials that underscore the political nature of impeachment. For example, the senators can overrule the presiding officer by a majority vote. Also, the senators' extensive knowledge of the case and political interest in its outcome would disqualify them from serving on the jury if the proceeding were a criminal trial. One member of the Senate in President Clinton's trial had a connection to the defendant that would certainly have disqualified her from serving as a juror in a criminal proceeding: Senator Barbara Boxer's daughter is married to Hillary Rodham Clinton's brother. Moreover, in all but the most routine impeachments the judge—that is, the vice president or the chief justice—is likely to be far more involved in the case than a judge in a criminal trial. Chief Justice Rehnquist, for example, who presided over President Clinton's trial, also selected the judges of the three-judge special division that selected Ken Starr to be Independent Counsel to investigate the president.

Rule XI, which the Senate adopted in 1935 but did not use until 1986, permits the Senate to appoint a committee of senators to gather evidence,

---

[39] *Rules of Procedure and Practice in the Senate When Sitting on Impeachment Trials,* from *Rules and Manual of the Senate;* revised pursuant to S. Res. 479,99–2, August 16, 1986.
[40] The vote was fifty-nine to forty-one. The Senate voted to allow individual senators to publish their remarks in the *Congressional Record* after the final vote. Some senators made their comments public even before the deliberations. Eric Pianin and Guy Gugliotta, "Senators Find Private Deliberations Create Public Confusion," *Washington Post,* February 11, 1999, A16.

take testimony, and otherwise exercise all the powers of the full Senate in an impeachment trial. After the committee completes its work and makes a report—including a full transcript of its proceedings—the full Senate may send for witnesses and even order the evidence resubmitted to the entire body. The Senate elected to use a committee of twelve senators in the impeachment trials of three federal judges in the 1980s: Harry Claiborne (1986), Alcee L. Hastings (1989), and Walter L. Nixon Jr. (1989). The Senate convicted all three. After his conviction, Judge Nixon challenged Rule XI, alleging that it violates the constitutional grant of authority to the Senate to "try" all impeachments insofar as it prohibits the whole Senate from taking part in the hearings. He argued that the full Senate is constitutionally mandated to hold a judicial trial—it cannot simply review the findings of a committee. In *Nixon v United States*, the justices unanimously rejected Judge Nixon's claim. Chief Justice Rehnquist's opinion in that case emphasized that the language of Article I, Section 3 (6), manifests a textual commitment of impeachment to the Senate. The Senate's power to try impeachments is subject only to the three limitations that the members must be under oath, a two-thirds vote is required to convict, and the chief justice presides when the president is tried. According to Rehnquist, the Framers did not intend to impose any additional limitations on the form of the Senate proceedings by inserting the word *try* in the first sentence of the clause. Moreover, he maintained that there are no judicially manageable standards for reviewing the Senate's actions. It would be impossible, and thus disruptive, for a court to determine whether the Senate had "tried" an impeached official within the meaning of the clause. Thus, he concluded that controversies concerning impeachment are political questions and as such are nonjusticiable—that is, they are not suitable for judicial resolution.[41] Three of the justices agreed with the decision to reject Nixon's claim but were not willing to give the Senate unreviewable authority to act on impeachments.[42] If the Senate were to dispense with all procedures and simply convict an official by a coin toss, Justice Souter noted, judicial review would clearly be warranted.

Is the Senate constitutionally obligated to try an official who has been impeached by the House? As the 106th Congress prepared to convene in the first week of 1999 a number of Republicans in both the House and the Senate argued that the "Power to try all Impeachments" mandates a full trial. The Constitution, they argued, leaves the Senate no discretion either to dispense with a trial altogether on the grounds that President Clinton's misconduct did not rise to the level of an impeachable offense or to conduct an abbreviated proceeding without witnesses. Two senators devised the following bipartisan plan.[43] House Judiciary Chair Henry Hyde would present evidence for one day. The White House would then have a day for rebuttal followed by a day of questioning by senators. Motions would then be offered asking the Senate to decide whether to proceed to a full-scale trial on each of the two articles of impeachment. The motions would provide, "assuming that all the facts alleged by the House are

---

[41]*Nixon v United States*, 506 US 224 (1993).
[42]The three concurrences came from White joined by Blackmun, and Souter, who wrote his own opinion.
[43]Senator Slade Gorton, Republican from Washington, and Senator Joseph I. Lieberman, Democrat from Connecticut, worked out the plan.

correct, they constitute sufficient grounds for conviction and removal from office."[44] The senators would debate the motions for at least two days and then
vote. Only if two-thirds of those voting agreed would the Senate proceed to a
full-scale trial. Otherwise, the Senate would vote on whether to dismiss the
case. A majority vote on that motion would result in dismissal. That plan failed
to receive support from Senate Republicans.

The language giving the Senate the "Sole power to try" might be interpreted
to bestow on the Senate the power to forgo a trial. Indeed, Rehnquist's opinion
in Judge Nixon's case implies as much. Even so, the Senate has never chosen to
ignore the House's decision to impeach by declining to hold a trial and there may
be some good—albeit more political than constitutional—reasons the Senate
would not wish to do so. First, the Senate's decision not to hold a trial could have
the effect of lowering the House's standard for impeachment. In future cases, the
House could adopt a position that impeaching a political opponent is appropriate because the Senate can bring an end to the matter by simply declining to proceed with a trial. Second, comity between the two houses of Congress may well
require that the Senate show its respect for the House's decision to impeach by
proceeding with a trial.

The televised trial of President Clinton—the first impeachment trial of an
elected president—lasted for five weeks in early 1999. The day after the opening of the trial, the Senate unanimously approved a resolution providing the
time periods for each side to submit their materials and specifying that the arguments presented by first, the House prosecutors, and then the president,
could not exceed twenty-four hours. The senators would then be allowed to
question the parties for no longer than sixteen hours. Following the questioning, the senators agreed, a motion to dismiss could be considered. Additionally,
a motion could be made to subpoena witnesses. If the Senate agreed to allow
either side to call witnesses, the witnesses would be deposed and then the Senate would decide which witnesses would testify.

After six days of opening speeches by the House managers and the White
House lawyers, the senators had their first opportunity to participate in the trial
by asking questions through Chief Justice Rehnquist. As January drew to a
close, a series of partisan votes determined the course that the rest of the trial
would take. Although a majority rejected Senator Robert Byrd's motion to dismiss the case, the fact that senators voted for it indicated that conviction was
not a possibility. But at the same time Democratic senators were seeking to end
the trial, the Republican House managers, with the help of Ken Starr, sought
and obtained a court order compelling Monica Lewinsky to talk with them.
That maneuver violated the Senate's agreement on procedures for deciding
whether to call witnesses. Then by a vote of fifty-six to forty-four, the Senate
approved prosecution subpoenas for Monica Lewinsky, presidential friend Ver-
non Jordan, and White House aide Sidney Blumenthal.[45] Two days of behind-
the-scenes negotiations while the senators met in party caucuses failed to bring

---

[44]Guy Gugliotta, "Two Senators Drew Up Plan for Trial Hoping to Rise above Partisan Rancor," *Washington Post*, January 5, 1995, A5.
[45]Peter Baker and Helen Dewar, "Senate Votes to Subpoena Three Witnesses," *Washington Post*, January 28, 1999, A1.

any bipartisan agreement over how to proceed with the trial. A series of votes along party lines followed. The Republican majority rejected a Democratic motion to move directly to a vote on the articles of impeachment and turned down a Democratic proposal that would have kept witnesses off the Senate floor and barred display of videotaped testimony. The majority adopted instead the Republican trial plan that left open the possibility of showing videotaped testimony on the Senate floor. In their only concession, the Republicans agreed that a motion for more witnesses could only be made jointly by the majority and minority leader. Because that arrangement gave the Democrats a veto over any effort by House prosecutors to call additional witnesses, it guaranteed that neither the House prosecutors nor the White House would call any more witnesses. The Republican plan also left open the possibility of a motion for "findings of fact," which would allow the Senate to judge the president guilty by a simple majority without removing him from office.[46]

By the first week in February, three days of depositions of Lewinsky, Jordan, and Blumenthal had reputedly failed to reveal any new information that would convince a dozen Democrats to join the fifty-five Republicans to vote for conviction. Senate Republicans, therefore, began to express a desire to bring the trial to an end. Twenty-five of the Senate's fifty-five Republicans voted with the Democrats to deny the House managers' request to summon Lewinsky to the Senate floor to testify. The Republicans remained united, however, in their determination to authorize the parties to show excerpts of the videotaped depositions. After some behind-the-scenes negotiations, the Republicans backed away from the "findings-of-fact" proposal, which not only Democrats but also the conservative Republicans opposed.

It seems probable that television viewers who did not look at any other portion of the impeachment trial eagerly watched Monica Lewinsky answer the House managers' questions. But when neither her testimony nor that of the other two witnesses provided any support to the House managers' case against the president, the trial moved toward the conclusion that had been expected virtually from the beginning—the acquittal of President Clinton.

Section 3

6. [continued] When the President of the United States is tried, the Chief Justice shall preside.

The vice president, who has the right to sit as President of the Senate as provided by Article I, Section 3 (4), is disqualified from doing so when the president is the subject of an impeachment trial. The Framers must have understood that the vice president, who would stand to gain the presidency in the event of a conviction, would have a conflict of interest in presiding over the Senate in an impeachment trial of a president. If a tie occurs, the chief justice casts a vote to break the tie. A majority of the senators can overrule the chief justice on any matter.

---

[46]Guy Gugliotta and Dan Morgan, "The Majority Rules in Trial Votes," *Washington Post,* January 29, 1999, A17; Alison Mitchell, "Senate Plan Opens Door to Testimony by Lewinsky," *New York Times,* January 29, 1999, National/Politics Section.

Section 3

6. [continued] And no Person shall be convicted without the Concurrence of two thirds of the Members Present.

Of the sixteen officials impeached by the House, the Senate has convicted seven—all judges of the lower federal courts—acquitted six, dismissed two because of doubts that the Senate had jurisdiction,[47] and declined to proceed against one who had resigned before the beginning of the trial.[48]

The two most well-known impeachment trials in the nineteenth century, those of Associate Justice Samuel Chase in 1805 and President Andrew Johnson in 1868, resulted in acquittal.[49] By a partisan vote, the Republican-controlled House impeached Justice Chase, a zealous Federalist, essentially for using his position for partisan purposes. Although the composition of the Senate— twenty-five Republicans and nine Federalists—gave the Republicans the necessary two-thirds majority to convict, a sufficient number of Republicans refused to go along with the House managers and Chase was acquitted. His acquittal has often been viewed as a victory for judicial independence that brought an end to the Republicans' antijudiciary campaign. Chase's impeachment, however, also served as a warning to federal judges that it would be prudent to limit their partisan activities.

Andrew Johnson, the first president to be tried by the Senate, was a Southern Democrat who ascended to the presidency when Abraham Lincoln was assassinated in April 1865. Johnson soon clashed with the Northern Republican-controlled Congress over policies for restoring the Union. He vetoed the Reconstruction Acts that dismantled his restored governments in the South and divided the South into five military districts. Congress overrode the vetoes and Johnson proceeded to enforce the laws as narrowly as possible. One of the acts that Congress passed to limit the president's authority was the Tenure of Office Act, which prohibited the president from removing executive officials confirmed by the Senate without the consent of that body. After three failed impeachment investigations, Republican House leaders were able to garner enough votes to impeach Johnson when he apparently violated the Tenure Act by removing Secretary of War Edwin M. Stanton.[50] Johnson's impeachment was not simply a dispute between the president and Congress over how Reconstruction should proceed. It also involved issues of whether the executive or legislative branch would make the policies, as well as president's power to veto

---

[47]The Senate acquitted Senator William Blount in 1799 in part because of doubt that a senator was a "civil officer." Two hours before the House's formal vote on his impeachment in 1876, Secretary of War William Belknap resigned from office. The Senate held a trial anyway but the vote fell short of the required two-thirds largely because a number of senators doubted that they retained jurisdiction after Belknap's resignation.

[48]District Judge George English, impeached for malperformance in 1926, resigned six days before his impeachment trial was scheduled to begin.

[49]For a more detailed discussion of the Chase and Johnson impeachments, see Alfred H. Kelly, Winfred A. Harbison, and Herman Belz, *The American Constitution: Its Origins and Development*, 7th ed. (New York: W. W. Norton, 1983), Vol. I, 168–170; Vol. II, 340–346.

[50]At his trial, Johnson's lawyers argued that he had not actually violated the law. The Tenure of Office Act provided that cabinet officers were to hold office only during the term of the president appointing them, and for one month thereafter. Because Stanton had been appointed by President Lincoln and Johnson had not reappointed him, the Tenure of Office Act did not apply. The prosecutors argued, however, that Johnson was completing Lincoln's unexpired term.

legislation and remove subordinate executive officials. At the outset of the two-month trial, Johnson's lawyers argued that the trial should be treated as a legal proceeding, bound by legal rules of evidence. The Republican prosecutors maintained that the nature of impeachment rendered the Senate more than a court. As such it could hear evidence that would be inadmissible in a criminal trial and it might convict the president for acting against the public interest. Although the Senate resolved the issue by adopting the form of a judicial proceeding, allowing the Chief Justice to settle all questions of law and evidence, the trial was, in substance, thoroughly political. With seven Republicans voting for acquittal, the Senate failed to muster the necessary two-thirds by only one vote.

The second impeachment trial of a president ended when the Senate—after four days of deliberations behind closed doors—voted to acquit President Bill Clinton by a vote of fifty-five to forty-five and fifty to fifty on the two articles of impeachment charging him with perjury and obstruction of justice. Although the trial took the form of a legal proceeding, in substance it was thoroughly political. The senators divided along party lines on nearly every procedural issue throughout the trial.[51] It was assumed from the outset of the trial that the House prosecutors would not be able to garner the sixty-seven votes needed for conviction. Nevertheless, a proposal for an abbreviated trial and a motion for dismissal were rejected in favor of carrying the trial through to its completion.

After the conclusion of Clinton's trial, California Democratic Senator Diane Feinstein moved to proceed with a resolution for censure. She asked that the rules be suspended so that the resolution could proceed even though it was not on the Calendar. The motion to suspend the rules failed by a vote of forty-three to fifty-six.

Section 3

7. Judgment in Cases of Impeachment shall not extend further than to removal from Office, and disqualification to hold and enjoy any Office of honor, Trust or Profit under the United States:

A vote of two-thirds or more on any article of impeachment results in conviction and automatic removal from office. The Senate's practice has been to vote separately or not at all on disqualification. The Senate has disqualified—by a majority vote—only two of the seven federal judges it has convicted. In the 1980s, the Senate declined to disqualify the three judges after convicting them, and one—Alcee L. Hastings—was elected to Congress in 1992. A Republican proposal to conclude President Clinton's trial with "findings of fact" would have allowed the Senate to judge the president guilty of perjury and obstruction of justice by a majority vote. That vote would have been followed by a formal vote on the articles of impeachment requiring two-thirds for conviction and removal. The possibility of "findings of fact" raised serious constitutional ques-

---

[51]The one exception was the unanimous vote to allow each side twenty-four hours to present its case and to postpone a decision on whether witnesses would be called.

tions. For example, such a procedure would have allowed a simple majority of the senators to condemn the president even though Article I, Section 3 (6), requires a vote of two-thirds for conviction.

Section 3

7. [continued] but the Party convicted shall nevertheless be liable and subject to Indictment, Trial, Judgment and Punishment according to Law.

Prosecution for criminal wrongdoing after conviction on impeachment does not constitute double jeopardy. Thus, although a president is not considered to be susceptible to criminal charges so long as he is in office, once he is convicted and removed there is no bar to prosecution. In December 1998, President Clinton stood fast in his refusal to admit that he had lied to the grand jury about his relationship with Monica Lewinsky. Although such an admission might have helped him to garner support from some wavering Republicans and thereby avoid impeachment, it was conceivable that such a maneuver would have provided the basis of a future prosecution for perjury. After he was acquitted by the Senate in February 1999, Clinton faced the prospect of possible criminal prosecution after he left office in January 2001. On his last full day in office, however, the president made a deal with Kenneth Starr's successor, Robert W. Ray, in which the Independent Council agreed not to pursue criminal charges against him. In return Clinton admitted that he gave false testimony under oath and agreed to surrender his license to practice law for five years.

Section 4

1. The Times, Places, and Manner of holding Elections for Senators and Representatives, shall be prescribed in each State by the Legislature thereof; but the Congress may at any time by Law make or alter such Regulations, except as to the Places of chusing Senators.

2. The Congress shall assemble at least once in every Year, and such Meeting shall be on the first Monday in December, unless they shall by Law appoint a different Day.

The first clause of Article I, Section 4, gave the states the authority to establish procedural regulations for Congressional elections but left Congress broad authority to protect the integrity of the constitutionally protected right to vote in those elections. The Seventeenth Amendment—ratified in 1913—which provides for the direct election of senators, negated the final phrase of Article I, Section 4 (1), "except as to the Places of chusing Senators."

We discussed *U.S. Term Limits, Inc. v Thornton* in the context of Article I, Section 2 (2). The Court also had an opportunity to interpret Article I, Section 4 (1), in that case. The first argument that U.S. Term Limits advanced in defense of the state's authority to impose limits on the number of terms that members of Congress may serve was that the state was simply acting under its power to prescribe the "Manner of holding Elections." Justice Stevens, who wrote for the five-member majority disagreed, reasoning that if the states could regulate the manner of congressional elections by imposing term limits, Congress could do so as well under its authority to "make or alter such Regulations." That result, Stevens maintained, was inconsistent with the Framers' determination not to allow Congress to set its own qualifications. Additionally, Stevens explained that the broad construction of the clause that U.S. Term Limits advanced was profoundly at odds with the Framers' understanding of its meaning. The Constitutional Convention "intended the . . . Clause to grant States authority to create procedural regulations, not to provide States with license to exclude classes of candidates from federal office."[52]

The Twentieth Amendment superseded Article I, Section 4 (2), by providing that Congress shall convene on January 3 or another date designated by law.

Section 5

1. Each House shall be the Judge of the Elections, Returns and Qualifications of its own Members,

Congress's authority under Article I, Section 5 (1), is limited to resolving disputed elections. The clause does not authorize either house to add to the age, citizenship, and residency qualifications specified in Article I, Section 2 (2), and Article I, Section 3 (3). Instead, it merely authorizes each house to determine whether a particular member possesses those qualifications.

For much of the nation's history, both the House and the Senate acted as if they were entitled to add qualifications, on twelve occasions denying properly elected members their seats.[53] For example, in 1919 and 1920 the House refused to admit Victor L. Berger, a member of the Socialist Party from Wisconsin who had been convicted of espionage. In the 1920s the Senate refused to seat two new members because of scandals in connection with campaign funds.

The Supreme Court refuted Congress's theory of its power to set qualifications in 1969 in *Powell v McCormack.*[54] The appellant, Adam Clayton Powell Jr., was a controversial legislator from Harlem who had been a member of Congress since 1944. The House refused to seat him in 1967 after a congressional investigation concluded that he had violated House rules by improperly using federal funds. The investigation found that he had, for example, paid his former wife a salary of $20,000 although she did not work either in his district or his office in Washington, D.C. A subsequent investigation concluded that Powell had tried to evade a fine connected with a defamation of character action against him, had misused public funds, and filed false expenditure reports. The House then adopted a resolution by a vote of 307–116 excluding Powell from the House and instructing the Speaker, John McCormack, to notify the Governor of New York that his seat was vacant. Powell and thirteen of his constituents filed suit against McCormack, alleging that the House had no authority to refuse to seat him because he met the age, citizenship, and residency requirements for office. McCormack contended that the House had the authority to exclude

---

[52]*U.S. Term Limits Inc. v Thornton*, 514 US 779 (1995).
[53]For the names and reasons for each exclusion, see Lee Epstein and Thomas G. Walker, *Constitutional Law for a Changing America, Institutional Powers and Constraints*, 2d ed. (Washington, DC: CQ Press, 1995), 116, Table 3-2.
[54]*Powell v McCormack*, 395 US 486 (1969).

members who met the constitutional requirements and that Article I, Section 5 (1), gave to the House the authority to determine Powell's qualifications, and that it was not appropriate for the Court to consider the question.[55]

Chief Justice Earl Warren, who wrote for the seven-member majority, engaged in various methods of constitutional interpretation in his attempt to discover the meaning of Congress's authority to judge the qualifications of its members. First, in an attempt to uncover the intent of the Framers, he examined the debates at the Constitutional Convention and inferred that the delegates to the Convention did not want Congress to have the power to establish qualifications. Second, Warren used a structural approach by considering the combined significance of three constitutional provisions: Article I, Sections 2 (2) and 3 (3), set forth the age, citizenship, and residency requirements; Article I, Section 5 (1), gave Congress the authority to judge the qualifications of its members; and Article I, Section 5 (2), provided that Congress could expel a member by a vote of two-thirds. The extent of Congress's authority to judge the qualifications of its members could not be discerned in isolation of the fact that the Constitution had defined age, citizenship, and residency requirements. Taken together, the provisions meant that Congress's power to judge the qualifications of its members was limited to a determination of whether a member had the requisite age, citizenship, and residency. Article I, Section 5 (2), considered in conjunction with the other two provisions, indicated to Warren that the Framers considered **expulsion** too serious to be determined by a majority vote and so required a vote of two-thirds. Third, Warren engaged in purposive analysis when he observed that if the intent of the Framers had been less clear, the "basic principles of our democratic system" and, more specifically, the principle "that the people should choose whom they please to govern them" would have persuaded the Court that the Constitution does not give Congress the authority to deny membership by a majority vote.[56]

Section 5

1. [continued] and a Majority of each [house] shall constitute a Quorum to do business; but a smaller Number may adjourn from day to day, and may be authorized to compel the Attendance of absent Members, in such Manner, and under such Penalties as each House may provide.

2. Each House may determine the Rules of its Proceedings, punish its Members for disorderly Behaviour, and, with the Concurrence of two thirds, expel a Member.

3. Each House shall keep a Journal of its Proceedings, and from time to time publish the same, excepting such Parts as may in their Judgment require Secrecy; and the yeas and Nays of the Members of either House on any question shall, at the Desire of one fifth of those Present, be entered on the Journal.

4. Neither House, during the Session of Congress, shall, without the Consent of the other, adjourn for more than three days, nor to any other place than that in which the two Houses shall be sitting.

---

[55]Epstein and Walker, 118.
[56]*Powell v McCormack*, 395 US 486, 548 (1969).

The provisions in Article 1, Section 5, cover routine procedural or "house-keeping" matters. The Constitution specified only the barest outline of congressional organization and operation. Important elements of congressional practices that have developed over the years but are not mentioned in the document include the function of political parties, the committees and their chairs, the seniority system, and the Senate filibuster.

Section 6

1. The Senators and Representatives shall receive a Compensation for their Services, to be ascertained by Law, and paid out of the Treasury of the United States.

The requirement that the salary of members of Congress be paid by the United States Treasury remedied one of the major problems that plagued the government under the Articles of Confederation: Congress's dependence on the states.

By the terms of Article 1, Section 6 (1), senators and representatives determine their own salaries. Such an arrangement was inconsistent with the overall design of the Constitution that limited the power of government officials by the mechanisms of the separation of powers and checks and balances. The First Congress proposed an amendment as part of the Bill of Rights that became the Twenty-seventh Amendment when it was ratified in 1992 effectively prohibiting members of Congress from giving themselves raises. Traditionally, however, legislators were reluctant to raise their salaries because doing so invariably invited public criticism. Between 1990 and 2002 congressional salaries increased from $98,400 to $150,000.[57]

Section 6

1. [continued] They shall in all Cases, except Treason, Felony and Breach of the Peace, be privileged from Arrest, during their Attendance at the Session of their respective Houses, and in going to and returning from the same; and for any Speech or Debate in either House, they shall not be questioned in any other Place.

Article I, Section 6 (1) confers two immunities on members of Congress. The first provides an extremely narrow privilege from arrest. In 1908, the Court found that "treason, felony, and breach of the peace," as those words were clearly understood at the time of the adoption of the Constitution embraced substantially all crimes.[58] Senators and representatives consequently have no privilege against arrest or prosecution in any criminal case. The immunity does, however, apply to arrests in civil suits. Although arrests for civil offenses were common when the Constitution was adopted, they have been virtually nonexistent for many years. The immunity, moreover, is limited to arrest and does not protect legislators from civil suits entirely.[59]

---

[57]"Salaries and Benefits of U.S. Congress Members" Available: http://usgovinfo.miningco.com/library/weekly/aa031200a.htm.
[58]*Williamson v United States*, 207 US 425 (1908).
[59]*Long v Ansell*, 293 US 76 (1934).

The second immunity, specified in the speech or debate clause, provides a broader protection against suits for libel or slander. The Framers wanted to protect legislators from the harassment and intimidation that parliamentary critics of the king suffered in England. The Court has held that the protection extends beyond formal debate to things "generally done in a session of the House by one of its members in relation to the business before it."[60] Elaborating on the reach of that immunity in 1972, Justice Byron White noted that matters are covered that are "an integral part of the deliberative and communicative processes by which Members participate in committee and House proceedings with respect to the consideration and passage or rejection of proposed legislation or with respect to other matters which the Constitution places within the jurisdiction of either House."[61] Thus, matters not essential to the deliberations of Congress are outside the scope of immunity. The same immunity enjoyed by members of Congress also extends to their aides.[62]

The Court elaborated further on the scope of the immunity offered by the speech or debate clause in several decisions in the 1970s. In one case, the Court held that members of Congress and their staff were immune from a suit for publishing and distributing a report on the Washington, D.C., school system that allegedly infringed on the privacy of students, who were identified by name. But the Court also held that a suit could proceed against the superintendent of documents, who printed and offered the report for sale because as a member of the executive branch he was not protected by the speech or debate clause. Moreover, the distribution of the report outside Congress was not a legislative function.[63] In another case, the Court allowed a libel suit to go forward against Senator William Proxmire for defamatory statements in press releases and constituent newsletters.[64] The justices again distinguished between the dissemination of materials within Congress, which would have been protected, and outside Congress, which was not essential to the legislative function.

Several cases have involved the criminal law. In a decision in 1972, noting that the speech or debate clause does not protect all conduct relating to the legislative process, the justices held that a senator could be prosecuted for bribery so long as that prosecution did not require inquiry into legislative acts or motivations.[65] In another case involving a prosecution of a member of Congress for bribery, the Court ruled that the speech or debate clause prohibits the introduction of evidence concerning past legislative acts.[66]

Section 6

2. No Senator or Representative shall, during the Time for which he was elected, be appointed to any civil Office under the Authority of the United States, which shall have been created, or the Emoluments whereof shall have been encreased during such time; and no person holding any Office under the United States, shall be a Member of either House during his Continuance in Office.

---

[60]*Kilbourn v Thompson*, 103 US 168, 204 (1881).
[61]*Gravel v United States*, 408 US 606, 625 (1980).
[62]*Ibid.*
[63]*Doe v McMillan*, 412 US 306 (1973).
[64]*Hutchinson v Proxmire*, 443 US 111 (1979).
[65]*United States v Brewster*, 408 US 501 (1972).
[66]*United States v Helstoski*, 442 US 477 (1979).

Article I, Section 6 (2), contains two clauses: the emoluments clause and the incompatibility clause. The first prevents members of Congress from profiting after they leave office by using their influence as legislators to create positions for themselves in the federal government or to increase the compensation of existing positions. The second clause prohibits members of Congress from simultaneously holding federal executive or judicial office. Both clauses are central to the doctrine of the separation of powers and distinguish the United States constitutional system from British parliamentary practice in which members of Parliament also serve as Cabinet ministers.

During the Vietnam War, some opponents of the United States' involvement alleged that the incompatibility clause prohibits members of Congress from serving in the military and sought to have members of Congress removed from the Reserves. The Court avoided addressing the issue by holding that the individuals who brought the action lacked standing to sue under the case or controversy requirement of Article III, Section 2 (1).[67]

Section 7

1. All Bills for raising Revenue shall originate in the House of Representatives; but the Senate may propose or concur with Amendments as on other Bills.

The origination clause was a crucial part of the Great Compromise. As the Committee of Eleven worked out the compromise over representation in the two houses of Congress, Ben Franklin proposed that the Senate be forbidden to originate or amend money bills.[68] Some of the delegates, including Madison, insisted that the provision would be meaningless—it would make no difference where a bill originated. Its defenders viewed the limitation as a concession to the large states, which would have more representatives and thus more power in the House as opposed to the Senate. Additionally, given the colonists' condemnation of taxation without representation, it was important to link taxation to representation by giving the House, the more democratic of the two chambers, primary responsibility for revenue-raising measures.

The delegates eventually softened the provision to allow the Senate to amend tax bills. As a result, the origination clause has had only a limited effect because senators are allowed to introduce what are essentially revenue bills in the form of amendments.

In 1990, the Supreme Court held that it is appropriate for the judiciary to consider challenges to laws on the grounds that they violate the origination clause. Further limiting the effect of the clause, the justices defined "revenue bill" as a "statute that raises revenue to support government generally." A statute that creates a specific governmental program and raises revenue to support it, the Court maintained, is not a bill for raising revenue and is therefore not subject to the limitations of the origination clause.[69] Moreover, the clause

---

[67]*Schlesinger v Reservists to Stop the War*, 418 US 208 (1974).
[68]Farber and Sherry, 128–129.
[69]*United States v Munoz-Flores*, 495 US 385 (1990).

does not apply to statutes that create fines or fees or that earmark funds for specific purposes; it applies only to those that raise general revenues.

Section 7

2. Every Bill which shall have passed the House of Representatives and the Senate, shall, before it becomes a Law, be presented to the President of the United States; if he approve he shall sign it, but if not he shall return it, with his Objections to that House in which it shall have originated, who shall enter the Objections at large on their Journal, and proceed to reconsider it. If after such Reconsideration two thirds of that House shall agree to pass the Bill, it shall be sent, together with the Objections, to the other House, by which it shall likewise be reconsidered, and if approved by two thirds of that House, it shall become a Law. But in all such Cases the Votes of both Houses shall be determined by yeas and Nays, and the Names of the Persons voting for and against the Bill shall be entered on the Journal of each House respectively. If any Bill shall not be returned by the President within ten Days (Sundays excepted) after it shall have been presented to him, the Same shall be a Law, in like Manner as if he had signed it, unless the Congress by their Adjournment prevent its Return, in which Case it shall not be a Law.

The procedures for making laws that are outlined in Article I, Section 7 (2), are one of the clearest manifestations of the constitutional principle of checks and balances. The requirement that both chambers must agree to the terms of a bill provides a mechanism whereby Congress checks itself—each house constrains the power of the other. The president then has the opportunity to veto the bill and thereby to check the power of the legislative branch. But then, to keep the power of the president within appropriate limits, Congress can pass the bill over the president's veto by a vote of two-thirds. Additionally, to limit the executive's ability to obstruct passage of a bill simply by ignoring it, it becomes law ten days after the president receives it. Finally, so that Congress may not arrange its recesses in order to deprive the president of the opportunity to veto a bill, the final clause of Article I, Section 7 (2), provides that if Congress adjourns before the ten days have passed, the bill will not become law. In that case the president is said to exercise a pocket veto and Congress has no opportunity to override it.

Although the pocket veto provision appears to be straightforward—the president may only exercise this absolute veto if Congress is not in session ten days after it sends him a bill—presidents have disagreed with Congress over what constitutes an "Adjournment." At the end of two sessions (two years—the length of a term for members of the House) Congress adjourns and its legislative existence terminates. There is no doubt that the president may exercise a pocket veto in that situation. There are two other situations that are not so clear, however. First, a session of Congress now runs from January until November or December. Does the break between the first and second session constitute an adjournment for purposes of the pocket veto? In 1929, when the Supreme Court construed the pocket veto provision for the first time the justices found that the determinative question was whether Congress, by virtue of not being in session, prevented the president from returning the bill, and thereby vetoing it, during the time allowed. The Court held that because there was no opportunity for the president to return the bill during Congress's break between sessions, that break constituted an adjournment for purposes of the pocket veto.[70] Despite that decision, there were several disputes during the 1970s and 1980s between Congress and the president as to whether the pocket veto can be used between sessions. President Gerald Ford adopted the position that he would not use a pocket veto when Congress was between sessions if the House and Senate designated officers to receive veto messages. President Ronald Reagan, however, insisted on using pocket vetoes during breaks between sessions. After he tried to kill a bill conditioning military aid to El Salvador on that country's progress in protecting human rights, thirty-three representatives filed suit. The Court of Appeals ruled that the president's use of the pocket veto was improper and the bill, therefore, had become law. The law expired a few weeks later. Although the Supreme Court subsequently heard the case, the justices managed to avoid addressing the issue by holding that because the statute had expired the case was moot and there was no case or controversy as required by Article III, Section 2 (1).[71]

A second situation that has been the source of disputes between the president and Congress arises when the legislature is in recess. In 1938, the Court ruled that during a short recess the secretary of the Senate had the authority to receive a veto message. Chief Justice Hughes's opinion in that case implied that a pocket veto could not be used during a recess of only a few days.[72] Nevertheless, President Richard Nixon tried to use a pocket veto in 1970 during a five-day Christmas recess. The Court of Appeals upheld the district court's invalidation of Nixon's action, noting that a recess does not prevent the president from returning a bill.[73] The Department of Justice decided not to appeal to the Supreme Court.

Section 7

3. Every Order, Resolution, or Vote to which the Concurrence of the Senate and House of Representatives may be necessary (except on a question of Adjournment) shall be presented to the President of the United States; and before the Same shall take Effect, shall be approved by him, or being disapproved by him, shall be repassed by two thirds of the Senate and House of Representatives, according to the Rules and Limitations prescribed in the Case of a Bill.

The presentment clause reinforces the president's role in the lawmaking process and thereby gives additional force to an important check on the power of Congress. Before a bill becomes a law the president must be "presented" with it so that he will have the opportunity to sign or veto it as provided by Article I, Section 7 (2). Congress cannot, by the terms of the presentment clause, sneak a bill into law by designating it an order, resolution, or vote, and thereby evade the president's veto power.

---

[70]*The Pocket Veto Case*, 279 US 655 (1929).
[71]*Burke v Barnes*, 479 US 361 (1987).
[72]*Wright v United States*, 302 US 583 (1938).
[73]*Kennedy v Sampson*, 364 F. Supp. 1075 (DDC 1973); 511 F 2d 430 (DC Cir. 1974).

The Supreme Court relied on the presentment clause when it invalidated the **legislative veto** in 1983. The legislative veto is a device that Congress has used to exert control over executive agencies and executive branch officials to whom it has delegated authority. In other words, in contrast to the normal procedure for making laws prescribed in Article I, Section 7 (2) and (3), with the legislative veto the executive branch makes policies that are subject to congressional disapproval.

The legislative veto originated when Congress agreed to allow President Herbert Hoover to reorganize the executive branch without submitting a bill to Congress on the condition that either House could reject a reorganization plan by passing a resolution of disapproval.[74] For a number of years Congress used the legislative veto sparingly—from 1932 until 1972 only fifty-one bills included a provision for a legislative veto. From 1972 to 1979, however, sixty-two statutes contained some form of legislative veto.[75] The precise form of legislative vetoes varied—presidential decisions were subject to disapproval by a vote of both houses, one house, a committee, or even a subcommittee.

Every president from Herbert Hoover to Ronald Reagan argued that the legislative veto was an unconstitutional infringement on the powers of the executive. In 1978 President Jimmy Carter informed Congress that he did not consider legislative vetoes to be binding. Although Ronald Reagan expressed his approval of the legislative veto during his campaign for the presidency in 1980, once he assumed office he instructed his Attorney General to proceed with a suit challenging a legislative veto in the Immigration and Nationality Act.[76] That provision allowed either the Senate or House to pass a resolution vetoing the Attorney General's decision to suspend deportation of an alien.

In a sweeping decision in 1983 that sounded "the death knell for nearly 200 other statutory provisions," as well as the one at issue in the case, the Supreme Court declared that legislative vetoes violate both the presentment clause of Article I, Section 7 (3), and the bicameral requirement of Article I, Section 7 (2).[77]

Although the legislative veto raised questions about the extent to which Congress may make policy without presidential review, the controversy over the line item veto was concerned with defining the limits of the president's role in the lawmaking process. The Line Item Veto Act of 1996 authorized the president to cancel spending and tax benefit measures after he had signed them into law. The law also authorized Congress to restore what the president canceled in "disapproval bills." Additionally, a provision of the law specified that any member of Congress or any individual adversely affected by the law could bring an action in United States District Court challenging its constitutionality. The day after the law went into effect six members of Congress filed suit, arguing that the law was unconstitutional. The members of Congress who challenged

---

[74]Epstein and Walker, 175–176.

[75]Melvin I. Urofsky, *A March of Liberty: A Constitutional History of the United States* (New York: Alfred A. Knopf, 1988), 945.

[76]*Ibid.*, 946–947. Earlier Carter had the Justice Department join a suit brought by the individual who was affected by the legislative veto. Epstein and Walker, 176.

[77]*Immigration and Naturalization Service v Chadha*, 462 US 919 (1983). Justice White, in his dissenting opinion made the "death knell" observation.

the law claimed that it injured them by altering the effect of the votes they cast on bills containing items subject to the president's cancellation. But the Supreme Court held that the members of Congress had failed to allege a sufficiently concrete injury to establish that they had standing to sue under the case or controversy requirement of Article III, Section 2 (1).[78]

President Clinton exercised his authority under the Line Item Veto Act by canceling a provision of the Balanced Budget Act of 1997, which gave money to healthcare providers in New York City, and a section of the Taxpayer Relief Act of 1997, which provided a tax break to farmers. Some individuals who were affected by the president's action brought suit, alleging that the law violated the Constitution. In 1998 in *Clinton v City of New York*, the Court invalidated the Line Item Veto Act, reasoning that nothing in either Article I, Section 7, or Article II of the Constitution authorizes the president to act unilaterally to repeal or amend parts of duly enacted statutes. The law, Justice Stevens noted in his opinion for a six-member majority, "would authorize the President to create a different law—one whose text was not voted on by either House of Congress or presented to the President for signature." The Line Item Veto Act, in short, authorized procedures that were clearly at odds with those that were so carefully designed by the Framers of Article I, Section 7.[79]

Section 8

The Congress shall have Power To . . .

Article I, Section 8, consists of eighteen paragraphs listing the powers granted to Congress that are commonly referred to as the enumerated powers.

A number of factors, including the Committee on Detail's decision to provide a list of Congress's powers, the emphasis the Framers placed on limiting the powers of government in the structure of the Constitution, and the initial opposition to a bill of rights on the ground that it was unnecessary to protect rights that the government had no power to regulate, suggest that the Framers expected that Congress would be able to exercise only those powers that were expressly enumerated in the text of the document. As we will see, however, the necessary and proper clause—the final paragraph of Section 8—served to bolster Congress's powers far beyond those that were enumerated.

1. lay and collect Taxes, Duties, Imposts and Excises, to pay the Debts and provide for the Common Defence and general Welfare of the United States; but all Duties, Imposts and Excises shall be uniform throughout the United States;

The absence of federal power to raise revenue was one of the most serious defects of the Articles of Confederation. Congress's authority to requisition the states for funds was grossly inadequate particularly given the fact that the states frequently simply refused Congress's requests. In 1786, a delegate to the Continental Congress wrote, "The Treasury now is literally without a penny."[80]

---

[78]*Raines v Byrd*, 521 US 811 (1997).
[79]*Clinton v City of New York*, 524 US 417 (1998).
[80]Rufus King to Elbridge Gerry, June 18, 1786, as quoted in Farber and Sherry, 24.

There was little disagreement among the delegates to the Constitutional Convention that Congress had to have the power to raise revenue. Even the New Jersey Plan proposed that the legislature be given increased power to raise revenue by import duties, stamp taxes, and postal charges, and to compel compliance with its requisitions.[81] As noted earlier, the Virginia Plan defined Congress's powers in the most general way—Congress was to have the power to "legislate in all cases for the general interest of the union, and also in those to which the states are separately incompetent." The Committee on Detail, however, devised a list of enumerated powers. That list provided the basis for what became Article I, Section 8.

The first paragraph of Article I, Section 8, confers sweeping authority on Congress to tax. It not only provides the general power to tax, but also grants the specific authority to collect taxes on imports—duties and imposts—and taxes on the manufacture, sale, or use of goods, and on certain activities—excises. The taxing power is limited by the geographic uniformity requirement—all items or activities that are taxed must be taxed at the same rate throughout the United States.[82]

From the beginning Congress used its taxing power for purposes other than raising revenue. In fact, in 1789 the first revenue act imposed import duties in part to encourage the growth of domestic industry and to protect it from foreign competition. In 1928, the first time the Supreme Court addressed the issue of whether Congress may use import taxes for regulatory purposes, the justices deferred to historical practice, holding "the existence of other motives" will not invalidate legislation "[s]o long as the motive of Congress and the effect of its legislative action are to secure revenue for the benefit of the general government."[83] Earlier, the Court upheld an excise tax—in this case a 10 percent tax on notes issued by state banks—that Congress had enacted to protect the new national bank from state competition.[84] In 1904, the Court upheld an excise tax on artificially colored oleomargarine. The purpose of the tax was clearly regulatory—to protect the dairy industry from competition. But the justices, emphasizing that it would be beyond the proper bounds of judicial power for the Court to consider the motives of Congress, ruled that the statute was on its face an excise tax and therefore within the scope of Congress's taxing power.[85] Thus, it appeared that the Court would not question Congress's motives in enacting excise taxes and would uphold such legislation so long as it conformed to the geographic uniformity requirement.

The Court sharply departed from that position during the period when a majority of the justices were determined to limit federal power vis-à-vis the states and to invalidate legislation that imposed regulations on business and

---

[81]Max Farrand, *The Framing of the Constitution of the United States* (New Haven, CT: Yale University Press, 1913), 85.

[82]The uniformity clause does not prevent Congress from defining a tax in geographic terms. Thus, a unanimous Court upheld the Crude Oil Windfall Profit Tax Act of 1980, which raised oil taxes except on wells located in a northerly section of Alaska. The exemption was not drawn on state political lines. Rather, it reflected a congressional judgment that unique climatic and geographic conditions make drilling wells in that region so much more costly than elsewhere that exempting that oil from the windfall profit tax in order to encourage further exploration in that area was justified. *Kraft Gen. Foods v Iowa Dept. of Revenue*, 505 US 71 (1992).

[83]*J.W. Hampton, Jr., & Co. v United States*, 276 US 394 (1928).

[84]*Veazie Bank v Fenno*, 8 Wall 533 (1869).

[85]*McCray v United States*, 195 US 27 (1904).

industry. In 1919, Congress attempted to grapple with the problem of child labor by imposing a tax of 10 percent on the net profits of any company that employed children. When an employer challenged the statute on the grounds that it was an attempt to regulate employment practices—a function reserved to the states—eight of the nine justices agreed. Chief Justice William Howard Taft, who wrote the opinion for the majority in *Bailey v Drexel Furniture Company*, reasoned that the statute exacted a penalty from employers who departed from its prescribed course of activity. It was, therefore, a regulation that was clearly beyond the authority of Congress. If the law were to stand, Taft maintained, Congress could take control of virtually any subject by enforcing extensive regulations "by a so-called tax."[86]

With the judicial revolution of 1937, the Court abandoned the restrictive interpretation of Congress's taxing power that it had adopted in *Drexel*. In 1953, the justices approved an excise tax that Congress imposed on gamblers.[87] The distinction between a tax for raising revenue and one for regulating behavior no longer constitutes a limit on Congress's taxing power. Still, there is an important limit on the taxing power that the Court continues to enforce. Congress may not use its power to tax in such a way as to violate other constitutional provisions. For example, in 1968 the Court held that tax laws requiring an individual to admit to criminal activities violate the self-incrimination clause of the Fifth Amendment.[88]

One of the results of the Depression and the New Deal was a major transformation in the understanding of the scope of government generally, and more specifically, the extent of Congress's power to tax and spend. Massive federal programs that Congress enacted in response to the economic disaster that began in 1929 and lasted until 1941 fundamentally altered the relationship between government and the economy, government and business, and government and the individual. The fact that 1937 marked the end of the "Constitution of limits" and the beginning of the "Constitution of powers" is particularly evident with regard to Congress's expanding power to tax and spend. Under the Constitution of limits the Court focused on the principle that the Constitution reserved powers to the states except where it expressly delegated authority to Congress. Under the Constitution of powers the Court generally defers to Congress, rarely invalidating legislation.

Article I, Section 8 (1), includes the power to spend as well as to tax, specifying that Congress may use the revenue it raises to pay government debts, to finance the nation's defense, and to provide for the general welfare. Although the power to raise revenue and spend it for the general welfare appears on its face to be extremely broad, it remained unclear until the late 1930s whether it authorized Congress to pay for programs that were not connected to an express grant of power listed elsewhere in Article I, Section 8. On the grounds that "[n]othing is more natural or common than first to use a general phrase, and then to explain and qualify it by a recital of particulars," James Madison ar-

---

[86]*Bailey v Drexel Furniture Co.*, 259 US 20 (1922).
[87]*United States v Kahriger*, 345 US 22 (1953).
[88]*Marchetti v United States*, 390 US 39 (1968).

gued in *Federalist 41* that spending for the general welfare was strictly limited to the enumerated powers that followed.[89] That is, Congress could only pay for programs that it had express authority to establish. In contrast, Alexander Hamilton argued in *Federalist 30* and *34* that the general welfare provision constituted an independent grant of authority, authorizing Congress to spend money for any purpose as long as it was in the general welfare of the nation.

When the Court began to address the scope of Congress's power to tax and spend for regulatory purposes in response to challenges to New Deal legislation, the justices adopted Hamilton's position. In 1936, for example, the Court noted that "the power of Congress to authorize expenditure of public moneys for public purposes is not limited by the direct grants of legislative power found in the Constitution." Nevertheless, in that case the justices invalidated the Agricultural Adjustment Act, which established a program whereby the federal government paid farmers to reduce the number of acres they planted in order to raise the prices of farm products and thereby boost the agricultural sector of the economy. The law was unconstitutional, Justice Roberts admonished in his opinion for the six-member majority, because it regulated agricultural production—a matter reserved to the states: "The tax, the appropriation of the funds raised, and the direction for their disbursement, . . . are but means to an unconstitutional end."[90] That was the last case in which the Court found that Congress had exceeded its constitutional spending powers.

In 1937, the justices upheld the unemployment and old-age provisions of the Social Security Act.[91] The unemployment provisions required employers to pay a tax based on the total amount of wages they paid. But employers could receive a tax credit of 90 percent of the tax if they made contributions to a state unemployment compensation program that met federal specifications. Thus, the law strongly encouraged businesses to pressure the states to create unemployment compensation programs. By a vote of five to four, the Court upheld the unemployment provisions against a challenge that they coerced the states. The old-age provisions imposed taxes on both employers and employees and provided that the federal government would hold the money in trust and pay it out when the employees retired. The justices upheld those provisions, noting that the program was clearly for the general welfare and that only the federal government could undertake such a massive program. The Social Security cases are significant because they established Congress's broad authority to tax and spend. Under the Constitution of powers since 1937 the Court has been particularly deferential to Congress's determination that a particular federal program is necessitated by the mandate to provide for the general welfare, only invalidating programs that violate constitutionally protected rights. Indeed, challenges to federal programs are now rare, as they are unlikely to be successful.

The Court has, however, addressed one issue pertaining to Congress's spending power since 1937. Federal grants programs that provide money to the

---

[89]*The Federalist Papers by Alexander Hamilton, James Madison and John Jay* (New York: Bantam Books, 1982), 210.
[90]*United States v Butler*, 297 US 1 (1936).
[91]*Steward Machine Co. v Davis*, 301 US 548 (1937) (unemployment); *Helvering v Davis*, 301 US 672 (1937) (old age).

states for a variety of purposes often make those funds conditional on state compliance with specified rules. In 1947, the Court affirmed that Congress had the authority to make such conditions when it upheld a provision of the Hatch Act that made Oklahoma's receipt of federal highway money contingent on the state's enforcement of the law's ban on participation by public employees in political activities.[92] Congress enacted legislation in 1984 requiring that federal highway funds be withheld from states in which the minimum drinking age was less than twenty-one. South Dakota objected that because Congress had no power to impose a national minimum drinking age directly, it should not be permitted to do so indirectly through a spending program. The Court disagreed, holding that Congress's method of encouraging the states to raise the drinking age was a valid use of the spending power. Writing for a seven-member majority, Chief Justice Rehnquist noted that Congress may use conditional spending provisions to accomplish objectives that it does not have the power to achieve directly. He pointed to an important limit on the spending power, however: Congress may not use the spending power "to induce states to engage in activities that would themselves be unconstitutional. Thus, for example, a grant of federal funds conditioned on invidiously discriminatory state action or the infliction of cruel and unusual punishment would be an illegitimate exercise of Congress's broad spending power."[93]

In 1991 the Court, by a vote of five to four, upheld federal regulations that restricted the speech of recipients of federal funds. Federal regulations issued in 1988 prohibited recipients of federal funding for family planning services from engaging in counseling or referrals and from encouraging, promoting, or advocating abortion. The regulations, in effect, made federal funding for family planning conditional on doctors and staff neither talking about abortions with their clients nor referring them to anyone else who would do so. In his opinion for the majority, Rehnquist maintained that the regulations did not constitute an abridgment on speech in violation of the First Amendment because the government had simply chosen to subsidize one form of family planning rather than another.[94] The decision did not turn directly on Congress's power to spend for the general welfare but rather on other issues including whether the regulations violated either freedom of speech or a woman's constitutionally protected right to terminate a pregnancy. The Court's decision, nevertheless, indicates that Congress's authority to place conditions on funding to regulate activities of states, organizations, and individuals is, indeed, extremely broad.

Section 8

2. To borrow money on the Credit of the United States;

---

[92]Specifically, the funds were conditional on the state's removing from office a member of the state highway commission who had engaged in improper political activities. *Oklahoma v Civil Service Commission*, 330 US 127 (1947).

[93]The state argued that the Twenty-First Amendment, which gave the states authority to regulate alcoholic beverages, prohibited Congress from determining the drinking age directly. Rehnquist did not concede this point, however. He maintained that it was not necessary for the Court to reach that issue because even if the Twenty-First Amendment prohibited Congress from acting directly to set the drinking age, it might still do so indirectly. *South Dakota v Dole*, 483 US 203, 210–211 (1987).

[94]*Rust v Sullivan*, 500 US 173 (1991).

Like the taxing and spending power, Congress's authority to borrow money is extremely broad. Congress borrows money by authorizing the sale of government securities to banks, businesses, and private individuals. The most important forms of government securities are bonds, Treasury certificates, and Treasury notes. The Constitution does not provide a limit on the amount of debt. When Congress enacted the Gramm-Rudman-Hollings Act in 1985 to limit deficit spending, the Court found that the law violated the doctrine of separation of powers insofar as it assigned the decisions on budget cuts—an executive function—to the comptroller general, an employee of Congress.[95]

Section 8

3. To regulate Commerce with foreign Nations, and among the several States, and with the Indian Tribes;

The absence of federal power to regulate commerce was another major defect of the Articles of Confederation that the delegates to the Constitutional Convention were determined to remedy. James Madison wrote in *Federalist 42* that experience under the Articles made clear that unless the national government had the power to regulate commerce between the states, they would continue to behave in ways that would be likely to "terminate in serious interruptions of the public tranquility."[96]

The Framers seem to have been primarily concerned with eliminating barriers to interstate and foreign trade that the states had devised to advance their own interests at the expense of the other states. Be that as it may, the understanding of the scope of Congress's authority to regulate commerce has changed profoundly over the years as the United States has grown from an agricultural society to a modern industrial state with overwhelming economic power. As we will see, the commerce clause not only has provided authority for far-reaching economic regulations but also, as the source of expansion of the national police powers, has given Congress the power to combat social problems.

The following discussion of the evolution of Congress's commerce power is organized around the three most important questions concerning the commerce clause: What is commerce? What constitutes commerce *among* the states? For what *purposes* may Congress regulate commercial activities?

Chief Justice John Marshall provided the initial answers in 1824 in *Gibbons v Ogden* when the Court held that Congress had the authority to prohibit the states from granting monopolies for steam navigation and thereby interfering with an important means of commercial transportation in the early nineteenth century. First, he noted that commerce includes more than buying and selling; it includes all commercial relations between nations and states. It was clear to Marshall that navigation was commerce. Indeed, he maintained that "The power over commerce, including navigation, was one of the primary objects for which the people of America adopted their government, and must have been contemplated in forming it. The convention must have used the word in

---

[95]*Bowsher v Synar*, 478 US 714 (1986).
[96]*The Federalist Papers*, 214.

that sense, because all have understood it in that sense."[97] Second, he shed some light on the meaning of commerce *among* the states. The word *among*, he observed, means intermingled with. Commerce *among* the states begins in one state and ends in another; it does not stop at the external boundary line of each state. Therefore, Congress may regulate commercial transactions within a state if it concerns more than that one state. But, he noted, it would be outside the bounds of the commerce power for Congress to regulate commercial activities that are "exclusively internal," do "not extend to or affect other States."[98] Third, Marshall did not explicitly identify the purposes for which Congress may regulate commerce. Still, his assertion that Congress's power of commerce is plenary was strongly suggestive: "This power, like all others vested in Congress, is complete in itself, may be exercised to its utmost extent, and acknowledges no limitations, other than are prescribed in the Constitution."[99] In short, he implied that, given Congress's complete authority over commerce, so long as Congress legislates on that subject the judiciary would not be concerned with the purpose of the legislation.

Marshall stood firm against efforts on the part of states to interfere with commerce across state lines. His opinion was more important, however, for the way that it laid the foundation for the subsequent development of the commerce power. Although he defined commerce broadly, he pulled back from the position that Daniel Webster advanced as counsel in *Gibbons v Ogden,* that "Almost all the business and intercourse of life may be connected, incidentally more or less, with commercial regulations."[100] The Chief Justice's proviso that commerce among the states does not include that which is completely internal to one state provided the basis for the distinction between interstate and intrastate commerce. Moreover, although Marshall by no means defined commerce *among* the states as that which crossed a state line, in later decisions the Court would use that as the test for distinguishing between interstate and intrastate commerce. For example, in 1849 the Court proclaimed, "All commercial action within the limits of a State, and which does not extend to any other State or foreign country, is exclusively under state regulation."[101]

Congress devised regulatory schemes in the late nineteenth century to combat the dangerous and unhealthy working conditions, child labor, and urban poverty that accompanied industrial expansion, commercial growth, and the emergence of large corporations, monopolies, and trusts. The Interstate Commerce Act of 1887 established the Interstate Commerce Commission to regulate railroads, and the Sherman Anti-Trust Act of 1890 was designed to break up monopolies that controlled a number of major industries. The earlier judicial decisions involving the commerce clause were concerned with whether state regulations interfered with interstate commerce, but with the growth of federal regulation the Court began to focus directly on the scope of Congress's power under the commerce clause.

---

[97]*Gibbons v. Ogden*, 9 Wheaton 1 (1824).
[98]*Ibid.*
[99]*Ibid.*
[100]As quoted in C. Herman Pritchett, *Constitutional Law of the Federal System* (Englewood Cliffs, NJ: Prentice Hall, 1984), 216.
[101]*The Passenger Cases*, 7 How. 283 (1849).

When the federal government took action under the Sherman Act to prevent the American Sugar Refining Company from acquiring additional refineries that would have given the company control of over 98 percent of the sugar refining business in the United States, the Court found the act to be inapplicable. In *United States v E.C. Knight Company,* the Court declared that commerce follows manufacturing, therefore, manufacturing is not commerce. Interstate commerce, according to the Court does not begin until goods "commence their final movement from the State of their origin to that of their destination." The justices also drew a distinction between direct and indirect effects on interstate commerce, noting that even though commerce might be indirectly affected by a sugar company merger that was not sufficient to justify a Sherman Act decree.[102] Production, in short, had only an incidental or indirect effect on commerce and therefore could not be regulated by federal law.

In *E.C. Knight,* the Court answered the three questions about the commerce clause very differently than Marshall had in *Gibbons v Ogden.* First, in determining that manufacturing was not commerce, Justice Melville Fuller who wrote the opinion for an eight-member majority, narrowed the definition of commerce considerably to include contracts to buy, sell, exchange, and transport but exclude manufacturing, agriculture, mining, and all forms of production, as well as wages and prices. Second, Fuller narrowed the definition of interstate commerce by limiting it to the movement of goods. The direct-indirect effect distinction, moreover, narrowed the portion of commerce that Congress may regulate to that which has a direct effect on interstate commerce. The Court used the same reasoning to render the Sherman Act inapplicable to mining, lumbering, fishing, farming, oil production, and the generation of hydroelectric power.[103]

The Court developed other, more flexible doctrines during the same period that allowed for a more expansive interpretation of Congress's commerce power. For example, in 1914 the justices announced the Shreveport doctrine when it upheld the power of the Interstate Commerce Commission to regulate railroads. Justice Charles Evans Hughes noted that when interstate and intrastate commercial activities are intertwined so that the regulation of one controls the other, Congress may regulate, "for otherwise [it] would be denied the exercise of its constitutional authority and the State, and not the Nation, would be supreme within the national field."[104] The Court also held that the Sherman Act applied to the meatpacking trust's control over meat production that began at the stockyards. In 1905, the Court held that what happens at stockyards is part of the "stream of commerce"—the commercial sale of beef began when the cattle left the range and did not terminate when the cattle stopped at the stockyards but with the final sale.[105] The Court also used the stream of commerce doctrine when it upheld the Packers and Stockyard Act, which prohibited unfair, deceptive practices and put the meatpacking industry under

---

[102]*United States v E.C. Knight,* 156 US 1 (1895).
[103]Pritchett, 221.
[104]*Shreveport Rate Case,* 234 US 342 (1914).
[105]*Swift & Company v United States,* 196 US 375 (1905).

regulations made by the Department of Agriculture. In his opinion for the majority, Chief Justice William Howard Taft observed that the "stockyards are but a throat through which the current flows. . . . Such transactions can not be separated from the movement to which they contribute and necessarily take on its character."[106] The Shreveport doctrine and the stream of commerce doctrine allowed Congress to regulate the economy far more than did the direct-indirect effects approach. The Court continued to use the latter approach in the early years of the twentieth century to invalidate the regulation of activities that purportedly did not have a sufficient direct effect on interstate commerce to justify federal regulation.

The Court reaffirmed the principle that manufacturing is not commerce and, therefore, is an activity to be regulated exclusively by the states when it invalidated the Child Labor Act in 1918.[107] That law, enacted by Congress in 1916, forbade the shipment in interstate commerce of factory products made by children under the age of fourteen or by children aged fourteen to sixteen who worked more than eight hours a day. In *Hammer v Dagenhart*, the Court contended that the power to regulate commerce does not include the authority "to forbid commerce from moving." Although the Court had previously established that Congress could forbid the transportation in interstate commerce of certain commodities including impure foods,[108] prostitutes,[109] and lottery tickets,[110] Justice William Day, who wrote the majority opinion in *Hammer v Dagenhart*, contended that although Congress did have the power to stop the movement of harmful goods it had no such authority to prohibit goods from moving that are harmless in themselves. Day addressed the third major question about the commerce power—for what purposes may Congress regulate—and found that the act's purpose was noncommercial and maintained that when Congress attempts to regulate for noncommercial purposes it invades the power reserved to the states to provide for the public health, safety, and morals.

In 1935 and 1936, the Court relied on *E.C. Knight*'s direct-indirect effect doctrine to invalidate some major New Deal programs. The National Industrial Recovery Act (NIRA), designed to stop the downward spiral in industrial wages and prices, called for codes of fair competition that would set minimum wages and maximum hours, regulate prices, and outlaw unfair competitive business practices. The codes were to be drafted by trade associations on an industry-by-industry basis and submitted to the president for approval. Once approved, the codes would have the force of law.[111] The Schechter Corporation, a slaughterhouse operation that purchased live poultry from other states but sold only to retailers in New York, not only violated the Poultry Code's wage and hour regulations, but also sold poultry that was unfit for human consumption. After

---

[106]*Stafford v Wallace*, 258 US 495 (1922).

[107]*Hammer v Dagenhart*, 247 US 251 (1918).

[108]*Hippolite Egg Co. v United States*, 220 US 45 (1911).

[109]*Hoke v United States*, 227 US 308 (1913).

[110]*Champion v Ames*, 188 US 32 (1903).

[111]There were several problems with the National Recovery Administration and the codes. The large corporations dominated and used their powers in devising the codes to increase their own profits. See William E. Leuchtenburg, *Franklin D. Roosevelt and the New Deal*, 1932–1940 (New York: Harper and Row, 1963) 64–70.

the owners were indicted, tried, and found guilty on nineteen counts of violating the code, they challenged the constitutionality of the NIRA.

In a unanimous decision in *Schechter Poultry Corp. v United States,* the Court found that the poultry dealer's activities—hours, wages, and local selling practices—were not transactions in interstate commerce. Chief Justice Hughes declined to apply the stream of commerce doctrine, noting that the poultry came to "a permanent rest within the State" and was not in the "flow" of interstate commerce. Because the stream of commerce doctrine was inapplicable, the regulation could only be justified if Schechter's activities had a direct effect on interstate commerce, which they clearly did not. Hughes, moreover, affirmed the validity of the indirect-direct effects doctrine: "The distinction between direct and indirect effects of intrastate transactions upon interstate commerce must be recognized as a fundamental one, essential to the maintenance of our constitutional system . . . Otherwise, there would be virtually no limit to federal power and for all practical purposes we should have a completely centralized government."[112]

In 1936 in *Carter v Carter Coal Company,* the Court again applied the indirect-direct effect doctrine to invalidate the coal industry codes established under the Bituminous Coal Conservation Act of 1935.[113] In the *Schechter* case the interstate commerce had come to an end, but in this case the five-member majority found that it had not yet begun. Production of goods within a state—here, the extraction of coal from the mine—even if the goods were intended to be sold or transported outside the state, was not interstate commerce. Moreover, local production had only an indirect effect on commerce. It did not matter if "the struggle between employers and employees over the matter of wages, working conditions, the right of collective bargaining . . . and the resulting strikes, curtailment and irregularity of production and effect on prices" had a great effect on interstate commerce because "the evils are all local evils over which the federal government has no legislative control. The relation of employer and employee is a local relation." The effect on commerce, however extensive, was nonetheless "secondary and indirect."[114] *Carter v Carter Coal* was to be the last major defeat for Roosevelt and the New Deal. Within a year, a majority of the Court would accept Justice Benjamin Cardozo's dissenting contention that the commerce power should be "as broad as the need that evokes it."[115]

The National Labor Relations Act of 1935 (NLRA), which was designed to protect the rights of workers to organize labor unions to improve wages and working conditions, delegated power to the National Labor Relations Board (NLRB) to issue orders against unfair labor practices. When the NLRB ordered Jones and Laughlin Steel, one of the nation's largest steel producers, to reinstate workers who had been fired for engaging in union activities, the company challenged the NLRA, alleging that manufacturing was a local activity beyond the scope of Congress's authority. By a vote of five to four, the Court upheld the

---

[112]*Schechter Poultry Corp. v United States,* 295 US 495 (1935).
[113]The Bituminous Coal Act replaced the NIRA coal codes after the Court's decision in *Schechter.*
[114]*Carter v Carter Coal Company,* 298 US 238 (1936).
[115]*Ibid.*

NLRA, emphasizing the size and complexity of the company—it was spread out over several states and shipped three-quarters of its products out of state—and the national character of the steel industry. Its activities, Justice Hughes observed, affect interstate commerce at every point; obstruction where production takes place would interfere with business throughout the country. Labor disputes clearly had an effect on commerce and thus could be regulated. Indeed, Hughes noted that Congress may regulate any activity that has a close and substantial relation to interstate commerce.[116]

Although Hughes was careful to distinguish the clearly national steel industry from other industries, the decision in *NLRB v Jones and Laughlin Steel* signaled the Court's expanding conception of interstate commerce. In subsequent cases, the justices would no longer use the distinctions between production and commerce and between indirect and direct effects on interstate commerce. The Court's unanimous decision in *Wickard v Filburn* in 1942 attests to sharp contrast between the pre-1937 conception of Congress's power to regulate economic activities and the conception that would prevail on the Court for nearly sixty years. Penalized for planting more wheat than he was allowed under the restrictions of the Agricultural Adjustment Act of 1938 (AAA), a farmer contended that because he intended to consume the wheat on his own farm it could not possibly be interstate commerce. The justices disagreed, noting that even if the activity was local it may still have a "substantial economic effect on interstate commerce" and thus come within the scope of Congress's power. The contribution of the farmer's homegrown wheat to the demand for wheat throughout the nation, Justice Robert H. Jackson pointed out, may be trivial by itself but "his contribution, taken together with that of many others similarly situated, is far from trivial."[117] Jackson captured the Court's new approach in a subsequent case when he stated: "If it is interstate commerce that feels the pinch, it does not matter how local the operation that applies the squeeze."[118]

In 1937, the Court formulated new answers to the first two questions about the commerce clause. The definition of commerce was no longer constrained as it had been earlier but had expanded to include the activities involved in manufacturing and production. The Court's conception of interstate commerce also expanded substantially when it discarded the distinction between direct and indirect effects and began to find that virtually all commercial activities have a sufficient relationship to interstate commerce to come within Congress's authority. The third question, however, for what purposes may Congress regulate, was not fully resolved until the 1960s. Although the Court firmly established that Congress could regulate extensively for economic purposes it was not clear whether it could use the commerce clause in the same way that states use their police powers to protect the public health, safety, and morals.

Title II of the Civil Rights Act of 1964 prohibits "discrimination or segregation on the ground of race, color, religion, or national origin" in the operation of "a place of public accommodation . . . if its operations affect

---

[116]*National Labor Relations Board v Jones and Laughlin Steel Corporation,* 301 US 1 (1937).
[117]*Wickard v Filburn,* 317 US 111 (1942).
[118]*United States v Women's Sportswear Manufacturing Association,* 336 US 460 (1949).

commerce."[119] The equal protection clause of the Fourteenth Amendment offers protection against discrimination, and Section 5 of the Amendment gives Congress the authority to enforce the other provisions with appropriate legislation. The Supreme Court has determined, however, that the Fourteenth Amendment, which provides, "Nor shall any state . . . deny to any person within its jurisdiction the equal protection of the laws," prohibits discrimination by government but not by private parties. Thus, Congress's authority to enforce the equal protection clause does not extend to regulating the behavior of private individuals. As a result of this rule, which is known as the "state action doctrine," Congress relied primarily on the commerce clause rather than the Fourteenth Amendment when it enacted legislation to prohibit discrimination by hotels, restaurants, movies, theaters, recreation areas, and transportation systems.

A hotel in Atlanta, Georgia, and a restaurant in Birmingham, Alabama, challenged the Civil Rights Act not long after it was enacted. The hotel conceded that it was involved in interstate commerce and, therefore, came within the provisions of the legislation but contended that Congress had exceeded its power to regulate commerce by attempting to prohibit racial discrimination. The restaurant contended that racial discrimination in restaurants did not have an effect on interstate commerce that was substantial enough to allow Congress to enact legislation regulating it. The Court upheld the Civil Rights Act against both challenges. Justice Tom Clark, who wrote the opinion for a unanimous Court in *Heart of Atlanta Motel v United States,* noted that there was overwhelming evidence that racial discrimination had a disruptive effect on interstate commerce and that "Congress was not restricted by the fact that the particular obstruction to interstate commerce with which it was dealing was also deemed a moral and social wrong."[120] Clark also noted that Congress could choose any reasonable method to eliminate the obstructions to interstate commerce that were caused by racial discrimination. Upholding the law as applied to restaurants in *Katzenbach v McClung,* Clark reasoned that there was a substantial relation between racial discrimination in restaurants and interstate commerce and that the act was therefore a valid exercise of Congress's power.[121]

Beginning in 1937 the Court interpreted the commerce clause to give sweeping powers to Congress to regulate for economic purposes activities that have a substantial impact on interstate commerce—and that includes virtually all commercial activities. The justices also allowed Congress to rely on the commerce power to legislate for noneconomic purposes to protect public health, safety, and morals. Further, the Court took an extremely deferential stance, allowing Congress not only to determine which activities need regulating but also to choose the methods by which it regulates. With few exceptions, the Court continued to adhere to that interpretation of Congress's commerce power[122] until the mid-1990s.

---

[119]42 U.S.C. Section 2000.

[120]*Heart of Atlanta Motel v United States,* 379 US 241 (1964).

[121]*Katzenbach v McClung,* 379 US 294 (1964).

[122]One notable exception was *National League of Cities v Usery* 426 US 833 (1976) in which a five-justice majority invalidated the 1974 amendments to the Fair Labor Standards Act, which extended minimum wage and maximum hours regulations to state and local government employees. The majority held that the commerce power is limited by state sovereignty, the states' ability to function as states in the federal system. The Court overruled that decision in *Garcia v San Antonio Metropolitan Transit Authority,* 469 US 528 (1985).

In 1995 in *United States v Lopez*, the Court invalidated the Gun-Free School Zones Act of 1990, which made the possession of a firearm in a school zone a federal offense. Writing for the five-member majority, Chief Justice Rehnquist noted that previous decisions have established that Congress may regulate three broad categories of activity: the use of the channels of interstate commerce, the instrumentalities or persons or things in interstate commerce, and those activities having a substantial relation to interstate commerce. He conceded that the Court's prior decisions do not make it clear whether an activity must "substantially affect" or merely "affect" interstate commerce in order to be within Congress's power to regulate. Nevertheless, the Chief Justice maintained that it was consistent with the "great weight of our case law" to require that a regulated activity substantially affect interstate commerce. He then assessed the Gun-Free School Zones Act in terms of the three categories. It was clearly neither a regulation of the use of the channels of interstate commerce nor an attempt to protect an instrumentality of interstate commerce or a thing in interstate commerce. Most important, in Rehnquist's analysis, the statute regulated activities that were not connected to any economic enterprise or any commercial transaction that substantially affects interstate commerce. The Chief Justice observed that there had been no congressional findings concerning the effects on interstate commerce of gun possession in school zones. If there had been, the Court would have been able to ascertain whether Congress had made a reasonable determination that guns in school zones substantially affect interstate commerce. He concluded that upholding the statute would constitute an unprecedented extension of Congress's commerce power "that would bid fair to convert congressional authority under the Commerce Clause to a general police power of the sort retained by the States."[123]

Rehnquist's opinion raised some intriguing questions about the Court's interpretation of the scope of Congress's power to regulate for noncommercial purposes. His comment about the lack of legislative findings showing that the possession of firearms substantially affects interstate commerce suggested that if Congress were to justify legislation by demonstrating a substantial connection between an activity—even a noneconomic activity—that it seeks to regulate and interstate commerce, then the Court might find the regulation acceptable. At the same time, the Chief Justice also seemed to signal an end to the Court's deferential attitude toward Congress's exercise of its commerce power with his assertion that Congress must demonstrate that the regulated activity has a *substantial* effect on interstate commerce. Moreover, the distinction that Rehnquist drew between commercial and noncommercial activities suggested that when Congress attempts to regulate activities that do not directly involve commercial transactions the Court will take a very careful look at the effect of the activity on interstate commerce. Additionally, the emphasis he placed on education as a matter reserved for the states suggested that the Court may be more likely to invalidate regulations that infringe on activities that are in and of themselves local even though they may have an obvious effect on interstate commerce.

---

[123]*United States v Lopez*, 514 US 549 (1995).

The narrow margin by which the Court invalidated the Gun-Free School Zones Act and the fact that there were six opinions underlined the uncertainty about the status of Congress's power under the commerce clause.[124] In his dissenting opinion Justice Stephen Breyer, emphasizing the Court's firmly established tradition of deferring to Congress, urged that when the justices are asked to determine whether there is a sufficient connection between a regulated activity and interstate commerce the Court should ask merely whether Congress could have had a rational basis for concluding that there was. In the case of the Gun-Free School Zones Act, Breyer noted, Congress could have determined that guns in and near schools undermines the quality of education in the nation's schools and that, given the economic links between education and business, "gun-related violence in and around schools is a commercial, as well as a human, problem."[125] In his separate dissent, Souter observed that "it seems fair to ask whether the step taken by the Court today does anything but portend a return to the untenable jurisprudence from which the Court extricated itself almost 60 years ago."

In another five-to-four decision in 1997 in *Printz v United States*, the Court invalidated a provision of the Brady Handgun Violence Prevention Act of 1993 that required local law enforcement officers to perform background checks on prospective gun purchasers.[126] The provision clearly involved interstate commerce, but the Court ruled that it violated the principle of state sovereignty by compelling state officers to execute federal laws. Justice Scalia, who wrote the opinion for the majority, did not address the extent of Congress's commerce power, relying instead on the rule that Congress cannot compel the states to enact or enforce a federal regulatory program.[127] Justice Thomas, however, in a concurring opinion went considerably further to argue that Congress lacks the authority to regulate the intrastate transfer of firearms. The four dissenters maintained that the commerce clause clearly provides support for the regulation of the sale of handguns and that the necessary and proper clause is adequate to support enlistment of local law enforcement officers.

In 2000 in *United States v Morrison* the justices divided along the same lines to invalidate the Violence Against Women Act of 1994.[128] In so doing, the Court, albeit by the narrowest possible margin, confirmed its determination to reverse the seventy-three-year-old tradition of deferring to Congress's use of its power under the commerce clause. In his opinion for the majority Rehnquist noted that gender-motivated crimes of violence are not economic activity and

---

[124]Both Kennedy and Thomas filed concurring opinions whereas Stevens, Souter, and Breyer each wrote a dissenting opinion.

[125]With Breyer in dissent were Stevens, Souter, and Ginsburg.

[126]*Printz v United States*, 521 US 98 (1997). The enlistment of local officials was a temporary measure that was to remain in effect only until a national system for checking prospective handgun purchasers' backgrounds went into effect.

[127]The Court established that rule in *New York v United States*, 505 US 144 (1992).

[128]*United States v Morrison*, 529 US 598 (2000). The Violence Against Women Act, Section 40302, 108 Stat. 1941–1942, provided in part that, "A person (including a person who acts under color of any statute, ordinance, regulation, custom, or usage of any State) who commits a crime of violence motivated by gender and thus deprives another of the right declared in subsection (b) of this section shall be liable to the party injured, in an action for the recovery of compensatory and punitive damages, injunctive and declaratory relief, and such other relief as a court may deem appropriate." Subsection (b) provided that, "[a]ll persons within the United States shall have the right to be free from crimes of violence motivated by gender." 42 U.S.C. § 13981(b).

suggested that even though Congress had buttressed the case for the statute with findings that gender-motivated violence has a serious impact on interstate commerce—something that it had not done with the Gun-Free School Zones Act—such findings were not sufficient. Indeed, Rehnquist made it clear that the majority would not allow Congress to regulate noneconomic activities unless they directly involve interstate commercial transactions or products. The Chief Justice emphasized the need to maintain a distinction between national and local authority, a distinction that in his view would be threatened if Congress were permitted to enter the state and local realm of regulating and punishing intrastate violence.

The final phrase of the commerce clause gives Congress extensive power over Indian affairs and serves as the primary source of federal authority over Native Americans. Because of the grant of power to Congress and the unique status of Indian tribes as quasi-sovereign entities, federal legislative power in this context is not constrained by principles of state sovereignty.

Section 8

4. To establish a uniform Rule of Naturalization, and uniform Laws on the subject of Bankruptcies throughout the United States;

Although the original Constitution did not specify criteria for citizenship, Article I, Section 8 (4), gave Congress the authority to make rules for granting citizenship to people from other countries. Congress also makes laws regarding admission of noncitizens to the United States. Neither Congress nor the states, however, may deprive noncitizens residing in the United States of rights that are protected in the Bill of Rights and elsewhere in the Constitution.

The Framers of the Constitution considered a national bankruptcy law to be essential to promoting a national commercial economy. Although bankruptcy rules provide some protection to debtors, their overarching purpose is to protect the interests of creditors. Article 1, Section 10 (1), which expressly prohibits state laws that impair the obligation of contracts, made it clear that states would not be allowed to interfere with the development of the national economy by simply canceling debts. Although the bankruptcy provision seemed to give Congress exclusive jurisdiction, in the early nineteenth century the Supreme Court allowed states to create their own bankruptcy systems in the absence of a federal law.[129] Congress enacted bankruptcy laws in 1800, 1841, and 1867, but they were all soon repealed. The law that Congress enacted in 1898 survived into the 1970s when the Bankruptcy Reform Act of 1978 went into effect.

Section 8

5. To coin Money, regulate the Value thereof, and of foreign Coin, and fix the Standard of Weights and Measures;

---

[129]*Ogden v Sanders*, 12 Wheat. 213 (1827).

Article I, Section 8 (5), remedied a weakness of the Articles of Confederation, which had given Congress the "right and power of regulating the alloy and value of coin struck by their own authority, or by that of the respective States— fixing the standard of weights and measures throughout the United States." The delegates to the Constitutional Convention declined to give Congress power to "emit bills of credit," reasoning that those whose wealth was in money rather than land would oppose a new Constitution that could issue paper currency and thereby devalue the worth of their money. But at any rate, the delegates thought that the power to borrow money would give Congress the authority to issue paper money.[130] The authority to make paper money legal tender for payment of debts is a "resulting power" derived from the enumerated powers to coin money, to regulate commerce among the states, and to borrow money (see Table 3-2, p. 126). In 1819, the Court upheld Congress's power to incorporate banks that could issue paper notes.[131] The justices later held that Congress may establish a federal reserve system to control currency and the money supply.[132]

Section 8

6. To provide for the Punishment of counterfeiting the Securities and current Coin of the United States;

Article I, Section 8 (6), together with Article I, Section 8 (5), which gives Congress the power to coin money, and the necessary and proper clause in Article I, Section 8 (18), give Congress the authority to make laws dealing with counterfeiting. The Court held in 1850 that Congress may criminalize the circulation and importation of counterfeit money.[133]

Section 8

7. To establish Post Offices and post Roads;

It remained unclear for almost a hundred years after the ratification of the Constitution whether Article I, Section 8 (7), gave Congress the power to appropriate funds to build post offices and post roads or only to designate existing roads and buildings for postal use. In 1876, the Court settled the issue when it held that the federal government could acquire land on which to build a post office.[134]

The justices have held that the postal power implies the authority to secure speedy delivery and protection of the mail.[135] After Eugene V. Debs and other labor leaders were convicted of contempt for violating an injunction prohibiting them from engaging in a railroad strike that would interrupt mail delivery, the Court upheld their convictions and the use of federal troops on the grounds

---

[130]Farrand, 147.
[131]*McCulloch v Maryland*, 17 US 316 (1819).
[132]*First National Bank v Fellows*, 244 US 416 (1917).
[133]*United States v Marigold*, 50 US 560 (1850).
[134]*Kohl v United States*, 91 US 367 (1876).
[135]*Ex parte Jackson*, 96 US 367 (1878).

that "[t]he strong arm of the national Government may be put forth to brush away all obstructions to the freedom of interstate commerce or the transportation of the mails."[136]

Congress may bar materials from the mail that it deems harmful, such as literature on lotteries and fraudulent solicitations or advertisements.[137] Although the postal power is broad, it is limited by other constitutional provisions. The First Amendment, for example, limits what can be excluded from the mails. In 1946, the Court held that the Post Office could not exclude *Esquire* from the mail.[138] The first time the Court struck down a federal law on the grounds that it violated the First Amendment it invalidated a statute allowing the Post Office not to forward "communist political propaganda" unless the addressee notified the Post Office Department that he or she wished to receive it.[139]

Section 8

8. To promote the Progress of Science and useful Arts, by securing for limited Times to Authors and Inventors exclusive Right to their respective Writings and Discoveries;

The copyright clause empowers Congress to grant monopolies on the use of intellectual property with copyrights and patents but makes it clear that they must not be permanent. The Court has interpreted the clause more as a means of benefiting the public than of protecting the creator. Thus, in devising copyright and patent laws, Congress seeks to balance two interests: "the interest of the public in being protected against monopolies and in having ready access and use of new items versus the interest of the country, as a whole, in encouraging invention by rewarding creative persons for their innovations.[140]

Congress has extensive power to set the standards and conditions for granting patents and copyrights. The Court, however, has found constitutional limits on the copyright power and thus has played a role in defining those standards. For example, the Court has found that copyright protection extends only to works with some degree of originality. In 1879, the justices held that trademarks could not be copyrighted, noting, "[W]hile the word writings may be liberally construed, as it has been, to include original designs for engraving, prints, &c., it is only such as are original, and are founded in the creative powers of the mind. The writings which are to be protected are the fruits of intellectual labor, embodied in the form of books, prints, engravings, and the like."[141] Originality remains central to copyright law and the Court continues to find that it is a constitutional requirement. Thus, facts are not subject to copyright protection as they are discovered rather than independently created

---

[136]*In re Debs*, 158 US 564, 582 (1895).
[137]*Ex parte Jackson*, 96 US 367 (1878); *Public Clearing House v Coyne*, 194 US 497 (1904).
[138]*Hannegan v Esquire, Inc.*, 327 US 146 (1946).
[139]*Lamont v Postmaster General*, 381 US 301 (1965).
[140]United States Congress, Library of Congress, Congressional Research Service, *The Constitution of the United States: Analysis and Interpretation* (Washington, DC: Government Printing Office, 1973), 316. As quoted in Elder Witt, *Congressional Quarterly's Guide to the United States Supreme Court*, 2d ed. (Washington, DC: Congressional Quarterly, Inc., 1990), 177.
[141]*Trademark Cases (United States v Steffens)*, 100 US 82, 94 (1879).

by an author. In 1991, following this principle, the Court held that alphabetically arranged names, towns, and phone numbers in a directory did not satisfy the originality requirement and could not be protected by copyright.[142]

The Court has also found constitutional limits on what Congress may protect with patents. Generally, patents may be issued only for new and useful inventions.[143] In 1966, the Court articulated the following standard: "Congress may not authorize the issuance of patents whose effects are to remove existent knowledge from the public domain, or to restrict free access to materials already available. Innovation, advancement, and things which add to the sum of useful knowledge are inherent requisites in a patent system which by constitutional command must 'promote the Progress of . . . useful Arts.'"[144] Consequently, to be eligible for a patent, an invention must be "nonobvious" to one who was reasonably skilled in the field in which the discovery was made.

Congress established a specialized tribunal in 1982, the Court of Appeals for the Federal Circuit, to hear patent appeals. The decisions of that court may be appealed to the Supreme Court.

Section 8

9. To constitute Tribunals inferior to the Supreme Court;

Article III, Section I, which vests the judicial power "in one Supreme Court, and in such inferior Courts as the Congress may from time to time ordain and establish," specifies that judges will hold their positions during good behavior, and that their salaries may not be reduced while they are in office. While that provision made it clear that Congress would have the authority to design the federal judicial system, Article I, Section 8 (9), also permits Congress to create "legislative courts" that do not exercise the "judicial power." Judges on such courts need not serve for life and their salaries may be reduced. "Legislative courts," also known as "Article I courts" are specialized tribunals, essentially administrative agencies, created to hear designated types of cases, such as tax, bankruptcy, and military. The territorial courts are also Article I courts.

Section 8

10. To define and punish Piracies and Felonies committed on the high Seas, and Offences against the Law of Nations;

In Article I, Section 8 (10), the Framers made clear that the United States would be bound by international law. Moreover, as construed by the Supreme Court since the early nineteenth century, the power "To define and punish," gives Congress broad authority. For example, Congress may prescribe punishments for acts that are in violation of international law without precisely codifying the prohibited acts.[145] The Supreme Court also pointed to Congress's

---

[142]*Feist Publications, Inc. v Rural Telephone Service Co.*, 499 US 340 (1991).
[143]*Hotchkiss v Greenwood*, 52 US 248 (1850).
[144]*Graham v John Deere Co.*, 383 US 1, 5–6 (1966).
[145]*United States v Smith*, 18 US 153 (1820); *The Marianna Flora*, 24 U.S. 1, 40–41 (1826); *United States v. Brig Malek Abhel*, 43 US 210 (1844).

power to punish offenses "against the Law of Nations" when it recognized the constitutional legitimacy of the trial by military tribunal of seven Germans who landed off the east coast of the United States by submarine in 1942 carrying explosives. In Article 15 of the Laws of War Congress had provided that military tribunals would have jurisdiction to try offenses against the law of war. Congress had thereby exercised its power to define and punish offenses against the law of nations and the president had invoked that law by means of his proclamation creating the military commission to try the saboteurs.[146]

In the aftermath of the terrorist attacks on the World Trade Center and the Pentagon on September 11, 2001, President George W. Bush issued a proclamation stating that noncitizens suspected of involvement in terrorist activities may be tried by military tribunal.[147] The president made it explicit that he was relying on provisions in the federal law giving military tribunals jurisdiction to try cases involving violations of the laws of war.[148] In March 2003 some 650 individuals remained in detention at the U.S. naval base in Guantánamo Bay, Cuba. These individuals, according to the Bush Administration, were subject to trial before military tribunals. Considering the Court's decision in 1942 upholding Congress's sweeping power to define infractions of the law of nations, in early 2003 it appeared that the president's determination to use military tribunals in cases against suspected terrorists and military leaders in Iraq, if challenged, would likely be given approval by the Supreme Court.

Although Congress has extremely broad authority under Section 8 (10) particularly in times of war the Court has consistently maintained that the power to define and punish acts against the law of nations has constitutional limits. For example, the justices held that in spite of the fact that the law prohibiting display of signs critical of a foreign government near the embassy of that country relied on Article I, Section 8 (10), it was incompatible with the First Amendment and thus was not a legitimate exercise of Congress's power.[149]

Section 8

11. To declare War, grant Letters of Marque and Reprisal, and make rules concerning Captures on Land and Water;

At the Philadelphia Convention, the Committee on Detail's enumeration of legislative powers gave Congress the power to *make* war. The final draft of the Constitution, however, designating that Congress had the power to *declare* war suggested that the legislative branch would share the war powers with the president. Article II, Section 2, which declares the president to be the commander in chief of the armed forces, gave the executive the responsibility for conducting war once Congress declared it. In the modern world, however, hostilities begin without a declaration of war and the president takes action without prior authorization from Congress. In fact, Congress has formally declared war in only five of over a hundred conflicts in which the United States has been in-

---

[146]*Ex parte Quirin*, 317 US 1 (1942).
[147]"Military Order: Detention, Treatment, and Trial of Certain Non-Citizens in the War Against Terrorism." Available: http://news.findlaw.com/hdocs/docs/terrorism/bushtribunalord111301.html.
[148]Sections 821 and 836, Title 10, United States Code.
[149]*Boos v Barry*, 485 US 312 (1988).

volved: the War of 1812, the Mexican War, the Spanish-American War, World War I, and World War II. One of the many military actions that have been conducted without a congressional declaration of war, the Vietnam War, sparked intense debate over the executive's alleged usurpation of Congress's power. The Court, generally reluctant to become involved in disputes between the president and Congress over the war powers, refused to rule on the issue of whether the war could be conducted without a formal declaration of war from Congress. Lower federal courts ruled that challenges to the war on the grounds that it was undeclared raised political questions that are not appropriately resolved by courts and the Supreme Court refused to review those decisions.[150] In 1973 Congress enacted the War Powers Act in an attempt to defend its constitutional authority to declare war. The War Powers Act provides that the president must file a formal report with Congress within forty-eight hours of initiating hostilities and limits military action to sixty days with a possible thirty-day extension unless Congress agrees to the military involvement.

Letters of marque and reprisal authorized private individuals to prey upon the shipping and property of enemy nations without being considered pirates. The Pact of Paris of 1856 banned such a practice.

Congress's authority to enact laws authorizing the seizure of enemy property in the United States during war is implied by the power to make "rules concerning Captures on Land and Water" as well as the power to declare war. In 1814 Chief Justice John Marshall held that although a declaration of war does not authorize either the executive or the judiciary to confiscate enemy property, Congress has broad authority to enact laws directing confiscations.[151] Subsequently, the Court has affirmed that during war Congress may authorize seizures of property believed to be owned by an enemy. Thus, seizures pursuant to legislation of property and assets of German corporations during World War I and World War II and of assets of Japanese business during World War II withstood constitutional challenges on the grounds that the confiscation of enemy property is a necessary element of waging war successfully.[152]

At the end of 2001 as a response to the terrorist attacks on September 11, Congress enacted the Uniting and Strengthening America by Providing Appropriate Tools Required to Intercept and Obstruct Terrorism Act of 2001, more commonly known as the USA Patriot Act. In this comprehensive attempt to combat terrorism Congress included provisions for freezing and confiscating assets of suspected terrorists. While a grand jury in Chicago was investigating two Islamic charities—the Benevolent International Foundation (BIF) and the Global Relief Fund—that receive funds and distribute food and clothing to Muslims in war-torn areas, the Office of Foreign Assets Control froze all funds and accounts of the organizations, relying on the authority of the USA Patriot Act. BIF filed a complaint in federal court arguing that the federal law did not authorize confiscation of property owned solely by U.S. citizens.[153]

---

[150]For example, *Holtzman v Schlesinger*, 361 F. Supp 553 (1973); *Holtzman v Schlesinger*, 414 US 1304 (1973).
[151]*Brown v US*, 12 U.S. 110 (1814).
[152]*Stoehr v Wallace*, 255 US 239 (1921); *Silesian-American Corp. v Clark*, 332 US 463 (1947); *Uebersee Finanz-Korp v McGrath*, 343 US 205 (1952).
[153]*Benevolence International Foundation v John Ashcroft*, Complaint, United States District Court for the Northern District of Illinois, Eastern Division, January 30, 2002. Available: http://news.findlaw.com/hdocs/docs/terrorism/bifashcroft013002cmp.pdf.

Section 8

12. To raise and support Armies, but no Appropriation of Money to that Use shall be for a longer Term than two Years;

13. To provide and maintain a Navy;

Under the Articles of Confederation, the states retained the power to raise and support the armed forces and the Continental Army was made up of forces recruited by the states. The Continental Congress, nevertheless, called on the states for military forces and most of the states instituted conscription to fulfill their quotas. The Framers gave Congress the express power to raise and support armies, including a two-year limit out of an aversion for a standing army during times of peace.

Congress's authority to draft people into the armed forces is an implied power based on the enumerated power to raise and support an army (see Table 3-2, p. 126). During the Civil War, both the Union and the Confederacy turned to conscription in 1862 making all healthy, white males between the ages of eighteen and thirty-five eligible for three years of service and requiring those who were already in the army to stay for the duration of the war. Although there was a great deal of resistance and protest—including several riots—to the draft during the Civil War, the constitutionality of conscription was not tested until World War I. In 1918, the Supreme Court unanimously upheld the Selective Service Act of 1917, noting that Article I, Section 8 (12), the necessary and proper clause, and historical practice firmly established Congress's authority to institute a draft.[154]

Congress eliminated the draft in 1973 and replaced it with an all-volunteer armed force. Registration for the draft was reactivated in 1980, however. In 1981, emphasizing that it accords greater deference to Congress in cases concerning military affairs, the Court upheld Congress's decision to require men but not women to register. Because women were excluded from combat service by statute or military policy, the seven-member majority noted, men and women were not similarly situated for purposes of a draft or registration for a draft.[155]

Congress's authority to impose extensive controls and regulations on the economy during war is an implied power stemming from the power to raise and support armies in conjunction with the power to declare war. During World War I, Congress delegated power to the president to take over factories and railroads and to fix prices. Congress enacted even more controls over the economy during World War II, including regulations on consumer prices and rationing. Congress also authorized the president to seize war-related factories that were threatened by labor strikes. There were more than sixty seizures of industrial plants or other facilities in response to labor disputes. In a series of legislative provisions known as the Renegotiation Act, Congress gave the executive branch authority to recover excessive profits from war industries. Upholding those pro-

---

[154]*Arver et al. v United States (Selective Service Draft Cases)*, 245 US 366 (1918).
[155]*Rostker v Goldberg*, 453 US 57 (1981).

visions, the Court indicated the broad sweep of Congress's powers during war when it

> [U]nquestionably has the fundamental power . . . to conscript men and to requisition the properties necessary and proper to enable it to raise and support its Armies. Congress furthermore has a primary obligation to bring about whatever production of war equipment and supplies shall be necessary to win a war.[156]

Congress's extraordinary war powers, moreover, continue after the actual hostilities end. The Court has held that the war powers continue for the duration of the emergency and do not necessarily end when hostilities cease. Thus, for example, in 1948 the justices upheld a 1947 law extending the rent control program that Congress had authorized in the Emergency Price Control Act of 1942. In his opinion for the majority in that case Justice William O. Douglas noted that "the effects of war under modern conditions may be felt in the economy for years and years." He also cautioned, "[I]f the war power can be used in days of peace to treat all the wounds which war inflicts on our society, it may not only swallow up all other powers of Congress but largely obliterate the Ninth and Tenth Amendments."[157]

Section 8

14. To make rules for the Government and Regulation of the land and naval Forces;

Congress's power to govern and regulate the armed services provides the basis of the separate system of military justice for members of the armed services. Congress specified the regulations for military justice in the Uniform Code of Military Justice, adopted in 1950. Courts-martial have jurisdiction to try any member of the armed forces for any crime.[158] Military justice procedures differ in some important respects from civilian criminal law. Generally, defendants in courts-martial proceedings are entitled to fewer procedural protections than are defendants in civilian criminal proceedings. For example, the grand jury indictment requirement in the Fifth Amendment specifically exempts cases involving the armed forces. In 1974, the Supreme Court upheld a conviction by a court-martial of an army physician who had made critical statements about United States' involvement in the Vietnam War for "conduct unbecoming an officer and a gentleman," against a challenge based on the First Amendment and the due process clause of the Fifth Amendment. Writing an opinion for the Court, Justice Rehnquist, emphasized that the military "is a specialized society separate from civilian society" with laws and traditions of its own whose business it is to "fight or be ready to fight wars should the occasion arise."[159] The Court has also held that the military authorities may prohibit civilians from distributing campaign literature and conducting political meetings on military bases.[160] In

---

[156]*Lichter v United States*, 334 US 742 (1948).
[157]*Woods v Miller Co.*, 333 US 138, 143–144 (1948).
[158]*Solorio v United States*, 483 US 435 (1987).
[159]*Parker v Levy*, 417 US 733, 743 (1974).
[160]*Greer v Spock*, 424 US 828 (1976).

1986, the Court held that the application of an Air Force regulation prohibiting the wearing of headgear indoors to prohibit a psychologist from wearing a yarmulke did not violate the free exercise clause of the First Amendment.[161]

Section 8

15. To provide for calling forth the Militia to execute the Laws of the Union, suppress Insurrections and repel Invasions;

16. To provide for organizing, arming, and disciplining the Militia, and for governing such Part of them as may be employed in the Service of the United States, reserving to the States, respectively, the Appointment of the Officers, and the Authority of training the Militia according to the discipline prescribed by Congress;

Article I, Section 8 (15), gives Congress authority over the state militias—citizens organized and armed by their states for defensive purposes. Congress first gave authority to call the militia to the president in 1795 providing:

> [W]henever the United States shall be invaded, or be in imminent danger of invasion from any foreign nation or Indian tribe, it shall be lawful for the President of the United States to call forth such number of the militia of the State or States most convenient to the place of danger, or scene of action, as he may judge necessary to repel such invasion, and to issue his order for that purpose to such officer or officers of the militia as he shall think proper.[162]

Congress has continued to delegate authority to the president. With that exception, the militias remained in the hands of the states until 1916 when Congress enacted the National Defense Act, bringing the militias under the control of the national government. Members of the militias—now the National Guard—may be called into the armed forces of the United States. In 1991, the Supreme Court, pointing out that the militia clauses must be interpreted in terms of "the supremacy of federal power in the area of military affairs," ruled that Congress may order the National Guard to train outside the United States without the consent of the state governor and without any declaration of national emergency.[163] Federal law also allows states to provide a defense force that is exempt from being called into the armed forces of the United States.

Section 8

17. To exercise exclusive Legislation in all Cases whatsoever, over such District (not exceeding ten Miles square), as may, by Cession of particular States, and the Acceptance of Congress, become the Seat of the Government of the United States, and to exercise like Authority over all Places purchased by the Consent of the Legislature of the State in which the Same shall be for the Erection of Forts, Magazines, Arsenals, dock-Yards, and other needful Buildings;

---

[161]*Goldman v Weinberger*, 475 US 503 (1986).
[162]As quoted in *Martin v Mott*, 25 US 19 (1827).
[163]*Perpich v Dept. of Defense*, 496 US 334 (1990).

The Constitutional Convention's decision to provide for a national seat of government completely removed from the control of any state was based partly on the experience of the Continental Congress. In 1783, some eighty soldiers, who had not been paid, marched on the Congress then meeting in Philadelphia and threatened the members. Neither the local or state authorities would provide protection and Congress fled the city.

The location of the capital in the District of Columbia was the result of a compromise over the assumption of the Revolutionary War debt. In 1790, President George Washington's Secretary of the Treasury, Alexander Hamilton, devised a plan to fund the remaining debt by allowing the government's creditors to exchange their depreciated securities at full value for new interest-bearing government bonds. He also proposed that the federal government assume responsibility for the state war debts. James Madison and other southern members of Congress voiced several objections. First, it would be unfair to fund depreciated securities at their face value, particularly since speculators had purchased most of them at a fraction of their initial worth. Second, because northern businessmen held most of the securities, the funding arrangement would be of little benefit to the South. Third, the problem with assumption of the state debts was that only the states with large unpaid obligations, such as Massachusetts, would benefit whereas those that had already retired most of their debt, such as Virginia, would have to help cover the more indebted states. Additionally, critics pointed out that because assumption would increase the central government's need for revenue, Hamilton's plan would require Congress to exercise its power to tax. To overcome the objections of the southerners, Hamilton's debt assumption proposal included an agreement to move the seat of government from New York to Philadelphia and then in 1800 to a swampy clearing on the Potomac River ceded by Maryland and Virginia. With the support of Madison and Secretary of State Thomas Jefferson, the plan won the approval of Congress.

Article I, Section 8 (17), gave Congress the authority to make the laws and appoint administrators for the District of Columbia or to delegate the lawmaking power to a locally elected government. In 1874, Congress provided that a three-member commission appointed by the president would administer the laws passed by Congress. A mayor and city council—both appointed by the president—replaced the commission in 1967. In 1973, Congress provided for a limited form of self-government in the District, with an elected mayor, city council, and school board. Congress retained authority to enact laws and continued to control the judicial system. In 1970, Congress authorized the District to elect one nonvoting delegate to the House of Representatives. A constitutional amendment to give the District a voting member in the House and representation in the Senate was approved by the House and Senate but was not ratified by the states.[164]

The final phrase of Article I, Section 8 (17), gave Congress authority over all structures that it considers necessary for carrying on the business of the

---

[164]Only sixteen states had ratified when the amendment expired seven years after it was sent to the states.

national government.[165] The Court has included in that category post offices, a hospital and a hotel located in a national park, and locks and dams for the improvement of navigation.

Section 8

18. And To make all Laws which shall be necessary and proper for carrying into Execution the foregoing Powers, and all other Powers vested by this Constitution in the Government of the United States, or in any Department or Officer thereof.

The necessary and proper clause—also known as the elastic clause and the coefficient clause—provides the textual justification for the doctrine that Congress has **implied powers** in addition to those that are expressly enumerated. Although there was virtually no discussion of the clause at the Constitutional Convention, it was the subject of much of the debate over ratification. The Antifederalists condemned it as a sweeping provision that could swallow up any limitations on federal power. Madison, defending the clause in *Federalist 44*, asserted:

> Had the Constitution been silent on this head, there can be no doubt that all the particular powers requisite as means of executing the general powers would have resulted to the government, by unavoidable implication. No axiom is more clearly established in law, or in reason, than that wherever the end is required, the means are authorised; wherever a general power to do a thing is given, every particular power necessary for doing it, is included.[166]

Early disagreement over the extent of the powers that the necessary and proper clause conferred on Congress focused on the issue of whether Congress had the power to establish a national bank. In 1791, Congress enacted a law creating the First Bank of the United States. With the bill on his desk, President Washington asked Secretary of State Thomas Jefferson and Secretary of the Treasury Alexander Hamilton for their opinions on its constitutionality and they responded with very different interpretations of the necessary and proper clause. Jefferson maintained that the clause empowered Congress to use only those means that are absolutely necessary to carry out an enumerated power. Indeed, for Jefferson, the necessary and proper clause constrained rather than expanded Congress's power: "[T]he Constitution restrained them to the necessary means, that is to say, to those means without the grant of power would be nugatory."[167] Hamilton charged that Jefferson misconstrued the meaning of the word *necessary* by, in effect, prefacing it with *absolutely*. Hamilton construed the necessary and proper clause as a broad grant of power to choose the means for giving force to the implied powers. As he explained, "The *relation* between the *measure* and the *end*; between the *nature* of the *means* employed towards

---

[165]*James v Dravo Contracting Co.*, 302 US 134, 143 (1937).
[166]*The Federalist Papers*, 229–230.
[167]"Opinion on the Constitutionality of a National Bank," in Melvin I. Urofsky, ed. *Documents of American Constitutional and Legal History, Volume One, From Settlement through Reconstruction* (New York: Alfred A. Knopf, 1989), 132–136, 134.

the execution of a power, and the object of that power, must be the criterion of constitutionality, not the more or less of *necessity* or *utility*."[168] Hamilton argued that establishing a bank clearly was related to the power to collect taxes, to borrow money, and to regulate trade between the states.

Washington took Hamilton's position and signed the bill creating the first Bank of the United States. The Bank's charter expired in 1811 but Congress established the Second Bank of the United States in 1816. A constitutional challenge to Maryland's attempt to tax the Bank brought the question of whether Congress had the power to charter a bank before the Supreme Court. Chief Justice John Marshall answered in the affirmative in *McCulloch v Maryland* in 1819. Adopting Hamilton's expansive construction, Marshall concluded that the necessary and proper clause endowed Congress with the authority to choose the means for carrying out its enumerated powers. He declared: "Let the end be legitimate, let it be within the scope of the Constitution, and all means which are appropriate, which are plainly adapted to that end, which are not prohibited, but consist with the letter and spirit of the Constitution, are constitutional."[169]

Hamilton's and Marshall's expansive interpretation of the necessary and proper clause has prevailed through the years, providing a major source of authority for Congress to legislate in areas that are not within its expressly enumerated powers. Indeed, the necessary and proper clause has supplied the constitutional basis for the expansion of nearly all the powers of the federal government. For example, Congress's authority to enact a large body of federal criminal law rests on the necessary and proper clause. Additionally, the extent to which Congress regulates the national economy is made possible by virtue of its authority to regulate the internal commerce of a state as necessary to promote interstate commerce. Monetary and fiscal controls also have their source in the necessary and proper clause as does Congress's authority to use appropriate means for collecting the revenue, including seizing property for federal taxes.

Inherent and Inherited Powers

Five types of congressional power are summarized in Table 3-2.

We have discussed the enumerated powers, the implied powers, and the resulting powers. The other two also merit some consideration. First, Congress has certain powers that do not depend on constitutional grants of power but instead derive from the nation's sovereignty. When the colonies declared their independence in 1776, certain powers passed from the Crown to the United States. The powers of a sovereign nation—that is, the powers regarding foreign affairs—existed prior to the Constitution, and when the Constitution was ratified, it did not constrain those powers. In his *Commentaries on the Constitution of the United States*, Justice Joseph Story defined the **inherent powers** as

---

[168]"Opinion as to the Constitutionality of the Bank of the United States," as quoted in Gerald Gunther, *Constitutional Law*, 11th ed. (Mineola, NY: Foundation Press, 1985), 86.
[169]*McCulloch v Maryland*, 4 Wheat. 316 (1819).

TABLE 3-2   The Types of Congressional Powers

Type	Definition	Example
Enumerated powers	Constitution expressly grants	The power to raise and support an army
Implied powers	May be inferred from power expressly granted	The power to raise and support an army implies the power to draft people into the armed forces
Resulting powers	Several enumerated powers added together *result* in another power	The enumerated powers to coin money + to regulate commerce among the states + to borrow money = the authority to make paper money legal tender for payment of debts
Inherent powers	Do not depend on constitutional grants but grow out of the nation's sovereignty	To discover and occupy territory, to make treaties with other nations, to send and receive representatives
Inherited powers	British Parliament and early state constitutions handed down to Congress	The power to investigate

those that result "from the whole mass of the powers of the National Government, and from the nature of political society, [rather] than a consequence or incident of the power specially enumerated."[170] Later, Justice George Sutherland explained the inherent powers in connection with the fundamental differences between the powers of the federal government in regard to foreign and domestic affairs:

> The broad statement that the federal government can exercise no powers except those specifically enumerated in the Constitution, and such implied powers as are necessary and proper to carry into effect the enumerated powers, is categorically true only in respect of our internal affairs. In that field, the primary purpose of the Constitution was to carve from the general mass of legislative powers then possessed by the states such portions as it was thought desirable to vest in the federal government, leaving those not included in the enumeration still in the states. That this doctrine applies only to powers which the states had is self-evident. And since the states severally never possessed international powers, such powers could not have been carved from the mass of state powers but obviously were transmitted to the United States from some other source.[171]

---

[170]As quoted in Witt, 74.
[171]*United States v Curtiss-Wright Corp.*, 299 US 304, 315–316.

Congress's power to conduct investigations to gather information on the need for legislation, the effectiveness of existing laws, and the activities of members of Congress and executive branch officials may be classified as an implied power based on the Constitution's conferral of the legislative power on Congress in Article I, Section 1. It may also be depicted as a resulting power derived from Congress's authority to legislate, to appropriate (Article I, Section 9 (7)), and to be the judge of the elections and returns (Article I, Section 5 (1)). The investigatory power has also been characterized as an inherited power that was handed down to Congress by the English Parliament and the early state legislatures. Regardless of whether it is an implied, resulting, or inherited power, Congress established the power to investigate early—the House of Representatives conducted an investigation in 1792—and reinforced it by summoning witnesses and punishing those who did not comply. In 1821, the Supreme Court held that although Congress could use its **contempt power** to punish nonmembers it could not extend imprisonment for contempt beyond adjournment.[172] Congress subsequently enacted a law that continues to remain in effect making it a criminal offense to refuse information demanded by either chamber of Congress. Although either house of Congress may cite a witness for contempt, the standard practice is to turn the witness over to the federal prosecutor who then brings an action under the criminal statute.

In 1881, the Court held that the House could not punish a witness for contempt when Congress had exceeded its authority to investigate. Congressional power to investigate, the justices noted, had three limits: investigations "could not invade areas constitutionally reserved to the courts or the executive; they must deal with subjects on which Congress could validly legislate; and the resolutions setting up the investigations must suggest a congressional interest in legislating on that subject."[173] In 1927, the justices affirmed that Congress has the power to conduct investigations and to compel witnesses to appear and answer relevant questions. Still, if the questions were not pertinent to the subject under inquiry or if the inquiry was beyond Congress's authority, the witness could refuse to answer.[174]

Investigations that congressional committees began to conduct in the late 1940s concerning communist activities and dissemination of propaganda by Americans raised important questions about the scope of Congress's investigatory power. When the House Committee on Un-American Activities asked witnesses about their past and present memberships in various organizations and that of their friends and associates, some refused to answer, claiming that the committee was violating the First Amendment by inquiring into and attempting to punish them for their beliefs and associations. When such claims reached the Supreme Court in 1957 the justices reversed a contempt conviction by a vote of six to one. Writing for the majority, Chief Justice Earl Warren acknowledged that "abuses of the investigative process may imperceptibly lead to abridgement of protected freedoms." He warned investigators that "there is no

---

[172]*Anderson v Dunn*, 6 Wheat. 204 (1821).
[173]*Kilbourn v Thompson*, 103 US 168 (1881), as quoted in Pritchett, 191.
[174]*McGrain v Daugherty*, 273 US 135 (1927).

congressional power to expose for the sake of exposure." The Court reversed the contempt conviction on the grounds that the authorization Congress had given to the Un-American Activities Committee was so broad that the witness had no way of knowing whether the questions he was asked were pertinent to the investigation.[175] Two years later, however, the Court rejected a similar challenge to a contempt conviction, holding that in contrast to the earlier case the witness had sufficient information about the pertinence of the questions.[176] In the early 1960s as the intense fear of communism subsided, the Court began to reverse contempt convictions by strictly enforcing the rules on the pertinence of questions and strictly observing the constitutional standards governing criminal prosecutions.[177]

Delegation of Legislative Power

As we have seen, the Constitution delegates certain powers to Congress in Article I, Section 8. According to an old legal doctrine, a power once delegated cannot be redelegated. Thus, it has been argued that Congress may not delegate its powers to another body (for example, the president or executive agencies). It has also been argued that when Congress delegates its authority to another branch of government it violates the doctrine of the separation of powers.

Although the Supreme Court has paid lip service to the nondelegation doctrine, it has invalidated legislation on the grounds that it constituted an unconstitutional delegation of legislative power in only three cases, all of which it decided in the 1930s when the Court was dismantling New Deal legislation.[178] Justice Thurgood Marshall writing in 1974 captured the Court's modern approach:

> The notion that the Constitution narrowly confines the Congress to delegate authority to administrative agencies, which was briefly in vogue in the 1930s, has been virtually abandoned by the Court for all practical purposes, at least in the absence of delegation creating the danger of overbroad, unauthorized, and arbitrary application of criminal sanctions in the area of constitutionally protected freedoms.[179]

Occasionally, however, legislation is still challenged alleging that it constitutes an unconstitutional **delegation of power.** In 1986 the justices warned Congress that it should not go too far in giving administrative agencies responsibility

---

[175]*Watkins v United States*, 354 US 178 (1957).

[176]*Barenblatt v United States*, 360 US 109 (1959).

[177]Pritchett, 194. The Supreme Court insisted that the federal law defining the offense of contempt of Congress be closely followed. Contempt of Congress, as defined by the law, is the refusal to answer pertinent questions. Before the Supreme Court will permit a conviction, the following must be met: (1) The parent chamber must have clearly authorized the committee to make the particular investigation (in the case of investigations by committees of the House of Representatives, since neither the House nor its committees are continuing bodies, the authorization must occur during the term of Congress in which the investigation takes place); (2) the committee must have authorized the investigation; (3) the committee must have made clear to the witness the subject under investigation, the pertinence of the question to the subject, and the reason the committee insisted that it be answered; and (4) the grand jury indictment must have specified the subject under committee investigation and the pertinent questions the defendant is charged with refusing to answer. *Gojack v United States*, 384 US 702 (1966); *Russell v United States*, 369 US 749 (1962).

[178]*Panama Refining Co. v Ryan*, 293 US 388 (1935); *Schechter Poultry Corp. v United States*, 295 US 495 (1935); *Carter v Carter Coal*, 298 US 238 (1936).

[179]*Federal Power Commission v New England Power Co.*, 415 US 345 (1974).

to deal with matters historically within the province of courts.[180] Although his position has not commanded a majority, Justice Antonin Scalia has expressed support for the nondelegation doctrine. In 1996, for example, he contended, "While it has become the practice in our opinions to refer to 'unconstitutional delegations of legislative authority' versus 'lawful delegations of legislative authority,' in fact the latter category does not exist. Legislative power is nondelegable."[181]

The prevailing view concerning delegation of legislative power is that Congress may engage in either of two types of delegation. In one, Congress sets an objective and authorizes an administrator to promulgate rules and regulations that will achieve that objective. In the other, Congress authorizes an administrator to take a specified course of action if and when he or she determines that certain conditions exist.[182] When the Court has heard challenges to legislative delegations of power, it has usually found that the guidelines and standards Congress provided were sufficient. The Court has also upheld delegations when the law provided no standards at all as it did in 1963 when it upheld a law that gave the Secretary of the Interior absolute discretion in allocating water to southwestern states during shortages.[183] Relatively recently, the Court has upheld legislation delegating the promulgation of sentencing guidelines for criminal offenses to appointees of the president[184] and conferring the responsibility to outlaw traffic in new drugs "when necessary to avoid an imminent hazard to the public safety" to the attorney general.[185]

The Court indicated in 1936 in *United States v Curtiss-Wright* that Congress may delegate power to the president in the area of foreign affairs.[186] Additionally, the Court has consistently affirmed all wartime delegations of legislative power since 1827 when it upheld an act of Congress delegating to the president the power to call out the militia.[187] In 1944, it sustained the delegation of price-fixing powers to the Office of Price Administration during World War II without specifying any standards for guidance except that the prices fixed be "fair and equitable."[188]

By sustaining the delegation of legislative powers, the Court has acknowledged that in the modern administrative state it is inevitable that executive agencies will exercise legislative power. As the Court has noted, "Delegation by Congress has long been recognized as necessary in order that the exertion of legislative power does not become a futility."[189] Additionally, by discarding the nondelegation doctrine, the Court has recognized that a system of rigidly separated powers is impossible and that it is more realistic to view the three branches of government as separate but overlapping institutions sharing powers.

Table 3-3 summarizes highlights of selected legislation enacted by Congress in the aftermath of September 11, 2001.

---

[180]*Commodity Futures Trading Commission v Schor*, 478 US 833 (1986).
[181]*Loving v United States*, 135 US 36 (1996).
[182]Witt, 75.
[183]*Arizona v California*, 373 US 546 (1963).
[184]*Mistretta v United States*, 488 US 361 (1989).
[185]*Touby v United States*, 500 US 160 (1991).
[186]*United States v Curtiss-Wright Export Corp.*, 299 US 304 (1936).
[187]*Martin v Mott*, 25 US 19 (1827).
[188]*Yakus v United States*, 321 US 414 (1944).
[189]*Sunshine Anthracite Coal Co. v Adkins*, 310 US 381, 398 (1940).

TABLE 3-3   Selected Laws Enacted by Congress in Response to the Terrorist Attacks on September 11, 2001

Name	Date	Major Provisions
Joint resolution to authorize the use of United States Armed Forces against those responsible for the recent attacks launched against the United States	September 18, 2001	Authorizes the use of United States Armed Forces against those responsible for the attacks launched against the United States.
Uniting and Strengthening America by Providing Appropriate Tools Required to Intercept and Obstruct Terrorism (USA PATRIOT) Act of 2001	October 26, 2001	(Sec. 106) Modifies provisions relating to presidential authority under the International Emergency Powers Act to (1) authorizes the president, when the United States is engaged in armed hostilities or has been attacked by a foreign country or foreign nationals, to confiscate any property subject to U.S. jurisdiction of a foreign person, organization, or country that he determines has planned, authorized, aided, or engaged in such hostilities or attacks (the rights to which shall vest in such agency or person as the president may designate); and (2) provide that, in any judicial review of a determination made under such provisions, if the determination was based on classified information such information may be submitted to the reviewing court ex parte and in camera.
		Title II: Enhanced Surveillance Procedures—Amends the Federal criminal code to authorize the interception of wire, oral, and electronic communications for the production of evidence of (1) specified chemical weapons or terrorism offenses; and (2) computer fraud and abuse.

TABLE 3-3 *(Continued)*

Name	Date	Major Provisions
		Title IV (Sec. 405) Directs the Attorney General to report on the feasibility of enhancing the Integrated Automated Fingerprint Identification System and other identification systems to better identify foreign individuals in connection with U.S. or foreign criminal investigations before issuance of a visa to, or permitting such person's entry or exit from, the United States. Authorizes appropriations.
		Subtitle B: Enhanced Immigration Provisions—Amends the Immigration and Nationality Act to broaden the scope of aliens ineligible for admission or deportable due to terrorist activities to include an alien who (1) is a representative of a political, social, or similar group whose political endorsement of terrorist acts undermines U.S. antiterrorist efforts; (2) has used a position of prominence to endorse terrorist activity, or to persuade others to support such activity in a way that undermines U.S. antiterrorist efforts (or the child or spouse of such an alien under specified circumstances); or (3) has been associated with a terrorist organization and intends to engage in threatening activities while in the United States.
		(Sec. 411) Includes within the definition of "terrorist activity" the use of any weapon or dangerous device.

(continued)

TABLE 3-3 *(Continued)*

Name	Date	Major Provisions
		Redefines "engage in terrorist activity" to mean, in an individual capacity or as a member of an organization, to (1) commit or to incite to commit, under circumstances indicating an intention to cause death or serious bodily injury, a terrorist activity; (2) prepare or plan a terrorist activity; (3) gather information on potential targets for terrorist activity; (4) solicit funds or other things of value for a terrorist activity or a terrorist organization (with an exception for lack of knowledge); (5) solicit any individual to engage in prohibited conduct or for terrorist organization membership (with an exception for lack of knowledge); or (6) commit an act that the actor knows, or reasonably should know, affords material support, including a safe house, transportation, communications, funds, transfer of funds or other material financial benefit, false documentation or identification, weapons (including chemical, biological, or radiological weapons), explosives, or training for the commission of a terrorist activity; to any individual who the actor knows or reasonably should know has committed or plans to commit a terrorist activity; or to a terrorist organization (with an exception for lack of knowledge).

TABLE 3-3   *(Continued)*

Name	Date	Major Provisions
		(Sec. 412) Provides for mandatory detention until removal from the United States (regardless of any relief from removal) of an alien certified by the Attorney General as a suspected terrorist or threat to national security. Requires release of such alien after seven days if removal proceedings have not commenced, or the alien has not been charged with a criminal offense. Authorizes detention for additional periods of up to six months of an alien not likely to be deported in the reasonably foreseeable future only if release will threaten U.S. national security or the safety of the community or any person. Limits judicial review to habeas corpus proceedings in the U.S. Supreme Court, the U.S. Court of Appeals for the District of Columbia, or any district court with jurisdiction to entertain a habeas corpus petition.
		Title VIII: Strengthening the Criminal Laws Against Terrorism—Amends the Federal criminal code to prohibit specific terrorist acts or otherwise destructive, disruptive, or violent acts against mass transportation vehicles, ferries, providers, employees, passengers, or operating systems.

(continued)

TABLE 3-3 *(Continued)*

Name	Date	Major Provisions
		Title IX: Improved Intelligence—Amends the National Security Act of 1947 to require the Director of Central Intelligence (DCI) to establish requirements and priorities for foreign intelligence collected under the Foreign Intelligence Surveillance Act of 1978 and to provide assistance to the Attorney General (AG) to ensure that information derived from electronic surveillance or physical searches is disseminated for efficient and effective foreign intelligence purposes. Requires the inclusion of international terrorist activities within the scope of foreign intelligence under such Act.
Homeland Security Act of 2002	November 25, 2002	Creates Cabinet-level department of Homeland Security comprised of four divisions: Border and Transportation; Security, Emergency Preparedness and Response; Chemical, Biological, Radiological and Nuclear Countermeasures; and Information Analysis and Infrastructure Protection. Department will analyze intelligence from various sources including the CIA; National Security Agency; FBI; Drug Enforcement Administration; Department of Energy; Customs Service, and Department of Transportation.*
		*"A Massive Federal Makeover," CNN.com./US Fact Sheet http://www.cnn.com/2002/US/11/20/facts.homeland/index.html
		For full text of the Homeland Security Act, see, HR 5005, http://www.nist.gov/director/ocla/HR_5005_Enrolled.pdf

Source: Library of Congress. "Legislation Related to the Attack of September 11, 2001." Available: http://thomas.loc.gov/home/terrorleg.htm. Visit this Web site for a complete listing of legislation passed in the aftermath of September 11.

Section 9

The eight paragraphs of Article I, Section 9, specify limits on Congress's powers.

1. The Migration or Importation of such Persons as any of the States now existing shall think proper to admit, shall not be prohibited by the Congress prior to the Year one thousand eight hundred and eight, but a Tax or duty may be imposed on such Importation, not exceeding ten dollars for each person.

The provision restricting Congress's authority to prohibit the importation of slaves was part of the compromise between the delegates from the North and South over the institution of slavery. Shortly before the Convention submitted its work to the Committee on Detail, South Carolina's Charles Pinckney warned that if the Committee "should fail to insert some security to the Southern States against an emancipation of slaves, and taxes on exports, he should be bound by duty to his State to vote against their Report."[190] Apparently out of regard for Pinckney's threat, the Committee on Detail included a provision forbidding Congress from either taxing or prohibiting the importation of "such persons as the several States shall think proper to admit." The committee's draft also included a proviso that navigation acts could be passed only with the assent "of two thirds of the members present in each House."[191] In response to Gouverneur Morris's charge that "Domestic slavery is the most prominent feature in the aristocratic countenance of the proposed Constitution,"[192] delegates from the Carolinas and Georgia threatened to take their states out of the Union if they were prohibited from carrying on slave importations. Connecticut's Oliver Ellsworth feared that South Carolina and Georgia would be lost "with such others as may be disposed to stand aloof, should fly into a variety of shapes and directions, and most probably into several confederations and not without bloodshed."[193] An ad hoc committee worked out the compromise that became Article I, Section 9 (1).

Section 9

2. The Privilege of the Writ of Habeas Corpus shall not be suspended, unless when in Cases of Rebellion or Invasion the public Safety may require it.

Habeas corpus is Latin for "have the body." The writ of habeas corpus is even older than the Magna Carta. By the sixteenth century, it had developed into the primary legal remedy for the arbitrary imprisonment of the monarch's enemies. A writ of habeas corpus ordered that a prisoner be brought before a judge for a determination of whether he or she was being lawfully detained.

The writ of habeas corpus developed in American law as a means by which individuals could appeal to the state judicial authorities charging that the state

---

[190]As quoted in Farber and Sherry, 165.
[191]As quoted in Farber and Sherry, 167.
[192]As quoted in Farber and Sherry, 165 and 166.
[193]As quoted in William M. Wiecek, "The Witch at the Christening: Slavery and the Constitution's Origins," in Leonard W. Levy and Dennis J. Mahoney, eds. *The Framing and Ratification of the Constitution* (New York: Macmillan Publishing Co., 1987), 167–184, 181.

was unlawfully detaining them. Article I, Section 9 (2), prevented the federal government from suspending the writ in state cases. But in the Judiciary Act of 1789, Congress gave the federal courts the authority to issue writs of habeas corpus against officers of the federal government.

In the 1850s, several northern states enacted personal liberty laws to protect fugitive slaves and those who helped them. Those state laws authorized state courts to issue writs of habeas corpus to free federal prisoners jailed for violating the Fugitive Slave Act of 1850.[194] It was in that context that the Supreme Court held that state courts may not interfere with the execution of federal law by issuing writs of habeas corpus against the federal government.[195] In the Judiciary Act of 1867, Congress gave the lower federal courts the authority to grant writs of habeas corpus to state prisoners who claimed to be detained in violation of the Constitution or the federal law. During the Warren era when the Court was expanding the constitutional protections for the criminally accused, the justices also greatly increased the availability of habeas corpus, construing it as a guarantee of broad independent review of state criminal proceedings.[196] The Burger and Rehnquist Courts subsequently severely limited the availability of federal habeas corpus review for state prisoners who claimed that their trials were marred by constitutional error.[197] The Rehnquist Court has been particularly determined to limit habeas corpus review of death sentences.[198] In 1996, Congress enacted comprehensive habeas reform legislation, the Antiterrorism and Effective Death Penalty Act, codifying some of the Court's restrictions and adding new ones. The Court upheld that law against a challenge that it was an unconstitutional suspension of the writ of habeas corpus.[199]

Article I, Section 9 (2), does not make it clear whether Congress or the president has the authority to suspend the writ of habeas corpus in emergencies. But the location of the provision in Article I suggests that the power belongs to Congress. When President Abraham Lincoln suspended the privilege on his own authority during the Civil War, critics charged that only Congress had the constitutional authority to suspend the writ. Congress subsequently enacted legislation authorizing the president to suspend the writ of habeas corpus in all cases in which he thought the public safety might require it. In 1866, five members of the Court held that neither the president nor Congress may suspend habeas corpus as long as the civilian courts remain open. Four justices argued that Congress had the power to suspend the privilege.[200] Congress authorized the suspension of habeas corpus in nine South Carolina counties in

---

[194]The Fugitive Slave Act of 1850 provided for the appointment, by federal courts, of federal commissioners who had jurisdiction over fugitive slave questions. Federal commissioners were authorized to permit a claimant who produced satisfactory proof of ownership to remove a fugitive slave. There was no provision for a jury trial nor could the alleged fugitive slave testify. The federal commissioner's decision also precluded the issuance of a state writ of habeas corpus.

[195]*Ableman v Booth*, 62 US 506 (1859).

[196]See, for example, *Fay v Noia*, 372 US 391 (1963) and *Townsend v Sain*, 372 US 293 (1963). See also, the earlier decision in *Brown v Allen*, 344 US 443 (1953).

[197]See, for example, *Stone v Powell*, 428 US 465 (1976); *Wainwright v Sykes*, 433 US 72 (1977); and *Sumner v Mata*, 449 US 539 (1981).

[198]See *McCleskey v Zant*, 499 US 467 (1991); *Keeney v Tamayo-Reyes*, 504 US 1 (1992).

[199]*Felker v Turpin*, 518 US 651 (1996).

[200]*Ex parte Milligan*, 71 US 2 (1866).

1871, in the Philippines during the 1905 insurrection, and in Hawaii during World War II. Immediately following the attack on Pearl Harbor, the Governor of Hawaii suspended the privilege of the writ of habeas corpus and placed the territory under martial law pursuant to a federal statute authorizing the territorial governor to take such action in cases of rebellion or invasion. The president quickly approved the governor's action. After the war ended, the Court rejected the suspension of habeas corpus on the grounds that it was not authorized by the federal statute in the situation where the civilian government and courts continued to function.[201]

Section 9

3. No Bill of Attainder or ex post facto Law shall be passed.

In England, a **bill of attainder** was an act of Parliament condemning an individual to death without the benefit of a trial. The Supreme Court has taken a broader view of the term, however, limiting it neither to the punishment of death nor to laws that single out a particular individual for punishment. For example, in 1867 the Court held that a law barring attorneys from practicing before federal courts unless they had sworn an oath that they had remained loyal to the Union throughout the Civil War was a bill of attainder.[202]

The Court has invalidated two other acts of Congress on the grounds that they were bills of attainder. In 1943 the chair of the House Un-American Activities Committee urged Congress to refuse to appropriate funds to pay the salaries of thirty-nine federal employees whom he labeled "irresponsible, unrepresentative, crackpot, radical bureaucrats" who were affiliated with "communist front organizations."[203] A subcommittee of the House Appropriations Committee then held hearings and pronounced three federal employees guilty of subversive activities and unfit to hold their positions. Congress then enacted a bill, which the president signed, barring appropriations for their salaries. The Court invalidated the law in 1946, noting, "Legislative acts, no matter what their form, that apply either to named individuals or to easily ascertainable members of a group in such a way as to inflict punishment on them without a judicial trial are bills of attainder."[204] The other law that the Court found to be a bill of attainder made it a crime for anyone to serve as an officer or employee of a labor union if he or she had been a member of the Communist Party within the previous five years.[205]

In 1977, the Court rejected Richard Nixon's challenge to the federal statute that gave control of his presidential papers to the administrator of general services, noting that Congress had not been motivated by a desire to punish the former president.[206] The justices also rejected a challenge to the Solomon Amendment, which required all men who applied for federal student financial

---

[201] *Duncan v Kahanamoku,* 327 US 304 (1946).
[202] *Ex parte Garland,* 71 US 333 (1867).
[203] As quoted in Witt, 76.
[204] *United States v Lovett,* 328 US 303 (1946).
[205] *United States v Brown,* 381 US 437 (1965).
[206] The law was the Presidential Recordings and Materials Preservation Act of 1974. *Nixon v Administrator of General Services,* 433 US 425 (1977).

aid to indicate that they had complied with the registration requirements for the military. In his opinion for the majority, Chief Justice Burger pointed out that the law did not single out an identifiable group—any student who wished to become eligible for aid could simply comply with the registration require- ments. Moreover, the Solomon Amendment did not impose punishment but only involved denial of a governmental benefit.[207]

An **ex post facto law** makes certain behavior illegal and provides for pun- ishment for engaging in that behavior before it became unlawful. In 1798, the Court established that the ex post facto clause applies only to criminal laws and outlined what it prohibits:

> Every law that makes an action done before the passage of the law, and which was innocent when done, criminal; and punishes such action. Every law that ag- gravates a crime, or makes it greater than it was, when committed. Every law that changes the punishment, and inflicts a greater punishment, than the law an- nexed to the crime, when committed. Every law that alters the legal rules of ev- idence, and receives less, or different, testimony, than the law required at the time of the commission of the offense, in order to convict the offender.[208]

Section 9

4. No Capitation, or other direct, Tax shall be laid, unless in Proportion to the Census or Enumeration herein before directed to be taken.

A capitation tax is a poll or head tax. The Committee on Detail added the prohibition as a gesture to the southern delegates who were threatening to vote against the Constitution if it allowed Congress to ban the importation of slaves. The prohibition on direct taxes was an effort to prevent Congress from taxing slaves. The Court's decision in 1895 that income taxes were direct taxes[209] was negated by the Sixteenth Amendment, which was ratified in 1913.

Section 9

5. No Tax or Duty shall be laid on Articles exported from any State.

6. No Preference shall be given by any Regulation of Commerce or Revenue to the Ports of one State over those of another: nor shall Vessels bound to, or from, one State, be obliged to enter, clear, or pay Duties in another.

The prohibition on export taxes was another provision that was important to the South as it relied heavily on income from agricultural exports. The Supreme Court has ruled that the clause forbids taxes on services and activities closely related to the export process as well as taxes on the exports themselves.[210]

Article I, Section 9 (6), reinforced Congress's control over commerce among the states. Addressing a problem that had been common under the Ar- ticles of Confederation, the provision prohibits Congress from favoring trade in one part of the country over others.

---

[207] *Selective Service v Minnesota Public Interest Research Group,* 468 US 841 (1984).
[208] *Calder v Bull,* 3 US 386 (1798).
[209] *Pollack v Farmers' Loan & Trust Co.,* 157 US 429 (1895).
[210] *United States v IBM Corp.,* 517 US 843 (1996).

Section 9

7. No money shall be drawn from the Treasury, but in Consequence of Appropriations made by Law; and a regular Statement and Account of the Receipts and Expenditures of all public Money shall be published from time to time.

Article I, Section 9 (7), is a limitation on the executive branch rather than on Congress. Indeed, it gives Congress substantial control over all the agencies of the federal government by specifying that money may only be drawn "in Consequence of Appropriations made by Law." The Court, however, has held Congress to the requirement that payment of money must be authorized by a statute.[211] In the course of appropriating funds, Congress passes a law authorizing an appropriation and then enacts another law appropriating the funds.

The Court underlined Congress's control over appropriations when it rejected the claim of a disabled civilian employee of the Navy who lost his pension because he followed the bad advice of a Navy pension specialist. The employee sued and recovered a judgment equal to his lost pension but the Court reversed, admonishing that "If agents of the Executive were able by their unauthorized oral or written statements to citizens, to obligate the Treasury for the payment of funds, the control over public funds that the Clause reposes in Congress in effect could be transferred to the Executive."[212]

Section 9

8. No Title of Nobility shall be granted by the United States: And no Person holding any Office of Profit or Trust under them, shall, without the Consent of the Congress, accept of any present, Emolument, Office, or Title, of any kind whatever, from any King, Prince, or foreign State.

The Committee on Detail took the provision that became Article I, Section 9 (8), from the Articles of Confederation. In *Federalist 39*, Madison observed that the prohibition on titles of nobility attested to the "republican complextion" of the design of the new government.[213] Similarly, Hamilton asserted in *Federalist 84* that the prohibition on titles of nobility "may truly be denominated the cornerstone of republican government; for so long as they are excluded, there can never be serious danger that the government will be any other than that of the people."[214]

Section 10

While Article I, Section 9, places limitations on the powers of Congress, Section 10 sets forth limits on the states. The provisions in Section 10 should be considered in conjunction with Article I, Section 8—particularly the commerce clause—and the supremacy clause of Article VI (2).

---

[211]*Office of Personnel Management v Richmond*, 496 US 414 (1990).
[212]*Ibid.*
[213]*The Federalist Papers*, 191.
[214]*Ibid.*, 436.

1. No State shall enter into any Treaty, Alliance, or Confederation; grant Letters of Marque and Reprisal; coin Money; emit Bills of Credit; make any Thing but gold and silver Coin a Tender in Payment of Debts; pass any Bill of Attainder, ex post facto Law,

The prohibitions listed in Article I, Section 10 (1), make clear that certain powers that the Constitution vested in Congress belong to the federal legislature exclusively and are forbidden to the states. The Articles of Confederation prohibited the states from entering any treaty, alliance, or confederation without the consent of Congress. At the Constitutional Convention, the Committee on Detail made the restriction into an absolute prohibition against states conducting international affairs. Additionally, Section 10 (1) barred the states from issuing their own money—a practice that had caused numerous problems under the Articles of Confederation.

The states, like Congress, were prohibited from enacting bills of attainder and ex post facto laws. Madison wrote in *Federalist 44* that bills of attainder, ex post facto laws, and laws impairing the obligation of contracts "are contrary to the first principles of the social compact, and to every principle of sound legislation."[215]

Section 10

1. [continued] or Law impairing the Obligation of Contracts, or grant any Title of Nobility.

The **contract clause** was designed to protect property rights from infringement by state legislatures. If states could cancel or alter contracts, such as agreements to repay loans or to pay for goods or services purchased on credit, the rights of property would never be secure. In the unstable economic environment following the American Revolution, some states acted to help farmers who were deeply in debt by enacting bankruptcy laws that modified their obligation to pay and by making paper money legal tender.

The contract clause was added to the Constitution late in the Convention and under odd circumstances. The Committee on Detail's draft did not include the clause, but Massachusetts delegate Rufus King proposed that the Convention add it. He modeled the clause after a similar provision in the Northwest Ordinance of 1787, which the Continental Congress had adopted several weeks earlier. The delegates rejected the proposal. The Committee on Style, however, reinserted it into the final draft of the Constitution. Thus, the contract clause seems to have been the work of the five-member Committee on Style and not the larger Convention or even the Committee on Detail.[216]

The general concern with debtor relief laws in the years preceding the Constitutional Convention has led some constitutional analysts to argue that the contract clause was aimed only at precluding legislation that interfered with private contracts. There was actually little agreement among the delegates at the

---

[215]*Ibid.*, 227.
[216]Forrest McDonald, *Novus Ordo Seclorum: The Intellectual Origins of the Constitution* (Lawrence, KS: University Press of Kansas, 1985), 272.

Convention and during the debates over ratification as to the precise meaning of the provision. Moreover, the Supreme Court's earliest application of the clause gave it a broader meaning to include public grants and charters—contracts made by the states—as well as private agreements. In 1810 in *Fletcher v Peck*, the Supreme Court invalidated a state law on constitutional grounds when Chief Justice John Marshall held that the Georgia legislature could not revoke previous public land grants even though the grants had been tainted with fraud.[217] In 1819 in *Dartmouth College v Woodward*, Marshall ruled that the contract clause prohibited New Hampshire from modifying the 1769 corporate charter that established Dartmouth College by altering the governing structure of the college.[218] Shortly after it decided *Dartmouth College*, the Court turned back to the issue of private contracts when it struck down New York's bankruptcy law, which absolved insolvent debtors of further obligation once they surrendered their property to their creditors.[219] In 1827, over Marshall's dissent, the Court declined to apply the contract clause to bankruptcy legislation that operated prospectively. That is, the states could pass bankruptcy laws that would affect contracts entered into after enactment of the law.[220]

When John Marshall died in 1835, President Andrew Jackson replaced him with Roger Brooke Taney. Jackson was also able to choose five associate justices during his two terms in office.[221] Although the Taney Court continued to use the contract clause to protect property rights and to prevent the states from bringing about redistributions of wealth, it was willing to allow the states to regulate grants and charters to promote industrial progress. Thus, in 1837 in *Charles River Bridge v Warren Bridge*, the justices refused to infer an exclusive grant in a contract that the state had awarded to a bridge company—the state, therefore, could grant a charter to another company to build a competing bridge.[222] Developing the principle that the inviolability of property rights must be balanced against the public good, in 1880 the Court fashioned a rule that the contract clause does not override the police power of the states to establish regulations to promote the health, safety, and morals of the community.[223]

Although the contract clause was the primary constitutional protection for property rights during the first half of the nineteenth century, it was eclipsed by the due process clause of the Fourteenth Amendment, which by the 1880s had become the basis for judicial invalidation of state economic regulations. In 1934, moreover, the Court intensified the dwindling importance of the contract clause when it upheld a Minnesota statute that allowed farmers who could not pay their mortgages to stay on their farms if they could pay some part of the value of the property. The mortgage moratorium was a temporary measure designed to alleviate the hardships of the Great Depression— at the end of two years the bank or other creditor could take the property if the farmer could not pay the mortgage. Chief Justice Charles Evans Hughes,

---

[217]*Fletcher v Peck*, 10 US 87 (1810).
[218]*Dartmouth College v Woodward*, 17 US 518 (1819).
[219]*Sturges v Crowinshield*, 17 US 122 (1819).
[220]*Ogden v Saunders*, 25 US 213 (1827).
[221]John McLean (1830), Henry Baldwin (1830), James Wayne (1835), Philip Barbour (1836), John Catron (1837).
[222]*Charles River Bridge Co. v Warren Bridge*, 36 US 420 (1837).
[223]*Stone v Mississippi*, 101 US 814 (1880).

writing for a five-member majority, emphasized the importance of the state's police power particularly in a time of economic emergency and noted that the moratorium was "not for the mere advantage of particular individuals but for the protection of a basic interest of society."[224] With that decision, the Court seemed to abandon the contract clause as a limitation on the states.

It was not until the late 1970s that the Court revived the contract clause by invalidating two state laws on the ground that they impaired the obligation of a contract. In 1977 by a vote of four to three, the Court held that New Jersey had violated the contract clause by setting aside a provision of an earlier law enacted to protect bondholders.[225] A year later the justices invalidated a Minnesota law—the Private Pension Benefits Protection Act—that required businesses that either terminated their pension plans or moved out of the state to contribute to a pension fund for former employees. Justice Potter Stewart, writing for a five-member majority, distinguished the mortgage moratorium legislation that the Court upheld in 1934 from the Private Pension Benefits Protection Act, noting that the latter was not enacted in response to a social or economic problem. He maintained that the contract clause limits the state's police powers and suggested that the crucial factor in contract clause analysis was the severity of the impairment—the more severe the impairment, the more careful the Court would be in examining the challenged legislation.[226] Although the Court to some extent rejuvenated the contract clause after a period of more than forty years, as Stewart's opinion suggested and as subsequent decisions confirmed, the justices were not willing to restore the clause to the position it held during the Marshall years.

During the 1980s, the Court upheld three regulations against challenges based on the contract clause. In 1983, a unanimous Court rejected challenges to Kansas legislation that regulated energy prices in a way that conflicted with existing contracts[227] and to Alabama's law prohibiting oil and natural gas producers from passing a tax increase on to purchasers, which was also at odds with existing contracts.[228] In the second case, the Court suggested that it would defer to legislation that imposes a "generally applicable rule of conduct designed to advance a 'broad societal interest'" that only incidentally disrupts existing contractual relationships.[229] In 1987, the justices upheld a Pennsylvania law requiring coal mine operators to leave 50 percent of the coal in the ground beneath certain structures to provide surface support—another provision that conflicted with existing contracts between mining companies and landowners. Justice Stevens, who wrote for the five-member majority, noted that "it is well-settled that the prohibition against impairing the obligation of contracts is not to be read literally."[230]

---

[224]*Home Building & Loan Association v Blaisdell*, 290 US 398 (1934).
[225]*United States Trust Co. v New Jersey*, 431 US 1 (1977).
[226]*Allied Structural Steel Co. v Spannaus*, 438 US 234 (1978).
[227]*Energy Reserves v Kansas Power and Light*, 459 US 400 (1983).
[228]*Exxon Corp. v Eagerton*, 462 US 176 (1983).
[229]*Ibid.*, 191.
[230]*Keystone Coal Association. v DeBenedictis*, 480 US 470 (1987).

Section 10

2. No State shall, without the Consent of the Congress, lay any Imposts or Duties on Imports or Exports, except what may be absolutely necessary for executing its inspection Laws: and the net Produce of all Duties and Imposts, laid by any State on Imports or Exports, shall be for the Use of the Treasury of the United States; and all such Laws shall be subject to the Revision and Controul of the Congress.

3. No State shall, without the Consent of Congress, lay any Duty of Tonnage, keep Troops, or Ships of War in time of Peace,

The import-export clause was designed to prevent the states from interfering with trade as they had done under the Articles of Confederation and to place the power to raise revenue from tariffs in the hands of the federal government. By explicitly precluding the states from regulating trade with other nations, the clause reinforces Congress's power to regulate foreign commerce under Article I, Section 8 (3). In 1827, Chief Justice John Marshall formulated a rule—the original package doctrine—that would last for nearly 150 years. According to that rule, a state could not tax imports so long as they remained in their original shipping packages.[231] In 1976, the Court held that so long as states do so in a nondiscriminatory manner—that is, they may not single out imported goods for taxation—they may tax foreign goods even if they are in their original package.[232]

Article I, Section 10 (3), forbids the states from imposing tonnage duties and from keeping troops during peacetime. A tonnage duty is a charge for bringing a ship into port or keeping it there. Although a tax on boats measured by their tonnage is prohibited, charges for actual services such as piloting and towing are not considered to be tonnage duties and are therefore allowed.[233] Article I, Section 8 (16), reserves some powers concerning the militia to the states and the Second Amendment gives the states the right to maintain a militia. Article I, Section 10 (3), makes it clear, however, that a state may not keep a standing army or maintain its own navy without the consent of Congress.

Section 10

3. [continued] enter into any Agreement or Compact with another State, or with a foreign Power, or engage in War, unless actually invaded, or in such imminent Danger as will not admit of delay.

Although it might seem to contradict the express terms of the compact clause, not all interstate agreements require the consent of Congress but only those "directed to the formation of any combination tending to the increase of political power in the states, which may encroach upon or interfere with the just

---

[231]*Brown v Maryland*, 25 US 419 (1827).
[232]*Michelin Tire Corp. v Wages*, 423 US 276 (1976). See also, *R.J. Reynolds Tobacco Co. v Durham County*, 479 US 130 (1986).
[233]*State Tonnage Tax Cases*, 79 US 204 (1871) (no taxes based on tonnage); *Cooley v Board of Wardens*, 53 US 299 (1851) (fees for services not a tonnage duty).

supremacy of the United States."[234] The states may enter into agreements resolving boundary disputes, for example, without congressional approval.[235]

The prohibition on agreements between a state and a foreign power except in emergencies reflects the conditions in the late eighteenth century when a state government might have had to assume responsibility for repelling a foreign invasion until the forces of the national government could be alerted and mobilized to do so.

QUESTIONS

1. In 1905, Justice John Marshall Harlan dismissed a claim that a state law violated the rights secured by the Preamble of the Constitution. He noted, "Although that Preamble indicates the general purposes for which the people ordained and established the Constitution, it has never been regarded as the source of any substantive power conferred on the Government of the United States or on any of its Departments."[236] How important is the Preamble in light of Harlan's dismissal?[237] Did he in effect eliminate the Preamble from the Constitution? Of what importance is that general prologue to the Constitution?

2. What is the difference between apportionment and districting? How was *Department of Commerce v United States House of Representatives* (1999) different from the earlier cases involving the apportionment of representatives as provided in Article I, Section 2 (3)? Should the Court have decided the case? Why or why not? What justification might the justices have used to avoid deciding the case?

3. We discussed briefly the methods of constitutional interpretation that Chief Justice Warren used in *Powell v McCormack* (1969). Examine that opinion and see if you can find any additional approaches. What did Warren's opinion suggest about the role of precedent in constitutional interpretation?

4. Was Justice Owen Roberts correct when he wrote the following: "The federal union is a government of delegated powers. It has only such as are expressly conferred upon it and such as are reasonably to be implied from those granted"?[238] See if you can find cases that support or refute Roberts's assertion.

5. Was the Court's decision in *Rust v Sullivan* (1991) consistent with the principle that Chief Justice Rehnquist set forth in *South Dakota v Dole* (1987), that Congress may not use its spending power to induce states to engage in activities that would be unconstitutional?

---

[234]*Virginia v Tennessee*, 148 US 503 (1893).
[235]See, for example, *New Hampshire v Maine*, 426 US 363 (1976).
[236]*Jacobson v Massachusetts*, 197 US 11 (1905).
[237]This question is raised in Walter F. Murphy, James E. Fleming, Sotirios A. Barber, *American Constitutional Interpretation*, 2d ed. (Westbury, NY: Foundation Press, 1995), 128.
[238]*United States v Butler*, 297 US 1 (1936).

6. In *United States v Lopez* (1995) Chief Justice Rehnquist asserted, "[E]ven these modern-era precedents which have expanded congressional power under the Commerce Clause confirm that this power is subject to outer limits." He was referring to cases such as *NLRB v Jones and Laughlin Steel Corporation* (1937) and, *Wickard v Filburn* (1942). What limits did those cases specify? Was *Lopez* and subsequently, *United States v Morrison,* consistent with those decisions? Or were they more consistent with the Court's decisions before 1937? Was it consistent with *Gibbons v Ogden* (1824)? Did the Gun-Free School Zones Act represent a further extension of Congress's commerce power insofar as it regulated noneconomic activities? Finally, was the Violence Against Women Act of 1994 significantly different from the Gun-Free School Zones Act? If so, why did the Court find it to be beyond Congress's commerce power?

7. What method of constitutional interpretation did Chief Justice John Marshall use in *McCulloch v Maryland* (1819)? What factors other than his understanding of the Constitution might help explain his expansive interpretation of federal power in that case?

8. Examine the various provisions of the USA Patriot Act of 2001 and consider whether these provisions expand in a significant way the powers of Congress. Consider also whether the Patriot Act may violate the Constitution insofar as it confers powers on Congress that go beyond those bestowed upon the legislative branch in Article I.

9. Has the Supreme Court been faithful to the original intent of the Framers in its interpretation of the contract clause? What was the Framers' intent? Assuming we know what it was, should the Court at the beginning of the twenty-first century follow the intent of the eighteenth-century designers of the Constitution?

KEY TERMS

Bicameralism
Qualifications for voters
Age, citizenship, and residency requirements
Term limits
One-person-one-vote
Three-fifths clause
Apportionment
Redistricting
Impeachment power
Expulsion

Legislative veto
Implied powers
Inherent powers
Contempt power
Delegation of power
Habeas corpus
Bill of attainder
Ex post facto law
Contract clause

SUGGESTIONS FOR FURTHER READING

Ackerman, Bruce. *Private Property and the Constitution.* New Haven, CT: Yale University Press, 1977.

Barber, Sotirios A. *On What the Constitution Means.* Baltimore, MD: Johns Hopkins University Press, 1984.

Benedict, Michael Les. *The Impeachment and Trial of Andrew Johnson.* New York: W.W. Norton, 1973.

Electronic Frontier Foundation. "USA Patriot Act as Passed by Congress." Available: http://www.eff.org/Privacy/Surveillance/Terrorism_militias/20011025_hr3162_usa _patriot_bill.html.

Farber, Daniel, and Suzanna Sherry. *A History of the American Constitution.* St. Paul, MN: West Publishing Co., 1990, Chapters 5 and 6.

FindLaw Legal News and Commentary. "Special Coverage: War on Terrorism." Available: http://news.findlaw.com/legalnews/us/terrorism/laws.html.

Horwitz, Morton J. *The Transformation of American Law, 1780–1860.* Cambridge, MA: Harvard University Press, 1977.

Kamisar, Yale, Wayne R. LaFave, and Jerold H. Israel. *Modern Criminal Procedure: Cases, Comments, Questions,* 8th ed. St. Paul, MN: West Publishing Co., 1994, Chapter 28.

Leuchtenburg, William E. *Franklin D. Roosevelt and the New Deal, 1932–1940.* New York: Harper and Row, 1963.

Leuchtenburg, William E. *The Supreme Court Reborn: The Constitutional Revolution in the Age of Roosevelt.* New York: Oxford University Press, 1995.

Levy, Leonard W. *Origins of the Bill of Rights.* New Haven, CT: Yale University Press, 1999, Chapters 2 and 3.

McCloskey, Robert G. *The American Supreme Court,* 2d ed. Revised by Sanford Levinson. Chicago, IL: University of Chicago Press, 1994.

McDonald, Forrest. *Novus Ordo Seclorum: The Intellectual Origins of the Constitution.* Lawrence, KS: University Press of Kansas, 1985.

McLoughlin, Merrill, ed. *The Impeachment and Trial of President Clinton: The Official Transcripts, from the House Judiciary Committee Hearings to the Senate Trial.* New York: Random House, 1999.

Pritchett, C. Herman. *Constitutional Law of the Federal System.* Englewood Cliffs, NJ: Prentice Hall, 1984.

"A Process Oriented Approach to the Contract Clause." *Yale Law Journal* 89 (1980): 1623–1651.

Rehnquist, William H. *Grand Inquests: The Historic Impeachments of Justice Samuel Chase and President Andrew Johnson.* New York: William Morrow, 1992.

"Revival of the Contract Clause: *Allied Structural Steel Co. v Spannaus* and *United States Trust Co. v New Jersey.*" *Virginia Law Review* 65 (1979): 377–402.

Swisher, Carl Brent. *The Growth of Constitutional Power in the United States.* Chicago, IL: University of Chicago Press, 1946.

Van Tassel, Emily Field, and Paul Finkelman. *Impeachable Offenses: A Documentary History from 1787 to the Present.* Washington, DC: Congressional Quarterly, Inc., 1999.

Volcansek, Mary L. *None Called for Justice: Judicial Impeachment.* Urbana, IL: University of Illinois Press, 1993.

Whittington, Keith E. *Constitutional Construction: Divided Powers and Constitutional Meaning.* Cambridge, MA: Harvard University Press, 1999, Chapters 2 and 4.

Wilkins, David E. *American Indian Sovereignty and the U.S. Supreme Court: The Masking of Justice.* Austin, TX: University of Texas Press, 1997.

Wilkins, David E., and Vine Deloria, Jr. *Tribes, Treaties, and Constitutional Tribulations.* Austin, TX: University of Texas Press, 2000.

Wright, Benjamin F. *The Contract Clause of the Constitution.* Cambridge, MA: Harvard University Press, 1938.

Wunder, John R. *'Retained by the People': A History of American Indians and the Bill of Rights.* New York: Oxford University Press, 1997.

4

ARTICLE II: THE EXECUTIVE BRANCH

Because of the colonists' experience under British rule, the Articles of Confederation and the early state constitutions deliberately and severely constrained executive power. In fact, the Articles did not even provide for a separate executive branch. Instead, Congress had the authority to create executive departments "as may be necessary for managing the general affairs of the United States under their direction." Congress was also permitted to "appoint one of their number to preside, provided that no person be allowed to serve in the office of President more than one year in any term of three years."[1] By 1787 some state constitutions had begun to provide for a stronger executive and there was widespread recognition that the lack of an executive was one of the major flaws of the Articles of Confederation.

A number of the delegates to the Constitutional Convention, nevertheless, had serious reservations about a strong executive. The initial draft of the Virginia Plan had only one provision concerning the executive branch. That provision left the nature of the executive uncertain, establishing only that the executive would be appointed by Congress, would be paid, and would be ineligible for a second term. Early discussions revolved around the number of the executive. Although some delegates argued that a single executive would too closely resemble a monarchy and advocated a two- or three-member executive from different parts of the country, the supporters of a single executive prevailed.

Later in the Convention after they had resolved some of the issues concerning the legislature, the delegates reached agreement on the general principle that "the executive should be independent enough to provide a check on the legislature, but not so strong that he would become a tyrant."[2] Disagreement remained over the mode of selection of the executive, eligibility for reelection, length of term, how the president was to be removed from office, the treaty-making power, and the veto power. The delegates resolved these issues during the Convention. A prominent constitutional scholar has remarked that the creation of the presidency was the Framers' "most creative act, and their achieve-

---

[1]"The Articles of Confederation," in Melvin I. Urofsky, ed. *Documents of American Constitutional and Legal History, Volume I, From Settlement through Reconstruction* (New York: Alfred A. Knopf, 1989), 69–76, 74.
[2]Daniel Farber and Suzanna Sherry, *A History of the American Constitution* (St. Paul, MN: West Publishing Co., 1990), 86.

TABLE 4-1 Constitutional Powers of the President

Type of Power	Constitutional Source
Executive powers	Executive power vested in president—Section 1 (1)
	Take care that the laws be faithfully executed— Section 3 (1)
	Appointment & removal power—Section 2 (2) & (3)
	Require opinions of officers of executive departments—Section 2 (1)
Legislative powers	Information to Congress; call special sessions & adjourn—Section 3 (1)
	Veto power—Article I, Section 7 (2) & (3)
Foreign affairs and military powers	Commander in chief of the armed forces—Section 2 (1)
	Make treaties; appoint ambassadors—Section 2 (2)
	Receive ambassadors—Section 3 (1)
Judicial powers	Appoint judges of the Supreme Court—Section 2 (2)
	Grant pardons and reprieves—Section 2 (1)

ment was all the more notable because leading Framers thought about the executive in notably divergent ways."[3]

Although Article I contains extensive lists of the powers and limitations of the legislative branch, Article II is far less attentive to outlining the powers of the executive and focuses instead on issues of selection and removal. As we examine the provisions in Article II, it will become evident that the powers of the executive have expanded tremendously during the twentieth century. Many factors have contributed to this trend including the emergence of the United States as a major international power, the consequent intertwining of international and domestic policy issues, and the rise of the administrative state. Although the powers of Congress have grown far beyond what the Framers could have envisioned, the expansion of the president's powers has been even more pronounced, giving force to Alexander Hamilton's contention in *Federalist 70*:

> Energy in the executive is a leading character in the definition of good government. It is essential to the protection of the community against foreign attacks: It is not less essential to the steady administration of the laws, to the protection of property against those irregular and high handed combinations, which sometimes

[3]Jack N. Rakove, *Original Meanings: Politics and Ideas in the Making of the Constitution* (New York: Alfred A. Knopf, 1996), 245.

interrupt the ordinary course of justice, to the security of liberty against the enterprises and assaults of ambition, of faction and of anarchy.[4]

Section 1

1. The executive Power shall be vested in a President of the United States of America.

Article I, Section 1 (1), states that "all legislative power *herein granted* shall be vested in a Congress." In contrast, Article II, Section 1 (1), *vests* executive power in a president. That language may be taken to suggest that the president possesses **inherent powers** not expressly granted in the Constitution. Thus, some presidents have claimed that certain executive powers are inherent in the nature of a sovereign government. Some have gone further to claim that their inherent powers include the prerogative to exercise extraordinary powers in an emergency.

The history of the presidency has been marked by debate about whether the initial phrase of Article II, Section 1, constitutes an affirmative grant of authority of general powers or whether it limits the president to the exercise only of those powers that appear in the remaining provisions in Article II. Presidents Theodore Roosevelt and William Howard Taft had sharply contrasting understandings of presidential power that capture the essentials of the debate. Roosevelt's **"stewardship" theory** posited that it was not only the president's "right but his duty to do anything that the needs of the nation demanded, unless such action was forbidden by the Constitution or by the laws."[5] In contrast, William Howard Taft argued that the president

> [C]an exercise no power which cannot be fairly and reasonably traced to some specific grant of power or justly implied and included within such express grant as proper and necessary to its exercise. Such specific grant must be either in the federal Constitution or in an act of Congress passed in pursuance thereof. There is no undefined residuum of power which he can exercise because it seems to him to be in the public interest.[6]

In 1936 when Justice George Sutherland distinguished between the federal government's sweeping inherent powers in foreign affairs and its limited authority in the domestic context, he also underlined the president's inherent power to conduct the nation's foreign affairs. The president, Sutherland proclaimed, possesses a "very delicate, plenary and exclusive power . . . as the sole organ of the federal government in the field of international relations."[7]

The Supreme Court has been careful to maintain limits on the powers of the president in the domestic realm. Nevertheless, the Court has endorsed the notion that the president possesses *some* inherent powers beyond those listed in Article II. When President Harry Truman seized the steel mills during the Ko-

---

[4]*The Federalist Papers* by Alexander Hamilton, James Madison, and John Jay (New York: Bantam Books, 1982), 355.
[5]*The Autobiography of Theodore Roosevelt* (New York: Macmillan, 1913) as quoted in Christopher H. Pyle and Richard M. Pious, *The President, Congress, and the Constitution: Power and Legitimacy in American Politics* (New York: Free Press, 1984), 69.
[6]William Howard Taft, *Our Chief Magistrate and His Powers* (New York: Columbia University Press, 1916), 139.
[7]*United States v Curtiss-Wright Export Corporation*, 299 US 304 (1936).

rean War to prevent a strike that would have disrupted the production of steel needed for military equipment, the justices held that the president did not have the constitutional power to take such action.[8] Justice Hugo Black, in his opinion for the majority, emphatically denied that the president had the power to act in the absence of express constitutional or statutory authorization. Each of the five justices who joined Black to hold that Truman could not seize the steel mills to avert a strike wrote a concurring opinion. Only one of those—William O. Douglas—agreed with Black that the president lacked inherent powers. The other four argued that the president lacked authority to seize the steel mills because Congress had prohibited such action in the Taft-Hartley Act, but they acknowledged the existence of inherent powers. Justice Robert Jackson, for example, argued, "Presidential powers are not fixed but fluctuate, depending upon their disjunction or conjunction with those of Congress."[9] In short, initial appearances to the contrary, the *Steel Seizure Case* actually supports rather than refutes the argument that the president has inherent powers.

Although the Court has rejected sweeping claims made by presidents and their lawyers, it has continued to acknowledge that the executive authority includes inherent powers in domestic affairs. For example, the justices conceded that a qualified **executive privilege** "is fundamental to the operation of Government" when they unanimously rejected President Nixon's claim of an absolute privilege of confidentiality for all presidential communications as a justification for refusing to produce the Watergate tapes pursuant to a judicial subpoena.[10] Although the need for the Watergate tapes as evidence in criminal proceedings prevailed over Nixon's interest in confidentiality, the Court noted that a president may have the right to claim executive privilege to protect military or diplomatic secrets. Moreover, the president must be able to explore policy alternatives with advisers with the assurance of privacy.

In 1982 the Court, by a vote of five to four, held that the president is "entitled to absolute **immunity** from damages liability predicated on his official acts." Writing for the majority, Justice Lewis Powell emphasized the unique position of the president in the constitutional scheme. He explained that the grant of authority in Article II, Section 1 (1)

> establishes the President as the chief constitutional officer of the Executive Branch, entrusted with supervisory and policy responsibilities of utmost discretion and sensitivity. These include the enforcement of federal law—it is the President who is charged constitutionally to "take Care that the Laws be faithfully executed"; the conduct of foreign affairs—a realm in which the Court has recognized that "[i]t would be intolerable that courts, without the relevant information, should review and perhaps nullify actions of the Executive taken on information properly held secret"; and management of the Executive Branch—a task for which "imperative reasons requir[e] an unrestricted power [in the President] to remove the most important of his subordinates in their most important duties."[11]

---

[8]*Youngstown Sheet & Tube Company v Sawyer*, 343 US 579 (1952).
[9]*Ibid.* The other justices in the majority were Harold Burton, Tom Clark, and Felix Frankfurter.
[10]*United States v Nixon*, 418 US 683 (1974).
[11]*Nixon v Fitzgerald*, 457 US 731, 750 (1982) (citations omitted).

In 1997, a unanimous Court held that such immunity did not extend to the president's unofficial conduct and rejected President Clinton's claim that proceedings concerning Paula Jones's suit against him for sexual harassment must be postponed until after the conclusion of his presidency. Nevertheless, the justices conceded that the presidency is "a unique office with powers and [vast and important] responsibilities."[12]

Section 1

1. [continued] He shall hold his Office during the Term of four Years, and, together with the Vice President, chosen for the same term, be elected, as follows:

The Philadelphia Convention deadlocked over the related issues of whether the president would be eligible for a second term, whether he would be impeachable, and the method by which the chief executive would be selected. Delegates who favored election by Congress preferred a long term—ranging from seven to twenty years—to protect the president from pressure from those to whom he owed his election. Those who supported election by the states wanted a short term to ensure the president's accountability to the electorate. Those delegates also argued that the president should be eligible for reelection as a reward for responsible service. The Convention appointed a Committee on Postponed Matters, composed of one delegate from each state, to resolve the issues. The Committee decided on a fixed term of four years and unlimited reeligibility. The Twenty-second Amendment, which became part of the Constitution in 1951, limited the president's tenure to two terms.

Section 1

2. Each State shall appoint, in such Manner as the Legislature thereof may direct, a Number of Electors, equal to the whole Number of Senators and Representatives to which the State may be entitled in the Congress: but no Senator or Representative, or Person holding an Office of Trust or Profit under the United States, shall be appointed an Elector.

3. The Electors shall meet in their respective States, and vote by Ballot for two Persons, of whom one at least shall not be an Inhabitant of the same State with themselves. And they shall make a List of all the Persons voted for, and of the Number of Votes for each; which List they shall sign and certify, and transmit sealed to the Seat of the Government of the United States, directed to the President of the Senate. The President of the Senate shall, in the Presence of the Senate and House of Representatives, open all the Certificates, and the Votes shall then be counted. The Person having the greatest Number of Votes shall be the President, if such Number be a Majority of the whole Number of Electors appointed; and if there be more than one who have such Majority, and have an equal Number of Votes, then the House of Representatives shall immediately chuse by Ballot one of them for President: and if no Person have a Majority, then from the five highest on the List the said House shall in like Manner chuse the President. But in chusing the President, the Votes shall be

---

[12]*Clinton v Jones*, 520 US 681 (1997).

taken by States, the Representation from each State having one Vote; A quorum for this Purpose shall consist of a Member or Members from two thirds of the States, and a Majority of all the States shall be necessary to a Choice. In every Case, after the Choice of the President, the Person having the greatest Number of Votes of the Electors shall be the Vice President. But if there should remain two or more who have equal Votes, the Senate shall choose from them by Ballot the Vice President.[13]

At the Philadelphia Convention, proponents of a weak executive argued that the legislature should choose the president, whereas advocates of a strong executive preferred direct popular election. There was little support for a popularly elected president and the delegates rejected a proposal—offered as a compromise—that the people of the states would choose presidential electors, who would meet and choose the president. The most important contribution of the Committee on Postponed Matters was a scheme—the **electoral college**—for choosing the president that the delegates found acceptable. Each state would choose its own electors "in such a Manner" as the legislature designated. The electors of each state were to meet and vote for two individuals, only one of whom could be from their own state—to avoid the deadlock that would result if electors voted for candidates from their own states. The recipient of the greatest number of votes, providing that number comprised a majority of all the electors, would be president. Because of the widely shared belief that in most elections no candidate would receive a majority, the Committee proposed that in such cases the election should shift to the Senate. But when fear that the Senate might become too powerful prompted several states to oppose such a plan the Committee shifted the choice to the House of Representatives with each state having one vote.

The most common explanations of the motives that lay behind the Constitutional Convention's decision to use the electoral college system as the method of choosing the president have been that the Framers did not consider most voters to be capable of making a reasoned and informed choice for president and that the electoral college was designed to ensure that the small states would have a role in choosing the president.[14] In the aftermath of the contested election of 2000 commentators began to point out the flaws in the traditional explanations and to note that Article II, Section 1 (2), made the number of electors to which each state would be entitled dependent on the number of representatives each state had in Congress. Thus, not only were the smaller states advantaged by the inclusion of the additional two electors based on the number of Senators but by linking the number of electors to representation in Congress the Framers gave a definite advantage to presidential candidates from the slave states where, for purposes of representation, each slave counted as three-fifths of a person as provided in Article I, Section 2. In short, the origins of the electoral college were undeniably proslavery and built a pro-Southern bias into the presidential election system.[15] Indeed, as law professor Akhil Reed Amar

---

[13]This paragraph of Article II, Section 1, was superseded by the Twelfth Amendment.
[14]Paul Finkleman, "The Murky Proslavery Origins of the Electoral College." *Jurist*, November 30, 2000. Available: http://jurist.law.pitt.edu/election/electionfink.htm.
[15]See, *ibid.*

pointed out, for thirty-two of the Constitution's first thirty-six years, a white slaveholding Virginian occupied the presidency.[16]

The electoral college played a prominent role in the disputed election of 2000, prompting a number of commentators to call for its abolition or at least for major reform. For the fourth time in the history of the United States, the candidate who lost the popular vote received a majority of electoral votes and consequently won the election. Currently, all the states except Maine and Nebraska use the winner-take-all or unit rule, which provides that a candidate who carries a state in the popular vote—even if only by one vote—receives all of its electoral votes. As a result, not only may a candidate lose the popular vote nationally and win the election under this system, but also the unit rule distorts the election results in such a way that a president who wins the popular vote by only a small margin may win by a landslide in the electoral college and thereby claim to have a popular mandate.

The first time that the presidential selection process resulted in a candidate who prevailed in the popular vote losing the election was in 1824 when no candidate received a majority of the electoral votes. Andrew Jackson, however, won a plurality of both the popular and the electoral college vote. Henry Clay, the candidate who was in fourth place, then gave his support to John Quincy Adams, who had run second in the popular vote. The election went to the House of Representatives, which decided in favor of Adams. The new president then named Clay his Secretary of State, prompting charges of a "corrupt bargain." In the election of 1876 Democrat Samuel Tilden prevailed over Republican Rutherford Hayes in the popular vote. Tilden received 184 undisputed electoral votes with 185 needed for election whereas Hayes received 165. Hayes, nevertheless, became president. The electoral vote was disputed in three Southern states and in Oregon—all four states submitted dual electoral returns to Congress. To settle the disputed returns a joint Senate-House committee created an Electoral Commission of Fifteen. As it turned out, the Commission was composed of eight Republicans and seven Democrats. Refusing to "go behind the election returns" the Commission did not investigate the popular vote in the disputed states but merely determined which electors had been certified in the proper manner. By a vote of eight to seven, the Commission decided every disputed return in favor of the Republicans. Hayes thereby received the requisite 185 electoral votes.[17] In 1888, Republican Benjamin Harrison lost the popular vote to incumbent Grover Cleveland, but won the electoral college vote and thus, the presidency.

Finally, when the Supreme Court intervened in the contested election of 2000 and prohibited further recounts of the votes in the contested state of Florida, the victory went to Republican governor George W. Bush of Texas. With the electoral votes in Florida, the latter received 271 electoral votes—one

---

[16]Akhil Reed Amar, "The Electoral College, Unfair From Day One." *The New York Times*, November 9, 2000.
[17]In the wake of the Hayes-Tilden election Congress enacted a federal statute that played an important role in the resolution of the contested election of 2000. What is now 3 USC Section 5 provides that if a state makes its final determination of who its electors shall be at least six days before the electoral college meets, that determination shall govern.

FIGURE 4-1

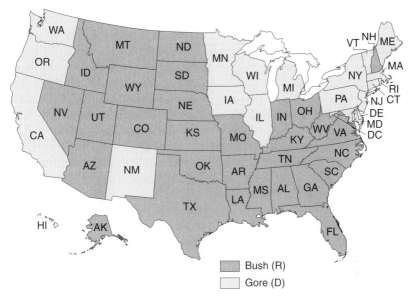

Source: NPR Online, "Election 2000. Available: http://www.npr.org/news/national/election2000/#.

more than the 270 he needed to win—whereas Democratic Vice President Al Gore received 266. The new president had received 50,455,156 votes while his opponent won the popular vote with 50,992,335 votes.[18] The disparity between the electoral and the popular vote revived the debate about whether the electoral college should continue to be used as a method of choosing the president, whether the system should be reformed to eliminate the winner-take-all rule, or whether the electoral college should be abolished in favor of direct election of the president. Figure 4-1 shows the distribution of the electoral votes in the 2000 election.

The original arrangement of voting for two candidates, specified in Article II, Section 1 (3), worked only until political parties emerged as a force in American politics. In the election of 1796, Federalist John Adams was elected president and Republican Thomas Jefferson became vice president. Then in 1800 Jefferson and Aaron Burr, who was also a Republican, each received seventy-three electoral votes. After thirty-six ballots, the House of Representatives chose Jefferson as president and Burr as vice president. The Twelfth Amendment, ratified in 1804, prevented another election like the Jefferson–Burr tie by providing that the electors vote separately for president and vice president.

The first phrase of Article II, Section 1 (2), also played an important role in the outcome of the disputed results in the crucial state of Florida. The provision gives to "Each State" the authority to "appoint, in such Manner as the

---

[18]For a state-by-state count see, "Presidential Election of 2000, Electoral and Popular Vote Summary." Available: http://www.infoplease.com/ipa/A0876793.html.

Legislature thereof may direct, a Number of Electors."[19] Although the details of the legal actions that the candidates filed in their attempts to resolve the election are too numerous and complex to recount here, we offer a chronology and summary of the legal actions in Table 4-2, and, at the end of this chapter, a separate list of suggested readings, including useful Internet resources.

We focus here on the justices' interpretation of Article II, Section 1 (2). The equal protection clause of the Fourteenth Amendment, which provided the justification for the majority's decision in *Bush v Gore*, is considered in Chapter 10.

Shortly before 8 P.M. on election night the Associated Press and the television networks announced that Gore was going to win in the "battleground" state of Florida. With his victories in the other key states of Michigan and Pennsylvania, winning in Florida would give him the requisite number of electoral votes to win the election. Within a few hours, however, the major networks withdrew their prediction and replaced it with the slogan that would soon become synonymous with the election: "Too close to call." Just after 2:00 A.M. the networks made another prediction: Bush would win Florida by 50,000 votes. The initial count, however, indicated that Bush had received some 1800 more votes than Gore out of a total of 5,800,000 votes cast. As required by state law when the margin is so close there was an automatic machine recount.[20] When that machine recount revealed Bush's lead to be in the vicinity of 300 votes, the Gore campaign asked for a hand recount of the votes in four counties that were heavily Democratic, including Palm Beach County where the controversial **"butterfly ballot,"** with its confusing placement of the candidates' names in relation to the holes that voters needed to punch, confused many voters (see Figure 4-2). As a result of that confusion, Pat Buchanan received a disproportionately high number of votes in the heavily Democratic county, almost 2,700 more than he had received in any other county in Florida. Additionally, there were around 19,000 ballots that had two votes for president.[21] On November 8 three Palm Beach County residents filed a complaint in state circuit court alleging that the election in their county had been illegal and demanded a new one. Although the controversy over the butterfly ballot would soon be overshadowed by other legal disputes, the claim that this confusing ballot violated Florida's law governing the permitted form of ballots was the issue that first took the 2000 election to court. On December 1, 2000, the Florida Supreme Court ruled that the ballot did not constitute substantial noncompliance with the statutory requirements.[22]

---

[19]Congress provided details of this process in Title 3 Ch. 1 of the United States Code. Title 3, section 5 of the U.S. Code: "If any State shall have provided, by laws enacted prior to the day fixed for the appointment of the electors, for its final determination of any controversy or contest concerning the appointment of all or any of the electors of such State, by judicial or other methods or procedures, and such determination shall have been made at least six days before the time fixed for the meeting of the electors, such determination made pursuant to such law so existing on said day, and made at least six days prior to said time of meeting of the electors, shall be conclusive, and shall govern in the counting of the electoral votes as provided in the Constitution, and as hereinafter regulated, so far as the ascertainment of the electors appointed by such State is concerned."

[20]Ch. 102.141 (4) provides: "If the returns for any office reflect that a candidate was defeated or eliminated by one-half of a percent or less of the votes cast for such office, . . . the board responsible for certifying the results of the vote . . . shall order a recount of the votes cast."

[21]Howard Gillman, *The Votes That Counted: How the Court Decided the 2000 Election* (Chicago, IL: University of Chicago Press, 2001), 23.

[22]*Fladell v Palm Beach County Canvassing Board*, 772 So 2d 1240 (2000).

TABLE 4-2   Choosing the President, 2000: Chronology of Legal Actions

November 7, 2000

Election Day

November 8, 2000

The first lawsuit (*Fladell v Palm Beach County Canv. Bd.* (PBCCB)) is filed in Florida by Palm Beach County voters who, alleging voter confusion over the county's butterfly ballot, are seeking to set aside all presidential votes in the county and order a new countywide election. Defendants include the PBCCB, Bush, Cheney, Gore, and Lieberman.

November 9, 2000

Palm Beach County voters file more voter lawsuits by challenging the constitutionality of the ballot and the presidential vote. U.S. Attorney General Janet Reno attempts to defer to state officials over the legality of the ballot.

November 10, 2000

The Democratic and Republican Parties attempt to show distance from the controversy. Governor Bush tells reporters he is making "low key" preparations for the White House in the midst of recount litigation.

November 11, 2000

The Bush campaign files a federal lawsuit in Miami (*Siegel v LePore*) seeking declaratory and injunctive relief to halt all manual recounts, on the grounds that they violate the due process and equal protection clauses of the Fourteenth Amendment.

November 13, 2000

Palm Beach and Volusia County Canvassing Boards sue Florida Secretary of State Katherine Harris to halt her just-announced 5:00 P.M. vote certification and recount deadline. They want to gain time so they can continue their recounts of presidential ballots and include the hand-counted votes that Harris seeks to prohibit.

U.S. District Court Judge Middlebrook, holding that Florida's vote-counting process appeared to be neutral without any necessity for federal intervention, denies the Bush campaign's request for injunctive relief to halt a manual recount of Florida voters' ballots. Middlebrook concludes, "The body of law is pretty pervasive that the federal courts ought to stay out of state elections."

November 14, 2000

The Palm Beach County Canvassing Board decides to continue manual recounts of presidential votes, even though a state court judge in Tallahassee upholds Harris's previously announced 5:00 P.M. deadline for counties to report ballot counts to the state.

Leon County Judge Terry Lewis upholds Harris's 5:00 P.M. deadline, but cautions that he will allow supplemental or corrected presidential vote totals after the deadline and that Harris may use them if she uses a "proper exercise of discretion."

(continued)

TABLE 4-2 *(Continued)*

November 15, 2000

Florida Secretary of State Katherine Harris sues in an effort to stop manual recounts. The Bush campaign appeals the U.S. District Court decision denying injunctive relief to the 11th Circuit Court of Appeals in Atlanta.

November 16, 2000

The Florida Supreme Court rejects the Secretary of State's request to halt manual recounts and allows them to continue.

November 17, 2000

Leon County circuit court Judge Terry Lewis denies the Gore campaign's emergency motion to compel Secretary of State Harris to comply with and enforce the court's earlier injunction, holding that it was within Secretary's discretion to refuse to include late-filed returns in the certified results of the election (*McDermott v Harris*).

The Gore campaign immediately appeals to the Florida Supreme Court and obtains a stay to enjoin Harris from certifying election recount. The court schedules oral argument at a Court hearing at 2:00 P.M. on Monday, November 20, 2000. The 11th Circuit Court of Appeals rejects the Bush campaign's emergency appeal.

November 18-19, 2000

All parties in the Florida Supreme Court appeal file briefs over the weekend.

November 20, 2000

The Florida Supreme Court listens to the parties' arguments on appeal. A Florida circuit judge rules that "it is not legally possible to have a revote or a new election for presidential electors in Florida" based upon voter confusion with, and constitutional challenges to, the butterfly ballot.

November 21, 2000

At 9:45 P.M. the Florida Supreme Court renders a unanimous decision, ordering that manual recounts must be added to the final certified count of presidential votes by Florida voters (*Palm Beach County Canvassing Board v Harris*).

November 22, 2000

Bush petitions the United States Supreme Court, seeking to have the decision of the Florida Supreme Court overruled.

November 23, 2000

Vice President Gore and the Florida Democratic Party file their own petition, opposing Bush's request for the Supreme Court to decide the case, arguing there is no federal question at issue for the Court to decide.

Florida's Supreme Court denies Gore's petition to order Miami-Dade County to resume their manual ballot recount.

TABLE 4-2   (Continued)

November 24, 2000

In a historic decision, the United States Supreme Court grants certiorari and decides to hear Bush's appeal of the Florida Supreme Court's decision of November 21. The country's highest court declines, however, to hear Bush's appeal of denials, by the Eleventh Circuit and the U.S. District Court in Miami, of the Republican presidential candidate's request for a temporary restraining order and injunction prohibiting any state-ordered manual recount of presidential ballots.

Attorneys in consolidated class action cases for Florida voters challenging the election results and the constitutionality of the butterfly ballots, file emergency appeals to the Florida Supreme Court, arguing that trial courts have the legal authority to order new presidential elections in Florida.

November 26, 2000

Florida Secretary of State Harris certifies George W. Bush as the Florida voters' choice for president, rejecting Palm Beach County Canvassing Board amended recounts. The Gore legal team announces that it will head to court the following day to contest the certification.

November 27, 2000

Gore and Lieberman commence a new lawsuit by filing a complaint and a request for an emergency hearing, contesting the Secretary of State's recount, in Leon County, Florida. The judge refuses to begin an immediate recount.

November 28, 2000

Bush, Gore, the Florida Secretary of State, and the Palm Beach County Canvassing Board file legal briefs with the United States Supreme Court outlining their respective arguments.

Leon County Circuit Court Judge N. Sanders Sauls is assigned to preside over Gore's election certification litigation. The Gore legal team makes emergency applications to commence a recount and impound votes in Miami-Dade and Palm Beach Counties. The Court orders the parties to file "proffers" from witnesses in support of their arguments.

November 29, 2000

Judge Sauls orders that Florida voter ballots from Miami-Dade and Palm Beach Counties be sent to Tallahassee, Florida, for a possible recount.

November 30, 2000

All parties to the United States Supreme Court litigation file reply briefs to oppose the arguments of the other parties.

December 1, 2000

The United States Supreme Court hears oral arguments from all parties in the case of *Bush v. Palm Beach County Canvassing Board*.

(continued)

TABLE 4-2 *(Continued)*

December 4, 2000

The United States Supreme Court sets aside the Florida Supreme Court's ruling and remands it so that the Florida justices may clarify the legal basis for their decision.

In Florida, Gore's plea for a recount of the undervote is rejected by the trial court. Immediately after the ruling, Gore's legal team files a notice of appeal asking Florida's First District Court of Appeal to certify the case to the Florida Supreme Court.

December 5, 2000

The U.S. Court of Appeals for the 11th Circuit listens to oral arguments on Bush's plea to stop the manual recounts. The request for an injunction had been rejected by the U.S. District Court.

December 6, 2000

The U.S. Court of Appeals for the 11th Circuit affirms the lower court decision and denies Bush's request for an injunction to stop the recounts.

December 8, 2000

The Florida Supreme Court overturns the trial court decision that rejected Gore's plea for a recount of the undervote[23] in certain Florida counties. A recount of the undervotes is ordered to begin immediately. Bush's legal team announces it will appeal the decision to the United States Supreme Court.

Lawsuits that sought to disqualify thousands of absentee ballots in Seminole and Martin Counties are rejected.

December 9, 2000

The United States Supreme Court stays the Florida recount. Oral arguments are scheduled for Monday, December 11.

December 12, 2000

The United States Supreme Court reverses the Florida Supreme Court in a 7-2 decision in *Bush v Gore.*

Source: Adapted from USATODAY.com. Guide to Government. "The Florida Recount: Chronology of Lawsuits." Available: http://usatoday.findlaw.com/election/election2000timeline.html.

Between November 8 and December 1 when the Florida Supreme Court put the controversy over the butterfly ballot to rest a number of other actions were filed in both state and federal court by both of the candidates as well as by voting officials in Florida. The part of the postelection litigation that began in the Florida courts and ended in the United States Supreme Court originally involved the issue of whether Secretary of State Katherine Harris had the authority to refuse to accept ballots after her deadline of November 14 at 5:00

---

[23]An undervote is a ballot that contains no vote for one or more office, as opposed to an overvote which is a ballot that contains more than one vote for the same office.

FIGURE 4-2   THE BUTTERFLY BALLOT

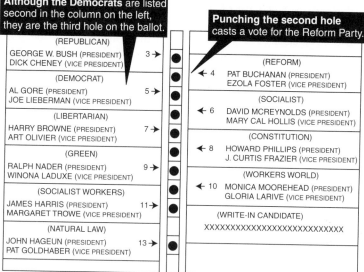

Source: Reprinted with permission from the *South Florida Sun-Sentinel.*

P.M.[24] The initial response, from the Leon County Circuit Court, was that she had the discretion to exclude returns that were filed after the deadline.[25] On appeal, however, the Florida Supreme Court on November 21 ruled unanimously that the secretary of state's discretion to ignore late-filed returns in certain circumstances did not extend to this case where recounts had been authorized but could not be completed by the deadline and where the delay would serve the voting rights of Florida citizens. Thus, the Court ordered Harris to accept results through 5:00 P.M. on November 26.[26]

In its appeal of the Florida high court's decision to the United States Supreme Court the Bush legal team argued that the Florida Supreme Court had violated Article II, Section 1 (2), of the Constitution because it had interfered with the legislature's exclusive authority to define the method of choosing electors both by using its equitable[27] powers to enjoin the certification of the election and by relying on the Florida constitution, which did not reflect the unrestrained choice of the legislature.[28] During the oral arguments on December 1 Chief Justice

---

[24]Harris relied on a state statute that provided, "if the county returns are not received by the Department of State by 5:00 P.M. of the seventh day following an election, all missing counties shall be ignored, and the results shown by the returns on file shall be certified." As quoted in Gillman, *The Votes That Counted,* 40.

[25]*McDermott v Harris.*

[26]*Palm Beach County Canvassing Board v Harris,* 772 So 2d 1200 (2000).

[27]Equitable powers refer to the power of the courts to issue orders to prevent or order some action in contrast to their authority to take action after a wrong has occurred.

[28]Gillman, *The Votes That Counted,* 81–82. The Bush lawyers also argued that the Florida Supreme Court had violated a federal statute, 3 USC Section 5, which clarifies the process of choosing electors. It provides, in part, that disputes regarding presidential electors must be resolved solely on the basis of laws enacted prior to election day. In other words, the Bush team argued, the Florida Supreme Court had altered preexisting law. The statutory argument was the one that the Bush team emphasized.

Rehnquist and Justice Scalia suggested that they agreed that the Florida court's reliance on the Florida constitution might well have constituted a violation of Article II. When the United States Supreme Court issued its decision, it did not find that the Florida Supreme Court had violated the Constitution or the federal law but it vacated the state high court's decision and remanded the case, asking the Florida justices to clarify the legal basis of their decision. More specifically, the justices wanted the Florida high court to explain whether its decision was based on the Florida statutes or on other components of the state law that had not been enacted by the legislature, such as the Florida constitution.[29]

In a second case, which the Florida Supreme Court decided on December 8, it authorized a recount—a manual recount of all possible uncounted legal votes in the state, not just the four counties that Gore had asked for—on the grounds that there was sufficient evidence that the certified election results did not include "a number of legal votes sufficient to change or place in doubt" the results of the presidential election.[30] In the majority opinion the Florida justices emphasized their reliance on state statutes, provided instructions on how the recount should proceed, and designated the legislative standard of determining "the intent of the voter."[31] Bush's legal team immediately appealed the Florida court's decision to the United States Supreme Court, relying on the same argument it had used in the earlier case to the effect that the Florida Supreme Court had changed the law enacted by the state legislature that provided the rules for contested elections in violation of Article II, Section 1 (2), as well as the federal statute, 3 USC Section 5, which requires that disputes regarding presidential electors must be resolved solely on the basis of laws enacted prior to the election.

The United States Supreme Court intervened once again, and less than twenty-four hours after the Florida high court issued its decision, a five-member majority issued an emergency injunction halting the recount, accepting the Bush lawyers' argument that the candidate would suffer irreparable harm if recounts were to resume before the case was resolved. The Court divided along ideological lines, with Rehnquist, Scalia, Thomas, O'Connor, and Kennedy in the majority. Stevens, Souter, Ginsburg, and Breyer dissented from the order. Commentators noted that, by issuing the order, the Court not only "all but cleared the way for" George W. Bush to win the election, but also "placed itself at the center of the partisan battling over the election."[32]

Three days later, on December 12, the same five-member majority permanently halted the recounts, holding that they violated the equal protection clause of the Fourteenth Amendment by virtue of the fact that the standard the state was using—determining the **"intent of the voter"**—made it possible for identical ballots to be treated in different ways by different counters. Thus, some voters would be treated differently than others. The Court held further that although the problem might have been remedied by clarifying the standard, such an option was not available because the Florida Supreme Court had im-

---

[29]*Bush v Palm Beach County Canvassing Board*, 531 US ___ (2000).
[30]These ballots were the "undervotes," ballots that contain no vote for one or more office—as read by the machine count. *Gore v Harris*, 772 So. 2d 1243 (2000).
[31]Gillman, *The Votes That Counted*, 124.
[32]As quoted in *ibid.*, 126.

plied that Florida law mandated that the deadline of December 12 had to be met—the deadline was only two hours away when the Supreme Court announced its decision.[33] By forbidding the recounts the justices resolved the election in favor of George W. Bush.[34]

Three of the justices in the majority—Chief Justice Rehnquist and Justices Scalia and Thomas—maintained that the Florida Supreme Court had violated Article II, Section 1 (2), insofar as it had changed the state law in departing from the legislative scheme by ordering the recounts of improperly marked ballots. Writing for this group of justices, Rehnquist pointed out that in most cases respect for federalism would compel deference "to the decisions of state courts on issues of state law. That practice reflects our understanding that the decisions of state courts are definitive pronouncements of the will of the States as sovereigns." In ordinary cases, he noted, matters concerning the distribution of powers among the branches of state government are left to the state. But in this case Article II, Section 1 (2), confers a power on the state legislature to choose the manner of selecting electors. In Rehnquist's view, the legislature had chosen to follow the federal statute requiring that states make rules concerning contested elections prior to the election and the Florida high court had tried to change those rules by ordering the recount.

The four dissenters argued that the Court should not have reviewed either of the decisions of the Florida Supreme Court. Article II, Section 1 (2), they argued, in four separate dissents, did not justify intervention in a state high court's resolution of a state election dispute. Stevens contended that Article II does not grant "federal judges any special authority to substitute their views for those of the state judiciary on matters of state law."[35] In short, the Florida Supreme Court had not violated Article II by ordering the recount; it had not changed the statutory scheme either with regard to the deadline or the matter of requiring the recount of improperly marked ballots. Indeed, as Stevens pointed out, the Court had endorsed a "federal assault" on the state court that had an underlying theme of "lack of confidence in the impartiality and capacity of the state judges who would make the critical decisions if the vote count were to proceed."[36] Stevens admonished that the Court's decision would seriously undercut confidence in judges:

> It is the confidence in the men and women who administer the judicial system that is the true backbone of the rule of law. Time will one day heal the wound to that confidence that will be inflicted by today's decision. One thing, however, is certain. Although we may never know with complete certainty the identity of the winner of this year's Presidential election, the identity of the loser is perfectly clear. It is the Nations' confidence in the judge as an impartial guardian of the rule of law.[37]

---

[33]*Ibid*, 142. The December 12 deadline was based on the Florida Supreme Court's interpretation of the state legislature's intended application to the election of federal statute, 3 USC Section 5.
[34]*Bush v Gore*, 531 US 98 (2000).
[35]*Ibid.*
[36]*Ibid.*
[37]*Ibid.*

Perhaps Stevens only meant to suggest that the majority's lack of respect for state judges would undermine the country's faith in judges in general but he could just as well have been castigating the majority's failure to act as "impartial guardians of the law" by acting in a blatantly partisan way to settle the contested election in favor of the Republican candidate.

Section 1

4. The Congress may determine the Time of chusing the Electors, and the Day on which they shall give their Votes; which Day shall be the same throughout the United States.

Congress has designated the first Tuesday after the first Monday in November in presidential election years for the selection of electors. On the first Monday after the second Wednesday in December the electors from each state meet in their state capitals and send their votes to Washington, D.C., where the votes are tabulated. Then in January the president of the Senate, in the presence of the Senate and the House of Representatives, opens the certificates and the electoral vote is counted; the winners are formally announced.

In the election of 2000 the date for the electors to send their votes to Washington was December 18. Thus, in order to meet the **"safe-harbor"** deadline required by the federal statute, 3 USC Section 5, Florida had to determine the outcome of its popular vote by December 12. Otherwise, as the federal provision specified, the state's determination would not be conclusive. Article 2, Section 1 (4), consequently, played an important role in the Court's decision in *Bush v Gore* prohibiting the recount that had been ordered by the Florida Supreme Court. Because the votes had to be in by December 12, the justices reasoned, a method of recounting that would overcome the equal protection problems that the Court found with the one that the Florida Supreme Court had ordered would not be possible with the time that remained before the deadline. Without any recounts Bush won the electors in Florida and on December 12 the electors sent their votes to Washington and on January 6 the votes were officially counted. George W. Bush became the forty-third president of the United States on January 20, 2001. It is important to be aware that the Constitution itself does not provide the dates but gives the power to Congress to do so. Thus, Congress could simply have changed the dates on which the electoral votes would be cast in order to allow sufficient time for Florida to complete a manual recount of the improperly marked ballots.

An additional criticism of the electoral college that is relevant to Article II, Section 1 (4), is referred to as the **"faithless elector"** problem. Nowhere does Article II specify that electors must vote for a particular candidate. What then prevents them from voting for any candidate they wish without regard to their previous commitment? Electors have—if only rarely—refused to vote for the candidate to whom he or she was pledged. Some jurisdictions do not, in fact, bind electors to vote according to the results of the popular election. Others bind their electors but do not impose a penalty on electors who do violate the rule.[38]

---

[38]Eight electors since 1789 have refused to vote for the candidate to whom he or she was pledged. Richard B. Bernstein with Jerome Agel, *Amending America: If We Love the Constitution So Much, Why Do We Keep Trying to Change It?* (New York: Times Books, 1993).

Section 1

5. No Person except a natural born Citizen, or a Citizen of the United States, at the time of the Adoption of this Constitution, shall be eligible to the Office of President; neither shall any Person be eligible to that Office who shall not have attained to the Age of thirty five Years, and been fourteen Years a Resident within the United States.

The Committee on Postponed Matters specified qualifications for the president that have been characterized as "slightly xenophobic."[39] All presidents after William Henry Harrison have been born in the United States. Although an individual who is born abroad to American parents is an American citizen, it has not been determined whether someone in that category would be a "natural born Citizen" within the meaning of the qualifications clause. When such an individual is nominated for the presidency, the Supreme Court may be called on to provide the answer. The election of President Herbert Hoover in 1928 established that an individual need not have been in the country for fourteen consecutive years immediately prior to his or her election.

Section 1

6. In Case of the Removal of the President from Office, or of his Death, Resignation, or Inability to discharge the Powers and Duties of the said Office,[40] the Same shall devolve on the Vice President, and the Congress may by Law provide for the Case of Removal, Death, Resignation or Inability, both of the President and Vice President, declaring what Officer shall then act as President, and such Officer shall act accordingly, until the Disability be removed, or a President shall be elected.

In 1841, William Henry Harrison, after only one month in office, became the first president to die in office. Although it was not clear whether the vice president would actually become president or merely "act" in that capacity, Harrison's vice president, John Tyler, settled the matter by assuming the title of president and signing all state papers "John Tyler, President of the United States." Seven other presidents have died in office and have been succeeded by the vice president. Vice President Gerald R. Ford succeeded Richard Nixon, the only president to resign from office, in 1974.

If the president is unable to "discharge the Powers and Duties" of the office, the vice president becomes the acting president. Ratified in 1967, the Twenty-fifth Amendment filled a gap in the constitutional provisions by providing a mechanism for handling a president's disability. Earlier when presidents became disabled, the vice president had no guidance on how to proceed. James Garfield was in a coma for eighty days after an assassination attempt, and Woodrow Wilson suffered an incapacitating stroke eighteen months before the end of his second term. Both Presidents Eisenhower and Kennedy had private agreements with their vice presidents on how to proceed in case of their disability.

---

[39]Clinton Rossiter, *1787: The Grand Convention* (New York: Macmillan, 1966), 218.
[40]The Twenty-fifth Amendment modifies this provision.

Pursuant to its authority to do so under Article II, Section 1 (6), Congress has specified the **line of succession** in the event that both the president and the vice president die or are unable to carry out the duties of the office. First is the Speaker of the House, followed by the president pro tempore of the Senate, then the Secretary of State, followed by the other cabinet officers in the order in which their departments were created. The individual who succeeds to the presidency or becomes acting president must possess the constitutional qualifications for the office. Additionally, the successor must resign his or her congressional seat or cabinet position.

Section 1

7. The President shall, at stated Times, receive for his Services, a Compensation, which shall neither be encreased nor diminished during the Period for which he shall have been elected, and he shall not receive within that Period any other Emolument from the United States, or any of them.

8. Before he enter on the Execution of his Office, he shall take the following Oath or Affirmation: "I do solemnly swear (or affirm) that I will faithfully execute the Office of President of the United States, and will to the best of my Ability, preserve, protect and defend the Constitution of the United States."

Article II, Section 1 (7), protects the independence of the executive by prohibiting Congress from trying to influence the president with promises of salary increases or cuts. The final phrase, "or any of them" protects the independence of the president from the individual states. The salary of the president, fixed by Congress, is now $200,000 a year.

Although any judicial officer may administer the oath of office, the Chief Justice of the United States usually does so. In 1923, after the death of President Warren G. Harding, Calvin Coolidge's father, a Justice of the Peace in Vermont, administered the oath to his son.

Section 2

1. The President shall be Commander in Chief of the Army and Navy of the United States, and of the Militia of the several States, when called into the actual Service of the United States;

The first clause in Article II, Section 2, guarantees civilian supremacy over the military by providing that the president shall be the commander of the U.S. military forces. Pursuant to such authority, the president appoints all military officers with the consent of the Senate. In *Federalist* 69, Alexander Hamilton maintained that the designation of the president as commander in chief "would amount to nothing more than the supreme command and direction of the military and naval forces, as first General and Admiral of the confederacy."[41] Hamilton also observed that Congress would have the authority to declare war and to raise and regulate the armed forces.

---

[41]*The Federalist Papers*, 350.

Early presidents conceived the **commander-in-chief power** as purely military in nature. During the Civil War, however, President Abraham Lincoln began to expand the president's war powers, relying on both the commander-in-chief clause and the president's duty set forth in Article II, Section 3—to take care that the laws are faithfully executed. Shortly after the Confederacy fired on Fort Sumter in 1861, Lincoln declared the existence of a rebellion, called out the state militia to suppress it, and imposed a naval blockade on southern ports without seeking approval from Congress and before Congress enacted a formal declaration of hostilities. When the Supreme Court addressed the issue of whether the president had the authority to institute a blockade, a majority of five justices upheld Lincoln's action, noting that although the president "does not initiate war, . . . [he] is bound to accept the challenge without waiting for any special legislative authority." Moreover, the Court noted that until Congress acts to declare war it is up to the president to determine what measures are necessary to respond to an emergency.[42] In contrast, the four dissenters argued that because the Constitution gave the power to declare war to Congress, the blockade was illegal from the time that Lincoln ordered it until Congress approved it. A civil war could exist, the dissenters maintained, only by an act of Congress.

The commander-in-chief clause has provided the basis for the continuing expansion of the president's authority to take action during an emergency. After American troops entered the conflict in Europe in 1917, President Woodrow Wilson, with broad authority delegated by Congress, constructed a massive bureaucracy to manage the economy. A series of war management and war production boards coordinated domestic production and supply. The War Industries Board, which Wilson created under his authority as commander in chief, set production schedules, allocated resources, standardized procedures, and coordinated government purchases. Although Wilson obtained congressional approval for his actions and the wartime bureaucracy was dismantled at the end of the war, his activities created an important precedent for the future expansion of the presidential **war powers.**

The growth of the war powers was even more pronounced during the twelve years of Franklin Delano Roosevelt's presidency. In his first inaugural address, Roosevelt announced that he would ask Congress "for the one remaining instrument to meet the crisis—broad Executive power to wage a war against the emergency as great as the power that would be given me if we were in fact invaded by a foreign foe."[43] The emergency to which he referred was the Great Depression. The New Deal legislative program included measures that were similar to those Wilson had used during World War I. The Supreme Court, however, invalidated major legislative measures on the grounds that they unconstitutionally delegated legislative powers to the president.[44] The Court was far more willing to approve Roosevelt's use of extraordinary powers in the area of foreign policy even before the United States entered the war.[45]

---

[42]*The Prize Cases*, 67 US 635 (1863).

[43]As quoted in Elder Witt, *Congressional Quarterly's Guide to the United States Supreme Court*, 2d ed. (Washington, DC: Congressional Quarterly, 1990), 190.

[44]See, for example, *Panama Refining Co. v Ryan*, 293 US 388 (1935); *Schechter Poultry Corp. v United States*, 295 US 495 (1935).

[45]*United States v Curtiss-Wright Export Corporation*, 299 US 304 (1936).

In September 1942, Roosevelt addressed Congress demanding repeal of a provision of the Emergency Price Control Act of 1942 that he believed was hampering the war effort. He asked Congress for legislation authorizing him to "stabilize the cost of living, including the price of all farm commodities." He announced that if Congress failed to act, he would be left "with an inescapable responsibility to the people of this country to see to it that the war effort is no longer imperiled by threat of economic chaos. In the event that the Congress should fail to act, and act adequately, I shall accept the responsibility, and I will act." Thus, he suggested that he would proceed to institute economic controls on the basis of his emergency powers without Congress's approval. Setting forth his view of the president's authority to take action in an emergency, Roosevelt proclaimed that the "President has the powers, under the Constitution and under congressional acts, to take measures necessary to avert a disaster which would interfere with the winning of the war." Conceding that he did not know "what power may have to be exercised in order to win this war," he assured the American people that he would "not hesitate to use every power vested in me to accomplish the defeat of our enemies in any part of the world where our own safety demands such defeat." Finally, Roosevelt noted that once the war was concluded the powers he was exercising would "automatically revert to the people—to whom they belong."[46]

During World War II, Roosevelt—just as Wilson had during World War I—created new administrative agencies to regulate the economy. In 1945, there were twenty-nine separate agencies grouped under the Office of Emergency Management.[47] In 1944, the Supreme Court upheld the Emergency Price Control Act of 1942 against the challenge that it was an unconstitutional delegation of legislative power to the executive. The law directed the Office of Price Administration to set price ceilings on rents and consumer goods and to ration some products. A majority of the Court found that Congress's delegation of power contained sufficient standards. In dissent, Justice Owen J. Roberts raised a fundamental issue about the nature of the **emergency powers.** Could Congress, he asked, suspend any part of the Constitution during war? He answered in the negative and went on to admonish the majority: "[I]f the court puts its decision on the war power I think it should say so. The citizens of this country will then know that in war the function of legislation may be surrendered to an autocrat whose 'judgment' will constitute the law; and that his judgment will be enforced by federal officials pursuant to civil judgments, and criminal punishments will be imposed by courts as matters of routine."[48] The Court also affirmed the president's authority to apply sanctions to individuals, labor unions, and industries that refused to comply with wartime guidelines even when the sanctions lacked a statutory basis. In a case involving sanctions for fuel rationing orders, the Court noted that so long as rationing supported the war effort, presidential sanctions requiring compliance were constitutional.[49]

---

[46]88 *Congressional Record* 7044 (September 7, 1942), as quoted in Pyle and Pius, 72–73.
[47]Witt, 190.
[48]*Yakus v United States*, 321 US 414 (1944).
[49]*Steuart & Bros. Inc. v Bowles*, 322 US 398 (1944).

In 1866, the Supreme Court held that civilians may not be tried by military tribunals so long as the civilian courts remain open.[50] But in 1942, in *Ex Parte Quirin*, the justices upheld President Roosevelt's use of military commissions to try eight German marines who entered the United States from a German submarine under orders to sabotage American war industries. Writing for the majority, Chief Justice Stone noted that Congress had declared war on Germany, had provided for military commissions for the trial of offenses against the law of war, and had authorized the president to designate procedures for those commissions. Because the eight Nazi saboteurs were enemy belligerents who had committed offenses against the law of war, Stone concluded, they could be tried without the procedural guarantees of indictment by a grand jury and trial by jury.[51]

In his Military Order of November 13, 2001, President Bush announced that noncitizens accused of terrorist activities would be tried by military tribunals with few of the procedural safeguards that are guaranteed in the Bill of Rights to individuals accused of crimes. Moreover, there would be no avenue of appeal to civilian courts. The Bush Administration and its supporters relied on *Quirin* to argue that the president had the authority to try suspected terrorists before military tribunals. There was a crucial distinction, however, that rendered the applicability of *Quirin* questionable. In the 1942 case Congress had declared war on Germany; thus, there was no question that the eight would-be saboteurs were enemy combatants. In contrast, Congress has not declared war on any country; consequently, suspected terrorists cannot be considered enemy combatants.[52] By the end of March 2003 it remained to be seen how the judiciary would view the matter, however, as no one had as yet been tried by a military tribunal. Thus, there had been no opportunity to challenge the president's power to authorize such trials.

On February 19, 1942, President Roosevelt issued **Executive Order 9066**, which authorized the Secretary of War and military commanders to prescribe military areas from which people could be excluded. On March 21, 1942, Congress made it a crime to violate military orders issued pursuant to the executive order.[53] Three days later, Lieutenant General John L. DeWitt, the military commander of the Western Defense Command, issued a curfew order, restricting "persons of Japanese ancestry" to their homes from 8:00 P.M. to 6:00 A.M. DeWitt then began issuing exclusion orders requiring evacuation and resettlement, and in early June more than 120,000 individuals of Japanese ancestry, two-thirds of whom were U.S. citizens, were in detention camps surrounded by barbed wire and guarded by armed troops; in some cases they remained there for nearly four years.[54]

---

[50]*Ex parte Milligan*, 71 US 2 (1866).

[51]*Ex parte Quirin*, 317 US 1 (1942).

[52]Ronald Dworkin, "The Trouble with the Tribunals." *The New York Review of Books*, April 25, 2002. Available: http://www.nybooks.com/articles/15284; "The Threat to Patriotism." *The New York Review of Books*, February 28, 2002. Available: http://www.nybooks.com/articles/15145.

[53]Public Law No. 503 made it a crime for anyone to "enter, remain in, leave, or commit any act in any military area or military zone prescribed . . . by any military commander . . . contrary to the restrictions applicable to any such area or zone or contrary to the order of . . . any such military commander."

[54]Roger Daniels notes that some officials who were involved in the decisions, including the president, publicly used the term *concentration camps* to describe the places where the Japanese were sent. After the discovery of the Nazi death camps, however, "many shied away" from the term. *Prisoners without Trial: Japanese Americans in World War II* (New York: Hill and Wang, 1993), 46.

The Supreme Court upheld both the curfew order and the detention program. In the curfew case, Chief Justice Stone, who wrote the opinion for the unanimous Court, indicated the justices' willingness to defer to the president and Congress under conditions of war:

> Since the Constitution commits to the Executive and to Congress the exercise of the war power in all the vicissitudes and conditions of warfare, it has necessarily given them wide scope for the exercise of judgment and discretion in determining the nature and extent of the threatened injury of danger and in the selection of the means for resisting it. . . . Where as they did here, the conditions call for the exercise of judgment and discretion and for the choice of means by those branches of the Government on which the Constitution has placed the responsibility of war-making, it is not for any court to sit in review of the wisdom of their action or substitute its judgment for theirs.[55]

Justice Hugo Black, writing the opinion for the six-member majority to justify upholding the detention program, emphasized the link between the exclusion order and the prevention of espionage and sabotage. Like Stone in the curfew case, Black deferred to the military authorities and to Congress, noting that the Court could not reject their judgment that the targets of exclusion "constituted a menace to the national defense and safety."[56] In their arguments before the Supreme Court in defense of the detention program, the War and Justice Departments made sweeping allegations of subversion that were unsupported by the facts, leading a majority of the justices to believe that exclusion was a military necessity.[57] The three dissenters were unconvinced. Justice Frank Murphy readily conceded that the judgments of the military authorities "ought not to be overruled lightly by those whose training and duties ill-equip them to deal intelligently with matters so vital to the physical security of the nation." He maintained, nevertheless, that individuals must not be left impoverished of their constitutional rights on a plea of military necessity that has neither substance nor support." In Murphy's view, the exclusion program crossed over "'the very brink of constitutional power' and falls into the ugly abyss of racism."[58] Justice Robert Jackson noted that military commands should not be required to comport with "conventional tests of constitutionality." But, he contended that even if DeWitt's orders were permissible military procedures, it did not follow that they were constitutional. If it did follow, he admonished, "then we may as well say that any military order will be constitutional and have done with it." Jackson pointed out that the Court's approval of the exclusion program established a dangerous precedent: "A military commander may overstep the bounds of constitutionality, and it is an incident. But if we review and approve, that passing incident becomes the doctrine of the Constitution. There it has a generative power of its own, and all that it creates will be in its own im-

---

[55]*Hirabayashi v United States*, 320 US 81 (1943).
[56]*Korematsu v United States*, 323 US 214 (1944).
[57]See, Peter Irons, *Justice at War: The Story of the Japanese-American Internment Cases* (New York: Oxford University Press, 1983), Chapters 8 and 9.
[58]*Korematsu v United States*, 323 US 214, 234 (1944).

age."[59] In a third case, without addressing the constitutionality of the detention program, a unanimous Court ruled that once an individual's loyalty had been determined, the War Relocation Authority was obligated to release her.[60]

Although Congress has the power to declare war, as commander of the nation's military forces the president has the authority to commit troops anywhere in the world and thereby—as President James Polk did by sending troops into disputed territory, precipitating the Mexican War—to push Congress into declaring war. The constitutional division of the war powers—giving Congress the decision to declare war and designating the president commander in chief—has always been a major source of tension between the two branches of government. As the role of the United States as a global power has grown, however, the separation of powers concerning the power to make war has grown increasingly blurred. Moreover, as the conduct of modern warfare has made immediate action imperative, the war powers have shifted dramatically to the president at the expense of Congress.

The accumulation of the president's war powers, which began with President Lincoln's actions during the Civil War, culminated during the Vietnam years in the "Imperial Presidency."[61] The U.S. military involvement in Southeast Asia did not begin with Lyndon Johnson or Richard Nixon. It began in 1950 when the Truman Administration decided to provide economic aid and military equipment to France for the war in Indochina. It was President Johnson, however, who escalated the war—there were 540,000 U.S. troops in Vietnam in 1968.

In August 1964, North Vietnamese torpedo boats attacked American ships conducting covert operations in the Tonkin Gulf. In response, President Johnson ordered the first aerial bombing of bases in North Vietnam. The president then asked Congress for a resolution making clear "[our] determination to take all necessary measures in support of freedom and in defense of peace in southeast Asia."[62] The **Tonkin Gulf Resolution** supported the determination of the president, as commander in chief, to take "all necessary measures to repel any armed attack against the forces of the United States and to prevent further aggression."[63] The president then used his authority pursuant to the Tonkin Gulf Resolution to escalate the Vietnam War. Johnson's successor, Richard M. Nixon, expanded the war into Cambodia and Laos. Congress responded in 1971 by prohibiting the introduction of U.S. ground combat troops or advisors into Cambodia and in 1973 by denying funds for all combat activities in Southeast Asia.

In 1973, to "ensure the collective judgment" of both the legislature and the executive, Congress passed the **War Powers Resolution** establishing consultation and reporting requirements and a sixty-day limit on the president's commitment of troops to hostilities without congressional authorization.[64] The

---

[59]*Ibid.*, 246.
[60]*Ex parte Endo*, 323 US 283 (1944).
[61]The term was first used by Arthur Schlesinger, Jr. in *The Imperial Presidency* (Boston: Houghton Mifflin, 1973).
[62]As quoted in Louis Fisher, *Presidential War Power* (Lawrence, KS: University Press of Kansas, 1995), 115–116.
[63]As quoted in *ibid.*, 116.
[64]As quoted in *ibid.*, 131.

purpose of the War Powers Resolution was to prevent future presidents from carrying on wars and escalating them without Congress's consent. The new law, however, failed to address the type of presidential war that grew increasingly common during the last twenty-five years of the twentieth century: short-term military strikes that could be completed in less than the sixty days at the end of which the president must secure congressional authorization for the commitment of troops or bring them home. Indeed, the War Powers Resolution in effect gave the president permission to commit troops to hostilities for a period of up to sixty days without authorization from Congress.

Thus, in 1975 President Gerald Ford sent troops to Cambodia to free the merchant ship *Mayaguez,* and in 1983 President Ronald Reagan sent forces to invade Grenada. Reagan also authorized air strikes against Libya in 1986 and sent troops into the Persian Gulf in 1987 and 1988. The first President George Bush sent troops into El Salvador, the Philippines, and Panama during his first year in office. In 1993, President Clinton ordered air strikes against Baghdad, sent troops as part of a United Nations force to Somalia, and sent troops to Haiti to restore the deposed government. In December 1998 while Congress was considering articles of impeachment against him, President Clinton ordered a series of air strikes against Iraq for its systematic refusals to allow the United Nations to conduct inspections for weapons pursuant to an agreement made in 1991.[65]

Not only did the War Powers Resolution fail to prevent short-term military actions initiated by the president without Congress's approval, it also failed to accomplish the major goal for which it was designed—preventing presidents from escalating the involvement of the United States in hostilities without Congress's approval. Presidents have been able to commit troops abroad and to keep them there far longer than the prescribed sixty days without congressional authorization. President Reagan, for example, sent troops to Lebanon in 1982 without prior consultation with Congress and kept them there until 1984. In 1987 during the Iran-Iraq war, an Iraqi missile hit the USS *Stark* and Reagan decided to provide U.S. naval escorts for Kuwaiti oil tankers through the Persian Gulf. The presence of U.S. naval forces significantly increased in the gulf with the introduction of warships, minesweepers, and small patrol boats. Despite the presence of hostilities and the potential for further hostilities in the Persian Gulf, the president did not report to Congress. He still did not file a report after a naval ship struck a mine and a United States fighter plane fired two missiles at an Iranian aircraft. Indeed, the administration did not begin to file reports pursuant to the War Powers Resolution until four months after the introduction of the naval escorts for the Kuwaiti oil tankers. Reagan claimed that he had constitutional authority for his actions as commander in chief. Although the Senate passed a bill imposing a sixty-day reporting requirement on the president, the House took no action. More than one hundred members of Congress filed suit in federal court contending that the use of naval escorts triggered the

---

[65]Harold Hongju Koh also points out that the War Powers Resolution did not address covert wars, in which intelligence operatives under civilian supervision carry on paramilitary activities against foreign governments. *The National Security Constitution: Sharing Power after the Iran-Contra Affair* (New Haven, CT: Yale University Press, 1990), 41.

reporting requirement of the War Powers Resolution, but a district court dismissed the suit as a nonjusticiable political question.[66]

Presidents have resisted the consultation and reporting requirements, and they have argued with Congress over the issue of what triggers the clock for the sixty-day time limit. Moreover, no president has acknowledged that the War Powers Resolution limits the power of the executive to commit troops to hostilities. In fact, presidents since Richard Nixon, who vetoed it, have argued that the War Powers Resolution unconstitutionally interferes with the president's ability to carry out the responsibilities of commander in chief. For example, a lawyer in the Reagan Administration argued, "Congress should not, as a matter of sound policy, and cannot, as a matter of constitutional law, impose statutory restrictions that impede the President's ability to carry out these responsibilities."[67] One commentator, summing up the ineffectiveness of the War Powers Resolution, noted, "Instead of the automatic control device the Congress apparently thought it was enacting, the WPR has become just another element in the political struggle between the branches."[68] Moreover, the political struggle over the war powers between the president and Congress is one that the president almost always wins because of a combination of executive initiative, congressional acquiescence, and judicial tolerance.[69]

The constitutional dynamic between Congress and the executive changes in important ways when Congress authorizes the president to send troops into hostilities. Moreover, the constitutional issues are further complicated when the president commits troops pursuant to a United Nations resolution authorizing the use of force. In such a situation, issues also arise concerning the relationship between international law and the United States Constitution.

On August 2, 1990, Iraq invaded Kuwait and the United Nations Security Council immediately passed a resolution demanding immediate withdrawal.[70] On August 6 the United Nations Security Council passed another resolution, this time imposing economic sanctions and full trade embargo on Iraq.[71] On the same day the administration of the first President George Bush announced "Operation Desert Shield," the purpose of which was to *defend* Saudi Arabia. It would be another three months before the United Nations Security Council authorized the use of all necessary means to expel Iraq from Kuwait and restore international peace and security in the area if Iraq had not withdrawn by January 15, 1991.[72] President Bush asserted that he was not obligated to consult with Congress under the War Powers Resolution because the United Nations Resolution provided a sufficient basis for the use of force by the United States. He reasoned that because the United States is a signatory of

---

[66]*Lowry v Reagan*, 676 F Supp 333 (D.D. 1987).
[67]As quoted in Robert A. Katzmann, "War Powers: Toward a New Accommodation," in Thomas E. Mann, ed., *A Question of Balance: The President, Congress, and Foreign Policy* (Washington, DC: Brookings Institution, 1990), 35–69, 53.
[68]Notes, "The Future of the War Powers Resolution," *Stanford Law Review* 36 (July 1984): 1407–1445, 1408.
[69]Koh, 117.
[70]United Nations Security Council Resolution 660.
[71]United Nations Security Council Resolution 661.
[72]United Nations Security Council Resolution 678. Approved November 29, 1990. Resolution 678 authorized action to implement Resolution 660, approved on August 2, 1990, which condemned Iraq's invasion of Kuwait, and called for immediate withdrawal.

the United Nations Charter—a binding treaty to which the Senate had given "advice and consent"—and a member of the Security Council that had issued the resolution authorizing the use of force, as commander in chief he had ample authority to use force. Congress objected but on January 12, some six weeks after the U.S. troops began to arrive in the Persian Gulf area, Congress authorized military action to expel Iraq from Kuwait in accordance with the United Nations Security Council Resolution. On January 16 Operation Desert Storm began with a bombing campaign against Iraq, and on February 23 the United States launched a ground war. Iraq retreated from Kuwait and within a few days there was a cease-fire. There is considerable doubt that the Senate, in approving the United Nations Charter, intended to give a priori authority to commit troops pursuant to a Security Council resolution. Indeed, Senate managers of the United Nations Charter and the enabling legislation rejected such a view.

In mid-March 2003, President George W. Bush had more than 225,000 troops in the Persian Gulf region preparing to attack Iraq to depose Saddam Hussein, install a new government, and search for biological and chemical weapons. About 1,000 Air Force, Navy, and Marine Corps aircraft also were ready to attack from aircraft carriers and land bases in the area.[73] Several armored units were scheduled to arrive in the Persian Gulf region in mid to late April. Air strikes had already begun—between November 2002 and March 2003 approximately 125 air strikes had been reported.[74]

Unlike his father twelve years earlier, President George W. Bush was not able to secure a United Nations Security Council resolution authorizing the use of force because of overwhelming international opposition to the use of military force in Iraq, although he was able to secure Congressional authorization for such action. In October 2002, Congress voted to give the president authority to use force against Iraq "as he determines to be necessary and appropriate."[75] Thus, President Bush appeared to have the authority to launch an attack on Iraq under the United States Constitution and was absolved from complying with the War Powers Resolution by virtue of Congress's authorization of the use of force.[76] But whether he had the authority under international law was highly problematic. Justifying its decision to take action without a Security Council resolution, the Bush Administration asserted that all the prior Security Council resolutions concerning Iraqi disarmament remained in effect and that Iraq was in material breach of those resolutions. Accordingly, he contended that

---

[73]Michael Gordon with Eric Schmitt, "U.S. Plan Sees GI's Invading Iraq as More Arrive." *New York Times,* March 16, 2003. Available: http://www.nytimes.com/2003/03/16/international/middleeast/16MILI.html?page wanted=1&th.

[74]Ken Moritsugu, S. Thorne Harper, and Fawn Vrazo, "Signaling Will to Oust Hussein, Bush Prepares to See War Allies." *The Miami Herald,* March 16, 2003. Available: http://www.miami.com/mld/miamiherald/news/world/5403460.htm.

[75]The vote was 296 to 133 in the House; the Senate approved it by a vote of 77 to 23. MSNBC News, "Court Denies Bid to Block War." Available: http://www.msnbc.com/news/884788.asp?cp1=1.

[76]See Section 3(C)(1): "Consistent with Section 8(a)(1) of the War Powers Resolution, the Congress declares that this section is intended to constitute specific statutory authorization within the meaning of section 5(b) of the War Powers Resolution." *Ibid.*

those resolutions gave the Administration all the authority it needed.[77] In contrast, a number of experts on international law argued that none of those resolutions authorized the use of force. Thus, the use of force by the Bush Administration absent a new Security Council resolution could not be legal under international law.[78]

As the Bush Administration stood poised to launch an attack on Iraq, three members of the military, six parents of U.S. troops, and a dozen members of Congress went to court arguing that the president lacked power to order an attack on Iraq without a declaration of war by Congress. They argued that Congress may not simply hand over to the president the power to declare war. On March 13, 2003, the Court of Appeals for the First Circuit upheld a district court's ruling rejecting the argument. The Court of Appeals noted that "the appropriate recourse for those who oppose war with Iraq lies with the political branches," rather than with the judiciary, and that judicial intervention was not warranted. A dispute between the president and Congress was not fully developed, the court reasoned, given that Congress had approved the resolution authoring the use of force.[79]

President Bush launched an air attack on targets in Iraq on March 19. Members of Congress who had been urging the president to continue diplomatic efforts to disarm Iraq began to issue statements expressing their support for Bush's decision to attack. Indeed, both houses began to consider resolutions expressing support for the troops and Bush as commander in chief.[80] In short, it appeared that the president's decision to attack Iraq, given that Congress had authorized such action, was constitutionally permissible. In contrast, however, the absence of one of the two circumstances recognized under international law in which the resort to force is legal—when the United Nations Security Council authorizes the use of force or self defense—made President Bush's action illegal under international law.[81]

---

[77]A concise elaboration of the argument is made by Ruth Wedgewood in "Legal Authority Exists for a Strike on Iraq." *The Financial Times*, March 13, 2003. Available: www.ft.com; and Lord Goldsmith, the British Attorney General, in "War and Law: Attorney General Statement" in *Times* on Line, March 17, 2003. Both Wedgewood and Lord Goldsmith argue that because 1441 finds that the Iraqis remain in material breach of the disarmament requirements of 678 and 687, the enforcement provisions of 678 and 687 are, therefore, "revived and so continues today" to use Lord Goldsmith's language.

[78]Specifically, United Nations Security Council Resolution 1441, which states that Iraq remains in material breach of council resolutions relating to Iraq's 1990 invasion of Kuwait and requires that Baghdad provide a complete and accurate declaration of all aspects of its chemical, biological, and nuclear weapons programs and ballistic missiles systems, as well as information on other chemical, biological, and nuclear programs that are supposed to be for civilian purposes, within 30 days. Approved on November 8, 2002. The resolution also warned that Iraq faced serious consequences if it continued to violate its obligations as provided in the resolution. U.S. Department of State, International Information Programs, November 8, 2002. Available: http://usinfo. state.gov/topical/pol/terror/02110803.htm. See also, Anne-Marie Slaughter, "Good Reasons for Going Around the UN." *The New York Times*, March 18, 2003. Available: http://www.nytimes.com/2003/03/18/opinion/18SLAU.html.

[79]"Court Denies Bid to Block War." MSNBC News, March 13, 2003. Available: http://www.msnbc.com/news/884788.asp?cp1=1.

[80]Vicki Allen, "Congress Unites Behind Troops, Iraq War." FindLaw Legal News and Commentary, March 20, 2003. Available: http://news.findlaw.com/news/s/20030320/iraqusacongressdc.html.

[81]Our comments concerning international law would not have been possible without the help of colleague James K. Oliver of the Department of Political Science and International Relations. The detailed commentary that he provided of the United Nations Security Council Resolutions regarding Iraq and the relationship of the president's authority to embark on hostilities and international law were infinitely helpful.

Section 2

1. [continued] he [the President] may require the Opinion, in writing, of the principal Officer in each of the executive Departments, upon any Subject relating to the Duties of their respective Offices,

The idea of a president conferring with a small group of advisors emerged from the power provided in Article II, Section 2 (1), to require written reports. Thus, although it does not contain the word *cabinet*, this provision supplies the basis for that body. Cabinet members serve at the president's pleasure, and presidential control over their official acts is complete. The executive departments, however, and usually their duties, are created by law, and the Congress authorizes the money needed for their operation.

Section 2

1. [continued] and he shall have Power to grant Reprieves and Pardons for Offenses against the United States, except in Cases of Impeachment.

The president's authority to grant reprieves and pardons is part of a broader **clemency power** that also includes commutation—replacing a greater penalty with a lessor one—and amnesty—a general pardon to a group. It also includes the power to grant conditional pardons. Although a reprieve merely postpones punishment, a pardon exempts an individual from punishment and restores all of his or her civil rights. The president's power to pardon extends to all federal offenses, including criminal contempt. The president may not pardon state crimes and the power does not extend to civil actions. The president may issue a pardon after a crime has been committed but before any formal charges have been made. Thus, in one of the most controversial exercises of the pardoning power, President Gerald Ford pardoned former President Richard Nixon for all crimes he may have committed while in office. President Jimmy Carter's decision to grant amnesty to all individuals who had violated the draft laws during the Vietnam War proved to be another controversial use of the pardoning power.[82]

The Supreme Court has held that a pardon is an "act of grace," and for it to take effect the recipient must agree to accept it.[83] The president may commute a sentence, however, without the recipient's consent.[84] The Court has upheld the president's pardoning power against challenges by Congress, noting that the "power flows from the Constitution alone, and not from any legislative enactments, and that it cannot be modified, abridged, or diminished by the Congress."[85] The president may attach conditions to pardons and commutations so long as they do not violate the Constitution.

In the summer of 1999, President Clinton commuted the sentences of sixteen members of FALN (*Fuerzas Armadas de Leberacion Nacional* or Armed

---

[82]Military deserters, employees of the selective service system, and individuals who had violated the draft laws through force or violence were not included.
[83]*United States v Wilson*, 32 US 150 (1833).
[84]*Biddle v Perovich*, 274 US 480 (1927).
[85]*Schick v Reed*, 419 US 256, 266–267 (1974).

Forces of National Liberation), a Puerto Rican group dedicated to the independence of Puerto Rico. Although FALN was involved in more than a hundred bombings in the 1970s and 1980s, the sixteen members to whom the president offered commutations were convicted of crimes such as possession of an unregistered firearm and interstate transportation of a stolen vehicle—none of their convictions were linked directly to bombings. Most of the FALN members were serving sentences of more than fifty years and had served more than nineteen of those. The president offered commutations on the condition that each individual renounce the use of violence and agree to comply with parole requirements including limiting association with other Puerto Rican nationalists. The terms of the commutations made eleven members eligible for immediate release from prison while two were required to serve more time. The other three had been released earlier and were to have their fines reduced. Two of the FALN members rejected the offer and two who were out of prison did not respond. The remaining twelve accepted.

The president's action aroused an unusual amount of controversy. A number of federal law enforcement agencies, including the FBI and the Bureau of Prisons, opposed the president's offer. Republicans criticized Clinton's action and suggested that it was a political ploy to garner support among Hispanic voters in New York for Hillary Rodham Clinton's Senate candidacy. The First Lady then announced her opposition to commutations, arguing that the FALN members had not shown sufficient contrition for their acts and those of others in the independence movement. Congressional Republicans launched investigations and issued a subpoena for White House records of the deliberations that led to the president's decision to make the offer. Although the White House rejected the subpoena, claiming executive privilege, it released some documents, which revealed that the case had been handled in a highly unusual way. For example, the prisoners had declined to apply for clemency and supporters applied on their behalf—the usual procedure is for prisoners to make their own requests. Moreover, the White House continued to pursue the matter even after the Justice Department's Pardon Attorney recommended against offering the commutations.[86]

Section 2

2. He shall have Power, by and with the Advice and Consent of the Senate, to make Treaties, provided two thirds of the Senators present concur;

The draft of the Constitution presented by the Committee on Detail at the Philadelphia Convention gave the power to make treaties to the Senate. Argument ensued among the delegates over whether the Senate or the president should have that power. The debate was linked to the method of selecting the president and although Madison argued that the president should have **the power to make treaties,** others objected because they disagreed with the method of selecting the president that the convention had adopted—appointment by the legislature. When they resolved the issue of presidential selection, the delegates

---

[86]Neil A. Lewis, "Records Show Puerto Ricans Got U.S. Help with Clemency." *New York Times*, October 21, 1999, A1.

also agreed to give the president the authority to make treaties. But the delegates did not contemplate giving the president exclusive power over treaties and gave the Senate a major role in the process by requiring its approval of a two-thirds vote. Thus, the president negotiates treaties with foreign governments, but only when the Senate gives its "advice and consent" by a vote of two-thirds do such treaties become binding on the United States.

Until the early 1940s, most disputes concerning treaties revolved around the supremacy of treaties over state law. The Supreme Court settled that matter by making it clear that treaties are "the law of the land" pursuant to the Supremacy Clause of Article VI and therefore supersede any contrary state laws. The Court also established that a treaty may bestow powers on Congress that it would not otherwise have. In *Missouri v Holland*, the Court upheld a federal law that implemented a treaty among the United States, Britain, and Canada to protect migratory birds even though lower federal courts had invalidated two earlier laws regulating hunting of migratory birds on the grounds that they infringed on matters reserved to the states. Justice Oliver Wendell Holmes Jr. noted in his opinion for the Court, "It is obvious that there may be matters of the sharpest exigency for the national well-being that an act of Congress could not deal with but that a treaty followed by such an act could."[87]

Since the 1940s, debates over the treaty power have been most concerned with the division of authority between the president and the Senate. The requirement that two-thirds of the Senate approve treaties has resulted in the defeat of some major international agreements. President Woodrow Wilson failed in 1919 to obtain Senate approval for the League of Nations, for example, and in 1980 Jimmy Carter withdrew the Strategic Arms Limitation Treaty that he negotiated with the Soviet Union from Senate consideration. More recently, in October 1999, by a vote of forty-eight (against) to fifty-one (for), the Senate rejected the Comprehensive Nuclear Test Ban Treaty, which prohibits underground tests of atomic weapons. The defeat of the Test Ban Treaty in the Senate meant that the United States would not join the fifty-one other nations that ratified it. Conflict between the president and the Senate over the treaty-making power heightened as presidents turned increasingly to the use of **executive agreements** rather than formal treaties to avoid defeat at the hands of the Senate.

The difference between treaties and executive agreements has never been clearly defined. Although it was traditionally assumed that executive agreements, which do not require Senate approval, were appropriate for matters that were less important than those requiring treaties, presidents have used executive agreements for major international compacts. For example, President Franklin Roosevelt made an agreement with England in 1940 authorizing the exchange of destroyers for bases—in exchange for fifty destroyers the United States received ninety-nine year leases for military bases on British-owned land. The Yalta and Potsdam agreements of 1945 were also executive agreements. Presidents continued to use executive agreements instead of treaties to carry out their foreign policy objectives through the Cold War years. During the Vietnam War, Congress began to object to the use of such agreements.

---

[87]*Missouri v Holland*, 252 US 416, 432 (1920).

Congress considered legislation calling for legislative review of all executive agreements but only managed to enact a law requiring the president to notify Congress of any international agreement.

The Supreme Court has approved the use of executive agreements. In 1933, the justices held that the executive agreement that gave effect to President Roosevelt's decision to recognize the Soviet Union was a valid international compact, had the effect of a treaty, and overruled conflicting state laws.[88] The Court also approved the executive agreement that President Carter negotiated with Iran to secure the release of the fifty-two American hostages whom Iran had held for more than fourteen months. In his opinion for the Court in that case, Justice William H. Rehnquist emphasized that Congress had, in effect, consented to the president's action. Rehnquist also underlined the narrowness of the decision, noting that in this case the agreement had been "determined to be a necessary incident to the resolution of a major foreign policy dispute between our country and another."[89]

Since the 1970s, presidents have increasingly reinterpreted treaties, in effect, amending them without congressional approval. In 1985, for example, the Reagan Administration broadened the terms of the 1972 Anti-Ballistic Missile Treaty to accommodate executive planning for a Strategic Defense Initiative. In response, Congress declared that no funds from the defense appropriation could be used for the new Strategic Defense Initiative tests. The Senate also attached as a condition to its approval of the Intermediate-Range Nuclear Forces Treaty a declaration that the United States shall not adopt a treaty interpretation that differs from the common understanding of that treaty shared by the executive and the Senate at the time the Senate gives its approval. The president responded by challenging the constitutionality of that condition, asserting that he could not "accept any diminution claimed to be effected by such a condition in the constitutional powers and responsibilities of the Presidency."[90]

Presidents in the post–Vietnam War years have also terminated treaties without consulting Congress. In 1979, President Carter terminated a mutual defense treaty with Taiwan as part of the United States' recognition of the People's Republic of China. President Reagan terminated the United States' acceptance of the compulsory jurisdiction of the International Court of Justice, the bilateral Friendship, Commerce, and Navigation Treaty with Nicaragua, and membership of the United States in the United Nations Educational Scientific and Cultural Organization.[91] The Supreme Court has not resolved the issue of whether the president has the authority to terminate treaties. After President Carter terminated the treaty with Taiwan, Senator Barry Goldwater brought suit in federal court charging that the president could not unilaterally abrogate a treaty. The Supreme Court declined to rule on the merits—four justices maintained that the case presented a political question whereas a fifth argued that the case was not ripe for review. Only Justice Brennan voted to uphold the president's power to terminate the treaty, noting that the case

---

[88] *United States v Belmont*, 310 US 324 (1936).
[89] *Dames & Moore v Regan*, 452 US 654, 688 (1981).
[90] As quoted in Koh, 43.
[91] *Ibid.*, 44.

involved recognition of foreign governments—a matter over which the president has complete authority.[92]

One of the most recent conflicts over a treaty arose in connection with the 1998 treaty setting up the **International Criminal Court** (ICC), which with the ratification of sixty nations established a permanent international court to investigate and prosecute acts by individuals of genocide, war crimes, and crimes against humanity.[93] Although President Bill Clinton signed the treaty in 2000 just before the deadline after which no more signatures would be accepted, the Senate did not give its advice and consent and the United States did not ratify it. Indeed, Clinton signed the treaty in order to make it possible for the United States to participate in future negotiations concerning its terms. The major concerns voiced by opponents were that U.S. soldiers or government officials might be subject to prosecution and that the ICC would infringe on the sovereignty of the United States. After conducting a policy review of the treaty in 2002, the Bush Administration announced that it would take the unprecedented step of "unsigning" it and then sought absolute immunity from the Court's jurisdiction for Americans.[94] It was the first time that a president had ever revoked a former chief executive's signature on a treaty. Bush's action raised the question of whether a president may revoke a decision of a previous president—something that could undermine the credibility of future presidents who sign treaties.

Section 2

2. [continued] and he shall nominate, and by and with the Advice and Consent of the Senate, shall appoint Ambassadors, other public Ministers and Consuls, Judges of the supreme Court, and all other Officers of the United States, whose Appointments are not herein otherwise provided for, and which shall be established by Law: but the Congress may by Law vest the Appointment of such inferior Officers, as they think proper, in the President alone, in the Courts of Law, or in the Heads of Departments.

The Appointments Clause, consistent with the doctrine of separation of powers, gives Congress the power to create offices and designates that the president shall share with the Senate the power to fill those offices. The president needs the approval of the Senate for the appointment of ambassadors, justices of the Supreme Court, and "all other Officers of the United States." The latter category includes judges on the lower federal courts, the heads of the fourteen executive branch departments and their chief assistants, and the heads of the independent agencies and regulatory commissions. The Appointments Clause provides that Congress may place the power to appoint **"inferior officers"** with the president, the courts, or the heads of departments. The Supreme Court shed some light on the category of inferior officers in 1988 when it held that the independent counsel, which Congress created in the Ethics in Government Act of 1978 to investigate and prosecute high-level executive officials for violation of federal laws, was an inferior officer. Therefore, the method of appointing the

---

[92]*Goldwater v Carter*, 444 US 996 (1979).
[93]As of March 2003, eighty-nine countries had accepted the ICC.
[94]"The International Criminal Court: Soon It Will Be Dispensing Justice." *The Economist*, March 15-21, 2003, 46.

independent counsel—the Attorney General asks a special federal court to appoint an independent counsel—did not violate the Appointments Clause. Writing for a majority of the Court, Chief Justice Rehnquist noted that the independent counsel is an inferior officer because he or she can be removed from office by the Attorney General, he or she has statutory authority to perform only limited duties, the office of independent counsel is limited in jurisdiction by statute and by the grant of authority conferred by the special federal court, and the independent counsel is limited in tenure.[95]

Senatorial courtesy, the Senate's long-established custom of deferring to members who object to appointees from their own states, constrains a president's choice of federal district judges. Indeed, it is because of senatorial courtesy that the president usually consults with senators of his party from the state in which an appointment is to be made before sending a nomination to the Senate. The **confirmation process** for federal judges involves not only the president and the Senate but also the American Bar Association's Committee on the Federal Judiciary, which issues a rating that may range from "exceptionally well qualified" to "not qualified" for each nominee.

Since the 1970s, increasing conflict has begun to dominate the confirmation process as it has become apparent that federal judges, who serve for life, can extend a president's influence on public policy far beyond that individual's term in office. The conflict is evidenced by the decrease in the percentage of nominations that the Senate has confirmed and the increase in the length of time it has taken for the Senate to decide for each administration from Nixon through the early Clinton years (see Table 4-3).[96]

Organized interests have taken an increasingly active role in judicial appointments since the 1970s, contributing to the conflict. For example, a coalition of labor, civil rights, and other liberal organizations opposed President Richard Nixon's appointments in 1969 and 1970 of Clement Haynsworth and G. Harold Carswell to the Supreme Court. The Senate rejected both nominees. In 1987, hundreds of organized interest groups rallied in opposition to President Ronald Reagan's nomination of Robert Bork. Groups made up of environmentalists, consumers, civil rights activists, mental health associations, the disabled, women, gays and lesbians, and labor unions used a variety of tactics, including advertising and grassroots events.[97] The Senate declined to confirm Bork's nomination.

Beginning with Jimmy Carter, presidents have placed a high priority on the selection of lower court judges and have thereby increased public awareness of their important role—another development that has promoted conflict in the confirmation process. President Carter, who appointed more than 250 federal

---

[95]*Morrison v Olson*, 486 US 654 (1988). See also, *Buckley v Valeo*, 424 US 1 (1976) (holding that the appointment procedures for members of the Federal Election Commission—they were appointed by Congress—were unconstitutional because the commissioners were not inferior officers and therefore could only be appointed by the president).

[96]Roger E. Hartley and Lisa M. Holmes, "Increasing Senate Scrutiny of Lower Federal Court Nominees," *Judicature* 80 (May–June 1997): 274–278, 275.

[97]Gregory A. Caldiera and John R. Wright, "Lobbying for Justice: The Rise of Organized Conflict in the Politics of Federal Judgeships," in Lee Epstein, ed. *Contemplating Courts* (Washington, DC: Congressional Quarterly, 1995), 44–71, 58.

TABLE 4-3   Conflict in the Confirmation Process: Confirmation Rate and Speed By Administration—through 1996

Presidential Administration	Percentage Confirmed	Average Days*
Nixon	92.5	25.4
Ford	87.3	27.7
Carter	88.2	46.5
Reagan	87.4	41.4
Bush	80.9	61.5
Clinton	83.3	56.0

*Average days from referral to confirmation.
Source: Roger E. Hartley and Lisa M. Holmes, "Increasing Senate Scrutiny of Lower Federal Court Nominees," *Judicature* 80 (May–June 1997): 274–278.

judges, deliberately increased the proportion of women, African Americans, and Hispanics on the lower federal courts. Subsequently, the Reagan Administration engaged in systematic screening of potential nominees in an effort to place young conservatives on the federal bench who opposed reproductive rights and school busing for purposes of achieving a racial balance and supported prayer in the schools. During his two terms, President Reagan appointed 385 federal judges, almost half of all federal judges—168 full-time appeals judges and 575 district judges.[98]

Divided government—the presidency and Congress were controlled by different parties—prevailed for most of the years from 1969 until the end of the twentieth century and was a major factor in the heightened conflict over judicial appointments. That conflict, though serious during the Reagan years, increased during the presidency of Bill Clinton. There were an unprecedented number of 115 federal judicial vacancies when Clinton became president in 1993.[99] Clinton had campaigned on the promise of selecting federal judges who would be sensitive to the concerns of minorities and who would protect the right to privacy, including a woman's right to choose to have an abortion. He also pledged to appoint federal judges who would be more representative of the ethnic composition of the United States. With the Democrats in control of both chambers of the Congress during his first two years, it seemed likely that Congress would expand the number of federal judgeships. In 1994, however, the Republicans took control of both houses of Congress and presidential candidate Bob Dole became Senate Majority Leader[100] and Orrin Hatch became chair of the Senate Judiciary Committee.

Facing the prospects of protracted battles over judicial selection, the White House engaged in frequent consultations with Senator Hatch and other sena-

---

[98]Stuart Taylor Jr., "The One-Pronged Test for Federal Judges: Reagan Puts Ideology First." *New York Times,* April 22, 1984, E5.
[99]Richard B. Schmitt, "Advocates for More Judges Feel Favorable Political Wind." *Wall Street Journal,* February 24, 1993, B2. See also Stephen Labaton, "Clinton Expected to Change Makeup of Federal Courts." *New York Times,* March 8, 1993, A1.
[100]Dole resigned from the Senate in June 1996 to campaign for the presidency.

tors from both parties, and the Administration declined to put forward candidates who were likely to arouse serious opposition.[101] Nevertheless, the confirmation process came to a virtual halt in 1996 when Dole used his power to control the flow of Senate business to prevent nominees sent forward by the Judiciary Committee from coming to a vote on the Senate floor. Dole made the federal judiciary a major theme in his campaign for the presidency, contending, for example, that Clinton was promoting "an all star team of liberal leniency" and that the president's reelection "could lock in liberal judicial activism for the next generation."[102]

Despite presidential politics and the traditional election-year slowdown in confirmations in 1996, President Clinton was able to appoint 198 judges during his first term. Additionally, despite the commitment to "play it safe" with the Republican Senate, at the end of his first term Clinton had appointed a higher percentage of women and racial minorities than had any of his predecessors.[103] An analysis of the voting behavior of Clinton's first term appointees refuted Bob Dole's charges of "liberal leniency." Clinton's appointees exhibited overwhelmingly moderate decision-making patterns; they were less liberal, in fact, than President Carter's judges.[104]

Increasing conflict with the Senate over the confirmation of lower court judges marked the first two years of Clinton's second term. The Senate Judiciary Committee delayed confirmations by refusing to schedule hearings on nominees, and when the Committee reported nominations favorably, they often failed to come to a vote on the Senate floor. The Senate confirmed only 36 judges in 1997 compared with 101 in 1994.[105] As a result, there were nearly 100 vacancies on the federal bench in late 1997. President Clinton accused Senate Republicans of putting politics above justice in refusing to act on his nominees. Senator Hatch rejoined that the problem resulted from the president's delays in sending nominations to the Senate. Chief Justice Rehnquist, in his annual year-end report on the state of the judiciary, criticized the Senate for failing to move on judicial appointments, warning, "[V]acancies cannot remain at such high levels indefinitely without eroding the quality of justice."[106] Although not obligated to confirm any particular nominee, the Chief Justice noted, the Senate should vote the nominee up or down after it has conducted an inquiry. Rehnquist's pointed complaint prompted Senator Hatch to contend that the problems on the courts were due to the caliber of the president's nominees and to their excessive liberal activism.[107]

Veteran conservative activist Paul Weyrich organized the Judicial Selection Monitoring Project to raise money to prevent the confirmation of President Clinton's nominees. Designed to alarm conservatives by recounting stories of

[101]Sheldon Goldman and Elliot Slotnick, "Clinton's First Term Judiciary: Many Bridges to Cross." *Judicature* 80 (May–June 1997): 254.
[102]As quoted in *ibid.*, 257.
[103]*Ibid.*, 261, 269.
[104]Ronald Stidham, Robert A. Carp, and Donald R. Songer, "The Voting Behavior of President Clinton's Judicial Appointees." *Judicature* 80, (July–August 1996): 20.
[105]John H. Cushman, Jr., "Senate Imperils Judicial System, Rehnquist Says." *New York Times,* January 1, 1998.
[106]*Ibid.*
[107]Neil A. Lewis, "Hatch Defends Senate Action on Judgeships." *New York Times,* January 2, 1998.

outrageous decisions by Clinton appointees—one had allegedly released a murderer from prison, for example—the Project pressured Republican Senators to block Clinton's nominations.[108] Despite such efforts, perhaps in part because of the Chief Justice's comments, in early 1998 the Senate Judiciary Committee acted on several nominations. By the end of 1998, forty-seven judges had been confirmed while fifty-four were still waiting for a decision.[109] A little more than a year later, at the beginning of March 2000, there were still seventy-six vacancies with thirty-seven nominees pending.[110]

When President George W. Bush took office in January 2001 some one hundred vacancies remained and he withdrew all forty-four Clinton nominations on which the Senate had not acted.[111] In May 2002, the anniversary of President Bush's nomination of his first eleven candidates to the Courts of Appeals, the Democratic Senate had confirmed only three and had not scheduled hearings for the remaining eight. Of Bush's one hundred judicial nominees, fifty-two had been confirmed; and of the forty-eight not confirmed, only nine had been granted hearings; eighty-nine vacancies remained on the federal courts. The Senate Judiciary Committee actually rejected only one nominee—Charles Pickering—a federal district judge from Mississippi with an "ambiguous" record on race.[112]

Republicans voiced the same complaint as the Democrats had during the Clinton years: the Senate was obstructing judicial nominees in such a way as to undermine the president's prerogative to choose federal judges. The Democrats defended their reluctance to hold hearings on the grounds that Bush's choices were extremists of the far right whose presence on the bench would threaten basic individual rights including a woman's right to terminate a pregnancy, would reverse the progress the country has made regarding racial equality, and would allow excessive intermingling of religion and government. Senator Charles Shumer, a Democratic member of the Senate Judiciary Committee, argued that it is appropriate for the Senate to consider the ideology of the nominees because the president himself was using ideology as the basis of his nominations.[113] Commentators in 2002 called for a compromise whereby Democrats would hold hearings and vote to confirm nominees they deemed "acceptably moderate" and the president would drop his most conservative nominees in favor of more moderate jurists.[114] The ongoing stalemate prompted Jeffrey Rosen to proclaim that the "confirmation process for federal

---

[108]The Judicial Selection Monitoring Project circulated a videotape that described a case in which Stewart R. Dalzell, a Federal District Judge in Pennsylvania, ordered the release of a young woman on a habeas corpus petition. Dalzell, however, was appointed by President Bush. Anthony Lewis, "Abroad at Home; The War on the Courts." *New York Times*, October 27, 1997.

[109]James Bennet, "225 Clinton Nominees Wait for Unlikely Senate Approval." *New York Times*, October 9, 1998.

[110]Vacancy Summary, November 1, 1999 and March 1, 2000. Available: http://www.uscourts.gov/vacancies/summary.html.

[111]Jesse J. Holland, "Bush Withdraws Clinton Nominees for Federal Bench, *LexisOne: The Resource for Small Law Firms.*" March 20, 2001. Available: http://www.lexisone.com/news/ap/ap_b032001h.html.

[112]Jason Zengerle, "Don't Give Bush's Judges a Hearing." *The New Republic*, May 20, 2002. Available: http://www.tnr.com/doc.mhtml?i=20020520&s=zengerle052002. The vote to defeat Pickering was 10-9—a straight party-line vote.

[113]Charles E. Schumer, "Judging by Ideology." *The New York Times*, June 26, 2001. Editorial Desk.

[114]Zengerle.

judges is in something of a meltdown. Appellate nominations are now provoking a level of partisan warfare that used to be reserved for the Supreme Court."[115]

Despite calls for compromise, Bush declined to submit more moderate candidates to the Senate, and in January 2003 renominated the thirty-one individuals who had not been approved by the Senate Judiciary Committee in the previous year.[116] With Republicans holding fifty-one seats in the Senate the nominees had a second and better chance to be confirmed. One of the nominees that the president resubmitted to the Senate was Miguel Estrada, a former Assistant Solicitor General, who Bush nominated to the Court of Appeals for the D.C. Circuit. Democrats charged that the officials in the Justice Department had information about Estrada's record in the Solicitor General's office that they were refusing to reveal to the Senate. After the Judiciary Committee approved his nomination in a party-line vote, Democrats began a filibuster to prevent an up or down vote in which the fifty-one Republicans were certain to prevail.[117]

There can be no doubt that the selection process at the lower court level has become increasingly politicized. Both Democratic and Republican presidents select judicial nominees on the basis of their policy preferences and the Senate Judiciary Committee splits along party lines, as the members of the opposing party attempt to block confirmation of nominees whose views are fundamentally incompatible with theirs. In 2003 when Bush was president, just as in the 1980s when Reagan was in the White House, Democrats charged the Republicans with attempting to pack the federal judiciary with right-wing ideologues. Likewise in the 1990s when Clinton was president, Republicans blocked judicial nominees, claiming that Clinton's choices were extreme liberals.

Although Article II, Section 2, says nothing about the president's power to remove officials from office, such authority grows out of the appointment power as well as the president's duty, specified in Article II, Section 3, to take care that the laws be faithfully executed. In 1926 in *Myers v United States* Chief Justice William Howard Taft proclaimed that the **authority to remove officials** appointed by the president and confirmed by the Senate rested with the president alone. The president, in Taft's view, must have the power to remove all subordinates in order to carry out the responsibility for seeing that the laws are faithfully executed.[118] In *Myers*, the majority invalidated a law that prohibited the president from removing postmasters during their four-year terms without the consent of the Senate. The three dissenters, pointing to a number of statutes that imposed restrictions on removals, argued that Congress had the authority

---

[115]Jeffrey Rosen, "Obstruction of Judges." *The New York Times Magazine*, August 11, 2002.
[116]ABA Network, American Bar Association 2002 Legislative and Governmental Priorities. "Independence of the Judiciary: Judicial Vacancies." Available: http://www.abanet.org/poladv/priorities/judvac.html. By the end of 2002 the president had nominated 131 individuals to the federal courts. The Senate Judiciary Committee held hearings for 103 of those nominees and approved 100—the Senate confirmed all of those individuals.
[117]Neil A. Lewis, "Judicial Nominee Gets Second Chance." *The New York Times*, March 13, 2003. Available: http://www.nytimes.com/2003/03/14/politics/14JUDG.html?th. On March 22, 2003, there were fifty-four vacancies with thirty-eight nominations pending. U.S. Department of Justice, Office of Legal Policy, Judicial Nominations. Available: http://www.usdoj.gov/olp/judicialnominations.htm.
[118]*Myers v United States*, 272 US 52 (1926).

to limit the president's authority to remove inferior officials. In 1935 in *Humphrey's Executor v United States*, the Court held that the unqualified removal power that Taft proclaimed in *Myers* did not extend to officers who have quasi-legislative or quasi-judicial functions, such as members of the Federal Trade Commission. Thus, Congress may limit the president's authority to remove such officials.[119]

Although the distinction between quasi-legislative or quasi-judicial and executive officials has never been made clear, the Court shed some light on the issue of Congress's constitutional authority to restrict the president's ability to remove an official when it upheld a legislative constraint on the president's authority to remove the independent counsel in 1988.[120] Chief Justice Rehnquist noted that the question

> cannot be made to turn on whether or not that official is classified as "purely executive." The analysis contained in our removal cases is designed not to define rigid categories of those officials who may or may not be removed at will by the President, but to ensure that Congress does not interfere with the President's exercise of the "executive power" and his constitutionally appointed duty to "take care that the laws be faithfully executed."[121]

Section 2

3. The President shall have Power to fill up all Vacancies that may happen during the Recess of the Senate, by granting Commissions which shall expire at the End of their next Session.

The president may fill any vacancy that exists when the Senate is not in session. A brief adjournment does not constitute a recess, but an adjournment that is "protracted enough to prevent that body from performing its functions of advising and consenting to executive nominations" allows the president to make recess appointments.[122] Recess appointments are temporary and expire at the end of the following session of the Senate.

Section 3

He shall from time to time give to the Congress Information of the State of the Union, and recommend to their Consideration such Measures as he shall judge necessary and expedient; he may, on extraordinary Occasions, convene both Houses, or either of them, and in Case of Disagreement between them, with Respect to the Time of Adjournment, he may adjourn them to such Time as he shall think proper;

Shortly after Congress convenes each January, the president delivers the State of the Union message. Although not constitutionally required to deliver the

---

[119] *Humphrey's Executor v United States*, 295 US 602 (1935).
[120] The president may remove an independent counsel only for good cause, physical disability, mental incapacity, or any other condition that substantially impairs the performance of duties.
[121] *Morrison v Olson*, 487 US 654, 689–690 (1988).
[122] As quoted in Louis Fisher, *Constitutional Conflicts between Congress and the President*, 3d ed. (Lawrence, KS: University Press of Kansas, 1991), 41.

message in person, presidents since Woodrow Wilson have appeared before a joint meeting of the two houses of Congress. Federal law also requires the president to send a budget message and an economic report to Congress. Additionally, throughout the session the president communicates with Congress, making recommendations for legislation. Article II, Section 3, is important insofar as it gives the president a role in initiating legislation and allows him to shape the national agenda.

The president may call a special session of Congress. Once in session, it has full powers. The president has never been called on to adjourn Congress.

Section 3

[continued] he shall receive Ambassadors and other public Ministers;

The authority to receive ambassadors and other public ministers is a source of the president's power as the sole official spokesperson for the United States in foreign affairs. Other nations must channel their communications with the United States through the president. The power to receive ambassadors includes the power to recognize new foreign governments.

Section 3

[continued] he shall take Care that the Laws be faithfully executed, and shall Commission all the Officers of the United States.

The Take Care Clause, which gives the president the responsibility for administering and enforcing the laws, is the source of considerable executive power. As noted, the **duty to take care that the laws be faithfully executed** gives the president the power to remove executive officials and severely limits Congress's authority to interfere. An important question concerning the Take Care Clause was whether it bestowed on the chief executive the power to initiate action in the absence of specific legislation. In 1890, the Court held that it did, noting that the power extends to vindicating "the rights, duties and obligations growing out of the Constitution itself, our international relations, and all the protection implied by the nature of the government under the Constitution."[123] In that case, the Court held that President Benjamin Harrison had the authority to assign a federal marshal as a bodyguard to protect a Supreme Court justice against a death threat in the absence of legislation empowering him to do so. Similarly, in 1895 the justices sustained President Grover Cleveland's decision to send federal troops to Chicago to break a railway strike that threatened to obstruct delivery of the mails. The Court indicated that a president may act pursuant to the Take Care Clause whenever the federal government has authority to take action and that the executive power is particularly extensive in an emergency:

> The entire strength of the nation may be used to enforce in any part of the land the full and free exercise of all national powers and the security of all rights intrusted by the constitution to its care. The strong arm of the national government

---

[123]*In re Neagle*, 125 US 1 (1890).

may be put forth to brush away all obstructions to the freedom of interstate commerce or the transportation of the mails. If the emergency arises, the army of the nation, and all its militia, are at the service of the nation, to compel obedience to its laws.[124]

When President Harry Truman seized the steel mills in 1952 to avert a strike and to ensure the uninterrupted production of military equipment during the Korean War, however, the Court found that his action could not be sustained by the executive's authority to see that the laws be faithfully executed. In that case, the Court designated a limit on the president's power under the Take Care Clause, noting that the president's power to see that the laws are faithfully executed "refutes the idea that he is to be a lawmaker."[125] Thus, the fact that Congress had rejected governmental seizure of property as a method of settling labor disputes clearly placed the president's action beyond the bounds of executing the laws.

Although the duty to take care that the laws be faithfully executed endows the president with considerable power to initiate action not explicitly authorized by Congress, the responsibility to enforce the laws also imposes a constraint on the chief executive. In 1974, President Richard Nixon refused to spend billions of dollars for programs he disapproved of even though Congress had authorized the spending and appropriated the funds. Although presidential impoundment—refusal to spend—of funds would seem to be directly contrary to the Take Care Clause, the Court has not ruled directly on the issue. Instead, federal courts have thus far resolved conflicts over impoundment on statutory grounds.[126] Presidents have also exercised considerable discretion by executing some laws more forcefully than others—the Reagan Administration did not place a high priority on enforcing civil rights laws, for example. President Reagan went considerably further when he claimed that the Boland Amendment forbidding all executive assistance to support the Contras, the group working to overthrow the government in Nicaragua, did not apply to him or his direct agents.[127]

Section 4

The President, Vice President and all civil Officers of the United States, shall be removed from Office on Impeachment for, and Conviction of, Treason, Bribery, or other High Crimes and Misdemeanors.

Article II, Section 4, addresses two of the most important issues concerning the impeachment power. First, which officials may be impeached? The phrase "civil Officers" includes federal judges and cabinet members but not members of

---

[124]*In re Debs*, 158 US 564, 578–579 (1895).
[125]*Youngstown Sheet & Tube Company v Sawyer*, 343 US 579, 587 (1952).
[126]See, for example, *Train v New York*, 420 US 35 (1975).
[127]The language of the Boland Amendment, in effect from October 1984 to October 1986, was as follows: "During fiscal year 1985, no funds available to the Central Intelligence Agency, the Department of Defense, or any other agency or entity of the United States involved in intelligence activities may be obligated or expended for the purpose of which would have the effect of supporting directly or indirectly, military or paramilitary operations in Nicaragua by any nation, group, organization, movement, or individual." As quoted in Fisher, *Constitutional Conflicts between Congress and the President*, 211.

Congress. Why are members of Congress excluded? Several provisions in the Constitution suggest that civil officers are officials appointed by the president who occupy positions created by Congress.[128] Additionally, Article I, Section 5, which provides Congress with a method of removing its members, renders impeachment for legislators unnecessary. Congress's practice also indicates that legislators are not impeachable. After the House impeached Senator William Blount in 1797 for conspiring to aid England in its war with Spain despite the neutrality of the United States, the Senate expelled him but dismissed the impeachment resolution for lack of jurisdiction. Congress has treated Blount's case as establishing the proposition that members of Congress are not civil officers of the United States.

The second issue addressed in Article II, Section 4, concerns the character of an impeachable offense. Treason is defined in Article III, Section 3, of the Constitution and bribery is defined in statutory provisions. The meaning of "other High Crimes and Misdemeanors," however, has been at the center of all the major cases of impeachment in American history. The defenders of Justice Samuel Chase in 1804–1805 and President Andrew Johnson in 1868 maintained that only a serious, indictable crime constituted an impeachable offense. In contrast, the proponents of Chase's and Johnson's impeachment argued for a broader construction of "High Crimes and Misdemeanors" that would include political abuses. Thus, for example, Republican House managers argued that Chase should be impeached for his zealous conduct as presiding judge in trials for violations of the Sedition Act and for delivering "an intemperate and inflammatory political harangue" to a grand jury. Senator Charles Sumner took an even more extreme position in Andrew Johnson's trial when he declared that "an act of evil example or influence committed by the President," was impeachable.[129] The more moderate interpretation that prevailed in both cases was that willful misconduct in office or violation of fundamental constitutional principles would constitute an impeachable offense even in the absence of a technical violation of the law.

Representative Gerald Ford's unsuccessful attempt to convince the House to impeach Justice William O. Douglas in 1970 reflected the broadest construction of the scope of impeachable offenses. Ford stated that an impeachable offense "is whatever a majority of the House [considers it] to be at a given moment in history; conviction results from whatever offense or offenses two-thirds of the other body considers to be sufficiently serious to require removal of the accused from office."[130] Richard Nixon's lawyers took the other extreme in 1974, contending that only a serious infraction of a criminal statute amounts to an impeachable offense.

Representatives who opposed President Clinton's impeachment in 1998 took the middle position, arguing that only serious misconduct involving the president's duties and performance in office would be impeachable. During Clinton's trial, the House managers contended that the president's perjury and

---

[128]See Article II, Section 3: the president shall "commission all the Officers of the United States." Article I, Section 6: "no person holding any office under the United States shall also be a member of either house during his continuance in office." Article II, Section 2 distinguishes between officers of the United States, appointed by the president and inferior officers, whose appointment Congress may vest in other bodies.
[129]As quoted in Whittington, 151.
[130]As quoted in Gerhardt, 103.

obstruction of justice had a devastating effect on the office of the presidency and on the judicial system and were, therefore, impeachable, even though they did not arise directly out of his official duties. More specifically, the House Brief asserted that lying under oath and obstructing justice "undermined the integrity and credibility of the Office of the President" and "affected the truth seeking process which is the foundation of our legal system." Further, "by mounting an assault in the truth seeking process, he has attacked the entire Judicial Branch of government."[131] In contrast, the White House lawyers maintained that the articles of impeachment alleged conduct that, even *if* proved, was not impeachable. In the context in which it occurred—trying to keep an inappropriate sexual relationship secret—Clinton's wrongdoing did not involve "the most serious public misconduct, aggravated abuse of Executive power," and thus did not rise to the level of high crimes and misdemeanors.[132]

Congress's practice over the years has reflected the moderate position. Most commentators have argued that criminal conduct is of very little use in defining an impeachable offense. Constitutional scholar Laurence H. Tribe has pointed out that a president's violation of the law by jaywalking would not be grounds for removal from office. On the other hand, a "deliberate presidential decision to emasculate our national defenses or to conduct a private war in circumvention of the Constitution" would probably not violate any criminal code but would, nevertheless, be grounds for impeachment.[133]

The moderate position with regard to the scope of impeachable offenses does not complete the inquiry as it does not answer the question of when official misconduct or abuse of power is serious enough to rise to the level of an impeachable offense. It has often been suggested that impeachment should be reserved for the most serious official misconduct: "[A]buses of power . . . that attack the constitutional order itself and endanger our system of government."[134] Yet such a standard is so subjective that it does not prevent legislators from using impeachment as a partisan weapon against their political enemies, something that is confirmed by the House managers' arguments in President Clinton's trial. To prevent abuse of the impeachment power, it might seem like a good idea to compile a list of acts that would warrant removal from office. But placing a list of impeachable offenses alongside an official's conduct could never take into account the political context against which impeachments invariably take place. Tribe suggested that a solution might be found by using the following as a guide: "Congress may properly impeach and remove a President only for conduct amounting to a gross breach of trust or serious abuse of power, and only if it would be prepared to take the same action against any President who engaged in comparable conduct in similar circumstances."[135]

---

[131]"House Brief for Impeachment Trial." *Washington Post*, January 11, 1999. Washingtonpost.com Special Report: Clinton Accused.

[132]See Nicole Seligman's argument, "The Impeachment Trial, January 25: White House Argues for Dismissal." *Congressional Record*, January 25, 1999. Washingtonpost.com Special Report: Clinton Accused.

[133]Laurence H. Tribe, *American Constitutional Law*, 2d ed. (Mineola, NY: Foundation Press, 1988), 294.

[134]Tribe, *Boston Globe*, Editorials/Opinions, September 16, 1998.

[135]Committee on Federal Legislation, Association of the Bar of the City of New York, The Law of Presidential Impeachment (released January 21, 1974), as quoted in Laurence H. Tribe, *American Constitutional Law*, 2d ed. (Mineola, NY: Foundation Press, 1988), 294.

In early 2003 President Bush's determination to secure a United Nations Security Council resolution to authorize the use of force against Iraq and then to unilaterally attack when he could not secure such a resolution prompted calls for the president's impeachment. John Conyers of Michigan, the ranking Democrat on the House Judiciary Committee, and former Attorney General Ramsey Clark met with some fifty attorneys and legal scholars in March to discuss the possibility that Bush's pending preemptive strike against Iraq constituted "high crimes and misdemeanors." Both Ramsey Clark and University of Illinois law professor Francis Boyle drew up articles of impeachment charging that Bush's proposed military action violated both international law and the United States Constitution and condemning the impact of the **USA Patriot Act** on constitutionally protected rights, blaming the president for its passage.[136]

QUESTIONS

1. Which provisions in Article II provide a basis for the argument that the president has inherent powers? Examine the cases in which the Court has addressed the existence of inherent powers. What do those cases reveal about the status of such powers? What are the limits of those powers?

2. What purpose did the electoral college serve in the early nineteenth century? What is its function today? What problems do you see with the electoral college? Should it be abolished? What are the arguments for retaining it? How might its abolition affect the way candidates conduct their campaigns? What effect might the change to direct election have on the party system?

3. On what specific provisions have presidents relied in justifying their use of emergency powers? Under what conditions is the president's exercise of such powers justified?

4. Does the War Powers Resolution amount to an unconstitutional infringement on the president's authority as commander in chief?

5. When President Clinton nominated former Senator Carol Moseley-Braun in 1999 to be Ambassador to New Zealand, Senator Jesse Helms, chair of the Senate Foreign Relations Committee, postponed confirmation hearings until the White House delivered documents pertaining to allegations of ethical misconduct. Once the Committee had the documents, the hearings proceeded although Helms continued to oppose Moseley-Braun's confirmation. In what way did Helms's behavior represent a departure from traditional Senate norms regarding presidential appointments?[137]

6. How does the Take Care Clause reinforce the doctrine of separation of powers?

---

[136]Francis Boyle's articles of impeachment can be found at http://www.counterpunch.org/boyle01172003.html. For Ramsey Clark's articles of impeachment see, http://www.VotetoImpeach.org/articles_rc.htm.
[137]See Lizette Alvarez "Confirmation 'Courtesy' Not a Given for Ex-Senator," *New York Times*, November 5, 1999.

7. Would the president be acting within the bounds of the constitutional authority of the executive if he were to refuse to enforce a federal law on the grounds that it was unconstitutional? If not, what recourse would be available? May the president refuse to enforce the federal law based on a determination that the legislation is bad policy?

8. Did President Clinton's conduct regarding his relationship with Monica Lewinsky amount to an impeachable offense? How might the impeachment of Clinton by the House of Representatives affect the institution of the presidency?

9. After reading Paul Finkleman's article "The Murky Proslavery Origins of the Electoral College," how has your perception of the origins of the electoral college changed? Does Finkleman's argument seriously challenge the legitimacy of the electoral college?

10. Why did the Court in *Bush v Gore* find it inappropriate to allow a recount that would take place with sufficient standards to remedy the equal protection problem? How is that related to the state legislature's authority to choose the manner of selecting electors pursuant to Article II, Section 1 (2)?

11. The majority's reasoning in *Bush v Gore* with regard to Article II, Section 1 (2), is complex but is important to understand in order to assess the strength of the constitutional argument and the interpretation of the provision that the justices developed. Can you explain that interpretation and how it could forbid a state supreme court from interpreting the state constitution? Can you also explain how the federal statute 3 USC Section 5 came into play? What is the "safe harbor" provision and what was its significance in the case?

12. In what sense might the Court's decision in *Bush v Gore* be a reflection not of ideological division "but professional self-interest"?[138]

13. Are there any similarities between Chief Justice John Marshall's opinion in *Marbury v Madison* (1803) and the per curium opinion in *Bush v Gore?*

KEY TERMS

inherent powers
"stewardship" theory
executive privilege
president's immunity
electoral college
"butterfly ballot"
"intent of the voter" standard
"safe-harbor"
"faithless elector"
line of succession
commander-in-chief power
war powers
emergency powers
Executive Order 9066

Tonkin Gulf Resolution
War Powers Resolution
clemency power
president's power to make treaties
executive agreements
International Criminal Court
"inferior officers"
Senatorial courtesy
confirmation process
president's authority to remove
  officials
duty to take care that the laws be
  faithfully executed
USA Patriot Act

---

[138]Ronald Dworkin, as quoted in Gillman, *The Votes That Counted*, 123.

SUGGESTIONS FOR FURTHER READING

Bronner, Ethan. *Battle for Justice: How the Bork Nomination Shook America*. New York: Doubleday, 1989.

Caldiera, Gregory A., and John R. Wright. "Lobbying for Justice: The Rise of Organized Conflict in the Politics of Federal Judgeships." In Lee Epstein, ed. *Contemplating Courts*. Washington, DC: Congressional Quarterly, 1995, 44–71.

Daniels, Roger. *Prisoners without Trial: Japanese Americans in World War II*. New York: Hill and Wang, 1993.

Dorf, Michael C. "Is the War on Iraq Lawful?" *Writ: FindLaw's Legal Commentary*, March 19, 2003. Available: http://writ.news.findlaw.com/dorf/20030319.html.

Dorf, Michael C. "Why Congressional Power to Declare War Does Not Provide an Effective Check on the President." *Writ: FindLaw's Legal Commentary*, March 6, 2002. Available: http://writ.news.findlaw.com/dorf/20020306.html.

Ely, John Hart. *War and Responsibility: Constitutional Lessons of Vietnam and Its Aftermath*. Princeton, NJ: Princeton University Press, 1993.

Farber, Daniel A., and Suzanna Sherry. *A History of the American Constitution*. St. Paul, MN: West Publishing Co., 1990, Chapter 4.

Fisher, Louis. *Constitutional Conflicts between Congress and the President*, 3rd ed. Lawrence, KS: University Press of Kansas, 1991.

Fisher, Louis. *Presidential War Power*. Lawrence, KS: University Press of Kansas, 1995.

Goldman, Sheldon. *Picking Federal Judges: Lower Court Selection from Roosevelt through Reagan*. New Haven, CT: Yale University Press, 1997.

Irons, Peter. *Justice at War: The Story of the Japanese-American Internment Cases*. New York: Oxford University Press, 1983.

Katzmann, Robert A. "War Powers: Toward a New Accommodation." In Thomas E. Mann, ed. *A Question of Balance: The President, Congress, and Foreign Policy*. Washington, DC: Brookings Institution, 1990, 35–69.

Koh, Harold Hongju. *The National Security Constitution: Sharing Power after the Iran-Contra Affair*. New Haven, CT: Yale University Press, 1990.

Maltese, John Anthony. *The Selling of Supreme Court Nominees*. Baltimore, MD: Johns Hopkins University Press, 1995.

Pius, Richard M. *The American Presidency*. New York: Basic Books, 1979.

Rakove, Jack N. *Original Meanings: Politics and Ideas in the Making of the Constitution*. New York: Alfred A. Knopf, 1996, Chapter 9.

Rossiter, Clinton. *Constitutional Dictatorship*. Princeton, NJ: Princeton University Press, 1948.

Schlesinger, Arthur M., Jr. *The Imperial Presidency*. Boston: Houghton Mifflin, 1973.

Westin, Alan. *The Anatomy of a Constitutional Law Case*. New York: Macmillan, 1959.

THE PRESIDENTIAL ELECTION OF 2000

Abbott, David W., and James P. Levine. *Wrong Winner: The Coming Debacle in the Electoral College*. New York: Praeger, 1991.

Ackerman, Bruce, ed. *Bush v. Gore: The Question of Legitimacy*. New Haven, CT: Yale University Press, 2002.

Best, Judith A. *The Case against Direct Election of the President*. Ithaca, NY: Cornell University Press, 1975.

CNN/AllPolitics.Com-Election 2000 Archive. Available: http://www.npr.org/news/national/election2000

Dershowitz, Alan M. *Supreme Injustice: How the High Court Hijacked Election 2000.* New York: Oxford University Press, 2001.

Dover, Edwin D. *The Disputed Presidential Election of 2000: A History and Reference Guide.* Westport, CT: Greenwood Press, 2003.

FindLaw Legal News and Commentary. "Election 2000, The Florida Recount: Chronology of Lawsuits." Available: http://news.findlaw.com/legalnews/us/election/election2000timeline.html.

Finkleman, Paul. "The Murky Proslavery Origins of the Electoral College." *Jurist,* November 30, 2000. Available: http://jurist.law.pitt.edu/election/electionfink.htm.

Gillman, Howard. "Materials Relating to the Role of Courts, Law, and Politics in Election 2000." Available: http://www.usc.edu/dept/polsci/gillman/election2000.html.

Gillman, Howard. *The Votes That Counted: How the Court Decided the 2000 Presidential Election.* Chicago, IL: University of Chicago Press, 2001.

Greene, Abner. *Understanding the 2000 Election: A Guide to the Legal Battles That Decided the Presidency.* New York: New York University Press, 2001.

NPR Online. "Election 2000." Available: http://www.npr.org/news/national/election2000/.

Posner, Richard. *Breaking the Deadlock: The 2000 Election, the Constitution, and the Courts.* Princeton, NJ: Princeton University Press, 2001.

Rakove, Jack N. *The Unfinished Election of 2000.* New York: Basic Books, 2002.

Rosen, Jeffrey. "Obstruction of Judges." *The New York Times Magazine,* August 11, 2002.

Sabato, Larry. *Overtime! The Election 2000 Thriller.* New York: Longman, 2001.

Sunstein, Cass R., and Richard Allen Epstein, eds. *The Vote: Bush, Gore, and the Supreme Court.* Chicago, IL: University of Chicago Press, 2001.

Supreme Court of the United States. "Florida Election Cases." Available: http://www.supremecourtus.gov/florida.html.

Toobin, Jeffrey. *Too Close to Call: The Thirty-Six-Day Battle to Decide the 2000 Election.* New York: Random House, 2001.

5

ARTICLE III: THE JUDICIARY

Because the delegates at the Philadelphia Convention, most of whom were trained in the law, were familiar with the judicial systems of Great Britain and of their states, they found relatively little on which to disagree in devising Article III. Indeed, Article III proved to be the least controversial of any constitutional provision.[1] The colonial courts and later the state courts as well as the federal judicial system that existed under the Articles of Confederation had very limited authority in relation to both state and federal legislatures. Early experience, in fact, prompted Alexander Hamilton in *Federalist 78* to describe the judiciary as **the least dangerous branch,** for unlike the executive, which holds "the sword of the community," and the legislature, which holds the "purse . . . and prescribes the rules by which the rights and duties of every citizen are to be regulated," it has "neither Force nor Will, but merely judgment."[2] Consequently, the delegates were intent on establishing an independent judiciary that would be equal to the other two branches of the federal government.

Section 1

The Judicial Power of the United States shall be vested in one supreme Court, and in such inferior Courts as the Congress may from time to time ordain and establish.

The delegates at the Philadelphia Convention agreed that there should be "one supreme Court," but they divided over whether the Constitution should establish a system of lower federal courts. The initial draft of the Virginia Plan provided for a national judiciary made up of "one or more supreme tribunals, and of inferior tribunals,"[3] but some delegates argued that state courts should decide cases initially with the possibility of appeal to the United States Supreme Court. The delegates compromised by leaving the matter to Congress—Congress may create lower federal courts but is not constitutionally required to do so. The First Congress created a three-tiered system of federal courts with the **Judiciary Act of 1789.** At the bottom were the thirteen district courts—federal trial courts each with one judge. The second tier was made up of three circuit courts (eastern, middle, and southern), each of which was presided over by one district judge and two Supreme Court justices. The circuit courts were author-

---

[1]Daniel A. Farber and Suzanna Sherry, *A History of the American Constitution* (St. Paul, MN: West Publishing Co., 1990), 51.
[2]*The Federalist Papers by Alexander Hamilton, James Madison and John Jay* (New York: Bantam Books, 1982), 393–394.
[3]Farber and Sherry, 54 and 416.

TABLE 5-1   The Structure of the Federal Judiciary

```
                     ┌────────────────────────┐
                     │  Supreme Court of the  │
                     │     United States      │
                     └────────────────────────┘
                        ▲                  ▲
        ┌───────────────────────┐   ┌───────────────────────┐
        │ United States Courts of│   │ United States Courts of│
        │  Appeals (12 Circuits) │   │  Appeals Appeals       │
        │                        │   │  for the Federal Circuit│
        └───────────────────────┘   └───────────────────────┘
              ▲                        ▲        ▲        ▲
```

| 94 United States District Courts | United States Tax Court | United States Claims Courts | United States Court of Veterans' Appeals | United States Court of International Trade |

ized to hear appeals of certain types of cases from the district courts, but these courts were primarily trial courts with jurisdiction over cases involving citizens from different states. At the top of the system was the Supreme Court with five associate justices and one chief justice.

The federal judiciary is still organized in three levels although the system differs in some important ways from the one that Congress established in 1789. In 1891, Congress created the circuit courts of appeals with their own judges to hear all appeals from the district and circuit courts. In 1911, Congress abolished the old circuit courts. The **courts of appeals,** as they have been called since 1949, are the courts of last resort for the vast majority of all federal cases. There are now thirteen courts of appeals including the twelve regional circuits and the United States Court of Appeals for the Federal Circuit, which hears appeals relating to patents, trademarks, and copyrights. There are 167 authorized judgeships for the twelve regional courts of appeals. There are ninety-four district courts for which there are 636 authorized judgeships. The Supreme Court has comprised nine justices since 1869. The structure of the federal courts is illustrated in Table 5-1.

Section 1

[continued] The Judges, both of the supreme and inferior Courts, shall hold their Offices during good Behavior, and shall, at stated Times, receive for their Services, a Compensation, which shall not be diminished during their Continuance in Office.

Determined to create an independent judiciary, the delegates to the Philadelphia Convention agreed that federal judges should serve "during good Behavior." The fact that federal judges serve for life has been a major source of the increasing politicization of judicial selection at the level of both the Supreme Court and the lower federal judiciary. Presidents at least since Ronald

Reagan have chosen young jurists who can be expected to serve for many years and to, therefore, have a significant impact on the decision making of the courts. In turn, members of the Senate from the opposing party have sought to block such nominations.[4]

The Framers provided that judges serve "during good Behavior." Consequently, Congress has devised various mechanisms for their discipline and removal. In the **Judicial Councils Reform and Judicial Conduct and Disability Act of 1980,** for example, Congress established a system within the federal judiciary to investigate complaints against judges and to curtail judicial misbehavior that falls short of impeachable offenses. The law allows the judicial councils—composed of judges—within each circuit to censure a judge and even to recommend impeachment.

An important and unresolved question concerning the impeachment of federal judges is whether a different standard should apply to them because they serve on good behavior rather than for a limited term. While other federal officials eventually leave office at the end of a specified term, the only way to remove a federal judge is by impeachment. Thus, it is arguable that judges should be impeached for behavior that does not amount to high crimes and misdemeanors. In 1970 when Gerald Ford tried to get his colleagues in the House of Representatives to impeach Justice William O. Douglas, he distinguished between the standards of impeachment for judges and for other officials:

> In my view, one of the specific or general offenses cited in Article II [of the Constitution: Treason, bribery, or other high crimes and misdemeanors] is required for removal of the indirectly elected President and Vice President and all appointed civil officers of the executive branch of the Federal Government, whatever their terms of office. But in the case of members of the judicial branch, Federal judges and justices, I believe an additional and much stricter requirement is imposed by Article III, namely "good behavior."[5]

The delegates to the Philadelphia Convention also sought to ensure judicial independence by prohibiting Congress from decreasing judicial salaries during the term of any particular judge.

Section 2

1. The judicial Power shall extend to all Cases, in Law and Equity, arising under this Constitution, the Laws of the United States, and Treaties made, or which shall be made, under their Authority;—to all Cases affecting Ambassadors, other public Ministers and Consuls;—to all Cases of admiralty and maritime Jurisdiction;—to Controversies to which the United States shall be a Party—to Controversies between two or more States;—between a State and Citizens of another State;[6]—between Citizens of different States;—between Citizens of the same State claiming Lands under Grants of different States, and between a State, or the Citizens thereof, and foreign States, Citizens or Subjects.

---

[4]See Chapter 4 for a discussion of judicial selection at the lower federal court level. Chapter 2 includes a consideration of presidents' nominations to the Supreme Court.
[5]As quoted in Emily Field Van Tassel and Paul Finkelman, *Impeachable Offenses: A Documentary History for 1787 to the Present* (Washington, DC: Congressional Quarterly, 1999), 8.
[6]The Eleventh Amendment modified this provision.

The words *Cases* or *Controversies* in Article III, Section 2 (1), reflect the decision of the Philadelphia Convention to limit the federal courts to the exercise of judicial power. The Virginia Plan initially provided for a Council of Revision composed of "the Executive and a convenient number of the National Judiciary . . . with authority to examine every act of the National Legislature before it shall operate."[7] James Madison and other delegates who advocated such an arrangement proposed a **Council of Revision** four separate times but it was defeated each time. The Convention also rejected Charles Pickney's suggestion that the legislature and the executive be given the authority to require the opinion of the judiciary "upon important questions of law."[8] Accordingly, the case or controversy requirement prohibits courts from acting as advisers to the legislature or the executive or rendering advisory opinions.

Because of the case or controversy requirement, a dispute is **justiciable**—suitable for judicial resolution—only if it fulfills several prerequisites. First, the legal interests of the parties must actually be in conflict. A case in which there is no real adversity between the litigants or one in which they are merely testing the law would be nonjusticiable.[9] Second, a dispute must be **ripe**—it must have matured into a threat to an individual's rights. Thus, courts usually will not hear a challenge to the constitutionality of a law that has not been enforced against the claimant.[10] Third, a dispute must not be **moot**—if a dispute no longer constitutes a live controversy because it has been resolved by time or intervening events, a court will not hear it.[11] Fourth, for a dispute to be justiciable, the party seeking relief must have **standing**. That is, a litigant must have suffered an actual injury that a court can redress.[12] Finally, the courts do not resolve cases that involve **political questions**—issues that are best left to the other branches of government. Although the Supreme Court used the political question doctrine for some time to avoid intervening to solve the problem of state legislative malapportionment,[13] the justices narrowed their conception of political questions as they moved into new areas to protect the rights of individuals during the Warren Era. Nevertheless, the Court has continued to find that certain types of cases, particularly those involving disputes between the president and Congress over the president's commitment of military forces abroad, are political questions. American courts do not have separate proceedings for cases in law and equity—a distinction inherited from England. Generally, cases in law involve remedies for something that has already occurred, whereas in **equity** the claimant asks the court to order the opposing party to either refrain from taking action or to carry out some action to prevent an injury.

Article III, Section 2 (1), outlines the bounds of federal judicial power—the **jurisdiction of the federal courts.** As outlined in Table 5-2, either the subject matter of a suit or the nature of the parties involved can give the federal courts jurisdiction. If the subject matter of a case involves the Constitution, federal law, or treaties, it is commonly referred to as raising a federal question and can

---

[7] As quoted in Farber and Sherry, 66.
[8] As quoted in *ibid.,* 60.
[9] See, for example, *Muskrat v United States* 219 US 346 (1911).
[10] See, for example, *United Public Workers v Mitchell* 330 US 75 (1947).
[11] See, for example, *DeFunis v Odegaard*, 416 US 312 (1974).
[12] See, for example, *Simon v Eastern Kentucky Welfare Rights Organization,* 426 US 26 (1976).
[13] *Colgrove v Green*, 328 US 549 (1946).

TABLE 5-2   Article III, Section 2 (1) & (2)—The Jurisdiction of the Federal Courts

Federal jurisdiction based on:

  Subject matter

  The Constitution, federal laws, and treaties

  Ambassadors, public ministers, and consuls

  Admiralty and maritime

  Parties

  United States

  Between two or more states

  Between a state and citizens of another state[*]

  Between citizens of different states

  Between citizens of the same state claiming lands under grants of different states

  Between a state, or the citizens thereof, and foreign states, citizens, or subjects

  Jurisdiction of the Supreme Court

  Original jurisdiction

  Cases affecting ambassadors, public ministers, and consuls

  Cases to which a state is a party

  Appellate jurisdiction

  Cases subject to the judicial power of the United States, "with such Exceptions, and under such Regulations as the Congress shall make."

[*]Modified by the Eleventh Amendment.

be brought in federal court. The purpose of extending federal power to cases involving federal questions was to promote uniformity in the interpretation of the federal law and to ensure that federal rights would be protected. Federal jurisdiction based on the nature of the parties reflects the Philadelphia Convention's wish to guarantee that certain categories of litigants would not be confined to state courts. For example, a federal forum when the U.S. government is a party to a legal action guards against possible state hostility just as federal jurisdiction in disputes involving two or more states and between citizens of different states guarantees a neutral forum.

Congress, beginning with the Judiciary Act of 1789, has provided more precise details about the jurisdiction of all three tiers of the federal courts. The **Removal Act of 1875** expanded access to the federal judicial system considerably by providing that any action asserting a federal right could begin in federal district court or if it began in state court it could be removed to a federal court. Additionally, because cases involving disputes between citizens of different states, which are known as diversity cases, comprise such a large portion of the federal caseload, in 1988 Congress set a jurisdictional amount on such cases, requiring that only disputes involving amounts of more than fifty thousand dollars may be filed in federal court.[14] Additionally, the Supreme Court

[14]Judicial Improvements and Access to Justice Act, 1988.

has recognized a "domestic relations exception" according to which diversity jurisdiction does not extend to divorce, alimony, or child custody cases.[15] Opponents of diversity jurisdiction argue that diversity cases needlessly crowd the federal dockets and that the state judiciaries are now capable of resolving such disputes fairly. Nevertheless, attempts to abolish diversity jurisdiction have not been successful.

Section 2

2. In all Cases affecting Ambassadors, other public Ministers and Consuls, and those in which a State shall be Party, the Supreme Court shall have original Jurisdiction. In all the other Cases before mentioned, the Supreme Court shall have appellate Jurisdiction, both as to Law and Fact, with such Exceptions, and under such Regulations as the Congress shall make.

The constitutional grant of **original jurisdiction** does not prohibit Congress from giving concurrent original jurisdiction to other federal courts. Thus, Congress has granted concurrent original jurisdiction to the federal district courts in all controversies except those between states where the Supreme Court has exclusive jurisdiction. As a result, the Court hears very few cases in its original jurisdiction. Most of those that it does hear involve border disputes between states. In such cases, the justices usually appoint a special master to determine the facts and recommend a decision. The Court considers the special master's report and issues a final decision. The Court will not accept a case in its original jurisdiction if a "state is only nominally a party and in reality is standing in to vindicate grievances of individuals."[16] Nevertheless, the justices have held that a state may act as a representative of its citizens when the alleged injury affects the general population of a state in a substantial way.[17]

Article III, Section 2 (2), provides that in all "the other cases" the Court shall have **appellate jurisdiction.** This provision provided the basis for the decision in *Marbury v Madison* (1803) in which Chief Justice John Marshall exercised the power of judicial review for the first time when he declared that Section 13 of the Judiciary Act of 1789 was unconstitutional. According to Marshall, Section 13 expanded the original jurisdiction of the Supreme Court and thus violated Article III, Section 2.[18]

The cases that come to the Court for review after they have been decided by a lower federal court or state court are appellate cases. The vast majority of cases that reach the Court in its appellate jurisdiction do so through a petition for a **writ of** *certiorari*. Any party to a case in which a final decision has been rendered by a lower federal court or a state court of last resort (if a federal question is involved) may petition the Court for a writ of certiorari, and if at least four justices agree that the case merits review, it will "grant cert" and schedule the case for oral argument. The decision to grant cert is completely at the discretion of the justices. Before 1925, most of the Supreme Court's docket consisted of cases that

---

[15]*Barber v Barber*, 21 Howard 582 (1859); *Ankenbrandt v Richards*, 504 US 689 (1992).
[16]*Illinois v Michigan*, 409 US 36 (1972).
[17]*Maryland et al. v Louisiana*, 451 US 725 (1981).
[18]*Marbury v Madison* is discussed at length in Chapter 2.

it was required to review. In the **Judges' Bill,** however, Congress gave the Supreme Court discretionary jurisdiction over broad categories of cases. By the 1970s, about 90 percent of the Court's cases came to it by a writ of certiorari, and in 1988 Congress made almost all of the Court's workload discretionary when it eliminated almost all the categories of cases in which the Court was mandated to hear appeals. Consequently, although the Court receives some seven thousand petitions for review, it heard only seventy-four cases in its 1999–2000 term. While that number increased to ninety in the 2000-2001 term, it nevertheless marked a drastic decline from the 175 cases decided in the 1984 term.[19]

By specifying that Congress shall have the authority to make exceptions to the Supreme Court's appellate jurisdiction, Article III, Section 2 (2), bestowed broad authority on the federal legislature to determine the scope of the Supreme Court's power to review cases. Congress relied on that authority when it enacted a law in 1868 eliminating the Court's appellate jurisdiction in cases involving petitions for federal habeas corpus with the goal of preventing the justices from curtailing the authority of military tribunals over civilians in the South pursuant to Reconstruction legislation.[20] In the twentieth century, Congress has proposed, although it has not enacted, legislation curbing the Court's appellate jurisdiction in areas such as school prayer, abortion, school busing, and criminal confessions—all areas in which some members of Congress strongly disagreed with the substance of the Court's decisions. The extent to which Congress may use the **Exceptions Clause** to limit or even eliminate the Supreme Court's jurisdiction over controversial subjects in order to prevent the justices from making decisions with which the legislative branch disagrees remains unresolved.

The **Antiterrorism and Effective Death Penalty Act of 1996** allows the courts of appeals to deny state prisoners permission to file second or successive petitions for habeas corpus and provides that such decisions are not reviewable by the Supreme Court. The justices unanimously rejected the argument that the law violated the Exceptions Clause, noting that the law did not deprive the Supreme Court of the power to consider habeas corpus petitions. In a concurring opinion, however, Justice David Souter contended that if Congress were to attempt to limit the Supreme Court's ability to hear habeas petitions "the question whether the statute exceeded Congress' Exceptions Clause power would be open."[21] Although the Supreme Court has not yet directly addressed the issue of Congress's authority to eliminate portions of the Supreme Court's appellate jurisdiction under the Exceptions Clause, scholars have argued that Congress may not eliminate the Court's appellate jurisdiction in such a way as to interfere with the Court's essential functions of resolving federal questions and protecting constitutional rights.[22]

---

[19]Judicial/Legislative Watch Report, Supreme Court in Review, October 2002. Available: http://www.nlcpi.org/books/pdf/jlwr_October02.pdf.

[20]The Court acquiesced to Congress in *Ex Parte McCardle*, 7 Wall. 506 (1869). But see *Ex parte Yerger*, 8 Wall. 85 (1869) in which the Court held that it did have jurisdiction to hear a habeas corpus appeal.

[21]*Felker v Turpin*, 518 US 1051 (1996).

[22]See, for example, Henry Hart, "The Power of Congress to Limit the Jurisdiction of Federal Courts: An Exercise in Dialectic." *Harvard Law Review* 66 (1953): 1362, 1364–1365; Leonard Ratner, "Congressional Power over the Appellate Jurisdiction of the Supreme Court." *University of Pennsylvania Law Review* 109 (1960): 157, 160–1673.

Section 2

3. The Trial of all Crimes, except in Cases of Impeachment, shall be by Jury; and such Trial shall be held in the State where the said Crimes shall have been committed; but when not committed within any State, the Trial shall be at such Place or Places as the Congress may by Law have directed.

Article III, Section 2 (3), attests to the importance of trial by jury in the American system of justice. The provision also guaranteed that individuals would not be transported to some far-off place for trial—as had been the practice under British rule—by specifying that the trial be held in the state where the crime was committed.

Section 3

1. Treason against the United States, shall consist only in levying War against them, or in adhering to their Enemies, giving them Aid and Comfort. No person shall be convicted of Treason unless on the Testimony of two Witnesses to the same overt Act, or on Confession in open Court.

2. The Congress shall have Power to declare the Punishment of Treason, but no Attainder of Treason shall work Corruption of Blood, or Forfeiture except during the Life of the Person attainted.

Under British law, treason was defined loosely enough that the government could use it to suppress individuals or groups deemed to be enemies of the state. To prevent the development of such a practice in the United States, the delegates at the Philadelphia Convention were careful to define treason narrowly, limiting it to levying war against the United States and giving aid and comfort to an enemy. By defining treason so narrowly and by requiring strict procedural safeguards for treason trials—no one may be convicted of treason unless there are two witnesses or if the accused confesses in open court—the Constitution ensured that the charge of treason could not be levied against the political opponents of the ruling regime or those who voice opposition to governmental policies. Although it may enact laws that make it a crime to use force against the government or to conspire to do so, Congress is constitutionally prohibited from expanding the definition of treason.

Presiding over **Aaron Burr's trial for treason** in 1807 in the United States Circuit Court for Virginia, Chief Justice John Marshall interpreted the Treason Clause in a way that made it impossible for Thomas Jefferson's administration to secure a conviction. Marshall maintained that the administration could not establish that Burr had engaged in an act of levying war without proof of the use of force. Marshall also distinguished between the act of levying war and the act of advising such action. Only the former constituted treason—the latter was merely "constructive treason." The indictment against Burr charged that he had levied war against the United States by arranging a gathering of an armed force on Blennerhassett's Island in the Ohio River. According to the common law doctrine of constructive treason if a group assembles for a treasonable purpose, anyone who participated in any way would be guilty of treason. Without directly addressing the issue of whether constructive treason comports with the constitutional definition of treason, Marshall found that the indictment of Burr was faulty because he had not been present on the island. By interpreting the Treason Clause as he did, and effectively discarding the doctrine of constructive treason, Marshall set a precedent that made it virtually impossible for future administrations to use treason as a political weapon.

The final provision in Article III, Section 3, barred an attainder of treason and corruption of blood, two closely related legal disabilities in English law. An attainder of treason was the loss of all legal protection pursuant to a conviction for treason including the right to pass on property. The legal disability, known as "corruption of blood," deprived descendants of a right to inherit from an individual convicted of treason. When Congress gave the president the power to confiscate the property of rebels in the Confiscation Act of 1862, Lincoln insisted that Congress limit the forfeiture of property to the owner's lifetime so that heirs would regain ownership after the death of the traitor. In 1875, the Supreme Court noted that the Attainder of Treason Clause was intended to protect heirs in such a situation.[23]

QUESTIONS

1. How might the American constitutional system have been different if the delegates to the Philadelphia Convention had agreed that (a) Article III should provide for a system of federal courts in addition to the Supreme Court or (b) Article III should forbid Congress from setting up federal courts other than the Supreme Court, thus leaving all judicial business except appeals of last resort to the state judiciaries or (c) there should be a Council of Revision or (d) that federal judges should serve a single term of four years?

2. In *Baker v Carr*, Justice Brennan defined a political question as follows:

   Prominent on the surface of any case held to involve a political question is found a textually demonstrable constitutional commitment of the issue to a coordinate political department; or a lack of judicially discoverable and manageable standards for resolving it; or the impossibility of deciding without an initial policy determination of a kind clearly for nonjudicial discretion; or the impossibility of a court's undertaking independent resolution without expressing lack of the respect due coordinate branches of government; or an unusual need for unquestioning adherence to a political decision already made; or the potentiality of embarrassment from multifarious pronouncements by various departments on one question.[24]

   Should the courts continue to rely on the political question doctrine to decline to resolve disputes between the president and Congress over the war powers? Which part of the definition is most applicable to such disputes?

---

[23]*Wallach v Van Riswick*, 92 US 202 (1875).
[24]*Baker v Carr*, 369 US 186, 217 (1962).

3. Does Congress have the power to eliminate the Supreme Court's entire appellate jurisdiction under the Exceptions Clause? If it were to do that, what do you think would be the likely outcome?

4. How might the history of the United States have been different if John Marshall had not interpreted the Treason Clause as narrowly as he did in *United States v Burr?*

KEY TERMS

the least dangerous branch
Judiciary Act of 1789
courts of appeals
Judicial Councils Reform and Judicial
    Conduct and Disability Act of 1980
Cases or Controversies
Council of Revision
a justiciable dispute
ripeness
mootness
standing
political questions

equity
jurisdiction of the federal courts
Removal Act of 1875
original jurisdiction
appellate jurisdiction
writ of certiorari
Judges' Bill
Exceptions Clause
Antiterrorism and Effective Death
    Penalty Act of 1996
Aaron Burr's trial for treason

SUGGESTIONS FOR FURTHER READING

Bator, Paul. "Judicial System, Federal." In Leonard W. Levy, Kenneth L. Karst, and Dennis J. Mahoney, eds. *Judicial Power and the Constitution:* Selections from the *Encyclopedia of the American Constitution.* New York: Macmillan, 1990, 122–134.

Bator, Paul M., Daniel J. Meltzer, Paul J. Mishkin, David L. Shapiro, and Richard H. Fallon, eds. Hart and Wechsler's *The Federal Courts and the Federal System,* 4th ed. Mineola, New York: Foundation Press, 1996.

Carp, Robert A., and Ronald Stidham. *Judicial Process in America,* 4th ed. Washington, DC: Congressional Quarterly Press, 1998, Chapter 2.

Farber, Daniel A., and Suzanna Sherry. *A History of the American Constitution.* St. Paul, MN: West Publishing Co., 1990, Chapter 3.

Gunther, Gerald. "Congressional Power to Curtail Federal Court Jurisdiction: An Opinionated Guide to the Ongoing Debate," 36 *Stanford Law Review* (1984), 895, 896–899.

Hart, Henry. "The Power of Congress to Limit the Jurisdiction of Federal Courts: An Exercise in Dialectic." *Harvard Law Review* 66 (1953): 1362, 1364–1365.

Howard, J. Woodford. *Courts of Appeals in the Federal Judicial System: A History of the Second, Fifth, and District of Columbia Circuits.* Princeton, NJ: Princeton University Press, 1981.

Ratner, Leonard. "Congressional Power over the Appellate Jurisdiction of the Supreme Court." *University of Pennsylvania Law Review* 109 (1960): 157, 160–167.

Richardson, Richard J., and Kenneth N. Vines. *The Politics of Federal Courts.* Boston, MA: Little, Brown, 1970.

6

ARTICLES IV–VII

While the first three articles of the Constitution outlined the powers of the legislative, executive, and judicial branches of the national government, Article IV focused on the obligations of the states to one another. Article VI, the most prominent part of which is the Supremacy Clause, clarified the relationship between the national government and the states. The Tenth Amendment, which is discussed in Chapter 9, shed further light on the nature of that relationship. Article V outlined the procedures for amending the Constitution, and Article VII provided the method for putting the new Constitution into effect.

ARTICLE IV: RELATIONS AMONG THE STATES

Section 1

Full Faith and Credit shall be given in each State to the public Acts, Records, and judicial Proceedings of every other State. And the Congress may by general Laws prescribe the Manner in which such Acts, Records and Proceedings shall be proved, and the Effect thereof.

The **Full Faith and Credit Clause** requires each state to recognize as legally binding the "public Acts, Records, and judicial Proceedings" of the other states. Neither the language of the clause nor the discussions at the Philadelphia Convention made clear whether it was meant to require only that public records be admitted into evidence in other states or whether it was intended to go further to give such records legal effect in other states. Congress soon provided clarification by enacting legislation requiring that records and judicial proceedings shall have the same faith and credit "in every court of the United States, as they have by law or usage in the courts of the State from whence the said records are or shall be taken."[1] Congress also enacted legislation providing that the same full faith and credit extend to the territories and possessions of the United States. In 1948, Congress revised the statutory provision regarding full faith and credit to require that full faith and credit be given to state laws as well as records and judgments.[2] The Supreme Court has also clarified the

---

[1] As quoted in Thomas O. Sargentich, "Full Faith and Credit," in Kermit L. Hall, ed. *The Oxford Companion to the Supreme Court of the United States* (New York: Oxford University Press, 1992), 322.
[2] The legislation is in United States Code, Title 28.

terms of the clause by holding that federal courts must grant full faith and credit to state court judgments.[3]

The Full Faith and Credit Clause is particularly important in the context of state court judgments. In the early nineteenth century, the Court held that a judgment rendered in one state or territory has effect in other states or territories provided that the court in the first state had jurisdiction and the judgment was final.[4] Thus, if a court in Pennsylvania resolves a dispute between Shashi and Tarun by ordering Shashi to pay Tarun $150,000, Shashi will not be able to avoid paying by moving to California. The California courts will recognize the Pennsylvania judgment just as if it were a California decision. Nevertheless, California may determine the method of enforcing the judgment in accordance with its own laws.[5]

Litigation in Hawaii began in 1991 challenging the state's marriage laws that confined marriage to two people of the opposite sex. In 1993, the state supreme court held that the restriction on same-sex marriage constituted sex discrimination under the state constitution's equal protection clause and could only be upheld if the state could show that the law served a compelling interest.[6] In December 1996, a trial court judge found that the state had not provided a sufficiently compelling reason to continue the ban on same-sex marriages. Although it appeared that the state of Hawaii would be the first state to recognize same-sex marriages, subsequent developments resulted in continuation of the prohibition on such unions.[7]

Nevertheless, the Hawaii Supreme Court's suggestion in 1993 that the prohibition on same-sex marriage might violate the state constitution raised the question of whether other states would be required under the Full Faith and Credit Clause to recognize same-sex marriages validly performed in Hawaii or any other state that might decide to permit them. Congress intervened with the Defense of Marriage Act (DOMA), which President Clinton signed into law in September 1996. The Act defines marriage for federal purposes as an arrangement between a man and a woman and gives the states the right not to recognize same-sex marriages from other states.[8]

DOMA raises intriguing constitutional questions. First, if the Full Faith and Credit Clause would not require other states to recognize Hawaiian marriages, would not Congress's unprecedented action in legislating to negate the application of one state's judgment in other states be unnecessary and unjustified? Con-

---

[3]*Stoll v Gottlieb*, 3051 US 165 (1938) and *St. John v Wisconsin Employment Relations Board*, 340 US 411 (1951).
[4]*Mills v Duryee*, 11 US 481 (1813) and *Hampton v McConnell*, 16 US 234 (1818).
[5]*Sistare v Sistare*, 218 US 1 (1910).
[6]Hawaii's equal protection clause provides that "[n]o person shall . . . be denied the equal protection of the laws, nor be denied the enjoyment of the person's civil rights or be discriminated against in the exercise thereof because of race, religion, sex or ancestry." As quoted in *Baehr v Lewin*, Supreme Court of Hawaii, P2d 44 (Haw. 1993).
[7]*Baehr v Miike*, First Circuit Court, State of Hawaii, December 3, 1996. Available: http://starbulletin.com/96/12/03/news/index.html. The court stayed its decision pending appeal. In November 1998, the voters in Hawaii approved an amendment to the state constitution that gives legislators the power to limit marriage to opposite-sex couples. Mike Yuen, "Same Sex Marriage Strongly Rejected." *Honolulu Star-Bulletin*, November 4, 1998. In late 1999, the Hawaii Supreme Court held that the amendment rendered the case moot.
[8]Defining marriage for federal purposes limits benefits such as Social Security and government pensions to heterosexual unions.

stitutional scholars have argued that states are not obligated to recognize marriages that violate the public policy of the state.[9] Second, if the Full Faith and Credit Clause obligates states to recognize Hawaiian same-sex marriages, can Congress relieve them of such an obligation? Scholars have contended that it cannot and even if it can do so under the Full Faith and Credit Clause, by singling out same-sex marriage, it creates constitutional problems under the equal protection component of the due process clause of the Fifth Amendment. Supporters of DOMA, on the other hand, pointed to the word *effects* in the Full Faith and Credit Clause, arguing that Congress's power to prescribe the effects of a judgment provides constitutional authorization for DOMA. The controversy over the meaning of the Full Faith and Credit Clause in the context of marriage between two people of the same sex cannot be resolved until a state permits same-sex marriage. Only then will it be possible for parties who marry in that state and move to another state that refuses to recognize their union to challenge that state's action on Full Faith and Credit Clause grounds.

Section 2

1. The Citizens of each State shall be entitled to all Privileges and Immunities of Citizens in the several States.

The delegates at the Philadelphia Convention borrowed the **Privileges and Immunities Clause** of Article IV, Section 2, from the Articles of Confederation as a means of creating unity among the newly independent states. Its enigmatic language left it open to several different interpretations. First, it might require Congress to guarantee equal treatment to citizens of different states. Second, it might be a guarantee of fundamental rights, which no state may deny to individuals from other states. In that case, Article IV, Section 2, would have given the Supreme Court the authority to invalidate state laws and other policies that deny such rights. The clause, in other words would have a similar effect on the states as the due process and equal protection clauses of the Fourteenth Amendment would come to have later.[10] This was the interpretation that Justice Bushrod Washington on circuit in *Corfield v Coryell* suggested when he declared that the clause protected privileges and immunities "which are, in their nature, fundamental; which belong of right to the citizens of all free governments."[11] Third, the Privileges and Immunities Clause may guarantee that individuals carry their rights as citizens of their own state with them when they reside temporarily in another state. That is, individuals carry their rights as state citizens throughout the union and other states may not deprive them of those rights. Fourth, the narrowest interpretation of the clause is that it merely prohibits states from discriminating against citizens from other states.

---

[9]See, for example, Cass Sunstein, "Don't Panic." In Andrew Sullivan, ed., *Same-Sex Marriage Pro and Con: A Reader* (New York: Vintage Books, 1997), 209–212. But see, Larry Kramer, "Same-Sex Marriage, Conflict of Laws, and the Unconstitutional Public Policy Exception." *Yale Law Journal* 106 (1997): 1965–2008 (arguing that the Full Faith and Credit Clause prohibits states from making decisions about whether to recognize other states' laws based on judgments about the substance of the policy).
[10]See Chapter 10.
[11]*Corfield v Coryell*, F. Cas. 546 (No. 3,230) (E.D. Pa. 1823).

The Supreme Court has firmly rejected the first three possibilities and has given the Privileges and Immunities Clause the most restrictive meaning possible. Thus, it is simply a requirement that states provide substantial justification for state laws that discriminate against people from other states and then only in limited contexts. The Court has, for example, invalidated state policies that discriminate against out-of-state residents in their ability to conduct business in the state. In so doing the Court has maintained that the Privileges and Immunities Clause has a reinforcing relationship with the Commerce Clause and "was intended to create a national economic union."[12]

Using such an approach, the Court invalidated an Alaska law giving preference to Alaska residents for construction jobs on the oil pipelines[13] and substantially higher license fees for out-of-state commercial fishermen.[14] The justices also held that states may not exclude nonresidents from admission to the practice of law.[15] Conversely, the Court has upheld policies that involve "disparity of treatment in the many situations where there are perfectly valid independent reasons for it."[16] Accordingly, it has approved higher fees for hunting on the ground that local citizens pay taxes for the upkeep of the public lands.[17] The Court has also held that states may charge higher tuition for state universities to out-of-state students.[18]

Section 2

2. A Person charged in any State with Treason, Felony, or other Crime, who shall flee from Justice, and be found in another State, shall on Demand of the executive Authority of the State from which he fled, be delivered up, to be removed to the State having jurisdiction of the Crime.

Article IV, Section 2 (2), provides for what is known as **extradition.** In 1861, in a case involving Kentucky's attempt to extradite a free black man who had been indicted for theft for helping a slave to escape to Ohio, the Supreme Court held that it lacked the power to coerce a state to comply with its constitutional obligation.[19] Accordingly, governors have sometimes refused to honor extradition requests. For example, in 1976 California's Governor Jerry Brown refused to extradite Native American activist Dennis Banks to South Dakota. Banks had fled the state after being convicted of "felony riot." In 1984, Governor Scott M. Matheson of Utah rejected an extradition request from Illinois for a business official wanted for murder because of an industrial accident in one of his company's plants. In 1987, however, the Court held that federal

---

[12]*Supreme Court of New Hampshire v Piper*, 470 US 274, 280 (1985).

[13]*Hicklin v Orbeck*, 437 US 518 (1978).

[14]*Toomer v Witsell*, 334 US 385 (1948).

[15]*Supreme Court of New Hampshire v Piper*, 470 US 274 (1985); *Supreme Court of Virginia v Friedman*, 487 US 59 (1988); *Barnard v Thorstenn*, 488 US 921 (1989).

[16]*Hicklin v Orbeck*, 437 US 518 (1978).

[17]*Baldwin v Montana Fish and Game Commission*, 436 US 371 (1978).

[18]In *Sturgis v Washington*, 414 US 1057 (1973), the Court upheld a one-year residency requirement for in-state tuition. In *Vlandis v Kline*, 412 US 441 (1973), however, the justices invalidated a state law requiring students admitted to state universities as nonresidents to pay nonresident tuition for the entire time of their enrollment.

[19]*Kentucky v Dennison*, 65 US 66 (1861).

courts have the power to order governors to fulfill a state's obligation under the Extradition Clause.[20]

Once the governor of the asylum state has issued the warrant of arrest and rendition, the courts of that state have four procedural issues to consider before delivering up the fugitive: whether the extradition documents are in order, whether the petitioner has been charged with a crime in the demanding state, whether the petitioner is the person named in the request, and whether the petitioner is a fugitive. They have no authority to inquire whether the demanding state had probable cause for an arrest, whether the charges are substantial, or whether the prison conditions of the demanding state violate the Eighth Amendment prohibition against cruel and unusual punishment.[21]

Section 2

3. No Person held to Service or Labour in one State, under the Laws thereof, escaping into another, shall, in Consequence of any Law or Regulation therein, be discharged from such Service or Labour, but shall be delivered up on Claim of the Party to whom such Service or Labour may be due.

Late in the Philadelphia Convention Pierce Butler, a delegate from South Carolina, proposed what came to be known as the **Fugitive Slave Clause.** The Convention adopted it without discussion or recorded dissent. Its location in Article IV suggests that the Convention thought that enforcement would be by state and local governments. Congress nevertheless passed a **Fugitive Slave Law** in 1793 allowing masters or their agents who captured fugitives to bring them to any magistrate to obtain a "certificate of removal" and to take the runaway back to the state where the slave owed service. The law provided fines for anyone who interfered with that process and allowed masters to seek damages from those who assisted fugitives.[22] In 1842, the Supreme Court held that the Fugitive Slave Law was constitutional. It also held that Pennsylvania's personal-liberty law, which protected black people from kidnapping and prescribed procedures for the return of genuine fugitives, was in violation of the Fugitive Slave Clause. In his opinion for the majority, Justice Joseph Story described the Fugitive Slave Clause as a "fundamental article" of the Constitution that was necessary for its adoption.[23]

Congress enacted a harsher law to enforce the Fugitive Slave Clause as part of the Compromise of 1850. The law not only deprived accused fugitives of the benefit of trial by jury, but also provided federal commissioners to enforce the law. Despite substantial northern resistance, more than nine hundred fugitives were returned between 1850 and 1861 under the law.[24] In 1859 Justice Roger B. Taney declared that the 1850 law was fully authorized by the Constitution.[25]

[20] *Puerto Rico v Branstad*, 483 US 219 (1987).

[21] *Michigan v Doran*, 439 US 282 (1978); *Pacileo v Walker*, 449 US 86 (1980); *California v Superior Court of California*, 482 US 400 (1987).

[22] Paul Finkelman, "Fugitive Slaves," in Kermit L. Hall, ed. *The Oxford Companion to the Supreme Court of the United States* (New York: Oxford University Press, 1992), 320.

[23] *Prigg v Pennsylvania*, 41 US 539 (1842).

[24] Finkelman, 320.

[25] *Ableman v Booth*, 62 US 506 (1859).

The Thirteenth Amendment, which was ratified in 1865, abolished slavery thereby nullifying the Fugitive Slave Clause.

Section 3

New States may be admitted by the Congress into this Union; but no new State shall be formed or erected within the Jurisdiction of any other State; nor any State be formed by the Junction of two or more States, or Parts of States, without the Consent of the Legislatures of the States concerned as well as of the Congress.

The Confederation Congress provided for the transition of the Northwest Territory into states in the Northwest Ordinance of 1787, stipulating that the new states would enter the union on an equal footing with the original states. In anticipation that the country would continue to expand westward, the Philadelphia Convention included such a provision in Article IV of the Constitution. Although the delegates at the Convention declined to use the "equal footing" language, the principle of equality has prevailed. Thus, the Court held that Congress could not prevent Oklahoma from moving its capital in legislation providing for its admission to the Union.[26]

The standard procedure for admission of a new state is as follows. First, the inhabitants of a territory file a petition for admission to the Union. Second, the president approves a congressional resolution authorizing the inhabitants of the territory to draw up a constitution. Third, a majority of both houses of Congress and then the president approve the proposed constitution. Finally, the territory is admitted to the Union.

Five states were formed from land that was initially part of the original thirteen states. Vermont from New York in 1791, Kentucky from Virginia in 1792, Tennessee from North Carolina in 1796, and Maine from Massachusetts in 1820—the ceding states readily agreed to the division. West Virginia was formed when the western counties of Virginia that wanted to remain in the Union split off from the rest of the state. A rump legislature convened for that purpose gave its approval to the split in 1863, but Virginia did not formally agree until after the Civil War. Texas was an independent nation before its admission to the Union in 1845, and California was part of a region ceded by Mexico in 1848. The other thirty states were all territories before they became states.

In the early 1980s when it became clear that the proposed constitutional amendment to extend additional representation to the District of Columbia was not going to be ratified, its proponents advocated that the district be admitted as a state.[27] Under their plan a small part of the district would be retained as the seat of government of the United States, as required by the Constitution, while the remainder would become a state. Such action would give the people of the district everything that the proposed amendment would have and could be done with only the vote of a majority of both houses of Con-

---

[26]*Coyle v Smith*, 221 US 559 (1911).
[27]The proposed amendment expired in 1985.

gress and the approval of the president. The District of Columbia held a constitutional convention, adopted a proposed constitution, and petitioned Congress for admission under the terms of Article IV, Section 3. Additionally, the Democratic Party endorsed the District of Columbia's admission as a state. Republicans in Congress, however, remained opposed, at least in part because admission would add two Democratic members to the Senate and one Democratic representative to the House.[28]

Section 3

2. The Congress shall have Power to dispose of and make all needful Rules and Regulations respecting the Territory or other Property belonging to the United States; and nothing in this Constitution shall be so construed as to Prejudice any Claims of the United States, or of any particular State.

Article IV, Section 3 (2), gave Congress complete legislative authority over territories. The Court has held that Congress may exercise its power directly just as if it were a state legislature[29] or it may delegate its authority to a territorial legislature.[30] As the United States began acquiring territories in the late nineteenth century, the question arose as to whether the Constitution would fully apply to those territories. The Court provided an answer in 1901 in the *Insular Cases* by making a distinction between incorporated and unincorporated territories. In incorporated territories—those that Congress anticipates admitting as states in the future—Congress must give to the people all the rights of the Constitution. But in unincorporated territories, Congress may limit its protection to fundamental rights such as fair trial and free speech.[31] The Court reaffirmed that distinction in 1990, noting that, "Only 'fundamental' constitutional rights are guaranteed to inhabitants of . . . territories."[32]

Section 4

The United States shall guarantee to every State in this Union a Republican Form of Government, and shall protect each of them against Invasion; and on Application of the Legislature, or of the Executive (when the Legislature cannot be convened) against domestic Violence.

In the late eighteenth century, the phrase "**republican form of government**" was used to describe a form of government derived from the consent of the people and which operates through representative institutions rather than direct democracy. The delegates at the Philadelphia Convention, however, did not specify how much popular participation in state government would be required to maintain the requisite republican form, nor did they identify which branch of the federal government would be responsible for enforcing the guarantee.

---

[28]Kent Jenkins Jr., "House Turns Down Statehood for D.C." *Washington Post*, November 22, 1993, A01.
[29]*First National Bank v Yankton County*, 101 US 129 (1880); *Simms v Simms*, 175 US 162 (1899).
[30]*Binns v United States*, 194 US 486 (1904).
[31]*DeLima v Bidwell*, 181 US 1 (1901); *Downes v Bidwell*, 181 US 244 (1901); *Dooley v United States*, 182 US 222 (1901).
[32]*United States v Verdugo-Urquidez*, 494 US 259 (1990).

Beginning in 1849 with **Luther v Borden,** the Supreme Court has consistently treated issues arising under the **Guaranty Clause** as political questions, to be resolved by Congress rather than the courts. In 1842, some Rhode Islanders who were disenfranchised under the state's original colonial charter, called a constitutional convention, drafted a new state constitution, submitted the document for popular ratification, and held elections. The government organized under the colonial charter refused to cede power and declared martial law. Soldiers, acting under authority of martial law, entered and searched the home of Martin Luther, one of the supporters of the reform government. To resolve the immediate issue of whether the soldiers' action constituted trespass, the Supreme Court had to consider whether a federal court could independently determine which of the two competing governments was the true government of state. The Court declared that "sovereignty in every State resides in the people [but this] . . . is a political question to be settled by the political power."[33] In short, a federal court could not decide which of the two governments had authority. The Guaranty Clause gave Congress the authority to decide the matter and in this case Congress had delegated the power to the president.

Later when Oregon's adoption of direct democracy[34] was challenged on the grounds that it departed from a republican form of government, the Court again held that a court was not the proper forum for resolving the issue. Chief Justice Edward White declared that to recognize federal judicial power under the Guaranty Clause would expand judicial power so as to "obliterate the division between judicial authority and legislative power."[35] In 1962 when advocates of reapportionment argued that the courts had a duty to guarantee republican governments to the states by invalidating legislative malapportionment, the Court affirmed its earlier interpretation of the Guaranty Clause and relied on the Equal Protection Clause to invalidate malapportioned legislatures.[36]

Some constitutional scholars have argued that the Court's refusal to decide which government in Rhode Island was the real government in *Luther v Borden* should not be understood to mean that all cases brought under the Guaranty Clause present political questions and are thus unsuitable for judicial resolution. John Hart Ely, for example, referred to the Court's inference as a "gross mistake in logic" and found it likely that the "unfortunate doctrine—that all Republican Form cases are necessarily cases involving political questions—will wholly pass from the scene one of these days."[37] Additionally, in 1992 in a case involving New York's challenge to a federal statute regulating the disposal of radioactive waste, Justice Sandra Day O'Connor rejected the state's argument that the law violated the Guaranty Clause but acknowledged the possibility that not all such claims present political questions.[38]

---

[33]*Luther v Borden,* 48 US 1 (1849).
[34]Oregon adopted the initiative and referendum, enabling its citizens to legislate directly.
[35]*Pacific States Tel. & Tel. Co. v Oregon,* 223 US 118 (1912).
[36]*Baker v Carr,* 369 US 186 (1962).
[37]John Hart Ely, *Democracy and Distrust: A Theory of Judicial Review* (Cambridge, MA: Harvard University Press, 1980), 118 note, and 123. Ely argued that the Court should have relied on the Guaranty Clause in the reapportionment decisions of the 1960s.
[38]*New York v United States,* 505 US 144 (1992).

The federal government's duty to protect the states against invasion and domestic violence provides additional authority for the president in the exercise of emergency powers particularly when the executive has the support of Congress. Thus, presidents have sent federal troops to curb disorder at the request of the state and even over the objection of state officials.

ARTICLE V: PROCEDURES FOR AMENDING THE CONSTITUTION

> The Congress, whenever two thirds of both Houses shall deem it necessary, shall propose Amendments to this Constitution, or, on the Application of the Legislatures of two thirds of the several States, shall call a Convention for proposing Amendments, which, in either Case, shall be valid to all Intents and Purposes, as Part of this Constitution, when ratified by the Legislatures of three fourths of the several States, or by Conventions in three fourths thereof, as the one or the other Mode of Ratification may be proposed by the Congress; Provided that no Amendment which may be made prior to the Year One thousand eight hundred and eight shall in any Manner affect the first and fourth Clauses in the Ninth Section of the first Article; and that no State, without its Consent, shall be deprived of its equal Suffrage in the Senate.

Several of the revolutionary state constitutions contained some mechanism for amendments either by giving the power to the legislature or providing for constitutional conventions.[39] But the Articles of Confederation made amendments virtually impossible by requiring the ascent of the legislature of every state. All attempts to amend the Articles to give Congress independent authority failed. Thus, it was clear to the delegates at the Philadelphia Convention that they needed to make the amending process easier but not so easy that the new document could be changed at the whim of a temporary majority or reduced to a catalog of "special provisos." It was James Madison who suggested that the amending process be initiated by two-thirds of Congress or two-thirds of the state legislatures and completed by three-fourths of the states.[40]

The prohibition on amendments before 1808 that would alter the provisions protecting the slave trade in Article I, Section 9 (1) and (4), was inserted at the insistence of John Rutledge of South Carolina. To overcome the objection that "the whole people of America can't make, or even propose Alterations," the delegates agreed to add the provision requiring Congress to call a constitutional convention on the request of two-thirds of the states. Finally, at

---

[39]Maryland's constitution of 1776, for example, provided that amendments would be effective only when passed by two successive separately elected legislatures. The Massachusetts constitution of 1780 provided for calling constitutional conventions at twenty-year intervals. Pennsylvania's constitution of 1776 provided that every seven years the legislature would name a Council of Censors to investigate how the government and constitution had been working. The Council would report to the legislature, which would then decide whether to call a convention. Richard B. Bernstein with Jerome Agel, *Amending America: If We Love the Constitution So Much, Why Do We Keep Trying to Change It?* (New York: Random House, 1993), 8–9.

[40]Clinton Rossiter, *1787: The Grand Convention* (New York: Macmillan, 1966), 224.

the urging of the small states, the Convention added the proviso that no state shall be deprived of its equal suffrage in the Senate.[41]

Madison's defense of the amending process in *Federalist 43* underlines that Article V not only struck a balance between making constitutional change too easy and rendering it impossible but also was consistent with the principles of federalism:

> The mode preferred by the convention seems to be stamped with every mark of propriety. It guards equally against that extreme facility, which would render the Constitution too mutable; and that extreme difficulty, which might perpetuate its discovered faults. It, moreover, equally enables the general and the State governments to originate the amendment of errors, as they may be pointed out by the experience on one side, or on the other.[42]

Article V also proved to be essential to the ratification of the new Constitution as seven of the state ratifying conventions agreed to approve the document on the condition that amendments to protect the rights of individuals be considered by the first Congress.[43]

Table 6-1 summarizes the four methods of amending the Constitution. All but one of the twenty-seven amendments to the Constitution have been proposed by a two-thirds vote of both houses of Congress and ratified by the state legislatures in three-fourths of the states. The Twenty-first Amendment, which repealed prohibition in 1933, was ratified by conventions called for that purpose in three-fourths of the states. When Congress proposes an amendment, it specifies which of these two procedures for ratification will be used. With the Twenty-first Amendment, Congress allowed each state to determine the manner of selecting delegates to its ratifying convention.

Although a constitutional convention for the purposes of proposing a constitutional amendment has never been called, there have been several attempts to do so. Indeed, even before the Philadelphia Convention had concluded its work, Edmund Randolph, delegate from Virginia, urged that a second convention be called to review the proposed Constitution. James Madison's proposal of the Bill of Rights in the first Congress ended the movement for a second convention, however. Later, a movement to call a second convention helped convince the Senate to agree to propose the Seventeenth Amendment, which provides for the direct election of Senators. In the spring of 1967, thirty-two state legislatures—only two short of the requisite two-thirds of the states—petitioned Congress to call a convention to propose an amendment to reverse Supreme Court rulings requiring both chambers of state legislatures to be apportioned on the basis of population. At the end of the 1980s, thirty-two states had passed resolutions calling for a national convention to propose an amendment requiring that the federal budget be balanced each year.

---

[41]Bernstein, 20–21. George Mason of Virginia made the statement about the inability of the whole people to propose alterations.

[42]*The Federalist Papers by Alexander Hamilton, James Madison and John Jay* (New York: Bantam Books, 1982), 223.

[43]Massachusetts, South Carolina, New Hampshire, Virginia, New York, North Carolina, Rhode Island.

TABLE 6-1   The Process of Amending the Constitution

Proposed By	Ratified By	Used
Two-thirds vote in both houses of Congress	State legislatures in three-fourths of the states or,	Twenty-six amendments
	Ratifying conventions in three-fourths of the states	Twenty-first Amendment (repealing prohibition, 1933)
Constitutional convention called at the request of two-thirds of the states	State legislatures in three-fourths of the states or,	Never used
	Ratifying conventions in three-fourths of the states	Never used

A number of questions about the untried mechanism of calling a second constitutional convention remain unresolved. For example, may Congress set conditions for determining when the constitutional prerequisites for calling a convention have been met? How long would petitions for a convention remain valid? How similar must the petitions from different states be for them to be joined into a single petition for a convention? Most importantly, can Congress limit the convention? Is there any recourse if a convention casts aside limits that Congress has imposed? In other words, is there any way for Congress to prevent a convention, called for the purpose of proposing a specific amendment, from proposing an entirely new constitution?

Some scholars have argued that Article V does not allow states to call for conventions limited to a single amendment or subject area but rather provides for a general convention for "proposing such amendments it decides to propose."[44] Thus, although Congress may not limit a constitutional convention, state requests for a convention to deal with a single issue such as a balanced budget would be invalid because they call for something that Article V does not make possible.[45] Others have countered that not only may the states request a convention for a limited purpose but also that Congress may limit the agenda of such conventions.[46]

There are also several intriguing issues surrounding the ratification process. First, the question of whether an amendment proposed without a time deadline must be ratified within a limited period of time was answered when the Twenty-seventh Amendment, which Congress proposed in 1789 as one of the original Bill of Rights, became part of the Constitution in 1992 when the

---

[44]Charles L. Black, Jr., "Amending the Constitution: A letter to a Congressman." *Yale Law Journal* 82 (1972) 198–225.
[45]Walter Dellinger, "The Recurring Question of the 'Limited' Constitutional Convention." *Yale Law Review* 88 (1979), 1623–1640.
[46]William Van Alstyne, "The Limited Constitutional Convention—The Recurring Answer." *Duke Law Journal* (1979): 988–1003.

thirty-eighth state ratified it, the Archivist of the United States certified it, and Congress voted to confirm the certification.[47]

A second question—whether a state may rescind its decision to ratify an amendment and, conversely, whether a state may ratify an amendment after first voting not to do so—first arose in connection with the Fourteenth Amendment. On July 20, 1868, the Secretary of State certified to Congress that the required twenty-eight states had ratified the Fourteenth Amendment.[48] Ohio and New Jersey, however, both of which had ratified, had subsequently "withdrawn their earlier assent." On July 21, Congress declared the Amendment to be a part of the Constitution. On July 28, the Secretary of State certified it. The prevailing view based on that experience is that once a state rejects an amendment, it may reconsider and ratify it but once a state ratifies, it may not rescind that ratification. The rationale for that limitation is that a state's decision to ratify an amendment provides the basis for other states' decisions to ratify or reject. Thus, to allow a state to rescind would confuse and possibly derail the orderly functioning of the amending process. On the other hand, for a state to reverse its rejection of an amendment does not undercut the basis for subsequent states' decisions.[49]

That issue along with the question of whether Congress may change a time limit for a proposed amendment's ratification arose in connection with the **Equal Rights Amendment** (ERA), which would have prohibited the denial of equal rights on the basis of sex. Congress proposed the ERA in 1972 and by mid-1973 thirty of the required thirty-eight states had ratified it. But after the thirty-fifth state ratified it in 1977 no additional states voted to do so. Anti-ERA activists persuaded state legislatures in five states to rescind their ratifications, but Congress refused to authorize their rescissions.[50] In 1978, Congress, by a majority vote, extended the deadline for ratification from 1979 to 1982.[51] When no additional states ratified the ERA during the extended period, the questions of whether Congress had the authority to revise its resolution containing the time limit and whether the five states could rescind their ratifications became moot.

The Supreme Court has suggested that at least some issues involving the amending process are political questions that are constitutionally committed to Congress.[52] Four justices who concurred in that decision, however, went much further, contending:

---

[47]The Twenty-seventh Amendment prohibits changes in the compensation of Senators and Representatives from taking effect until a congressional election intervenes. The Archivist of the United States has had the statutory responsibility for certifying amendments since 1984. But see *Dillon v Gloss*, 256 US 368 (1921) in which the Supreme Court cited that amendment as an example of long-forgotten proposals that had failed to pass the test of being ratified in a time "sufficiently contemporaneous in that the number of States to reflect the will of the people in all sections at relatively the same period."

[48]At that time there were thirty-seven states.

[49]Bernstein, 254.

[50]Idaho, Nebraska, Tennessee, Massachusetts, and South Dakota.

[51]The seven-year time limit for ratification did not appear in the text of the Amendment but in Congress's authorizing resolution accompanying it.

[52]*Coleman v Miller*, 307 US 433 (1939).

> Article V . . . grants power over the amending of the Constitution to Congress alone. Undivided control of that process has been given by the Article exclusively and completely to Congress. The process itself is "political" in its entirety, from submission until an amendment becomes part of the Constitution, and is not subject to judicial guidance, control or interference at any point.[53]

Some constitutional scholars have argued that the courts should address the issues surrounding the amending process. Judicial review, one commentator noted, is sometimes essential to vindicate the rights of litigants.[54] Walter F. Murphy urged judicial intervention of an amendment contrary to the preeminent constitutional value of human dignity. An amendment endorsing racial discrimination, for example, would be constitutionally invalid on the ground that it sought to "contradict the basic purpose of the whole constitutional system."[55] Others maintain that courts should stay out of the amending process. Laurence H. Tribe, for example, cautioned that judicial review of constitutional amendments might provide the Court with the opportunity to invalidate amendments designed to overturn decisions of the Court.[56]

The twenty-seven amendments that have been ratified and the six that Congress has proposed but that the states did not ratify constitute only about one-third of one percent of the more than eleven thousand amendments that have been introduced in Congress since the Constitution went into effect (see Table 6-2). Those figures testify to the difficulty of amending the Constitution and suggest that the delegates to the Philadelphia Convention were at least partly successful in striking the right balance between making formal constitutional change too easy on the one hand, too difficult on the other.

ARTICLE VI: THE STATES AND THE FEDERAL GOVERNMENT

> 1. All Debts contracted and Engagements entered into, before the Adoption of this Constitution, shall be as valid against the United States under this Constitution, as under the Confederation.

By 1787 when the Philadelphia Convention met, the securities and currencies issued by the Confederation and the several states had depreciated in value to such an extent that they were practically worthless. Moreover, the state governments and the Confederation had borrowed money during the Revolutionary War and owed over $79,000,000 to domestic and foreign creditors. Article

---

[53]*Ibid.* But two district court decisions questioned the applicability of the political questions doctrine to the amending process. See *Dyer v Blair*, 390 F. Supp. 1291 (1975) and *Idaho v Freeman*, 529 F. Supp. 1107 (1981).
[54]Walter Dellinger, "The Legitimacy of Constitutional Change: Rethinking the Amending Process." *Harvard Law Review* 97 (1983): 380–432.
[55]Walter F. Murphy, "An Ordering of Constitutional Values." *Southern California Law Review* 53 (1980): 703–760.
[56]Laurence H. Tribe, "A Constitution We Are Amending: In Defense of a Restrained Judicial Role." *Harvard Law Review* 97 (1983): 433–445.

TABLE 6-2   The Six Amendments Proposed by Congress but Not Ratified by the States

Year Proposed	Provision
1789	Reapportionment Amendment: Congress would be empowered to regulate the proportion of members of the House of Representatives once the proportion went beyond 100,000 per Representative.
1810	Stripped anyone who received a title of nobility of citizenship and prohibited from holding office.
1861	Corwin Amendment: An unamendable amendment providing, "No amendment shall be made to the Constitution which will authorize or give to Congress the power to abolish or interfere, within any State, with the domestic institutions thereof, including that of persons held to labor or service by the laws of said State."
1924	Child Labor Amendment: Would have given Congress the power to "limit, regulate, and prohibit the labor of persons under 18 years of age" and would have suspended any state laws that might contravene regulations established by Congress.
1972	Equal Rights Amendment: "equality of rights under the law shall not be denied or abridged by the United States or by any State on account of sex." Expired in 1982.
1978	"For purposes of representation in the Congress, election of the President and Vice President, and Article V of this Constitution, the District [of Columbia] . . . shall be treated as though it were a State." Expired in 1985.

Source: Joseph T. Keenan, *The Constitution of the United States: An Unfolding Story*, 2nd ed. (Chicago, IL: Dorsey Press, 1988), 45–46.

VI (1) assured those to whom the previous government owed money that the debt would be paid. Later, Alexander Hamilton, President George Washington's Secretary of the Treasury, convinced Congress to assume the debts incurred by the states and pay the debts of the Confederation.

> 2. This Constitution, and the Laws of the United States which shall be made in Pursuance thereof; and all Treaties made, or which shall be made, under the Authority of the United States, shall be the supreme Law of the Land; and the Judges in every State shall be bound thereby, any Thing in the Constitution or Laws of any State to the Contrary notwithstanding.

The delegates at the Philadelphia Convention added the **Supremacy Clause** after discarding a proposal to give Congress a veto over state laws.[57] The Committee on Detail placed it at the end of the enumeration of Congress's powers and the Committee on Style moved it to Article VI. Subsequently, the Conven-

---

[57]Clinton Rossiter, *1787: The Grand Convention* (New York: Macmillan, 1966), 197.

tion strengthened it by changing the following language: "The Acts of the Legislature of the United States made in pursuance of this constitution, and all treaties made under the authority of the United States shall be the supreme law of the several States, and of their citizens and inhabitants; and the judges in the several States shall be bound thereby in their decisions; any thing in the Constitutions of laws of the several States to the contrary notwithstanding" so that the Supremacy Clause began with "This Constitution."[58]

The Supremacy Clause underscores one of the key principles of the Constitution. The Constitution, the federal laws that are consistent with it, and treaties made under the authority of the United States are supreme. Any conflicting provision of a state constitution or any state law is null and void. State courts are, moreover, bound to uphold the supremacy of the Constitution and of the national government.

The Supremacy Clause provides important support for judicial review particularly when state legislation is challenged as a violation of the Constitution and when state laws conflict with those of the national government and are thereby preempted.

Treaties, like national laws, must conform to the Constitution. A treaty, or a law implementing a treaty, that infringed on First Amendment freedoms would be just as unconstitutional as any law that did so. Thus the Court noted in 1957, "This Court has regularly and uniformly recognized the supremacy of the Constitution over a treaty."[59] Nevertheless, the Court made clear that the treaty-making power is more extensive than Congress's lawmaking power when Justice Oliver Wendell Holmes, Jr., upholding a law regulating the hunting of migratory birds that Congress had enacted to fulfill the obligations of the United States pursuant to a treaty with Canada, noted:

> Acts of Congress are the supreme law of the land only when made in pursuance of the Constitution, while treaties are declared to be so when made under the authority of the United States. . . . We do not mean to imply that there are no qualifications to the treaty-making power; but they must be ascertained in a different way. . . . The only question is whether it is forbidden by some invisible radiation from the general terms of the Tenth Amendment. . . . We see nothing in the Constitution that compels the Government to sit by while a food supply is cut off and the protectors of our forest and our crops are destroyed.[60]

3. The Senators and Representatives before mentioned, and the Members of the several State Legislatures, and all executive and judicial Officers, both of the United States and of the several States, shall be bound by Oath or Affirmation, to support this Constitution; but no religious Test shall ever be required as a Qualification to any Office of public Trust under the United States.

Article VI (3) reinforced the spirit of the Supremacy Clause by making it clear that federal and state officials owe their allegiance to the Constitution.

---

[58]Daniel Farber and Suzanna Sherry, *A History of the American Constitution* (St Paul, MN: West Publishing Co., 1990), 425. Also, Rossiter, 214.
[59]*Reid v Covert*, 354 US 1 (1957).
[60]*Missouri v Holland*, 252 US 416 (1920).

The final sentence, prohibiting religious tests as a qualification for federal office testifies to the Constitution's opposition to an established religion prior to the addition of the Bill of Rights.

ARTICLE VII: RATIFICATION OF THE CONSTITUTION

> The Ratification of the Conventions of nine States, shall be sufficient for the Establishment of this Constitution between the States so ratifying the Same.

Toward the end of the Philadelphia Convention when the Committee on Detail completed its draft of the Constitution, it required that the document would be "laid before the United States in Congress assembled, for their approbation," and then ratified by state conventions. The Committee left the number of states required for ratification blank. When the Convention discussed the issue of how many states should be required, the delegates suggested seven, eight, nine, ten, and thirteen. They agreed to require nine states for ratification after George Mason suggested that it was a number that was familiar to the people because it had been required "in all great cases under the Confederation."[61] Table 1-2 shows the order in which the states ratified the Constitution as well as the dates, the terms, and the vote.

QUESTIONS

1. Does the Defense of Marriage Act of 1996 violate the Full Faith and Credit Clause? What recent developments may render the legislation unnecessary? What other constitutional provisions might be violated if states do not recognize same-sex marriages validly performed in other states?

2. What distinctions may the states make between in-state and out-of-state residents without violating the Privileges and Immunities Clause of Article IV, Section 2? What is the basis for the Court's demarcation between what is acceptable and what is prohibited?

3. If Congress were to propose and the states to ratify a constitutional amendment making Christianity the nation's official religion, would the amendment be constitutional?[62] Would the political questions doctrine prohibit judicial resolution of a challenge to that amendment?

4. What if Congress proposed and the states ratified an amendment repealing the Fourteenth Amendment and making the new amendment unamendable? Would that amendment be unconstitutional?

5. Could Article V be amended to place additional restrictions on the amending power?

---

[61]Farber and Sherry, 45.
[62]This suggestion appears in Bernstein, 255.

KEY TERMS

Full Faith and Credit Clause
Privileges and Immunities Clause
Corfield v Coryell
extradition
Fugitive Slave Clause
Fugitive Slave Law of 1793

Insular Cases
republican form of government
Luther v Borden
Guaranty Clause
Equal Rights Amendment
Supremacy Clause

SUGGESTIONS FOR FURTHER READING

Bernstein, Richard B., with Jerome Agel. *Amending America: If We Love the Constitution So Much, Why Do We Keep Trying to Change It?* New York: Random House, 1993.

Berry, Mary Francis. *Why ERA Failed: Politics, Women's Rights, and the Amending Process of the Constitution.* Bloomington: Indiana University Press, 1986.

Bonfield, Arthur E. "The Guarantee Clause of Article IV, Section 4: A Study in Constitutional Desuetude." *Minnesota Law Review* 46 (1962): 513–572.

Caplan, Russell L. *Constitutional Brinkmanship: Amending the Constitution by National Convention.* New York: Oxford University Press, 1988.

Dellinger, Walter. "The Legitimacy of Constitutional Change: Rethinking the Amending Process." *Harvard Law Review* 97 (1983): 380–432.

Finkelman, Paul. *Slavery and the Founders: Race & Liberty in the Age of Jefferson,* 2d ed. Armonk, NY: M.E. Sharpe, 1999.

Kramer, Larry. "Same-Sex Marriage, Conflict of Laws, and the Unconstitutional Public Policy Exception." *Yale Law Journal* 106 (1997): 1965–2008.

Levinson, Sanford, ed. *Responding to Imperfection: The Theory and Practice of Constitutional Amendment.* Princeton, NJ: Princeton University Press, 1995.

Murphy, Walter F. "An Ordering of Constitutional Values." *Southern California Law Review* 53 (1980): 703–760.

Sunstein, Cass. "Don't Panic." In Andrew Sullivan, ed. *Same-Sex Marriage Pro and Con: A Reader.* New York: Vintage Books, 1997, 209–212.

"Symposium on Interjurisdictional Marriage Recognition." *Creighton Law Review* 32 (1998).

Tribe, Laurence H. "A Constitution We Are Amending: In Defense of a Restrained Judicial Role." *Harvard Law Review* 97 (1983): 433–445.

Vile, John R. *Contemporary Questions Surrounding the Constitutional Amending Process.* Westport, CT: Praeger, 1993.

Weber, Paul J., and Barbara Perry. *Unfounded Fears: Myths and Realities of a Constitutional Convention.* New York: Praeger, 1989.

Wiecek, William. *The Guarantee Clause of the U.S. Constitution.* Ithaca, NY: Cornell University Press, 1972.

PART THREE

THE AMENDMENTS

7

THE BILL OF RIGHTS I: PROTECTING INDIVIDUAL LIBERTIES

THE BILL OF RIGHTS

Although several of the delegates to the Philadelphia Convention either proposed specific guarantees—such as liberty of the press—or expressed support for a more extensive list of rights, their proposals were defeated. Why did the Convention omit a bill of rights? One reason was that many of the delegates shared Alexander Hamilton's view "that the Constitution is itself in every rational sense, and to every useful purpose, a Bill of Rights."[1] The Constitution provided for the election of public officials, a republican form of government, a prohibition on titles of nobility, and separation of powers and checks and balances—all of which would serve to limit the power of government to infringe on the liberty of the people. Moreover, the document included some specific guarantees such as trial by jury in criminal cases and a clear definition of treason that would make convictions difficult. It also contained clear prohibitions on bills of attainder, ex post facto laws, and suspension of the writ of habeas corpus except when the public safety required it. Thus, the delegates could well have concluded that a bill of rights was unnecessary.

A second reason for omitting a bill of rights was, as some of the delegates argued, that it would be dangerous. Emphasizing that the federal government derived its authority from positive grants of power enumerated in the Constitution, they pointed out that a bill of rights would be absurd because it would, in effect, prohibit the government from doing what it did not have the power to do. Additionally, some delegates reasoned that a bill of rights would be dangerous because such an attempt to limit power might imply that some power had been granted where it, in fact, had not. For example, a provision declaring freedom of the press might be used to support the argument that the Constitution gave Congress the authority to regulate the press.

A bill of rights would also be dangerous, in the view of some delegates, because an enumeration of rights would be presumed to be exhaustive—people

---

[1]Alexander Hamilton, *Federalist 84. The Federalist Papers by Alexander Hamilton, James Madison and John Jay* (New York: Bantam Books, 1982), 438.

might assume that rights not enumerated had been surrendered to the federal government. There was also skepticism at the Convention about the effectiveness of a bill of rights. The delegates were well aware that violations of liberties frequently occurred in states that had constitutions with bills of rights.

The omission of a bill of rights aroused some of the most serious opposition to ratification to the new document. Indeed, the Constitution was ratified with the understanding that the first business of the first Congress would be consideration of a bill of rights in the form of amendments. Congress proposed twelve such amendments on September 25, 1789, ten of which were ratified and became part of the Constitution on December 15, 1791. One that was not ratified prescribed the ratio of representation to population in the House of Representatives; the other, which prohibited any increase in compensation to members of Congress until an election for representatives intervened, was ratified 202 years later and became the Twenty-seventh Amendment.

THE BILL OF RIGHTS AND THE STATES

The initial version of the Bill of Rights, prepared by James Madison and approved by the House of Representatives, restricted both the federal and state governments. The Senate, however, altered the language, removing any mention of state government.[2] In 1833 when the Supreme Court addressed the question of whether the Bill of Rights applied to the states, Chief Justice John Marshall answered with a resounding "no." The Constitution, Marshall argued, was "ordained and established by the people of the United States for themselves, for their own government, and not for the government of the individual states." He also emphasized that at the time the Constitution was ratified most states had their own bills of rights and that it was "universally understood" that it was the federal government rather than the states that posed a threat to liberty.[3]

The prevailing belief that the people had more to fear from the federal government than from state and local governments proved to be misplaced. States commonly disregarded the rights of individuals. Although most state constitutions included their own bills of rights, state judges who interpreted those provisions rarely did so in a way that effectively protected the liberties of individuals. Because the states have the primary responsibility for the administration of justice, the failure of the Constitution to restrain state and local authorities left large segments of governmental activity without constitutional supervision.

The adoption of the Fourteenth Amendment in 1868 with its express proscriptions on states might have fundamentally changed the relationship between the Bill of Rights and the states. Some lawyers argued that the Fourteenth Amendment "incorporated" the Bill of Rights; more specifically, they urged the Court to adopt the view that the provisions forbidding states from abridging

---

[2]Leonard W. Levy, *Original Intent and the Framers' Constitution* (New York: Macmillan, 1988), 169–170.
[3]*Barron v Baltimore*, 7 Peters 243 (1833).

privileges or immunities and from depriving persons of life, liberty, or property without due process of law subsumed all the restrictions listed in the Bill of Rights. The Bill of Rights, according to that view, constituted restrictions on the states, if only indirectly, via the Fourteenth Amendment. The Court construed the Fourteenth Amendment narrowly, however, although it held in 1895 that the due process clause of the Fourteenth Amendment included the Fifth Amendment's prohibition on taking private property without just compensation.[4]

Although the states remained beyond the reach of the Bill of Rights in the late nineteenth and early twentieth centuries, the Supreme Court eventually began to find that the due process clause of the Fourteenth Amendment subsumed specific protections in the Bill of Rights. In 1925, for example, it held that the word *liberty* in the due process clause includes liberty of speech.[5] By the early 1940s, the Court had found that the due process clause included all the provisions of the First Amendment. Thus, the First Amendment restricted the states (or applied to the states) by virtue of the essential connection between freedom of religion, speech, the press, and the liberty protected by the due process clause. In short, the Court had "incorporated" the First Amendment.

What about the other provisions in the Bill of Rights? If the due process clause of the Fourteenth Amendment imposes on state governments the same limitations that the First Amendment places on the national government, does the rest of the Bill of Rights also come within the scope of the Fourteenth Amendment? For some time, a persistent minority of justices argued that it did; they would have construed the due process clause of the Fourteenth Amendment to mean that the states should follow precisely the same procedures that the Bill of Rights requires of the national government. What national authorities cannot do because of a provision in the Bill of Rights, these justices contended, state authorities could not do because of the due process clause of the Fourteenth Amendment.

The view that prevailed on the Court until the early 1960s—which we refer to as the **"fundamental fairness" approach**—held that although it did not incorporate the specific provisions in the Bill of Rights, the due process clause required the states to comport with a standard of fairness. Principles of fairness might overlap with some of the rules of the Bill of Rights.[6] Thus, the police could not engage in "conduct that shocks the conscience" by forcibly pumping a man's stomach to obtain evidence of narcotics violations.[7]

Although a majority of the Supreme Court has never adopted the doctrine of **"total incorporation,"** it rejected the fundamental fairness approach and *selectively incorporated* nearly all the provisions in the Bill of Rights. In *Palko v Connecticut*,[8] Justice Benjamin Cardozo noted that the provisions in the Bill of Rights that should be incorporated by the due process clause of the Fourteenth Amendment were those that protected rights that were fundamental—"implicit in the concept of ordered liberty." Cardozo's reasoning provided the basis for

---

[4]*Chicago B & O RR Co v City of Chicago*, 166 US 226 (1895).
[5]*Gitlow v New York*, 268 US 652 (1925).
[6]See Frankfurter's concurring opinion in *Adamson v California*, 332 US 46, 59–68 (1947).
[7]*Rochin v California*, 342 US 165 (1952).
[8]302 US 319 (1937).

Table 7-1   Provisions in the Bill of Rights That the Supreme Court Has Not Incorporated

Amendment	Provision
Second	Right to keep and bear arms.
Third	Prohibition on quartering soldiers.
Fifth	Right to indictment by grand jury.
Seventh	Right to trial in civil cases.
Eighth	Prohibition on excessive bail and fines.

the **doctrine of selective incorporation,** which the Court used to extend the protections of the First Amendment to the states in the 1940s.

It was not until the 1960s, however, that the Court began to incorporate the provisions that protect the rights of the criminally accused. Proceeding provision by provision, the Court selectively incorporated the Fifth Amendment's protection against self-incrimination[9] and double jeopardy,[10] and the Sixth Amendment's guarantees of right to counsel[11] and trial by jury.[12] The only provisions concerning the rights of the accused that have not been incorporated are the right to indictment by a grand jury in the Fifth Amendment, the right to a jury trial in civil cases in the Seventh Amendment, and the right against excessive bail and fines in the Eighth Amendment (see Table 7-1). The incorporation controversy was settled by the late 1960s and remains so today. Some justices, however, would like to see the Court return to the fundamental fairness approach. Chief Justice William H. Rehnquist, for example, has characterized the incorporation of the Bill of Rights as a "mysterious process of transmogrification."[13]

POSTINCORPORATION ISSUES

The incorporation of the Bill of Rights was the most important development in the criminal justice revolution of the 1960s. The decisions we have discussed established that one set of standards would govern both state and federal criminal justice systems. No longer would states be free to disregard the procedural protections offered to the criminally accused in the Fourth, Fifth, and Sixth Amendments. Nevertheless, incorporation left a number of questions unsettled about the meaning of the protections guaranteed to the criminally accused. Although the Court might have continued to expand the rights of the accused after incorporation, it has generally refrained from doing so. The Warren Court expanded rights, but the Burger Court and subsequently the Rehn-

---

[9]*Malloy v Hogan,* 378 US 1 (1964).
[10]*Benton v Maryland,* 395 US 784 (1969).
[11]*Gideon v Wainwright,* 372 US 355 (1963).
[12]*Duncan v Louisiana,* 391 US 145 (1968).
[13]*Carter v Kentucky,* 450 US 288 (1981).

quist Court developed devices for drawing limits. We discuss two of those devices here: **dilution of the Bill of Rights** and the **harmless error doctrine.**

As a result of incorporation, the states may not offer less protection to the criminally accused than does the federal government. The rule that states and the federal government must comply with the same standard does not, however, define that standard. Thus, because the Sixth Amendment requires trial by jury for federal trials, it also requires trial by jury for state trials. But how many jurors are required? Although Americans adopted the long-standing British tradition of a twelve-person jury, after the Court incorporated the jury provision of the Sixth Amendment, it ruled that the twelve-person jury was a historical accident and not constitutionally required.[14] Similarly, Americans adopted the British tradition requiring a unanimous jury verdict for a criminal conviction. In 1972, however, the Court held that a nine-to-three verdict did not violate the Sixth Amendment.[15] Those decisions upheld state practices that were inconsistent with long-established rules regarding federal constitutional requirements. And because the Supreme Court has held that the standard must be the same for the state and federal systems, the effect of the decisions is to dilute the protection offered by the Sixth Amendment. Thus, although the Federal Rules of Criminal Procedure—proposed by the Court and accepted by Congress—require twelve-person juries and unanimous verdicts, they are no longer constitutionally required.

A second device that the Court has developed to limit the rights of the accused is the **harmless error doctrine,** which holds that not all constitutional errors necessarily render a trial fundamentally unfair.[16] Certain errors are per se grounds for reversal and are not subject to harmless error analysis. That is, if the defense shows that such an error occurred, the conviction must be reversed. Such errors include complete denial of the right to counsel,[17] lack of an unbiased judge,[18] denial of the right to trial by jury,[19] conviction by a jury that acted on an indictment by a grand jury from which individuals were excluded because of race,[20] a judge's failure to instruct the jury properly on the "reasonable doubt" standard,[21] and conviction and death sentence by a jury from which a juror was improperly dismissed because of opposition to the death penalty.[22] Such errors render it impossible for a trial to determine guilt or innocence reliably. Thus, no criminal punishment that resulted from a trial containing such errors could possibly be fair.[23] The Court has held, however, that a number of other constitutional errors can be harmless. When a conviction is challenged on the grounds that a constitutional error occurred at trial, the Court may find

---

[14]*Williams v Florida,* 399 US 78 (1970).
[15]*Johnson v Louisiana,* 406 US 356 (1972). Taking the fundamental fairness approach, Justice Lewis Powell, who supplied the crucial fifth vote for that decision, maintained that the Sixth Amendment requires unanimous verdicts in federal prosecutions.
[16]*Faby v Connecticut,* 375 US 85 (1963); *Chapman v California,* 386 US 18 (1967).
[17]*Gideon v Wainwright,* 372 US 335 (1963).
[18]*Tumey v Ohio,* 273 US 510 (1927).
[19]*Duncan v Louisiana,* 391 US 145 (1968).
[20]*Vasquez v Hillery,* 474 US 254 (1986).
[21]*Sullivan v Louisiana,* 508 US 275 (1993).
[22]*Gray v Mississippi,* 481 US 648 (1987).
[23]*Rose v Clark,* 478 US 570 (1986).

that the error does not constitute per se grounds for reversal. In that situation, the Court applies the harmless error analysis to determine whether the error influenced the outcome of the trial. If it did not, then the conviction is not reversed. The errors subject to harmless error analysis include use of evidence obtained in violation of the Fourth Amendment,[24] admission of statements obtained in violation of the Sixth Amendment right to counsel,[25] comments about a defendant's failure to testify,[26] improper jury instructions,[27] denial of a defendant's right to be present at a trial,[28] and violation of the right to confront witnesses.[29] Until 1991, the introduction of a coerced confession constituted per se grounds for reversal.[30] That year, however, a five-member majority held that a coerced confession, if not obtained by physical violence, is subject to harmless error analysis.[31]

The Court has held that when harmless error analysis is used, the proper standard is that reversal of a conviction is required unless the state can show that the error was "harmless beyond a reasonable doubt."[32] The standard for determining whether habeas corpus relief must be granted is more difficult, however. It depends on whether the error "had substantial and injurious effect or influence in determining the jury's verdict."[33] In 1995, the Court declared that petitioners for habeas corpus are not entitled to relief based on trial error unless they can establish that it resulted in actual prejudice.[34]

Justices have repeatedly defended the harmless error doctrine on the grounds that it is essential to preserving the central purpose of a criminal trial—to determine guilt or innocence—and to maintain a focus on the underlying fairness of the trial rather than on "the virtually inevitable presence of immaterial error."[35] Some errors are harmless, the Court reasons, because they are not relevant to the truth-finding function of the trial. In any case the harmless error doctrine has the effect of seriously undermining the protections expressly provided in the Bill of Rights.

STATE CONSTITUTIONS AND INDIVIDUAL RIGHTS

State constitutions seemed to have been forgotten in the 1960s as the Supreme Court expanded protections for individual rights by applying federal constitutional provisions to the states. Litigants relied on federal rather than state constitutional guarantees and chose the federal judiciary as the forum most likely to protect their rights.[36] But in the 1970s, the Burger Court's retreat from

---

[24]*Chambers v Maroney*, 399 US 42 (1970).
[25]*Moore v Illinois*, 434 U.S. 220 (1977); *Milton v Wainwright*, 407 US 371 (1972).
[26]*United States v Hasting*, 461 US 499 (1983).
[27]*Rose v Clark*, 478 US 570 (1986). Specifically, in this case an instruction creating a presumption of malice that had the effect of shifting the burden of proof of intent to the defendant was held to be harmless error.
[28]*Rushen v Spain*, 464 US 114, 118 (1983)
[29]*Delaware v Van Arsdall*, 475 US 673 (1986).
[30]*Payne v Arkansas*, 356 US 560 (1958).
[31]*Arizona v Fulminante*, 499 US 279 (1991).
[32]*Chapman v California*, 386 US 18 (1967).
[33]*Brecht v Abrahamson*, 507 US 619 (1993).
[34]*O'Neal v McAninch*, 513 US 432 (1995).
[35]*Arizona v Fulminante*, 499 US 279 (1991) quoting *Delaware v Van Arsdall*, 475 US 673, 681 (1986).
[36]See Bert Neuborne, "The Myth of Parity," *Harvard Law Review* 90 (1977): 1105.

the Warren Court's protective approach sparked renewed interest in state constitutions. A number of legal scholars as well as judges began to urge state supreme courts to take a more active role in protecting individual rights by relying on their own state constitutional provisions. Justice William J. Brennan, for example, invited state courts to "thrust themselves into a position of prominence in the struggle to protect the people of our nation from governmental intrusions in their freedoms."[37] He underlined the importance of state constitutions by noting that they often offer protections that extend beyond those required by the Supreme Court's interpretation of the federal Constitution.

State courts have tremendous potential for expanding protections for individual rights beyond those offered by the United States Supreme Court by interpreting their own constitutions. Although the Supreme Court has jurisdiction to review decisions of a state's highest court when a question of federal law is raised, the Court does not review state court decisions that rest on **adequate and independent state grounds.** Thus, a state high court may determine, without the prospect of a reversal from the United States Supreme Court, that a provision in its own bill of rights offers more protection than does the federal Bill of Rights. Some state courts have done so. Notably, the supreme courts of California, New Jersey, and Washington have ruled that the free speech provisions of their own constitutions protect expressive activities on privately owned property,[38] even though the United States Supreme Court has ruled that the First Amendment does not guarantee freedom of expression in privately owned shopping centers.[39] It is imperative for state courts to make clear that they are relying solely on their own constitutions, for the United States Supreme Court has declared that unless state courts indicate "clearly and expressly" that they are relying solely on the own constitutions, their decisions will be subject to review.[40]

In 1986, Justice Brennan noted that during the 1970s and the early 1980s, state courts published over 250 opinions "holding that the constitutional minimums set by the United States Supreme Court were insufficient to satisfy the more stringent requirements of state constitutional law."[41] Although the high courts of California, New Jersey, Washington, Oregon, Wisconsin, and Massachusetts have expanded rights by interpreting their constitutions independently of the United States Constitution, states with more conservative constituents have continued to follow the decisions of the United States Supreme Court. For example, the ten states that were least active in developing their state constitutional criminal procedure law were South Carolina, Arkansas, Nevada, Alabama, Indiana, Minnesota, New Mexico, Virginia, Georgia, and North Dakota.[42]

---

[37]William J. Brennan Jr., "State Constitutions and the Protection of Individual Rights," *Harvard Law Review* 90 (1977): 489, 491, 503.

[38]*Robins v Pruneyard Shopping Center*, 23 Cal. 3d 899, 592 P 2d 341 (1979); *State v Schmid*, 84 NJ 535, 423 A 2d 615 (1980); *Alderwood Associates v Washington Environmental Council*, 96 Wash. 2d 230, 635 P 2d 108 (1981).

[39]*Lloyd Corp. v Tanner*, 407 US 551 (1972); *Hudgens v NLRB*, 424 US 507 (1976).

[40]*Michigan v Long*, 463 US 1032 (1983).

[41]William J. Brennan, Jr., "The Bill of Rights and the States: The Revival of State Constitutions as Guardians of Individual Rights," *New York University Law Review* 61 (1986): 535, 548.

[42]Barry Latzer, "Whose Federalism? Or, Why 'Conservative' States Should Develop Their State Constitutional Law," *Albany Law Review* 61 (1998), 1402, note 18.

State constitutional law may also have advantages for conservatives who are interested in reviving a state-centered federalism. State courts may be more responsive to local needs than the distant United States Supreme Court.[43] One commentator has encouraged state high court judges to rely on their own constitutions to narrow procedural protections by relying on the principles of state autonomy and the independence of state constitutional law. State courts, according to this line of reasoning, could confront the United States Supreme Court to overrule outright old Warren Court precedents—such as the *Miranda* Warnings.[44]

Despite the importance of state constitutional law, the United States Supreme Court and the United States Constitution are likely to remain the primary source for the protection of individual rights. There are many reasons for this but among the most important is that a majority of state judges lack life tenure and must be careful not to anger the voters.[45] The removal of California's Chief Justice Rose Bird and Associate Justices Joseph R. Grodin and Cruz Reynoso in 1986 suggests the dimensions of this problem.

AMENDMENT I: FREEDOM OF RELIGION, SPEECH, ASSEMBLY, AND PETITION

The First Amendment prohibited the government from establishing a religion, interfering with religious activities, abridging the right to speak or publish, or limiting the right to assemble and to petition the government for a redress of grievances. Considered together, the First Amendment's guarantees stand for the principles of freedom of belief and conscience; they also imply the existence of a realm of personal privacy that government may not breach. When the first two amendments failed to be ratified, the Third Amendment became the First—that accident has had tremendous symbolic implications. The First Amendment is often said to protect the first—that is, the most important and fundamental—freedoms of individuals.

The Establishment Clause

Congress shall make no law respecting an establishment of religion

Over the years, the Court has been called on to apply the Establishment Clause to a wide variety of situations, including challenges to public funding and other assistance for religious schools, prayer in schools, holiday displays, and laws requiring the teaching of creationism in the public schools. As the justices have endeavored to develop a coherent set of standards, they have divided over what the Framers of the First Amendment intended to prohibit. One interpretation of the Establishment Clause, which is known as the **separationist**

---

[43]Stanley Mosk, "State Constitutionalism: Both Liberal and Conservative," *Texas Law Review* 63 (1985): 1081.
[44]Latzer, 1399.
[45]See, for example, Melinda Gann Hall, "Electoral Politics and Strategic Voting in State Supreme Courts," *Journal of Politics* 54 (1992): 427.

approach, relies heavily on the argument that the Framers intended the clause to erect "a wall of separation" between church and state.[46] In 1947, Justice Hugo Black outlined the separationist view when he wrote that the Establishment Clause

> means at least this: Neither a state nor the Federal Government can set up a church. Neither can pass laws which aid one religion, aid all religions, or prefer one religion over another. Neither can force nor influence a person to go to or to remain away from church against his will or force him to profess a belief or disbelief in any religion. No person can be punished for entertaining or professing religious beliefs or disbeliefs, for church attendance or non-attendance. No tax in any amount, large or small, can be levied in support of any religious activities or institutions, whatever they may be called, or whatever form they may adopt to teach or practice religion. Neither a state nor the Federal Government can, openly or secretly, participate in the affairs of any religious organizations or groups and vice versa.[47]

The contrasting view, known as **nonpreferentialism,** holds that the Framers intended only to prohibit Congress from creating a national religion or preferring one religion over another. Nonpreferentialists take a considerable more accommodationist stance toward public support for religion and are unlikely to vote to invalidate programs challenged under the Establishment Clause.

Applying the separationist approach, the Court held in 1948 that "released time" programs in which students in public schools were sent to another part of the school to receive religious instruction from teachers who came to the school for that purpose violated the Establishment Clause.[48] But four years later, the justices found that a program in which students left the school buildings for religious instruction did not breach the wall of separation.[49] Then in 1962 and 1963 the Court held that the policies of reciting a prayer and reading verses from the Bible at the beginning of school day violated the Establishment Clause.[50]

Congress responded with more than a hundred proposals for a constitutional amendment to overturn the Court's decisions by allowing prayer in the schools. Critics of the school prayer decisions continued to introduce constitutional amendments and bills designed to limit the Supreme Court's jurisdiction in the 1970s and 1980s. In 1983, the Court seemed to retreat from the separationist position when it upheld a state legislature's practice of having a chaplain open each session with a prayer,[51] but in 1992 in *Lee v Weisman,* the justices invalidated an arrangement whereby public school principals invited local clergy to offer invocation and benediction prayers at graduation ceremonies for middle schools and high schools.[52] Registering its displeasure with

---

[46]Thomas Jefferson used the metaphor in his letter to the Danbury Baptist Association in 1802.
[47]*Everson v Board of Education,* 330 US 1 (1947).
[48]*Illinois ex rel McCollum v Board of Education,* 333 US 203 (1948).
[49]*Zorach v Clauson,* 343 US 306 (1952).
[50]*Engel v Vitale,* 370 US 421 (1962); *Abington School District v Schempp* and *Murray v Curlett,* 374 US 203 (1963).
[51]*Marsh v Chambers,* 463 US 783 (1983).
[52]*Lee v Weisman,* 505 US 577 (1992).

that decision and others involving aid to religious schools, a majority of the House of Representatives—but not the requisite two-thirds—approved a constitutional amendment in 1998 guaranteeing "the people's right to pray and to recognize their religious beliefs, heritage, or traditions on public property, including schools."[53] In *Lee v Weisman* the Court left unresolved the issue of whether student-led prayers at graduation would be permissible, but in 2000 held that the Establishment Clause prohibits student-led prayers at the beginning of high school football games.[54]

In 1971 in *Lemon v Kurtzman*, the Court fashioned the following three-pronged test for determining the validity of a challenged policy. First, the policy must have a secular purpose. Second, its primary effect must neither advance nor inhibit religion. Third, the policy must not result in excessive governmental entanglement with religion.[55] During the later years of the Burger Court, some of the justices began to question the usefulness of the **Lemon Test.** Subsequently, several justices on the Rehnquist Court have continued to criticize the *Lemon* Test although the Court has expressly not overruled it. For example, in 1985 in *Wallace v Jaffree* when a six-member majority held that Alabama's law authorizing a minute of silence in the public schools lacked the requisite secular purpose, four of the justices objected to the Court's use of the test.[56] Justice Rehnquist argued that the "wall of separation" is a "metaphor based on bad history, a metaphor which has proved useless as a guide to judging." He argued further that the test has divided the Court and has yielded inconsistent, unprincipled results.

Although neither the five-member majority in *Lee v Weisman* nor the six-member majority in *Santa Fe Independent School District v Doe* overruled the *Lemon* Test, the majority did not rely on it in either case. In *Lee,* the Court focused instead on the element of coercion—the practice of inviting local clergy to graduation ceremonies to lead prayers created a state-sponsored and state-directed religious exercise in which the students were coerced into participating.[57] The four opinions in that case help to illustrate the division on the Court over the proper standard for deciding Establishment Clause cases. Justice Anthony Kennedy, who wrote the opinion for the majority, took the position that government may not coerce anyone to support or participate in any religion or its exercise. Justice Sandra Day O'Connor, who wrote a concurring opinion, argued that the Establishment Clause prohibits government endorsement of religion. Rehnquist, in his dissenting opinion, argued that the clause prohibits the government from "asserting a preference for one religious denomination or sect over others." Scalia also wrote a dissenting opinion in which he endorsed the nonpreferentialist approach and characterized the *Lemon* Test as irrelevant.[58] Then in an opinion he wrote in a case decided in 1993 in which

---

[53]Religious Freedom Amendment (H.J. Res. 78, June 4, 1998). The vote in the House was 224–203. The Senate failed to act on the proposed amendment.
[54]*Santa Fe Independent School District v Doe,* 530 US 290 (2000).
[55]*Lemon v Kurtzman,* 403 US 602 (1971).
[56]*Wallace v Jaffree,* 472 US 38 (1985). The four justices who objected to the *Lemon* Test were O'Connor (concurring), White, Rehnquist, and Burger (in separate dissenting opinions).
[57]*Lee v Weisman,* 505 US 577 (1992).
[58]*Ibid.*

the majority used a combination of the *Lemon* Test and the endorsement approach, he condemned the *Lemon* Test as a "creature" that is "[l]ike some ghoul in a late-night movie that repeatedly sits up in its grave and shuffles abroad, after being repeatedly killed and buried." Scalia contended that a majority of the justices had "personally driven pencils through the creature's heart."[59] The *Lemon* Test has continued to endure, however. In 1994, Justice David Souter implicitly reaffirmed it when he referred to "a principle at the heart of the Establishment Clause that government should not prefer one religion to another, or religion to irreligion."[60] Finally, in 1997 O'Connor applied the *Lemon* Test when she wrote the majority opinion allowing state assistance for religious schools.[61]

The contrasting positions that the current justices have taken regarding the proper standard for deciding Establishment Clause cases are summarized in Table 7-2. Even though a majority of the current justices continue to endorse the *Lemon* Test, as Table 7-3 shows, the results of some the most recent decisions indicate that the Court has shifted to a more accommodationist position. Table 7-3 also reveals that the complexities of the different facts of each case have had a major impact on the outcome.

The Court's decision in 1995 that the University of Virginia may not deny a Christian student organization funds from student fees for printing its religious newspaper provides another indication of the Court's growing **accommodationism**.[62] Moreover, during the same term the Court also held that there was no Establishment Clause problem for Ohio to allow the Ku Klux Klan to erect a cross in a state-owned park during Christmas season. Indeed, the Court found that the state violated the free speech rights of the Klan by refusing to allow the display of the cross. Scalia's opinion, which was joined by three other members of the Court, suggested that all religious expression in public places is protected by the freedom of expression provision of the First Amendment. Indeed, for Scalia, freedom of expression seemed to prevail over the Establishment Clause.[63] Similarly, in 2001 Justice Thomas led a six-member majority in its decision that a public school violated the free speech rights of a Christian student club by denying that group access to the school's public forum. Here, as in the Ohio case, the Court held that the Establishment Clause does not allow a state to discriminate against a particular group "simply because of its religious viewpoint."[64]

In a decision in 2002 that could have profound implications for the future of public education, the Court ruled that Ohio's school voucher program, giving tuition aid to certain students to allow them to attend the public or private

[59]Concurring in *Lamb's Chapel v Center Moriches Union Free School District*, 508 US 384 (1993).
[60]*Board of Education of Kiryas Joel Village School District v Grumet*, 512 US 687 (1994).
[61]*Agostini v Felton*, 521 US 203 (1997).
[62]*Rosenberger v Rector and Visitors of University of Virginia*, 515 US 819 (1995).
[63]*Capital Square Review Board v Pinette*, 515 US 753 (1995). The three other justices were Rehnquist, Thomas, and Kennedy. Previous cases in which the Court has addressed the issue of religious symbols in holiday displays in public places are *Lynch v Donnelly*, 465 US 668 (1984); *Allegheny County v Greater Pittsburgh ACLU*, 492 US 573 (1989). Generally, the rule prior to *Pinette* seemed to be that the display must give the appearance that state is endorsing a religion.
[64]*Good News Club v Milford Central School*, 533 US 98 (2001).

Table 7-2 The Division on the Current Court regarding the Proper Standard in Establishment Clause Cases

Justice	Standard	Definition	Cases Illustrating
Rehnquist, Scalia, Thomas	Nonpreferentialism	The Establishment Clause allows the government to accommodate religion; it only prohibits government from preferring one religious denomination over others.	Scalia's concurring opinion in *Lamb's Chapel v Center Moriches Union Free School District*, 508 US 384 (1993) Scalia's plurality opinion in *Capital Square Review and Advisory Board v Pinette*, 515 753 (1995) Rehnquist's dissenting opinion in *Wallace v Jaffree*, 472 US 38 (1985)
O'Connor	Endorsement	The Establishment Clause prohibits government from endorsing a religion or conveying a message of endorsement.	O'Connor's concurring opinions in *Lynch v Donnelly*, 472 US 38 (1985) and *Wallace v Jaffree*, 465 US 668 (1984)
Kennedy	Coercion	Government may not coerce anyone to support or participate in any religion or its exercise; and it may not . . . give direct benefits to a religion in such a degree that it in fact "establishes a religion or religious faith, or tends to do so."	*County of Allegheny v ACLU*, 492 US 573 (1989)
Stevens, Souter, Ginsburg, Breyer,	*Lemon* Test	Policy violates the Establishment Clause if it fails any part of the following: 1. Must have a secular purpose. 2. Effect must neither advance nor inhibit religion. 3. Must not result in excessive entanglement with religion.	*Lemon v Kurtzman*, 403 US 602 (1971) *Edwards v Aguillard*, 482 US 578 (1987) *Wallace v Jaffree*, 472 US 38 (1985)

Note: The idea for this table came from Lee Epstein and Thomas G. Walker, *Constitutional Law for a Changing America: Rights, Liberties, and Justice* (Washington, DC: CQ Press, 1998), 169. Reprinted by permission.

Table 7-3   The Shift from the "Wall of Separation" to Accommodationism—Aid to Religious Schools

Case	Outcome and Vote	Aid Upheld	Aid Invalidated
Everson v Board of Education (1947)	Accommodation 5–4	Transportation reimbursements	
Board of Education v Allen (1968)	Accommodation 6–3	Textbook loans	
Lemon v Kurtzman (1971)	Separation 8–0		Reimbursements for teacher salaries, textbooks, instructional materials
Early v DiCenso (1971)	Separation 8–1		Teacher salary supplements
Tilton v Richardson (1971)	Accommodation 5–4	Funds for secular buildings at colleges	
Levitt v CPEARL (1973)	Separation 8–1		Reimbursements for administering and grading tests required by state
CPEARL v Nyquist (1973)	Separation 6–3		Grants for maintenance and building repair, tax benefits, tuition reimbursements
Meek v Pittenger (1975)	Mixed	Textbook loans	"Auxiliary services" such as counseling, testing, speech therapy; loans of "instructional materials and equipment" such as maps, films, photographs, periodicals
Roemer v Maryland Public Works Board (1976)	Accommodation 5–4	General-purpose funds to colleges and universities for secular purposes	
New York v Cathedral Academy (1977)	Separation 6–3		Direct reimbursement for record keeping and testing
CPEARL v Regan (1980)	Accommodation 5–4	Reimbursements for meeting state requirements for regents examinations, "pupil attendance reporting"	

Continued

Table 7-3 The Shift from the "Wall of Separation" to Accommodationism—Aid to Religious Schools—Concluded

Case	Outcome and Vote	Aid Upheld	Aid Invalidated
Mueller v Allen (1983)	Accommodation 5–4	Tax deductions for tuition, textbooks, transportation	
Grand Rapids School District v Ball (1985)	Separation 5–4		Community Education Program offering courses (chess, home economics, languages) at end of school day; employing private school teachers and using public and private school facilities. Shared Time Program offering secular classes to private school children in private school facilities (leased by the state) during regular school hours and taught by public school teachers, many of whom had previously taught in private schools
Aguilar v Felton (1985)	Separation 5–4		Teacher/counselor salaries and supplies/materials for remedial instruction to private school students in private school facilities
Witters v Washington Service for the Blind (1986)	Accommodation 9–0	Disabled student at Christian college cannot be denied state vocational rehabilitation assistance	
Zobrest v Catalina Foothills School District (1993)	Accommodation 5–4	Disabled student at Roman Catholic high school can be furnished with a state-funded sign-language interpreter	
Board of Education of Kiryas Joel Village School District v Grumet (1994)	Separation 6–3		School district created to accommodate handicapped children of particular sect
Agostini v Felton (1997)	Accommodation 5–4	Special education classes taught in parochial schools; overruled *Aguilar v Felton* (1985)	

Source: Adapted from Lee Epstein and Thomas G. Walker, *Constitutional Law for a Changing America: Rights, Liberties, and Justice* (Washington, DC: CQ Press, 1998), 171–172. Reprinted by permission.

school of their choice, did not violate the Establishment Clause. Chief Justice Rehnquist, writing the opinion for the five-member majority, emphasized that the purpose of the program was to serve general state interests in providing educational opportunities to children. He found that the program was "entirely neutral with respect to religion," and "provides benefits directly to a wide spectrum of individuals, defined only by financial need and residence." The program, in Rehnquist's assessment, allowed for "genuine choice among options public and private, secular and religious."[65]

The Free Exercise Clause

[continued] or prohibiting the free exercise thereof;

Although the Establishment Clause and the Free Exercise Clause together stand for the principle of religious freedom, the two clauses are potentially in conflict. If, for example, the state were to grant an exemption from a law to members of a religious group on free exercise grounds, that exemption could constitute favoritism toward that religion and thus would be a violation of the Establishment Clause. Thus, Justice Harry Blackmun noted in 1989 that "The Free Exercise Clause value suggests that a State may not impose a tax on spreading the gospel. . . . The Establishment Clause value suggests that a state may not give a tax break to those who spread the gospel that it does not also give to others who actively might advocate disbelief in religion."[66]

The starting point for understanding the Court's decision making in the area of the Free Exercise Clause is the distinction between beliefs and actions.[67] Although freedom of belief is protected from government interference, conduct may be regulated. The Court underlined this distinction in 1879 when it upheld Congress's prohibition on polygamy in federal territory against the claim that Mormon men had a religious right and duty to practice it. The Court noted that Congress had the authority to prohibit actions that were "in violation of social duties or subversive of good order."[68]

Once the Court applied the Free Exercise Clause to the states in 1940,[69] the justices continued to use the distinction between beliefs and actions while they also began to develop a standard for determining what actions are protected by the Clause. Thus, the Court developed the **valid secular policy test** to determine whether a policy violated the Free Exercise Clause. Under that test, if a state had a valid secular reason for its policy and the policy was not directed at any particular religion, then no exemption from the policy would be granted even if it burdened religious practices. Using that standard, the Court upheld, against a challenge by Jehovah's Witnesses, a requirement that schoolchildren must salute the flag and a prohibition on minors selling magazines on the streets.[70]

---

[65]*Zelman v Simmons-Harris*, ____ US ____ (2002).
[66]Concurring in *Texas Monthly Inc. v Bullock*, 489 US 1 (1989).
[67]Thomas Jefferson's letter to the Danbury Baptist Association supports the distinction: "[R]eligion is a matter which lies solely between man and his God; that he owes account to none other for his faith or his worship; that the legislative powers of the Government reach actions only, and not opinion." As quoted in *Reynolds v United States*, 98 US 145 (1879).
[68]*Reynolds v United States*.
[69]*Cantwell v Connecticut*, 310 US 296 (1940).
[70]*Minersville School District v Gobitis*, 310 US 586 (1940); *Prince v Massachusetts*, 321 US 296 (1944).

The Court adopted a more protective approach in the early 1960s when it began to require that if a policy infringes on religious practices the state must show that it has a compelling interest that it cannot achieve with any less restrictive means. Thus, in 1963 the justices held that a state could not deny unemployment compensation to a Seventh Day Adventist who refused to accept employment that would require her to work on Saturday. Justice William J. Brennan, who wrote the opinion for the seven-member majority, noted that the state had no compelling interest in forcing the claimant to choose between losing her unemployment benefits to follow her religion or abandoning the requirements of her religion to accept work.[71]

Applying the **compelling state-interest–least-restrictive-means test,** the Court in 1972 held that requiring the Amish to comply with compulsory school attendance laws beyond the eighth grade violated their Free Exercise rights. Chief Justice Warren Burger found that the compulsory school attendance interfered with the traditional way of life of the Amish. Their way of life, he found, was inextricably bound up with their religious beliefs. Therefore, compulsory school attendance interfered with the Amish exercise of their religion. He concluded that the state lacked an interest in providing universal education that was sufficiently compelling to overcome the free exercise interests of the Amish.[72]

In the early 1980s, the Court began to hint that it might be retreating from the compelling state interest standard in favor of a less protective approach. First, in 1982 the justices held that Amish employers must participate in the Social Security system by collecting and paying taxes for their employees even though such a practice violated their religious principles. Chief Justice Burger, writing for the majority, reasoned that compulsory participation was essential to accomplishing government's overriding interest in maintaining the Social Security system.[73] Second, in 1986 the majority declined to use the test when it held that a captain in the Air Force whose religion required him to wear his yarmulke while in uniform was not entitled to an exemption from the Air Force dress code regulation forbidding all head coverings other than military headgear.[74] The Court's position was not clear, however. In the first case, the Court used the test but found that the government had a compelling interest. Moreover, the Court may have declined to apply the compelling interest test simply because the case involved a military decision—to which the Court typically defers.

In 1990 in *Employment Division v Smith,* however, Justice Antonin Scalia, speaking for five members of the Court, announced that it would no longer use the compelling state interest standard. A state need not have a compelling interest in the situation where a neutral generally applicable law burdens religious practices.[75] Indeed, Scalia contended that the compelling interest test never had any relevance beyond the context of challenges to the denial of unemployment

---

[71]*Sherbert v Verner,* 375 US 398 (1963).
[72]*Wisconsin v Yoder,* 406 US 205 (1972).
[73]*United States v Lee,* 455 US 252 (1982).
[74]*Goldman v Weinberger,* 475 US 503 (1986).
[75]There were six justices in the majority but only four other justices agreed with Scalia's new approach. O'Connor wrote a concurring opinion defending the compelling interest test. *Employment Division, Department of Human Resources of Oregon v Smith,* 494 US 872 (1990).

compensation.[76] Thus, the Court ruled that Oregon could apply its criminal law against the use of controlled substances to Native Americans who used peyote as part of their religious rituals. Two years later, however, the Court made clear that it would continue to apply the compelling interest test to laws that are not neutral but instead target religious conduct when the justices unanimously invalidated ordinances forbidding animal sacrifice. The city had enacted the ordinances only after Santerians, who use animal sacrifice in their religious ceremonies, moved into the area and opened a church.[77]

In response to the Court's rejection of the compelling interest test in *Employment Division v Smith*, Congress passed and President Bill Clinton signed the **Religious Freedom Restoration Act of 1993** (RFRA). Designed to reverse the *Smith* decision and to require the courts to use the compelling interest test, RFRA prohibited government from burdening religious practices even if the burden results from a rule of general applicability, unless it demonstrates that the burden (1) is in furtherance of a compelling governmental interest; and (2) is the least restrictive means of furthering that compelling governmental interest.[78] Asserting that it had the power to enact RFRA, Congress relied on Section 5 of the Fourteenth Amendment, which gives it the authority to enact legislation to enforce the other provisions of that Amendment. Because the due process clause of the Fourteenth Amendment incorporates all the provisions in the First Amendment, Section 5 bestows on Congress the authority to enact legislation to enforce the Free Exercise Clause.

In 1997 in *City of Boerne v Flores*, the Court invalidated RFRA. The case arose out of a Catholic parish's attempt to build a new church building. The city denied permission for the project because the existing church was covered by the city's historical preservation program. The Archbishop of San Antonio brought suit in federal court claiming that denial of the permit infringed on free exercise rights that were protected by RFRA. By a vote of six to three, the Court held that Congress's power under Section 5 of the Fourteenth Amendment authorized it to enact laws that are remedial and preventive but it cannot change the meaning of constitutional provisions. Writing for the majority, Justice Anthony Kennedy contended that Congress could not prevent states from action that the Supreme Court has held to be constitutional. RFRA constituted, according to the majority, a violation of principles of separation of powers—Congress was trying to tell the judiciary how to interpret the Constitution—and federalism—Congress was trying to require the states to show that they had a compelling state interest to justify any legislation that burdens religious practices.[79] The dissenters argued that RFRA only appeared to change the meaning of the Free Exercise Clause if one accepted the Supreme Court's interpretation in *Employment Services v Smith*, and they took the opportunity to reiterate their support for the compelling state interest test.[80]

---

[76]Those cases were, in addition to *Sherbert v Vernor, Thomas v Indiana Employment Security Review Board*, 450 US 707 (1981); and *Hobbie v Unemployment Appeals Commission of Florida*, 480 US 136 (1987).
[77]*Church of Lukumi Babalu Aye v City of Hialeah*, 508 US 520 (1993).
[78]Religious Freedom Restoration Act of 1993, 107 Stat. 1488.
[79]*City of Boerne v Flores*, 521 US 507 (1997).
[80]The dissenters in *City of Boerne v Flores* were Breyer, O'Connor, and Souter.

Disappointed supporters of RFRA, including Utah Republican Senator Orrin Hatch and Massachusetts Democratic Senator Edward Kennedy, countered the Supreme Court's decision with a proposal for the **Religious Liberty Protection Act.** Signed into law in September 2000, the Act builds on Congress's powers to regulate interstate commerce and to spend for the general welfare. The law specifies that a government will lose federal funds for a program if it substantially burdens a person's religious exercise unless the government can demonstrate that the burden furthers a compelling governmental interest and is the least restrictive means of achieving that compelling interest. Passage of the Religious Liberty Protection Act virtually guarantees more constitutional challenges to policies that burden religious practices.[81]

Freedom of Speech
or abridging the freedom of speech,

The rights of speech, press, assembly, and petition together provide a guarantee of freedom of expression. Such rights are recognized as essential to a democratic form of government—the free exchange of ideas is necessary if individuals are to be able to participate in governing. Freedom of expression may also be crucial to individual self-fulfillment as it may not be possible for human beings to fulfill their potential or to achieve happiness without the ability to acquire information, learn, express their views, disagree, develop their beliefs, and attempt to discover the truth.[82]

Since 1925 when the Court applied freedom of expression to the states, it has elevated freedom of expression to a preferred position, treating it as a fundamental right because of its importance to the democratic process.[83] Consequently, the Court has drawn lines between expression that is protected and that which is unprotected. Protected expression bears some connection to public affairs and thus to a democratic form of government. The Court has noted, for example, "Not all speech is of equal First Amendment concern." Political speech about matters of public concern is "at the heart of the First Amendment's protection."[84] Such speech is so important that "in public debate our own citizens must tolerate insulting, and even outrageous, speech in order to provide adequate breathing space to the freedoms protected by the First Amendment."[85]

On the other hand, speech that has no relation to public affairs, has no role in a search for truth, or political speech that is harmful or dangerous is left outside the protection of the First Amendment and therefore may be regulated,

---

[81]Jeremy Learning, "Senators Told New Religious-Protection Act Is Needed and Constitutional," *The Freedom Forum OnLine,* June 25, 1998. Available: http://www.freeddomforum.org/religion.
[82]See, generally, John Stuart Mill, *On Liberty* (New York: W. W. Norton, 1975), 3–106. Mill published *On Liberty* in 1859.
[83]The Court held that freedom of speech and of the press are fundamental rights that apply to the states through the due process clause of the Fourteenth Amendment to the states in *Gitlow v New York,* 268 US 652 (1925). The Court signaled the beginning of the preferred freedoms doctrine in the Carolene Products footnote in 1938 (*United States v Carolene Products Co.,* 304 US 144 (1938)) and explicitly designated freedom of expression a preferred freedom in the 1940s. See, for example, *Thomas v Collins,* 323 US 516 (1945).
[84]*Dun & Bradstreet v Greenmoss Builders,* 472 US 749 (1985).
[85]*Boos v Barry,* 485 US 312 (1988).

possibly even prohibited. In one of its many attempts to ascertain just what kind of expression does not enjoy the protection of the First Amendment the Court asserted,

> There are certain well-defined and narrowly limited classes of speech, the prevention and punishment of which have never been thought to raise any Constitutional problem. These include the lewd and obscene, the profane, the libelous, and the insulting or "fighting" words—those which by their very utterance inflict injury or tend to incite an immediate breach of the peace. It has been well observed that such utterances are no essential part of any exposition of ideas, and are of such slight social value as a step to the truth that any benefit that may be derived from them is clearly outweighed by the social interest in order and morality.[86]

Identifying unprotected categories of expression, however, is only the beginning of the matter, for the Court must determine just what expression fits into each category. For example, after entering the area of **obscenity** in 1957,[87] the justices spent sixteen years trying to define it, finally settling on the following in the case of *Miller v California* in 1973. A work may be considered obscene, provided (1) the average person, applying contemporary standards of the community in which the court sits, finds that the work, taken as a whole, appeals to a prurient interest in sex. Because of the differences in community standards, it is possible for a book, a movie, or record album to be legally obscene in one state or city but not in another. The Court has never defined prurient interest in sex although it has made clear that a work that appeals to a normal interest in sex or that merely promotes "lust" cannot be declared obscene; (2) the work depicts in a patently offensive way sexual conduct specifically defined by the law or by decisions of the courts; and (3) the work, taken as a whole, lacks serious literary, artistic, political, or scientific value.[88] Three justices—Brennan, Marshall, and Stevens—subsequently concluded that the Court's attempts to define obscenity were futile as it would be impossible to develop a definition without endangering protected speech and miring the Court in a "case-by-case determination of obscenity." Their solution to the problem was to let adults see or read whatever they wish and to permit only narrowly drawn statutes designed to prevent pornography from being forced on people or made available to minors.[89]

The Court's failure to develop a precise definition of obscenity was at the center of the justices' difficulties in determining what materials were obscene and therefore outside of the protection of the First Amendment. Important exceptions to the rule that nonobscene sexually explicit expression is protected include regulations on materials that are either produced by or directed at children. Thus, in 1982 the Court upheld a New York statute that prohibited the

---

[86]*Chaplinsky v New Hampshire*, 315 US 568 (1942).
[87]*Roth v United States*, 354 US 476.
[88]*Miller v California*, 415 US 15 (1973).
[89]*Miller v California*, 413 US 15 (1973); *Paris Adult Theatre I v Slaton*, 413 US 49 (1973). Justice Stevens argued for some latitude for civil regulations that would treat panderers of obscenity as public nuisances and would find acceptable some time, place, and manner regulations for the sale and distribution of pornography. *Young v American Mini Theatres*, 427 US 50 (1976).

distribution of material depicting a sexual performance by a child under the age of sixteen, noting that the standard provided by *Miller v California* for determining what is obscene is not satisfactory in the context of child pornography, in large part because the state has a strong interest in protecting children from exploitation and in prosecuting those who produce such materials. Moreover, because the production of child pornography is motivated by economic objectives it is not fully protected by the First Amendment. Accordingly, even though the material that the statute prohibited was not legally obscene, it was nevertheless, outside the protection of the First Amendment.[90] In 2002, however, the Court held that material that conveys the impression of depicting children engaging in sexually explicit conduct but is actually "virtual child pornography," which is produced either with youthful adults or with computer-generated images of children, is protected by the First Amendment.[91]

Fighting words constitutes a second category that lies outside the protection of the First Amendment. Since 1942 when the Court first proclaimed that fighting words are not protected, the justices have limited the category so severely so as to virtually eliminate it. The Court, for example, has maintained that fighting words are limited to those that "have a direct tendency to cause acts of violence by the person to whom, individually, the remarks are addressed"—words that are merely abusive, harsh, or insulting are not sufficient and therefore remain protected.[92] Moreover, the fighting words exception "requires an even narrower application in cases involving words addressed to a police officer, because a properly trained officer may reasonably be expected to exercise a higher degree of restraint 'than the average citizen, and thus be less likely to respond belligerently to fighting words.'"[93] Nonetheless, the Court has reaffirmed that fighting words—those that "provoke immediate violence"—are not protected by the First Amendment. In fact, the Court has emphasized that "words that create an immediate panic"—apparently another way of referring to fighting words—are not entitled to constitutional protection.[94]

In the 1990s, cities, colleges, and universities began to attempt to protect individuals from rising incidents of **hate speech**—verbal assaults based on race, religion, sex, or sexual orientation—by devising hate speech codes that made certain fighting words punishable.[95] Several teenagers were charged for violating the St. Paul Bias-Motivated Crime Ordinance after they made a cross out of chair legs and burned it in the backyard of an African American family. The ordinance provided in part that,

> Whoever places on public or private property a symbol, object, appellation, characterization or graffiti, including, but not limited to, a burning cross or Nazi swastika, which one knows or has reasonable grounds to know arouses anger,

---

[90]*New York v Ferber*, 458 U.S. 747 (1982).
[91]*Ashcroft v Free Speech Coalition*, ____ US ____ (2002).
[92]*Cohen v California*, 403 US 15 (1971); *Gooding v Wilson*, 405 US 518 (1972).
[93]Justice Powell concurring in *Lewis v City of New Orleans*, 415 US 180 (1974), as quoted approvingly by Justice Brennan in the opinion of the Court in *Houston v Hill*, 482 US 451 (1987).
[94]*NAACP v Clairborne Hardware*, 458 US 886 (1982).
[95]Calvin R. Massey, "Hate Speech, Cultural Diversity, and the Foundational Paradigms of Free Expression," *UCLA Law Review* 40 (1992): 155–197.

alarm or resentment in others on the basis of race, color, creed, religion or gender commits disorderly conduct and shall be guilty of a misdemeanor.

The Supreme Court of Minnesota construed the ordinance to reach only expressions that constitute fighting words. The United States Supreme Court, however, invalidated the ordinance. Although all the members of the Court agreed that the ordinance was unconstitutional, they disagreed over the reason. Justice Scalia, who wrote the opinion for himself and four others, held that even though the ordinance made only fighting words punishable, it was unconstitutional because it applied only to the type of fighting words that "insult, or provoke violence, on the basis of race, color, creed, religion, or gender," and did not apply, for example, to "[t]hose who wish to use 'fighting words' in connection with other ideas—to express hostility, for example, on the basis of political affiliation, union membership, or homosexuality."[96] According to Scalia, the ordinance was a **content-based regulation**—forbidden by the First Amendment—insofar as it made expression punishable based on the substance of the message it conveyed. The four justices who concurred in the judgment argued that the ordinance was unconstitutionally overbroad.

An apparent flaw in Scalia's reasoning is that it is inconsistent with previous cases in which the Court has held that fighting words are not protected by the First Amendment. Because such expression is not protected, it may be regulated and whether the regulation is content-based on not would be irrelevant. To reconcile his rationale with the principle that fighting words are not protected Scalia contended that what the Court meant when it said that certain categories of expression are "not within the area of constitutionally protected speech" was that "these areas of speech can, consistently with the First Amendment, be regulated because of their constitutionally proscribable content, not that they are categories of speech entirely invisible to the Constitution."[97] Therefore, fighting words may not be made punishable with a content-based regulation.

Although the Court has also designated **libelous speech** as an unprotected category, it has issued some constitutional rules that protect people who engage in such expression under a variety of circumstances. For example, in 1964 in *New York Times v Sullivan*, the Court announced the rule that plaintiffs who are public officials cannot prevail in a libel action unless they can demonstrate that the statement was made with "actual malice," that is, with knowledge that it was false or with reckless disregard for whether it was false or not.[98] Emphasizing that the new standard was necessary because of "a profound national commitment to the principle that debate on public issues should be uninhibited, robust, and wide-open,"[99] the Court expanded First Amendment protection to the media by making it considerably more difficult for public officials to win libel actions. Subsequently, the Court held that not only public officials but also public figures must comply with the *New York Times* standard.[100]

---

[96]*R.A.V. v City of St. Paul, Minnesota*, 505 US 377 (1992).
[97]*Ibid.*
[98]*New York Times v Sullivan*, 376 US 254 (1964).
[99]*Ibid.*
[100]*Curtis Publishing Company v Butts*, 388 US 139 (1967); *Associated Press v Walker*, 388 US 130 (1967).

Then in 1971, the Court shifted ground, announcing that the *New York Times* standard is triggered not so much by whether plaintiff is a public figure but rather whether the allegedly defamatory publication concerns a matter of public or general interest.[101] In so doing, the Court extended further First Amendment protection to the media—it would be extremely difficult for any individual mentioned in a story that had public interest to prevail in a libel action. Only three years later, however, the Court withdrew that protection when it repudiated that standard and held by a vote of five to four that states may define the appropriate standard of liability for a publisher or broadcaster of a defamatory falsehood of a private individual.[102]

In subsequent decisions regarding libel, the Court has held that the First Amendment precludes public figures from recovering damages for the tort of intentional infliction of emotional distress caused by the publication of an offensive parody of an advertisement. Thus, the head of the Moral Majority, Jerry Falwell, could not recover damages from *Hustler* Magazine for its parody of an advertisement for Campari Liqueur in which Falwell talked about his "first time"—an incestuous sexual encounter with his mother in an outhouse.[103] That decision serves to protect political cartoonists and satirists from being subjected to damage awards without any showing that their work falsely and with actual malice defamed its subject. Finally, in 1991 in the case involving prominent psychoanalyst Jeffrey Masson's libel action against journalist Janet Malcolm and the *New Yorker,* the Court rejected the argument that any alteration of a quotation beyond correction of grammar or syntax equates with actual malice under the *New York Times* standard. But the justices held that if the alteration gives a different meaning to the statement than the one conveyed by the speaker in a way that makes the statement defamatory, the alteration of quotations may be tantamount to actual malice.[104]

Seditious speech—advocating the use of force as a political tactic or as a means to overthrow the government—is a fourth category of expression that is outside the protection of the First Amendment. Since 1919, the Supreme Court has addressed the issue of when speech that is critical of the government becomes sufficiently dangerous or crosses over into conduct to justify punishment.[105] In 1951, in *Dennis v United States*, the Court sustained the application of the Smith Act, a federal statute making it illegal to advocate the violent overthrow of the government, to the leaders of the Communist Party of the United States, even though there was no evidence that they actually urged people to commit specific acts of violence.[106] Although it has never been expressly overruled, *Dennis* has been fatally undermined by subsequent rulings in which the Court has made it clear that the Smith Act can be applied only to individuals who incite imminent lawless action. Seditious incitement, if narrowly defined

---

[101]*Rosenbloom v Metromedia, Inc.,* 403 US 29 (1971).
[102]*Gertz v Welch,* 418 US 323 (1974).
[103]*Hustler Magazine v Falwell,* 485 US 46 (1988).
[104]*Masson v New Yorker Magazine Inc.,* 501 US 496 (1991).
[105]See, for example, *Schenck v United States,* 249 US 47 (1919); *Abrams v United States,* 250 US 616 (1919); *Gitlow v New York,* 268 US 652 (1925); *DeJonge v Oregon,* 229 US 353 (1937); *Thomas v Collins,* 323 US 516 (1945); *Dennis v United States,* 341 US 494 (1951); *Brandenburg v Ohio,* 395 US 444 (1969).
[106]*Dennis v United States,* 341 US 494 (1951).

by statute and narrowly applied by the courts, is another exception to the protection of the First Amendment. Most importantly, the First Amendment protects the abstract advocacy of violence and prohibits government from making it a crime or punishing persons for what they advocate, except "where such advocacy is directed to inciting or producing imminent lawless action and is likely to incite or produce such action."[107]

In the realm of protected speech, the Court has taken the position that freedom of expression is a fundamental right. Thus, when the government infringes on that right, it bears a heavy burden of demonstrating that its action serves a compelling interest that cannot be achieved by any other less restrictive means. Although the Court generally subjects regulations of protected expression to such an exacting standard of strict scrutiny, it has also articulated more specific guidelines to determine the constitutionality of regulations. Those guidelines are summarized in Table 7-4.

We now turn to several areas of freedom of expression that occupy a prominent place in the free speech doctrine and raise difficult questions about the extent and limits of the protections offered by the First Amendment. **Symbolic speech** combines elements of both speech and action. When the Court has been called on to determine the constitutionality of regulations on such expression, it has sought to balance the protection of symbolic speech with the government's interest in preventing harmful conduct. In so doing, the central question for the Court has been whether the regulation suppresses the communicative aspect of the expression or simply regulates the conduct. Thus, the Court upheld a federal law prohibiting the destruction of draft registration cards on the grounds that the law served a legitimate governmental interest in administering national conscription effectively and was not intended to infringe the free speech rights of antiwar protesters.[108] Similarly, the Court upheld a National Park Service regulation prohibiting overnight sleeping on the Mall and in Lafayette Park even though it interfered with demonstrators' ability to convey their message about homelessness because the regulation was not directed at expression but rather at the destructive effects that camping would have on the area.[109] In contrast, a majority of the justices held that the suspension of two high school students who wore black armbands to protest the Vietnam War violated their First Amendment rights because the school authorities intended to suppress the message of the protest rather than prevent disruptive conduct.[110]

In 1989 and 1990, the Court invalidated state and federal statutes prohibiting flag desecration. In the first case, by a vote of five to four, the justices held Texas's conviction of a demonstrator who burned the flag as part of a protest against the policies of the Reagan Administration violated the First Amendment. Justice Brennan, speaking for the Court, emphasized the expressive elements of the flag burning. There was no evidence that the expression threatened a disturbance of the peace and the flag desecration statute's protection

---

[107]*Yates v United States*, 354 US 298 (1957); *Brandenburg v Ohio*, 395 US 444 (1969).
[108]*United States v O'Brien*, 391 US 367 (1968).
[109]*Clark v Community for Creative Non-Violence*, 468 US 288 (1984).
[110]*Tinker v Des Moines School District*, 391 US 367 (1968).

Table 7-4 Guidelines for Determining Constitutionality of Regulations on Expression

Name	Guideline and Example	Cases
Prior restraint	Approval, in the form of a license or permit, required before publication. Or prohibition, in the form of an injunction against a speech or publication. The Court regards prior restraint as the most objectionable, almost always unconstitutional restriction on speech—there is a "heavy presumption against its constitutionality."	*Nebraska Press Association v Stuart*, 427 US 539 (1976) *New York Times v United States*, 403 US 713 (1971) *United States v CBS Inc. v Davis*, 510 US 1315 (1994) *Snepp v United States*, 444 US 507 (1980)
Vagueness	Laws that restrict expression must be drawn with sufficient precision to give fair notice of what is prohibited. *Example:* Prohibition on indecent Internet transmissions would be "void for vagueness."	*Reno v American Civil Liberties Union*, 521 US 844 (1997) *National Endowment for Arts v Finley*, 524 US 569 (1998)
Overbreadth	Laws that restrict expression must be narrowly drawn to meet the government's needs. A statute is fatally overbroad if it restricts constitutionally protected speech as well as unprotected speech. *Example:* Prohibition on interrupting a police officer would be fatally overbroad.	*NAACP v Button*, 371 US 415 (1963) *Board of Airport Commissioners v Jews for Jesus*, 482 US 569 (1987) *Houston v Hill*, 482 US 451 (1987) *Forsythe County v Nationalist Movement*, 505 US 123 (1992) *Ashcroft v Free Speech Coalition*, _____ US _____ (2002)
Least restrictive means	In regulating the content of expression, government must use the least restrictive means possible for achieving its goal. *Example:* If a state wants to protect the public from unscrupulous lawyers, it may not do so by forbidding attorneys to advertise—that would not be the least restrictive means for achieving the state's purpose.	*Bates v State Bar of Arizona*, 433 US 450 (1977) *Boos v Barry*, 485 US 312 (1988)

Name	Guideline and Example	Cases
Content discrimination	A regulation that discriminates on the basis of viewpoint or that forbids all discussion on a particular topic is presumptive invalid. *Examples:* A law prohibiting posting any signs that discuss racial discrimination on telephones poles; denial of parade permits to Democrats but not Republicans.	*R.A.V. v City of St. Paul, Minnesota,* 505 US 377 (1992) *Turner Broadcasting Systems v FCC,* 512 US 622 (1994) *Smith v Collin,* 436 US 953 (1978) *Republican Party of Minnesota v White,* ___ US___ (2002)
Time, place, and manner doctrine	Government may regulate expression to limit harmful incidental effects but such regulation must meet the following requirements: 1. It must be neutral concerning the content of expression and must be applied evenhandedly. 2. It must leave open ample alternative channels for communication of the information. 3. It must be narrowly tailored to serve a significant governmental interest. Time, place, and manner doctrine assumes that distinctions can be drawn between the message of speech and its medium—substance and form. *Examples:* Regulations on noise, litter, obstruction of traffic; rules concerning conditions under which groups may solicit funds.	*Consolidated Edison Co. v Public Service Commission of New York,* 447 US 530 (1980) (Blackmun's criticism of the rule) *Clark v Community for Creative Non-Violence,* 468 US 288 (1984) *Frisby v Schultz,* 487 US 474 (1988) *City of Renton v Playtime Theaters, Inc.,* 475 US 41 (1986) *Madsen v Women's Health Center,* 512 US 753 (1994)

of the flag as a symbol was improperly directed at the communicative message involved in the flag burning.[111] President Bush greeted the decision with a call for a constitutional amendment. Congress responded by passing a law making it a crime to burn or deface the flag whatever one's purpose or intent. The president allowed the bill to become law without his signature, insisting that a constitutional amendment was preferable. The law was promptly tested. Two federal judges, relying on the 1989 decision, declared the law unconstitutional. Thus, in the second case—again by a five-to-four vote—the Supreme Court declared the federal law unconstitutional. Justice Brennan, who spoke for the majority, noted that "Congress cast the Flag Protection Act in somewhat broader terms than the Texas statute . . . , the Act still suffers from the same fundamental flaw: it suppresses expression out of concern for its likely communicative impact." The government's interest was related to the suppression of free expression and concerned with the content of such expression, and was consequently "foreign to the First Amendment."[112] President Bush called for a constitutional amendment and Congress introduced one that provided the following: "The Congress and the states shall have power to prohibit the physical desecration of the flag of the United States." The House of Representatives failed, however, to muster the necessary two-thirds vote, as did the Senate a few weeks later. The Republican Congress introduced similar amendments regularly beginning in 1995. In 1997 and again in 1999 the House passed a proposed amendment by more than the required two-thirds margin. The Senate failed to vote on the measure in 1997, however, and in 1999 a poll of the one hundred senators showed that the amendment had sixty-five supporters—two short of the necessary two-thirds.

Traditionally, the Court relegated **commercial speech** to a special category of expression that received less protection than other types of protected speech. In 1942, the Court ruled that commercial advertising was not protected by the First Amendment.[113] In the 1970s, however, the Court began to extend greater protection to commercial speech. Thus, in 1976 the Court invalidated a state law prohibiting the advertisement of prescription drug prices, reasoning that such advertisements relayed important information to consumers.[114] The Court was careful to point out, however, that states may ban deceptive and misleading advertising. A year later, the justices held that state restrictions on lawyers' advertising are unconstitutional, again emphasizing the consumers' need for information.[115] Several of the Court's decisions concerning advertising by lawyers are summarized in Table 7-5.

In 1980 in *Central Hudson Gas v Public Service Commission of New York*, the Court invalidated a statute banning certain types of advertising by utilities and announced a four-part test for determining whether a regulation on com-

---

[111]*Texas v Johnson*, 488 US 884 (1989).
[112]*United States v Eichman*, 496 US 310 (1990).
[113]*Valentine v Christensen*, 316 US 52 (1942).
[114]*Virginia State Board of Pharmacy v Virginia Citizens Consumer Council*, 425 US 748 (1976).
[115]*Bates v State Bar of Arizona*, 433 US 350 (1977). A state may not prohibit professionals including doctors, lawyers, pharmacists, and accountants from advertising their prices, listing their fields of specialization, or sending targeted advertisements. See *In re RMJ*, 455 US 191 (1982); *Ibanez v Florida Board of Accountancy*, 512 US 136 (1994).

Table 7-5   Commercial Speech: Some Decisions on Advertising by Lawyers

Case	Ruling	Vote
Bates v State Bar of Arizona, 433 US 350 (1977)	Lawyers may advertise prices for routine legal services in newspaper.	6–3. Burger, Powell, Rehnquist dissented.
Ohralik v Ohio State Bar, 436 US 447 (1978)	Bar associations may sanction face-to-face solicitation.	8–0. Marshall concurred in the judgment, Rehnquist concurred in the judgment. Brennan did not participate.
In re Primus, 436 US 412 (1978)	Mail solicitations, not for financial gain, to express political beliefs may not be disciplined.	8–1. Rehnquist dissented.
Shapero v Kentucky Bar Association, 486 US 466 (1988)	State may not categorically bar lawyers from generating business by mailing truthful, nondeceptive letters to potential clients known to be facing particular legal problems.	6–3. Rehnquist, O'Connor, and Scalia dissented.
Florida Bar v Went for It, Inc., 515 US 618 (1995)	Upheld prohibition on personal injury lawyers sending targeted direct-mail solicitations to accident victims and their relatives within thirty days of the accident or injury.	5–4. Stevens, Souter, Ginsburg, Kennedy dissented.

mercial speech violates the First Amendment. First, is the activity lawful and is the expression misleading? Second, is the governmental interest in the regulation substantial? Third, does the regulation directly advance the governmental interest? Finally, is there a less restrictive means of advancing the government's interest? The four-part test reflects the Court's primary concern with the informational function of advertising and the emphasis it has placed on the interests of the audience. Thus, the issue that has informed the Court's decisions has been whether commercial messages accurately inform the public.

The Court continued to emphasize the same concerns in 1999 when it applied the *Central Hudson* test in a challenge to a section of the Federal Communications Act of 1934 prohibiting broadcast advertising of lotteries and casino gambling. The law exempted advertisements for state-operated casinos and lotteries and Native American tribal-owned and operated casinos, but not advertisements for gaming at privately owned for-profit casinos even in areas where such activity is legal. The Court found that the restrictions on advertising were unconstitutional. The advertisements were about legal activities and were not misleading, and although the ban may have advanced a substantial governmental interest in reducing the social costs of gambling, the law had so many exemptions and inconsistencies that it could not be effective and there-fore failed the third part of the test.[116] Similarly, in 2002 the Court held that provisions in the Food and Drug Administration Modernization Act of 1997, which placed restrictions on the solicitation and advertisement of "com-pounded drugs,"[117] was unconstitutional. Again using the *Central Hudson* test, the five-member majority found that although there was clearly a governmen-tal interest in the restriction on advertising compounded drugs—to make such custom-made drugs available to those who need them while protecting integrity of the government's drug approval process as well as the health of the public—the government had not shown that there were no other means of achieving those interests that would not impose on freedom of speech.[118]

The thrust of the commercial speech cases is that commercial speech does not enjoy the same level of protection as other types of protected speech. Still, governments bear the burden of showing that the regulation advances a substan-tial governmental interest that cannot be accomplished by any method that would not impose restrictions on the expression. Some members of the Court—most enthusiastically, Justice Thomas—would like to give commercial speech the full protection of the First Amendment. He argued, for example, in the 2002 case that the *Central Hudson* test should not be applied to restrictions on commercial speech when the result of those restrictions is to keep "would-be recipients of the speech in the dark."[119] In January 2003 the Court agreed to hear an important commercial speech case in which Nike had been sued under a California law for making false and misleading statements about working conditions in its overseas factories. An important issue in the case is the definition of commercial speech and whether it extends to expression that is not advertising in its traditional sense. If the Court decides that Nike's statements do not constitute commercial speech, it will almost certainly find that the First Amendment protects them.[120]

Just as the Burger Court began to expand First Amendment protection for commercial speech in the 1970s, it also increased the protection of **corporate speech** in the political process. In 1978, the Court invalidated a Massachu-setts law that prohibited business corporations from spending corporate funds to influence votes on referendum proposals.[121] Subsequently, the jus-tices held that public utilities may include statements about public issues in the bills they mail to customers.[122] In 1986, the justices held that nonprofit corporations whose purpose is advocacy on public issues have a First Amend-ment right to make independent expenditures in political campaigns.[123] In

---

[116]*Greater New Orleans Broadcasting Association v United States*, 527 US 123 (1999).

[117]Compounded drugs are mixed by a doctor or pharmacist to create a custom-made drug. The law provided that such drugs would be exempt from the requirements for approval by the Food and Drug Administration if they were not advertised.

[118]*Thompson v Western States Medical Center*, ____ US ____ (2002).

[119]*Ibid.*, quoting *Liquormart v Rhode Island*, 517 US 484, 523 (1996).

[120]*Nike v Kasky*, No. 02-575.

[121]*First National Bank of Boston v Bellotti*, 435 US 765 (1978).

[122]*Consolidated Edison v Public Service Commission*, 447 US 530 (1980); see also *Pacific Gas & Electric Co. v Public Utilities Commission of California*, 475 US 1 (1986) ruling that a state agency could not require a utility to include as an insert with its bills a statement from a consumer advocacy group responding to statements the utility company had made in its previous bill inserts.

[123]*FEC v Massachusetts Citizens for Life*, 479 US 238 (1986).

March 2003 the justices heard a challenge to a federal ban, in place since 1990, that prohibited corporations from giving contributions to candidates in federal elections. The specific issue is whether the ban can be applied to nonprofit advocacy organizations that are organized as corporations. Opponents of the ban argued that it should be the nature of the organization rather than the mere fact that it is a corporation that determines whether the ban on contributions should apply, as many organizations pose no threat of corrupting the political process.[124]

Like corporate speech, **campaign finance reform** raises serious questions about the extent to which the First Amendment allows the electoral process to be influenced by enormous amounts of money. The Federal Election Campaign Act of 1971 as amended in 1974 in the wake of Watergate contained a number of provisions limiting campaign contributions. In a complicated ruling in 1976 in *Buckley v Valeo*, the Court invalidated several provisions of that law.[125] The law's major provisions and the Court's disposition of them are presented in Table 7-6.

The most controversial aspect of *Buckley* was the distinction that the Court made between **contributions** to candidates, which may be limited, and **expenditures**, which are an important form of political speech and, therefore, may not be limited. Consequently, the amounts that individuals and groups may spend to help candidates, so long as the expenditures are "independent" of the candidate and the candidate's campaign committee, are unlimited. In subsequent decisions the Court has adhered to this distinction. For example, the justices invalidated the Presidential Election Campaign Fund Act's limitation on independent expenditures by political committees.[126] In two subsequent decisions the Court held that independent expenditures by political parties are not contributions and, therefore, cannot be limited but that a party's "coordinated expenditures" may be restricted because they are not truly independent and restricting them may "minimize circumvention of contribution limits."[127] The distinction between contributions and expenditures is widely blamed for the flood of **"soft money"** to political parties that is used to aid candidates and "issue ads" that are, in reality, barely disguised campaign ads. Although there was immense popular support for major campaign finance reform in the final years of the twentieth century, prospects for major change seemed dim in light of *Buckley* and its progeny. It appeared that any attempt to limit expenditures were doomed because they would be challenged and invalidated on First Amendment grounds regardless of the detrimental effect that the flood of money was having on the electoral process.

In the fall of 1999 it appeared that the Court might let stand a decision by a federal court of appeals holding that the Missouri campaign finance law,

---

[124]*FEC v Beaumont*, No. 02-403. See, Linda Greenhouse, "Justices Hear Arguments on Campaign Finance," *The New York Times*, March 26, 2003. Available: http://www.nytimes.com/2003/03/26/politics/26SCOT.html.
[125]*Buckley v Valeo*, 424 US 1 (1976).
[126]*FEC v National Conservative Political Action Committee*, 470 US 480 (1985).
[127]*Colorado Republican Federal Campaign Committee v Federal Election Commission*, 518 U. S. 604 (1996); *FEC v Colorado Republican Federal Campaign Committee*, 533 US 431 (2001).

Table 7-6 Key Provisions in the Federal Election Campaign Act of 1971

Provision	Disposition in Buckley v Valeo (1976)	Reason
Limited contributions by individuals and groups to $1,000 each and by political committees to $5,000 each for any single candidate in any one election, with an annual limit of $25,000 on any individual contribution	Upheld	Serves governmental interest in safeguarding the integrity of the electoral process without directly impinging on First Amendment rights
Limited independent spending by an individual or a group "relative to a clearly identified candidate" to $1,000 each per election	Invalidated	Restriction on political expression violated First Amendment
Set limits, which vary with the office, on personal contributions by both the candidate himself and his family toward his campaign	Upheld	Serves governmental interest in safeguarding the integrity of the electoral process without directly impinging on First Amendment rights
Established a ceiling on overall primary and general election expenditures by a candidate in any one election according to the office sought	Invalidated	Restriction on political expression violated First Amendment
Created an eight-member commission to oversee enforcement of the regulations: two to be appointed by the president, two by the president pro tempore of the Senate, and two by the Speaker of the House, all to be confirmed by both Houses of Congress, and the Secretary of the Senate and Clerk of the House to be ex officio members	Invalidated	Violation of the Appointments Clause—only the president may nominate such officers
Required political committees to keep detailed contribution and expenditure records, publicly disclosing the identity of the contributors and the nature of the expenditures above a certain level	Upheld	Serves governmental interest in safeguarding the integrity of the electoral process without directly impinging on First Amendment rights
Amended the Internal Revenue Code to provide for some financing of primary and general election campaigns from public funds: Major party candidates were to receive "full" funding, and "minor" and "new" party candidates were to receive a reduced proportion of funding (the funding to be on a dollar-matching basis)	Upheld	Congress's power to spend under the General Welfare Clause. Candidate must agree to expenditure ceiling as a condition for receiving funding.

Source (left-hand column): Craig R. Ducat, *Constitutional Interpretation: Rights of the Individual*, Vol. II, 7th ed. (Belmont, CA: West Wadsworth/Thomson Learning, 2000), 941–942.

which set a $1,000 cap (the same amount set by the federal law) on contributions was unconstitutional because the amount was too low and the state had not demonstrated that problems resulted from large contributions. By a vote of six to three, however, the justices overturned the lower court. As a result, states may impose a $1,000 limit or, if they choose, a lower cap, so long as it is not so low "as to render political association ineffective, drive the sound of a candidate's voice below the level of notice, and render contributions pointless."[128] In short, the majority reaffirmed the principle that political contributions are not protected speech. Although the case did not require the justices to consider modifying or overruling *Buckley,* several of them discussed the question of whether that case should continue to control campaign finance rules. The dissenters—Kennedy, Thomas, and Scalia—argued that *Buckley* should be overruled. Although these three justices want fewer limits on contributions, the other justices criticized *Buckley* for the rigidity with which it condemns limits on expenditures. Justice Breyer suggested that the Court should allow Congress ample room to work out the difficult issues of campaign finance. Various regulations, for example, limits on soft money, Breyer noted, could be upheld within the framework of *Buckley.* Another possibility, he said, would be to reinterpret *Buckley* to make the distinction between contributions and expenditures less absolute, "particularly in respect to independently wealthy candidates, whose expenditures might be considered contributions to their own campaigns."[129] Breyer also contended that if *Buckley* proves to be inflexible, the Constitution might require the Court to reconsider it.

On November 6, 2002, the Bipartisan Campaign Reform Act, more commonly known as McCain-Feingold, went into effect with sweeping new campaign finance rules. Among the most prominent and controversial reforms of the new law are a prohibition on "soft money" and a ban on "issue advertising." With the passage of the law, a variety of individuals and groups, including but not limited to conservative interest groups, immediately filed actions challenging it on constitutional grounds. To facilitate the resolution of the anticipated challenges to the law, its sponsors provided that such challenges will be heard by a special three-judge federal district court in Washington, D.C. and then the Supreme Court will be required to hear the appeal. As of this writing the three-judge district court had heard a challenge but had not yet issued a decision.

Freedom of the Press
or of the press;

Freedom of the press, like freedom of speech, is a fundamental right and serves essentially the same functions—it is crucial to a democratic form of government and to individual self-fulfillment. The Framers of the First Amendment may have given the press its own separate clause to affirm the fundamentally important role of a free press in a free society. The press must be free of government

---

[128]*Nixon v Shrink Missouri Government PAC,* 528 US 377 (2000).
[129]*Ibid.*

control not only so that it may report abuses of power by government officials but also so that the people can receive news and exchange information and opinions about public affairs. Freedom of the press, even more than freedom of speech, is intended to function as a check on the powers of government by alerting the public when other rights are threatened. Accordingly, some legal scholars as well as several justices have argued that the press is entitled to special constitutional protection. Justice Potter Stewart, for example, emphasizing the special role of the press argued that to treat the Press Clause as a guarantee of the same freedom of expression as the Speech Clause renders the former a "constitutional redundancy" and gives "insufficient weight to the institutional autonomy of the press that it was the purpose of the Constitution to guarantee."[130] Chief Justice Burger presented the opposing view when he declared:

> Those interpreting the Press Clause as extending protection only to, or creating a special role for, the "institutional press" must either (a) assert such an intention on the part of the Framers for which no supporting evidence is available; (b) argue that events after 1791 somehow operated to "constitutionalize" this interpretation; or (c) candidly acknowledging the absence of historical support, suggest that the intent of the Framers is not important today.[131]

Today "the press," which includes print and electronic media, comprises powerful business organizations that operate for a profit. Thus, in the contemporary context freedom of the press operates to protect the media conglomerate.

A good place to begin the discussion of freedom of the press is with **prior restraint** and censorship—something that was foremost in the minds of the Framers of the First Amendment. In the late 1760s, William Blackstone wrote in his *Commentaries on the Laws of England* that "The liberty of the press is indeed essential to the nature of a free state; but this consists in laying no previous restraint upon publications and not in freedom from censure for criminal matter when published."[132]

In 1931 in *Near v Minnesota*, the Supreme Court took issue with that, noting that immunity from previous restraints could not be all that the First Amendment secures. Nevertheless, *Near* made clear that hostility to prior restraint is at the core of the First Amendment by invalidating a state law that permitted a judge to enjoin the future publication of a newspaper on finding that it was "obscene, lewd, and lascivious" or "malicious, scandalous, and defamatory."[133] Writing the opinion for the majority in *Near*, Chief Justice Charles Evans Hughes noted that the prohibition on previous restraint has certain exceptions: the government might prevent publication of information that con-

---

[130]Potter Stewart, "Or of the Press," *Hastings Law Journal* 26 (1975): 631. As quoted in Gerald Gunther, *Constitutional Law*, 11th ed. (Mineola, NY: Foundation Press, 1985), 1418.
[131]Burger's concurring opinion in *First National Bank of Boston v Bellotti*, 435 US 765 (1978).
[132]*Blackstone's Commentaries on the Laws of England*, as quoted in *Near v Minnesota*, 283 US 697 (1932).
[133]*Near v Minnesota.*

stitutes a threat to the nation's security during war, enjoin publications that are obscene, and prohibit expression that incites violence.

Forty years later, the Court lifted the injunction against publication of the "Pentagon Papers," the classified, seven-thousand-page study of the process of United States' decision making on Vietnam, noting that the government had not met the heavy burden of proving the need for a prior restraint.[134] The strong presumption against prior restraints is also illustrated by the Court's decision in 1976 invalidating a state court order prohibiting the publication or broadcasting of an accused mass murderer's statements prior to his trial.[135]

The Court upheld a prior restraint, however, against a high school student newspaper, reasoning that educators have some authority over school-sponsored publications. Justice Byron White, writing for the six-member majority, proclaimed, "[E]ducators do not offend the First Amendment by exercising editorial control over the style and content of student speech in school-sponsored expressive activities so long as their actions are reasonably related to legitimate pedagogical concerns."[136]

A second major issue concerning freedom of the press is a journalist's right to maintain the confidentiality of his or her sources when the government—usually in the interest of law enforcement—demands such information. Journalists have argued that freedom of the press entails special immunity for governmental inquiries. The Court has held that the First Amendment does not provide such immunity. In 1976, the justices held that journalists could not refuse to answer questions before a grand jury about their stories on the manufacture of hashish and the Black Panthers. Writing for the five-member majority, Justice White maintained that a reporter's responsibility to a grand jury was the same as that of any other individual. The four dissenters pointed out that the ability to protect the confidentiality of sources is essential to newsgathering. Therefore, a showing of a compelling interest should be required before a grand jury could obtain privileged information from reporters.[137] Two years later, a five-member majority held that newspapers do not enjoy special protection against police searches of its offices, rejecting the argument that such searches would interfere with the newspapers' sources and would lead to self-censorship. The dissenters contended that the search placed an unacceptable burden on freedom of the press insofar as it threatened physical disruption of newspaper operation and forced disclosure of confidential sources essential to newsgathering.[138] Congress responded by prohibiting the use of searching newspaper offices where neither the organization nor its members were suspected of wrongdoing. A majority of five justices also held that the First Amendment does not protect a newspaper from litigation if an editor, on the grounds that the public has a right to the information, violates a report's promise of confidentiality to a source.[139]

---

[134]*New York Times Co. v United States*, 403 US 713 (1971).
[135]*Nebraska Press Association v Stuart*, 427 US 539 (1976).
[136]*Hazelwood School District v Kuhlmeier*, 484 US 260 (1988).
[137]*Branzburg v Hayes*, 408 US 665 (1972).
[138]*Zurcher v Stanford Daily*, 436 US 547 (1978).
[139]*Cohen v Cowles Media Co.*, 501 US 663 (1991).

A third issue that is central to freedom of the press is the right of access to places such as jails and courtrooms to obtain newsworthy information, and more generally, the right of access to information. In the 1970s, the Court upheld state and federal rules prohibiting press interviews with individual prisoners. Justice Stewart, who subsequently advanced the argument that the Press Clause bestows special rights on the print and broadcast media, wrote majority opinions in which he reasoned that the rules did not violate the First Amendment because they did not "deny the press access to sources of information available to members of the general public"; the rules did not discriminate against the press but merely eliminated a special privilege.[140] Then in 1978, Stewart cast the decisive vote to affirm that the press has a right to access that is equal to the public's—a sheriff could not allow monthly tours of the jail to the public but deny access to the press.[141]

In 1979, the Court upheld an order barring the press and the public from a pretrial hearing on suppression of evidence in a murder case. The trial judge, the prosecutor, and the defendant had all agreed to close the hearing to ensure a fair trial.[142] A year later, however, in *Richmond Newspapers v Virginia* the Court held that the trial of a criminal case must be open to the public.[143] By a vote of seven to one, the Court ruled that "[a]bsent an overriding interest" the trial judge could not close a criminal trial even with the consent of the prosecutor and the defendant. Since *Richmond,* the Court has been more positive about the value of open judicial proceedings, extending the right of access to preliminary hearings, for example.[144] The justices also refused to allow a trial judge in a rape and murder case to close the jury selection process to protect the privacy of potential jurors.[145]

Although the claim of a right of access is usually made by journalists in pursuit of information, it has also been made by individuals seeking access to newspapers. Florida enacted a "right to reply" statute that required any newspaper attacking a candidate for public office to make equal space available to the candidate to counter the criticism. The underlying rationale for the law was that by guaranteeing that a wide variety of views could reach the public, the government would promote the democratic function of freedom of expression. Supporters of the law pointed out that the press had "become noncompetitive and enormously powerful and influential in its capacity to manipulate popular opinion and change the course of events." Further, in many cities the only newspaper is owned by the same interest that owns a television station and radio station so that only one perspective is conveyed to the public. But the Court rejected that argument and invalidated the law on the grounds that it violated the First Amendment by intruding on the function of editors.[146]

A fourth issue concerning freedom of the press is whether the First Amendment protects the media from laws that single out the press for taxes or regu-

---

[140]*Pell v Procunier,* 417 US 817 (1974); *Saxbe v Washington Post,* 417 US 843 (1974).
[141]*Houchins v KQED,* 438 US 1 (1978).
[142]*Gannett v DePasquale,* 443 US 368 (1979).
[143]*Richmond Newspapers v Virginia,* 448 US 555 (1980).
[144]*Globe Newspaper Co. v Superior Court,* 457 US 596 (1982).
[145]*Press Enterprise Co. v Superior Court,* 464 US 501 (1984).
[146]*Miami Herald Publishing Co. v Tornillo,* 418 US 241 (1974).

lations. The Court has adopted the position that although government may subject the media to generally applicable economic regulations it may not create a special tax that applies only to newspapers even if it does so with no hostile or discriminatory purpose. Thus, in *Minneapolis Star v Minnesota Commissioner of Revenue* the Court found that a "use tax" on the cost of paper and ink consumed in the production of a publication ran afoul of the First Amendment.[147] In a similar vein, the Court struck down an Arkansas sales tax that applied to general-interest magazines but exempted newspapers and magazines published in the state, as well as religious, professional, trade, and sport magazines.[148] Subsequently, however, the Court sustained a general gross receipt sales tax in Arkansas that applied to cable television but exempted newspapers, magazines, and satellite television. In her opinion for the majority, Justice O'Connor contended, "[D]ifferential taxation, of speakers, even members of the press, does not implicate the First Amendment unless the tax is directed at, or presents the danger of suppressing, particular ideas."[149]

Important questions also arise in the context of the regulation of the broadcast media. Congress created the Federal Communications Commission (FCC) to implement its policies regarding the broadcast industry. The FCC issues broadcast licenses and mandates that radio and television stations follow strict codes of operation. The federal government maintains that the differences between the print media and the broadcast media justify extensive regulation of the latter. The finite number of broadcast frequencies means that the airwaves can accommodate only a limited number of broadcasters. Moreover, radio and television can easily intrude on the privacy of the home. Thus, the government argues that it needs to regulate the broadcast industry to make sure that it operates effectively, fairly, and consistently with the interest of viewers and listeners.

In 1969 in *Red Lion Broadcasting v FCC*, the Court sustained the FCC's **"fairness doctrine,"** which requires broadcasters to allow reply time to individuals subjected to personal attacks or political editorials.[150] Although the FCC repealed the fairness doctrine in 1987, *Red Lion* established that the differences between broadcast and print journalism merit different treatment under the First Amendment. In short, government may subject the broadcast media to more extensive regulation than the print media without running afoul of the First Amendment. The Court, for example, upheld the fairness doctrine whereas it invalidated the nearly identical "right to reply" law that applied to newspapers.[151] Additionally, emphasizing that radio and television intrude into the home, a five-member majority held that the FCC could regulate indecent language on the public airwaves when there is a reasonable risk that children may be watching or listening.[152] Although the Court has upheld restrictions on the broadcast media that would not have been permissible if they had been imposed on the print media, it has not completely abandoned the broadcast industry to

---

[147]*Minneapolis Star & Tribune v Minnesota Commissioner of Revenue*, 460 US 575 (1983).
[148]*Austin v Michigan Chamber of Commerce*, 494 US 652 (1990); *Arkansas Writer's Project v Ragland*, 481 US 221 (1987).
[149]*Leathers v Medlock*, 499 US 439 (1991).
[150]*Red Lion Broadcasting v Federal Communications Commission*, 395 US 367 (1969).
[151]*Miami Herald Publishing Co. v Tornillo*, 418 US 241 (1974).
[152]*Federal Communications Commission v Pacifica Foundation*, 438 US 726 (1978).

legislative and administrative control. In *FCC v League of Women Voters of California*, the Court invalidated a federal statute that prohibited "editorializing" by noncommercial educational broadcasting stations that receive funds from the Corporation for Public Broadcasting. Writing for the majority, Justice Brennan noted the special concerns of the broadcast media that warrant regulation but announced that regulation of the content of broadcasting would be upheld "only when we [are] satisfied that the restriction is narrowly tailored to further a substantial governmental interest, such as ensuring adequate and balanced coverage of public issues." Restriction on editorial opinion, Brennan noted, lies "at the heart of First Amendment protection."[153] Three of the four dissenters argued that recipients of federal funds should be subject to reasonable regulations that are designed to prevent government subsidies for editorials to which many taxpayers might object.

The introduction of newer electronic means of communication, including cable television and the Internet, raises more questions about the extent to which regulation may be justified for media that do not have the same physical limitations of radio and broadcast television. In a challenge to the "must-carry" provisions of the Cable Television Act of 1992, which required cable television systems to devote a portion of their channels to local and public outlets, the justices agreed that cable television systems are entitled to more First Amendment protection than broadcast television and radio but less than the print media. To justify that approach, the Court pointed to the fact that cable television is not constrained by the limited frequencies available in the electromagnetic spectrum, noting that "soon there may be no practical limitation on the number of speakers who may use the cable medium. Nor is there any danger of physical interference between two cable speakers attempting to share the same channel."[154] Five of the justices voted to send the case back to the lower court for consideration in light of the new standard. The case came before the Court again in 1996 and a five-member majority upheld the law, finding that the government had met the requirement of showing that the law furthered an important governmental interest without unnecessarily burdening free speech.[155]

Congress's initial attempt to regulate the Internet with the **Communications Decency Act of 1996** (CDA) prohibited online communication of material that is indecent or obscene to anyone under the age of eighteen.[156] The Court found only the ban on obscene materials acceptable. The prohibition on indecent transmissions was so vague and overbroad that it would extend to protected expression received by adults as well as children.[157] The Court's initial

---

[153]*FCC v League of Women Voters of California*, 468 US 364 (1984).

[154]*Turner Broadcasting System v FCC*, 512 US 622 (1994).

[155]Lee Epstein and Thomas G. Walker, *Constitutional Law for a Changing America: Rights, Liberties, and Justice* (Washington, DC: CQ Press, 1998), 349. Also in 1996, the Court upheld a provision of the Cable Television Act of 1992 that permits cable operators to refuse to allow indecent programming by operators of leased channels, struck down the provision permitting cable operators to ban indecent programming by public access channels, and struck down a provision requiring that if a cable operator allows such programming that it be blocked and unscrambled only through special devices. *Denver Area Educational Telecommunications Consortium v FCC*, 518 US 727 (1996).

[156]Congress defined indecent communication as "any message that, in context, depicts or describes, in terms patently offensive as measured by contemporary community standards, sexual or excretory activities or organs."

[157]*Reno v American Civil Liberties Union*, 521 US 844(1997).

attempt to grapple with the myriad of issues involving freedom of expression in cyberspace made clear that the Internet, in part because it "provides relatively unlimited, low-cost capacity for communications of all kinds"[158] will merit more First Amendment protection than the broadcast media. After the Court found the CDA to be inconsistent with the First Amendment, Congress made another attempt to protect children from exposure to sexually explicit materials on the Internet in the **Child Online Protection Act of 1998** (COPA). The COPA was narrower than its predecessor insofar as it proscribed only material displayed on the World Wide Web and covered only material made for commercial purposes. Moreover, in contrast to CDA's prohibition on indecent materials, COPA restricted only "material that is harmful to minors." To render that restriction sufficiently narrow and precise, Congress specified that whether or not a transmission contained "material that is harmful to minors" would be determined using the "contemporary community standards" of the test set forth in *Miller v California*. By a vote of eight to one, but with only a plurality opinion and three concurring opinions, the Court found that the statute's reliance on "community standards" to determine whether material is harmful to minors does not by itself render the statute overbroad. The Court, however, remanded the case to the Court of Appeals, leaving the lower court to resolve the other questions about overbreadth.[159] On remand, the Court of Appeals found that both the "harmful to minors" provision and the "commercial purposes" provision to be overbroad.[160]

Freedom of Assembly
or the right of the people peaceably to assemble,

The guarantee of the right of assembly, like the other guarantees in the First Amendment, is not absolute. Moreover, almost all exercises of the right to assemble peacefully involve conduct as well as speech and as the Court has often noted, the First Amendment does not "afford the same kind of freedom" for speech that includes conduct as it does for pure speech.[161] Just as it has with protected speech, the Court has developed a number of guidelines for determining when regulations violate the right to assemble.

First, the extent of government's power to regulate assembly depends on where the assembly takes place. In 1939 in *Hague v Congress of Industrial Organizations,* the Court established the **public forum doctrine** when it held that government may not prohibit speech-related activities such as demonstrations, leafleting, and speaking in public areas traditionally provided for speech.[162] The justices developed the concept of a public forum further in the ensuing years particularly during the 1960s as large numbers of individuals ventured outside traditional political channels in their pursuit of social change. The Court uses doctrine to determine whether an area where expressive activity

---

[158]*Ibid.*
[159]*Ashcroft v ACLU,* ____ US ____ (2002).
[160]*ACLU v Ashcroft,* US Court of Appeals, Third Circuit, March 6, 2003.
[161]*Cox v Louisiana,* 379 US 536 (1965).
[162]*Hague v Congress of Industrial Organizations,* 307 US 496 (1939).

takes place is a public forum. If the Court determines that it is, the expression will still be subject to regulation as to **time, place, and manner** in order to alleviate harmful incidental effects of the expression including noise, congestion, and disorder. There cannot be any regulation of the content of the expression, however, nor may the regulation substantially restrict the communication.

In 1983, the Court identified three types of public forum. First, traditional public forums are those established by historical practice. Access to all speakers, regardless of the content of their message, is required in such areas. Moreover, controversial speech in traditional public forums cannot be restricted by a hostile audience—a "heckler's veto"—unless police have reason to believe that disorder is imminent.[163] The areas that the Court has designated traditional public forums include streets and sidewalks adjoining public buildings,[164] courthouses,[165] schools,[166] parks,[167] and residential neighborhoods.[168] Government may restrict speech in such areas only if it can show that the regulation is narrowly drawn to achieve a compelling interest. Additionally, content-neutral time, place, and manner regulations are permissible, but they must leave open ample alternative channels of communication. Using this guideline, the Court held that the law forbidding display in the Supreme Court building or on its grounds of flags or banners was unconstitutional as applied to sidewalks surrounding the building. In so doing, the justices rejected the government's contention that since judges, unlike legislators and executives, are supposed to decide cases on the basis only of the record before them, Congress had a compelling reason for outlawing conduct that might create the appearance that judges are subject to outside influences.[169] The Court also invalidated a ban on political signs within five hundred feet of an embassy.[170] But it sustained an ordinance forbidding picketing "before or about any residence" construing it to apply only to picketing against a single residence. The justices reasoned that the government had an interest in protecting residential privacy.[171]

The second type of public forum is one that is created by government designation. Although not constitutionally required to do so, the government may open up areas "for use by the public as a place for expressive activity." Such limited public forums include public theaters,[172] public fair grounds,[173] and school facilities that are opened generally to student group activities.[174] Although the government may close such forums, so long as it allows them to remain open, it may only regulate as to time, place, and manner. Thus, the Court held that once a state university opens its facilities to student groups, it may not exclude religious groups without a compelling reason.[175]

---

[163]*Gregory v City of Chicago*, 394 US 111 (1969).
[164]*Edwards v South Carolina*, 372 US 229 (1963).
[165]*United States v Grace*, 461 US 171 (1983).
[166]*Police Department of Chicago v Mosley*, 408 US 92 (1972).
[167]*Niemotko v Maryland*, 340 US 268 (1951).
[168]*Frisby v Schultz*, 487 US 474 (1988).
[169]*United States v Grace*, 461 US 171 (1983).
[170]*Boos v Barry*, 485 US 312 (1988).
[171]*Frisby v Schultz*, 487 US 474 (1988).
[172]*Southeastern Promotions v Conrad*, 420 US 546 (1975).
[173]*Heffron v International Society for Krishna Consciousness*, 452 US 640 (1981).
[174]*Widmar v Vincent*, 454 US 263 (1981).
[175]*Ibid.*

The third type of forum is a **nonpublic forum** or "off-limits" public property. Such areas are substantially less protected than the first two and the government may even regulate expression there based on its content by showing that the regulation is reasonably related to the property's function. Areas in this category include the grounds of jails,[176] military bases,[177] home mail boxes,[178] and public utility poles.[179]

In 1972 and again in 1976, the justices ruled that the First Amendment does not require owners of private shopping centers to provide access to people who want to distribute handbills or engage in picketing on matters unrelated to the shopping center's operations.[180] The Court's refusal to recognize shopping centers as a public forum raised an important question of how meaningful the right to communicate on public streets and in parks will be if the audience is far away in shopping centers where such expression is prohibited.

Freedom of association is not mentioned in the First Amendment or anywhere in the Constitution. Nevertheless there is a constitutionally protected right to associate, derived from the right to assemble as well as from freedom of speech and petition.[181] It means at least that the government may not prohibit individuals from forming or joining organizations nor may it interfere in the internal activities of private associations to the extent that they are engaged in activities protected by the First Amendment. During the McCarthy era, the Court upheld punishments for membership and activities in proscribed organizations that the government deemed to be subversive,[182] but it eventually moved toward a more protective position, rejected the notion of "guilt by association," and focused on individual rather than group action and responsibility.[183]

In the late 1950s and early 1960s, the Court established that groups not engaged in illegal activities are protected by the right of association. In 1958, the Court upheld the right of the National Association for the Advancement of Colored People (NAACP) to refuse to turn over their membership lists to Alabama officials who were seeking such lists under the state's foreign corporation registration law. Justice John M. Harlan, writing for a unanimous Court, noted that privacy in groups espousing dissident ideas is "indispensable to preservation of freedom of association."[184] In 1963, the Court invalidated a Virginia attack on the NAACP's use of agents to solicit parents of school children to file desegregation lawsuits, noting that this method of accomplishing political goals is a "mode of expression and association" that the First Amendment protects.[185] Using the same line of reasoning almost twenty years later, the Court held that an Ohio campaign law could not be applied to require the Socialist Workers' Party to report the names and addresses of campaign

---

[176]*Adderley v Florida*, 385 US 39 (1966).
[177]*Greer v Spock*, 424 US 828 (1976).
[178]*United States Postal Service v Council of Greenburgh Civic Association*, 453 US 114 (1981).
[179]*City Council of Los Angeles v Taxpayers for Vincent*, 466 US 789 (1984).
[180]*Lloyd Corporation v Tanner*, 407 US 551 (1972); *Hudgens v NLRB*, 424 US 507 (1976).
[181]*Healy v James*, 408 US 169 (1972).
[182]See, for example, *Dennis v United States*, 341 US 494 (1951); *Barenblatt v United States*, 360 US 109 (1959).
[183]See, for example, *Yates v United States*, 354 US 298 (1957); *DeGregory v New Hampshire*, 383 US 825 (1966).
[184]*NAACP v Alabama*, 357 US 449 (1958).
[185]*NAACP v Button*, 371 US 415 (1963).

contributors, or even the names and addresses of those with whom it did business: "The First Amendment prohibits a state from compelling disclosures by a minor party that will subject those persons identified to the reasonable probability of threats, harassment, or reprisals. Such disclosures would infringe the First Amendment rights of the party and its members and supporters."[186]

In the 1980s, the Court heard several cases in which organizations invoked their right to associate as a justification for excluding or discriminating on the basis of race or sex. In 1984, for example, the Court rejected a law firm's contention that it was not required to comply with prohibition on sex discrimination in employment in Title VII of the Civil Rights Act of 1964, because of its constitutional right of association.[187] The justices also sustained the application of the Minnesota Human Rights Act to compel the Minnesota Junior Chamber of Commerce (Jaycees) to admit women as members. The Jaycees argued that the law interfered with their constitutionally protected right to associate with individuals of their own choice for the purpose of expressing their views. Justice Brennan, writing for the majority, conceded, "There can be no clearer example of an intrusion into the internal structure or affairs of an association than a regulation that forces the group to accept members it does not desire." But the right of association of a large, nonselective group like the Jaycees, Brennan noted, could be overridden by a compelling governmental interest and Minnesota's interest in prohibiting sex discrimination was just such an interest. As such, it was sufficient to override the associational interests of the male Jaycee members.[188] The Court has implied that antidiscrimination laws might not override the associational rights of groups organized for religious, cultural, or social purposes. Small organizations that have an expressive component are more likely to prevail if they claim the right to exclude people than large, nonexclusive groups that are engaged primarily in commercial activities. In 1995, a unanimous Court upheld the right of the South Boston Allied War Veterans Council, sponsor of Boston's annual Saint Patrick's Day parade, to exclude the Irish-American Gay, Lesbian, and Bisexual Group (GLIB) from marching in the parade. The Court noted that the First Amendment protects a private group from being forced to be associated with messages with which it disapproves.[189]

In an important and controversial decision in 2000, the justices held by a vote of five to four that applying a state public accommodations law, which prohibited discrimination on the basis of sexual orientation, to require the Boy Scouts to admit a gay man violated the Boy Scouts' First Amendment right of expressive association.[190] In his opinion for the majority Chief Justice Rehnquist explained that the Boy Scouts is a group that engages in expressive association and the presence of gay members would burden the expression of the group's views. Defending its policy of expelling gay members and refusing to admit new members who are openly gay, the Boy Scouts claimed that the val-

---

[186]*Brown v Socialist Workers*, 459 US 87 (1983).
[187]*Hishon v King & Spalding*, 467 US 69 (1984).
[188]*Roberts v United States Jaycees*, 468 US 609 (1984). See also, *Board of Directors of Rotary International v Rotary Club of Duarte*, 481 US 537 (1987).
[189]*Hurley v Irish-American Gay, Lesbian and Bisexual Group of Boston*, 515 US 557 (1995).
[190]*Boy Scouts of America v Dale* 530 US 640 (2000).

ues embodied in the Scout Oath, namely to be "morally straight" and "clean," demonstrated that gay conduct is inconsistent with the organization's values. The majority deferred to that claim and noted that even though the Boy Scouts is not an association that exists solely for the purpose of disseminating a message, it nevertheless engages in expressive activity and has the right not to have that activity disrupted. The dissenters objected that the Boy Scouts had by no means shown that its ability to express its views would be burdened by gay members. Indeed, Justice Stevens suggested that linking a belief that homosexuality is wrong with the Scouts' expressive goals was merely a pretext. The Scouts' policy, he admonished, was "the product of a habitual way of thinking about strangers" for which the Court had created "a constitutional shield," which would only exacerbate the harms of intolerance.

A troubling question arises out of the conflict between the constitutional right to engage in political activity, to join political organizations, and to speak freely, on the one hand, and the right of the government to regulate the conditions of public employment on the other. Justice Oliver Wendell Holmes, Jr., as a member of the Supreme Judicial Court of Massachusetts, dismissing the First Amendment objection of a policeman who was fired after making public remarks criticizing the police department made the following comment:

> The petitioner may have a constitutional right to talk politics, but he has no constitutional right to be a policeman. There are few employments for hire in which the servant does not agree to suspend his constitutional right of free speech, as well as of idleness, by the implied terms of his contract. The servant cannot complain, as he takes the employment on the terms which are offered him.[191]

The Supreme Court followed that approach, which is known as the **right-privilege doctrine,** until the early 1950s when it began to replace it with the **unconstitutional conditions doctrine,** which held that what government cannot do directly, it cannot do indirectly by offering a trade, such as a job.[192] Thus, the Court has remarked, "[I]t is clearly established that a State may not discharge an employee on a basis that infringes an employee's constitutionally protected interest in freedom of speech."[193]

Although individuals who are unwilling to take an oath to support the Constitution may be disqualified from public employment, neither the national nor state governments may make it a condition of employment that employees abandon their constitutional rights of freedom of speech or of association. The Court has invalidated all but the most narrowly drawn loyalty oath requirements, including those that bring within their net individuals who are members of organizations that have unlawful purposes but who themselves do not participate in those unlawful activities or share the unlawful purposes.[194]

Still, the First Amendment does not limit the government's authority as an employer to the same extent as it does its power as a sovereign: "The government

---

[191]*McAuliffe v Mayor of New Bedford,* 155 Mass 216 (1892).
[192]See William W. Van Alstyne, "The Demise of the Right-Privilege Distinction in Constitutional Law," *Harvard Law Review* 83 (1968): 1415.
[193]*Rankin v McPherson,* 483 US 378 (1987).
[194]*Elfbrandt v Russell,* 384 US 11 (1966); *Connell v Higginbotham,* 403 US 207 (1971).

cannot restrict the speech of the public at large just in the name of efficiency. But where the government is employing someone for the very purpose of effectively achieving its goals, such restrictions may well be appropriate."[195] Although public employees do not relinquish the right to speak about matters of public interest, they may nevertheless be dismissed for insubordination or for disrupting their offices when they write or speak about matters of merely personal interest that relate to their jobs. As the Court has noted, "First Amendment protections extend to public employees only for speech on matters of public concern, and then only to employees who serve no confidential, policy making, or public contact role."[196] Employees who occupy key policy roles may be dismissed for policy differences and for failing to support the positions of the department while pursuing their duties.

The First Amendment rights of speech and association do not protect government employees from federal and state regulations forbidding civil servants to take "an active part in the political management of political campaigns." The Court has sustained the Hatch Act against the challenge that it is overbroad and vague and interferes with the right of association, concluding that it is a reasonable measure to free employees from political pressures and to ensure that they are not coerced into political action in behalf of the party in power.[197] A state may also require certain officeholders to resign if they wish to run for other offices and may make certain officeholders ineligible for other posts until after their current term in office expires.[198]

The political patronage system had a long tradition, but the Court began to dismantle it in 1976 when it held that non-civil-service employees may not be fired solely for reasons of patronage. A five-to-four majority held that only policymaking officials may be dismissed because of their party affiliation.[199] In 1980, the Court rejected a Democratic county public defender's claim that he had the right to fire Republican assistant public defenders, noting that whether a public employee may be fired for patronage reasons depends on "whether the hiring authority can demonstrate that party affiliation is an appropriate requirement for the effective performance of the public office involved."[200] In 1990, by a vote of five to four, the Court extended the limitation on patronage further, holding that transfers, promotions, and hiring may not be conditioned on party affiliation.[201]

In 1996, the Court extended its antipatronage doctrine to cover independent contractors who do business with governments, holding that they could not be dropped or denied contracts for political disloyalty or expressing their opinions on public issues.[202]

---

[195] *Waters v Churchill*, 511 US 661 (1994).
[196] *Connick v Myers*, 461 US 138 (1983).
[197] *United Public Workers v Mitchell*, 330 US 75 (1947); *Civil Service Commission v Letter Carriers*, 413 US 548 (1973); *Broadrick v Oklahoma*, 413 US 601 (1973).
[198] *Clements v Flashing*, 457 US 957 (1982).
[199] *Elrod v Burns*, 427 US 347 (1976).
[200] *Branti v Finkel*, 445 US 507 (1980).
[201] *Rutan v Republican Party of Illinois*, 497 US 62 (1990).
[202] *Board of County Commissioners v Umbehr*, 518 US 668 (1996). See also *O'Hare Truck Service Inc. v City of Northlake*, 518 US 712 (1996).

The right to associate also protects the right to form a political party, vote for candidates of one's choice in a general election, and register and vote in a party primary. Additionally, it includes the right to be able to vote for independent candidates, and to make that right effective, independent candidates have a right to get onto ballots. State laws regulating the way independent candidates can get on a ballot relate not only to the candidates' rights but also to the rights of association of those who would vote for them. Thus, cases relating to ballot access often involve the same questions as voting rights cases, since "the rights of voters and the rights of candidates do not lend themselves to neat separation."[203]

Freedom to Petition Government
and to petition the Government for a redress of grievances.

The Court has paid far less attention to the **Petition Clause** than to the other provisions in the First Amendment. In fact, the Court has often treated it as though it is subsumed under the rights of assembly and association. The right to petition may take the form of direct petitioning of legislators or executive officials or circulating petitions to be signed and delivered to policymaking as evidence of popular support for the proposed change in policy. In 1836, the House of Representatives curbed the right to petition with the "gag rule" under which it refused to consider any of the many antislavery petitions it was receiving. The "gag rule" remained in effect for eight years.

Lobbying is an important means of "petitioning the government for the redress of grievances." Lobbying, like other activities that involve both speech and conduct, is subject to some regulation. Congress and most states require associations that spend considerable sums of money to influence legislation to register, keep records, and make them available to the public. These laws have been upheld, provided "lobbying" is narrowly defined. Although lobbying is protected by the First Amendment, Congress is not required to subsidize it. A nonprofit group may lose its tax-exempt status and contributions to the group may no longer be deductible if "a substantial part of the activities" is "carrying on propaganda, otherwise attempting to influence legislation."[204]

Litigation is also an important means of "petitioning Government for a redress of grievances." The Petition Clause provided the basis for the Court's decision in 1963 holding that states could not prohibit the NAACP from soliciting plaintiffs for cases challenging segregation.[205] The Court maintains that the "right of access to the courts is an aspect of the First Amendment right to petition the Government for redress of grievances," and although governments may regulate to prevent "baseless litigation," they may not halt the prosecution of lawsuits unless these suits lack any reasonable basis in fact or law.[206]

---

[203]*Bullock v Carter*, 405 US 134 (1972).
[204]*Regan v Taxation with Representation*, 461 US 540 (1983).
[205]*NAACP v Button*, 371 US 415 (1963).
[206]*Bill Johnson's Restaurants v NLRB*, 461 US 731 (1983).

AMENDMENT II: THE RIGHT TO BEAR ARMS

> A well regulated Militia, being necessary to the security of a free State, the Right of the people to keep and bear Arms, shall not be infringed.

The Supreme Court has unequivocally ruled that the Second Amendment does not protect an individual's right to possess a firearm. The Court has never departed from its initial interpretation of the Amendment as a guarantee of the right of states to equip and maintain a militia.[207] Justice James McReynolds explained in 1939 that although Article I, Section 8, of the Constitution gave Congress the power to provide for organizing, arming, and disciplining the militia, it reserved certain responsibilities to the states: the appointment of officers and training of the militia. The Second Amendment was designed to prohibit Congress from interfering with the ability of the states to carry out those functions. In the late eighteenth century, militias typically included all free able-bodied males—civilians who were expected to appear with arms if called on to do so. It was generally believed that the militia was necessary to the security of a free state because, in contrast to a standing army, the militia made it possible for ordinary citizens to participate in defending their country.[208] Adhering to that interpretation of the Amendment as a protection for states rather than individuals, the Court has held that unless defendants can show that possession of firearms in violation of a federal statute has some connection to the preservation or efficiency of a well-regulated militia, they cannot challenge a gun statute on Second Amendment grounds.[209] In 1980, the Court cited the 1939 decision with approval when it upheld federal restrictions on the possession of firearms against a due process and equal protection challenge. In a footnote, Justice Harry Blackmun commented, "These legislative restrictions on the use of firearms are neither based upon constitutionally suspect criteria, nor do they trench upon any constitutionally protected liberties."[210]

Because the Second Amendment protects the states rather than individuals against actions by Congress, it could not logically be a restriction on the power of the states to regulate the possession of firearms. In other words, the Fourteenth Amendment cannot incorporate the Second Amendment. Although the Supreme Court has not addressed this issue directly, Justice William O. Douglas, in a dissenting opinion on another matter, offered the following observation: "There is under our [Second Amendment] decisions no reason why stiff state laws governing the purchase and possession of pistols may not be enacted. There is no reason why pistols may not be barred from anyone with a police record. There is no reason why a State may not require a purchaser of a pistol to pass a psychiatric test. There is no reason why all pistols should not be barred to everyone except the police."[211] On the other hand, in a concurring

---

[207] *United States v Cruikshank*, 92 US 542 (1875).
[208] *United States v Miller*, 307 US 174 (1939).
[209] *Ibid.*
[210] *Lewis v United States*, 445 US 55, 67, note 8 (1980).
[211] *Adams v Williams*, 407 US 143 (1973).

opinion in 1997 in a case in which the Court invalidated part of a federal gun control law on Tenth Amendment grounds, Justice Thomas commented that although the parties in this case had not raised a Second Amendment claim, "perhaps, at some future date, this court will have the opportunity" to reinterpret the Second Amendment.[212]

There has been a recent surge of scholarly interest in the Second Amendment. Some academic commentators have challenged the Court's interpretation, contending that there is evidence that the Framers intended to protect not only the existence of state militias but also the right of private citizens to possess firearms. This interpretation emphasizes that the Framers feared the power of centralized government and believed the private possession of guns was an important protection against tyranny. In this view—sometimes referred to as **"an intermediary view"**—the Second Amendment may well have been designed to prevent the national government from abolishing—though not regulating—the private ownership of firearms.[213]

In May 2001 Attorney General John Ashcroft, in a letter to the chief lobbyist for the National Rifle Association, expressed "unequivocally" his belief that the Second Amendment protects the **right of individuals to own firearms.** Although Ashcroft indicated his agreement with gun-owner groups, he stopped short of endorsing the position that the Second Amendment prohibits all gun control laws. In fact, he maintained that Congress could legitimately enact gun control laws if there are compelling state interests.[214] It was unclear whether Ashcroft's letter actually signaled a reversal in the Justice Department's position or whether he was simply expressing his own opinion. A year later, however, two Justice Department briefs to the Supreme Court asserted that the Constitution protects an individual's right to own firearms.

In a decision in December 2002 that did not address the nature of the Second Amendment but rather a related issue, the justices held that federal judges may not restore gun ownership rights to convicted felons who have been deprived of those rights by the Federal Firearms Act.[215] Neither the Justice Department's brief nor Justice Thomas addressed the Second Amendment issue.[216]

AMENDMENT III: QUARTERING OF SOLDIERS

> No Soldier shall, in time of peace be quartered in any house, without the consent of the Owner, nor in time of war, but in a manner to be prescribed by law.

A nearly forgotten provision, the Third Amendment has aroused virtually no political or legal controversy. The Supreme Court has never addressed the issue of forced quartering of troops and the Amendment remains one of the

---

[212]*Printz v US,* 521 US 98 (1997).
[213]Sanford Levinson, "The Embarrassing Second Amendment," *Yale Law Journal* 99 (1989): 637.
[214]Fox Butterfield, "Broad View of Gun Rights Is Supported by Ashcroft," *The New York Times,* May 24, 2001, National Desk.
[215]*United States v Bean,* ____ US ____ (2002).
[216]Linda Greenhouse, "Supreme Court, 9–0, Rebuffs a Gun-Seeking Felon," *The New York Times,* December 11, 2002, National Desk.

provisions of the Bill of Rights that has not been incorporated into the Fourteenth Amendment.

The prohibition on the nonconsensual quartering of soldiers in private homes during peacetime was, however, of major importance to the Framers. It became part of the Bill of Rights largely in response to the presence of British troops just prior to and during the American Revolution, which was viewed as a violation of the colonists' fundamental rights as English people.

Justice Douglas included the Third Amendment when he articulated his theory that a constitutionally protected right to privacy is based on the penumbras of several provisions of the Bill of Rights.[217] Although the Court has not continued to rely on Douglas's penumbras to support a right to privacy, his argument suggested that the Third Amendment provided one of the foundations of the right to privacy.

QUESTIONS

1. What are the implications for the future of public education of the Court's approval of school vouchers?

2. In the area of the Free Exercise Clause, what do you think the prospects are for a return to the compelling state interest test? Is the majority likely to adopt such an approach?

3. How might the Court's decision in *Federal Election Commission v Beaumont* (2003) have an impact on the legal challenges to McCain-Feingold?

4. In light of *Buckley* and its progeny, as well as what you know about the different justices' positions on campaign finance regulations, how would you expect the Court to resolve the challenges to McCain-Feingold?

5. The Court established in *Miller v California,* and has since reaffirmed, that the standards for determining what is obscene are to be those of the community from which the jury comes, rather than what the jury might believe to be the standards of the nation.[218] How might this standard work as the Court faces challenges to Congress's attempts to regulate offensive communication on the Internet?

6. In 1943, the Supreme Court invalidated as overbroad a municipal ordinance that made it unlawful "for any person distributing handbills, circulars or other advertisements to ring the door bell, sound the door knocker, or otherwise summon the inmate or inmates of any residence to the door for the purpose of receiving such handbills, circulars or other advertisements they or any person with them may be distributing."[219] In light of that ruling, what might the Court do with a challenge to the Telephone Consumer Protection Act of 1991, a law that made it unlawful for anyone "to initiate any telephone call to any residential telephone line using an artificial or prerecorded voice to deliver a message without the prior express

---

[217]*Griswold v Connecticut*, 381 US 479 (1965). See page 371.
[218]*Hamling v United States*, 418 US 87 (1974).
[219]*Martin v City of Struthers*, 319 US 141 (1943).

consent of the party called, unless the call is initiated for emergency purposes or is exempted by rule or order of the [Federal Communications] Commission."[220]

7. Because of the heavy presumption against prior restraints, would the government be able to justify prohibiting publication of a magazine article with instructions for building a nuclear weapon? Consider the Court's position and the various opinions in *New York Times v United States* as well as the federal district court judge's opinion in United States v Progressive.[221]

8. In light of the Court's decision in *R.A.V. v St. Paul* (1992) as well as other free speech guidelines that we have considered in this chapter, what is the constitutional status of campus hate speech codes that make punishable expression that insults people on the basis of their race, sex, sexual orientation, or religion?

9. Do nonstudents have a right to give speeches and hand out leaflets on college and university campuses? If so, what is the constitutional basis of such a right? Does it make any difference whether a university is public or private?

10. In light of the Justice Department's shift regarding the Second Amendment, what is the likelihood that the Court will reconsider its interpretation of the Amendment in the near future? If it does address the meaning of the Amendment, is it likely to endorse the individual rights theory of the right to bear arms?

KEY TERMS

Incorporation of the Bill of Rights
"fundamental fairness" approach
total incorporation
doctrine of selective incorporation
dilution of the Bill of Rights
harmless error doctrine
adequate and independent state
  grounds
separationist approach
nonpreferentialism
Lemon Test
accommodationism
valid secular policy test
compelling state-interest–least-
  restrictive-means test
religious Freedom Restoration Act
  of 1993

Religious Liberty Protection Act
obscenity
fighting words
hate speech
content-based regulation
libelous speech
seditious speech
symbolic speech
commercial speech
corporate speech
campaign finance reform
contributions
expenditures
"soft money"
prior restraint
"fairness doctrine"

---

[220]47 USCA Sect. 227 (b)(1)(B).
[221]*United States v Progressive*, 467 F Supp 900 (W D Wis 1979).

Communications Decency
  Act of 1996
Child Online Protection Act of 1998
public forum doctrine
time, place, and manner regulation
nonpublic forum
freedom of association

right-privilege doctrine
unconstitutional conditions doctrine
Petition Clause
intermediary view of Second
  Amendment right of individuals
  to bear arms

SUGGESTIONS FOR FURTHER READING

Amar, Akhil Reed. *The Bill of Rights: Creation and Reconstruction.* New Haven, CT: Yale University Press, 1998.

Amar, Akhil Reed, and Vikram David. "Breaking Constitutional Faith: President Bush and Campaign Finance Reform." *FindLaw's Writ,* April 5, 2002. Available: http://writ.news.findlaw.com/amar/20020405.html.

Choper, Jesse H. *Securing Religious Liberty: Principles for Judicial Interpretation of the Religion Clauses.* Chicago, IL: University of Chicago Press, 1995.

Curtis, Michael Kent. *Free Speech, "The People's Darling Privilege": Struggles for Freedom of Expression in American History.* Raleigh-Durham, NC: Duke University Press, 2000.

Dean, John W. "Let the Next Fight Begin: Campaign Finance Reform Goes to Court." *FindLaw's Writ,* March 29, 2002. Available: http://writ.news.findlaw.com/dean/20020329.html.

Downs, Donald Alexander. *The New Politics of Pornography.* Chicago, IL: University of Chicago Press, 1989.

Farber, Daniel, and Suzanna Sherry. *A History of the American Constitution.* St. Paul, MN: West Publishing Co, 1990, Chapter 8.

Fish, Stanley. *There's No Such Thing as Free Speech and It's a Good Thing Too.* New York: Oxford University Press, 1994.

Godwin, Mike. *Cyber Rights: Defending Free Speech in the Digital Age.* Cambridge, MA: MIT Press, 2003.

Graber, Mark. *Transforming Free Speech: The Ambiguous Legacy of Civil Libertarianism.* Berkeley, CA: University of California Press, 1991.

Greenhouse, Linda. "Justices Hear Arguments on Campaign Finance." *The New York Times,* March 25, 2003.

Grimes, Alan P. *Democracy and the Amendments to the Constitution.* Lexington, MA: Lexington Books, 1978.

Heumann, Milton, Thomas Church, and David P. Redlawsk. *Hate Speech on Campus: Cases, Case Studies, and Commentary.* Boston, MA: Northeastern University Press, 1997.

Hilden, Julie. "The First Amendment and Campaign Finance Reform: The Fallacious Supreme Court Reasoning that Puts McCain-Feingold in Jeopardy." *FindLaw's Writ,* April 16, 2001. Available: http://writ.news.findlaw.com/hilden/20010416.html.

Levy, Leonard W. *Origins of the Bill of Rights.* New Haven, CT: Yale University Press, 1999.

Levy, Leonard W. *The Establishment Clause: Religion and the First Amendment,* 2d ed. Chapel Hill, NC: University of North Carolina Press, 1994.

MacKinnon, Catharine A. *Feminism Unmodified: Discourses on Life and Law.* Cambridge, MA: Harvard University Press, 1987.

Miller, William Lee. *Arguing about Slavery: The Great Battle in the United States Congress.* New York: Alfred A. Knopf, 1995.

Murphy, Walter F., James E. Fleming, and Sotirios Barber. *American Constitutional Interpretation.* Westbury, NY: Foundation Press, 1995, Chapter 12.

Smith, Steven D. *Foreordained Failure: The Quest for a Constitutional Principle of Religious Freedom.* New York: Oxford University Press, 1995.

Sorauf, Frank J. *The Wall of Separation.* Princeton, NJ: Princeton University Press, 1976.

Van Alstyne, William W. *First Amendment: Cases and Materials.* Westbury, NY: Foundation Press, 1991.

8

THE BILL OF RIGHTS II: PROCEDURAL BOUNDARIES

AMENDMENT IV: SEARCHES AND SEIZURES

The Reasonableness Clause

The right of the people to be secure in their persons, houses, papers, and effects, against unreasonable searches and seizures, shall not be violated.

The first clause of the Fourth Amendment demands that searches and seizures be *reasonable*. That mandate has led the Supreme Court to try to strike a balance between two competing values. Although the Court has sought to protect individuals from overzealous, intrusive governmental authorities, it has also tried to further the goals of controlling crime and punishing criminals. The results have often been less than clear; the Court has articulated general rules that are often so vague that they offer little guidance and has carved out exceptions that, some argue, render the rules useless. The Court, for example, has often explained that the "touchstone of the Fourth Amendment is reasonableness"[1] and that reasonableness is measured by examining the totality of the circumstances.[2] One critic has characterized the Court's decisions as "a vast jumble of judicial pronouncements that is not merely complex and contradictory, but often perverse."[3] We begin by explaining some general principles of the Fourth Amendment and then proceed to consider some of the specific rules (and their exceptions) that have emerged from the Supreme Court's efforts to interpret the reasonableness clause.

First, because the Fourth Amendment applies to the states through the due process clause of the Fourteenth Amendment,[4] the prohibition on unreasonable searches and seizures restricts state and local as well as federal officials. Private individuals, associations, and corporations, however, are not constrained by the Fourth Amendment unless they are operating as agents of the government.

---

[1] *Florida v Jimeno*, 500 US 248, 250 (1991).
[2] *Ohio v Robinette*, 519 US 33 (1996).
[3] Akhil Reed Amar, *The Constitution and Criminal Procedure: First Principles* (New Haven, CT: Yale University Press, 1997), 1.
[4] *Wolf v Colorado*, 338 US 25 (1949).

Thus, the railroads, acting pursuant to federal regulations in administering blood and urine tests, are limited by the Amendment.

Second, the "people" who are protected against unreasonable searches and seizures include American citizens wherever they may be and all others who are in the territory of the United States and have substantial connections with this country. Although the Court has never unequivocally declared that the Fourth Amendment protects illegal aliens, it has assumed as much.[5] The Amendment, however, does not apply to a search and seizure by U.S. agents of property owned by a nonresident alien and located in a foreign country.[6]

Third, the answer to the question of what areas are protected by the prohibition on unreasonable searches turns on the notion of a legitimate **expectation of privacy**. Thus, the Fourth Amendment offers us considerably more protection when we are in our home—whether rented or owned—even the home of a friend where we are staying[7] than it does in a car, the curb where we leave our trash,[8] open fields, or a barn.[9] The Court has often repeated the requirement that Justice John Marshall Harlan explained in a concurring opinion in 1967: one must have exhibited a subjective expectation of privacy and the expectation must "be one that society is prepared to recognize as 'reasonable.'"[10] The protection against unreasonable seizures (of persons or property) is based on slightly different interests—those of the possession of property and liberty of person.

Police Detentions and Arrests

There are three categories of encounters between the police and citizens.[11] First, an interaction may not even constitute a seizure within the meaning of the Fourth Amendment. The Court has noted, for example, that law enforcement officers do not engage in a seizure "by merely approaching an individual on the street or in another public place, by asking him if he is willing to answer some questions, by putting questions to him if the person is willing to listen, or by offering in evidence in a criminal prosecution his voluntary answers to such questions."[12] Under such circumstances, the individual may decline to answer questions; indeed, he or she may walk away. The Court has held that police officers may approach individuals at random in airport lobbies and other public places to ask them questions and to request consent to search their luggage, but they must make it clear that cooperation is purely voluntary. In 1991, the justices extended this rule to the practice whereby police officers enter a bus and request permission to search the passengers' luggage. Such a practice does not constitute a detention, the Court held, so long as the police advise the passengers that they have the right to refuse consent.[13] The heightened security at airports

---

[5]*INS v Lopez-Mendoza*, 468 US 1032 (1984).
[6]*United States v Verdugo-Urquidez*, 494 US 259 (1990).
[7]*Minnesota v Olson*, 495 US 91 (1990).
[8]*California v Greenwood*, 486 US 35 (1988).
[9]*United States v Dunn*, 480 US 294 (1987).
[10]*Katz v United States*, 389 US 347, 361 (1967).
[11]See *United States v Puglisi*, 723 F2d 779 (1984). Citizen as used here does not denote citizen of the United States but is meant only to distinguish between the police and other people they encounter in carrying out their duties.
[12]*Florida v Royer*, 460 US 491, 498 (1983).
[13]*Florida v Bostick*, 501 US 429 (1991).

in the aftermath of the events of September 11, 2001, however, have served to eliminate such limits on federal officials to search travelers and their luggage.

Second, although the Fourth Amendment is activated once a police officer detains an individual, under certain limited circumstances such detentions may be justified by **reasonable suspicion,** short of **probable cause** to arrest. To determine at what point police conduct constitutes a seizure, the Court has relied on the following: "A person is 'seized' only when by means of physical force or a show of authority, his freedom of movement is restrained."[14] The justices have elaborated that the test for a "show of authority is an objective one": not merely the subjective perception of the individual "but whether the officer's words and actions would have conveyed . . . to a reasonable person" that he was being ordered to restrict his movement.[15] The second category—limited seizure based on reasonable suspicion—constitutes a major exception to the general rule that seizures of a person require probable cause to arrest. The Court has repeatedly been faced with the task of clarifying the nature and extent of that exception.

In *Terry v Ohio*, the Court announced that individuals in public places may be detained for a limited, investigatory stop—a stop and frisk—when a "police officer observes unusual conduct [that] leads him reasonably to conclude . . . that criminal activity may be afoot" and that the individual is armed even though the officer does not have probable cause to make an arrest.[16] That decision made clear that the Fourth Amendment applies to "seizures" that do not result in arrest or prosecution. Yet at the same time, the justices carved out a major exception to the general rule that searches and seizures are reasonable only if justified by probable cause. As the Court has examined police stops and detentions under a variety of circumstances, it has begun to provide some idea of when a *"Terry* stop" is justified.

In 1981, Chief Justice Warren Burger tried to expand the "*Terry* exception" beyond the specific facts that justified a stop-and-frisk in *Terry* when he stated in a footnote: "Of course, an officer may stop and question a person if there are reasonable grounds to believe that person is wanted for *past* criminal conduct."[17] Later, the Court directly addressed the issue of whether people suspected of completed crimes as well as ongoing or pending criminal activity could be detained without probable cause. The justices held that so long as "police have a reasonable suspicion, grounded in specific and articulable facts, that a person they encounter was involved in or is wanted in connection with a completed felony, then a *Terry* stop may be made to investigate that suspicion."[18] The justices also extended the *Terry* exception by upholding investigatory stops based on an informant's tip rather than solely on the officer's own suspicions.[19] Noting difficulties in policing the border and the important government interest in preventing illegal entry of aliens, the Court approved brief stops by the

---

[14]*United States v Mendenhall*, 446 US 544 (1980).
[15]*California v Hodari D.*, 499 US 621 (1991).
[16]*Terry v Ohio*, 392 US 1, 30 (1968).
[17]*United States v Cortez*, 449 US 411, 417, note 2 (1981), emphasis added.
[18]*United States v Hensley*, 469 US 221, 228 (1985).
[19]*Adams v Williams*, 407 US 143 (1972); *Alabama v White*, 496 US 325 (1990).

Border Patrol when officers' observations lead them reasonably to suspect that a vehicle may contain illegal aliens.[20] Additionally automobiles may be stopped at fixed checkpoints for questioning of the occupants about their citizenship and immigration status.[21] The Court has also upheld brief stops at checkpoints for sobriety tests.[22] Still, it is important to be aware that such stops are exceptions to the rule that a search or seizure is unreasonable without individualized suspicion of wrongdoing. That is, as the Court held in 1981, based on the **totality of circumstances,** the detaining officers must have a particularized and objective basis for suspecting the individual of criminal activity.[23] Accordingly, stopping automobiles randomly to check drivers' licenses and vehicle registration without some reasonable suspicion that the car is being driven in violation of the laws or that occupants of the car have violated the law is prohibited.[24] Moreover, the justices have made clear that the police may not detain an individual—"even momentarily"—without some articulable objective grounds for suspecting criminal activity.[25] In 2000 the Court held that a checkpoint program whose primary purpose was to detect evidence of ordinary criminal activity—in this case, illegal drugs—violated the Fourth Amendment.[26]

In some cases the Court has found that even though the police had sufficient justification to stop and detain suspects, their treatment of those suspects was so much like a full-scale arrest that it required probable cause. For example, the police may not forcibly transport a person to the police station, detain him there, place him in an interrogation room for questioning,[27] or take his fingerprints without probable cause.[28] Another situation that the Court found to be closely akin to an arrest was one in which narcotics detectives in the Miami International Airport approached a man whom they believed fit the "drug courier profile," asked him to accompany them to a small room where they detained him while they retrieved his luggage and searched it. The justices held that the conduct of the detectives was more intrusive than necessary to carry out an investigative detention authorized by the *Terry* line of cases.[29] Writing for the majority, Justice Byron White explained that an investigative detention must be temporary and last no longer than is necessary to accomplish the purpose of the stop. Moreover, the police must employ investigative methods that are the least intrusive means reasonably available to verify or dispel the officer's suspicion.

The third category of encounter between the police and citizens is a full-scale arrest and requires probable cause. When police act without a warrant, they make the probable cause decision themselves although it may be reviewed subsequently by a court. The general rule is that an arrest requires probable cause to believe that an offense has been committed and that the person to be

---

[20]*United States v Brignoni-Ponce*, 422 US 873 (1975).
[21]*United States v Martinez-Fuerte*, 428 US 543 (1976).
[22]*Michigan Department of State Police v Sitz*, 496 US 444 (1990).
[23]*United States v Cortez*, 449 US 411, 417 (1981).
[24]*Delaware v Prouse*, 440 US 648 (1979).
[25]*Florida v Royer*, 460 US 491 (1983).
[26]*City of Indianapolis v Edmond*, 531 US 32 (2000).
[27]*Dunaway v New York*, 442 US 200 (1979).
[28]*Hayes v Florida*, 470 US 811 (1985).
[29]*Florida v Royer*, 460 US 491 (1983).

arrested committed it. Probable cause refers to the amount of evidence that would lead a reasonable person to believe that the defendant is likely to have committed a crime. Although the concept purports to be objective, it has never been clear precisely how much evidence constitutes probable cause. In 1949 the Court noted that the probabilities with which probable cause deals "are not technical; they are the factual and practical considerations of everyday life on which reasonable and prudent men, not legal technicians, act."[30] More than thirty years later, the justices' attempt to elucidate probable cause was similarly obscure: "a fluid concept—turning on the assessment of probabilities in particular factual contexts—not readily, or even usefully, reduced to a neat set of legal rules."[31] What the Court has made clear, however, is that probable cause is "more than bare suspicion" and "less than evidence which would justify conviction."[32] The police are allowed to rely on certain factors to establish probable cause including flight, furtive gestures, presence in the company of a known offender at or near the time of the offense, or false or contradictory answers to police questions.[33]

Warrantless Searches

The general rule on which the Court has relied since 1967 is that searches require warrants if they are to be consistent with the Fourth Amendment's demand for reasonableness. Construing the two clauses of the Amendment as inseparable—the warrant clause provides an explanation of the reasonableness clause—the Court has declared that it is a cardinal principle that "searches conducted outside the judicial process, without prior approval by judge or magistrate, are per se unreasonable under the Fourth Amendment—subject only to a few specifically established and well-delineated exceptions."[34] As the last phrase suggests, the Court recognizes exceptions to the general rule. Moreover, over the years the justices have amassed a voluminous catalog of exceptions that, according to some commentators, threatens to devour the rule.[35] We consider seven of the major exceptions in the following subsections.

Consent

One of the exceptions to the warrant requirement is a search conducted pursuant to consent. The consent must not be obtained through coercion or intimidation. In 1973 the Court held that explicit notice of the right to refuse was not necessary. In that case, the justices adopted the rule that voluntariness of con-

---

[30]*Brinegar v United States*, 338 US 160, 175 (1949).
[31]*Illinois v Gates*, 462 US 213, 232 (1983).
[32]*Brinegar v United States*, 338 US 160, 175 (1949).
[33]James B. Haddad, James B. Zagel, Gary L. Starkman, and William J. Bauer, *Criminal Procedure*, 3d ed. (Mineola, NY: Foundation Press, 1987), 287.
[34]*Mincey v Arizona*, 437 US 385, 389 (1978), quoting *Katz v United States*, 389 US 347, 357 (1967); *Thompson v Louisiana*, 469 US 17, 20 (1984).
[35]Craig R. Ducat, *Constitutional Interpretation: Rights of the Individual*, Vol. II, 7th ed. (Belmont, CA: Wadsworth/Thomson Learning, 1999), 665.

sent is a question to be determined from the totality of all the circumstances—knowledge of the right to refuse consent is one factor to be taken into account. The Court rejected an alternative rule—that the state has the burden of proving that an individual knows he or she has a right to refuse consent.[36] Thus, the Court held in 1991 that the search of bus passengers' suitcases was voluntary because in that situation where the police advised the passengers that they could refuse and did not take any threatening actions a reasonable person would have felt free to decline the requests.[37] More recently, the justices went further to hold that a detaining officer need not advise a detainee that he or she is "free to go" for the consent to search to be recognized as voluntary.[38] Finally, in 2002 the justices were even more explicit when they held that knowledge of the right to refuse is a factor to be taken into account in the totality of the circumstances of a search but that explicit notification that the search is voluntary is not necessary.[39]

Incident to Arrest

A search conducted incident to a valid arrest is another exception to the warrant requirement. The Court established this exception in 1950[40] without specifying limits on the extent of such searches. As a result, lower courts routinely approved searches of an entire house in which a person was arrested. In 1969 in *Chimel v California,* the justices specified that the areas that could be searched pursuant to an arrest included only the arrestee's person and those within his or her immediate control.[41] The Court justified such searches on the grounds that they protect the safety of the officer by allowing a search for weapons and they prevent the destruction of evidence. The Court, however, soon expanded the area that may be searched incident to arrest beyond the justifications underlying *Chimel.* A majority of the Court held that a container—a crumpled cigarette package—that could neither have held a weapon nor evidence of the criminal conduct for which the suspect was arrested was nevertheless within the proper scope of the search. In fact, a full search of the person was justified. Justice Rehnquist reasoned that "the authority to search the person incident to a lawful custodial arrest, while based upon the need to disarm and to discover evidence, does not depend on what a court may later decide was the probability in a particular arrest situation that weapons or evidence would in fact be found upon the person of the suspect. A custodial arrest of a suspect based on probable cause is a reasonable intrusion under the Fourth Amendment; that intrusion being lawful, a search incident to the arrest requires no additional justification."[42] Subsequently, the justices extended the scope of searches incident to arrest to passenger compartments of automobiles—including containers

---

[36]*Schneckloth v Bustamonte,* 412 US 218 (1973).
[37]*Florida v Bostick,* 510 US 429 (1991).
[38]*Ohio v Robinette,* 519 US 33 (1996).
[39]*US v Drayton,* __US __ (2002)
[40]*United States v Rabinowitz,* 339 US 56 (1950).
[41]*Chimel v California,* 395 US 752 (1969).
[42]*United States v Robinson,* 414 US 218, 235 (1973).

found there—finding that "articles inside the relatively narrow compass of the passenger compartment of an automobile are in fact generally, even if not inevitably, within 'the area into which an arrestee might reach in order to grab a weapon or evidentiary item.'"[43]

Exigent Circumstances

Searches conducted in emergencies are also considered to be reasonable in the absence of a warrant. When the police enter a person's home in "hot pursuit" of a suspect, they may search the premises because if they had to wait to obtain a warrant, evidence could be destroyed and lives could be endangered. Thus, in 1967 the Court upheld a search of all areas of the house where the suspect could have been hiding or where he might have hidden a weapon.[44] The Court has limited the "hot pursuit" exception to situations in which speed is essential. Accordingly, the police may not enter a suspect's home without a warrant in order to make a nonemergency arrest.[45] The justices, for example, rejected the state's argument that exigent circumstances justified entry into the home of a man who, apparently drunk, had driven his car off the road and walked away. Writing for the majority, Justice William Brennan noted that the facts failed to suggest any need for quick action by the police: there was no immediate or continuous pursuit of the suspect from the scene of a crime. When the police entered the house, the suspect was already inside and had abandoned his car at the scene of the accident; thus, there was no threat to the public safety. The only possible emergency was the need to determine the suspect's blood-alcohol level. But Brennan found that was not sufficient to justify entry without a warrant. In that case, the Court added a new element to the "hot pursuit" exception with the following statement: "[A]n important factor to be considered when determining whether any exigency exists is the gravity of the underlying offense for which the arrest is being made . . . application of the exigent-circumstances exception in the context of a home entry should rarely be sanctioned when there is probable cause to believe that only a minor offense, . . . has been committed."[46]

Loss of Evidence

Police may conduct a warrantless limited search to prevent the loss of evidence. This exception to the warrant requirement is closely related to the "incident to arrest" exception. It applies, however, to the situation in which the police do not make an arrest immediately even though they have probable cause to do so. Such searches are limited by their justification: they must not reach beyond what is necessary to prevent the loss or destruction of evidence. The Court upheld the scraping of a murder suspect's fingernails—"a very limited

---

[43]*New York v Belton*, 453 US 454 (1981), quoting *Chimel v California*, 395 US 752, 763 (1969).
[44]*Warden v Hayden*, 387 US 294 (1967).
[45]*Payton v New York*, 445 US 573 (1980).
[46]*Welsh v Wisconsin*, 466 US 740, 753 (1984).

search necessary to preserve the highly evanescent evidence."[47] The justices have also found that it is reasonable for the police to force an individual to submit to a blood test to ascertain alcohol level[48] but that it is unreasonable to compel a suspect to undergo surgery to remove a bullet that could be used as evidence of his participation in a robbery.[49]

Motor Vehicles

We have noted that the police may search an automobile incident to a lawful arrest of one of its occupants. Even without an arrest, however, police may search an automobile as long as they have probable cause to believe that the car contains contraband or evidence of a crime, that it is being used to commit a crime, or that its occupants have committed a crime. The Court has declared that, "a search is not unreasonable if based on facts that would justify the issuance of a warrant, even though a warrant has not actually been obtained."[50] In 1996, the justices declared that when the police stop a car with probable cause to believe there has been a traffic violation but when it is not likely that they would have done so without some additional objective, such as a search for drugs, there is no Fourth Amendment violation. Justice Antonin Scalia explained that the Court does not attempt to delve into the motivations of the police.[51]

The Court first recognized the automobile exception to the warrant requirement in 1925, reasoning that automobiles do not merit the same degree of protection against searches and seizures as houses because of their mobility: the vehicle might easily be moved out of the jurisdiction in which the warrant must be issued.[52] Subsequently, the justices expanded the exception to apply to situations where the police had impounded a car, removing its mobility. Indeed, since 1970 the Court has repeatedly noted that if police officers have probable cause to search an automobile at the scene where it was stopped, they may do so later at the station without obtaining a warrant.[53] Thus, the Court has moved away from mobility as the justification for the automobile exception to the warrant requirement. The justices have focused instead on the decreased expectation of privacy that one has in an automobile. As Justice Harry Blackmun explained, "One has a lesser expectation of privacy in a motor vehicle because its function is transportation and it seldom serves as one's residence or as the repository of personal effects. A car has little capacity for escaping public scrutiny. It travels public thoroughfares where both its occupants and its contents are in plain view."[54]

Additionally, the police may search all containers in the car. The Court has explained that "the scope of a warrantless search of an automobile . . . is not

---

[47]*Cupp v Murphy*, 412 US 291, 296 (1973).
[48]*Schmerber v California*, 384 US 757 (1966).
[49]*Winston v Lee*, 470 US 753 (1985).
[50]*United States v Ross*, 456 US 798, 809 (1982).
[51]*Whren v United States*, 517 US 806 (1996).
[52]*Carroll v United States*, 267 US 132, 154 (1925).
[53]*Chambers v Maroney*, 399 US 42; *Texas v White*, 423 US 67 (1975); *Michigan v Thomas*, 458 US 259, 261 (1982); *Florida v Meyers*, 466 US 380 (1984).
[54]*Cardwell v Lewis*, 417 US 583, 590 (1974).

defined by the nature of the container in which the contraband is secreted. Rather, it is defined by the object of the search and the places in which there is probable cause to believe that it may be found."[55] Accordingly, the police may search every part of the vehicle and its contents that might conceal what the police are looking for, including passengers' belongings.[56] Finally, the automobile exception applies to motor homes "being used on the highways, or . . . readily capable of such use." The Court pointed out that motor homes in such circumstances are "readily mobile by the turn of an ignition key" and, probably more important, have a reduced expectation of privacy because they are subject to regulations that are not applicable to a fixed dwelling.[57]

Safety

We considered the *Terry* exception earlier in the context of seizures. The exception also applies to searches: the stop-and-frisk includes a quick pat-down for weapons that may pose a danger to the officers or others. The Court has allowed safety searches to expand over the years so that they are no longer limited to a quick pat-down. For example, in 1990 the Court approved a protective sweep of a house after a suspect was arrested and, therefore, could not pose a threat to the officers. The sweep was justified, the justices reasoned, to make sure that the house did not harbor another individual who posed a danger to the arresting officers.[58] Despite the expansion of *Terry* searches, the Court has maintained some important limits. In 1993, for example, the justices held that in keeping with the purpose of a protective search—to allow the officer to pursue an investigation without fear of violence—officers must not go beyond what is necessary to determine whether the suspect is armed. In that case, a police officer stopped and frisked a man who had just left a building known for cocaine traffic. The officer did not find a weapon but felt a small lump in the suspect's jacket. After squeezing, sliding, and otherwise manipulating the lump, the officer removed it from the pocket and found that it was a small bag of cocaine. The justices reasoned that the officer's continued exploration of the pocket after he concluded that it did not contain a weapon was not related to the justification for the search.[59]

Plain View

The final exception to the warrant requirement that we will consider here allows officers who are engaged in a lawful search to seize items that are in view so long as they have probable cause to believe that those items are contraband or evidence of a crime. It is important to be aware that the plain-view exception applies only when police are already engaged in a lawful search either pursuant to a warrant or one of the other exceptions to the warrant requirement.[60] The

---

[55]*United States v Ross*, 456 US 798, 824 (1982).
[56]*Wyoming v Houghton*, 526 US 295 (1999).
[57]*California v Carney*, 471 US 386, 393 (1985).
[58]*Maryland v Buie*, 494 US 325 (1990).
[59]*Minnesota v Dickerson*, 508 US 366 (1993).
[60]*Coolidge v New Hampshire*, 403 US 443, 468 (1971).

plain-view exception also differs from the other exceptions to the warrant requirement because it actually applies to seizures rather than searches. The justification for the exception is that if an article is in plain view, the police do not engage in any invasion of privacy when they seize it.

In 1971, a four-member plurality of the Court asserted that the discovery of evidence in plain view must be inadvertent.[61] That is, if police have a warrant to search an armed robbery suspect's home for stolen money and they also expect to find weapons, a search for and discovery of weapons will be in violation of the constitutional requirement that a warrant must describe the items to be seized. Subsequently, however, the Court abandoned that limit on the plain-view exception. Justice John Paul Stevens reasoned that the requirement that evidence must be discovered inadvertently relied on assumptions about the subjective state of mind of the officers rather than on objective standards of conduct. Stevens also pointed out that the warrant clause of the Fourth Amendment and the requirement that warrantless searches be limited to the exigencies that justify such searches supply limits on searches; thus, the requirement of inadvertence is not necessary.[62]

A decision in 1987 provides an illustration of the limits of the plain-view exception. When a bullet came through the ceiling and injured a man in his apartment, the police entered the apartment above to search for the shooter, for other victims, and for weapons. Discovering expensive-looking stereo equipment in the squalid and ill-appointed apartment, the officers moved the equipment so that they could see the serial numbers. They recorded the numbers and subsequently learned that the equipment was stolen. The Court found that moving the equipment constituted a separate search that was beyond the bounds of the plain-view exception. Although the officers had reason to suspect that the stereo equipment was stolen, they needed probable cause to render a search valid.[63]

Searches by Other Authorities than the Police

Because the purpose of the Fourth Amendment is to protect the privacy and security of individuals against arbitrary invasions by governmental officials, it applies to civil as well as criminal investigations. Thus, inspections conducted by Internal Revenue agents; probation officers; fire, health, and safety inspectors; supervisors of government employees; and public school officials are limited by the prohibition on unreasonable searches and seizures. Whether such searches are reasonable, however, is determined by a standard that is different from the one to which police are held. Rather than require a warrant or probable cause for all inspections, the Court has engaged in a balancing of the individual's privacy expectations against the government's interests to determine whether searches have been reasonable in particular situations.

Because fire, health, and housing inspections are significant intrusions on the interests protected by the Fourth Amendment, the Court has held, such

---

[61]*Ibid.*, 469.
[62]*Horton v California*, 496 US 128, 139 (1990).
[63]*Arizona v Hicks*, 480 US 321 (1987).

searches may not be conducted without a warrant. Thus, in a nonemergency situation, if a property owner refuses to admit inspectors to his or her home or business, the inspectors must secure a warrant. To secure such a warrant, however, the inspectors need not show probable cause to believe that a particular dwelling contains violations. They need only show that an inspection is authorized by law, that it is based on a general administrative plan for the enforcement of the law, and that they are acting reasonably to enforce it.[64]

An important exception to that rule allows warrantless searches of businesses with a tradition of close government supervision. By engaging in such a business, the Court has reasoned, an individual implicitly agrees to submit to regulation and has a diminished expectation of privacy. Moreover, heightened governmental interests are involved. For example, emphasizing Congress's extensive and long-established power to regulate the liquor industry, the Court noted the inapplicability of the warrant requirement to situations where federal agents inspect the premises of alcoholic beverage dealers.[65] Similarly, the government has an important interest in regulating firearms and ammunitions to prevent violent crime as well as to assist the states in regulating firearms traffic within their borders. For any regulatory scheme concerning firearms to succeed, inspections are necessary. Thus, warrants are not required for inspections of the premises of dealers in firearms.[66] Subsequently, the Court has approved warrantless searches for mines[67] and automobile junkyards[68] on the same grounds. In those two cases, the justices pointed out that the exception to the warrant requirement is not limited to businesses with a long tradition of pervasive regulation. Indeed, Justice Harry Blackmun, writing for the majority in the case involving junkyards, outlined three criteria that must be met for a warrantless inspection to be judged reasonable. First, the inspection must be made pursuant to a regulatory scheme that is informed by a "substantial" government interest. Second, warrantless inspections must be necessary to the regulatory scheme. Third, the regulatory scheme must provide a constitutionally adequate substitute for a warrant—that is, the inspections must be regular both in their timing and scope.[69]

Although the Fourth Amendment applies to searches conducted by school authorities just as it does to administrative searches, neither a warrant nor probable cause is required. Instead, the Court has held that limited searches are allowed if there are reasonable grounds for suspecting that they will uncover evidence of a violation of law or school regulation. The search must not be excessively intrusive considering the age and sex of the student and the nature of the infraction.[70]

Although the searches discussed in this section occur outside the criminal justice system, evidence that may be seized as a result of such searches can be used to support criminal charges. Consider, for example, the case of automo-

---

[64]*Camara v Municipal Court of San Francisco,* 387 US 523 (1967); *See v City of Seattle,* 387 US 541 (1967).
[65]*Colonnade Catering Corp. v United States,* 397 US 72 (1970).
[66]*United States v Biswell,* 406 US 311 (1972).
[67]*Donovan v Dewey,* 452 US 594 (1981).
[68]*New York v Burger,* 482 US 691 (1987).
[69]*Ibid.,* 702–709 (1972).
[70]*New Jersey v T.L.O.,* 469 US 325 (1985).

bile junkyards. Warrantless administrative searches, the Court noted, serve the state's interest both in eradicating automobile theft and ensuring that junkyard operators follow the rules established for the conduct of such businesses. The discovery of crime in the course of a proper administrative inspection did not render that search illegal. Likewise, when school officials discover evidence of illegal drug use in a student's purse or locker, that evidence may be used in a criminal prosecution. Although police officers may conduct inspections when authorized to do so by a regulatory statute (as they were in the junkyard regulatory scheme), the Court has not made clear whether police may take the place of school officials in searches of students.

Drug Testing

Mandatory drug testing programs that are conducted in the absence of probable cause—even without individualized reasonable suspicion—and outside the criminal justice process raise serious constitutional questions. Does a requirement that federal employees produce urine samples for chemical testing invade reasonable expectations of privacy? Is random drug testing of public school students as a condition for participation in athletics consistent with the Fourth Amendment's mandate that searches be reasonable?

In 1989, the Court upheld the United States Customs Service's drug screening program that requires testing of applicants for positions that involve drug enforcement, the carrying of a firearm, or access to classified information.[71] The justices also upheld the Federal Railroad Administration's regulations mandating blood and urine testing of employees who have been involved in train accidents and authorizing tests for employees who have violated safety rules.[72] In 1995, a majority of the Court approved a school district's program that required all students who participate in sports to consent to drug testing. All student athletes were tested at the beginning of each season and 10 percent chosen at random were tested each week thereafter.[73] In 2002, the justices upheld a school district's program whereby all students who participated in extracurricular activities were required to consent to testing for drugs.[74]

The justices were divided in all four cases. The majority, however, emphasized that in situations like these the government has "special needs, beyond the normal need for law enforcement, [that] make the warrant and probable cause requirement impracticable."[75] Thus, the Court engages in a balancing analysis of the government's special needs against the privacy concerns of the individuals in each particular context. The majority agreed that the government's interest in ensuring that drug users do not occupy sensitive positions in the enforcement of drug laws outweighs the privacy interests of customs agents. Likewise, the government's need to ensure the safety of the traveling public and

---

[71]*National Treasury Employees Union v Von Raab*, 489 US 656 (1989).
[72]*Skinner v Railway Labor Executives' Association*, 489 US 602 (1989).
[73]*Vernonia School District 47J v Acton*, 515 US 646 (1995).
[74]*Board of Education of Independent School District of Pottawatomie County v Earls*, __US __ (2002).
[75]*Skinner v Railway Labor Executives' Association*, 489 US 602, 619 (1989), quoting *New Jersey v T.L.O.*, 469 US 325, 351 (1985).

of the employees themselves by deterring and diagnosing train accidents outweighs the privacy interests of railroad workers. The government's interest in ensuring that athletes do not use drugs outweighs the privacy concerns of students, particularly in light of the fact that students have a lesser privacy expectation with regard to medical examinations and procedures than the general population. In short, the Court's **balancing analysis** enabled it to find that the tests were reasonable even though they proceeded in the absence of a warrant, probable cause, or individualized reasonable suspicion.

The majority opinions in the cases involving customs agents and railroad workers provoked an angry dissent from Justice Thurgood Marshall who warned that the majority's use of the manipulable "special needs" balancing analysis to justify searches of the human body without any evidence of wrongdoing threatens the core protections of the Fourth Amendment by eliminating the probable-cause requirement. The majority, Marshall admonished, was disregarding the explicit text of the Fourth Amendment and interpreting it as though there were a drug exception to the Constitution.[76] In the case involving drug testing for student athletes, Justice O'Connor pointed out, "For most of our constitutional history, mass, suspicionless searches have been generally considered per se unreasonable within the meaning of the Fourth Amendment."[77] She argued that searches without individualized suspicion can only be justified in the very limited circumstances where searches of selected individuals are ineffective in preventing grave harm. In the more recent case involving drug testing of students who participate in extracurricular activities, Justice Ginsburg's dissent drew attention to the fact that although the majority claimed that the earlier case provided the authority for upholding the policy, that policy was much broader in that it included a much larger population of students and was thus not governed by the earlier case.

An additional case that concerned the constitutionality of drug testing arose in a different context and involved a policy that differed in important ways from those that were challenged and upheld in the other four cases. *Ferguson v City of Charleston* involved a challenge to a city's drug testing policy that subjected pregnant women receiving prenatal treatment to tests for cocaine use without their consent. The results were used by law enforcement and women who tested positive were arrested and charged with illegal drug use. The justices, by a vote of six to three, held that the policy violated the Fourth Amendment. Distinguishing the policy in this case from those that the Court upheld in the earlier drug testing cases, the majority opinion noted that in those cases individuals who tested positive were disqualified from eligibility for particular benefits. Here, however, the results were used by the police to prosecute women for illegal drug use. Consequently, the "special needs" that justified drug testing in the absence of consent or probable cause in the earlier cases did were not present here.[78]

---

[76]Brennan joined Marshall in *Skinner* and *Von Raab*.
[77]*Vernonia School District 47J v Acton*, 515 US 646 (1995), 2. Stevens and Souter joined O'Connor's dissent.
[78]*Ferguson v City of Charleston* __US __ (2001).

The Warrant Clause

And no Warrants shall issue, but upon probable cause, supported by Oath or affirmation, and particularly describing the place to be searched, and the persons or things to be seized.

The immediate evil at which the Framers aimed the Fourth Amendment was the old Writ of Assistance, a general search warrant authorized by Parliament, granting British customs officials unlimited discretion to search without probable cause and without a description of the places to be searched. Thus, the second part of the Fourth Amendment mandates that an independent authority, acting as a buffer between the police and the people, control the warrant process. It is that independent authority who makes the determination of requisite probable cause and specifies the scope of the search.

The two clauses of the Fourth Amendment are inextricably linked. As we noted earlier, in most of its decisions since 1967 the Court has considered the warrant clause as explanatory of the reasonableness clause. Thus, while the first part of the Amendment forbids unreasonable searches and seizures, the second part provides that a properly issued warrant renders a search reasonable. A search conducted without such a warrant is unreasonable. As the justices have often repeated, "[S]earches conducted outside the judicial process without prior approval by judge or magistrate, are *per se* unreasonable under the Fourth Amendment, subject to a few specifically established and well-delineated exceptions."[79] Additionally, the term *probable cause* appears in the warrant clause, but the requirements of probable cause are essential to a determination of the reasonableness of a search or seizure. As discussed earlier, many warrantless searches and seizures are considered to be reasonable only if they are supported by probable cause.

Despite the connection between the two clauses, it is useful to examine some of the cases in which the Court has interpreted the warrant clause. As we have explained, the justices are guided by the reasonableness clause when they are faced with the issues of when a warrant is required to render a particular search reasonable, how much information is necessary to make a particular search or seizure reasonable, and whether the warrant was executed properly (if one was used). It is the warrant clause, however, that guides the Court in determining whether a warrant was issued properly and whether it adequately described the objects of the search.

To obtain a warrant, the police must appear before an official—usually a judge or magistrate—and present data under oath establishing that there is probable cause to believe that a search will yield evidence of a crime. A warrant may only be issued by a neutral and detached judicial officer. Thus, the Court has invalidated warrants issued by officials directly involved in an investigation. For example, the justices held invalid a warrant issued by the state attorney general who directed the investigation.[80] Similarly, the Court held that a magistrate who issued a warrant, went with the police on a raid of an adult bookstore, and

---

[79]*Katz v United States*, 389 US 347, 357 (1967).
[80]*Coolidge v New Hampshire*, 403 US 443 (1971).

acted as if he were the supervising investigative officer was not sufficiently detached.[81] The Court also found the requisite neutrality to be lacking where the officer who issued the warrant received a fee for issuing a warrant but no fee if he declined to issue one.[82] So long as the official is neutral, he or she need not be a judge or magistrate but can be a court clerk.[83]

A warrant must describe the place to be searched and the items to be seized. An address is required except in rural areas where property might be identified in a more general way, by rural route or township. In multiple occupancy buildings, the unit to be searched must be identified by occupant, room number, or apartment number unless the officers who applied for the warrant did not know that the building they wanted to search had multiple units. The requirement that a warrant must describe the things to be seized prevents the general search warrants that were so feared and abhorred by the Framers. Thus, a warrant that authorizes a search of certain premises without specifying what is to be seized is invalid. Exactly how specific a warrant must be depends on the materials to be seized. Generally, contraband may be described in less detail than property the possession of which is not a crime. The latter must be described more specifically so that the police conducting the search will be able to distinguish between the items they are seeking and others that may be similar. Although searches for documents carry the potential for serious intrusions into privacy, the Court has upheld warrants with quite general descriptions. For example, in a case involving an investigation of real estate fraud, the warrant contained a list of specific items appended with "together with other fruits, instrumentalities and evidence of crime at this [time] unknown."[84] Finally, warrants must be specific when the items to be seized raise First Amendment concerns—where "unrestricted power of search and seizure could also be an instrument for stifling liberty of expression."[85] Thus the Court has found warrants to be insufficiently specific where the police were searching for obscene magazines[86] and books pertaining to the Communist Party.[87]

Technology and the Fourth Amendment: Electronic Searches

Developments in technology made it possible for law enforcement officials to combat crime during Prohibition with new devices for gathering evidence. In its initial attempt to answer the question of whether a wiretap is subject to the constraints of the Fourth Amendment, the Court, interpreting the language of the Amendment literally, held that a search only occurs if there is trespass and search of a place. Likewise, a seizure occurs only if officials remove physical things. In *Olmstead v United States*, the Court, by a vote of five to four, held that a wiretap on telephone lines was not a search or seizure—"the evidence

---

[81] *Lo-Ji Sales, Inc. v NY*, 442 US 319 (1979).
[82] *Connally v Georgia*, 429 US 245 (1977).
[83] *Shadwick v City of Tampa*, 407 US 345 (1972).
[84] *Andresen v Maryland*, 427 US 463, 479 (1976).
[85] *Marcus v Search Warrant*, 367 US 717, 729 (1961).
[86] *Marcus v Search Warrant*, 367 US 717 (1961).
[87] *Stanford v Texas*, 379 US 476 (1965).

was secured by the use of the sense of hearing and that only."[88] In his dissenting opinion, Justice Louis Brandeis argued that the Constitution confers a right to privacy: "the right to be let alone—the most comprehensive of rights and the right most valued by civilized men. To protect that right, every unjustifiable intrusion by the government upon the privacy of the individual, whatever the means employed, must be deemed a violation of the Fourth Amendment."[89]

Congress subsequently included a provision in the Federal Communications Act of 1934 prohibiting any "person not being authorized by the sender . . . [from] intercept[ing] any communication and divulg[ing] or publish[ing] the existence, contents, substance, . . . of such intercepted communication to any person." The Court interpreted that language to forbid federal agents from tapping telephone conversations.[90] Nevertheless, a majority of the justices continued to hold that electronic eavesdropping did not constitute a search under the Fourth Amendment. In 1942, for example, the Court held that there was no trespass and thus no constitutional violation when federal officers placed a dictaphone—a sensitive listening device—against the outer wall of a private office in order to hear conversations revealing illegal business practices.[91] Similarly, in 1952 the Court held that there was no Fourth Amendment violation when an acquaintance of the defendant who was an undercover agent carrying a concealed radio transmitter relayed incriminating statements to federal agents.[92]

It was not until 1967 in *Katz v United States* that the Court explicitly rejected the *Olmstead* approach and made it clear that wiretapping and electronic eavesdropping are subject to the limitations of the Fourth Amendment. In *Katz,* the justices found that FBI agents violated the Fourth Amendment by attaching an electronic listening and recording device to the outside of a public telephone booth to obtain recordings of the defendant's end of telephone conversations. Writing for the majority, Justice Potter Stewart explained, "[T]he Fourth Amendment protects people, not places. What a person knowingly exposes to the public, even in his own home or office, is not a subject of Fourth Amendment protection. But what he seeks to preserve as private, even in an area accessible to the public, may be constitutionally protected."[93] By acknowledging that the Fourth Amendment's restrictions on searches and seizures involve a right to privacy, the Court finally adopted the position that Brandeis had advanced forty years earlier. The Court's decision in *Katz* established that warrants are required for electronic surveillance. It also directed justices when faced with the question of whether a particular type of surveillance constituted a search for Fourth Amendment purposes to focus on whether the defendant had a reasonable expectation of privacy. Thus, the Court would consider whether the defendant could have reasonably expected his or her communication not to be heard by others and whether society would consider the defendant to have a legitimate expectation of privacy.

---

[88]*Olmstead v United States,* 277 US 438, 464 (1928).
[89]*Olmstead v United States,* 277 US 438, 478 (1928).
[90]*Nardone v United States,* 302 US 379 (1937).
[91]*Goldman v United States,* 316 US 129 (1942).
[92]*On Lee v United States,* 343 US 747 (1952).
[93]*Katz v United States,* 389 US 347, 351 (1967).

In **Title III of the Federal Omnibus Crime Control and Safe Streets Act of 1968,**[94] Congress prohibited wiretapping and electronic surveillance without judicial authorization and outlined procedures that federal and state law enforcement officials must follow to obtain such authorization. The law specifies grounds on which an order for surveillance may be issued. For example, a judge must determine that there is probable cause to believe that an individual is committing, has committed, or is about to commit one of the offenses enumerated in the statute. There must be probable cause to believe that communications about the offense will be obtained with the surveillance and that other investigative procedures have been tried and have failed, are unlikely to succeed, or are too dangerous. Title III permits law enforcement officials to act without a warrant for forty-eight hours in an emergency situation that poses an immediate danger of death or serious physical injury. Electronic surveillance may also proceed without judicial authorization in situations involving conspiratorial activities that pose a threat to the national security or are characteristic of organized crime. Very important, the law also excepts from the warrant requirement electronic eavesdropping and recording of communications when one party consents to the surveillance. The law specifically left intact the president's constitutional authority to authorize electronic surveillance to obtain foreign intelligence information to protect national security. That authority, the Court made clear, does not extend to warrantless wiretapping in domestic security cases.[95]

In contrast to the 1968 Crime Control law, which provided restrictions on the use of electronic surveillance for gathering evidence for a criminal prosecution, the **Foreign Intelligence Surveillance Act of 1978** (FISA) provided rules for gathering information on the activities of foreign agents.[96] The law authorizes special courts to issue warrants and requires agents applying for warrants to produce evidence of criminal activity when they seek to engage in surveillance of an American citizen, a resident alien, or various domestic organizations believed to be involved in intelligence operations on behalf of a foreign power. When agents apply for a warrant authorizing surveillance of a foreign power or an agent of a foreign power, however, they need only show probable cause to believe that the target is an agent of a foreign power. FISA allows the president to authorize electronic surveillance without a court order to acquire the contents of communications transmitted between foreign powers or from property or premises under the open and exclusive control of a foreign power. It also allows the president to authorize surveillance to acquire foreign intelligence for up to fifteen days following a declaration of war by Congress. The special courts created by FISA, the Foreign Intelligence Surveillance Act Court and the Foreign Intelligence Surveillance Court of Review, meet in secret, normally do not publish their decisions, and allow only the government to appear before them.

The **USA Patriot Act,** enacted in response to the terrorist attacks on September 11, 2001, allows surveillance of U.S. citizens without probable cause

---

[94]18 U.S.C. Sec. 2510–2520.
[95]*United States v United States District Court,* 407 US 297 (1972).
[96]50 U.S.C. Sec. 1801–1811.

and with only the most minimal judicial involvement. For example, the 2001 law extended the wiretap regulations under the Crime Control Act to authorize the use of roving wiretaps—allowing an individual's conversations to be monitored on any phone—under the procedures used for intelligence wiretaps under FISA, that is without probable cause. Even before the Patriot Act was enacted the government had the authority to order a telephone company to provide a list of numbers that are dialed to and from a particular telephone, but the new law extends such authority to computers. The upshot is that the government may obtain access to lists of e-mails sent and received as well as the identities of Web sites visited on a particular computer.[97]

In March 2003 the Supreme Court declined to allow an appeal from a decision of the Foreign Intelligence Surveillance Court of Review brought by civil liberties groups to challenge that court's decision granting broad authority for wiretaps to gather information to prosecute suspected terrorists.[98] The decision of the FISA Court of Review indicated its disagreement with the traditional distinction between intelligence gathering and criminal investigations that make it more difficult to secure authorization for surveillance for criminal investigations.[99]

The Exclusionary Rule

What if police disregard the rules and violate the Fourth Amendment? If police officers break into an individual's home without a warrant and no exigent circumstances are present, search the entire house, and seize personal belongings, what recourse does the individual have? Similarly, if the police conduct a search pursuant to a warrant that was issued by an official who had a personal vendetta against the suspect, is there a remedy? Although individuals can initiate a civil suit against the police for violations of the Fourth Amendment, such remedies are highly ineffective, in large part because victims of illegal searches are rarely in a position to sue the police.

We rely on **the exclusionary rule** to enforce the Fourth Amendment.[100] Created by judges, the exclusionary rule forbids evidence that has been obtained illegally from being introduced in court, thus removing any incentive law enforcement officials might have for violating the rights of criminal suspects. The rule was established in 1914 when the Court noted that if illegally seized documents could be used as evidence, the protection of the Fourth Amendment would be of no value and might as well be stricken from the Constitution.[101] The exclusionary rule initially applied only to material obtained by a federal official in a

---

[97]See, Susan Herman, "The USA Patriot Act and the U.S. Department of Justice: Losing Our Balances?" *Jurist*, December 3, 2001. Available: http://jurist.law.pitt.edu/forum/forumnew40.htm.
[98]Linda Greenhouse, "Groups Lose Challenge to Government's Broader Use of Wiretaps," *The New York Times*, March 25, 2003. Available: http://www.nytimes.com/2003/03/25/politics/25SCOT.html?tntemail1.
[99]David Stout, "Supreme Court Refuses to Review Wiretaps Ruling," *The New York Times*, March 24, 2003. Available: http://www.nytimes.com/2003/03/24/politics/24CND-SCOT.html?tntemail1.
[100]The exclusionary rule is used to enforce the Fifth Amendment's protection against self-incrimination and the Sixth Amendment's guarantee of right to counsel as well.
[101]*Weeks v United States*, 232 US 383 (1914).

federal case. In 1949, when the Court held that the Fourth Amendment protected individuals against state as well as federal action, it declined to extend the exclusionary rule to the states. Thus, it was possible for state officials to obtain evidence illegally and turn it over to federal officials for prosecution. According to the "silver platter" doctrine, if the evidence was obtained without federal participation, the exclusionary rule did not come into play.[102] Similarly, federal prosecutors could seize evidence without regard to the Fourth Amendment and turn it over to state prosecutors for use in state courts.[103]

In 1949, the Court pointed out that the states were overwhelmingly opposed to the rule and that there were other means of giving force to the Fourth Amendment than excluding evidence. But in 1961, noting that states had begun to adopt it and that other remedies had proved to be ineffective, the Court extended the exclusionary rule to the states.[104] Writing for the six-person majority, Justice Tom Clark conceded that a guilty person might go free because of the exclusionary rule but pointed out "another consideration—the imperative of judicial integrity. The criminal goes free, if he must, but it is the law that sets him free. Nothing can destroy a government more quickly than its failure to observe its own laws, or worse, its disregard of the charter of its own existence."[105]

The exclusionary rule has always been controversial. Critics argue that its consequences are unacceptable. As Benjamin Cardozo complained in 1926, "The criminal is to go free because the constable has blundered."[106] When Warren Burger replaced Earl Warren as Chief Justice, it seemed likely that the Court would overrule the exclusionary rule. Although that has not come to pass, the Burger and Rehnquist Courts have carved out major exceptions, seriously narrowing the reach of the rule. Since the 1970s, a majority of the Court has embraced the deterrence theory of the exclusionary rule, emphasizing that the rule is not a personal constitutional right but a judicially created remedy designed to safeguard Fourth Amendment guarantees through its deterrent effect. The Court has emphasized deterrence to such an extent that it has neglected another major rationale for the exclusionary rule: judicial integrity—the government must play fair and must not be permitted to profit from its own illegal behavior. Because it is difficult to demonstrate that the exclusionary rule deters police misconduct in particular circumstances, it has been easy for the Court to narrow the scope of the rule by engaging in a cost-benefit analysis. Typically, the Court has found that in particular situations where the exclusionary rule is not likely to deter police misconduct, the benefit of deterrence is outweighed by the cost of losing reliable evidence.

Using such reasoning, the Court has held that the exclusionary rule does not apply to grand jury proceedings,[107] to civil tax proceedings,[108] or to de-

---

[102]The "silver platter" doctrine was laid to rest in *Elkins v United States,* 364 US 206 (1960).
[103]The Court closed this loophole in *Rea v United States,* 350 US 214 (1956).
[104]*Mapp v Ohio,* 367 US 642 (1961).
[105]*Mapp v Ohio,* 367 US 643, 659, quoting *Elkins v United States,* 364 US 206, 222 (1960).
[106]*People v Defore,* 242 NY 13 (1926).
[107]The grand jury may consider illegally obtained evidence although such evidence may not be used in a subsequent criminal trial. *United States v Calandra,* 414 US 338 (1974).
[108]*United States v Janis,* 428 US 433 (1978).

portation proceedings.[109] Again relying on the deterrence rationale and cost-benefit analysis, in 1998 the Court held that the exclusionary rule does not bar the introduction at parole revocation hearings of evidence seized in violation of parolees' Fourth Amendment rights. The rule, the majority noted, "applies only in contexts where its remedial objectives are thought most efficaciously served."[110]

The most important exception to the exclusionary rule is the **"objective good faith" exception** established by a six-person majority in *United States v Leon* in 1984. Evidence need not be excluded if the police conduct a search pursuant to a warrant that they have reasonable grounds to believe was properly issued even if it is subsequently found to be invalid. The majority reasoned that the exclusionary rule cannot be expected to deter law enforcement activity that is objectively reasonable. "Penalizing the officer for the magistrate's error, rather than his own, cannot logically contribute to the deterrence of Fourth Amendment violations." In short, there is "no police illegality and thus nothing to deter."[111] In that case, the Court allowed evidence to be introduced that had been gathered pursuant to a warrant that had been issued without probable cause. In his opinion for the majority, Justice Byron White outlined some limits to the good faith exception. It will not apply, he explained, if the police mislead the magistrate or judge when they apply for the warrant with information that they either know to be false or would know if they did not recklessly disregard the truth. Evidence will also be suppressed in situations where the police know that the official who issues the warrant has abandoned his or her neutral and detached role and where a warrant is so obviously not based on probable cause that it would be unreasonable for a police officer to believe that it was. Finally, White noted that a warrant may be "so facially deficient—i.e., in failing to particularize the place to be searched or the things to be seized—that the executing officers cannot reasonably presume it to be valid."[112]

Subsequently, the Court has held that the good faith exception applied where evidence was seized by an officer who relied on a computer printout—later found to be erroneous—indicating the existence of an outstanding arrest warrant. The error was the result of clerical errors by court employees rather than the police. In a concurring opinion, Justice David Souter noted that the Court may eventually have to reach the question of "how far, in dealing with fruits of computerized error, our very concept of deterrence by exclusion of evidence should extend to the government as a whole, not merely the police, on the ground that there would otherwise be no reasonable expectation of keeping the number of resulting false arrests within an acceptable minimum limit."[113]

---

[109]*INS v Lopez-Mendoza*, 468 US 1032 (1984).
[110]*Pennsylvania Board of Probation & Parole v Scott*, 524 US 357 (1998).
[111]*United States v Leon*, 468 US 897, 921 (1984).
[112]*Ibid.*, 923.
[113]*Arizona v Evans*, 514 US 1 (1995).

AMENDMENT V: GRAND JURIES, DOUBLE JEOPARDY, SELF-INCRIMINATION, DUE PROCESS, EMINENT DOMAIN

> No person shall be held to answer for a capital, or otherwise infamous crime, unless on a presentment or indictment of a Grand Jury,

The **grand jury** has a long history. Toward the end of the tenth century in England, leading citizens were summoned to court to report crimes that had occurred in their communities. In the twelfth century, Henry II established the Clarendon jury of inquest, an accusatory body of "good and lawful men" to report all offenses that had been committed. Those reports became the key instrument for initiating criminal proceedings. The grand jury in its modern form dates from 1368, when Edward III appointed twenty-four men to an inquisitorial and accusatory board in each English county.[114] It was not until the seventeenth century, however, that the grand jury acquired the function of protecting individuals from politically motivated prosecution by the crown. The colonists brought the grand jury to America as part of the common law. In the eighteenth century, as conflicts with England increased, it became an instrument of resistance when the colonists refused to allow prosecutions of patriots by royal officials. The colonists also used the grand jury to investigate wrongdoing by government officials and to report its findings through the "presentment"—a public document stating the grand jury's accusations.

The Fifth Amendment reflects the Framers' belief that the grand jury was essential to protect individuals against unfounded criminal prosecutions. Thus, before the government can subject an individual to the ordeal of a serious criminal prosecution, it must first obtain the consent of a panel of ordinary citizens. The Supreme Court has explained the importance of the grand jury in the following way:

> [A]s a primary security to the innocent against hasty, malicious and oppressive persecution; it serves the invaluable function in our society of standing between the accuser and the accused, whether the latter be an individual, minority group, or other, to determine whether a charge is founded upon reason or was dictated by an intimidating power or by malice and personal ill will.[115]

Most federal grand juries are composed of twenty-three members. Sixteen constitute a quorum and twelve must agree to issue an indictment. Federal law requires that grand jurors be chosen from a cross-section of the community, without regard to religion, race, sex, national origin, or economic status.

A grand jury is responsible for determining whether a crime has been committed and whether criminal proceedings should be instituted. To fulfill that responsibility, grand juries are endowed with considerable power. They deliberate in secret, and normally testimony is kept secret to aid prosecutors conducting

---

[114]Peter W. Sperlich, "Grand Juries." In Kermit L. Hall, ed. *The Oxford Companion to the Supreme Court of the United States* (New York: Oxford University Press, 1992), 344–345.
[115]*Wood v Georgia*, 370 US 375 (1962).

investigations and to protect witnesses and the subjects of investigations.[116] They may compel witnesses to appear, to testify under oath, and to produce documents.[117] Those who appear before grand juries are not protected by the rules that govern the conduct of criminal trials. An accused has no right to confront and cross-examine his or her accusers. No warnings are required regarding self-incrimination.[118] The possibility of criminal prosecution need not be pointed out.[119] Moreover, the exclusionary rule does not apply.[120] Although a witness may leave the room to consult with a lawyer, he or she has no right to be advised by an attorney in the grand jury room.[121] Additionally, the prosecutor may grant witnesses immunity against their will, and thereby compel their testimony. Witnesses who are granted immunity may not rely on the privilege against self-incrimination to refuse to answer questions. A prosecutor may grant a witness **"transactional"** immunity, which means that the witness may not be prosecuted for any offenses to which his or her testimony relates. More commonly, prosecutors grant the narrower **"use"** immunity, which has the effect of prohibiting prosecutors from using the compelled testimony (as well as information directly or indirectly derived from that testimony) as the basis of a prosecution.[122] "Use" immunity leaves room for prosecutors to prosecute a witness based on evidence obtained independently of the testimony.

The requirement for indictment by a grand jury is the one provision of the Bill of Rights concerning criminal prosecutions that the Court has not applied to the states through the due process clause of the Fourteenth Amendment. States are, therefore, free to proceed against an accused by other means, and about one-half of the states do so. In those states, the prosecuting attorney simply files an affidavit, called an information, that there is sufficient evidence to justify a trial. To hold a person in custody, however, the prosecutor's information must be followed by a hearing before a magistrate for presentation of evidence showing probable cause.[123]

The events of the summer of 1998 involving President Clinton's relationship with Monica Lewinsky revived a long-standing debate about grand juries. Critics of the grand jury have argued, at least since the 1970s, that "It is, indeed, common knowledge that the grand jury, having been conceived as a bulwark between the citizen and the Government, is now a tool of the

---

[116]*United States v Procter & Gamble Co.*, 356 US 677 (1958). Rule 6 (e) of the Rules of Criminal Procedure provides in part: "A grand juror, an interpreter, a stenographer, an operator of a recording device, a typist who transcribes recorded testimony, an attorney for the government, or any person to whom disclosure is made under paragraph (3)(A)(ii) of this subdivision shall not disclose matters occurring before the grand jury, except as otherwise provided for in these rules. No obligation of secrecy may be imposed on any person except in accordance with this rule. A knowing violation of Rule 6 may be punished as a contempt of court." Rule 6 also provides for disclosure with permission of the judge who presides over the grand jury: "(C) Disclosure otherwise prohibited by this rule of matters occurring before the grand jury may also be made—(i) when so directed by a court preliminarily to or in connection with a judicial proceeding; (ii) when permitted by a court at the request of the defendant, upon a showing that grounds may exist for a motion to dismiss the indictment because of matters occurring before the grand jury."
[117]*United States v Dionisio*, 410 US 1 (1973).
[118]*United States v Wong*, 431 US 174 (1977).
[119]*United States v Washington*, 431 US 181 (1977).
[120]*United States v Calandra*, 414 US 338 (1974).
[121]*United States v Mandujano*, 425 US 564 (1976).
[122]Use immunity was authorized in 1970 in 18 U.S.C. Sec. 6002.
[123]*Gerstein v Pugh*, 420 US 103 (1975).

[prosecutor]."[124] The grand jurors who heard the testimony of numerous presidential advisers, Secret Service personnel, the president's secretary, Monica Lewinsky, and, finally, the president himself, seemed to serve as little more than backdrop for Independent Counsel Ken Starr's vigorous campaign to uncover presidential wrongdoing.[125] Not only did the prosecutors manage the event but also the secrecy rules went largely unheeded as testimony was constantly leaked to the press. Moreover, with the permission of United States District Judge Norma Holloway Johnson, who was formally in charge of the grand jury, the Office of the Independent Counsel released its extensive report containing President Clinton's testimony and summaries of other testimony to the House of Representatives. The House quickly voted to release *The Starr Report,* which became available over the Internet within minutes. In a partisan move, Republicans in the House then voted to release the videotape of President Clinton's testimony, which was then aired on national television and viewed by millions.[126] Thus, the long-standing tradition of grand jury secrecy seems to have been seriously eroded. One commentator even referred to the secrecy requirement as a "flexible rule."[127]

> except in cases arising in the land or naval forces, or in the Militia, when in actual service in time of War or public danger;

The significance of this exception goes far beyond merely eliminating the requirement of indictment by a grand jury for individuals in the armed forces. This clause, along with Article I, Section 8 (authorizing Congress to make "rules for the government and regulation of the land and naval forces"), means that individuals who are members of the armed forces are not entitled to the same procedural protections as civilians. The Court has held, however, that Congress is "subject to the requirements of the Due Process Clause when legislating in the area of military affairs, and that Clause provides some measure of protection to defendants in military proceedings."[128] The Court of Appeals for the Armed Forces has construed the Uniform Code to extend to military personnel the rights to speedy trial and to confront witnesses, protection against unreasonable searches and seizures, public trial, compulsory service of process, *Miranda*-like warnings, and the privilege against self-incrimination.[129] Additionally, the Supreme Court has held that the restrictions on the imposition of the death penalty required by the Eighth Amendment extend to military proceedings.[130]

---

[124]Justice William O. Douglas, dissenting in *United States v Mara,* 410 US 19, 23 (1973).
[125]Neil A. Lewis, "Only a Modest Role for Clinton Grand Jurors," *New York Times,* August 17, 1998, National Politics.
[126]President Clinton's lawyers permitted his testimony to be videotaped so that any jurors who were absent could view it later.
[127]William Glaberson, "Tape Release Challenges Secrecy of Grand Jury," *New York Times,* September 17, 1998, National Politics.
[128]*Weiss v United States,* 510 US 163 (1994).
[129]*McLucas v De Champlain,* 421 US 21 (1975).
[130]*Loving v United States,* 517 US 748 (1996).

Since 1960,[131] only members of the armed forces have been subject to military trials and from 1969 to 1987, only for service-connected crimes. But in 1987 in *Solorio v United States*,[132] the Court held that the jurisdiction of military tribunals extends to members of the armed services for crimes they commit during their military service regardless of whether the crime is service-connected.

> nor shall any person be subject for the same offence to be twice put in jeopardy of life or limb;

In 1937, eight members of the Court agreed that the protection against double jeopardy was not "of the very essence of the scheme of ordered liberty."[133] Thus, the states were left free to ignore the Fifth Amendment's prohibition so long as they complied with general principles of due process. It was not until 1969 that the Court held that the double jeopardy clause applied to the states through the due process clause of the Fourteenth Amendment.[134]

The underlying idea of the double jeopardy clause, as the Court has explained,

> is that the State with all its resources and power should not be allowed to make repeated attempts to convict an individual for an alleged offense, thereby subjecting him to embarrassment, expense and ordeal and compelling him to live in a continuing state of anxiety and insecurity, as well as enhancing the possibility that even though innocent he may be found guilty.[135]

The double jeopardy clause consists of three constitutional protections. It prohibits a second prosecution for the same offense after acquittal, a second prosecution for the same offense after conviction, and multiple punishments for the same offense.[136] In light of the underlying rationale for the clause, those three prohibitions would seem to render the protection against double jeopardy simple and straightforward. As the Court has been called on to apply the clause to a wide variety of circumstances, however, the protection against double jeopardy has proved to be one of the most puzzling provisions in the Bill of Rights. A consideration of some of the questions that the Court has addressed reveals the complexities and confusion regarding the meaning of the prohibition on putting a person "twice . . . in jeopardy of life and limb" for the "same offence." A great deal of the uncertainty stems from the phrase "same offence," the meaning of which is "deceptively simple in appearance but virtually kaleidoscopic in application."[137] It is quite common, for example, for a defendant's actions in the course of a single criminal episode to violate several statutory provisions. May the government prosecute each violation in a separate trial? If a terrorist bombs

---

[131]*Kinsella v Singleton*, 361 US 234 (1960).
[132]483 US 435 (1987).
[133]*Palko v Connecticut*, 302 US 319 (1937).
[134]*Benton v Maryland*, 395 US 784 (1969).
[135]*Green v United States*, 355 US 184, 187–188 (1957).
[136]*North Carolina v Pearce*, 395 US 711 (1969).
[137]Rehnquist, dissenting in *Whalen v United States*, 445 US 684, 700 (1980).

a building and kills twenty people, may the government try him for twenty crimes or only one? Similarly, is a trial court in violation of the prohibition on multiple punishments for the same offense if it imposes consecutive or concurrent sentences for multiple crimes that occurred in a single transaction?

In 1932 in *Blockburger v United States*, the Court articulated the "**same-elements**" **test** and continues to rely on it as a guide for determining when multiple prosecutions for one criminal transaction are permitted: "Where the same act or transaction constitutes a violation of two distinct statutory provisions, the test to be applied to determine whether there are two offenses or only one is whether each provision requires proof of an additional fact which the other does not."[138] Thus, an individual who was convicted of joyriding could not subsequently be prosecuted for theft because the conviction for joyriding would not have been possible without proof of theft—a conviction for theft would, therefore, involve the same element as the conviction for joyriding.[139] Conversely, a single act of reckless driving can result in convictions for reckless driving and vehicular homicide if that act causes death. A conviction for reckless driving would not bar prosecution for vehicular homicide because conviction for the latter would require proof of a different element—death. Moreover, there might be multiple prosecutions for vehicular homicide because a separate element for each one would have to be proved.

The Court addressed a related question about the extent to which the double jeopardy clause prohibits multiple prosecutions for the same crime in *Ashe v Swenson*.[140] If a defendant is acquitted of one offense based on a factual element, does the double jeopardy clause prohibit a subsequent prosecution on a related offense for which that same factual element is essential to a conviction? Ashe was charged with armed robbery after three or four masked, armed men broke into the basement of a private residence and robbed six men who were playing poker. He was tried for the robbery of one of the poker players but was acquitted due to insufficient evidence identifying him as one of the robbers. Six weeks later Ashe was tried for the robbery of another poker player and this time he was convicted. In the second trial, the poker players testified with more certainty that Ashe had been one of the robbers and the state did not call the witness whose testimony had been most favorable to Ashe at the first trial. The Court held that the second prosecution violated the double jeopardy clause because the state relied on the same critical facts in the second trial—the identification of Ashe. *Ashe v Swenson* prohibits the prosecution from using the same facts in multiple prosecutions—the state, the court noted, may not use one trial as a dry run for a second prosecution.[141]

---

[138]*Blockburger v United States*, 284 US 299, 304 (1932).

[139]Another way of stating the rule is that the government may not prosecute for a greater offense after a prosecution for a lesser included offense. There is an exception to the rule, however, "where the State is unable to proceed on the more serious charge at the outset because the additional facts necessary to sustain that charge have not occurred or have not been discovered despite the exercise of due diligence." *Brown v Ohio*, 432 US 161 (1977).

[140]*Ashe v Swenson*, 397 US 436 (1970).

[141]In *Ashe*, the Court held that collateral estoppel is part of the Fifth Amendment's guarantee against double jeopardy. Collateral estoppel means that when an issue of ultimate fact has once been determined by a valid and final judgment, that issue cannot again be litigated between the same parties in any future lawsuit.

The Court has confronted the issue of the extent to which the double jeopardy clause prohibits multiple punishments in a series of challenges to a trial court's imposition of consecutive or concurrent sentences when a defendant has been found guilty in one trial of several criminal violations. A majority of the justices has adopted the position that the double jeopardy clause offers very limited protection against multiple punishments. The Court has held that multiple sentences are constitutionally permissible so long as they are authorized by legislation: "[T]he question of what punishments are constitutionally permissible is not different from the question of what punishments the Legislative Branch intended to be imposed. Where Congress intended, . . . to impose multiple punishments, imposition of such sentences does not violate the Constitution."[142] Where legislative intent is not clear, the Court has presumed that a legislature does not intend to authorize multiple punishments where two statutory provisions proscribe the "same offense" as defined by the *Blockburger* test.[143] Thus, the Court's task is to determine whether a second criminal violation requires additional proof that the first one did not—a matter of statutory interpretation. The Court does not consider the constitutional issue of whether the legislation runs afoul of the double jeopardy clause by authorizing too many punishments. Consequently, the constitutional protection against multiple punishments is nearly nonexistent. Some justices, including Antonin Scalia and Clarence Thomas, would go further to eliminate the protection against multiple punishments entirely. They argue that the double jeopardy clause, properly understood, limits only multiple prosecutions.[144]

The phrase "put twice in jeopardy" is a second source of confusion about the protection against double jeopardy. If a defendant is tried and acquitted based on a jury verdict of not guilty, may the government bring a second prosecution? The Court has answered that a second trial is not permitted following an acquittal even when the basis for the acquittal was "egregiously erroneous."[145] The Court has explained the significance that the double jeopardy clause assigns to an acquittal: "To permit a second trial after an acquittal, however mistaken the acquittal may have been, would present an unacceptably high risk that the Government, with its vastly superior resources, might wear down the defendant so that 'even though innocent he may be found guilty.'"[146] Other outcomes that are equivalent to acquittal are treated the same way. No reprosecution is permitted when a judge dismisses a case or directs a verdict of acquittal on the grounds that the evidence is legally insufficient to justify a conviction.[147] Neither may the government subject an individual to a second trial after an appellate court has determined that the evidence did not justify a verdict of guilty.[148]

---

[142]*Albernaz v United States,* 450 US 333, 344 (1981). *Whalen v United States,* 445 US 684 (1980). In this case, a majority found that Congress did not intend to allow consecutive sentences for felony-murder and the underlying felony. But in *Albernaz v United States,* 450 US 333 (1980), the Court upheld multiple punishment of one conspiracy with two criminal objectives because Congress had authorized it. See also, *Missouri v Hunter,* 459 US 359 (1983); *Garrett v United States,* 471 US 773 (1985).

[143]*Rutledge v United States,* 517 US 292 (1996).

[144]*Department of Revenues of Montana v Kurth Ranch,* 511 US 767 (1994).

[145]*Fong Foo v United States,* 369 US 141, 143 (1962).

[146]*United States v Scott,* 437 US 82, 91 (1978), quoting *Green v United States,* 355 US 184, 188 (1957).

[147]*Hudson v Louisiana,* 450 US 40 (1981).

[148]*Burks v United States,* 437 US 1 (1978). Essentially, lacking legally sufficient evidence means that the government's case was so lacking that it should have not even been submitted to the jury.

Although the rule against subsequent prosecution after acquittal is fairly straightforward, a number of other issues are considerably more complicated. For example, if a prosecution does not end with a verdict but instead with a mistrial, is the state allowed to institute another prosecution? If a defendant is found guilty, appeals, and has the conviction overturned by an appellate court on grounds of trial error, may the state prosecute again? The protection against double jeopardy applies only if "jeopardy has attached." Thus, one of the most important questions is, "when does jeopardy attach?" Jeopardy attaches when the jury is impaneled; in a case tried by a judge jeopardy attaches when the first witness is sworn in;[149] and in cases where a defendant pleads guilty jeopardy attaches when the court accepts the plea. Those propositions would appear to bar subsequent prosecutions even when the trial ended without a verdict. Indeed, the Court has declared that "as a general rule, the prosecutor is entitled to one, and only one, opportunity to require an accused to stand trial."[150] But the Court has also maintained that the double jeopardy clause "does not guarantee a defendant that the Government will be prepared, in all circumstances, to vindicate the social interest in law enforcement through the vehicle of a single proceeding for a given offense."[151] As one may well expect, the Court has developed a complicated set of rules to determine when the double jeopardy clause bars a second prosecution by carving out a number of exceptions to the general rule.

Thus, even though jeopardy has attached, if a prosecution results in a mistrial under certain circumstances, the state may prosecute the defendant again. When a trial judge declares a mistrial over the objection of the defendant, a second trial is permitted if there was a **"manifest necessity" for a mistrial.**[152] On the other hand, if the trial judge declares a mistrial without the consent of the defendant and in the absence of "manifest necessity," the judge is considered to have abused his or her discretion. A case in which a judge declares a mistrial with the purpose of helping the prosecution by giving it another opportunity to convict the defendant is a prime example of such abuse.[153] The most common situation in which a "manifest necessity" exists is where the jury is unable to reach a verdict. The Court has also found that the judge exercised proper discretion in declaring a mistrial because the indictment contained a defect that would have been the basis for reversing a conviction[154] and where the defense counsel made improper and prejudicial remarks during his opening statement to the jury.[155]

The "manifest necessity" standard applies only when a judge declares a mistrial over the objection of the defendant. A second trial is not barred when the defendant requests a mistrial unless the prosecution engages in misconduct to provoke the defendant into moving for a mistrial.[156] Similarly, the Court has

---

[149]*Crist v Bretz*, 437 US 28 (1979).
[150]Stevens, writing for the majority in *Arizona v Washington*, 434 US 497, 505 (1978).
[151]Harlan, writing for the plurality in *United States v Jorn*, 400 US 47, 483–484 (1971).
[152]*United States v Perez*, 9 Wheat. 579, 580 (1824).
[153]See *Gori v United States*, 367 US 364 (1961); *United States v Jorn*, 400 US 47, 484 (1971).
[154]*Illinois v Somerville*, 4;10 US 458 (1973).
[155]*Arizona v Washington*, 434 US 497 (1978).
[156]*Oregon v Kennedy*, 456 US 667 (1982).

held that when a defendant seeks termination of a trial on grounds other than lack of evidence and the judge dismisses the case, an appeal by the government that may result in a new trial does not violate the double jeopardy clause.[157]

When a trial ends in a conviction that is subsequently reversed on appeal, a second prosecution does not violate the double jeopardy clause so long as the reversal was based on trial error and not on lack of sufficient proof of guilt.[158] The Court has offered two rationales for imposing this limit on the protection against double jeopardy. First, the government has an important interest in punishing those whose guilt is clear after a trial: "It would be a high price indeed for society to pay were every accused granted immunity from punishment because of any defect sufficient to constitute reversible error in the proceedings leading to conviction."[159] Second, the justices have maintained that retrial after reversal of a conviction is not the type of governmental oppression that the double jeopardy clause targets.[160]

A majority of the Court has also drawn a distinction between appellate reversals based on insufficiency of the evidence and appellate reversals based on weight of the evidence. When a reviewing court reverses on the grounds of lack of sufficiency of the evidence, it makes a determination that no rational fact-finder could have voted to convict the defendant—acquittal was the only proper verdict. In contrast, with "weight" reversals the appellate court disagrees with the jury's resolution of the conflicting testimony; however, "this difference of opinion no more signifies acquittal than does a disagreement among the jurors themselves."[161] A weight reversal, according to the majority, gives the defendant a second chance to seek a favorable judgment; "that second chance, does not create 'an unacceptably high risk that the Government, with its superior resources, [will] wear down [the] defendant' and obtain conviction solely through its persistence."[162]

The Court has noted that the double jeopardy clause is one of the least understood and one of the most frequently litigated provisions in the Bill of Rights. Moreover, the justices, by their own admission, have done little to alleviate the confusion.[163] At its strongest when used as a shield against a second prosecution after acquittal, the protection offered by the double jeopardy clause declines sharply in other contexts. As discussed, it is seriously limited as a protection against subsequent prosecution after conviction and against multiple punishments. Additionally, the prohibition on double jeopardy does not protect against prosecutions by both the state and federal governments[164] or by two or more states for the same offense.[165] Neither does it offer protection

[157]United States v Scott, 437 US 82 (1978).
[158]United States v Ball, 163 US 662, 671–672 (1896); United States v Tateo, 377 US 463 (1964).
[159]United States v Tateo, 377 US 463, 466 (1964).
[160]United States v Scott, 437 US 82, 91 (1978).
[161]Tibbs v Florida, 457 US 31, 43 (1982).
[162]Ibid., 44.
[163]Whalen v United States, 445 US 684, 699 (1980).
[164]Bartkus v Illinois, 359 US 121 (1959) (upholding a state conviction for bank robbery after an unsuccessful federal prosecution for the same offense). Abbate v United States, 359 US 187 (1959) (upholding a federal conviction after a state conviction). Successive state and municipal prosecutions are barred, however. Waller v Florida, 387 US 387 (1970).
[165]Heath v Alabama, 474 US 82 (1985).

against appeals by the prosecution to obtain an increased sentence[166] nor against statutory schemes that authorize enhancement of a sentence for one crime based on evidence of related criminal conduct.[167] Double jeopardy protections are inapplicable to sentencing proceedings except in capital cases.[168]

Finally, a major limitation of the double jeopardy clause is that it does not apply to civil cases. The Court has held that civil penalties may amount to punishment and thus be limited by the double jeopardy clause.[169] In 1997, the Court held that state legislation establishing procedures for the institutionalization of violent sexual predators after they complete a prison term did not amount to punishment because it had neither a retributive nor a deterrent function. Its purpose was simply to protect the community from harm.[170]

> nor shall be compelled in any criminal case to be a witness against himself,

The self-incrimination clause prohibits the government from forcing an individual to provide evidence that can be used against him or her in a criminal proceeding. The protection applies only to evidence of a testimonial nature not to physical evidence.[171] Accordingly, one may not rely on the right against self-incrimination to refuse to submit handwriting samples, to provide voice samples, to be fingerprinted, to appear in a police lineup, to submit to a breath test, or to give a blood sample.[172] The protection is most obviously applicable to criminal trials and police interrogations: a defendant cannot be required to take the witness stand and confessions may not be secured by coercion. But the right against self-incrimination extends beyond the context in which an individual is a suspect or a defendant in a trial. If called to testify at another person's trial, one may not refuse to testify but may refuse to answer particular questions on the ground of self-incrimination. The clause also protects those who are called to testify before civil, administrative, and legislative proceedings.

For most of its history the self-incrimination clause only protected an accused who refused to answer incriminating questions in federal trials. In 1908, the Court held that the guarantee against self-incrimination was not essential to the concept of due process embodied in the Fourteenth Amendment.[173] The Court upheld a state law in 1947 that permitted the judge and prosecutor to comment on the defendant's failure to take the witness stand, again reasoning that a state does not necessarily violate principles of due process by requiring an accused to provide testimony at trial.[174] The Fourteenth Amendment's due process clause required the states to comply with the general principles of fun-

---

[166]*United States v DiFrancesco*, 449 US 117 (1980).
[167]*Witte v United States*, 515 US 389 (1995); *Monge v California*, 524 US 721 (1998).
[168]*Bullington v Missouri*, 451 US 430 (1981).
[169]See *United States v Halper*, 490 US 435 (1989) (disproportionate civil fine amounted to punishment); *Department of Revenue of Montana v Kurth Ranch*, 511 US 767 (1994) (state tax on marijuana struck down); *United States v Ursery*, 518 US 267 (1996) (civil forfeiture upheld).
[170]*Kansas v Hendricks*, 521 US 346 (1997).
[171]*Pennsylvania v Munitz*, 496 US 582 (1990).
[172]*Schmerber v California*, 384 US 757 (1967); *South Dakota v Neville*, 459 US 553 (1983).
[173]*Twining v New Jersey*, 211 US 78 (1908). In *Twining*, the Court held that principles of due process were not violated by the judge's comment on defendant's refusal to testify at his trial.
[174]*Adamson v California*, 332 US 46 (1947).

damental fairness, which mandated that the accused be given a fair trial. Thus, when it was faced with challenges to state convictions on grounds that testimony was compelled or a confession was coerced, the Court proceeded on a case-by-case basis, asking not whether the state had violated the right against self-incrimination but whether it had behaved in a way that was consistent with fundamental fairness. It was not until 1964 that the Court held that the due process clause of the Fourteenth Amendment incorporated the self-incrimination clause. Writing for the majority in *Malloy v Hogan*, Justice William J. Brennan explained, "It would be incongruous to have different standards determine the validity of a claim of privilege based on the same feared prosecution, depending on whether the claim was asserted in a state or federal court. Therefore, the same standards must determine whether an accused's silence in either a federal or state proceeding is justified."[175]

Custodial Interrogations and Coerced Confessions

Although the Supreme Court relied in one case on the Fifth Amendment privilege against self-incrimination to consider the admissibility of confessions in the federal courts,[176] in subsequent decisions it relied instead on legislation requiring prompt presentment of federal arrestees before a judicial officer. The Court grounded its authority to require that evidence obtained in violation of that rule be excluded in its responsibility to supervise the administration of criminal justice in federal proceedings.[177] It was not until 1936 that the justices reviewed the use of a confession in the state courts.[178] In *Brown v Mississippi*, the justices considered whether the use of the confessions of three black men to convict them of the murder of a white farmer violated the Fourteenth Amendment due process clause. The confessions provided the only basis for the convictions, and the methods the police used to extract those confessions were shocking. The sheriff and a group of vigilantes hung one of the suspects from a tree until he was near death, let him down and did it again; then they tied him to a tree and whipped him. The other two suspects were taken to the police station where they were stripped and whipped with a leather belt and metal buckle. The police made it clear to all three of the suspects that the beatings and torture would continue until they confessed. Those facts were not disputed; indeed, the deputy sheriff admitted the beatings in his testimony at the trial. In his opinion for the majority, Chief Justice Charles Evans Hughes reiterated that the Fifth Amendment's self-incrimination clause was not binding on the states but noted, "It would be difficult to conceive of methods more revolting to the sense of justice" than those used to obtain the confessions. All of the justices agreed that those methods and the use of the confessions to convict constituted an obvious denial of due process.[179]

---

[175]*Malloy v Hogan*, 378 US 1, 11 (1964).
[176]*Bram v United States*, 168 US 532 (1897).
[177]*McNabb v United States*, 318 US 332 (1943) and *Mallory v United States*, 354 US 449 (1957).
[178]*Brown v Mississippi*, 297 US 278 (1936).
[179]*Ibid.*, 286.

With *Brown v Mississippi*, the Court began to develop a standard for determining whether a confession violated the requirements of due process that it continued to use for almost thirty years. The standard revolved around the question of whether, considering the "totality of the circumstances" in each case, a confession was voluntary or whether the defendant had been deprived of the power to resist.[180] If a confession failed the **"voluntariness" test**, the Court would rule it inadmissible and reverse the conviction. A primary factor in the "totality of the circumstances" was the conduct of the police. Although the justices found physical mistreatment to be most obviously impermissible, they also began to find that extremely long interrogation sessions in which the police questioned the suspect in isolation without advice from counsel, family, or friends were inconsistent with due process.[181] The Court also began to hold that the use of psychological coercion to obtain a confession was constitutionally unacceptable. In one case, the police had a state-employed psychiatrist pose as a doctor brought in to treat the suspect's painful sinus condition. The psychiatrist was successful in obtaining a confession. The Court found that the suspect's ability to resist had been broken by the psychiatrist's use of his considerable skills.[182] In another case after the defendant declined to answer questions without his attorney present, detectives brought in a young police officer who was the defendant's close friend to conduct the interrogation. The officer told the defendant that if he did not get a statement, he would lose his job, bringing hardship to his wife and children. After an all-night session, the defendant confessed. The Court found that official pressure, fatigue, and sympathy falsely aroused overcame the defendant's will; thus, the confession failed the voluntariness test.[183] The characteristics of the accused were also important to the Court's determination of the voluntariness of a confession. Thus, finding a confession to have been coerced, the Court commonly emphasized such characteristics as the youthfulness of an accused,[184] intelligence and education,[185] and mental illness.[186]

The voluntariness standard had a number of problems. Its focus on the suspect's response to police interrogation methods made it highly subjective. It was also no easy task for the justices to examine all the facts surrounding each challenged confession because in most cases those facts were not clear. Although the brutality under which the confessions were obtained in *Brown* was not in dispute, conflicting testimony at trial, particularly as to what happened in the interrogation room, was far more common. Additionally, the case-by-case analysis failed to produce a consistent set of rules. For example, in a case it decided in 1941, the Court held that a confession was voluntary even though the suspect was held in police custody for eleven days and subjected to periodic in-

---

[180]*Fikes v Alabama*, 352 US 191, 197 (1957).
[181]*Ashcraft v Tennessee*, 322 US 143 (1944).
[182]*Leyra v Denno*, 347 US 556 (1954).
[183]*Spano v NY*, 360 US 315 (1959).
[184]*Haley v Ohio*, 332 US 596 (1948).
[185]*Davis v North Carolina*, 384 US 737 (1966). In *Crooker v California*, 357 US 433 (1958), the Court found the confession to be voluntary and noted that the accused was a college graduate who had attended law school and studied criminal law.
[186]*Blackburn v Alabama*, 361 US 199 (1960).

terrogation, including an all-night session, with no counsel, and his arraignment was illegally delayed.[187] Only a year earlier, the Court had found another confession obtained under similar circumstances to be involuntary.[188] One of the factors in the totality of circumstances—the conduct of the police—was similar, but another—the characteristics of the suspect—was not. The suspects in the earlier case were, according to the majority opinion, ignorant tenant farmers, whereas in the later case the suspect was intelligent and experienced. The Court seemed to suggest that more severe police tactics would be allowed for suspects who, because of education and experience, would be more likely to resist pressure to confess. The most serious problem with the voluntariness test was its connection to the due process clause of the Fourteenth Amendment, which the Court continued to rule, required only that state criminal proceedings comply with a standard of fundamental fairness. The vague standard left the states free of an objective, specific rule. It also made federal supervision over the state courts and police practices impossible. Thus, police interrogation practices continued to vary from state to state and no one could be certain exactly what was permissible.

In 1958, four justices proposed an alternative to the voluntariness standard. In a dissenting opinion Justice Douglas, joined by Warren, Black, and Brennan, argued that the denial of the suspect's request for an attorney during the interrogation constituted a violation of due process required by the Fourteenth Amendment.[189] In a subsequent case, all of the justices agreed that a confession obtained through psychological coercion was inadmissible. But while the majority relied on the voluntariness test, Douglas, Black, Brennan, and Stewart argued that the defendant was entitled to consult with a lawyer during the interrogation.[190]

In three cases that the Court decided in the spring of 1964, the majority decidedly cast aside the voluntariness test. In the first of those cases, the majority turned to the Sixth Amendment right to counsel as the basis for finding a defendant's postindictment statements inadmissible.[191] In that case, the defendant had already been indicted and had retained an attorney. Thus, it was not clear whether the new rule applied either to interrogations that took place before indictment or to a suspect who had not retained an attorney. It seemed plausible that, if confronted with such facts, the Court would return to the voluntariness test. The Court would soon provide an answer. Before it did, however, the Court announced that the right against self-incrimination applied to the states.[192] Although *Malloy v Hogan* did not involve a confession, Justice Brennan asserted in his opinion for the majority that the admissibility of confessions must be tested by the same standard in state and federal proceedings. In the third case, decided only a week later, the Court again relied on the Sixth Amendment and clarified the conditions under which the accused must be

---

[187]*Lisenba v California*, 314 US 219 (1941).
[188]*Chambers v Florida*, 309 US 227 (1940).
[189]*Crooker v California*, 357 US 433 (1958). See also, *Cicenia v LaGay*, 357 US 504 (1958).
[190]*Spano v NY*, 360 US 315 (1959).
[191]*Massiah v United States*, 377 US 201 (1964).
[192]*Malloy v Hogan*, 378 US 1, 11 (1964).

availed of the right to counsel. In *Escobedo v Illinois*, Justice Arthur Goldberg wrote for a five-member majority explaining that the right to counsel is violated where

> The investigation is no longer a general inquiry into an unsolved crime but has begun to focus on a particular suspect, the suspect has been taken into police custody, the police carry out a process of interrogations that lends itself to eliciting incriminating statements, the suspect has requested and been denied an opportunity to consult with his lawyer, and the police have not effectively warned him of his absolute constitutional right to remain silent.[193]

While Goldberg explicitly grounded his exclusion of Escobedo's confession on the right to counsel, he also referred to "the right of the accused to be advised by his lawyer of his privilege against self-incrimination.[194]

Two years later in *Miranda v Arizona*, Chief Justice Warren, writing for a five-member majority, announced that the Fifth Amendment right against self-incrimination is fully applicable to custodial interrogations.[195] The majority thereby incontrovertibly abandoned both the case-by-case due process analysis and the Sixth Amendment approach. The Court replaced the subjective "totality of the circumstances" voluntariness approach with an objective set of procedural safeguards that the police must use. If they fail to use the safeguards, all statements they obtain from suspects will be deemed inadmissible in criminal proceedings; all convictions in which such statements were used will be reversed.

The Court was very precise about what safeguards are required: "Prior to any questioning, the person must be warned that he has a right to remain silent, that any statement he does make may be used as evidence against him, and that he has a right to the presence of an attorney, either retained or appointed."[196] Further, although the defendant may waive those rights, so long as the waiver is made voluntarily, knowingly, and intelligently, if he or she indicates in any manner and at any stage of the process a wish to consult with an attorney before speaking, there can be no questioning.

Miranda brought a barrage of criticism from the four dissenting justices as well as law enforcement officials and numerous commentators. Perhaps the most oft-repeated criticism was that the new rules would make it impossible for law enforcement officials to obtain confessions and other information from suspects—information that is crucial to the investigation and punishment of crimes.

Miranda raised a number of questions that the Court has answered in subsequent decisions. One issue of crucial importance was whether the requirements set forth in *Miranda* amounted to a constitutional rule or whether they constituted instead a "prophylactic" rule going beyond the constitutional

---

[193]*Escobedo v Illinois*, 378 US 478, 490–491 (1964).
[194]*Ibid.*, 488.
[195]*Miranda v Arizona*, 384 US 436 (1966) was decided with three other cases: *Vignera v New York*, *Westover v United States*, and *California v Stewart*.
[196]*Ibid.*, 444–445.

requirement—a safeguard to protect Fifth Amendment rights. If the *Miranda* warnings were not required by the Constitution, then Congress could legislate to guarantee the protection against self-incrimination through other means and, in effect, could overrule *Miranda*. This issue came before the Court in 2000, and it was widely expected that the Rehnquist Court would take the opportunity to overrule *Miranda*. A seven-member majority, however, declined to do so and instead held that Congress did not have the authority to replace the *Miranda* requirements with a case-by-case test of whether a confession was voluntary.[197] In his opinion for the majority, Chief Justice Rehnquist emphasized that there was no justification for overruling *Miranda*, a ruling that had become embedded in routine police practice. Thus, although the *Miranda* rule still stands, between 1966 and 2003 both the Burger and Rehnquist Courts narrowed it considerably. We consider some of the clarifications of and modifications to *Miranda* in the next two sections.

Clarifications of *Miranda*

At first glance *Miranda* appears to provide the most straightforward rule possible: no statements will be admissible unless the police first give the proper warnings and receive a valid waiver. Further scrutiny, however, reveals a variety of unresolved issues. "When is a suspect in custody?" has been among the most frequently litigated of those issues.

In his opinion in *Miranda*, Chief Justice Warren defined **custodial interrogation** as "questioning initiated by law enforcement officers after a person has been taken into custody or otherwise deprived of his freedom of action in any significant way."[198] In 1969, the Court confirmed what Warren's opinion suggested: law enforcement officials must provide the *Miranda* warnings to all individuals who are deprived of their freedom of action. It makes no difference whether a suspect is deprived of freedom at the police station or at home in bed.[199] Subsequently, however, the Court held that an interview conducted by Internal Revenue Service agents in a private home did not constitute custodial interrogation even though the interviewee was the focus of a criminal investigation.[200] In another case the Court rejected the Oregon Supreme Court's contention that the office of the state police was a coercive environment and therefore interrogation of a robbery suspect who appeared voluntarily at the police station required the *Miranda* warnings. The Court ruled that under such conditions a suspect is not in custody so long as he or she is free to leave at any time.[201] In 1983 in a case with similar facts, the justices reaffirmed their position that interrogation at a police station, though it may have coercive aspects,

---

[197]*Dickerson v US* 530 US 428 (2000). The law that replaced the *Miranda* warnings with a test of voluntariness was 18 U.S.C. Section 3501. Enacted in 1968, the law had not been challenged previously because it had not been applied. That is, no prosecutor had sought a conviction without *Miranda* warnings, with the claim that they were unnecessary under the law.
[198]*Miranda v Arizona*, 444.
[199]*Orozco v Texas*, 394 US 324 (1969).
[200]*Beckwith v United States*, 425 US 341 (1976).
[201]*Oregon v Mathiason*, 429 US 492 (1977); *California v Beheler*, 463 US 1121 (1983).

does not amount to custody unless there is a " 'formal arrest or restraint on freedom of movement' of the degree associated with a formal arrest."[202]

In 1984 and again in 1988, the Court held that a moderate amount of questioning pursuant to a routine traffic stop does not amount to custodial interrogation.[203] Thus, statements the police elicited from the drivers without *Miranda* warnings indicating intoxication were admissible. A majority of the Court has also held that incriminating statements a man made to his probation officer in her office were admissible because there was no formal arrest or restraint on freedom of movement of the degree associated with formal arrest. In short, the probationer was not in custody.[204]

It is common for prisoners to petition for federal habeas corpus review after a state court of last resort determines that an incriminating statement made in the absence of *Miranda* warnings was admissible because it was made when the defendant was not in custody. A troubling question that the Court did not resolve until 1995 was how much deference federal courts should give to state trial court determinations that a defendant was not in custody at the time he or she made incriminating statements. Some of the Courts of Appeals followed the rule that a state court determination of whether a person was in custody is a factual matter and thus, under federal statute,[205] entitled to a presumption of correctness. Other circuits adopted the position that in-custody determinations are mixed questions of law and fact and, therefore, warrant independent review by the federal court in a habeas corpus proceeding.

The Supreme Court adopted the latter view.[206] Justice Ruth Bader Ginsburg, writing for a seven-member majority, contended that providing for independent review of in-custody determinations "should serve legitimate law enforcement interests as effectively as it serves to insure protection of the right against self-incrimination."[207] She expressed confidence that the federal courts will make legal determinations that will guide police, unify precedent, and stabilize the law. Justice Clarence Thomas, who was joined by Chief Justice Rehnquist in dissent, argued that the state trial judge is in a far better position than a federal court to decide the issue of *Miranda* custody.

Warren's statement in *Miranda* that linked custody to the deprivation of "freedom of action in any significant way" remains central to the Court's determination of whether a suspect was in custody and therefore entitled to the *Miranda* warnings. Nevertheless, the justices, attempting to clarify the definition of custody, have constructed a rule with several elements. First, to make the in-custody determination, a court must examine all the circumstances surrounding the interrogation. Still, the Court has maintained that "the ultimate inquiry is simply whether there [was] a 'formal arrest or restraint on freedom of movement' of the degree associated with a formal arrest."[208] Second, the justices have

---

[202]*California v Beheler*, 463 US 1121, 1125 (1983) quoting *Oregon v Mathiason*, 429 US 492, 495 (1977).
[203]*Berkemer v McCarty*, 468 US 420 (1984). The Court held that *Miranda* applies to custodial interrogation for misdemeanor traffic offenses. *Pennsylvania v Bruder*, 488 US 9 (1988).
[204]*Minnesota v Murphy*, 465 US 420 (1984).
[205]28 U.S.C. 2254(d).
[206]*Thompson v Keohane*, 516 US 99 (1996).
[207]*Ibid.*, 16.
[208]*Stansbury v California*, 511 US 318 (1994).

insisted that whether a suspect was in custody is to be determined by the objective circumstances of the interrogation rather than the subjective views of the interrogating officers or the person being questioned. Thus, it is not determinative that the police have focused an investigation on the particular suspect whom they are questioning or that the suspect believes that he or she is not free to leave. Finally, given the objective circumstances, would a reasonable person have felt he or she was not at liberty to terminate the interrogation and leave?

A second issue *Miranda* did not fully resolve was "What constitutes interrogation?" In his opinion, Chief Justice Warren defined **interrogation** as "questioning initiated by law enforcement officers."[209] He also noted:

> Any statement given freely and voluntarily without any compelling influences is, of course, admissible in evidence. The fundamental import of the privilege while an individual is in custody is not whether he is allowed to talk to the police without the benefit of warnings and counsel, but whether he can be interrogated. There is no requirement that police stop a person who enters a police station and states that he wishes to confess to a crime, or a person who calls the police to offer a confession or any other statement he desires to make.[210]

Thus, incriminating statements made outside the context of interrogation do not require the *Miranda* warnings. Frequently, however, questions arise concerning whether the interaction between police and a suspect constituted interrogation. Consider, for example, the following situation. On Christmas Eve, a ten-year-old girl disappeared from the YMCA in Des Moines, Iowa. Shortly after her disappearance, Robert Williams, a resident of the YMCA and an escapee from a mental hospital, was seen placing a bundle with two legs sticking out of it into his car. His abandoned car was found the following day in Davenport, about 160 miles from Des Moines. A warrant was then issued in Des Moines for Williams's arrest. The next day, Williams's lawyer went to the Des Moines police station and informed the officers that he had advised Williams to turn himself in to the police. Williams surrendered the same morning in Davenport and was booked and given the *Miranda* warnings. An arrangement was made between the police and Williams's lawyer for two Des Moines police detectives to drive to Davenport to pick up Williams and bring him back to Des Moines and not to question him during the trip. Williams's lawyer also spoke to his client and advised him not to talk about the missing child until they could consult back in Des Moines. Another lawyer who conferred with Williams in Davenport reiterated to the police and to Williams that there was to be no interrogation on the journey to Des Moines.

During the trip one of the detectives and the prisoner engaged in a wide-ranging conversation. The detective, who knew not only that Williams was a mental patient but also that he was deeply religious, delivered what came to be known as the "Christian Burial Speech":

> I want to give you something to think about while we're traveling down the road
> . . . Number one, I want you to observe the weather conditions, it's raining, it's

---

[209]*Miranda v Arizona*, 384 US 436, 444 (1966).
[210]*Ibid.*, 478.

sleeting, it's freezing, driving is very treacherous, visibility is poor, it's going to be dark early this evening. They are predicting several inches of snow for tonight, and I feel that you yourself are the only person that knows where this little girl's body is, that you yourself have only been there once, and if you get a snow on top of it you yourself may be unable to find it. And, since we will be going right past the area on the way into Des Moines, I feel that we could stop and locate the body, that the parents of this little girl should be entitled to a Christian burial for the little girl who was snatched away from them on Christmas [E]ve and murdered. And I feel we should stop and locate it on the way in rather than waiting until morning and trying to come back out after a snow storm and possibly not being able to find it at all.[211]

Williams offered to show the officers where the body was and then directed them to it.

Despite objections from his lawyer, Williams's statements and the evidence derived from those statements were admitted at his trial. In *Brewer v Williams*, by a vote of five to four, the Court found that the police had violated Williams's Sixth Amendment right to counsel. The question of whether the police had interrogated Williams was crucial to the decision. Writing for the majority, Justice Stewart noted that the constitutional guarantee of assistance of counsel came into play only because the "Christian burial speech" was tantamount to interrogation.

Three years later in *Rhode Island v Innis*, the Court held that a conversation between police and a suspect that was quite similar to the one that occurred between Williams and the detectives did not constitute interrogation. The body of a taxicab driver who had disappeared on his way to pick up a passenger was found with a shotgun wound in the back of the head. Another taxi driver reported that a man with a sawed-off shotgun had robbed him. The taxi driver saw a picture of Thomas Innis at the police station and identified him as his assailant. A patrolman found Innis, arrested him, and advised him of his *Miranda* rights. Two other officers arrived and also both gave Innis the warnings. Innis responded that he understood his rights and wanted to speak with a lawyer. He was then placed in a police car with three officers. A fourth officer instructed the others not to question Innis or intimidate or coerce him in any way on the way to the police station. Traveling to the station, two of the officers in the car engaged in a conversation that one explained in his testimony as follows.

At this point, I was talking back and forth with Patrolman McKenna stating that I frequent this area while on patrol and [that because a school for handicapped children is located nearby,] there's a lot of handicapped children running around in this area, and God forbid one of them might find a weapon with shells and they might hurt themselves.[212]

---

[211]*Brewer v Williams*, 430 US 387, 392–393 (1977).
[212]*Rhode Island v Innis*, 446 US 291, 294–295 (1980).

The second officer testified that he had agreed and had suggested that they continue to try to find the weapon. The third officer testified that he heard one of the others say that "it would be too bad if the little—I believe he said a girl—would pick up the gun, maybe kill herself."[213] Innis then interrupted the officers and told them to turn the car around so he could show them where the gun was located. Before Innis led them to the gun, one of the officers gave him the *Miranda* warnings again. Innis responded that he understood but "wanted to get the gun out of the way because of the kids in the area in the school."[214]

Relying heavily on *Brewer v Williams*, the state supreme court reversed Innis's conviction. The state court found that the officers had engaged in subtle coercion that was the equivalent of interrogation after Innis invoked his right to counsel and, therefore, had violated *Miranda's* mandate that once a suspect asks for counsel all interrogation must cease. A six-member majority of the United States Supreme Court disagreed. Writing for the majority, Justice Stewart announced that "the *Miranda* safeguards come into play whenever a person in custody is subjected to either express questioning or its functional equivalent."[215] The functional equivalent of express questioning, he went on to explain, consists of any words or actions on the part of the police that they should know are reasonably likely to elicit an incriminating response from the suspect. Stewart emphasized that the police did not expressly question Innis but simply engaged in a conversation among themselves and did not invite any response from him. Nor was there any indication that the police should have known their conversation was reasonably likely to elicit an incriminating response. Nothing in the record suggested either that the police knew that Innis was unusually susceptible to an appeal to his conscience about the safety of handicapped children or that he was unusually disoriented or upset at the time of his arrest.

In 1987, the Court had an opportunity to elaborate further on what constitutes interrogation in a case that involved the following facts. A man named Mauro was arrested and advised of his *Miranda* rights after he freely admitted that he had killed his son and led the police to the body. Advised of his rights again at the police station, Mauro stated that he did not wish to make any more statements without having a lawyer present. All questioning ceased, but the officers allowed Mauro to speak with his wife, who was also a suspect, at her request. The meeting took place in the presence of an officer and was recorded. During the brief conversation, Mauro told his wife not to answer questions until a lawyer was present. At Mauro's trial, the prosecution used the conversation to rebut his insanity defense. Mauro's lawyer argued that the recording was a product of police interrogation in violation of the *Miranda* requirements. The Arizona Supreme Court agreed, relying on the statement in *Innis* defining interrogation as a practice that the police should know is reasonably likely to evoke an incriminating response from a suspect. The officers' testimony at Mauro's trial, the Arizona court noted, revealed that they both knew that incriminating

---

[213]*Ibid.*, 295.
[214]*Ibid.*
[215]*Ibid.*, 300–301.

statements were likely to be made if the conversation between Mauro and his wife took place. Therefore, the tape recording should not have been admitted at Mauro's trial. A five-member majority of the United States Supreme Court disagreed, holding that the behavior of the police did not constitute interrogation. The police did not question Mauro about the crime or his conduct nor was there any suggestion that the officers' decision to allow Mauro's wife to see him was a psychological ploy. There was no evidence that the officers allowed the meeting for the purpose of eliciting incriminating statements. Moreover, it was unlikely that Mauro felt that he was being coerced when he was allowed to see his wife. Even if the officers were aware of the possibility that Mauro would make some incriminating statements to his wife, "Officers do not interrogate a suspect simply by hoping that he will incriminate himself."[216]

A third issue that needed clarification after *Miranda* concerned the portion of the requirements that allow for a knowing, voluntary, and intelligent waiver of the right to remain silent and to speak with an attorney. What constitutes a valid waiver? In his opinion in *Miranda*, Warren cautioned that when an interrogation continues without an attorney present, "a heavy burden rests on the government to demonstrate that the defendant knowingly and intelligently waived his privilege against self-incrimination and his right to retained or appointed counsel."[217] Moreover, an express statement that a suspect is willing to make a statement and does not want an attorney followed closely by a statement could constitute a waiver. Nevertheless, Warren noted, "a valid waiver will not be presumed simply from the silence of the accused after warnings are given or simply from the fact that a confession was in fact eventually obtained."[218] Those comments gave rise to the question of whether an express statement of a waiver was required for the prosecution to meet its burden. The Court provided an answer in 1979 when a majority declined to adopt a rule requiring an express written or oral statement from the suspect to establish the validity of that waiver.[219] An explicit statement is not always required and a suspect's silence, though not alone sufficient, can help to support a finding of waiver when considered in conjunction with the particular facts and circumstances of the case, including the background, experience, and conduct of the accused.

Miranda made it clear that once a suspect asserts his or her right to remain silent all interrogation must cease. It was not clear, however, under what conditions—if at all—it would be possible for a suspect subsequently to waive the right and, thus, for interrogation to resume. In 1975, the justices provided some clarification by rejecting the claim that the assertion of *Miranda* rights creates a prohibition of "indefinite duration upon any further questioning by any police officer on any subject, once the person in custody has indicated a desire to remain silent."[220] The crucial issue in determining whether statements that result from subsequent rounds of interrogation after the suspect has indicated a wish not to answer questions, the Court held, is whether the

---

[216]*Arizona v Mauro*, 481 US 520, 529 (1987).
[217]*Miranda v Arizona*, 384 US 436, 475 (1966).
[218]*Ibid.*
[219]*North Carolina v Butler*, 441 US 369 (1979).
[220]*Michigan v Mosley*, 423 US 96, 102–103 (1975).

defendant's right to cut off questioning was "scrupulously honored." The police in this case had complied with that standard as they had immediately ceased the interrogation, resumed questioning only after the passage of a significant period of time and a new set of warnings, and restricted the second interrogation to a crime that had not been a subject of the earlier interrogation.

The "scrupulously honored" test applies when a defendant has invoked the right to silence but not the right to counsel. In *Edwards v Arizona*, the Court adopted the rule that when a defendant invokes the right to counsel he or she is not subject to further questioning until a lawyer has been made available or the suspect reinitiates conversation.[221] Clarifying the phrase "made available," the Court held that it did not mean merely the opportunity to consult with an attorney outside the interrogation room. The accused must have counsel present during the questioning.[222] Thus, once a suspect asserts the right to counsel, he or she cannot validly waive that right during any interrogation that the police initiate.

Edwards v Arizona created an objective rule that once a suspect requests an attorney, the police must end the interrogation. What if a suspect does not explicitly request an attorney but instead only makes some reference to a lawyer? The Court has answered that in such a situation if the reference was ambiguous or equivocal to the extent that "a reasonable officer, in light of the circumstances, would have understood only that the suspect might be invoking the right to counsel," questioning need not cease.[223] Finally, can a suspect who did not know that a lawyer was trying to contact him properly waive his rights when he talks to the police? Does the fact that the police failed to notify him that a lawyer had called render the waiver invalid? The Court provided an answer in *Moran v Burbine* when it held that such a confession was admissible, reasoning that "events occurring outside the presence of the suspect and entirely unknown to him surely can have no bearing on the capacity to comprehend and knowingly relinquish a constitutional right."[224]

Modifications to *Miranda*

Without directly addressing modifications to *Miranda,* the preceding discussion indicated that the Burger and Rehnquist Courts' clarifications of *Miranda* have resulted in relaxing constraints on law enforcement. The Court has used other means as well to narrow *Miranda*. Beginning in the early 1970s, a majority of the Court began to carve out exceptions to the *Miranda* rules. In 1971, a six-person majority held that statements preceded by defective *Miranda* warnings could be used to impeach the defendant's credibility if he chose to testify at his trial.[225] In subsequent cases involving the use of statements obtained in violation of *Miranda* for impeachment purposes, the Court has held that statements can be used that were obtained when the police continued to

---

[221]*Edwards v Arizona,* 451 US 477 (1981).
[222]*Minnick v Mississippi,* 498 US 146 (1990).
[223]*Davis v United States,* 512 US 452, 459 (1994).
[224]*Moran v Burbine,* 475 US 412, 422 (1986).
[225]*Harris v NY,* 401 US 222 (1971).

question a suspect after he requested a lawyer.[226] Also, a defendant's silence after he was arrested but not under custodial interrogation could be used to impeach his testimony.[227]

The Court created a major exception to *Miranda* in 1984 in *New York v Quarles* when Justice Rehnquist announced that "the need for answers to questions in a situation posing a threat to public safety outweighs the need for the . . . rule protecting the FifthAmendment."[228] The Court reached that conclusion in a case involving the following facts: a woman approached two police officers and reported that she had just been raped by a man who had then gone into a supermarket nearby and that he was carrying a gun. The officers drove the woman to the supermarket, one of them entered the store and spotted the suspect who ran to the rear of the store, briefly disappearing from the view of the officer. When the officer reached the suspect he frisked him and found that he was wearing an empty holster. After handcuffing him, the officer asked him where the gun was, and the suspect responded, "The gun is over there," pointing to some empty cartons. The officer then retrieved a loaded .38-caliber revolver, formally placed the defendant under arrest, and read him his *Miranda* rights.

In Quarles's prosecution for criminal possession of a weapon, the judge excluded the statement, "the gun is over there," because the officer had not given Quarles the *Miranda* warnings before asking him where the gun was. The state appellate courts agreed but the United States Supreme Court ruled that when police officers "ask questions reasonably prompted by a concern for the public safety,"[229] the *Miranda* warnings are not required. The **public safety exception** requires the police to distinguish between questions that are necessary to secure their own safety or the safety of the public and questions designed solely to elicit testimonial evidence from a suspect. Only the latter require *Miranda* warnings.

In the context of the Fourth Amendment, the exclusionary rule prohibits the use not only of evidence obtained directly from an unconstitutional search but all evidence subsequently obtained through the use of information acquired during that search. Such evidence is considered to be "tainted" by the unconstitutional search and the rule that it must be excluded is known as the "fruit of the poisonous tree" doctrine or the fruits doctrine.[230] In 1985, the Court held that the fruits doctrine does not apply to *Miranda* violations. That case originated with an investigation of a burglary in which Michael Elstad was implicated. Police officers went to his home and without giving him the *Miranda* warnings conveyed their belief that he had been involved in the burglary.

Elstad responded, "Yes, I was there." He was arrested, taken to police headquarters and about one hour later was advised of his rights. He indicated that he understood his rights and that he wished to speak with the officers, gave a full statement, and signed a confession explaining his participation in the bur-

---

[226]*Oregon v Hass*, 420 US 714 (1975).
[227]*Fletcher v Weir*, 455 US 603 (1982).
[228]*New York v Quarles*, 467 US 649 (1984).
[229]*Ibid.*
[230]The doctrine began with *Silverthorne Lumber Co. v United States*, 251 US 385 (1920).

glary. At his trial, Elstad's lawyer argued that the initial statement "let the cat out of the bag" and tainted the subsequent confession. The trial judge, nevertheless, admitted the confession and Elstad was convicted of burglary. The Oregon Court of Appeals reversed, holding that the period separating the questioning in Elstad's home from his interrogation at police headquarters was so brief that the initial statement letting "the cat out of the bag" had a coercive impact on his subsequent admission.

In *Oregon v Elstad*, Justice O'Connor, writing for six members of the Court, emphasized the "fundamental differences between the role of the Fourth Amendment exclusionary rule and the function of *Miranda* in guarding against the prosecutorial use of compelled statements as prohibited by the Fifth Amendment."[231] She explained that the purpose of the Fourth Amendment exclusionary rule is to deter unreasonable searches. In contrast, the *Miranda* rule serves the Fifth Amendment prohibition on the use of compelled statements and "sweeps more broadly than the Fifth Amendment itself"[232] by establishing an irrebuttable presumption that statements obtained under conditions of custodial interrogation without warnings are compelled. But that presumption, she reasoned, extends only to the state's use of an unwarned statement in its case in chief—that is, Elstad's initial statement could not be used as evidence against him. But the initial statement did not render his subsequent confession inadmissible. Because his initial statement was voluntary though technically in violation of *Miranda*, Elstad's later statement after he had been given the proper warnings was admissible so long as it was voluntary in light of all the surrounding circumstances.[233]

Justice Brennan argued in his dissent that the majority had delivered "a potentially crippling blow to *Miranda*." The Court, he noted, cast aside an important and long-recognized presumption that an illegally obtained confession may cause an accused to confess again out of a belief that "he already has sealed his fate" and discarded the requirement that the prosecution affirmatively rebut that presumption before the subsequent confession.[234]

In 1991, the Court adopted another device to limit *Miranda* when, by a vote of five to four, it held that the erroneous admission of a coerced confession is subject to harmless-error analysis.[235] The Court held that the admission of the coerced confession in the circumstances of that particular case was not harmless and, therefore, reversed a conviction for murder. More important, however, by exempting coerced confessions from the rule of automatic reversal, the Court opened the way for reviewing courts to find that confessions obtained in violation of *Miranda* are admissible so long as the confession is deemed not to have caused any inaccuracy in the determination of guilt. Thus, if the prosecution has sufficient evidence for a conviction that is independent of the coerced confession, a reversal will not be necessary.

---

[231]*Oregon v Elstad*, 470 US 298, 304 (1985).
[232]*Ibid.*, 306.
[233]The Court suggested the inapplicability to *Miranda* of the fruits doctrine in 1974 when it held that information gained from statements a suspect made after incomplete *Miranda* warnings could be used to assist the prosecution in developing its case. *Michigan v Tucker*, 417 US 433 (1974).
[234]*Oregon v Elstad*, 470 US 298, 319 (1985).
[235]*Arizona v Fulminante*, 499 US 279 (1991).

The more conservative justices on the Burger Court and subsequently the Rehnquist Court have commonly taken the opportunity in dicta to alter *Miranda*'s constitutional basis and its central purpose, and, thereby, diminish its effect. For example, in *Michigan v Tucker*, Justice Rehnquist characterized the *Miranda* rights as merely "prophylactic standards," "procedural safeguards," "designed to safeguard or to provide practical reinforcement for the privilege against self-incrimination" that "were not themselves rights protected by the Constitution."[236] Similarly, Justice O'Connor emphasized that *Miranda* goes beyond what the Fifth Amendment requires.[237] Several justices have also helped to pave the way for limiting *Miranda* by emphasizing that its purpose is to prevent coercion. If so, then the warnings need only be given in contexts that are potentially coercive.[238] Moreover, if a confession obtained in violation of *Miranda* may nevertheless be voluntary, as O'Connor argued in *Oregon v Elstad*, it may be possible to conclude that warnings were not required. By such means, the Court has been able to avoid expressly repudiating *Miranda* but nevertheless to depart from one of its central presumptions: that custodial interrogations inherently involve compulsion and, therefore, require specific safeguards.

In *Miranda*, the Court replaced the old voluntariness-totality of the circumstances standard with the per se rule that incriminating statements will not be admissible in the absence of specific warnings. Nevertheless, the Court has spent the years since the early 1970s moving away from that rule back toward a more flexible, less exacting approach that gives the police more room to maneuver in their efforts to obtain confessions.

Testimony and Self-Incrimination

Because of the vast amount of litigation and the complexity of the issues surrounding police interrogation, *Miranda* and its progeny tend to dominate discussions of the self-incrimination clause. There are other important aspects of the protection against self-incrimination that need to be considered, however.

At the center of the protection against compulsory self-incrimination is the defendant's right in a criminal trial to refuse to take the witness stand. The Court has given force to that right by providing guidelines concerning what prosecutors and trial judges are allowed to say about a defendant's failure to take the stand. A federal statutory provision first enacted in 1878[239] specified that failure to take the stand could create no presumption of guilt and the Court held in 1893 that jurors must not hear any comment on a defendant's choice not to testify.[240] The self-incrimination clause did not apply to the states until 1964.[241] But less than a year later in *Griffin v California*, the Court held that "either comment by the prosecution on the accused's silence or instructions by the court that such silence

---

[236]*Michigan v Tucker*, 417 US 433, 444 (1974).
[237]*Oregon v Elstad*, 470 US 298, 304, 306 (1985).
[238]See, for example, *Illinois v Perkins*, 496 US 292 (1990) (Jail cell with undercover officer not coercive).
[239]18 U.S.C. 3481.
[240]*Wilson v United States*, 149 US 60 (1893).
[241]*Malloy v Hogan*, 378 US 1, 11 (1964).

is evidence of guilt" is forbidden in both state and federal proceedings.[242] The rationale for such a rule, as Justice William O. Douglas explained, is that such statements by judges and prosecutors would be "a penalty imposed by courts for exercising a constitutional privilege. [They would] cut . . . down on the privilege by making its assertion costly."[243] In subsequent decisions, the Court answered some questions left open in *Griffin*. It held, for example, that a judge's instruction to the jury not to draw an unfavorable inference from a defendant's failure to testify when given over the defendant's objection does not violate the prohibition on compulsory self-incrimination.[244] Then in *Carter v Kentucky*, the Court held that when the defendant requests it, the trial judge must instruct the jury not to draw an inference of guilt from defendant's silence at trial.[245]

The Court's holding in *Griffin* that "either comment by the prosecution on the accused's silence or instructions by the court that such silence is evidence of guilt" violate the Fifth Amendment might be interpreted to ban all references by the prosecution to a defendant's decision not to testify. A majority of the Court has chosen to read *Griffin* considerably more narrowly, however. Chief Justice Rehnquist's opinion for five members of the Court in *United States v Robinson*[246] in 1988 illustrates the way the Court has narrowed *Griffin*. In a federal trial for mail fraud, defense counsel stated several times in his closing argument that the prosecution had not allowed the defendant to explain his side of the story. In his summation, the prosecutor remarked that the defendant "could have taken the stand and explained it to you." The judge then admonished the jury that no inference could be drawn from a defendant's decision not to testify. The Court of Appeals, relying on *Griffin*, held that the prosecutor's reference to the defendant's failure to testify violated the Fifth Amendment.

The Supreme Court disagreed. Noting that *Griffin* requires that a prosecutor's comments be examined in context, Rehnquist characterized the comments in this case as a "fair response" to a claim made by the defendant's counsel that did not violate the right against compulsory self-incrimination. He distinguished the situation here from the one condemned in *Griffin* where the prosecutor "on his own initiative asks the jury to draw an adverse inference from a defendant's silence, or to treat the defendant's silence as substantive evidence of guilt."[247] Here, Rehnquist explained, the prosecutor's comment merely "referred to the possibility of testifying as one of several opportunities which the defendant was afforded, contrary to the statement of his counsel, to explain his side of the case."[248] In short, according to the Court, *Griffin* did not ban all "comment by the prosecution on the accused's silence" but only comments by the prosecution that silence is evidence of guilt.

---

[242] *Griffin v California*, 380 US 609 (1965).

[243] *Ibid.*, 380 US 609, 614 (1965).

[244] *Lakeside v Oregon*, 435 US 333 (1978).

[245] *Carter v Kentucky*, 450 US 288 (1981).

[246] *United States v Robinson*, 485 US 25 (1988).

[247] *Ibid.*, 485 US 25 (1988).

[248] *Ibid.* See also, *Lockett v Ohio*, 438 US 586 (1978), where prosecutor repeatedly referred to the state's evidence as "unrefuted" and "uncontradicted." The Court held that there was no violation of the right against self-incrimination because the comments added nothing to the impression that had already been created by the defendant's refusal to testify after her lawyer had told the jury that she would take the stand.

Even if a prosecutor's comments or a judge's instructions violate the rules, the violation may be considered harmless error.[249] Under the Court's harmless-error doctrine, certain constitutional violations, including violations of the *Griffin* rules, do not require reversal if the prosecution can demonstrate beyond a reasonable doubt that the error did not contribute to the verdict. The Court clarified the impact of applying the harmless-error rule to comments on a defendant's failure to testify when it noted that such comments cannot be labeled harmless error where the comment "is extensive, where an inference of guilt from silence is stressed to the jury as a basis of conviction, and where there is evidence that could have supported acquittal."[250] In *Carter v Kentucky*, the Court in dicta alluded to the possibility that a judge's refusal to honor the defendant's request to instruct the jury not to infer guilt from the defendant's decision not to testify might never be harmless."[251]

A number of questions about the right against self-incrimination have arisen in the context of investigations by legislative committees. In the early 1950s, at the height of the McCarthy era both state and federal legislative committees were engaged in investigating "communist subversion" in virtually all realms of American life including the highest levels of government, labor unions, education, and the entertainment industry. Individuals called to testify about their beliefs, activities, and associations were vulnerable to prosecution under both state and federal laws that made it a crime to organize, to conspire to organize, or to belong to groups engaged in advocating the violent overthrow of the government.[252] Thus, they were clearly entitled to refuse to answer questions on self-incrimination grounds.[253] Those who did so, however, paid a high price in practical terms. Labeled "Fifth Amendment Communists," their reputations and careers were destroyed. "Taking the Fifth" also proved to be quite limited in a legal sense. Witnesses often found that once they answered questions they were considered to have waived their right against self-incrimination so could not refuse to answer related questions. Moreover, because the self-incrimination clause cannot be used to protect others, witnesses who were asked to provide the investigators with names of people allegedly engaged in subversive activities could not rely on the Fifth Amendment to refuse to do so. Even during the McCarthy era, however, the right against self-incrimination was not entirely devoid of meaning. In 1956, for example, a majority of the Court held that a provision of the New York City Charter requiring the termination of any city employee who relied on the privilege against self-incrimination to avoid an-

---

[249]*Chapman v California*, 386 US 18 (1967). See also, *United States v Hasting*, 461 US 499, 507 (1983), holding that the Court of Appeals should have applied the harmless-error doctrine.
[250]*Anderson v Nelson*, 390 US 523, 524 (1968).
[251]*Carter v Kentucky*, 450 US 288, 304 (1981).
[252]The Smith Act, 18 U.S.C. 2385, made it a crime to advocate knowingly the desirability of overthrow of the Government by force or violence, to organize or help to organize any society or group that teaches, advocates, or encourages such overthrow of the government, to be or become a member of such a group with knowledge of its purposes.
[253]In *Quinn v United States*, 349 US 155, 161 (1955), the Court noted that "limitations on the power to investigate are found in the specific individual guarantees of the Bill of Rights, such as the Fifth Amendment's privilege against self-incrimination."

swering a question before a legislative committee could not be applied to all employees who invoked the Fifth Amendment before investigating committees.[254]

In a series of decisions in the late 1960s and early 1970s, the Court extended broad protection to public employees who refuse to answer questions on Fifth Amendment grounds. The Court held that statements obtained under threat of removal from office may not be used in a subsequent prosecution.[255] Subsequently, the justices ruled that a police officer could not be discharged for his refusal to waive his right against self-incrimination before a grand jury.[256] The justices later extended the same protection to public contractors, holding that a state cannot cancel existing contracts nor deny future contracts to those who refuse to testify before a grand jury without immunity.[257] The Court has made clear, however, that public employees may be dismissed for refusing to answer questions "specifically, directly, and narrowly relating to the performance of [their] official duties"[258] if their answers cannot be used against them in subsequent criminal prosecutions. Finally, the justices have continually affirmed that lying is never protected. Most recently, the Court held that a federal agency may punish employees for making false statements regarding employment-related misconduct.[259]

Compelled Testimony and Immunity

We considered immunity briefly in our discussion of the grand jury provision of the Fifth Amendment. The rules concerning immunity for testimony before grand juries apply to other government hearings as well. Thus, when individuals who are called to testify before legislative committees are offered immunity—and usually the arrangement is involuntary—they may not rely on the Fifth Amendment to refuse to answer questions. Under such circumstances refusal to answer can result in prosecution for criminal contempt.[260] Also, consistent with the principle that lying is never protected, even when immunity has been granted, any testimony may be used in a prosecution for perjury.

When the government grants immunity, it must be as broad as the protection provided by the self-incrimination clause. As noted earlier, the Court has approved "use immunity," which bars the prosecution from use of a witness's compelled testimony and any information derived directly or indirectly from that testimony.[261] Use immunity leaves open the possibility for a witness

---

[254]*Slochower v Board of Education*, 350 US 551 (1956). During this time, the Court did allow dismissal of public school teachers who belonged to organizations that advocated the violent overthrow of the government by unlawful means, or who were unable to explain satisfactorily membership in certain organizations found to have that aim. *Adler v Board of Education*, 342 US 485 (1952).
[255]*Garrity v New Jersey*, 385 US 493 (1967).
[256]*Gardner v Broderick*, 392 US 273 (1968). In *Uniformed Sanitation Men Assn, Inc. v Commissioner of Sanitation*, 392 US 280 (1968), the Court reached the same conclusion with regard to sanitation workers.
[257]*Lefkowitz v Turley*, 414 US 70 (1973).
[258]*Gardner v Broderick*, 392 US 273, 278 (1968).
[259]*La Chance v Erickson*, 522 US 262 (1998). In *Bryson v United States*, 396 US 64, 72 (1969), the Court stated, "Our legal system provides methods for challenging the Government's right to ask questions—lying is not one of them. A citizen may decline to answer the question, or answer it honestly, but he cannot with impunity knowingly and willfully answer with a falsehood."
[260]*Piemonte v United States*, 367 US 556 (1961).
[261]*Kastigar v United States*, 406 US 441 (1972).

to be prosecuted for criminal violations related to the testimony, but the government must prove that the evidence was gathered completely independent of that testimony.

Prosecutions resulting from the Iran-Contra scandal raised some intriguing questions about use immunity. In early 1987, Congress established two committees to investigate allegations that the United States had secretly sold arms to Iran, used the proceeds to provide illegal support to the Contras in Nicaragua, and then attempted to cover up those activities. Lieutenant Colonel Oliver L. North, a former member of the National Security Council, called to testify before the committees, was granted use immunity. His testimony, which lasted six days, was carried live on national television and radio and replayed widely on news broadcasts. As a result of the investigation by Independent Counsel Lawrence E. Walsh, of criminal activities by government officials in the Iran-Contra affair, North was prosecuted in 1989 and convicted of three criminal violations, including lying to Congress. In his appeal, North argued that the trial court had violated his right against self-incrimination by not requiring the prosecution to establish independent sources for the testimony of witnesses before the grand jury and at trial and to demonstrate that witnesses did not use North's compelled testimony. A number of witnesses "had their memories refreshed by" and "were thoroughly soaked in" North's immunized testimony. The Court of Appeals admonished that *any* use of immunized testimony to refresh the memories of witnesses "or otherwise to focus their thoughts, organize their testimony, or alter their prior or contemporaneous statements," constitutes prohibited use in violation of the federal use immunity statute and the Fifth Amendment.[262] The rules are violated anytime the prosecution puts on a witness whose testimony is shaped directly or indirectly by compelled testimony, regardless of whether the prosecution or the witnesses themselves did the shaping. Because the trial court could not establish that witnesses' testimony had not been influenced by the immunized testimony, North's convictions could not stand. The Court of Appeals shortly thereafter reversed John M. Poindexter's criminal convictions for his role in the Iran-Contra affair, relying on its decision in *North*.[263]

The Court of Appeals rulings in *North* and *Poindexter* placed a formidable—possibly, insurmountable—obstacle in the path of the government's attempts to prosecute public officials accused of criminal activities who have previously testified either before a grand jury or a congressional committee under a grant of use immunity. In the increasingly common situation in which such testimony is made public, it may be impossible for the prosecution to find useful witnesses who have not been exposed to the immunized testimony. Forced to use such witnesses, the prosecution may find it impossible to meet the heavy burden of demonstrating that the immunized statements of the defendant did not have any

---

[262]*United States v North*, 910 F2d 843, 860 (1990), modified, *United States v North*, 920 F2d 940 (1990).

[263]Poindexter, National Security Advisor in 1985, also testified before Congress under a grant of use immunity. He was subsequently convicted of five criminal violations including lying to Congress. His convictions were reversed on appeal on the grounds that the Independent Counsel had not carried the burden of showing that Poindexter's compelled testimony was not used against him at his trial. *United States v Poindexter*, 951 F2d 369 (1991).

effect on their testimony. Consequently, congressional committees and prosecutors will need to develop strategies for obtaining information without precluding criminal convictions. It seems likely that public figures who are clearly guilty of criminal violations but who have information crucial to an investigation of widespread official wrongdoing will be virtually immune from any criminal sanction either for the criminal misconduct itself, for covering it up, or even for lying to the investigators.

Personal Papers

As noted earlier, the protection against compulsory self-incrimination applies to testimonial rather than physical evidence. An individual's private papers, however, protected by the Fourth Amendment prohibition on unreasonable searches and seizures, also implicate the self-incrimination clause of the Fifth Amendment. As the Court noted in *Boyd v United States,* "[W]e have been unable to perceive that the seizure of a man's private books and papers to be used in evidence against him is substantially different from compelling him to be a witness against himself."[264]

Although the Court has expressly recognized that the very act of production of papers and records can be incriminating,[265] the extent to which the Fifth Amendment offers protection in this context is quite limited. First, consistent with the principle that the self-incrimination clause applies only to testimonial evidence, the protection of personal papers does not apply to their contents but only to their production and then only under certain conditions. An individual may rely on the right against self-incrimination to refuse to produce papers only if there are testimonial aspects of their production that would be incriminating. More specifically, the protection applies only if the production of the documents would supply incriminating evidence that the government would not otherwise have that the records exist, that they are in his or her possession, and that they are authentic.[266] Second, the protection does not apply to the production of records of corporations, labor unions, or business partnerships but only of individuals.[267] Finally, the protection extends only to the person who is compelled to produce the records. Accordingly, a taxpayer could not rely on the right against self-incrimination when his accountant was required to produce records in the accountant's possession.[268]

The Due Process Clause

▮ nor be deprived of life, liberty, or property, without due process of law;

Due process is one of the most important concepts in American constitutional law. The Constitution includes two due process clauses. The due process

---

[264]*Boyd v United States,* 116 US 616 (1886).
[265]*Fisher v United States,* 425 US 391 (1976).
[266]*Fisher v United States,* 425 US 391 (1976); *United States v Doe,* 465 US 605 (1984).
[267]*Bellis v United States,* 417 US 85 (1974).
[268]*Couch v United States,* 409 US 322 (1973).

clause of the Fourteenth Amendment expressly applies to the states, whereas the due process clause of the Fifth Amendment applies to actions of the federal government.

When James Madison proposed the language in the first Congress, no state had a due process clause in its own constitution. But it was far from a new concept as it was identified with a phrase in the thirty-ninth chapter of the Magna Carta (1215) requiring that the King abide by the "law of the land." That great charter of English liberties promised that "no freeman shall be arrested, or imprisoned, or disseized, or outlawed, or exiled, or in any way molested; nor will we proceed against him, unless by the lawful judgment of his peers or by the law of the land."[269] The Framers understood due process to mean in accordance with regularized common law procedures.[270] In England, the king was limited by due process whereas Parliament was not, but in the nineteenth century the Supreme Court held that due process was a limitation on the legislature as well as the executive and the judiciary.[271]

The primary purpose of due process is to ensure fair procedures when the government imposes a burden on an individual.[272] Particularly relevant to the burdens imposed by the criminal justice system, the due process clause makes clear that the government can deprive individuals of liberty and property—and perhaps life—so long as it follows the proper procedures. Although the guarantee of fair procedures is central to due process, the Court has also used a **substantive concept of due process** to protect property rights. In *Dred Scott v Sandford* in 1857, for example, seven members of the Court agreed that the due process clause prohibited Congress from regulating slavery in the territories in large part because that would interfere with the property rights of slaveholders.[273] Additionally, early in the twentieth century the Court used the due process clause of the Fourteenth Amendment to invalidate state legislation that imposed limits on businesses including minimum wage and maximum hours regulations.[274]

Several recent and current justices have argued that the Court should adhere to the early understanding of due process as no more and no less than the regularized common law procedures. Justice Scalia, for example, has frequently urged that due process is defined by those processes known to the English Common Law at the time of our independence, as modified by the consensus of American experience, reflected in the practices of our legislatures and courts

---

[269]As quoted in C. Herman Pritchett, *Constitutional Civil Liberties* (Englewood Cliffs, NJ: Prentice Hall, 1984), 9.
[270]In *Murray's Lessee v Hoboken Land and Improvement Co.*, 59 US 272 (1856), Justice Benjamin Curtis attempted to articulate the principles on which the Court would rely in deciding whether a particular process fulfilled the requirements of due process. First, did it comport with the Constitution? Second, was it consistent with "those settled usages and modes of proceeding existing in the common and statute law of England, before the emigration of our ancestors, and which are shown not to have been unsuited to their civil and political condition by having been acted on by them after the settlement of this country"?
[271]*Ibid.*
[272]Thomas O. Sargentich, "Due Process, Procedural." In Kermit L. Hall, ed. *The Oxford Companion to the Supreme Court* (New York: Oxford University Press, 1992), 236.
[273]*Scott v Sandford*, 60 US 393 (1857).
[274]See, for example, *Lochner v New York*, 198 US 45 (1905), in which the Court invalidated a maximum hours regulation for bakers; *Adkins v Children's Hospital*, 261 US 525 (1923). *Adkins* involved a regulation on wages for women and children in Washington, D.C. and therefore the Fifth Amendment rather than the Fourteenth.

during the past two hundred years. Chief Justice Rehnquist and Justices Kennedy and Thomas agree. In contrast, Justice Brennan advanced an **evolving concept of due process,** arguing that judges have a responsibility to make an independent inquiry to determine whether government has acted in accordance with standards of fairness. Similarly, Justices O'Connor and Souter have objected to Scalia's static "historical status quo" understanding of due process.[275] The justices' disparate conceptions of due process reflect the divisions on the Court regarding the proper method of interpreting the Constitution and the role of the judiciary in the American constitutional system.

Most of the Supreme Court's major decisions regarding due process have been challenges to state or local rather than federal practices and have, therefore, involved the Fourteenth rather than the Fifth Amendment. We discuss many of those cases in Chapter 10.

The Takings Clause

▪   nor shall private property be taken for public use, without just compensation.

The takings clause protects property by limiting government's power of eminent domain—that is, its authority to take private property for public use. The first provision in the Bill of Rights to be applied to the states through the due process clause of the Fourteenth Amendment,[276] the takings clause obligates the government to pay "just compensation" when it takes property.[277]

Two major questions that the Court has been called on to answer in regard to the takings clause are, first, whether **a taking** has occurred and, second, if it has, whether the government took the property for public use. The takings clause prohibits the actual physical takeover by the government of private property without just compensation. One commentator summarized that requirement as follows: "If the government wants to convert a private house into a post office, or run a new highway through a farm, or build a dam which will flood nearby land, it is going to have to compensate the losses sustained as a result of these activities."[278]

A more difficult question arises, however, when a property owner contends that a regulation, such as a zoning restriction, constitutes a taking. The Court has established the general rule that governmental regulation of property amounts to a taking when it actually takes the property or prevents its use in such a way that the value is virtually destroyed. On the other hand, if the regulation is an exercise of the police power to protect the health, safety, and morals of the community, the resulting economic loss is not a taking and compensation is not required.

In 1978 in *Penn Central Transportation Company v City of New York,* a six-member majority held that the application of New York City's Landmarks

---

[275]*Medina v California,* 505 US 437 (1992).

[276]*Chicago, Milwaukee & St. Paul Ry. v Minnesota,* 134 US 418 (1890).

[277]Just compensation is considered to be fair value: "[T]he owner is entitled to receive what a willing buyer would pay in cash to a willing seller at the time of the taking." *United States v 564.54 Acres of Land,* 441 US 506 (1979).

[278]Joseph L. Sax, "Takings and the Police Power," *Yale Law Journal* 74 (1964): 36–75.

Preservation Law to prohibit the construction of a fifty-three-story office building on top of Grand Central Station was not a taking. Writing for the majority, Justice Brennan noted that the Landmarks Law did not interfere with the uses of the building as a railroad terminal, with office space and concessions, and that not all development was prohibited and concluded that the restrictions were "substantially related to the general welfare and permit reasonable beneficial use of the landmark site."[279] In 1980, the Court unanimously upheld land-use regulations that restricted residential development by limiting the number and type of houses that could be built on land in Tiburon overlooking San Francisco Bay.[280] Justice Powell reasoned that the ordinance substantially advanced legitimate governmental interests in protecting the residents of the city from the ill effects of urbanization and that the restrictions did not completely deny the use of the land. Then-Justice Rehnquist vigorously disagreed, arguing that when the value of property decreases as a result of a regulation, it constitutes a taking.[281] When Scalia joined the Court in 1986 he led the Court's effort to transform the takings clause into a powerful tool to protect the interests of property owners.

Three cases that the Court decided between 1987 and 1994 provide a clear illustration of the reinvigoration of the takings clause. In *Nollan v California Coastal Commission*, by a vote of five to four, the Court held that a state land-use commission could not require waterfront property owners to set aside a strip of their property for the public to walk across as a condition of building a larger house without a showing that there was a substantial relation between the governmental purpose and the condition.[282] The majority could not find any relationship between requiring public access to the beach and the governmental purpose of increasing the view of the beach. Then by a vote of six to three in *Lucas v South Carolina Coastal Commission*, the justices held that if a new land regulation enacted since the owner purchased the land prohibits economically productive or beneficial uses of the land, compensation must be paid even if the government has a compelling interest in enacting the regulation. In that case after Lucas purchased oceanfront lots, the state enacted a law giving the coastal council authority to protect shoreline areas from erosion. The council then decided that building on Lucas's lot would be dangerous to the environment and prohibited any construction rendering his land worthless.[283] Finally, in *Dolan v City of Tigard* the justices reviewed a claim by a property owner that the City Planning Commission's decision to condition permission for the enlargement of her business site on leaving a portion of the property open for a bicycle/pedestrian path and devoting some of it to a public green space constituted a taking. The Commission was acting pursuant to a municipal land-use ordinance that—for environmental and flood control purposes—

[279]*Penn Central Transportation Company v City of New York*, 438 US 104 (1978).
[280]*Agins v City of Tiburon*, 447 US 255 (1980).
[281]See, for example, *San Diego Gas and Electric Company v City of San Diego*, 450 US 621 (1981); *United States v Security Industrial Bank*, 459 US 70 (1982). See also, Rehnquist's opinion for the majority in *Kaiser Aetna v United States*, 444 US 164 (1979).
[282]*Nollan v California Coastal Commission*, 483 US 825 (1987).
[283]*Lucas v South Carolina Coastal Commission*, 505 US 1003 (1992).

required owners in the central business district to leave a portion of their space open or landscaped. A five-member majority agreed that the conditions constituted a taking in the absence of a more specific showing that there was a relationship between the conditions on the proposed development and the impact of that development on traffic congestion and flooding hazards. The Court's use of a heightened level of scrutiny in that case prompted Justice Stevens to compare the majority's approach with the discredited doctrine of substantive due process as well as to comment that "property owners have surely found a new friend today."[284]

In 2002 Justices O'Connor and Kennedy, who were both in the majority in *Dolan*, joined Stevens and three other justices to uphold Tahoe Regional Planning Agency's moratoria on development in the Lake Tahoe Basin for two and one-half years pending completion of a comprehensive land-use plan for the area.[285] In his opinion for the majority Stevens distinguished between a physical taking—an acquisition of property for public use—and a regulation prohibiting private uses. The latter constitutes a regulatory taking, which, in contrast to a physical taking, falls outside the categorical rule that a taking of property requires compensation. Stevens emphasized that cases involving physical takings should not be treated as precedent for cases in which a regulatory taking has been challenged. Instead, when there has been a regulatory taking, the Court should examine all the relevant circumstances carefully to determine whether compensation is required. Accordingly, in this case the Court held that because the moratoria had only a temporary impact on the value of the land it did not constitute a taking that required compensation.

Since the 1940s, the Court has regularly allowed legislatures to decide what constitutes public use.[286] The Court's deference to legislative determinations was particularly clear in its unanimous decision in 1984 upholding the Hawaii Land Reform Act. To redress problems created by concentrated land ownership, the act set up a condemnation scheme according to which long-term renters of certain designated property could ask the Hawaii Housing Authority to require owners to sell their land to them. The landowners who lost their property argued that the act violated the takings clause because it took property from one party and made it available to others for private—rather than public—use. In her opinion for the Court, Justice O'Connor noted that the exercise of the power of eminent domain need only be rationally related to a conceivable public purpose. She concluded that the Hawaii legislature had enacted the law in an attempt to reduce the social and economic evils of land concentration and had adopted a rational approach in doing so.[287] In 1992, the Court had no difficulty in finding a public purpose when the government took 48.8 miles of railroad track from the Boston and Maine Railway and gave it to Amtrak to facilitate its passenger railroad service.[288]

---

[284]*Dolan v City of Tigard*, 512 US 374 (1994).
[285]*Tahoe-Sierra Preservation Council v Tahoe Regional Planning Agency*, __ US __ (2002). Souter, Ginsburg, and Breyer were the other three members of the majority.
[286]See, for example, *United States ex rel. Tennessee Valley Authority v Welch*, 327 US 546 (1946), and *Berman v Parker*, 348 US 26 (1954).
[287]*Hawaii Housing Authority v Midkiff*, 467 US 229 (1984).
[288]*National Railroad Passenger Corp. v Boston & Maine Corp.*, 503 US 407 (1992).

The Court has declined to extend its support for property owners to forfeitures imposed on property used in criminal activity even when an owner is not involved in the criminal behavior and has no knowledge of it. In 1996 in a case in which a woman lost the value of her part ownership of the family car when her husband was caught having sex in it with a prostitute, the Court upheld a state law that mandated forfeiture of the car. By a vote of five to four, the justices rejected the claim that the law violated the takings clause pointing to the governmental interest in preventing further illicit use of the property and in making crime unprofitable.[289]

AMENDMENT VI: CRIMINAL COURT PROCEDURES

The Sixth Amendment identifies seven rights that pertain to "all criminal prosecutions": speedy trial, public trial, trial by jury, notice of the accusation, confrontation of opposing witnesses, compulsory process for obtaining favorable witnesses, and the assistance of counsel. All of these rights have been incorporated into the due process clause of the Fourteenth Amendment and are, therefore, applicable to the states.[290]

▊ In all criminal prosecutions, the accused shall enjoy the right to a speedy . . . trial

A defendant's right to a speedy trial attaches at the time of arrest or formal charge, whichever comes first.[291] The right to a speedy trial, as the Court has explained, involves three interests. It prevents oppressive incarceration prior to trial, alleviates anxiety and concern accompanying public accusation, and avoids the delay that will impair the ability of an accused to construct a viable defense.[292] The Court has repeatedly characterized the right to a speedy trial as a fundamental right—"one of the most basic rights preserved by our Constitution."[293] But it has also noted that the right to speedy trial "is a more vague concept than other procedural rights" and described the provision as amorphous and slippery.[294]

In *Barker v Wingo*,[295] the Court declined to adopt a precise rule for determining when the right to a speedy trial has been violated.[296] Instead, the justices identified four factors that courts are to consider in an ad hoc balancing analysis: the length of delay, the reason for the delay, the defendant's assertion

---

[289]*Bennis v Michigan*, 516 US 442 (1996).
[290]*Klopfer v North Carolina*, 386 US 213, 226 (1967) (speedy trial); *In re Oliver*, 333 US 257 (1948) (public trial); *Duncan v Louisiana*, 391 US 145 (1968) (trial by jury); *Pointer v Texas*, 380 US 400 (1965) (confrontation of opposing witnesses); *Washington v Texas*, 388 US 14 (1967) (compulsory process for obtaining favorable witnesses); *Gannett Co., Inc. v DePasquale*, 443 US 368 (1979) (notice of the accusation); *Gideon v Wainwright*, 372 US 335 (1963) (assistance of counsel).
[291]*Doggett v United States*, 505 US 647 (1992).
[292]*United States v Ewell*, 383 US 116, 120 (1966).
[293]*Klopfer v North Carolina*, 386 US 213, 226 (1967).
[294]*Barker v Wingo*, 407 US 514, 521–522 (1972).
[295]*Ibid.*
[296]The Court declined to adopt either a rule requiring a trial within a specified time or a demand-waiver rule whereby an accused would be deemed to have waived the right for any period prior to which he or she did not demand it.

of his or her right, and prejudice to the defendant as a result of the delay. First, after some period of time—how much time depends on the circumstances—the delay is sufficient to require further inquiry into the other circumstances. Second, the Court pointed to three categories of reasons for delay. A deliberate attempt by the prosecution to delay in order to hinder the defense should be counted heavily against the government, a more neutral reason "such as negligence or overcrowded courts" would count less heavily, and a valid reason, such as a missing witness, should serve to justify appropriate delay. Third, although it is not determinative, the defendant's assertion of the right to a speedy trial is so important that "failure to assert the right will make it difficult for a defendant to prove that he was denied a speedy trial."[297] The fourth factor is prejudice—that is, disadvantage—to the defendant's interests, particularly the interest in avoiding impairment in his or her ability to mount a successful defense. The death or disappearance of witnesses for the defense during the delay would be an obvious example of such prejudice. Although all four factors need to be considered, the Court made clear that the presence of any one factor by itself is neither necessary nor sufficient for finding a denial of the right to a speedy trial. Rather, "they are related factors and must be considered together with such other circumstances as may be relevant . . . these factors have no talismanic qualities; courts must still engage in a difficult and sensitive balancing process."[298] The Court's announcement in 1973 that dismissal is the only possible remedy for denial of the right to speedy trial underlines just how difficult and sensitive the balancing process is.[299]

The justices applied the four-part balancing analysis in *Doggett v United States*[300] and agreed with the defendant that his right to a speedy trial had been violated. Marc Doggett was indicted in 1980 on federal drug charges while he was out of the country. He had no knowledge of the indictment and two years later returned to the United States. Another six years passed before Doggett was arrested when a credit check on several thousand people subject to outstanding arrest warrants revealed his name and address. The Court found that the period of eight and a half years between indictment and arrest was clearly sufficient to trigger further inquiry into the other three factors. The delay occurred as a result of official negligence—a reason that weighs against the government though not as heavily as a deliberate attempt to delay in order to hamper the defense. Because Doggett did not know that he had been indicted, he could not have asserted his right to a speedy trial before his arrest. The government argued that Doggett had failed to show how he was disadvantaged by the delay. More specifically, he had not demonstrated how the delay weakened his ability to mount an effective defense.

A five-member majority, however, noted that even though Doggett "came up short" in regard to demonstrating specific prejudice, "excessive delay presumptively compromises the reliability of a trial in ways that neither party can

---

[297] *Ibid.*, 532.
[298] *Ibid.*, 533.
[299] *Strunk v United States*, 412 US 434 (1973).
[300] *Doggett v United States*, 505 US 647 (1992).

prove or, for that matter, identify. While such presumptive prejudice cannot alone carry a Sixth Amendment claim without regard to the other criteria, it is part of the mix of relevant facts, and its importance increases with the length of delay."[301] In a dissenting opinion that both Rehnquist and Scalia joined, Justice Thomas argued that the speedy trial clause does not protect defendants from the harm of prejudice to their ability to defend themselves resulting from the passage of time. In his view, the clause is limited to guaranteeing protection from "undue and oppressive incarceration" and the "anxiety and concern accompanying public accusation;" it does not extend to prejudice to the defense. The Court's contention in a decision in 1994 that a showing of prejudice is required to establish a violation of the speedy trial clause prompted some commentators to speculate that the Court may have revised the *Barker* four-part test.[302]

▮   and public trial,

The purpose of the requirement of a public trial, Justice Hugo Black wrote, was to protect the accused. He explained:

> The traditional Anglo-American distrust for secret trials has been variously ascribed to the notorious use of this practice by the Spanish Inquisition, to the excesses of the English Court of Star Chamber, and to the French monarchy's abuse of the lettre de cachet. . . . Whatever other benefits the guarantee to an accused that his trial be conducted in public may confer upon our society, the guarantee has always been recognized as a safeguard against any attempt to employ our courts as instruments of persecution.[303]

The right to a public trial applies not only to the entire trial but also to all pretrial proceedings that resemble a criminal trial. The right is considered to be adequately protected when the public has access to the trial even if everyone who wants to attend is not accommodated. To show a violation of the right, the defendant need not show a specific prejudice.

Despite its importance, the right to a public trial is not absolute. There may be overriding interests that justify closing a trial such as the defendant's right to a fair trial or the government's interest in preventing disclosure of sensitive information. In determining whether a trial should be closed, the trial court must balance the defendant's interest in a public trial against the reasons for closing it. If there is sufficient reason for closing a trial, the closure must not be any broader than necessary and the trial court must consider reasonable alternatives to closing the proceeding; it must also make specific findings adequate to support the closure.[304] Applying that test, the Court found that in a case involving prosecutions for violation of a state racketeering statute, the closing of a suppression hearing to everyone other than witnesses, court personnel, the parties, and the lawyers was unjustified.[305] The grounds on which the trial court based the decision to close the hearing—that because the evidence that the defendants

---

[301]*Ibid.*, 655–656.
[302]*Reed v Farley*, 512 US 339 (1994).
[303]*In re Oliver*, 333 US 257, 268–270 (1948), as quoted in *Estes v Texas*, 381 US 532, 539 (1965).
[304]*Waller v Georgia*, 467 US 39 (1984).
[305]*Ibid.*

sought to have suppressed related to alleged offenders not then on trial, the evidence would be tainted and could not be used in future prosecutions—were not specific enough to support closing the entire hearing.

The increasingly common practice of televising criminal trials underlines the tension between the constitutional requirements of fair trial and free press.[306] Although a state may permit the televising of a trial over the objections of the defendant,[307] a defendant may challenge his or her conviction on the grounds that televising the trial compromised the ability of the jury to decide fairly and, therefore, constituted a violation of due process. We considered the issue of media coverage of trials at some length in our discussion of the First Amendment.

■   by an impartial jury

The English colonists brought trial by jury to America. Later, as the Revolution approached, Americans fiercely resisted British attempts to restrict the right to a jury trial. The value that early Americans attached to trial by jury is evidenced by the fact that it is guaranteed in Article III, Section 2; in the Sixth Amendment; and in the context of civil proceedings, in the Seventh Amendment. Justice White explained the importance of trial by jury when he held that the right to a jury trial was fundamental and, therefore, applied to the states through the due process clause of the Fourteenth Amendment:

> A right to jury trial is granted to criminal defendants in order to prevent oppression by the Government. Those who wrote our constitutions knew from history and experience that it was necessary to protect against unfounded criminal charges brought to eliminate enemies and against judges too responsive to the voice of higher authority. . . . Providing an accused with the right . . . gave him an inestimable safeguard against the corrupt or overzealous prosecutor and against the compliant, biased, or eccentric judge.[308]

Dimensions of the Right to Trial by Jury

The right to a jury trial applies to all serious offenses—those that are punishable by imprisonment for more than six months.[309] It also applies to criminal contempt cases where a judge imposes more than six months' imprisonment even when that punishment is for multiple acts of contempt, each of which is punished by less than six months.[310]

The right to a jury trial does not extend to criminal offenses that the Court presumes to be petty—punishable by six months or less. Nevertheless, a defendant is entitled to a jury trial if he or she can demonstrate that additional statutory penalties considered along with the maximum authorized period of

---

[306]Federal rules of criminal procedure forbid radio or photographic coverage of criminal cases in federal courts, but most states now permit electronic, including television, coverage of courtroom proceedings. Susanna Barber, *News Cameras in the Courtroom: A Free Press-Fair Trial Debate* (Norwood, NJ: Ablex Publishing Corp., 1987), 9.
[307]*Chandler v Florida,* 449 US 560 (1981).
[308]*Duncan v Louisiana,* 391 US 145, 155–156 (1968).
[309]*Baldwin v New York,* 399 US 66 (1970).
[310]*Codispoti v Pennsylvania,* 418 US 506 (1974). In this case, the legislature had not set a maximum penalty for criminal contempt.

imprisonment are so severe that they reflect a legislative determination that the offense is a serious one. As Justice Marshall explained, "[T]his standard, albeit somewhat imprecise, should ensure the availability of a jury trial in the rare situation where a legislature packs an offense it deems 'serious' with onerous penalties that nonetheless 'do not puncture the 6-month incarceration line.'"[311]

In 1996, the Court held that a defendant who is prosecuted in a single proceeding for multiple petty offenses for which the aggregate potential punishment is more than six months does not have right to a jury trial.[312] Justice O'Connor, who wrote an opinion for five members of the Court, reasoned that by setting the maximum authorized prison term for obstructing the mail at six months Congress had categorized the offense as petty. That legislative assessment "is used to determine whether a jury trial is required, not the particularities of an individual case." Charging a defendant with two counts of a petty offense, she claimed, "does not revise the legislative judgment as to the gravity of that particular offense, nor does it transform the petty offense into a serious one, to which the jury-trial right would apply."[313] Further, she distinguished the case in which the Court held that multiple contempt sentences adding up to more than six months require a jury trial pointing out that in that case the legislature had not set a specific penalty for criminal contempt, leaving the determination to the judge.[314] Thus, a jury trial was needed to limit the judge's discretion particularly considering the pressures that a judge experiences when faced with sentencing for acts of criminal contempt in his or her own courtroom. In contrast, in this case Congress had set the maximum penalty at six months, thereby designating the offense as petty, and eliminating the need for a jury trial. Four justices disagreed with O'Connor's analysis. Kennedy, in a concurring opinion that Breyer joined, argued that the defendant in this case did not have a right to a jury trial only because the judge explained at the outset of the proceedings that she would not impose a sentence of more than six months. If she had not provided that guarantee, the defendant would have had the right to a jury trial. In a dissenting opinion, Stevens, who was joined by Ginsburg, argued that the legislature's determination of the severity of the charges against a defendant should be measured by the maximum sentence authorized for the prosecution as a whole rather than each individual offense.

Under the common law, a jury was composed of twelve members. In 1898, the Court noted that "the word 'jury' and the words 'trial by jury' were placed in the [C]onstitution . . . with reference to the meaning affixed to them in the law as it was in this country and in England at the time of the adoption of that instrument." Consequently, juries must be composed of twelve persons.[315] Af-

[311]*Blanton v North Las Vegas*, 489 US 538 (1989) (there is no right to a trial by jury for individuals charged under Nevada law with driving under the influence of alcohol, for which maximum punishment is six months incarceration or forty-eight hours of community work while identifiably dressed as a DUI offender, and a fine of $1,000, mandatory attendance at an alcohol abuse education course, and loss of license for 90 days). *United States v Nachtigal*, 507 US 1 (1993) (no right to a jury trial for individual charged with DUI in a national park, which carries a maximum penalty of six months' imprisonment and a $5,000 fine, and as an alternative to a term of imprisonment a term of probation of up to five years).
[312]*Lewis v United States*, 518 US 322 (1996).
[313]*Ibid.*
[314]*Codispoti v Pennsylvania*, 418 US 506 (1974).
[315]*Thompson v Utah*, 170 US 343, 350 (1898). At the time of the defendant's trial, Utah was a territory to which the Bill of Rights was fully applicable.

ter the incorporation of the right to trial by jury in 1968, it appeared that the juries in state courts, like those in federal courts, would have to be composed of twelve members. Thus, it came as quite a surprise two years later when the Court approved Florida's law providing that six individuals would constitute the jury to try all criminal cases except for capital crimes.[316] Justice White, who wrote for six members of the Court, claimed that the twelve-person jury was a "historical accident," "unnecessary to effect the purposes of the jury system and wholly without significance "except to mystics."[317] White emphasized the importance of preserving the essential feature of the jury, which he explained,

> obviously lies in the interposition between the accused and his accuser of the commonsense judgment of a group of laymen, and in the community participation and shared responsibility that results from that group's determination of guilt or innocence. . . . the number should probably be large enough to promote group deliberation, free from outside attempts at intimidation, and to provide a fair possibility for obtaining a representative cross-section of the community. But we find little reason to think that these goals are in any meaningful sense less likely to be achieved when the jury numbers six, than when it numbers 12— particularly if the requirement of unanimity is retained.[318]

In 1978, the justices invalidated Georgia's five-person jury relying heavily on research showing that reducing the size of the jury impairs its ability to carry out its essential functions.[319] Smaller juries, the studies suggested, are less likely to engage in effective group deliberation and may produce "inaccurate fact-finding and incorrect application of the common sense of the community to the facts." Additionally, as the size of the jury decreases, the risk of convicting an innocent person increases and verdicts of guilty increase. Finally, a smaller jury drastically reduces the likelihood that it will represent a cross-section of the community. Although the justices conceded that it was impossible to "discern a clear line between six members and five," they concluded that "the assembled data raise substantial doubt about the reliability and appropriate representation panels smaller than six"—problems that are so serious that they "attain . . . constitutional significance."[320]

Like the twelve-person jury, unanimity was traditionally considered to be an integral part of criminal procedure under the common law and was a constitutional requirement for federal jury trials.[321] In 1972, however, the Court held that unanimity is not required for conviction in state courts.[322] Upholding a guilty verdict based on a nine-to-three vote, Justice White maintained that unanimity was not necessary to give effect to the "reasonable doubt" standard. He rejected the argument that if nine jurors found guilt beyond a reasonable doubt, they would ignore the reasonable doubts of the remaining

---

[316] *Williams v Florida*, 399 US 78 (1970).
[317] *Ibid.*, 89, 102.
[318] *Ibid.*, 100.
[319] *Ballew v Georgia*, 435 US 223 (1978).
[320] *Ibid.*, 239.
[321] *Patton v United States*, 281 US 276 (1930).
[322] *Johnson v Louisiana*, 406 US 356 (1972); *Apodaca v Oregon*, 406 US 404 (1972).

three and terminate their deliberations. White also dispensed easily with the argument that unanimity is necessary for the jury to represent a cross-section of the community: "No group, . . . has the right to block convictions; it has only the right to participate in the overall legal processes by which criminal guilt and innocence are determined."[323] Five justices agreed that unanimity was not constitutionally required in state criminal trials. One of those five, however—Justice Powell—joined the other four justices to preserve the requirement for unanimity in federal trials. Although the Court has approved verdicts of nine to three when there are twelve jurors, it has held that the decisions of six-member juries must be unanimous.[324]

A Representative Jury: A Fair Cross-Section of the Community

There is a historical as well as a logical link between the mandate of an impartial jury and a representative jury drawn from a **cross-section** of the community. If a jury is not drawn from a broad-based representative pool but instead excludes certain groups in the community, it cannot be impartial. The constitutional prohibition on exclusion from juries is located not only in the Sixth Amendment, but also in the equal protection clause of the Fourteenth Amendment.

Many years before the Sixth Amendment applied to the states, the Court relied on the equal protection clause of the Fourteenth Amendment to condemn racial discrimination in jury selection.[325] The Court has extended that prohibition to discrimination on the basis of ethnicity.[326] More recently, a majority of the justices have held that the prohibition against racial, ethnic, and gender discrimination applies not only to the selection of the jury venire,[327] but also to the selection of individual jurors through the exercise of peremptory challenges.[328] Subsequently, the Court held that a defendant who was a member of a different race than that of the excluded juror could raise an equal protection objection. The guarantee of equal protection, the Court reasoned, precludes potential unfairness to a defendant who is tried by a jury from which members of his or her race are excluded. But the equal protection clause also prohibits the harm to the community at large and to the excluded prospective jurors who are prevented because of their race from an opportunity to participate in civil life.[329] Although the two constitutional protections are very different, there is an important overlap between the equal protection clause's prohibition of discrimination in jury selection and the Sixth Amendment's mandate that a jury be impartial.

---

[323]*Apodaca v Oregon*, 406 US 404, 413 (1972).
[324]*Burch v Louisiana*, 441 US 130 (1979).
[325]*Strauder v West Virginia*, 100 US 303 (1879).
[326]*Castaneda v Partida*, 430 US 482 (1977).
[327]The venire is the panel of individuals from which a jury is drawn.
[328]*Batson v Kentucky*, 476 US 79 (1986) (race); *Georgia v McCollom*, 505 US 42 (1992) (race); *J.E.B. v Alabama Ex Re. T.B.*, 511 US 127 (1994) (gender). The lawyers for each side in a criminal case have a specified number of peremptory challenges that they may use to eliminate a juror without giving any reason. The number of challenges for cause is not limited—most states have specified the permissible grounds for challenge for cause in statutes. One cause, for example, is that the juror is related to the defendant or others involved in the case.
[329]*Powers v Ohio*, 499 US 400 (1991).

The Court has held that the Sixth Amendment requires juries to be drawn from a "fair cross-section of the community."[330] All defendants are entitled to a jury that complies with the cross-section requirement. Consequently, as with equal protection challenges, a defendant may object to the composition of the jury on the grounds that it fails to comply with the requirement regardless of whether the defendant is a member of the class allegedly excluded. In 1975, the Court held that the cross-section requirement is violated by the systematic exclusion of women from jury panels.[331] The Court has articulated a three-part test that a defendant must pass to establish a prima facie violation of the cross-section requirement. The defendant must show that the excluded group is a distinctive group in the community, that the group is underrepresented in the pools from which juries are selected in relation to the group's size in the community, and that systematic exclusion of the group in the jury-selection process produced the under representation.[332]

The cross-section requirement has a major limitation in that a representative jury *pool* satisfies it. A representative *jury* is not required. The Court carefully limited the holding that juries must be drawn from a source fairly representative of the community by noting that "we impose no requirement that petit juries actually chosen must mirror the community and reflect the various distinctive groups in the population. Defendants are not entitled to a jury of any particular composition."[333] Subsequently, the Court made clear that, in contrast to the equal protection prohibition, the cross-section requirement applies only to the selection of the venire; it does not extend to peremptory challenges or challenges for cause.[334] In his opinion for a five-member majority Justice Scalia maintained that such a rule was the only plausible reading of the text of the Sixth Amendment and that "it best furthers the Amendment's central purpose . . . jury impartiality with respect to both contestants: neither the defendant nor the State should be favored. This goal, it seems to us, would positively be obstructed by a petit jury cross-section requirement which . . . would cripple the device of peremptory challenge."[335] He explained that although the "Sixth Amendment deprives the State of the ability to 'stack the deck' in its favor [that] is not to say that each side may not, once a fair hand is dealt, use peremptory challenges to eliminate prospective jurors belonging to groups it believes would unduly favor the other side."[336]

As noted, the Sixth Amendment requirement of an **impartial jury** does not require constraints on peremptory challenges. Neither has the Court imposed

---

[330]*Taylor v Louisiana*, 419 US 522 (1975).
[331]*Taylor v Louisiana*, 419 US 522 (1975). In this case, a male defendant objected to the exclusion of women. Under the Louisiana system, a woman could not serve on a jury unless she filed a written declaration of her willingness to do so. In *Duren v Missouri*, 439 US 357, 364 (1979), the Court held that provisions in Missouri law granting women an automatic exemption from jury service on request, which resulted in less than 15 percent women on jury venires violated the cross-section requirement.
[332]Establishing a prima facie violation does not invariably result in decision that the Sixth Amendment was violated. Once such a violation is established, the burden shifts to the government to demonstrate that there was a significant state interest in establishing criteria that produced the under-representation.
[333]*Taylor v Louisiana*, 419 US 522, 538 (1975).
[334]*Lockhart v McCree*, 476 US 162 (1986); *Holland v Illinois*, 493 US 474 (1990).
[335]*Holland v Illinois*, 493 US 474, 483–484 (1990).
[336]*Ibid.*, 481.

major limits on challenges for cause.[337] The constitutional regulation on both types of challenges is primarily limited to prohibiting racial discrimination under the equal protection clause of the Fourteenth Amendment.[338] Consequently, the Sixth Amendment's potential to guarantee a representative jury at the actual selection stage is severely limited.

Important questions about the Sixth Amendment requirement of an impartial jury have arisen in the context of the exclusion of certain prospective jurors in capital cases. In *Witherspoon v Illinois* the Court held that the defendant had been denied his right to an impartial jury by virtue of the fact that state law authorized the prosecution to exclude "from the jury all who expressed conscientious or religious scruples against capital punishment and all who opposed it in principle." The result—"a death qualified jury"—was an unrepresentative jury that was "uncommonly willing to condemn a man to die."[339] The Court announced that no one may be put to death by such a jury. Although *Witherspoon* limited the grounds on which prospective jurors may be excluded for cause from capital sentencing juries, in a footnote the Court left room for the exclusion of those whose views would interfere with their ability to serve as impartial jurors:

> [N]othing we say today bears upon the power of a State to execute a defendant sentenced to death by a jury from which the only veniremen who were in fact excluded for cause were those who made unmistakably clear (1) that they would automatically vote against the imposition of capital punishment without regard to any evidence that might be developed at the trial of the case before them, or (2) that their attitude toward the death penalty would prevent them from making an impartial decision as to the defendant's guilt.[340]

Several decisions after *Witherspoon* further established the general rule that a juror may only be excused for cause from a sentencing jury based on his or her views about capital punishment if those views would clearly interfere with his or her ability to perform the duties of a juror.[341] Thus, it seemed that a prospective juror could not be excluded merely for expressing uncertainty about the death penalty. Additionally, the Court held that even if only a single prospective juror is improperly excluded the death penalty cannot stand.[342]

In a subsequent case, a lower federal court, relying on the language of the footnote in *Witherspoon*, held that a prospective juror in a capital sentencing proceeding who expressed personal reservations but did not make it "unmistakably clear" that she would "automatically vote" against a sentence of death had been improperly excused. The Supreme Court reversed in *Wainwright v Witt*, noting that the proper standard for excluding jurors from sentencing in capital cases was whether the juror's views would "prevent or substantially im-

---

[337]But see, *Dennis v United States*, 339 US 162 (1950), and *Smith v Phillips*, 455 US 209 (1982).
[338]*Ham v South Carolina*, 409 US 524 (1973).
[339]*Witherspoon v Illinois*, 391 US 510, 520–521 (1968).
[340]*Ibid.*, 522–523, Note 21.
[341]See *Boulden v Holman*, 394 US 478, 483–484 (1969); *Lockett v Ohio*, 438 US 586, 595–596 (1978); *Adams v Texas*, 448 US 38 (1980).
[342]*Davis v Georgia*, 429 US 122 (1976).

pair the performance of his duties as a juror in accordance with his instructions and his oath."[343] Writing for the majority, Justice Rehnquist revised the *Witherspoon* rule, eliminating both the reference to automatic decision making and the standard that required a juror's bias to be unmistakably clear. Over the objection of Justices Brennan and Marshall, the Court considerably narrowed the reach of the rule by allowing prospective jurors whose views about the death penalty are merely ambiguous or vacillating to be excluded.

The justices addressed the application of the *Witherspoon-Witt* standard in a series of subsequent decisions. In 1986, the Court held that removal for cause of prospective jurors from the *guilt* phase of a trial who state that they could not under any circumstances vote for the death penalty—that is, those who are excludable under the *Witherspoon-Witt* standard from the *sentencing* phase of a trial—does not violate the Sixth Amendment.[344] In that case, Justice Rehnquist, who wrote for a six-member majority, proclaimed that even if the cross-section requirement applied to petit juries, the Constitution would not prohibit the states from "death qualifying" juries because doing so does not result in the exclusion of any distinctive group in the community. In 1987, the Court reaffirmed the rule that even a single improperly excluded juror negates a death sentence and held that *Witherspoon* violations cannot be subjected to harmless-error review.[345] The Court also has made clear that prospective jurors who express unwillingness to consider any penalty short of death must not sit on sentencing juries.[346] Moreover, the defendant has a right to have prospective jurors questioned to determine if they would automatically vote to impose the death penalty.[347]

Pretrial Publicity and the Impartial Jury

The Sixth Amendment also plays an important role in cases where extensive media coverage threatens to make the selection of an impartial jury impossible. The Court has not insisted that prospective jurors be completely unaware of all publicity, noting that such a standard would be impossible considering the speed and reach as well as the diverse methods of mass communication. Nevertheless, jurors in such cases must be able to set aside their impressions or opinions and "render a verdict based on the evidence presented in court."[348] The case in which the Court made that statement in 1961 marked the first time that the justices invalidated a state conviction solely on the basis of prejudicial pretrial publicity.

The facts of that case were as follows. Six murders, committed near Evansville, Indiana, were covered extensively by the local news media. Shortly after Irvin was arrested, the prosecutor and local police officials issued press releases stating that he had confessed to the six murders. After Irvin was indicted for

[343] *Wainwright v Witt*, 469 US 412, 424 (1985).
[344] *Lockhart v McCree*, 476 US 162 (1986).
[345] *Gray v Mississippi*, 481 US 648 (1987).
[346] *Ross v Oklahoma*, 487 US 81 (1988).
[347] *Morgan v Illinois*, 504 US 719 (1992).
[348] *Irvin v Dowd*, 366 US 717 (1961).

one of the murders, his lawyer sought a change of venue, which was granted, but only to the adjoining county. Irvin's lawyer's subsequent requests for a change of venue to a more distant county were denied. Newspaper, radio, and television coverage prior to and during the trial was extensive and extremely adverse. For example, stories revealed the details of Irvin's background, including his convictions for arson and burglary and a court-martial. The stories frequently described him as the confessed killer of six, a parole violator, and fraudulent-check artist. Three hundred seventy prospective jurors, or almost 90 percent of those who were asked,[349] expressed some opinion as to the defendant's guilt. Eight of the twelve jurors had an opinion that Irvin was guilty. One went so far as to say that he "could not . . . give the defendant the benefit of the doubt that he is innocent."[350] The Court concluded that, given the pervasiveness of the publicity, even though all the jurors said that they would be fair and impartial the jury pool was tainted by the publicity and Irvin was entitled to a change of venue.

In a case that arose out of a different set of circumstances, the Court found that a defendant had not been denied the right to an impartial jury. There, news articles appeared several months before jury selection and the community atmosphere was not inflammatory, only one-fourth of the potential jurors examined had to be excused because their opinions were firmly established, and the statements of the jurors during voir dire[351] revealed no hostility that would raise doubts about their professed impartiality.[352]

In 1991, Chief Justice Rehnquist, speaking for a five-member majority, held that in a case dominated by extensive publicity the judge was not required to question the prospective jurors about the content of their knowledge of the case.[353] It was sufficient, Rehnquist maintained, that the judge questioned the jurors in small groups and asked whether the information they had would affect their impartiality. The Chief Justice emphasized that a trial judge must be given "great latitude" in voir dire questioning. Moreover, the determining question was whether the trial court's finding that the jurors' claims of impartiality was so lacking in credibility as to constitute "fundamental unfairness." Although the depth and extent of publicity in *Irvin* might have required more extensive examination of the jurors than the judge conducted, neither the publicity nor the mood of the community in this case were anywhere near as extreme. In a dissenting opinion, Justice Marshall, joined by Blackmun and Stevens,[354] argued that the majority had turned the right to an impartial jury "into a hollow formality."[355] Marshall reasoned that when a prospective juror has been exposed to prejudicial pretrial publicity, a trial court cannot adequately assess the juror's impartiality without first establishing what the juror

---

[349]Ten members of the panel were never asked whether or not they had any opinion.
[350]*Irvin v Dowd*, 366 US 717, 728 (1961).
[351]*Voir dire* is term used to refer to selection of the jury during which the judge and the lawyers question the prospective jurors.
[352]*Murphy v Florida*, 421 US 794 (1975).
[353]*Mu'Min v Virginia*, 500 US 415 (1991).
[354]Kennedy wrote a separate dissenting opinion.
[355]*Ibid.*, 433.

has already learned about the case. Under such circumstances, he asserted, merely asking the jurors whether they thought they could be fair would not eliminate the possibility that they would be predisposed against the defendant.

> of the State and district wherein the crime shall have been committed, which district shall have been previously ascertained by law,

One of the colonists' grievances against England was that Parliament forced them to stand trial in England for offenses alleged to have been committed in America. To prevent the new government from using such procedures, both Article III and the Sixth Amendment require trials to be held in the state (and district) in which the crime was committed. As noted, however, the impartial jury provision requires that a trial be removed from the area in which the crime took place if publicity has pervaded the community so as to make a fair trial impossible.

> and to be informed of the nature and cause of the accusation;

A defendant must be provided with notice of the charges against him or her. Charges—whether in an indictment by a grand jury or an information filed by a prosecutor—must be specified so that the accused can prepare a defense. The Court ruled in 1895 that an indictment must contain "every element of the offense intended to be charged" and must "sufficiently apprise . . . the defendant of what he must be prepared to meet."[356] The justices have repeatedly reaffirmed that rule.[357] The Federal Rules of Criminal Procedure have also included it since 1946.[358]

In 1962, the Court held that the indictments of six individuals who had refused to answer questions before a congressional subcommittee failed to provide adequate notice to the defendants. The individuals were convicted of violating a federal statute that made it a crime to refuse to answer questions before a legislative committee.[359] The Court had previously made it clear that refusal to answer questions could not be punishable under the statute unless the questions were pertinent to the subject under investigation.[360] The indictments in this case did not identify the subject under investigation at the time of the subcommittee's interrogation of the defendants, but stated only that the questions "were

---

[356]*Cochran v United States*, 157 US 286, 290 (1895).

[357]See, for example, *United States v Debrow*, 346 US 374, 377–378 (1953); *Russell v United States*, 369 US 749, 763 (1962).

[358]Rule 7 (c) of the Federal Rules of Criminal Procedure provides: "The indictment or the information shall be a plain, concise and definite written statement of the essential facts constituting the offense charged. It shall be signed by the attorney for the government. It need not contain a formal commencement, a formal conclusion or any other matter not necessary to such statement. Allegations made in one count may be incorporated by reference in another count. It may be alleged in a single count that the means by which the defendant committed the offense are unknown or that he committed it by one or more specified means. The indictment or information shall state for each count the official or customary citation of the statute, rule, regulation or other provision of law which the defendant is alleged therein to have violated. Error in the citation or its omission shall not be ground for dismissal of the indictment or information or for reversal of a conviction if the error or omission did not mislead the defendant to his prejudice." As quoted in *Russell v United States*, 369 US 749, 762–763 (1962).

[359]2 U.S.C. Sec. 192.

[360]*Sinclair v United States*, 279 US 263 (1929).

pertinent to the question then under inquiry" by the subcommittee. It was, therefore, impossible to determine whether the questions that the defendants refused to answer were pertinent to the subject under investigation. Consequently, the indictments "failed to sufficiently apprise the defendant 'of what he must be prepared to meet.'"[361] Writing for the majority, Justice Stewart outlined the unacceptable consequences of such indictments: "A cryptic form of indictment in cases of this kind requires the defendant to go to trial with the chief issue undefined. It enables his conviction to rest on one point and the affirmance of the conviction to rest on another. It gives the prosecution free hand on appeal to fill in the gaps of proof by surmise or conjecture."[362]

Criminal statutes must be specific enough to define and provide adequate notice of the conduct they forbid. The Court has explained this rule as follows:

> That the terms of a penal statute creating a new offense must be sufficiently explicit to inform those who are subject to it what conduct on their part will render them liable to its penalties is a well-recognized requirement, consonant alike with ordinary notions of fair play and the settled rules of law; and a statute which either forbids or requires the doing of an act in terms so vague that men of common intelligence must necessarily guess at its meaning and differ as to its application violates the first essential of due process of law.[363]

A statute that fails to meet this standard is vulnerable to a challenge on due process grounds rather than the Sixth Amendment although the same principle—the requirement of adequate notice—applies. Although the Court has often declared statutes to be "void for vagueness" on due process grounds, in a number of cases the issue was not the constitutionality of the statute but rather the specificity of the charges under a less than precise statute. In those cases, the Court has relied on the Sixth Amendment to hold that a charge that repeated the language of the statute was not adequately specific to afford adequate notice to the accused. As the Court has explained, "It is an elementary principle of criminal pleading, that where the definition of an offence, whether it be at common law or by statute, 'includes generic terms, it is not sufficient that the indictment shall charge the offence in the same generic terms as in the definition; but it must state the species—it must descend to particulars.'"[364]

▪ to be confronted with the witnesses against him;

In 1895, the Court explained the purpose of the **confrontation clause** as follows:

> [It] was to prevent depositions or ex parte affidavits, such as were sometimes admitted in civil cases, being used against the prisoner in lieu of a personal examination and cross-examination of the witness, in which the accused has an opportunity, not only of testing the recollection and sifting the conscience of the

witness, but of compelling him to stand face to face with the jury in order that they may look at him, and judge by his demeanor upon the stand and the manner in which he gives his testimony whether he is worthy of belief.[365]

In 1965, the Court held that a defendant's right to confront witnesses is a fundamental right applicable to the states through the due process clause of the Fourteenth Amendment.[366] The defendant's right to confront adverse witnesses plays a major role in ensuring the "accuracy of the truth-determining process."[367] Consistent with that role, the confrontation clause provides two important protections for criminal defendants: the right to face prosecution witnesses and the right to conduct cross-examination of those witnesses.

Although the protection of those rights necessarily includes a defendant's right to be present at trial, the Court has noted that a primary interest of the confrontation clause is the right of cross-examination. Consequently, the right to be present at trial in situations where the defendant is not actually confronting witnesses or evidence is protected by requirements of due process.[368] The right to be present at trial, moreover, is not absolute. For example, a defendant can lose the right to be present "if, after he has been warned by the judge that he will be removed if he continues his disruptive behavior, he nevertheless insists on conducting himself in "a manner so disorderly, disruptive, and disrespectful of the court that his trial cannot be carried on with him in the courtroom.[369] The right to be present can also be waived by a defendant who, knowing that the trial is going to continue, is voluntarily absent from the proceedings."[370]

In 1988, the Court noted that the right to face adverse witnesses physically in court is at the core of the confrontation clause and "so essential to fairness that the right can be overcome by other important interests only when necessary to further an important public policy."[371] In that case, a majority held that a screen placed between the defendant and witnesses during the testimony of the two thirteen-year-old girls whom he was charged with sexually assaulting violated the confrontation clause. The procedure of using the screen was authorized by a statute that presumed sexual abuse victims would be traumatized if they were required to testify in the presence of their abuser. There were no individualized findings that the witnesses needed special protection. Consequently, in his opinion for the majority Justice Scalia maintained that the state had failed to show that it was necessary to deny the defendant's right to face his accusers. Although Scalia declined to reach the question of whether there are

---

[365]*Mattox v United States*, 156 US 237, 242–243 (1895).
[366]*Pointer v Texas*, 380 US 400 (1965).
[367]*Dutton v Evans*, 400 US 74, 89 (1970).
[368]*United States v Gagnon*, 470 US 522 (1985).
[369]*Illinois v Allen*, 397 US 337, 343 (1970).
[370]*Taylor v United States*, 414 US 17 (1973). Rule 43 of the Rules of Criminal Procedure provides that a defendant must be present at every stage of trial "except as otherwise provided" by the Rule. Rule 43 lists situations in which a right to be present may be waived, including when a defendant, initially present, "is voluntarily absent after the trial has commenced." The Court held that Rule 43 does not permit a trial in absentia of a defendant who is not present at the beginning of trial but did not address the issue of whether the Sixth Amendment requires such a rule. *Crosby v United States*, 506 US 255 (1993).
[371]*Coy v Iowa*, 487 US 1012, 1021 (1988).

exceptions to the right to face adverse witnesses, he commented that *if* there are exceptions, "they would surely be allowed only when necessary to further an important public policy."[372]

Two years later, a five-member majority upheld Maryland's special procedure whereby alleged child abuse victims are allowed to testify by one-way closed-circuit television. Writing for the majority, Justice O'Connor emphasized that such a procedure did not violate the confrontation clause because the state made an adequate showing of necessity in that particular case: the children testified under oath, were subject to full cross-examination, and were able to be observed by the judge, jury, and defendant as they testified. Under those conditions the state's interest in protecting child witnesses from the trauma of testifying in child abuse cases was sufficiently important to overcome the defendant's right to a face-to-face confrontation.[373] In the earlier case, Scalia contended that the right to face adverse witnesses is the right most clearly protected by the confrontation clause as evidenced by the text of the clause. In contrast, in the more recent case O'Connor noted that the Court's previous decisions concerning the confrontation clause reflects a "preference for face-to-face confrontation at trial." But she emphasized that other rights are guaranteed by the confrontation clause, including the right to conduct a cross-examination. In fact, the Court has noted that an adequate opportunity for cross-examination may satisfy the clause even in the absence of physical confrontation.[374] At any rate, O'Connor was considerably more willing than was Scalia to allow other interests to overcome the defendant's right to confront witnesses. Indeed, Scalia, writing for the four dissenters, in the more recent case condemned the majority opinion for subordinating explicit constitutional text to currently favored public policy.

What is the scope of the defendant's right to cross-examine adverse witnesses? The Court has held that restrictions imposed by the trial court on the scope of the defense's cross-examination of key witnesses where the credibility of the witness is at issue violate the confrontation clause. In a case in which the state's key witness was an informer who testified that he had purchased heroin from the defendant, the justices held that the trial court's refusal to allow the defense to ask the witness for his real name violated the defendant's right to confront adverse witnesses.[375] In another case, the Court held that a protective order barring cross-examination of a juvenile witness in a burglary case relating to his record—he was on probation—violated the confrontation clause. The Court noted that the defense sought to show that the witness was biased by the fear that his probation would be revoked if he did not testify favorably for the prosecution and that, consequently, his testimony identifying the defendant should not be believed. A majority concluded that under such circumstances the defendant's right to confront the witness outweighed the state's policy of protecting a juvenile offender.[376] Rehnquist has summarized the rule as follows: "[A] crimi-

---

[372] *Ibid.*
[373] *Maryland v Craig*, 497 US 836 (1990).
[374] *Douglas v Alabama*, 380 US 415 (1965).
[375] *Smith v Illinois*, 390 US 129 (1968).
[376] *Davis v Alaska*, 415 US 308 (1974).

nal defendant states a violation of the Confrontation Clause by showing that he was prohibited from engaging in otherwise appropriate cross-examination designed to show a prototypical form of bias on the part of the witness, and thereby 'to expose to the jury the facts from which jurors . . . could appropriately draw inferences relating to the reliability of the witness.'"[377] Additionally, a defendant need not demonstrate that the cross-examination would have revealed a witness's bias or raised doubts about his or her credibility. Denial of the right to cross-examine and a proper challenge to that denial are sufficient to establish a constitutional violation.

There are limits to the right to conduct cross-examination. Indeed, the very terms of the rule stated previously imply its limits; namely, trial courts may prohibit cross-examination that is not appropriate or is not designed to show bias. Indeed, the Court has adhered to the proposition that "a trial court may, . . . impose reasonable limits on defense counsel's inquiry into the potential bias of a prosecution witness, to take account of such factors as 'harassment, prejudice, confusion of the issues, the witness safety, or interrogation that [would be] repetitive or only marginally relevant.'"[378] Additionally, the scope of cross-examination is limited by the witness's constitutional right against compulsory self-incrimination. The Court has also limited the scope of the confrontation clause by holding that the right to attempt to discredit a witness for the prosecution applies only to the actual cross-examination at trial. It does not extend to pretrial disclosure of material that the defense might be able to use to impeach a witness.[379]

In 1986, the Court held that a violation of the right to conduct cross-examination is subject to harmless-error analysis. The Court announced that to determine whether the error had been harmless in a particular case, it would consider several factors, including the importance of the witness's testimony, whether the testimony was cumulative, the presence or absence of corroborating or contradictory testimony on material points, the extent of cross-examination otherwise permitted, and the overall strength of the prosecution's case.[380] Applying those factors in a subsequent decision, the Court found that the trial court violated the confrontation clause by refusing to allow the defense to attempt to impeach a witness's testimony. The defense hoped to show that the female complainant had a motive to charge falsely that the defendant had raped her. According to the defense, she had constructed her story to deceive her boyfriend about the reason for her presence in the company of the defendant. The trial judge barred cross-examination to reveal that the complainant and her boyfriend were living together on the grounds that the fact that she was in an interracial relationship could bias the jury against her. The Court held that forbidding cross-examination to reveal that information violated the confrontation clause and considering that her testimony was crucial to the prosecution's case, that her story was corroborated only by her

---

[377]*Delaware v Van Arsdall*, 475 US 673, 680 (1986).
[378]*Olden v Kentucky*, 488 US 227, 232 (1988).
[379]*United States v Bagley*, 473 US 667 (1985); *Pennsylvania v Richie*, 480 US 39 (1987).
[380]*Delaware v Van Arsdall*, 475 US 673 (1986).

boyfriend, and was directly contradicted by the defendant, it was not harmless error.[381] The Court has also held that denial of face-to-face confrontation is subject to harmless-error analysis.[382]

The confrontation clause also limits the prosecution's use of statements of individuals who do not testify at trial and therefore cannot be cross-examined. Such statements ordinarily constitute hearsay and are not admissible under federal and state rules of evidence unless they fall within a recognized "hearsay exception."[383] Admission of evidence that would be admissible under exceptions to the hearsay rule might, nevertheless, violate the confrontation clause. Indeed, a literal interpretation of the confrontation clause would negate all hearsay exceptions, thereby barring the use of any out-of-court statement made by an individual who is not present at trial. The Court, however, has consistently rejected that view.[384] Instead, it has adopted a general approach according to which prior statements may be admitted only if they were obtained under conditions very likely to have rendered the statements trustworthy. As the Court has termed its approach, such testimony must bear adequate "indicia of reliability." That requirement can be fulfilled, the Court has explained, where the testimony falls within a firmly rooted hearsay exception.[385] Otherwise it must be supported by "a showing of particularized guarantees of trustworthiness." Accordingly, the Court has held that testimony obtained in a preliminary hearing must have been obtained at a prior proceeding that resembled a trial in that the witness was under oath, and the defense was represented by counsel and had an adequate opportunity for cross-examination or the equivalent of significant cross-examination.[386] Subsequently, the Court held that admission of the testimony of a pediatrician who had questioned a three-year-old child in his office about alleged sexual abuse violated the confrontation clause. The pediatrician's questions and the child's answers were not recorded, he asked leading questions, and he had a preconceived notion of how he wanted her to respond. In her opinion for a five-member majority in that case, O'Connor elaborated on the requirement of "particularized guarantees of trustworthiness," noting that they "must be drawn from the totality of circumstances that surround the making of the statement and that render the declarant particularly worthy of belief."[387] Evidence admitted under that requirement must be so trustworthy that subjecting it to cross-examination would add little to its reliability. In this case, O'Connor maintained, the circumstances in which the child answered questions did not render her particularly likely to be telling the truth. Over the objection of the four dissenters, O'Connor also declared that the existence of corroborating evidence could not be included in the consideration of the relia-

---

[381]*Olden v Kentucky*, 488 US 227 (1988).

[382]*Coy v Iowa*, 487 US 1012 (1988).

[383]Testimony of a co-conspirator, spontaneous declarations, and statements made in the course of receiving medical care are all exceptions to the hearsay rule.

[384]See, for example, *Mattox v United States*, 156 US 237, 243 (1895), and *Bourjaily v United States*, 483 US 171 (1987).

[385]For example, spontaneous statements and those made in the course of receiving medical care are considered to be trustworthy. *White v Illinois*, 502 US 346 (1992). Also, dying declarations are presumed to be trustworthy because in such circumstances a person is unlikely to lie.

[386]*Ohio v Roberts*, 448 US, 56, 66 (1980). See also, *California v Green*, 399 US 149 (1970).

[387]*Idaho v Wright*, 497 US 805, 820 (1990).

bility of the child's statements. Corroborating evidence, in other words, did not enhance the trustworthiness of the child's statements.

▌   to have compulsory process for obtaining witnesses in his favor,

Under the common law in England those accused of treason or other serious crimes were not allowed to introduce witnesses in their defense. England abolished that absolute prohibition by statute well before 1788 when the Constitution went into effect. Nevertheless, when it drafted the Bill of Rights, the first Congress included the confrontation clause at least partly in reaction to the common law rule.

Despite the Sixth Amendment, the federal rules of evidence maintained many of the common law restrictions on the theory that only witnesses "presumably honest, appreciating the sanctity of an oath, unaffected as a party by the result, and free from any of the temptations of interest" should be allowed on the witness stand.[388] In 1918, the Court held that the rules of evidence should not be bound by the common law rules that were in force in 1789.[389] Without relying on constitutional grounds the Court noted, "the conviction of our time that the truth is more likely to be arrived at by hearing the testimony of all persons of competent understanding who may seem to have knowledge of the facts involved in a case, leaving the credit and weight of such testimony to be determined by the jury or by the court."[390]

It was not until 1967 that the Court made it explicit that "arbitrary rules that prevent whole categories of defense witnesses from testifying on the basis of a priori categories that presume them unworthy of belief" are inconsistent with the **compulsory process clause.**[391] In that case, the justices invalidated the disqualification of defendants who were indicted together from testifying for each other. Moreover, in the same decision the Court announced that a defendant's right to call witnesses was fundamental to a fair trial and therefore obligatory on the states through the due process clause of the Fourteenth Amendment. The Court has made it clear that the compulsory process clause does not invalidate testimonial privileges, including the lawyer-client, priest-penitent, doctor-patient, and psychotherapist-patient privilege[392] nor the privilege against self-incrimination.

The compulsory process clause includes the defendant's right not only to offer the testimony of witnesses but also to compel their attendance—that is, the right to subpoena witnesses. The few cases that the Court has ruled on this issue suggest that the right is limited. For example, the Court rejected a challenge under the compulsory process clause brought by a man who was convicted for violating the federal law prohibiting the transportation of illegal aliens. The justices held that, in light of the federal government's responsibility

---

[388]*Benson v United States*, 146 US 325, 336 (1892).
[389]The Court held that the rules of evidence in the federal courts were those in force in the states at the time of the passage of the Judiciary Act of 1789 in *United States v Reid*, 12 How 361 (1852).
[390]*Rosen v United States*, 245 US 467, 471 (1918).
[391]*Washington v Texas*, 388 US 14, 22 (1967).
[392]Testimonial privileges are provided by federal (Rule 501 of the Federal Rules of Evidence) and state rules of evidence. The Court established the psychotherapist-patient privilege in *Jaffee v Redmond*, 518 US 1 (1996).

to regulate immigration, the deportation of two of the three individuals who had been passengers in the defendant's car did not violate the Sixth Amendment absent a showing that their testimony would have been both material and favorable to the defense.[393]

Another guarantee included in the compulsory process clause is the defendant's right to testify.[394] The right to testify, the Court has noted, may be restricted to accommodate other legitimate interests in the criminal trial process, but those restrictions must not be disproportionate to the purposes they are designed to serve. Accordingly, the Court held that the state's legitimate interest in imposing evidentiary restrictions to exclude unreliable evidence could not justify a per se rule excluding a defendant's hypnotically refreshed testimony. The majority reasoned that a per se rule was excessive because it operated without regard either to procedural safeguards used in the hypnosis process to reduce inaccuracies or to the availability of corroborating evidence and other means of assessing the accuracy of testimony.[395]

and to have the Assistance of Counsel for his defence.

The list of grievances in the Declaration of Independence included the denial of the right to counsel. The guarantee of the right to assistance of counsel in the Sixth Amendment represented a departure from the English common law, which prohibited attorneys from appearing on behalf of defendants in felony cases. The Sixth Amendment established the right of a defendant who possessed the financial resources to retain counsel. But until well into the twentieth century the Amendment's guarantee of assistance of counsel did not include government's obligation to appoint an attorney for individuals who could not afford to retain their own.

Until 1938, the federal courts were not required to assign counsel to represent defendants except in capital cases. In *Johnson v Zerbst*, emphasizing the inability of even an intelligent and educated "layman" to prepare an adequate defense, the Court held that the Sixth Amendment required federal courts to provide indigent defendants with appointed counsel in all felony cases.[396]

Addressing the issue of the **right to counsel** in state courts for the first time in 1932 in *Powell v Alabama*, the Court held that the due process clause of the Fourteenth Amendment required counsel to be appointed for defendants in capital cases who are "incapable adequately of making [their] own defense because of ignorance, feeble-mindedness, illiteracy, or the like."[397] Ten years later in *Betts v Brady*, the justices declined to hold that the due process clause of the Fourteenth Amendment incorporated the Sixth Amendment right to counsel. Instead, a six-member majority adopted the **"special circumstances" rule** and held that due process required appointment of counsel only in those cases

---

[393] *United States v Valenzuela-Bernal*, 458 US 866 (1982).
[394] The defendant's right to testify is also protected by due process and by the Fifth Amendment's prohibition on compulsory self-incrimination.
[395] *Rock v Arkansas*, 483 US 44 (1987).
[396] *Johnson v Zerbst*, 304 US 458 (1938).
[397] *Powell v Alabama*, 287 US 45, 71 (1932).

where the absence of counsel would result in a trial lacking fundamental fairness.[398] Thus, due process did not require the state to furnish counsel for a defendant in a robbery case who "was not helpless, but was a man forty-three years old, of ordinary intelligence and ability to take care of his own interests."[399] During the years following *Betts,* the Court proceeded on a case-by-case basis, examining the circumstances of trials in which the defendant had not been furnished with counsel. The justices found that due process demanded the appointment of counsel in cases in which the defendant was accused of a capital crime, the conduct of the trial judge appeared to be questionable, the defendant was young or ignorant, and the points of law involved were too technical for a nonlawyer to grasp.[400] After 1950, the justices never affirmed a state conviction where the defendant claimed denial of counsel.

In 1963 in *Gideon v Wainwright,* the Court overruled *Betts v Brady,* discarded the "special circumstances" rule, and held that the due process clause of the Fourteenth Amendment incorporates the Sixth Amendment's guarantee of assistance of counsel.[401] Justice Black, who wrote the majority opinion, emphasized that assistance of counsel is essential to a fair trial:

> [R]eason and reflection require us to recognize that in our adversary system of criminal justice, any person haled into court, who is too poor to hire a lawyer, cannot be assured a fair trial unless counsel is provided for him. This seems to us to be an obvious truth. Governments, both state and federal, quite properly spend vast sums of money to establish machinery to try defendants accused of crime. Lawyers to prosecute are everywhere deemed essential to protect the public's interest in an orderly society. Similarly, there are few defendants charged with crime, few indeed, who fail to hire the best lawyers they can get to prepare and present their defenses.[402]

Gideon required the states to make appointed counsel available to indigent defendants in all felony cases. Subsequently, the Court declined to extend assistance of counsel to the six-month-imprisonment rule that the Court fashioned to determine when a defendant is entitled to a jury trial. The justices held that counsel must be appointed to all indigent defendants who are sentenced to a jail term.[403] In 1994, the Court held that a prior misdemeanor conviction in which the defendant did not have counsel may be used to enhance the sentence on a subsequent offense so long as the prior conviction did not result in a sentence of imprisonment.[404]

The Fifth Amendment's self-incrimination clause guarantees the right to counsel at the interrogation stage whereas the Sixth Amendment's assistance of counsel clause applies to the formal stages of the criminal prosecution. Thus, the Sixth Amendment right to counsel attaches with the initiation of criminal

---

[398]*Betts v Brady,* 316 US 455 (1942).
[399]*Ibid.,* 472.
[400]C. Herman Pritchett, *Constitutional Civil Liberties.* Englewood Cliffs, NJ: Prentice-Hall, 1984, 210.
[401]*Gideon v Wainwright,* 372 US 335 (1963).
[402]*Ibid.,* 344.
[403]*Argersinger v Hamlin,* 407 US 25 (1972); *Scott v Illinois,* 440 US 367 (1979).
[404]*Nichols v United States,* 511 US 738 (1994), overruling *Baldasar v Illinois,* 446 US 222 (1980).

charges, whether by indictment, information, at a preliminary hearing, or arraignment. From that point on, defendants are entitled to have a lawyer present at all the "critical stages" in the criminal prosecution—that is, whenever substantial rights of the accused may be affected by the absence of counsel.[405] The Court has held that the following are critical stages: preliminary hearing, postindictment lineup, guilty plea negotiation, and sentencing hearing, as well as the trial and the proceeding at which formal charges are initiated. Attempts by police or prosecutor to elicit incriminating statements are also critical stages.

After sentencing, the criminal prosecution comes to an end for Sixth Amendment purposes. Thus, the right to counsel on appeal is based on due process and equal protection considerations. Moreover, probation and parole revocation proceedings that were not part of the initial sentencing are not a stage in the criminal prosecution and, therefore, require assistance of counsel only in limited circumstances as required by due process.[406]

A defendant may waive the right to assistance of counsel, but the Court has insisted on strict standards for establishing that a waiver was made competently and intelligently. The Court has maintained that, as with other fundamental rights, there is a strong presumption against waiver of the right to counsel. As Justice Brennan explained, "Presuming waiver from a silent record is impermissible. The record must show, or there must be an allegation and evidence which show, that an accused was offered counsel but intelligently and understandingly rejected the offer. Anything less is not waiver."[407] Moreover, the Court has extended the rules governing waiver after the suspect has asserted the right to counsel during interrogation[408] to the later stages of the process when formal charges have been instituted. Thus, "if police initiate interrogation after a defendant's assertion, at an arraignment or similar proceeding, of his right to counsel, any waiver of the defendant's right to counsel for that police-initiated interrogation is invalid."[409]

In a ruling that paralleled the Court's decisions in the Fifth Amendment *Miranda* area, the justices held that the prohibition on police-initiated questioning is a prophylactic rule designed to ensure voluntary, knowing, and intelligent waivers of the right to counsel, which does "not mark the exact the boundary of the Sixth Amendment right itself." Therefore, the Court reasoned, statements obtained as a result of questioning initiated by the police after the defendant asserted the right to counsel can be used to impeach a defendant's testimony.[410] Additionally the Court has held that assertion of the right to counsel under the Sixth Amendment is "offense-specific." Thus, although no questioning is allowed concerning the offense for which a defendant has been charged, there is no bar to questioning about other offenses.[411]

---

[405]*Mempa v Rhay*, 389 US 128 (1967).

[406]*Gagnon v Scarpelli*, 411 US 778 (1973).

[407]*Carnley v Cochran*, 369 US 506, 515 (1962).

[408]Relying on the Fifth Amendment, the Court announced that once a suspect who is under custodial interrogation asserts the right to counsel police may not initiate questioning. *Edwards v Arizona*, 451 US 477 (1981).

[409]*Michigan v Jackson*, 475 US 625 (1986).

[410]*Michigan v Harvey*, 494 US 344 (1990).

[411]*McNeil v Wisconsin*, 501 US 171 (1991). Compare rule under the Fifth Amendment: The *Edwards* rule, moreover, is not offense-specific: once a suspect invokes the *Miranda* right to counsel for interrogation regarding one offense, he or she may not be reapproached regarding any offense unless counsel is present. *Arizona v Roberson*, 486 US 675 (1988).

The Court has held that the Sixth Amendment implies a defendant's right to proceed *pro se*—that is, without the assistance of counsel. The right to assistance of counsel, Justice Stewart wrote for six members of the Court, should "be an aid to a willing defendant—not an organ of the State interposed between an unwilling defendant and his right to defend himself personally."[412] Stewart emphasized the importance of consent in the right to assistance of counsel, noting that if the accused has not agreed to be represented, "the defense presented is not the defense guaranteed him by the Constitution, for, in a very real sense, it is not his defense."[413] The Court made it clear that a defendant who proceeds pro se must "knowingly and intelligently" forgo the benefits of the right to counsel. Additionally, the defendant should be made aware of the dangers and disadvantages of self-representation so that the record will show "he knows what he is doing and his choice is made with eyes open."[414] So long as a defendant knowingly and intelligently gives up the benefit of counsel it does not matter that he or she lacks the skills and experience of a lawyer. Despite the right to proceed pro se, the trial court may appoint standby counsel over the defendant's objection to help the accused if requested to do so and to relieve the judge of the responsibility of explaining basic rules of courtroom procedure. Standby counsel must not, however, deprive the defendant of actual control over the organization and content of the defense and must not alter the jury's perception that the accused is engaged in self-representation.[415] A defendant who chooses to proceed pro se cannot later complain that he or she was denied effective assistance of counsel.

Even before it held that government must appoint counsel for defendants who cannot to retain their own, the Court recognized an essential connection between the right to counsel and the right to *effective* assistance of counsel. In *Powell v Alabama*, Justice Sutherland noted that the trial judge's appointment of all members of the local bar to represent the defendants failed to impose a substantial or definite obligation on any individual lawyer and indicated that the defendants did not have the aid of counsel in any real sense.[416] In a series of subsequent decisions, the Court made clear that the right to counsel includes the **effective assistance of competent counsel.**[417]

But what constitutes effective representation of counsel? Rather than provide a specific checklist, the Court has underlined that counsel's assistance must be reasonable considering all the circumstances of a given case. Thus, if counsel makes mistakes, his or her conduct will, nevertheless, be deemed acceptable unless it rendered the trial unfair by severely undermining the operation of the adversarial process rendering the verdict suspect. In *Strickland v Washington*, Justice O'Connor, writing for a seven-member majority, announced that to prevail on a claim of ineffective assistance of counsel, a defendant must meet two requirements. The defendant must demonstrate that counsel's performance was

---

[412]*Faretta v California*, 422 US 806, 820 (1975).
[413]*Ibid.*, 821.
[414]*Ibid.*, 835 quoting *Adams v United States ex rel. McCann*, 317 US 269, 279 (1942).
[415]*McKaskle v Wiggins*, 465 US 168 (1984).
[416]*Powell v Alabama*, 287 US 45, 57 (1932).
[417]*McMann v Richardson*, 397 US 759 (1970); *Reece v Georgia*, 350 US 85 (1955); *Glasser v United States*, 315 US 60 (1942); *Avery v Alabama*, 308 US 444 (1940).

deficient and that the deficient performance prejudiced the defense to the extent that there is a reasonable probability that the result would have been different had it not been for counsel's errors. She explained, "[T]his requires showing that counsel's errors were so serious as to deprive the defendant of a fair trial, a trial whose result is reliable. Unless a defendant makes both showings, it cannot be said that the conviction or death sentence resulted from a breakdown in the adversary process that renders the result unreliable."[418] More specific guidelines are not appropriate, O'Connor maintained, because the Sixth Amendment refers only to "counsel," and does not specify particular criteria for effective assistance: "It relies instead on the legal profession's maintenance of standards sufficient to justify the law's presumption that counsel will fulfill the role in the adversary process that the Amendment envisions."[419] In another case decided the same day, the Court held that neither counsel's inexperience nor the lack of time he had to prepare rendered defendant's trial for "check-kiting" unfair. In his opinion for the majority, Justice Stevens noted that so long as the process maintains "its character as a confrontation between adversaries" the Sixth Amendment is not violated.[420] The Court's deferential "objective standard of reasonableness" approach is "highly demanding" and makes it difficult for defendants to prevail. In her opinion in *Strickland*, O'Connor expressed concern that if the Court were to provide detailed guidelines for the evaluation of counsel, it would "encourage the proliferation of ineffectiveness challenges." A number of adverse effects would ensue, including

> Criminal trials resolved unfavorably to the defendant would increasingly come to be followed by a second trial, this one of counsel's unsuccessful defense. Counsel's performance and even willingness to serve could be adversely affected. Intensive scrutiny of counsel and rigid requirements for acceptable assistance could dampen the ardor and impair the independence of defense counsel, discourage the acceptance of assigned cases, and undermine the trust between attorney and client.[421]

Justice Marshall argued in dissent that to require counsel to behave reasonably "is to tell them almost nothing" and discourages the development of standards governing the performance of defense counsel. He contended that although counsel must have ample room to make tactical decisions regarding trial strategy much of the work of the criminal defense attorney is amenable to judicial oversight. Some uniform standards for evaluating defense counsel, Marshall argued, would benefit not only defendants but also lawyers and lower courts.

The Court's subsequent application of the *Strickland* standard illustrates the burden that its two-pronged requirement imposes on a defendant who challenges counsel's performance. For example, all of the justices agreed that defense counsel's threat to withdraw and reveal defendant's perjury if the latter

---

[418]*Strickland v Washington*, 466 US 668, 687 (1984).
[419]*Ibid.*, 688.
[420]*United States v Cronic*, 466 US 648, 656 (1984).
[421]*Strickland v Washington*, 466 US 668, 690 (1984).

carried out his plan to testify falsely did not diminish confidence in the reliability of the trial. Thus, the defendant had not established the prejudice required by *Strickland*. Noting that counsel's conduct was well within accepted standards of professional conduct, five of the justices also argued that the defendant's claim did not demonstrate any deficiency in counsel's assistance.[422]

In another case the defendant challenged his death sentence on the grounds that his counsel had failed to raise on appeal an objection to the admission of a psychiatrist's testimony recounting the defendant's revelation of prior criminal behavior. Admission of that testimony violated the defendant's Fifth Amendment right against self-incrimination. The Court easily disposed of the defendant's claim, noting that counsel's conscious decision not to pursue the objection may have appeared to be unwise with the benefit of hindsight but was not an error of such magnitude that it rendered counsel's performance constitutionally deficient.[423]

A five-member majority also rejected a defendant's challenge to his death sentence that was based on his counsel's failure either to investigate adequately or present at the sentencing hearings mitigating circumstances relating to the defendant's troubled background. Writing for the majority, Justice Stevens observed that the defendant's lawyer had learned of some of the mitigating evidence while interviewing the defendant, his mother, and a psychologist who examined him but had made a reasonable professional judgment that presenting it would not serve his client's interests. Thus, the lawyer's conduct fell well within the range of professionally competent assistance and there was no breakdown of the adversarial testing process. The dissenters, however, perceived the circumstances of this case quite differently. They argued that considering the importance of background information in capital sentencing proceedings and that the defendant was an adolescent with psychological problems and apparent diminished mental capabilities, defense counsel's failure to conduct a thorough investigation of possible mitigating factors was clearly not within the realm of professional reasonable judgment. Moreover, the dissenters argued, there was a reasonable probability that if the sentencer had possessed more information about the defendant's background he would have determined that the defendant should not receive the death penalty.[424]

In another case, the Court found that the defense counsel had committed an error that was sufficiently serious to satisfy the first requirement of the *Strickland* standard. Counsel failed to file in a timely fashion a motion to suppress evidence that police obtained illegally. As a result, the trial court refused to consider the merits of the motion. Counsel had no knowledge of the illegal search because he had not conducted pretrial discovery as he had assumed that the state was required to turn over all of its evidence to the defense. Although the Court was careful to note that failure to file a suppression motion does not invariably constitute ineffective assistance of counsel, in this case it was not based on strategic considerations but instead resulted from counsel's "startling

---

[422]*Nix v Whiteside*, 475 US 157 (1986).
[423]*Smith v Murray*, 477 US 527, 535 (1986).
[424]*Burger v Kemp*, 483 US 776 (1987).

ignorance" of the law. In short, counsel's errors were not the result of strategic or tactical decisions but errors based on lack of understanding of the law and, therefore, were outside the boundaries of reasonable professional conduct.[425]

As noted, the *Strickland* rule requires a defendant to demonstrate that prejudice resulted from counsel's errors. That is, the defendant bears the burden of establishing that there was a reasonable probability that the verdict or sentence would have been different had it not been for counsel's errors. In 1993 in *Lockhart v Fretwell*, Chief Justice Rehnquist wrote an opinion that suggested the Court has revised the *Strickland* standard to make it even more difficult for defendants to succeed with ineffective assistance of counsel claims. In that case, the defense lawyer in a capital sentencing proceeding failed to make any objection to the jury's use of an aggravating factor that was clearly prohibited by the law at the time although the law had been changed by the time the case reached the appellate stage.[426] The lower courts found in favor of the defendant on the grounds that if defense counsel had made the objection, the trial judge would have sustained it and the jury would not have sentenced the defendant to death.

The Supreme Court disagreed. Rehnquist maintained that the prejudice portion of the *Strickland* rule does not revolve solely around "outcome determination" but is primarily concerned with "whether the result of the proceeding was fundamentally unfair or unreliable." Thus, he reasoned that "to set aside a conviction or sentence solely because the outcome would have been different but for counsel's error may grant the defendant a windfall to which the law does not entitle him."[427] Rehnquist's language strongly suggests a revision of the prejudice part of the *Strickland* rule. Moreover, the two dissenters complained that the majority had modified the rule. Justice O'Connor, however, wrote a concurring opinion contending that the rule remained unchanged. The narrow holding in *Lockhart v Fretwell*, in her view, was merely that a court making the determination as to whether defense counsel's failure to raise an objection resulted in prejudice may not consider the effect that such an objection would have had if the court knows it would be completely without merit under current governing law.

AMENDMENT VII: TRIAL BY JURY IN CIVIL CASES

> In suits at common law, where the value in controversy shall exceed twenty dollars, the right of trial by jury shall be preserved,

At the Philadelphia Convention in 1787 a proposal to include in Article III, Section 2, of the Constitution a guarantee of the right to trial by jury in civil cases was rejected on the grounds that it would be too difficult to fashion a rule that would cover the widely divergent state practices. The absence of a guaran-

---

[425]*Kimmelman v Morrison*, 477 US 365 (1986).
[426]*Collins v Lockhart*, 754 F2d 258 (1985), held that an aggravating factor could not duplicate an element of the underlying felony—murder in the course of a robbery. Overruled in 1989 in *Perry v Lockhart*, 871 F2d 1384, (8th Cir. 1989).
[427]*Lockhart v Fretwell*, 506 US 364, 369–370 (1993).

tee of trial by jury in civil cases subsequently provided fuel for the Antifederalists' arguments against the new Constitution. The controversy was resolved by including the jury trial provision for civil cases in the Bill of Rights.

The Seventh Amendment is one of the few provisions in the Bill of Rights that has not been incorporated into the due process clause of the Fourteenth Amendment.[428] Thus, it applies only to litigation in the federal courts. It does apply, however, to diversity of citizenship cases—based on state law but decided by a federal court because the parties reside in different states. The phrase "suits at common law" includes suits that are analogous to those recognized by the common law in 1791 when the Seventh Amendment became part of the Constitution.[429] Generally, such actions are for recovery of money as compensation for injury or damage. The Court has also extended the guarantee to civil actions to enforce statutory rights.[430]

The Seventh Amendment does not apply to equity proceedings, which are actions to compel or prohibit conduct or to require the performance of a contract.[431] In cases that involve both a legal and an equitable claim, the right to trial by jury applies to the legal claim. The trial court may not deny the right to a jury trial by characterizing the legal claim as merely incidental to the equitable relief sought.[432] Additionally the Seventh Amendment does not apply to cases heard by administrative tribunals rather than Article III courts. The Court has held, moreover, that Congress may create "a seemingly 'private' right that is so closely integrated into a public regulatory scheme as to be a matter appropriate for agency resolution with limited involvement by the Article III judiciary."[433] Thus, Congress may, in effect, withdraw certain subjects of litigation from the realm of Article III courts and thus from the Seventh Amendment's guarantee of trial by jury. Finally, the Court has made it clear that the right to trial by jury does not extend to actions against the federal government.[434]

As noted, parties in actions at law that are analogous to those recognized by the common law in 1791 are entitled to a trial by a jury. Nevertheless, particular issues may arise in jury trials that are not suitable for a jury. To make that determination, the Court has explained, it is necessary to examine historical practices. Where that proves inconclusive, the Court noted that it would turn to precedent and consider "both the relative interpretive skills of judges and juries and the statutory policies that ought to be furthered by the allocation."[435] Using such an approach, the justices found that the interpretation of terms in a patent claim was properly decided by a judge.

---

[428] *Walker v Sauvinet*, 92 US 90 (1876).

[429] The "Thrust of Seventh Amendment is to preserve right to jury trial as it existed in 1791." *Parklane Hosiery Co. v Shore*, 439 US 322 (1979).

[430] "The Seventh Amendment does apply to actions enforcing statutory rights, and requires a jury trial upon demand, if the statute creates legal rights and remedies, enforceable in an action for damages in the ordinary courts of law." *Curtis v Loether*, 415 US 189, 194 (1974). The Court had previously held the guarantee of trial by jury applicable to statutory actions in cases going back to 1909. See *Hepner v United States*, 213 US 103 (1909).

[431] "The phrase 'common law' . . . is used in contradistinction to equity, admiralty, and maritime jurisprudence." *Parsons v Bedford*, 3 Pet. 433, 446–447 (1830).

[432] *Tull v United States*, 481 US 412 (1987).

[433] *Thomas v Union Carbide*, 473 US 568 (1985).

[434] *Lehman v Nakshian*, 453 US 156 (1981).

[435] *Markman v Westview*, 517 US 370 (1996).

In 1973, the Court ruled that six-member federal civil juries meet the Seventh Amendment requirement of trial by jury.[436] The five-member majority reasoned that the goal of the Seventh Amendment was to preserve "the substance of the common law right of trial by jury, as distinguished from mere matters of form or procedure." Because the civil jury's performance as a fact-finder like that of the criminal jury was not a function of its size, the number of jurors was simply a matter of form or procedure.

> and no fact tried by a jury, shall be otherwise re-examined in any Court of the United States, than according to the rules of the common law.

The function of appellate courts is to make certain that trial courts apply the law correctly. But if reviewing courts could also reject the factual determinations of juries, the latter could all too easily lose their function as fact finders. Thus, the second part of the Seventh Amendment protects the role of the jury in the American judicial system by prohibiting appellate courts from reversing or altering juries' decisions based on alleged errors of fact. It guarantees that judges may not simply cancel jurors' factual determinations and substitute their own. The reexamination clause clearly prohibits an appellate court from reversing a jury's verdict on the grounds that it was contrary to the evidence. It is not always easy, however, to separate issues of law and fact. In one decision for example, the justices disagreed about whether a challenge to the amount of a jury's award of damages on the grounds that it departed from what would be reasonable compensation according to state law was an issue of fact or law.[437]

Although the Seventh Amendment does not apply to the states, the prohibition on the reexamination of facts applies to cases that are tried by a jury in state court and are ultimately reviewed by the United States Supreme Court.[438] It also applies to diversity of citizenship cases, which are based on state law but tried in federal court because the parties reside in different states. In 1996, the Court limited the reexamination clause when it held that the Court of Appeals could vacate a jury's verdict on the grounds that under controlling state law the amount of damages it awarded was excessive.[439] That holding, Justice O'Connor acknowledged in her opinion for the majority, was inconsistent with the Court's previous decisions. But she pointed out that all of the circuits of the Courts of Appeals had adopted the position that the Court took here.[440] In dissent, Justice Scalia argued that the Court had abandoned precedent without justification and that when appellate courts decide whether an award is excessive or inadequate they are engaging in the reexamination of facts found by a jury—a practice that the Seventh Amendment expressly prohibits.[441]

---

[436]*Colegrove v Battin*, 413 US 149 (1973).
[437]*Gasperini v Center for Humanities*, 518 US 415 (1996).
[438]*Chicago, B.&Q.R. Co. v Chicago*, 166 US 226 (1897).
[439]This was a diversity case, based on state law, but in federal court because the parties resided in different states.
[440]*Gasperini v Center for Humanities*, 517 US 1102 (1996).
[441]Rehnquist and Thomas joined Scalia's dissent.

Amendment VIII: Bail, and Cruel and Unusual Punishments

Excessive bail shall not be required, nor excessive fines imposed,

The general rule regarding excessive bail is that bail may be set only high enough to guarantee the defendant's appearance for trial.[442] A defendant who is accused of a capital crime or one who presents a threat to the judicial process by intimidating witnesses may, however, be refused bail.

In 1987 in *United States v Salerno*, the Court modified that rule when it upheld the provisions of the Bail Reform Act of 1984 allowing federal trial judges to deny bail to individuals accused of certain crimes[443] if the government demonstrates by clear and convincing evidence after an adversary hearing that no release conditions "will reasonably assure . . . the safety of any other person and the community." The claimants argued that setting bail at an infinite amount for reasons unrelated to the risk of flight violated the excessive bail clause. A six-member majority rejected that reasoning. Writing for that majority, Chief Justice Rehnquist noted that the clause "says nothing about whether bail shall be available at all." He suggested that the prohibition on excessive bail applies when the government's interest is in preventing flight but here Congress had authorized preventive detention on the basis of a different interest—that of protecting the community. Thus, the Eighth Amendment did not require release on bail. The dissenters rejoined that the Eighth Amendment and the due process clause prohibit Congress from advancing the interest of protecting the community by denying bail to individuals who have not been convicted of any crime. The preventive detention statute, in their analysis, violated the due process and the excessive bail clauses because it was "an abhorrent limitation of the presumption of innocence."[444]

The Court addressed the excessive fines clause for the first time in 1989 when it held that the clause did not limit the award of punitive damages in a civil suit—the clause applies only to fines levied by the government "as punishment for some offense."[445] In 1993, the Court concluded that the clause limits the government's power to extract payments, whether in cash or in kind as punishment, including civil procedures for the forfeiture of property.[446]

[continued] nor cruel and unusual punishments inflicted

The prohibition on cruel and unusual punishments, which is by far the most important of the three provisions in the Eighth Amendment, has been

---

[442] *Stack v Boyle*, 342 US 1 (1951); *Schlib v Kuebel*, 404 US 357 (1971).

[443] The statute specified that detention without bail would be possible if the case involved crimes of violence, offenses for which the sentence was life imprisonment or death, serious drug offenses, and for certain repeat offenders.

[444] *United States v Salerno*, 481 US 739 (1987). Marshall wrote a dissenting opinion, in which Brennan joined. Stevens also wrote a dissenting opinion.

[445] *Browning-Ferris v Kelco Disposal*, 492 US 257 (1989).

[446] *Austin v United States*, 502 US 849 (1993).

one of the bases for challenging the death penalty in the second half of the twentieth century. The limited evidence concerning the original understanding of the Framers of the Bill of Rights suggests that they wanted to ensure that barbaric punishments involving torture or lingering death—boiling in oil, disembowelment, pressing with weights, drawing and quartering, burning alive, for example—would not be available. But the death penalty was common in the late eighteenth century and the Framers assumed it would be used. Indeed, in its earliest interpretation of the cruel and unusual punishments clause in the nineteenth century the Court held that torture and punitive atrocities such as burning at the stake, crucifixion, or breaking on the wheel would be cruel and unusual.[447] But the justices upheld execution by public shooting in Utah[448] and electrocution in New York.[449]

The Court declared a punishment to be cruel and unusual for the first time in 1910 when it reversed a sentence of fifteen years at hard labor chained at ankle and wrist imposed on a Coast Guard official for falsifying government pay records. Although the Court conceded that the meaning of cruel and unusual punishment was not clear, it maintained that a prison sentence might be so disproportionate to the crime as to be unconstitutional.[450] It was not until almost fifty years later in 1958 that the Court again held a punishment to be cruel and unusual. In *Trop v Dulles* the justices held that it was cruel and unusual punishment to make loss of citizenship the penalty for desertion. In that case, Chief Justice Warren suggested that the meaning of the Eighth Amendment could be discerned from "**evolving standards of decency** that mark the progress of a maturing society."[451] Then in 1962, the Court held the cruel and unusual punishments clause applicable to the states through the due process clause of the Fourteenth Amendment. In that case the Court also reversed a conviction under a California law that made drug addiction a crime on the grounds that criminal statutes can impose liability only on the basis of conduct not status or condition.[452]

Those early cases suggest that the cruel and unusual punishments clause might require a standard of proportionality—the punishment must fit the crime—and that it might have an evolving rather than a static meaning so that it could prohibit punishments that were not considered cruel or unusual in 1791. Nevertheless, before the 1960s the Court declined to get involved in constitutional challenges to the death penalty. For example, in 1947 after Willie Francis survived electrocution in Louisiana as a result of a mechanical malfunction, he alleged that it would be cruel and unusual punishment for the state to subject him to a second execution. The Court dismissed his argument, concluding that the state had not attempted to inflict unnecessary pain—"accidents happen for which no man is to blame."[453] In 1963 prior to the conference

---

[447] *Wilkerson v Utah*, 99 US 130 (1879).
[448] *Ibid.*
[449] *In re Kemmler*, 136 US 436 (1890).
[450] *Weems v United States*, 217 US 349 (1910).
[451] *Trop v Dulles*, 356 US 44 (1958).
[452] *Robinson v California* (1962).
[453] *Louisiana ex rel. Francis v Resweber*, 329 US 459 (1947).

in which the justices met to decide whether to review a case in which a young African American man had been sentenced to death for the rape of a white woman, Justice Arthur Goldberg circulated a memo informing the others that he would raise the question of "Whether and under what circumstances, the imposition of the death penalty is proscribed by the Eighth and Fourteenth Amendments."[454] When the Court decided not to grant *cert* in that case, Goldberg wrote a dissenting opinion in which Brennan and Douglas joined, contending that the Court needed to consider the following questions: Does the imposition of the death penalty for rape violate "evolving standards of decency that mark the progress of [our] maturing society"? Is the taking of human life to protect a value other than human life consistent with the proscription against punishments that are disproportionate to the crime? And can goals of punishment such as deterrence, isolation, and rehabilitation be achieved by punishing rape less severely than by death? If so, does the imposition of the death penalty for rape constitute "unnecessary cruelty"?[455]

In 1969, the Court began to hear cases involving challenges to the death penalty on Eighth Amendment grounds, partly in response to the organized campaign that the NAACP Legal Defense Fund launched in 1965 to challenge all death sentences on any possible constitutional grounds. The moratorium strategy was effective in bringing executions to a halt—from 1968 until 1977 there were no executions although hundreds of condemned individuals remained on death row. The Supreme Court needed to take a position of whether the death penalty constituted cruel and unusual punishment, but at first the justices managed to duck the issue. In one case, for example, the Court invalidated a death sentence for robbery on the grounds that the defendant pleaded guilty without understanding that he could receive the death penalty. The Court held merely that before accepting a defendant's guilty plea, a trial judge must inquire into a defendant's understanding of the consequences of such a plea.[456] By 1971, the Court had ruled on six capital cases but had not addressed the cruel and unusual punishments issue.[457]

The Court struck down the death penalty under the cruel and unusual punishments clause for the first time in *Furman v Georgia* in 1972. A jury in Georgia had convicted Furman of murder and juries in Georgia and Texas had convicted two other men of rape. All three juries imposed the death penalty without any specific guidelines. The lawyers for the condemned men argued that systems in which the jury that determined guilt also determined punishment without any standards led to disparities in sentencing. Specifically, blacks who were convicted of murdering whites were more likely to be sentenced to death than whites convicted of a similar crime. In a short *per curiam* opinion, the Court announced that "the imposition and carrying out of the death

[454]As quoted in Lee Epstein and Joseph F. Kobylka, *The Supreme Court and Legal Change: Abortion and the Death Penalty* (Chapel Hill, NC: University of North Carolina Press, 1992), 42.
[455]*Rudolph v Alabama*, 375 US 889 (1963).
[456]*Boykin v Alabama*, 395 US 238 (1969).
[457]*United States v Jackson*, 390 US 570 (1968); *Witherspoon v Illinois*, 391 US 510 (1968); *Boykin v Alabama*, 395 US 238 (1969); *Maxwell v Bishop*, 398 US 262 (1970); *Crampton v Ohio* and *McGautha v California*, 402 US 183 (1971).

penalty in these cases constitutes cruel and unusual punishment." The Court was divided five to four on the result and the majority could not agree on the reasoning. There were nine separate opinions. Three of the justices—White, Stewart, and Douglas—maintained that capital punishment, as it was then imposed, violated the Constitution. Two—Brennan and Marshall—argued that it was unconstitutional in all circumstances. The dissenters—Blackmun,[458] Burger, Rehnquist, and Powell—contended that the Court should leave such decisions to legislatures. Chief Justice Burger suggested that state legislatures could refashion their laws and provide standards for judges and juries to follow or by defining crimes for which the death penalty is imposed more narrowly.[459]

Almost every state that had the death penalty prior to *Furman* responded just as Burger suggested and reinstated it within four years. Consequently, the Court confronted the issue again in 1976. In *Gregg v Georgia*, by a vote of seven to two, the Court held that the death penalty is not unconstitutional per se and approved statutes that provided standards for judges and juries in imposing death sentences. Writing for the majority, Justice Potter Stewart noted that in light of evolving standards of decency the death penalty is constitutional when it is proportional to the severity of the crime. Stewart conceded that the death penalty may or may not actually deter crime, but legislatures rather than courts are the appropriate forums for making such a determination.

Stewart also suggested that Georgia's statute prevented arbitrary and disproportionate death sentences with its bifurcated trial procedure—guilt and sentence are determined in separate proceedings—its requirement that the sentencing body must make specific factual findings to support the result, and the requirement for state supreme court review.[460] In another case decided the same day, however, the Court held that mandatory death sentence laws—requiring the death penalty for certain crimes—were unconstitutional.[461] The procedures that the Court addressed in the 1976 cases are summarized in Table 8-1.

During the next few terms, the Court clarified the standards for the imposition of the death penalty, holding in one case that the death sentence for the crime of rape is disproportionate and therefore violates the cruel and unusual punishments clause.[462] In another, the justices reasoned that because "the imposition of death by public authority is so profoundly different from all other penalties" an "individualized decision is essential." Therefore, Ohio's requirement that if a murder was aggravated by at least one of seven enumerated factors, the death penalty had to be imposed unless the trial judge found at least one of a specifically enumerated mitigating factors was invalid.[463] In 1982, the justices held that a trial judge could not refuse to hear mitigating evidence pointing to the defendant's youth, troubled childhood, and history of mental problems.[464]

---

[458]In 1994, his final term on the Court, Blackmun adopted the position that the Court's attempt to eliminate arbitrariness while maintaining fairness in imposition of the death penalty had failed and that the death penalty could not be constitutionally imposed.
[459]*Furman v Georgia*, 408 US 238 (1972).
[460]*Gregg v Georgia*, 428 US 153 (1976).
[461]*Woodson v North Carolina*, 428 US 280 (1976).
[462]*Coker v Georgia*, 433 US 584 (1977).
[463]*Lockett v Ohio*, 438 US 586 (1978).
[464]*Eddings v Oklahoma*, 455 US 104 (1982).

Table 8-1 The 1976 Death Penalty Cases

Case	Facts	State Law
Gregg v Georgia, 428 US 153	Gregg was convicted of murdering and robbing two men who had picked him up while hitchhiking.	Bifurcated trial after which the jury weighs evidence in mitigation and aggravation. The Georgia law specifies ten aggravating circumstances; factors in mitigation are not codified. Automatic appeal to state supreme court.
Jurek v Texas, 428 US 262	Jurek was convicted of murder (by strangulation and drowning), while committing a forcible rape.	Bifurcated trial after which attorneys may introduce any relevant evidence for/against a sentence of death. The judge, then, presents the jury with questions that are defined by law. If a unanimous jury responds positively, judge must sentence defendant to death.
Profitt v Florida, 428 US 242	Profitt was convicted of murder (by stabbing) during the course of a burglary.	Same as Georgia law, except specifies eight aggravating and seven mitigating circumstances.
Roberts v Louisiana, 428 US 325	Roberts was convicted of murder during the course of a robbery.	Mandatory death for first-degree murder. But under a provision for "responsive verdicts," juries are to be instructed on second-degree murder. They can reach a verdict of guilt on a lesser offense.
Woodson and Waxton v North Carolina, 428 US 280	Woodson and Waxton were convicted of murder while committing armed robbery.	Mandatory death sentence for first-degree murder.

Source: Lee Epstein and Joseph F. Kobylka, *The Supreme Court and Legal Change: Abortion and the Death Penalty* (Chapel Hill, NC: University of North Carolina Press, 1992), 101.

During the ten years between *Gregg v Georgia* in 1976 and William Rehnquist's elevation to Chief Justice in 1986 many of the death penalty challenges that the Court heard involved procedural questions about the standards that juries and judges could use and what factors could be considered. A majority of the Rehnquist Court, however, has taken a position that is accurately described as prodeath penalty. In 1987, for example, the justices expanded the range of offenses punishable by death when it held that an individual who does not intend to commit murder and who does not actually do so can be executed when he or she participates in a felony that results in murder and is found to have shown "reckless indifference" for human life.[465] In another case that same year, a majority held that statistical evidence of racial discrimination in capital sentencing cannot, without more, establish a violation of the Eighth Amendment.[466] Moreover, the Court has upheld the imposition of the death penalty on individuals who were sixteen or seventeen years old at the time they committed murder.[467] Additionally, a mentally retarded defendant who was found competent to stand trial and whose insanity defense was rejected, the Court held, could also be sentenced to death.[468]

The Rehnquist Court has also made appeals to death sentences more difficult. A majority in 1991 limited the use of habeas corpus petitions by state prisoners[469] and in 1996 upheld the Antiterrorism and Effective Death Penalty Act of 1996, which places constraints on district courts to hear second and successive petitions for habeas corpus.[470] Additionally, in 1993 the Court held that a state prisoner's claim of actual innocence based on newly discovered evidence does not constitute grounds for federal habeas corpus relief.[471]

In 1987 and again in 1989 the Court held that statements and evidence about the character of the victim and the impact that a murder had on the victim's family could not be considered at the time of sentencing.[472] In 1991, however, the Court overruled those decisions and upheld the practice of admitting victim impact evidence at the penalty phase of capital trials.[473]

Finally, by the end of 1999, the Court had at least three times refused to hear appeals by death row inmates who argued that their decades-long waits for death sentences to be carried out amounted to cruel and unusual punishment. In 1995, a Texas inmate argued that seventeen years on death row was cruel and unusual. In that case Justices Stevens and Breyer both argued that the question deserved the attention of the state and lower federal courts. In the fall of 1998 when the Court declined to hear the appeal of man who had spent twenty-three years on death row in Florida, Justice Steven Breyer wrote a dissenting opinion in which he admonished that "After such a delay, an execution may well cease to serve the legitimate penological purposes that otherwise provide a necessary constitutional justification for the death penalty." He added, "The Eighth Amendment forbids punishments that are 'cruel' and 'unusual.' Twenty-three years under sentence of death is unusual whether one takes as a measuring rod current practices or the practice in this country and in England at the time our Constitution was written."[474] Again in the fall of 1999, the justices turned down appeals by two convicted murderers, one who had been on death row in Nebraska for nearly twenty years and the other who had been on

---

[465]*Tison v Arizona*, 481 US 137 (1987).
[466]*McCleskey v Kemp*, 481 US 279 (1987).
[467]*Stanford v Kentucky*, 492 US 361 (1989). By a five-to-three vote, the Court held that a fifteen-year-old could not be executed. *Thompson v Oklahoma*, 487 US 815 (1988).
[468]*Penry v Lynaugh*, 492 US 302 (1989).
[469]*McCleskey v Zant*, 499 US 467 (1991).
[470]*Felker v Turpin*, 518 US 651 (1996).
[471]*Herrera v Collins*, 506 US 390 (1993).
[472]*Booth v Maryland*, 482 US 496 (1987); *South Carolina v Gathers*, 489 US 805 (1989).
[473]*Payne v Tennessee*, 501 US 808 (1991).
[474]*Elledge v Florida*, 98-54210. Richard Carelli, "Justice Speaks Out on Executions," *AP*, October 13, 1998.

Florida's for nearly twenty-five. Justice Breyer repeated his objections of the previous year. Justice Thomas, who did not want the Court to take the cases expressed his disagreement with Breyer, asserting that "It is incongruous to arm capital defendants with an arsenal of 'constitutional' claims with which they may delay their executions, and simultaneously to complain when executions are inevitably delayed."[475]

In 2002 the justices revisited the issue of whether the death penalty may be imposed on the mentally retarded. As noted previously, the Court concluded in 1989 that a mentally retarded defendant could be sentenced to death.[476] In 2002, however, Stevens, writing for a six-person majority, held that the Eighth Amendment prohibits executions of the mentally retarded. He emphasized that since 1989 the consistency with which eighteen states have enacted legislation prohibiting capital punishment for mentally retarded criminals indicates that a national consensus has developed. That is, society has come to perceive mentally retarded offenders as categorically less culpable than the average criminal. Stevens noted that questions of whether the justifications for the death penalty are applicable to the mentally retarded led the majority to agree with the legislative consensus. One justification for capital punishment, retribution, Stevens pointed out, depends on the offender's culpability; given the diminished culpability of the mentally retarded, such severe retribution cannot be justified. The other justification for the death penalty, deterrence, clearly cannot justify execution of a mentally retarded offender who is not likely to understand the possibility of execution as a punishment for their behavior.[477]

Although the death penalty invariably dominates discussions of the cruel and unusual punishments clause, two other issues merit brief consideration. First, do mandatory life sentences that are disproportionate to the crime violate the cruel and unusual punishments clause? In 1991 in *Harmelin v Michigan*, the Court held that a mandatory life sentence without the possibility of parole for possession of over 650 grams of cocaine did not constitute cruel and unusual punishment. Justices Rehnquist and Scalia argued that the prohibition on cruel and unusual punishments is not even applicable to alleged disproportionate sentences. Outside of the context of the death penalty, they contended, decisions about severity of punishment should be left to the discretion of the legislature. O'Connor, Kennedy, and Souter maintained that the Eighth Amendment provides only a narrow **proportionality guarantee** in noncapital cases, forbidding "only extreme sentences that are 'grossly disproportionate' to the crime."[478] In two previous cases, the Court upheld a mandatory life sentence for a third nonviolent felony[479] and a forty-year prison term for possession and distribution of nine ounces of marijuana.[480] The Court has only once found a mandatory life sentence to violate the Eighth Amendment. In that case,

---

[475]Linda Greenhouse, "Court's Refusal to Hear Cases Preserves Delays on Death Row," *New York Times*, November 9, 1999.
[476]*Penry v Lynaugh*, 492 US 302 (1989).
[477]*Atkins v Virginia*, __ US __ (2002).
[478]*Harmelin v Michigan*, 501 US 957 (1991).
[479]*Rummel v Estelle*, 445 US 263 (1980).
[480]*Hutto v Davis*, 454 US 370 (1982).

a slim majority adopted a three-part framework for measuring disproportion-ality: "(i) the gravity of the offense and the harshness of the penalty; (ii) the sentences imposed on other criminals in the same jurisdiction; and (iii) the sentences imposed for the commission of the same crime in other jurisdictions."[481] The dissenters in *Harmelin*—White, Marshall, Blackmun, and Stevens—argued that the life term violated that framework. Indeed, they complained, the Court seemed to have cast it aside. In March 2003, by a vote of five to four, the justices upheld California's "three-strikes" law, rejecting arguments that a sentence of twenty-five years without parole for a man who stole three golf clubs and fifty years without parole for another for the theft of $150 worth of children's videotapes were so disproportionate that they violated the Eighth Amendment.[482]

The second issue outside of the context of the death penalty that arises in connection with the cruel and unusual punishments clause is whether treatment of prisoners and prison conditions can constitute violations of the Eighth Amendment. Before 1976, the Court took the position that the prohibition on cruel and unusual punishments applied only to punishments and not to conditions of prisons or treatment at the hands of prison officials and guards. In that year, however, the Court held that "deliberate indifference" by prison personnel to a prisoner's serious illness or injury constitutes cruel and unusual punishment.[483] Since then, the Court has reviewed prisoner complaints about conditions and treatment. In 1993, for example, a seven-member majority held that a prisoner had stated an Eighth Amendment claim by alleging that prison officials treated him with "deliberate indifference" by forcing him to be exposed to high levels of environmental tobacco smoke, which posed an unreasonable risk to his health.[484] The Court has also held that "unnecessary and wanton" infliction of pain and "maliciously and sadistic" use of force may support an Eighth Amendment claim.[485]

CIVIL LIBERTIES AND THE RESPONSE TO SEPTEMBER 11, 2001

Table 3-3 summarizes the major provisions of the USA Patriot Act of 2001 and the other measures that Congress enacted in the aftermath of the terrorist attacks on September 11, 2001. Earlier in this chapter we considered the impact on the protection against unreasonable searches and seizures of the USA Patriot Act's endorsement of roving wiretaps as well as the fact that the new law makes it easier for investigators to obtain authorization for electronic surveillance. In Chapter 7 we also considered briefly the potential impact that a national crisis like that brought on by the terrorist attacks can have on freedom

---

[481]*Solen v Helm*, 463 US 277 (1983).
[482]*Ewing v California* __ US __ (2003); *Lockyer v Andrade*, __ US__ (2003).
[483]*Estelle v Gamble*, 429 US 97 (1976).
[484]*Helling v McKinney*, 509 US 25 (1993).
[485]*Wilson v Seiter*, 501 US 299 (1991); *Whitley v Albers*, 475 US 312 (1986).

of expression. In this section we consider the impact of the government's response to the events of September 11 on other procedural rights.

First, more than twelve hundred people were detained immediately following the attacks for violating immigration laws, being material witnesses to terrorist activities, or working with the enemy. The majority of those detained were men from the Middle East with immigration problems, and some spent up to seven months in jail before being cleared of terrorist connections and released or deported.[486] Their cases were heard in secret pursuant to rules promulgated by the executive branch. Additionally, people who were held as material witnesses were detained pending grand jury investigations in which they would be required to testify. Two Americans who were labeled "enemy combatants" were not allowed to consult with their lawyers, were detained without being charged with a crime, and faced the prospect of trial by a military tribunal. Several federal district courts held that the identities of detainees must be made public and that deportation proceedings may not be conducted in secrecy. But their rulings had not been tested on appeal by the summer of 2003.

Second, President Bush's Executive Order of November 2001 provided that at the president's discretion, noncitizens accused of acts of terrorism would be tried by military tribunals. The following March the president changed some of the details of his military tribunal plan, leaving more procedural safeguards in place than had the original. For example, defendants will be presumed innocent until proved guilty beyond a reasonable doubt; they will be assigned, at government expense, defense lawyers from a trained legal staff of the military; and the trials will be open to journalists and to the public. Defendants will not be required to testify and will have advance information about evidence that will be used against them. Two-thirds vote of the tribunal will be required for a finding of guilt and for the imposition of any sentence except the death penalty, which will require a unanimous vote. Still, a number of problems remained even with the modified plan. The proceedings may be closed to the public as well as the press if the presiding officer or the Secretary of Defense determines that it is necessary to protect classified information or other national security interests. Defendants and their lawyers may be excluded from the closed part of the trial. Moreover, the rules provide that there can be no appeal from a military tribunal to the civilian courts. Additionally, pursuant to the new rules the government might not release accused terrorists after they are acquitted by a military tribunal but instead might detain them indefinitely if the authorities believe that they are dangerous.[487]

Finally, President Bush made clear that the government would seek the death penalty in its prosecution of some suspected terrorists. As Ronald Dworkin pointed out, the significantly heightened risk that innocent people would be convicted as a result of the relaxed procedural safeguards made the punishment of death seem particularly inappropriate "because that penalty is unnecessary for safety and magnifies the horror of an unjust conviction. We

---

[486]Adam Liptak, Neil A. Lewis, and Benjamin Weiser, "After Sept. 11, a Legal Battle on the Limits of Civil Liberty," *The New York Times,* August 4, 2002.
[487]Ronald Dworkin, "The Trouble with the Tribunals," *The New York Review of Books,* April 25, 2002. Available: http://www.nybooks.com/articles/15284.

may need to incarcerate suspected terrorists to avoid great danger, but we do not need to kill them."[488]

In conclusion, the responses to the events of September 11, including the Executive Order and the USA Patriot Act, threaten some of the major protections guaranteed by the Fourth, Fifth, and Sixth Amendments. Although the roving wiretaps authorized by the Patriot Act seem to be problematic in light of the prohibition on unreasonable searches and seizures in the Fourth Amendment, the detention of aliens secretly and without trial, as well as the president's plan to try suspected terrorists by military tribunal are even more glaringly inconsistent with the right to a speedy and public trial by an impartial jury and assistance of counsel, as well as the broader guarantee of due process. The Bill of Rights applies to noncitizens as well as citizens. Indeed, in 2001 Justice Breyer noted that "once an alien enters the country, the legal circumstance changes, for the Due Process Clause applies to all 'persons' within the United States, including aliens, whether their presence here is lawful, unlawful, temporary, or permanent."[489] It remains to be seen how the Supreme Court will define the delicate balance between national security and civil liberties in the face of continuing widespread fear of further terrorist attacks.

QUESTIONS

1. If the Court continues to use the deterrence theory of the exclusionary rule, emphasizing that the rule is not a constitutional right but a judicially created remedy designed to safeguard Fourth Amendment guarantees through its deterrent effect, what is the future of the rule likely to be? If the exclusionary rule is, on the other hand, a personal constitutional right that has the effect of allowing criminals to go free and that in turn results in higher rates of crime, should the Court overrule it?

2. In light of the Court's most recent cases involving the takings clause, *Nollan v California Coastal Commission* (1987), *Lucas v South Carolina Coastal Commission* (1993), *Dolan v City of Tigard* (1994), and *Tahoe-Sierra Preservation Council v Tahoe Regional Planning Agency* (2002), what sort of land-use regulations is the Court likely to uphold? Do you agree with Justice Stevens that different standards should apply to physical takings as opposed to regulatory takings? Do the previous cases involving takings support Stevens or Rehnquist and Scalia on this issue?

3. Considering the use of the grand jury for Ken Starr's investigation of President Clinton, what seem to be some of the most serious problems with the institution of the grand jury?

4. Can you explain the reason behind the Court's position that the double jeopardy clause offers only minimal protection against multiple punishments? Does that position make sense in terms of the purpose of the pro-

---

[488]Ronald Dworkin, "The Threat to Patriotism," *The New York Review of Books*, February 28, 2002. Available: http://www.nybooks.com/articles/15145.
[489]*Zadvydas v Davis*, 533 US 678 (2001).

hibition on double jeopardy? Does it make more sense as a policy of keeping criminals off the streets?

5. If the Court looks to "evolving standards of decency" to discern the meaning of the prohibition on cruel and unusual punishments, how might Justice Scalia, on the one hand, and Justices Brennan, Marshall, and Blackmun, on the other, have reached opposite conclusions about the constitutionality of the death penalty?

6. What parallels can you find between the government's response to the Japanese military's attack on Pearl Harbor, December 7, 1941 (see Chapter 10), and the response to the terrorist attacks of September 11, 2001? What do the differences and similarities suggest about the U.S. government's ability to define the balance between civil liberties and national security?

KEY TERMS

expectation of privacy
reasonable suspicion
probable cause
"*Terry* stop"
totality of circumstances
balancing analysis
Title III of the Federal Omnibus
   Crime Control and Safe Streets
   Act of 1968
Foreign Intelligence Surveillance Act
   of 1978
USA Patriot Act
exclusionary rule
good faith exception
grand jury
"transactional" immunity
"use" immunity
"same-elements" test
"manifest necessity" for a mistrial

"voluntariness" test
custodial interrogation
interrogation
public safety exception
substantive concept of due process
evolving concept of due process
taking
jury drawn from a fair cross-section
   of the community
impartial jury
confrontation clause
compulsory process clause
right to counsel
"special circumstances" rule
effective assistance of competent
   counsel
evolving standards of decency
proportionality guarantee

SUGGESTIONS FOR FURTHER READING

Abramson, Jeffery. *We, the Jury: The Jury System and the Ideal of Democracy.* New York: Basic Books, 1994.

Ackerman, Bruce. *Private Property and the Constitution.* New Haven, CT: Yale University Press, 1977.

Amar, Akhil Reed. *The Constitution and Criminal Procedure: First Principles.* New Haven, CT: Yale University Press, 1997.

Arenella, Peter. "Foreword: O.J. Lessons." *Southern California Law Review* 69 (1996): 501.

Baker, Liva. *Miranda: Crime, Law, and Politics*. New York: Atheneum, 1983.

Baldus, David C., George G. Woodworth, and Charles A Pulaski Jr. *Equal Justice and the Death Penalty*. Boston: Northeastern University Press, 1990.

Banner, Stuart. *The Death Penalty: An American History*. Cambridge, MA: Harvard University Press, 2002.

Bedau, Hugo Adam, ed. *The Death Penalty in America: Current Controversies*. New York: Oxford University Press, 1997.

Black, Charles L., Jr. *Capital Punishment: The Inevitability of Caprice and Mistake*, 2d ed. New York: W. W. Norton, 1981.

Bradley, Craig M. *The Failure of the Criminal Procedure Revolution*. Philadelphia: University of Pennsylvania Press, 1993.

Coleman, James E., Jr. ed. "The ABA's Proposed Moratorium on the Death Penalty." *Law and Contemporary Problems* 61 (1998).

Colgrove v Battin, 413 US 149 (1973). Justice Brennan's opinion provides a useful discussion of the history of the Seventh Amendment.

Dworkin, Ronald. "The Trouble with the Tribunals." *The New York Review of Books*, April 25, 2002. Available: http://www.nybooks.com/articles/15284.

Dworkin, Ronald. "The Threat to Patriotism." *The New York Review of Books*, February 28, 2002. Available: http://www.nybooks.com/articles/15145.

Ely, James W., Jr. *The Guardian of Every Other Right: A Constitutional History of Property Rights*. New York: Oxford University Press, 1992.

Epstein, Lee, and Joseph F. Kobylka. *The Supreme Court and Legal Change: Abortion and the Death Penalty*. Chapel Hill: University of North Carolina Press, 1992, Chapters 3 and 4.

Epstein, Richard A. *Takings: Private Property and the Power of Eminent Domain*. Cambridge, MA: Harvard University Press, 1985.

Gasperini v Center for Humanities, 135 L Ed 2d 659 (1996). Justice Scalia's dissent provides a historical overview of the re-examination clause.

Haas, Kenneth C., and James A. Inciardi, eds. *Challenging Capital Punishment: Legal and Social Science Approaches*. Newbury Park, CA: Sage Publications, 1988.

Henderson, "The Background of the Seventh Amendment." *Harvard Law Review* 80 (1966): 289.

Kamisar, Yale. "The Warren Court (Was It Really So Defense-Minded?), The Burger Court (Is It Really So Prosecution-Oriented)? And Police Investigatory Practices." In Vincent Blasi, ed. *The Burger Court: The Counter-Revolution That Wasn't*. New Haven, CT: Yale University Press, 1983, 62–91.

Kamisar, Yale, Wayne R. LaFare, and Jerold H. Israel. *Modern Criminal Procedure: Cases, Comments, Questions*. St Paul, MN: West Publishing Co., 1994.

Levy, Leonard. *Against the Law: The Nixon Court and Criminal Justice*. New York: Harper and Row, 1974.

Levy, Leonard. *Origins of the Fifth Amendment*. New York: Oxford University Press, 1968.

Lewis, Anthony. *Gideon's Trumpet*. New York: Vintage Books, 1964.

Meltsner, Michael. *Cruel and Unusual: The Supreme Court and Capital Punishment*. New York: Random House, 1973.

Neier, Aryeh. "The Military Tribunals on Trial." *The New York Review of Books*, February 14, 2002. Available: http://www.nybooks.com/articles/15122.

Note. "Article III Implications for the Applicability of the Seventh Amendment to Federal Statutory Actions." *Yale Law Journal* 95 (1986): 1459.

Orth, John V. *Due Process of Law: A Brief History.* Lawrence, KS: University Press of Kansas, 2003.

Sager, Kelli L., and Karen N. Frederiksen. "Televising the Judicial Branch: In Furtherance of the Public's First Amendment Rights." *Southern California Law Review* 69 (1996).

9

CLARIFYING AND MODIFYING

Although the Ninth and Tenth Amendments were part of the Bill of Rights proposed by the First Congress in 1789 and ratified by the states in 1791, we have placed them in this chapter with the Eleventh and Twelfth Amendments. The latter two amendments followed soon after the Bill of Rights—they were ratified in 1798 and 1804, respectively—and no additional amendments were added to the Constitution until 1865. In fact, the Eleventh and Twelfth Amendments may be viewed as early supplements to the Bill of Rights.[1] The Ninth Amendment did not add any rights to those set forth in the first eight amendments but instead provided some clarification by providing that the enumerated rights did not constitute an exhaustive list. Similarly, the Tenth Amendment reflected recognition that the federal government has the powers bestowed on it elsewhere in the Constitution, that the first eight amendments did not enlarge those powers, and that some powers are reserved to the states. Thus, the last two amendments of the Bill of Rights recognized that silence should not be taken as permitting a limitation on the rights of the people—the Ninth Amendment—or on the powers of the federal government—the Tenth Amendment. The Eleventh Amendment modified the Supreme Court's interpretation of Article III, Section 2, by prohibiting suits against states by citizens of other states. The Twelfth Amendment modified the original method of selecting the president.

AMENDMENT IX: RIGHTS RETAINED BY THE PEOPLE

The enumeration in the Constitution, of certain rights, shall not be construed to deny or disparage others retained by the people.

The Ninth Amendment responded to an objection to a bill of rights that was frequently expressed during the campaign for ratification by supporters of the Constitution: an enumeration of rights would be presumed to be exhaustive with the result that the government could violate any right that was not explicitly guaranteed. James Wilson argued, for example, "If we attempt an enumeration, everything that is not enumerated is presumed to be given. The

---

[1]George Anastaplo, *The Amendments to the Constitution: A Commentary* (Baltimore, MD: Johns Hopkins University Press, 1995), 104.

consequence is, that an imperfect enumeration would throw all implied powers into the scale of government; and the rights of the people would be rendered incomplete."[2] James Madison expressed the same argument at Virginia's ratifying convention. In the First Congress, Madison's proposal for what became the Ninth Amendment declared, "The exceptions [to power] here or elsewhere in the constitution made in favor of particular rights, shall not be so construed as to diminish the just importance of other rights retained by the people, or as to enlarge the powers delegated by the constitution; but either as actual limitations on such powers, or as inserted merely for greater caution."[3] The Ninth Amendment solved the problem of how to enumerate rights without endangering those not mentioned. Additionally, as Leonard W. Levy pointed out, it allowed the first Congress to frame a bill of rights without attempting to list every right that merited protection.[4]

The nature of the rights that the Ninth Amendment protects are suggested by the text of the Amendment and by the specific context in which it was framed, as well as the more general background of the political theory of the late eighteenth century. The latter included the notion that individuals have certain natural rights that are always beyond the reach of government, something that was expressed clearly in the Declaration of Independence as the inalienable rights to life, liberty, and the pursuit of happiness. Thus, it is quite plausible to argue that the **unenumerated rights the Ninth Amendment protects include natural rights** as well as rights that are essential to a democratic form of government such as the right to vote and hold office and the right to free elections. By such an interpretation, the Ninth Amendment also includes a commitment to the principle of equality—at least, equal treatment before the law.

It was not until 1965 that the Supreme Court relied on the Ninth Amendment to uphold a claim to an unenumerated right.[5] In *Griswold v Connecticut,* the justices held that a Connecticut law forbidding the use of contraceptives violated the right of marital privacy. Justice William O. Douglas, writing for the majority, proclaimed that zones of privacy are created by the penumbras of the specific guarantees of several amendments: the First, Second, Third, Fourth, Fifth, as well as the Ninth. Justice Arthur Goldberg wrote a concurring opinion in which Chief Justice Earl Warren and Justice William Brennan joined focusing expressly on the Ninth Amendment. Goldberg maintained that "to hold that a right so basic and fundamental and so deep-rooted in our society as the right of privacy in marriage may be infringed because that right is not guaranteed in so many words by the first eight amendments to the Constitution is to ignore the Ninth Amendment and to give it no effect whatsoever." **Justice Hugo Black presented the opposing view of the Ninth Amendment** in his dissenting opinion. He maintained that the amendment was added to the Constitution, "as every student of history knows, to assure the people that the Constitution in all its provisions was intended to limit the Federal Government to the powers granted

---

[2]As quoted in Leonard W. Levy, *Origins of the Bill of Rights* (New Haven, CT: Yale University Press, 1999), 246–247.
[3]*Ibid.,* 247.
[4]*Ibid.,* 249–250.
[5]The Court mentioned the Ninth Amendment in passing in *United Public Workers v Mitchell,* 330 US 75 (1947).

expressly or by necessary implication."[6] In other words, all the Ninth Amendment did was reiterate the principle that the people retain the rights that are not granted to the federal government.

Although state and federal courts considered the Ninth Amendment during the ensuing fifteen years in more than twelve hundred cases, the Supreme Court has used it only once, relying on it in part to protect the rights of the press to attend a public trial.[7] When the Court has protected unenumerated rights—such as the right to vote and the right to travel, and in subsequent cases involving the right to privacy—it has turned to the due process and equal protection clauses of the Fourteenth Amendment.[8] A number of justices as well as commentators have argued that the use of the Ninth Amendment to protect unenumerated rights that are deemed fundamental leaves too much discretion to the judiciary.

AMENDMENT X: POWERS RESERVED TO THE STATES

The powers not delegated to the United States by the Constitution, nor prohibited by it to the States, are reserved to the States respectively, or to the people.

While the Ninth Amendment was designed to eliminate the problem of unenumerated rights, the Tenth Amendment was aimed at avoiding the implication of unexpressed powers. During the ratification debates, supporters of the Constitution argued that a bill of rights would be dangerous because an attempt to limit power might imply that some power had been granted. For example, a provision declaring freedom of the press might support an argument that the Constitution gave Congress the authority to regulate the press. As Alexander Hamilton contended in *Federalist 84*, "They would contain various exceptions to powers which are not granted; and on this very account, would afford a colourable pretext to claim more than were granted. For why declare that things shall not be done which there is no power to do?"[9] Responding to such an objection, the Tenth Amendment makes it clear that the Bill of Rights did not add to the powers of the federal government that were granted by the Constitution of 1787.

Additionally, the Tenth Amendment did not constrain the powers of the federal government further than the limits imposed by the original Constitution. It does not, for example, curtail any of the powers of Congress enumerated in Article I, Section 8. If the First Congress had begun the Tenth Amendment, "The powers not *expressly* delegated to the United States," it would have been a different matter, but the members of Congress purposely re-

---

[6]*Griswold v Connecticut*, 381 US 479 (1965).
[7]*Richmond Newspapers, Inc. v Virginia*, 488 US 555 (1980).
[8]For example, *Shapiro v Thompson*, 394 US 618 (1969) (right to travel); and *Harper v Virginia State Board of Elections*, 383 US 663 (1966).
[9]Alexander Hamilton, James Madison, and John Jay, *The Federalist Papers* (New York: Bantam Books, 1982), 437.

jected proposals to include the word *expressly,* and in so doing affirmed that they did not want the Tenth Amendment to place additional limits on the federal government. Neither did they wish to alter the distribution of powers between the national government and the states.

The Supreme Court's interpretation of the Tenth Amendment, reflecting the Court's shifting conceptions of federalism, has sometimes been consistent with the meaning just suggested here, whereas at other times it has placed constraints on the powers delegated to Congress. During John Marshall's tenure as Chief Justice, the Court expanded the powers of the national government in relation to the states, finding in the Tenth Amendment no constraints on the constitutional powers of Congress. In *McCulloch v Maryland,* Marshall suggested that the Tenth Amendment prohibits only laws designed to invade state concerns and enacted under the pretext of an enumerated federal power—that is, "for the accomplishment of objects not entrusted to the government."[10] After the Civil War until the late 1930s, however, the Court invalidated a number of laws on the grounds that they invaded the reserved powers of the states. For example, in 1918 the Court invalidated the Child Labor Act of 1916, which barred from shipment in interstate commerce goods produced by children under the age of fourteen.[11] Congress, the Court held, had used its commerce power to regulate local trade and manufacture—a matter reserved to the states by the Tenth Amendment. Justice William R. Day inserted the word *expressly* into the amendment, when he proclaimed, "It must never be forgotten that the nation is made up of states, to which are entrusted the powers of local government. And to them and to the people the powers not expressly delegated to the national government are reserved."[12] The Court also found that the Tenth Amendment curtailed Congress's power to tax, invalidating a tax on child labor,[13] and an excise tax on certain agricultural products. In the latter case, Justice Owen Roberts noted that the law in question, by regulating agricultural production, invaded the reserved rights of the states.[14]

Subsequently, however, the Court returned to Marshall's view that the Tenth Amendment does not limit the powers delegated to the federal government by the Constitution. In 1941, Justice Harlan Fiske Stone observed:

> [T]he amendment states but a truism that all is retained which has not been surrendered. There is nothing in the history of its adoption to suggest that it was more than declaratory of the relationship between the national and state governments as it had been established by the Constitution before the amendment or that its purpose was other than to allay fears that the new national government might seek to exercise powers not granted, and that the states might not be able to exercise fully their reserved powers.[15]

---

[10]See, for example, *McCulloch v Maryland,* 4 Wheat. 316 (1819).
[11]The law also prohibited shipment in interstate commerce of goods produced in factories that allowed children between the ages of fourteen and sixteen to work more than eight hours a day or more than six days a week or at night.
[12]*Hammer v Dagenhart,* 247 US 251 (1918).
[13]*Bailey v Drexel Furniture Co.,* 259 US 20 (1922).
[14]*United States v Butler,* 297 US 1 (1936).
[15]*United States v Darby Lumber,* 312 US 100 (1941).

After 1956, the Court did not rely on the Tenth Amendment to invalidate federal legislation again until 1976 in *National League of Cities v Usery* when the justices invalidated the 1974 amendments of the Fair Labor Standards Act that extended minimum wage and maximum hours regulations to state and local government employees. Writing for the five-member majority, Justice Rehnquist emphasized that the Tenth Amendment prevents Congress from interfering with the ability of the states to perform their traditional governmental functions—Congress cannot act under its commerce power in a way that interferes with "the States' separate and independent existence."[16] It seemed clear that the Court was reviving the old dual federalism. Nine years later, however, in *Garcia v San Antonio Metropolitan Transit Authority*, the Court, again by a vote of five to four, found that attempts to determine the limits of Congress's power in terms of traditional governmental functions is unworkable as well as inconsistent with established principles of federalism and overruled *National League of Cities*. Writing for the majority in *Garcia*, Justice Harry Blackmun emphasized that the extent of Congress's commerce power must reflect the special position of the states in the constitutional system but that it is the political process rather than the judiciary that protects that position. He pointed out that federalism is structured into the political process: states are represented in the Senate, members of the House of Representatives champion their districts, and electoral votes for president are cast by states.

Three of the four dissenting justices wrote opinions expressing their disagreement with the majority's view of federalism. Justice Lewis Powell objected that the decision would allow the federal government to "devour the essentials of state sovereignty" despite the protection ensured by the Tenth Amendment. Justices Rehnquist and O'Connor, emphasizing that state autonomy is an essential component of federalism and that the courts have a responsibility to protect the states' ability to carry out their functions, expressed confidence that the principle of *National League of Cities* would "in time again command the support of a majority of this Court."[17]

The Rehnquist Court began to signal its move away from *Garcia* in 1991 when it refused to apply the Age Discrimination in Employment Act of 1967 to set aside a provision of the Missouri Constitution mandating the retirement of judges at the age of seventy. Congress, the Court noted, made the law applicable to state employees but had not stated plainly that it intended the law to apply to state judges.[18] Then in 1992 in *New York v United States*, the Court invalidated legislation that required states that failed to provide for disposal of their own radioactive waste to assume title to the waste and made them liable for all damages arising from failure to dispose of it. Justice O'Connor noted that whether one views the provision as "lying outside Congress' enumerated powers or as infringing upon the core of state sovereignty reserved by the Tenth Amendment, the provision is inconsistent with the federal structure of our Government established by the Constitution."[19] The three dissenters—White,

---

[16]*National League of Cities v Usery*, 426 US 833 (1976).
[17]*Garcia v San Antonio Metropolitan Transit Authority*, 469 US 528 (1985).
[18]*Gregory v Ashcroft*, 501 US 452 (1991).
[19]*New York v United States*, 505 US 144 (1992).

Blackmun, and Stevens—complained that the majority relied on an outdated interpretation of federalism.

In 1997 in *Printz v United States*, the Court invalidated a provision of the Brady Handgun Violence Prevention Act of 1993 that required local law enforcement officers to perform background checks on prospective gun purchasers.[20] By a vote of five to four, the justices ruled that the provision violated the principle of state sovereignty by compelling state officers to execute federal laws. Justice Scalia, who wrote the opinion for the majority, relied on the rule established in *New York v United States* that Congress cannot compel the states to enact or enforce a federal regulatory program. Justice O'Connor, in a concurring opinion, maintained that the Brady Act violated the Tenth Amendment insofar as it forced states and local law enforcement officers to perform background checks on prospective handgun owners and to accept Brady Forms from firearms dealers. In contrast, in 2000, the justices ruled unanimously that the regulatory scheme that Congress devised in the Driver's Privacy Protection Act of 1994 (DPPA), which restricts the states' ability to disclose the personal information that Departments of Motor Vehicles require from individuals as a condition of obtaining a driver's license or registering an automobile, without the driver's consent did not violate the Tenth Amendment. The Court distinguished *Printz*, noting that whereas the law invalidated in that case required state officials to assist in the enforcement of a federal statute regulating private individuals but the DPPA merely regulates the states as owners of databases.[21] Nevertheless, the confidence that O'Connor and Rehnquist expressed in *Garcia* that the Court would return to their conception of the nation-state relationship seems to have been well-founded as the majority has clearly returned the doctrine of dual federalism.

AMENDMENT XI: SUITS AGAINST STATES

> The Judicial power of the United States shall not be construed to extend to any suit in law or equity, commenced or prosecuted against one of the United States by Citizens of another State, or by Citizens or Subjects of any Foreign State.
>
> Proposed March 4, 1794; ratified by the states February 7, 1795; declared to be part of the Constitution by presidential message to Congress, January 8, 1798.[22]

The first amendment to be added to the Constitution after the Bill of Rights, the Eleventh Amendment also represents the first time the amending process was used to overturn a decision of the Supreme Court. One of the powers that Article III, Section 2 granted to the federal courts was the authority to hear cases involving a state and citizens of another state. During the campaign

---

[20]*Printz v United States*, 521 US 98 (1997). The enlistment of local officials was a temporary measure that was to remain in effect only until a national system for checking prospective handgun purchasers' backgrounds went into effect.

[21]*Reno v Condon*, 528 US 141 (2000).

[22]Because the president has no formal role in the process of amending the Constitution, 1795 may be considered the date on which the Eleventh Amendment became part of the Constitution.

for ratification of the Constitution, a number of people objected to that provision on the ground that it would permit a private individual to take a state to federal court. Alexander Hamilton and others noted reassuringly that the **doctrine of "sovereign immunity"** would protect a state from being sued without its consent. In 1793, however, in *Chisholm v Georgia* the Court permitted a citizen of one state to sue another state in a federal court.[23] That case involved a suit brought by some citizens of South Carolina against Georgia to recover confiscated property. Although Georgia denied that the Supreme Court had jurisdiction, and even refused to appear in court to argue the case, the justices ruled by a vote of four to one that the Constitution granted the Court jurisdiction. The Georgia house of representatives responded by passing a resolution that any federal marshal who sought to carry out the ruling of the Court would be declared a felon and suffer death by hanging.[24] Congress then proposed the Eleventh Amendment and the states ratified it, effectively overruling the Court's decision in *Chisholm*.

In 1890 in *Hans v Louisiana*, the Court extended the Eleventh Amendment to prohibit people from suing their own states in federal court.[25] The amendment is subject to several important exceptions. First, states may waive sovereign immunity and consent to suit, either by state statute or by agreement in an individual case. Second, Congress may abrogate the states' sovereign immunity and create private causes of action against states by virtue of its enforcement powers under the Fourteenth and Fifteenth Amendments. Third, and very important, as the Court held in *Ex Parte Young* in 1908, it is possible for individuals to bring federal suit to enjoin state officials from enforcing unconstitutional state laws.[26]

Although the Eleventh Amendment and the concept of state sovereign immunity may at first glance seem technical and obscure, they raise major questions concerning individual rights. A great deal of scholarship on the amendment has developed an argument to the effect that "the broad constitutional prohibition against suing states in federal court is unworkable in a federal system premised in important part on controlling state behavior by federal law in order to protect private individuals."[27] The amendment has the potential to render it impossible for individuals to bring suit in federal court when their states violate federal law. In such an event, individuals would be left without recourse when the states violate rights protected by the federal law. Congress's authority to enforce the federal law would thereby be severely curtailed.

The Court has decisively moved in that direction. In 1996, the justices held that Congress does not have the authority under Article I, Section 8, of the Constitution to abrogate the states' sovereign immunity and allow suits against

[23]*Chisholm v Georgia*, 2 US 419 (1793).
[24]Alan P. Grimes, *Democracy and the Amendments to the Constitution* (Lexington, MA: Lexington Books, 1978), 18.
[25]*Hans v Louisiana*, 134 US 1 (1890). The amendment does not prohibit suits by other states and suits by the United States. See, for example, *Blatchford v Native Village of Noatak*, 501 US 775 (1991).
[26]*Ex Parte Young*, 209 US 123 (1908).
[27]William A. Fletcher, "A Historical Interpretation of the Eleventh Amendment: A Narrow Construction of an Affirmative Grant of Jurisdiction Rather than a Prohibition against Jurisdiction," *Stanford Law Review* 35 (1983): 1033–1131, 1040–1041.

states in federal courts pursuant to its commerce power.[28] Then in 1999 in *Alden v Maine* the justices, by a vote of five to four, held that Congress cannot subject nonconsenting states to suit in their own courts by state employees for violations of the Fair Labor Standards Act. It would be inconsistent with principles of federalism, Justice Anthony Kennedy reasoned, to give Congress more power over state courts than the federal courts, which is what the result would be if Congress could require suits against states in state but not federal court.[29] Because such suits cannot be brought either in federal or state court, state employees are left without recourse if the state chooses to violate the federal labor laws. Writing for the four dissenters, Justice David Souter pointed out that although a remedy for state violation of the law is still available because the United States may bring suit in federal court against a state for damages, "unless Congress plans a significant expansion of the National Government's litigating forces to provide a lawyer whenever private litigation is barred by today's decision [and the 1996 decision], the allusion to enforcement of private rights by the National Government is probably not much more than whimsy."[30]

The Court has also construed the principle of *Ex parte Young*—that individuals may seek injunctions against state officials who are acting in violation of the federal law or Constitution—narrowly. For example, a majority refused to extend that principle to charges that state authorities are violating their own state constitutions and laws.[31]

In spite of the Court's holding in 1996 that Congress does not have the authority under Article I, Section 8, to abrogate the states' sovereignty, it was possible that such authority existed under Section 5 of the Fourteenth Amendment, which gives Congress the power to enforce the other provisions of that amendment. The Court acknowledged in 1976, for example, that the Fourteenth Amendment limits the protection for states offered by the Eleventh Amendment.[32] A narrow majority of the Court, however, has eliminated such a possibility. In 1999, when the justices held that the states are immune from patent infringement suits and trademark suits, it indicated that it would take a careful look at legislation in which Congress purports to be acting under Section 5 of the Fourteenth Amendment to determine whether Congress acted appropriately to remedy a constitutional violation.[33] That same year the Court agreed to hear a case that involved issues of whether Congress was sufficiently clear and whether it had the authority to waive sovereign immunity in the Age Discrimination in Employment Act. Several circuits of the Courts of Appeals had issued conflicting decisions in challenges brought by faculty members of universities who were attempting to sue their employers for age discrimination. The Courts of Appeals disagreed on whether the states could be sued. The

---

[28]*Seminole Tribe of Florida v Florida*, 517 US 44 (1996).
[29]*Alden v Maine*, 527 US 706 (1999).
[30]*Ibid.* Stevens, Ginsburg, and Breyer, the other dissenters, with Souter, reject the doctrine of sovereign immunity and argue that the Court should overrule *Hans v Louisiana*.
[31]*Pennhurst State School & Hospital v Halderman*, 465 US 89 (1984). See also, *Papasan v Allain*, 478 US 265 (1986).
[32]*Fitzpatrick v Bitzer*, 427 US 445 (1976).
[33]*Florida Prepaid v College Savings Bank*, 527 US 627 (1999) (patent infringement); *College Savings Bank v Florida Prepaid*, 527 US 666 (1999) (trademark).

Supreme Court, by a divided vote, held that although Congress's intent to abrogate the states' immunity was sufficiently clear, it was invalid because Congress had exceeded its authority under Section 5 of the Fourteenth Amendment.[34]

Following the same line of reasoning in 2001, the Court, again by a vote of five to four, held that the Eleventh Amendment prohibits federal suits by state employees for violations of the Americans with Disabilities Act. The majority reasoned that because the equal protection clause of the Fourteenth Amendment does not require the states to make special accommodations for the disabled, Congress may not rely on its power under Section 5 of that amendment to abrogate the states' sovereign immunity.[35] In 2003, the majority seemed to have shifted course when a six-person majority held that states can be sued for violating their employees' federal right, under the Family and Medical Leave Act, to take time off for family emergencies.[36]

In a book he published in 2002, federal judge and law professor John T. Noonan, expressed his disagreement with the Court's interpretation of the Eleventh Amendment, with the assertion that,

> The claim that the sovereignty of the states is constitutional rests on an audacious addition to the eleventh amendment, a pretense that it incorporates the idea of state sovereignty. Neither the text nor the legislative history of the amendment supports this claim, nor does an appeal to the history contemporaneous with the amendment. A rhetorical advantage is gained by the current court referring to state sovereignty as "an eleventh amendment" matter. The constitutional connection is imaginary.[37]

AMENDMENT XII: ELECTION OF THE PRESIDENT

The Electors shall meet in their respective states and vote by ballot for President and Vice-President, one of whom, at least, shall not be an inhabitant of the same state with themselves; they shall name in their ballots the person voted for as President, and in distinct ballots the person voted for as Vice-President, and they shall make distinct lists of all persons voted for as President, and of all persons voted for as Vice-President, and of the number of votes for each, which lists they shall sign and certify, and transmit sealed to the seat of the government of the United States, directed to the President of the Senate;—The President of the Senate shall, in the presence of the Senate and House of Representatives, open all the certificates and the votes shall then be counted;—The person having the greatest number of votes for President, shall be the President, if such number be a majority of the whole number of Electors appointed; and if no person have such majority, then from the persons having the highest numbers not exceeding three on the list of those voted for as

---

[34]*Kimel v Florida Board of Regents*, 530 US ___ (2000).
[35]*Board of Trustees of the University of Alabama v Garrett* 531US356 (2001).
[36]*Nevada Department of Human Resources v Hibbs*, ___ US ___ (2003). Linda Greenhouse, "In a Momentous Term, Justices Remake the Law, and the Court, *The New York Times*, July 1, 2003.
[37]John T. Noonan, Jr., *Narrowing the Nation's Power: The Supreme Court Sides with the States* (Berkeley, CA: University of California Press, 2002), 151–152. Reprinted by permission.

President, the House of Representatives shall choose immediately, by ballot, the President. But in choosing the President, the votes shall be taken by states, the representation from each state having one vote; a quorum for this purpose shall consist of a member or members from two-thirds of the states, and a majority of all the states shall be necessary to a choice. [And if the House of Representatives shall not choose a President whenever the right of choice shall devolve upon them, before the fourth day of March next following, then the Vice-President shall act as President, as in the case of the death or other constitutional disability of the President][38]—The person having the greatest number of votes as Vice-President, shall be the Vice-President, if such number be a majority of the whole number of Electors appointed, and if no person have a majority, then from the two highest numbers on the list, the Senate shall choose the Vice-President; a quorum for the purpose shall consist of two-thirds of the whole number of Senators, and a majority of the whole number shall be necessary to a choice. But no person constitutionally ineligible to the office of President shall be eligible to that of Vice-President of the United States.

Proposed December 8, 1803. Declared in force by the secretary of state September 25, 1804.

As discussed in Chapter 4, the delegates to the Philadelphia Convention expected electors to be distinguished citizens who would choose the president and the vice president. The failure of the electoral system was due in part to the rise of national political parties. By the election of 1800, electors were pledged in advance to vote for the candidates nominated by their respective parties and in that election, the Republican-Democratic electors were in a majority. Under the original provisions for selecting the president and the vice president, each elector voted for two individuals without specifying choices for president and vice president. As a result, Aaron Burr, the Republican-Democratic candidate for vice president, received the same number of electoral votes as Thomas Jefferson, the Republican-Democratic candidate for president. The election went to the House of Representatives, where the Federalists were in control. Although many Federalists favored Burr, Alexander Hamilton used his considerable influence to support Jefferson, who was elected on the thirty-sixth ballot. The Twelfth Amendment was designed to prevent such a situation from occurring again.

The two major differences between the Twelfth Amendment and the original provisions of the Constitution, which it repealed, are as follows. First, under the Twelfth Amendment, electors are required to cast separate votes clearly designating their choice for president and vice president. Second, in the event that no person receives a majority of the electoral votes for president, the House of Representatives chooses from the three candidates with the most electoral votes—rather than five, as in the original provision. Each state has one vote in the House. If no one receives a majority of the electoral votes for vice president, the Senate chooses between the two individuals with the most electoral votes, each senator having one vote.

---

[38]The portion of the Twelfth Amendment in brackets has been superseded by the Twentieth Amendment and modified by the Twenty-fifth.

The development of the two-party system had another consequence for the **electoral college** that the Framers of the Constitution did not anticipate. It greatly lessened the probability that the House of Representatives would be called on to make the final selection. Only once since 1801 has the House had to exercise this duty. In the election of 1824, before the party system had fully developed, Andrew Jackson, John Quincy Adams, and William Crawford received the most electoral votes, but none of them had a majority. The House, voting by states, chose John Quincy Adams. The only time the Senate has been called on to make the final selection for the vice presidency was in 1837, when it favored Richard M. Johnson over Francis Granger.

Whenever a strong showing by a third-party candidate develops, such as George Wallace's American Independent Party bid in the 1968 election, John Anderson's independent candidacy in 1980, Ross Perot's Reform Party candidacy in 1992 and 1996, and Ralph Nader's Green Party candidacy in 2000, the threat of final selection by the House and Senate increases.

All the states except Maine and Nebraska currently provide for the selection of electors on a general statewide, straight-ticket basis. Each voter casts one vote for all the electors of one party or independent candidate. This statewide, **straight-ticket voting** means that the party receiving the most popular votes in a state receives all that state's electoral votes—the winner-take-all principle. For example, in 1996 Bill Clinton received 51 percent of the popular vote in California, Bob Dole received 38 percent, and Ross Perot received 7 percent. Clinton nevertheless received all fifty-four of California's electoral votes. In the highly controversial election of 2000, after the Supreme Court intervened to prohibit the recounts in the contested state of Florida, Vice President Al Gore had 266 electoral votes whereas Texas Governor George W. Bush won the election with 271. The final count of the popular votes showed that the new president had received 50,455,156 votes whereas his opponent had garnered 50,992,335.[39] We discuss the electoral college and the election of 2000 at greater length in Chapter 4.

Despite the widely supported view that the electoral college needs to be reformed, it has been difficult to secure agreement about what reforms should be made. The 1980 and 1992 elections temporarily revived and intensified the concerns about the risks inherent in our present arrangements: if John Anderson in 1980, or Ross Perot in 1992 or 1996, had secured enough electoral votes to keep either major party candidate from obtaining a majority, electors might have been tempted to exercise some discretion. More probably, the election would have been thrown into the House of Representatives, where the Anderson supporters in 1980 or the Perot followers in 1992 or 1996 might have had the balance-of-power votes necessary to decide between the two major party candidates. If the Supreme Court had not halted the recounts in Florida in 2000, the House of Representatives might have determined the outcome of the election.

Representatives of the less populous states have opposed proposals to provide for direct popular election. Because states have as many electoral votes as

---

[39]For a state-by-state count, see "Presidential Election of 2000, Electoral and Popular Vote Summary." Available: http://www.infoplease.com/ipa/A0876793.html. Reprinted by permission.

they have senators and representatives, the smaller states carry greater weight in the electoral college than they would in a nationwide direct election. Some observers have proposed that individual electors be eliminated but that the system of electoral votes be retained with the distribution of a state's electoral vote in the same ratio as its popular vote. Such a change would eliminate any danger of an elector's disregarding the wishes of the voters (something that happened in 1956, 1960, 1968, and 1972), lessen the influence of strategically located minorities, weaken the one-party system where it now exists, and ensure the election of the candidate with the largest popular vote. Those who fear it would weaken the influence of people living in large cities, who often have the balance of power in presidential elections, have opposed such a change. The same objections hold even more strongly against proposals to have electors chosen by congressional districts rather than on statewide tickets.

QUESTIONS

1. Did Justice Black's dissenting opinion in *Griswold v Connecticut* provide a plausible interpretation of the Ninth Amendment? Or did he seem to confuse the Ninth Amendment with the Tenth? Does Black's interpretation of the Ninth Amendment eliminate its function? If Black's interpretation is correct, why did the First Congress include the Ninth Amendment in the Bill of Rights and why did the states ratify it?

2. In light of the Court's most recent decisions through 2001 regarding the Eleventh Amendment, what recourse remains for individuals who have been denied employment or promotion because of discrimination? What is the relationship between Section 5 of the Fourteenth Amendment and the Eleventh Amendment?

3. What is the relationship between the Court's decision in *City of Boerne v Flores* (discussed in Chapter 7) and the most recent decisions regarding the Eleventh Amendment? What do those decisions considered together suggest about Congress's authority to enforce constitutional rights against state infringement?

4. Do you think the electoral college should be abolished in favor of direct election of the president?

KEY TERMS

natural rights theory of the Ninth
   Amendment
Justice Hugo Black theory of the
   Ninth Amendment

doctrine of "sovereign immunity"
electoral college
straight-ticket voting

SUGGESTIONS FOR FURTHER READING

Abbott, David W., and James P. Levine. *Wrong Winner: The Coming Debacle in the Electoral College.* New York: Praeger, 1991.

Barnett, Randy E. "Ninth Amendment." *The Oxford Companion to the Supreme Court of the United States.* New York: Oxford University Press, 1992, 589–592.

Best, Judith A. *The Case against Direct Election of the President.* Ithaca, NY: Cornell University Press, 1975.

Fletcher, William A. "A Historical Interpretation of the Eleventh Amendment: A Narrow Construction of an Affirmative Grant of Jurisdiction Rather than a Prohibition against Jurisdiction." *Stanford Law Review* 35 (1983): 1033–1131.

Levy, Leonard W. *Origins of the Bill of Rights.* New Haven, CT: Yale University Press, 1999, Chapter 12.

Lofgren, Charles A. "The Origins of the Tenth Amendment: History, Sovereignty, and the Problem of Constitutional Intention." In Ronald K. L. Collins, ed. *Constitutional Government in America.* Durham, NC: Carolina Academic Press, 1980, 331–337.

Orth, John V. *The Judicial Power of the United States: The Eleventh Amendment in American History.* New York: Oxford University Press, 1987.

Noonan, John T., Jr. *Narrowing the Nation's Power: The Supreme Court Sides with the States.* Berkeley, CA: University of California Press, 2002.

Rappaport, Michael B. "Reconciling Textualism and Federalism: The Proper Textual Basis of the Supreme Court's Tenth and Eleventh Amendment Decisions." *Northwestern University Law Review* 93 (1999): 819–875.

Schwartz, Bernard. *The Great Rights of Mankind: A History of the Bill of Rights.* New York: Oxford University Press, 1977.

10

THE RECONSTRUCTION AMENDMENTS

After the ratification of the Eleventh and Twelfth Amendments, no new amendments were added to the Constitution for nearly half a century. During the Reconstruction period in the aftermath of the Civil War, three amendments were adopted. The Thirteenth Amendment abolished slavery, the Fourteenth Amendment established citizenship by birthright and guaranteed due process and equal protection of the laws, and the Fifteenth Amendment prohibited denial of the vote on the basis of race. The Reconstruction Amendments reflected the antislavery Republicans' belief in the principles of natural law and fundamental rights that included the equality of all men before the law. That the amendments fell far short of their potential was due in part to the narrow interpretation that the Supreme Court insisted upon until at least the middle of the twentieth century. The Reconstruction Amendments, nevertheless, transformed the original constitutional structure by placing limits on the states and authorizing Congress to enforce those limits. Perhaps most important, the Reconstruction Amendments placed the principle of equality before the law at the center of the Constitution.

AMENDMENT XIII: THE PROHIBITION ON SLAVERY

Section 1

Neither slavery nor involuntary servitude, except as a punishment for crime whereof the party shall have been duly convicted, shall exist within the United States, or any place subject to their jurisdiction.

Section 2

Congress shall have power to enforce this article by appropriate legislation.

Proposed: January 31, 1865   Declared in force by the Secretary of State, December 18, 1865.

In his first inaugural address in 1861, Abraham Lincoln endorsed the proposed constitutional amendment that protected the legal institution of slavery, not only by prohibiting legislation interfering with it but also by placing it beyond the reach of any future constitutional amendments. Although the Republicans may have had a strong ideological opposition to slavery, during the early stages of the Civil War they did not embrace abolition as a Northern war aim. Later, however, they came to believe that emancipation was necessary to preserve the Union. In 1862, Congress enacted the Confiscation Act, which provided for the seizure of rebel property including slaves. In that same year, Congress also prohibited slavery in the territories. President Lincoln issued a preliminary proclamation in September 1862 and the final **Emancipation Proclamation** on January 1, 1863. It did not free all the slaves because it applied only to the Confederacy. By mid-1863, Republicans were convinced that a constitutional amendment was needed to accomplish the crucial task of ridding the nation of the institution of slavery.

Both Houses of Congress debated the amendment in the spring of 1864. It passed the Senate but Republicans in the House were unable to attract enough Democratic votes to achieve the necessary two-thirds vote. The Republican victory in the fall of 1864 and a lobbying effort by the White House changed enough Democratic votes so that the amendment passed the House in 1865. Later that year, the requisite number of state legislatures ratified the amendment. Several southern states ratified with the understanding that Congress lacked the power to determine the future of the former slaves.[1]

The disagreement over the meaning of the prohibition on slavery and the extent of Congress's authority to enforce the prohibition marked the debates in Congress over the Thirteenth Amendment and continues among scholars today. Generally, in 1865 Democrats argued that the amendment merely ended the legal master-slave relationship and left all other legal inequalities intact. By that understanding, no more federal action would be needed nor warranted to enforce the amendment. President Andrew Johnson also argued that the amendment ended only formal slavery and did not affect other nation-state relationships. In contrast, many Republicans argued that the amendment required positive enforcement by the federal government of the full and equal rights of freedom. Harold M. Hyman and William M. Wiecek observed that there was a "vocabulary of freedom" among abolitionist-Republicans in 1865: "Freedom was much more than the absence of slavery. It was, like slavery, an evolving, enlarging matrix of both formal and customary relationships rather than a static catalog."[2]

In the *Civil Rights Cases* in 1883, the Supreme Court suggested that Section 2 of the Thirteenth Amendment gave Congress the authority to outlaw **"badges and incidents" of slavery** as well as the institution itself.[3] But the Court defined badges and incidents narrowly and held that Congress had no power to reach private action or to prohibit racial discrimination in public accommodations.[4] Because of this narrow interpretation it was not until 1944 that the Court held state peonage laws that made it a crime to fail to perform work after receiving money on the promise to do so to be contrary to the Thirteenth

---

[1]Eric Foner, *Reconstruction: America's Unfinished Revolution 1863–1877* (New York: Harper and Row, 1988), 199.
[2]Harold M. Hyman and William M. Wiecek, *Equal Justice under Law: Constitutional Development 1835–1875* (New York: Harper and Row, 1982), 391–392.
[3]*Civil Rights Cases*, 109 US 3 (1833).
[4]*United States v Harris*, 106 US 629 (1883), and *Civil Rights Cases*, 109 US 3 (1833).

Amendment. The justices reasoned that such laws established a condition of involuntary servitude.[5]

The Court revived the abolitionist-Republican interpretation of Section 2 of the Thirteenth Amendment in 1968 in *Jones v Alfred H. Mayer Company,* when it held that a provision of the federal law based on the Civil Rights Act of 1866, guaranteeing the same property rights as those that are "enjoyed by white citizens" prohibited discrimination by private individuals. The Court also held that Section 2 of the Amendment gave Congress the authority to prohibit private discrimination. Justice Potter Stewart, who wrote for the seven-member majority, announced:

> The Thirteenth Amendment authorized Congress to do more than merely dissolve the legal bond by which the Negro slave was held to his master; it gave Congress the power rationally to determine what are the badges and the incidents of slavery and the authority to translate that determination into effective legislation. . . .
>
> When racial discrimination herds men into ghettos and makes their ability to buy property turn on the color of their skin, then it too is a relic of slavery. . . .
>
> At the very least, the freedom that Congress is empowered to secure under the Thirteenth Amendment includes the freedom to buy whatever a white man can buy, the right to live wherever a white man can live. If Congress cannot say that being a free man means at least this much, then the Thirteenth Amendment made a promise the Nation cannot keep.[6]

The Court has upheld the principle of *Jones v Mayer* and, indeed, has expanded it to cover other groups in addition to African Americans in a number of decisions holding that federal legislation prohibits discrimination by private individuals.[7]

AMENDMENT XIV: CITIZENSHIP, PRIVILEGES, AND IMMUNITIES OF UNITED STATES CITIZENSHIP, DUE PROCESS, AND EQUAL PROTECTION OF THE LAWS

Proposed: June 13, 1866   Declared in force by the Secretary of State: July 28, 1868

The Fourteenth Amendment has been at the center of an overwhelming number of Supreme Court decisions since the 1930s. The vast array of cases include those that we discuss at some length here as well as those in which the Court interpreted the due process clause to incorporate most of the Bill of Rights, which we discuss in Chapter 7. The provisions in the Bill of Rights apply to the states not directly but through the due process clause of the Fourteenth Amendment. Consequently, the Fourteenth Amendment is implicated in

---

[5]*Pollock v Williams,* 322 US 4 (1944).
[6]*Jones v Alfred H. Mayer Co.,* 392 US 409 (1968).
[7]*Saint Francis College v Al-Khazraji,* 481 U.S. 604 (1987); *Shaare Tefila Congregation v Cobb,* 481 U.S. 615 (1987).

every case in which the Court is asked to determine whether a state has violated the First, Fourth, Fifth, Sixth, Seventh, or Eighth Amendments. In short, the Fourteenth Amendment is featured in the panorama of cases concerning the protection of individual rights against infringement by the states.

Historian Eric Foner remarked,

> The aims of the Fourteenth Amendment can only be understood within the political and ideological context of 1866: the break with the President, the need to find a measure upon which all Republicans could unite, and the growing consensus within the party around the need for strong federal action to protect the freedmen's rights, short of the suffrage. Despite the many drafts, changes, and deletions, the Amendment's central principle remained constant: a national guarantee of equality before the law."[8]

Foner contended in general terms that the Fourteenth Amendment "changed and broadened the meaning of freedom for all Americans."[9]

A detailed discussion of the historical and political context of the framing of the Fourteenth Amendment would consume far more space than is available here. Therefore, we summarize that context as briefly as possible but in a way that we hope will be useful to understanding the Supreme Court's interpretation of the Fourteenth Amendment. We strongly encourage readers to consult the Suggestions for Further Reading at the end of this chapter.

By the time the war ended in early April 1865, Congress had proposed the Thirteenth Amendment. It was not yet clear what shape Reconstruction would take or how the southern states would be readmitted to the Union. After President Lincoln's assassination on April 14, Andrew Johnson assumed office and at the end of May announced his extremely lenient Reconstruction plan, which allowed leading Confederates to dominate the state governments of the former Confederacy In the summer of 1865, southern localities began to adopt ordinances to coerce blacks in order to keep the plantation system of labor running in the absence of slavery. Opelousas, Louisiana, for example, established a pass system and curfew and barred blacks from living in town except as servants.[10] But local measures proved inadequate to solve the "labor problem" and the southern states enacted the **Black Codes**, a series of laws designed "for getting things back as near to slavery as possible."[11] The codes required blacks to sign labor contracts that barred them from leaving the plantation and provided for the arrest and return of those who breached contracts—Florida provided that blacks who broke labor contracts could be whipped, placed in the pillory, and sold for up to one year's labor. The codes also prohibited blacks from renting land in urban areas and made vagrancy punishable not only by fines but also by involuntary labor. South Carolina's laws forbade blacks from pursuing any occupation other than farmer or servant unless they paid an annual tax ranging from $10 to $100.

---

[8]Foner, 257.
[9]*Ibid.*, 258.
[10]*Ibid.*, 198.
[11]*Ibid.*, 199.

Republicans in the Thirty-Ninth Congress, which convened in December of 1865, were determined to provide more protection for blacks in the South. Thus, Congress established a **Joint Committee on Reconstruction** and passed the Civil Rights Bill, which declared blacks to be citizens of the United States and provided that all inhabitants of states or territories were to have the same rights as whites to contract, sue, and engage in personal property transactions.

It also provided that all inhabitants were to have "full and equal benefit of all laws and proceedings for the security of person and property"[12] and were to be subject to the same punishments. Finally, the law provided that any person who under color of law caused any such civil right to be denied would be guilty of a federal offense.

Congress overrode President Johnson's veto and the Civil Rights Bill became law in April 1866. There was a problem, however. It was not clear that Congress had the constitutional authority to enact legislation providing for such far-reaching federal intervention into areas that, prior to the Civil War, were assumed to be matters that the Constitution left to the discretion of the states. A number of Republicans argued that the Thirteenth Amendment provided the authority—that when the state deprived individuals of rights that the **Civil Rights Act** protected they were denying the freedom guaranteed by that amendment. Republicans also found authority for the Civil Rights Act in the privileges and immunities clause of Article IV, Section 2. Arguments were also advanced that Congress's power to provide for the general welfare in Article I, Section 8, supplied the necessary support for the Civil Rights Act. One member of Congress argued that the act did not create any new rights but merely enforced those that were "simply the absolute rights of individuals" or "the natural rights of man."[13] Some Republicans, however, expressed doubts that Congress had the authority to enact the law.

The Joint Committee on Reconstruction proposed the Fourteenth Amendment soon after the Civil Rights Bill was introduced in the Senate. It was designed in part to ensure the constitutionality of that legislation. An overwhelming majority of Republicans in the Thirty-ninth Congress also believed that it was imperative to constitutionalize the rights protected by the Civil Rights Act to place them beyond the power of shifting congressional majorities.

Section 1

All persons born or naturalized in the United States, and subject to the jurisdiction thereof, are citizens of the United States and of the State wherein they reside.

In *Dred Scott v Sandford* in 1857, Chief Justice Roger Brooke Taney proclaimed that blacks were not citizens of the United States and thus did not have the right to sue in federal court. The Court, therefore, had no jurisdiction to resolve Dred Scott's claim that he was entitled to his freedom by virtue of his

---

[12]As quoted in Daniel A. Farber and Suzanna Sherry, *A History of the American Constitution* (St. Paul, MN: West Publishing, Co, 1990), 299.
[13]As quoted in *ibid.*, 303.

travels to the free state of Illinois and free Wisconsin Territory. The Court went further, however, to hold that Congress lacked the authority to abolish slavery in the territories, that slaves were property protected by the Constitution, and that a slave's status depended on the law of the state in which he or she resided. For Dred Scott, since the Missouri Supreme Court had determined that he was a slave, the United States Supreme Court considered him to be a slave.[14]

Section 1 of the Fourteenth Amendment overturned the Supreme Court's decision in Dred Scott's case by making all individuals born in the United States citizens. It made the principle of *jus soli* an explicit part of the Constitution. According to *jus soli*—a term meaning "right of land or ground"—citizenship results from birth within a territory. But Section 1 of the Fourteenth Amendment did not prevent Congress from conferring citizenship by *jus sanguinis*—by descent—and it has done so for children born to American citizens outside the United States. The authors of the Fourteenth Amendment included the phrase "subject to the jurisdiction thereof" indicating the special status of Native Americans. The Court ruled in 1884 that Native Americans born in the United States were not automatically citizens.[15] Congress subsequently enacted legislation making all Native Americans citizens of the United States.

Although all black people who were born in the United States were citizens by virtue of Section 1 of the Fourteenth Amendment, those who were born elsewhere and brought to the United States illegally as slaves after 1808 were ineligible for naturalization because the legislation setting forth the rules for naturalization had since 1790 reserved naturalized citizenship to white persons. Likewise, Section 1 gave citizenship to individuals born in the United States whose parents were Chinese although their parents remained ineligible for naturalization.

Section 1

[continued] No State shall make or enforce any law which shall abridge the privileges or immunities of citizens of the United States;

Justice Bushrod Washington's interpretation in *Corfield v Coryell* of the privileges and immunities clause of Article IV, Section 2, was well known to the Framers of the Fourteenth Amendment. In that case, Washington asserted that the clause protected the privileges and immunities "which are, in their nature, fundamental; which belong of right to the citizens of all free governments; and which have, at all times, been enjoyed by the citizens of the several states." Among those rights, Washington noted, were "protection by the government; the enjoyment of life and liberty, with the right to acquire and possess property of every kind, and to pursue and obtain happiness and safety; subject nevertheless to such restraints as the government may justly prescribe for the general good of the whole."[16] The debates in Congress on the Thirteenth Amendment

---

[14]*Scott v Sandford*, 60 US 393 (1857).
[15]*Elk v Wilkins*, 112 US 94 (1884).
[16]*Corfield v Coryell*, F. Cas. 546 (No. 3,230) (E.D. Pa. 1823).

and the Civil Rights Bill as well as the Fourteenth Amendment reflected agreement with that interpretation of privileges and immunities. For example, in the debate on the Civil Rights Bill, Senator Lyman Trumbull argued that

> [T]he rights of a citizen of the United States were certain great fundamental rights, such as the right to life, to liberty, and to avail one's self of all the laws passed for the benefit of the citizen to enable him to enforce his rights; inasmuch as this was the definition given to the term as applied in that part of the Constitution, I reasoned from that, that when the Constitution had been amended and slavery abolished, and we were about to pass a law declaring every person, no matter of what color, born in the United States a citizen of the United States, the same rights would then appertain to all persons who were clothed with American citizenship.[17]

Other members of Congress also expressed the view that the clause in the original Constitution embodied equal fundamental rights for all citizens and maintained that Congress had the power to protect those rights. Although there was disagreement over the proposed Fourteenth Amendment's impact, the amendment's supporters generally agreed that it would give Congress the power to enforce protections that were already in the Constitution, including the privileges and immunities clause of Article IV, Section 2.

Interpreting the Fourteenth Amendment for the first time in the *Slaughterhouse Cases* in 1873, the Court interpreted the privileges or immunities clause so narrowly as to virtually eliminate it as a source of protection of individual rights against state infringement. A five-member majority upheld a Louisiana law that created a monopoly on slaughtering in the New Orleans area. Writing for the majority, Justice Samuel F. Miller, who took an excessively rigid literal approach, pointed to the phrase "the privileges or immunities of citizens of the United States" and the designation of citizens of the United States and citizens of states in the preceding citizenship clause to demonstrate that the rights that were protected against state infringement were only the rights of United States citizenship—those rights that pertained to the individual's relationship with the federal government—such as the right to protection on the high seas, the right to use the navigable waters of the United States, and the right to travel to the seat of government to assert a claim. All other rights, including the right to pursue one's chosen lawful profession—which, according to the butchers, was violated by the monopoly—remained under the control of the states. The four dissenters countered that the privileges or immunities clause protected the "natural and inalienable rights which belong to all citizens" against infringement by the states. What would be the point, Justice Field asked, to include a clause in the new amendment that did not protect any rights other than those that were already protected by provisions elsewhere in the Constitution? If that were the case, he admonished, "it was a vain and idle enactment, which accomplished" nothing.[18]

---

[17]As quoted in Farber and Sherry, 302.
[18]*Butchers' Benevolent Association v Crescent City Livestock Landing & Slaughterhouse Co* (the *Slaughterhouse Cases*), 83 US 36 (1873).

The Court's reasoning in the *Slaughterhouse Cases* stripped the privileges or immunities clause of virtually all significance. But in 1999 when the Court invalidated California's attempt to restrict welfare benefits for newcomers to the state, it relied in part on the clause, noting that "it has always been common ground that this Clause protects the third component of the right to travel"—the right of the newly arrived citizen to the same privileges and immunities enjoyed by other citizens of the same state. The two dissenters—Chief Justice William H. Rehnquist and Justice Clarence Thomas—objected that the majority was giving a meaning to the privileges or immunities clause that was not intended at the time the Fourteenth Amendment was framed and ratified. Thomas voiced his concern that the clause might become "yet another convenient tool for inventing new rights."[19]

Section 1

[continued] nor shall any State deprive any person of life, liberty, or property, without due process of law;

We discussed the concept of due process in Chapter 8. The due process clause of the Fourteenth Amendment imposes on the states the same limits that the corresponding clause in the Fifth Amendment imposes on the national government. In Chapter 7, we discussed the incorporation of the Bill of Rights—the process by which most of the provisions in the first nine amendments came to constitute restrictions on the states. The Court's interpretation of the privileges or immunities clause in the *Slaughterhouse Cases* precluded the possibility that the clause might serve as a vehicle for incorporating the Bill of Rights. Thus, claimants turned to the due process clause, and by the end of the 1960s the Court had selectively incorporated almost every provision in the Bill of Rights.

By the end of the nineteenth century, the Court had begun to find that the due process clause of the Fourteenth Amendment limited the substance of governmental action as well as the manner in which the government acts. Finding that liberty protected by the due process clause includes liberty of contract, the Court developed the **doctrine of substantive due process** to protect business from state economic regulations. In *Lochner v New York* in 1905, the justices invalidated a law that prohibited employers from employing workers in bakeries more than ten hours a day or sixty hours a week. Justice Rufus Peckham, who wrote the opinion for the five-member majority, noting that the "right to purchase or to sell labor is part of the liberty protected" by the due process clause, found that the maximum-hours law was an unreasonable, arbitrary intrusion on that right. The law could not be justified as an exercise of the state's police powers—the authority to legislate to protect the health, welfare, or morals—because the legislators were actually attempting to regulate private labor contracts, something that lay beyond the bounds of the state's police power.[20]

During the ensuing years, the Court upheld similar regulations on the hours of workers, finding them to be reasonable exercises of the states' police

---

[19]*Saenz v Roe*, 526 US 489(1999).
[20]*Lochner v New York*, 198 US 45 (1905).

powers.[21] But the justices also invalidated a variety of laws on the grounds that they interfered with liberty of contract. Regulations that the Court struck down included a law that fixed minimum wages for women and children,[22] a federal law barring dismissals of interstate common carrier workers because they joined unions,[23] and a state law prohibiting yellow dog contracts.[24]

In 1937 in *West Coast Hotel v Parish*, the justices upheld, by a vote of five to four, a Washington state minimum-wage law. Writing for the majority, Chief Justice Hughes pointed out that liberty of contract is not absolute:

> The Constitution does not speak of freedom of contract. It speaks of liberty and prohibits the deprivation of liberty without due process of law. In prohibiting that deprivation the Constitution does not recognize an absolute and uncontrollable liberty. Liberty in each of its phases has its history and connotation. But the liberty safeguarded is liberty in a social organization which requires the protection of law against the evils which menace the health, safety, morals and welfare of the people. Liberty under the Constitution is thus necessarily subject to the restraints of due process, and regulation which is reasonable in relation to its subject and is adopted in the interests of the community is due process.[25]

Hughes indicated that the Court would give the legislatures wide discretion to regulate relations between employer and employee to protect the liberty of workers who were in an unequal bargaining position and were consequently "relatively defenseless against the denial of a living wage."[26] *West Coast Hotel* signaled the demise of substantive due process. Since 1937 when the Court has had the occasion to consider challenges based on the Fourteenth Amendment to economic regulations, it has taken a deferential rational basis approach—the law may be unwise but if it is reasonably related to a legitimate governmental interest, the Court will let it stand.

The Court discarded the doctrine of substantive due process at the same time that it changed its position limiting the reach of Congress's commerce power and began to uphold New Deal legislation. In 1938 in **Footnote Four of his opinion in *Carolene Products*,** Justice Harlan Fiske Stone suggested that the Court was embarking on a new approach—it would take more responsibility for protecting the rights of individuals and would leave economic matters to legislators. Stone's footnote identified three sets of circumstances in which the Court would be justified in setting aside the normal presumption of constitutionality and taking a more careful look at challenged legislation. First, the Court would suspend that presumption of constitutionality when legislation appeared on its face to be within a specific prohibition of the Constitution, such as those in the Bill of Rights. Second, the Court might apply more exacting

---

[21]For example, *Muller v Oregon*, 208 US 412 (1908) (maximum hours for female laundry workers); and *Bunting v Oregon*, 243 US 246 (1917) (maximum hours for mill and factory workers).
[22]*Adkins v Children's Hospital*, 261 US 525 (1923). See also, *Morehead v New York ex. rel. Tipaldo*, 298 US 587 (1936).
[23]*Adair v United States*, 208 US 161 (1908).
[24]*Coppage v Kansas*, 236 US 1 (1915). Yellow dog contracts, used by employers to keep employees from joining labor unions, made it a condition of employment that the worker not belong to a union.
[25]*West Coast Hotel v Parrish*, 300 US 379 (1937).
[26]*Ibid.*

scrutiny under the general prohibitions of the Fourteenth Amendment to "legislation which restricts those political processes which can ordinarily be expected to bring about repeal of undesirable legislation." Third, Stone suggested that the same standard might apply to statutes that are directed at particular religions, or national, or racial minorities, or that are motivated by prejudice against "discrete and insular minorities."[27]

Once the Court began to focus on the protections for individual rights in the Bill of Rights and the Fourteenth Amendment, the justices took special care when they invalidated legislation to ground their action in an express constitutional provision lest they be accused of returning to the discredited doctrine of substantive due process. Nevertheless, that doctrine provided an important foundation for the protection of unenumerated individual rights insofar as it took the position that there are certain rights with which the government may not interfere. Although the Court no longer considered liberty of contract to be a fundamental right, substantive due process paved the way for the Court to protect other fundamental yet unenumerated rights such as the right to privacy. Moreover, the **Carolene Products footnote** strongly suggested that the Court might find protection for such rights in the Fourteenth Amendment.

The Court developed the foundations for a constitutionally protected **right to privacy** in a series of cases that began before it repudiated substantive due process. In *Meyer v Nebraska* in 1923, the justices invalidated a state law that prohibited schools from teaching foreign languages to students below the eighth grade, noting that liberty in the due process clause includes the individual's right "to engage in any of the common occupations of life, to acquire useful knowledge, to marry, establish a home and bring up children."[28] Two years later, the Court struck down an Oregon law that required children to attend public schools on the grounds that it interfered with the ability of parents to direct the upbringing and education of their children.[29] After it repudiated substantive due process, the Court continued to protect rights that involved deeply personal matters. In 1942, for example, the justices invalidated an Oklahoma's Habitual Criminal Sterilization Act, which authorized sterilization for individuals who were convicted two or more times of certain crimes that the law classified as involving moral turpitude. In his opinion for the Court, Justice William O. Douglas recognized the right to have children as a fundamental right and held that the state's classification of criminals, singling out only those who engaged in crimes of moral turpitude for sterilization violated the equal protection clause of the Fourteenth Amendment.[30] Then in 1961, Justice John Marshall Harlan dissented from the majority's decision to dismiss a challenge to Connecticut's law prohibiting the use of contraceptives. Harlan argued that the law ran afoul of the Fourteenth Amendment because it violated the "fundamental aspect of 'liberty,' the privacy of the home in its most basic sense."[31]

---

[27] *United States v Carolene Products Co.*, 304 US 144 (1938).
[28] *Meyer v Nebraska*, 262 US 390 (1923).
[29] *Pierce v Society of Sisters*, 268 US 510 (1925).
[30] *Skinner v Oklahoma*, 316 US 535 (1942).
[31] *Poe v Ullman*, 367 US 497 (1961).

Four years later, the Court invalidated Connecticut's prohibition on birth control. Although the seven justices who comprised the majority agreed that there is a constitutionally protected right to privacy, they located its source in different provisions. Justice Douglas found the right to privacy in the penumbras—literally, lighted areas around a space covered in shadow—of specific guarantees in the Bill of Rights. Those penumbras create zones of privacy, peripheral rights that make the specific guarantees more secure. Thus, for Douglas the right to privacy emerged from the explicit guarantees in the First, Third, Fourth, Fifth, and Ninth Amendments. Justice Arthur Goldberg argued that the Ninth Amendment protects the right to privacy. Finally, Justice Harlan argued, as he had in his earlier dissenting opinion, that the right to privacy is protected by the due process clause of the Fourteenth Amendment.

The actual holding in *Griswold* was quite narrow: because the Connecticut law prohibited the use of contraceptives by anyone, married or single, the Court held that it was unconstitutional for the state to make it a crime for married couples to use birth control—the law violated the right of marital privacy. In 1972, the Court held that Massachusetts' law prohibiting the sale of contraceptives to unmarried people violated the rights of single people. Writing for the majority, Justice Brennan made a comment that went beyond the Court's actual holding: "If the right of privacy means anything, it is the right of the individual, married or single, to be free from unwarranted governmental intrusion into matters so fundamentally affecting a person as the decision whether to bear or beget a child."[32]

In 1973, a seven-member majority held that the right to privacy encompasses a woman's right to terminate a pregnancy.[33] In his opinion for the majority, Justice Harry Blackmun did not locate the right in a specific constitutional provision but noted that the Court had recognized such a right in the context of marriage, procreation, family relationships, child rearing, and education. He also linked the right of privacy to liberty in the due process clause. The right, Blackmun established, is fundamental; therefore, any interference with it can be justified only by a showing that the state has a compelling interest. Reasoning that the state's interests increase as a pregnancy progresses, Blackmun formulated **the trimester scheme** to reconcile the woman's privacy rights with the state's interests. During the first trimester—the first twelve weeks—the state has no compelling interest and thus may not interfere with a woman's right to choose to have an abortion—the decision must be left to the woman and her physician. Blackmun linked the lack of a compelling state interest during the first trimester to the fact that abortion during that period was a safe medical procedure. During the second trimester, the state's interest in protecting the health of the woman becomes compelling. Thus, the state may regulate abortion procedures in order to promote the health of the woman. The state's interest in protecting potential life becomes compelling at the point of viability, roughly the beginning of the third trimester. Thus, during the third trimester, the state may proscribe abortion except when it is necessary to preserve the life or health of the woman.

---

[32]*Eisenstadt v Baird*, 405 US 438 (1972).
[33]*Roe v Wade*, 410 US 113 (1973).

In dissent, Justice Rehnquist objected that abortion—a transaction result-ing in an operation—does not involve a right to privacy. Because there was no fundamental right involved, he argued, the Court should require only that the law be reasonably related to a legitimate state interest. All restrictions on abor-tion would pass such a test, except those that prohibit abortion when continu-ation of the pregnancy would jeopardize a woman's life. Rehnquist accused the majority of reviving the old discredited doctrine of substantive due process.

Roe v Wade galvanized a countermovement that committed itself to chang-ing the law to prohibit abortion rights. Antiabortion groups were unsuccessful in their efforts to secure a constitutional amendment that would either allow state legislatures to regulate abortion or criminalize abortion permanently by extending constitutional protection to all human beings "from the moment of conception." But they helped to elect a president in 1980 who supported the goals of the right-to-life movement and who would use opposition to *Roe v Wade* as a litmus test for his nominations to the federal courts. During his eight years in office, Ronald Reagan was able to appoint three new justices to the Supreme Court, replacing three of the seven members who comprised the ma-jority in *Roe*. Antiabortion forces also lobbied state legislatures as well as Con-gress for legislation restricting abortion. When such legislation was enacted, prochoice groups quickly challenged it. Laurence H. Tribe described the pat-tern of litigation before the Court in the years following *Roe v Wade* as quite predictable: "Antiabortion legislatures would enact restrictions, ones less strin-gent than those previously invalidated, that would themselves ultimately be challenged and, in most cases, invalidated."[34] A number of states enacted laws requiring that a woman seeking an abortion obtain written consent from her husband or from her parents if she were unmarried. The Court invalidated that restriction in 1976.[35]

The major restrictions that the Court did not invalidate in the early years after *Roe* were state and federal limitations on the funding of abortions for needy women. In the late 1970s, more than half of the states enacted restric-tions on funding for abortions that are not necessary to protect the life or health of the woman. In 1976, Congress passed the Hyde Amendment—a rider to the Labor-Health, Education, and Welfare Appropriations Bill—prohibiting the use of federal funds for abortions except when the life of the woman is in danger. Prochoice groups challenged the laws, arguing that they were inconsis-tent with the fundamental right, established in *Roe*, to choose to have an abor-tion. In 1977, the Court upheld state and local restrictions on abortion funding.[36] In 1980, by a vote of five to four, the Court upheld the Hyde Amend-ment, reasoning that although *Roe* recognized a woman's right to terminate a pregnancy, "it simply does not follow that a woman's freedom of choice carries with it a constitutional entitlement to the financial resources to avail herself of the full range of protected choices . . . although government may not place ob-stacles in the path of a woman's exercise of her freedom of choice, it need not

---

[34]Laurence H. Tribe, *Abortion: The Clash of Absolutes* (New York: W. W. Norton, 1990), 15.
[35]*Planned Parenthood of Central Missouri v Danforth*, 428 US 52 (1976).
[36]*Beal v Doe*, 432 US 438 (1977); *Maher v Roe*, 412 US 464 (1977); *Poelker v Doe*, 432 US 519 (1977).

remove those not of its own creation."[37] The Court's abortion funding decisions seemed to be a serious retreat from the principle that a woman has a fundamental right protected by the due process clause to choose to terminate a pregnancy during the first two trimesters.

The Court's declining support for *Roe* was reflected in three major cases in which the Court considered challenges to state restrictions on abortions. First, in *Akron v Akron Center for Reproductive Health* in 1983, a six-member majority invalidated several provisions of a local ordinance including a requirement that all second trimester abortions be performed in a hospital, informed consent, and a twenty-four hour waiting period. The informed consent provision required physicians to tell women seeking abortions certain things including the "unborn child is a human life form from the moment of conception." It was in that case that Justice O'Connor, who dissented, soundly condemned *Roe*'s trimester system, arguing that it was tied to medical technology in 1973. As a result of medical advances, abortions were safe further into a pregnancy just as viability was possible sooner, putting the trimester system "on a collision course with itself." She urged the Court to adopt an alternative standard whereby the Court would apply strict scrutiny to any regulation that "imposes an undue burden" on a woman's fundamental right to seek an abortion.[38]

In the second case, *Thornburgh v American College of Obstetricians and Gynecologists* in 1986, the Court—this time by a vote of five to four—invalidated a series of restrictions in Pennsylvania that were similar to those it struck down in *Akron*. Justice Blackmun, in his opinion for the majority, reaffirmed the principles of *Roe* and proclaimed, "The States are not free, under the guise of protecting maternal health or potential life, to intimidate women into continuing pregnancies."[39] O'Connor, in dissent, again urged the Court to adopt the unduly burdensome standard.

In 1986, Chief Justice Burger retired and President Reagan chose Rehnquist to succeed him and filled the resulting vacancy with Antonin Scalia. Then in 1987, Reagan chose Robert Bork to replace Lewis Powell. After Bork's nomination failed in the Senate, Reagan nominated Anthony Kennedy. Scalia was expected to provide the crucial fifth vote to overrule *Roe*. Thus, when the Court agreed in the 1988 term to hear the third case, *Webster v Reproductive Services*, a challenge to a Missouri law that imposed more restrictions on abortions, including a law requiring testing for viability when a doctor believes that a woman is twenty weeks or more pregnant, observers predicted the demise of *Roe*. In *Webster*, however, the Court declined to overrule *Roe* although it sustained the challenged provisions by a narrow margin.[40] There was no majority opinion in that case, but the plurality comprised of Rehnquist, White, and Kennedy interpreted the testing requirement in such a way that it conflicted with the trimester framework of *Roe* and asserted that the government has an interest in protecting potential human life not just after viability but throughout the pregnancy.

---

[37]*Harris v McCrae*, 448 US 297 (1980).
[38]*Akron v Akron Center for Reproductive Health*, 462 US 416 (1983).
[39]*Thornburgh v American College of Obstetricians and Gynecologists*, 476 US 747 (1986).
[40]*Webster v Reproductive Health Services*, 492 US 490 (1989).

That interest, Rehnquist maintained, was sufficient to allow Missouri to restrict the right to abortion. A woman's right to choose to have an abortion, according to Rehnquist, was not a fundamental right but merely a liberty interest that can be regulated by reasonable means. Even though the plurality opinion attacked *Roe*, it did not overrule it, but noted instead that "we would modify and narrow" it. Justice Scalia argued that the Court should overrule *Roe* outright. Four other justices argued that *Roe* should be reaffirmed and voted to invalidate the regulations. They maintained that the right to decide whether to end a pregnancy is fundamental. O'Connor again reiterated her **undue burden standard** and cast her vote to uphold the regulations. Because she construed the viability-testing requirement not to conflict with *Roe*, she found it unnecessary to consider the question of whether it should be overruled.

When Justices William Brennan and Thurgood Marshall retired from the Court in 1990 and 1991, respectively, President George Bush replaced them with two justices who were expected to vote to repudiate *Roe*. Thus, in 1992 as the country waited for the Court to announce its decision in *Planned Parenthood of Southeastern Pennsylvania v Casey*, it seemed certain that this time the justices would overrule *Roe*. Pennsylvania's regulations on abortion included informed consent, a twenty-four-hour waiting period, and spousal notification. The majority voted to uphold the first two of those restrictions, but not the third. Most important, however, the majority did not agree to overrule *Roe*. Instead, a joint opinion written by O'Connor, Kennedy, and Souter announced, "The woman's right to terminate her pregnancy before viability is the most central principle of *Roe v Wade*. It is a rule of law and a component of liberty we cannot renounce."[41] Nevertheless, the plurality set aside the trimester framework and adopted the undue burden standard according to which regulations that place a substantial obstacle in the path of a woman's choice before viability are unconstitutional. The joint opinion indicated that regulations that do not impose an undue burden but merely attempt to persuade women not to choose abortion will be upheld so long as they are reasonably related to that goal. Although the joint opinion claimed to reaffirm the central holding of *Roe*, it actually modified it considerably. A number of regulations that would not be upheld under the trimester framework will be sustained—the twenty-four-hour waiting period is one of the best examples.

Four justices—Rehnquist, White, Scalia, and Thomas—argued that *Roe* should be overruled outright. They argued that the appropriate approach would be to allow states to regulate abortion in ways that are rationally related to a legitimate state interest. Justice Blackmun, who retired just two years later, bemoaned the precarious position of the right to reproductive choice and noted that although "now, just when so many expected the darkness to fall, the flame has grown bright. . . . I fear for the darkness as four Justices anxiously await the single vote necessary to extinguish the light."[42] Blackmun's comment highlighted that the status of reproductive rights is far from settled.

---

[41]*Planned Parenthood of Southeastern Pennsylvania v Casey*, 505 US 833 (1992).
[42]*Ibid.*

Is the right to choose fundamental so that the state must not impose an undue burden on that choice? Or is there merely a liberty interest in abortion that can be regulated by reasonable means? In late 1999, reproductive rights seemed to be somewhat more secure as a result of Bill Clinton's appointment of Ruth Bader Ginsburg and Steven Breyer in 1993 and 1994, respectively. Their presumed support for a woman's right to choose to terminate a pregnancy, with Stevens's adherence to *Roe,* and Kennedy's, O'Connor's, and Souter's support for the undue burden standard indicated six votes to maintain at least some protection for reproductive rights.

As antiabortion forces continued their efforts to reverse the principle of *Roe* and make abortion illegal, both Congress and the states began to consider legislation prohibiting a method of abortion known as "partial birth" abortion or "dilation and extraction," a procedure normally used when a pregnancy has progressed longer than sixteen weeks and there are serious problems with the fetus. Nebraska criminalized the procedure, making it a felony for a doctor to perform it except when necessary to save the life of the woman. When a doctor's challenge to the law came before the Court, the justices, by a vote of five to four, held that Nebraska's law violated the Constitution because it failed to provide an exception for the preservation of the health of the mother and it imposed an undue burden on a woman's decision to terminate a pregnancy.[43]

The right of privacy that the Court established in *Griswold v Connecticut* is most often associated with reproductive rights, but it is also important in other contexts. For example, one of the rules that the Court has developed concerning the prohibition on unreasonable searches and seizures is that the Fourth Amendment protects the areas in which an individual has an expectation of privacy. Also, in 1969 in *Stanley v Georgia* the justices held that the right of privacy in conjunction with the First Amendment forbids states from punishing individuals for possessing obscene materials in the privacy of their homes.[44] *Griswold* and *Stanley* arguably provided the basis for holding that laws forbidding consensual sexual acts between two people of the same sex violate the constitutionally protected right to privacy.

The Court rejected that claim by a vote of five to four in 1986 in *Bowers v Hardwick*—a case involving a challenge to Georgia's prohibition on the practice of oral or anal sex. Justice White, who wrote the opinion for the majority, proclaimed that there is no constitutional right of homosexuals to engage in acts of sodomy. He distinguished the earlier cases involving the right to privacy, noting that they were limited to issues pertaining to the family, marriage, and procreation. He also differentiated *Stanley,* noting that it protected otherwise illegal activities performed in the privacy of the home only if they involved the First Amendment. In dissent, Justice Blackmun formulated the issue very differently. In his view, the case was no more about a "fundamental right to engage in homosexual sodomy" than *Stanley* was about a fundamental right to watch obscene movies. Rather, the case was about the fundamental right of all individuals to be free of governmental intrusion in their intimate associations with

---

[43]*Stenberg v Carhart,* 530 US 913 (2000).
[44]*Stanley v Georgia,* 394 US 557 (1969).

others. In another dissenting opinion, Justice Stevens contended that the right to privacy "surely embraces the right to engage in nonreproductive, sexual conduct that others may consider offensive or immoral."[45] He noted that the statute prohibited all sodomy and that previous cases established that the state may not prohibit such conduct between married or unmarried heterosexuals. Thus, the law would be unconstitutional if it were applied to heterosexuals. If it were applied only to homosexual conduct, the state would need to identify a neutral and legitimate interest in selectively applying the law to one group.

A great deal had changed between the Court's decision in *Bowers* in 1986 and 2002 when the justices agreed to hear a challenge to a Texas law that made it a crime for people of the same sex to engage in oral or anal sex, characterized as "deviate sexual intercourse."[46] In 1986 half the states had sodomy laws, many of which applied to people of the opposite as well as the same sex; by 2002, only thirteen states had such laws. Nine states still had laws that applied to both gay and heterosexual activity. Four states criminalized conduct between partners of the same sex that would be legal if performed by members of the opposite sex.[47] Georgia's law, which the Supreme Court upheld in *Bowers*, was struck down by the Georgia Supreme Court in 1998.

In the case of *Lawrence v Texas*, a gay couple who were arrested in their home, charged, and convicted for violating the antisodomy statute challenged the law on both privacy and equal protection grounds; they also asked the Court to overrule *Bowers*. In his argument before the Court in late March 2003, Paul M. Smith, the attorney for Lawrence, contended that the protection of matters of sexual intimacy in the home have a long tradition going back to the country's beginnings. He emphasized that the trend toward decriminalization demonstrates that criminal sodomy laws are not consistent with "our basic American values about the relationship between the individual and the state." In response to Justice Scalia's question about whether a new consensus on any subject should "receive constitutional weight," he stressed that the issue at hand played a central role in the lives of real people. Asserting the necessity of overruling *Bowers*, Smith stated that the 1986 decision was based on faulty "assumptions that the court made . . . about the realities of gay lives and gay relationships." The Court must realize by now, he said, that "there are gay families, that family relationships are established, that there are hundreds of thousands of people registered in the 2000 Census who have formed gay families." For this part of the population the right to privacy in matters of sexual intimacy in their own homes "performs much the same function that it does in the marital context." The right to privacy in this context, he noted, should be protected for everyone.[48]

---

[45]*Bowers v Hardwick*, 478 US 186 (1986).

[46]*Lawrence v Texas*, No. 02-102

[47]Kansas, Oklahoma, and Missouri, in addition to Texas had laws that applied only to same-sex partners. Alabama, Florida, Idaho, Louisiana, Mississippi, North Carolina, South Carolina, Utah, and Virginia had laws that applied to both same-sex and opposite-sex couples. Linda Greenhouse, "Justices, 6–3, Legalize Gay Sexual Conduct in Sweeping Reversal," *The New York Times*, June 27, 2003.

[48]Linda Greenhouse, "Supreme Court Seems Set to Reverse a Sodomy Law," *The New York Times*, March 27, 2003.

A narrow majority of the Court agreed and overruled *Bowers v Hardwick,* condemning it as precedent that "demeans the lives of homosexual persons."[49] Writing for the majority, Justice Kennedy emphasized the right to privacy, noting that the state must respect the private lives of gays; "it cannot demean their existence or control their destiny by making their private sexual conduct a crime."[50] Five members of the Court agreed to overrule *Bowers.* Justice O'Connor, who was part of the majority in that case, provided the sixth vote for invalidating the Texas law. She relied on the equal protection clause, noting that the law "branded one class of persons as criminal solely based on the state's moral disapproval of the class and the conduct associated with that class."[51] Justice Scalia, in dissent, accused the majority of taking "sides in the culture war" and signing on "to the so-called homosexual agenda."[52] Chief Justice Rehnquist and Justice Thomas joined his opinion. The Court's decision rendered the laws in all thirteen states that had continued to make sodomy a crime invalid.

In 1986 in his majority opinion in *Bowers,* Justice White admonished the Court not to expand the reach of the due process clause, "particularly if it requires redefining the category of rights deemed to be fundamental. Otherwise, the Judiciary necessarily takes to itself further authority to govern the country without express constitutional authority."[53] Nevertheless, in 1990 in another five-to-four decision, Chief Justice Rehnquist indicated that patients have a constitutionally based right to refuse life-preserving medical treatment. He identified the right as a **protected liberty interest,** neither linking it to privacy nor characterizing it as fundamental. In that case, *Cruzan v Director, Missouri Department of Health,* the majority rejected the claim brought by parents of a woman who was in a persistent vegetative condition that the state's refusal to allow the withdrawal of feeding tubes violated her right to refuse unwanted medical treatment. The Missouri Supreme Court had ruled that in the absence of "clear and convincing" evidence of the patient's wishes, the parents could not authorize removal of the feeding tubes. Rehnquist held that it is reasonable for a state to require "clear and convincing" evidence of a patient's wishes before allowing a family member to authorize the withdrawal of medical treatment. While there is a constitutionally protected right to refuse medical treatment, states may formulate their own standards governing the issue of when others may make that decision for incompetent patients.[54]

In 1997, the Court addressed the controversial issue of assisted suicide for terminally ill but competent individuals. In *Washington v Glucksberg,* the justices unanimously sustained Washington's law that makes it a crime to "cause or aid another person to attempt suicide." Rehnquist held that the right to assistance in committing suicide is not a fundamental liberty interest

---

[49]Linda Greenhouse, *The New York Times,* June 27, 2003.
[50]As quoted in *ibid.*
[51]*Ibid.*
[52]*Ibid.*
[53]*Bowers v Hardwick,* 478 US 186 (1986).
[54]*Cruzan v Director, Missouri Department of Health,* 497 US 261 (1990).

protected by the due process clause. Such a right, he reasoned, is neither "deeply rooted in this Nation's history and tradition," nor "fundamental to our concept of constitutionally ordered liberty." Moreover, it cannot be inferred from previous cases such as *Cruzan* and *Casey*. Thus, the state's ban on assisted suicide need only be rationally related to legitimate government interests, a requirement that the law easily met. The law was related to the state's interests in preserving human life, protecting the integrity and ethics of the medical profession, protecting vulnerable groups, and preventing the development of a broader right to voluntary or even involuntary euthanasia. There were five concurring opinions, all of which allowed that an individual might in certain circumstances have a right to assisted suicide. Justice Breyer went furthest to develop that argument, noting that he would formulate the issue not as a right to assisted suicide but rather as something like a "right to die with dignity," with "personal control over the manner of death, professional medical assistance, and the avoidance of unnecessary and severe physical suffering—combined" at its core.[55]

In 2000, by a divided vote, the justices reaffirmed that parents have a fundamental right to make decisions concerning the care, custody, and control of their children when they invalidated a state statute that allowed anyone to petition for visitation rights and authorized the state courts to grant such rights whenever it may serve a child's best interest.[56] Thus, the Court has affirmed that there are certain liberty interests to make decisions regarding matters of the family that are protected by the due process clause of the Fourteenth Amendment. It is important to be aware, however, that beginning with *Cruzan* in 1990, the justices have avoided relying on a right to privacy and fundamental rights, relying instead on the principle that there are liberty interests in certain activities. Thus, the majority's return to privacy as the basis for its decision in *Lawrence v Texas* along with its numerous references to the Court's privacy precedents in 2003 represented a significant development.

Several justices and a number of commentators argue that the Court's use of the due process clause to protect fundamental rights that are not enumerated in the Constitution is no different from the discredited doctrine of substantive due process that prevailed from 1897 through 1936. Justice Black expressed that view in *Griswold v Connecticut*, as Justice White did in *Bowers*; Justices Scalia and Thomas as well as Chief Justice Rehnquist take that position today. Their argument is grounded on the notion that the meaning of the Constitution should be gleaned from its text or the original intent of the Framers, and they maintain that when the justices depart from those interpretive rules, they invariably end up relying on their own preferences. In so doing, they replace the preferences of the voters and elected representatives with their own and, thereby, defeat the democratic process. On the other hand, the justices and commentators who support the Court's protection of fundamental rights identify major differences between the old substantive due process to

---

[55] *Washington v Glucksburg*, 521 US 702(1997).
[56] *Troxel v Granville*, 530 US 57 (2000).

protect economic interests and the Court's use of the due process clause to protect fundamental individual rights. The driving force behind the doctrine of substantive due process was the justices' commitment to laissez-faire that was founded in political and economic theories of the nineteenth century. In contrast, the right of privacy has a firm basis in the structure and values of the Constitution.

It is important to be aware that the Court's interpretation of the due process clause takes it beyond a guarantee of fair process. Thus, it includes the principle that there are certain rights with which the government may not interfere. As Chief Justice Rehnquist noted in *Washington v Glucksburg*, the due process clause protects rights that are "deeply rooted in this Nation's history and tradition," and "implicit in the concept of ordered liberty."[57]

Section 1

[continued] nor deny to any person within its jurisdiction the equal protection of the laws.

The equal protection clause reflected the Republicans' commitment at the end of the Civil War to extend protection for equal rights to black people. In the House Debates on the Fourteenth Amendment in 1866, Representative Thaddeus Stevens, praising the proposed amendment, explained the equal protection clause as follows:

> This amendment . . . allows Congress to correct the unjust legislation of the States, so far that the law which operates upon one man shall operate *equally* upon all. Whatever law punishes a white man for a crime shall punish the black man precisely in the same way and to the same degree. Whatever law protects the white man shall afford "equal" protection to the black man. Whatever means of redress is afforded to one shall be afforded to all. Whatever law allows the white man to testify in court shall allow the man of color to do the same.[58]

Although the Framers of the equal protection clause wanted to combat inequality toward blacks, their deliberate use of general language has meant that the clause may provide protection for the equal rights of everyone.

State Action

By its terms, the Fourteenth Amendment applies only to the actions of state governments.[59] In the *Civil Rights Cases* of 1883, the Court invalidated the Civil Rights Act of 1875, which prohibited racial discrimination in public accommodations, on the grounds that the Act was beyond the power of Congress

---

[57]*Ibid.*
[58]As quoted in Farber and Sherry, 310.
[59]The Fifth Amendment contains no equal protection clause, but the Supreme Court has interpreted the due process clause of the Fifth Amendment to limit the national government in precisely the same way that the equal protection clause of the Fourteenth Amendment limits the state governments. *Bolling v Sharpe*, 347 US 497 (1954).

under the Fourteenth Amendment.[60] The justices interpreted the phrase, "No State shall" to mean that deprivation of due process or denial of equal protection by the government is forbidden while private action of the same nature is not, and, thereby, established a state-private distinction. That distinction provided a basic point of reference for determining whether the restrictions of the Fourteenth Amendment apply to challenged action. The Court thus created the **"state action" requirement,** which meant that if the justices did not find a challenged action to be governmental, they would hold that the Fourteenth Amendment was inapplicable, allowing the challenged action to stand. Additionally, if the justices found that challenged federal legislation attempted to regulate nonstate action, they would find that legislation to be beyond the powers of Congress.

The Court's early literal interpretation of the state action language in the Fourteenth Amendment considerably reduced the power of the amendment to protect the equal rights of blacks. The state action requirement has been most important in the context of equal protection although it is also relevant to challenges based on the due process clause. The state-private distinction of the *Civil Rights Cases* has survived, but the Court has significantly enlarged its understanding of what constitutes state action.

In the early twentieth century, the Court began to expand the concept of state action to include not only legislation but also the acts of state officials, even those who violated state law.[61] Situations in which a significant relationship existed between a private actor and the government and where the nature of the questioned activity was statelike—when the state had delegated its function to a private party—also began to fall under the rubric of state action. The main problem with the state action limitation on the Fourteenth Amendment is that states have used it in their attempts to circumvent the mandate of equal protection of the laws. Charles L. Black complained that the state action concept in the context of racial discrimination "has just one practical function; if and where it works, it immunizes racist practices from constitutional control."[62]

In numerous instances, individuals or groups have severed all ties with the state to avoid the restrictions of the equal protection clause. For example, Democratic Party groups in one-party states in the South severed formal ties to the state and excluded blacks from voting in their primaries.[63] Baconsfield Park in Macon, Georgia, was a tract of land left to the city by Senator Bacon with the specification that it was to be used as a park for white people only. By the 1950s, it was clear that a segregated public park would violate the equal protection clause so the city resigned as trustee of the estate and new private trustees were appointed to run the park. After the Supreme Court held that such an arrangement did not place the park beyond the bounds of the Four-

---

[60]*Civil Rights Cases*, 109 US 3 (1883).

[61]*Home Telephone & Telegraph Co. v City of Los Angeles*, 227 US 278 (1913).

[62]Charles L. Black, Jr., "The Supreme Court 1966 Term. Forward: 'State Action' Equal Protection, and California's Proposition 14," *Harvard Law Review* 81 (1967): 69–109.

[63]See *Grovey v Townsend*, 295 US 45 (1935) (the party convention was an organ of a voluntary, private group rather than the state). Some of the cases in which the Court addressed the issue of white primaries were decided under the Fifteenth Amendment, which also contains the "No State shall" language.

teenth Amendment,[64] the trust was terminated and the property reverted to the heirs of Senator Bacon.[65] Additionally, individuals and groups have claimed that any connection they have to the state is not sufficient to constitute state action. The Moose Lodge in Pennsylvania, which ran a restaurant that did not serve blacks, claimed to be a private entity with insufficient ties to government to be constrained by the equal protection clause. The Supreme Court agreed.[66]

The Court has used two different methods to determine whether the requisite state action is present. First, the Court has most often used the government involvement approach, in which it measures the extent of government entanglement with a private party whose activities have been challenged on equal protection grounds. There are several ways that the government involvement might occur that will justify imposing constitutional restraints. The government may be allocating aid to support private parties, for example, through grants of money, contracts, or tax exemptions of deductions. The government may be influencing private entities to act as agents in accomplishing government objectives. The judiciary may be enforcing private rights, or the government may be regulating private activities. Thus, in *Shelley v Kramer* in 1948 the justices held that although restrictive covenants—agreements between property owners not to allow nonwhites to purchase their homes—did not constitute state action, judicial enforcement of those agreements did and was therefore prohibited by the equal protection clause.[67]

The Court has also found that sufficient government involvement in private discrimination to activate the equal protection clause exists when the state acts in such a way as to encourage discrimination. In 1961 in *Burton v Wilmington Parking Authority,* for example, a restaurant claimed that it was not a state actor for equal protection purposes but the Court pointed out that it leased its space from and was located within a building owned and operated by the city parking authority. The parking authority constructed the restaurant, furnished it with heat, and provided maintenance. The Court held that the restaurant was subject to the constraints of the Fourteenth Amendment.[68]

Additionally, the Court has found that the state's involvement in racial discrimination may occur by virtue of the state's placing its power and prestige behind the allegedly private discrimination. In *Reitman v Mulkey,* the Court found that an amendment to the California state constitution, enacted by the voters through the initiative process, amounted to unconstitutional involvement by the state in discrimination. Proposition 14 repealed legislation that prohibited racial discrimination in real estate transactions, providing: "Neither the State nor any subdivision or agency thereof shall deny, limit or abridge, directly or indirectly, the right of any person who is willing or desires to sell, lease or rent such property to such person or persons as he in his absolute discretion, chooses."[69] The California Supreme Court found that

---

[64]*Evans v Newton,* 382 US 296 (1966).
[65]The Court allowed that arrangement in *Evans v Abney,* 396 US 435 (1970).
[66]*Moose Lodge v Irvis,* 407 US 163 (1972).
[67]*Shelley v Kramer,* 334 US 1 (1948).
[68]*Burton v Wilmington Parking Authority,* 365 US 715 (1961).
[69]*Reitman v Mulkey,* 387 US 369 (1967).

Proposition 14 expressly authorized racial discrimination and, indeed, made the right to discriminate one of the policies of the state. The United States Supreme Court agreed.

A second approach to state action is the public function analysis—which has been used only infrequently—in which the Court examines the activity in which the private actor is engaged. With this approach, the inquiry focuses on whether the private enterprise in question is sufficiently statelike to be treated as a state for Fourteenth Amendment purposes. Certain private enterprises may perform services delegated to them by the state that are so essential that in their absence the state would perform the services. Or the operation may be affected with the public interest. In 1946 in a case that involved freedom of expression, the Court held that a company-owned town is not exempt from the constraints of the First Amendment. Justice Black, who wrote the opinion for the majority, pointed out:

> The more an owner, for his advantage, opens up his property for use by the public in general, the more do his rights become circumscribed by the statutory and constitutional rights of those who use it. Thus, the owners of privately held bridges, ferries, turnpikes and railroads may not operate them as freely as a farmer does his farm. Since these facilities are built and operated primarily to benefit the public and since their operation is essentially a public function, it is subject to state regulation.[70]

Thirty years later, however, that Court declined to extend that reasoning when it held that shopping center owners were not engaged in state action and were therefore not obligated to allow expressive activities on their premises.[71] The Court also declined to use the public function analysis in a case involving a due process challenge to a privately owned utility for termination of service without adequate notice or a hearing.[72] In 1978, Justice Rehnquist underlined the limited context in which the Court would use the public function analysis when he held that a warehouse operator's proposed sale of goods entrusted to him for storage to satisfy a lien under the Uniform Commercial Code did not constitute state action even though the state authorized the warehouse operator to perform the state function of the nonconsensual transfer of property.[73]

Racial Segregation: The Separate but Equal Doctrine

In the late nineteenth century, the Court interpreted the equal protection clause narrowly just as it did the privileges or immunities clause, the due process clause—except in cases involving economic rights—and the concept of state action. As a result, the amendment that was designed to guarantee equality before the law for blacks had minimal effect. In 1883, the Court held that it was beyond the power of Congress to regulate the behavior of private individuals by prohibiting racial discrimination in hotels, theaters, inns, and public trans-

---

[70]*Marsh v Alabama*, 326 US 501 (1946).
[71]*Hudgens v NLRB*, 424 US 507 (1976).
[72]*Jackson v Metropolitan Edison*, 419 US 345 (1974).
[73]*Flagg Brothers v Brooks*, 436 US 14 (1978).

portation. Then in 1896 in *Plessy v Ferguson,* the Court, by a vote of seven to one, sustained a Louisiana law requiring the segregation of railroad passengers. Justice Henry B. Brown reasoned that the purpose of the Fourteenth Amendment was to guarantee absolute legal and political equality. It was not, however, intended to abolish distinctions based on color or to enforce social equality, or to force the commingling of the races. He contended that segregation by law does not interfere with legal or political equality and that it is a reasonable exercise of the state's police powers to preserve the public peace, and is based on custom and tradition. Brown denied Plessy's assertion that legally imposed segregation implies the inferiority of blacks. The law does not "stamp them with a badge of inferiority" and if black people see it that way, it is simply their own perception. Justice John Marshall Harlan, the sole dissenter, admonished, "Our Constitution is color-blind, and neither knows nor tolerates classes among citizens. In respect of civil rights, all citizens are equal before the law."[74]

In *Plessy,* the Court announced the **"separate but equal" doctrine,** which held that legally required segregation does not constitute inequality; therefore, so long as the facilities provided for the two groups are roughly similar, segregation does not raise a constitutional problem. By 1890, laws requiring segregation had become popular in the South, and when the Court gave a nod of approval in *Plessy,* southern states enacted laws requiring segregation in virtually all aspects of life from hospitals to schools to recreation areas to restaurants, funeral homes, and burial grounds. Thus, Jim Crow—the system of segregation—prevailed and blacks and whites were to have separate lives from birth to death. Under the "separate but equal" doctrine, facilities were separate although they were never equal.

In the 1930s, the NAACP and then the **NAACP Legal Defense and Educational Fund Inc.,** which became known as the LDF or the Inc Fund,[75] began an organized litigation campaign to challenge segregation in education. The LDF's strategy was to begin with graduate and professional schools, and not to challenge segregation *per se* as a violation of the equal protection clause but rather to challenge segregation as it was applied—that is, to demonstrate that the separate facilities were not equal. In one of the early cases, the University of Missouri Law School refused admission to a black applicant, Lloyd Gaines, because of his race. When he brought suit, Missouri offered to pay his tuition at an out-of-state school until a black law school could be established in Missouri. The Court rejected Missouri's offer, holding that the state was obligated to furnish Gaines "within its borders facilities for legal education substantially equal to those which the State offered for persons of the white race, whether or not other negroes sought the same opportunity." In the absence of such facilities, the Court held, Gaines was entitled to be admitted to the existing state law school.[76] In *Gaines* and other cases that the Court decided through the 1940s,

---

[74]*Plessy v Ferguson,* 163 US 537 (1896).
[75]Because the NAACP engaged in lobbying, it was not eligible for tax-exempt status. To keep the donors who might not contribute if their donations were not tax-deductible, the NAACP set up a separate arm of the organization for lobbying.
[76]*Missouri ex rel. Gaines v Canada,* 305 US 337 (1938).

the justices were able to hold that state graduate and professional schools had to admit black students on an equal basis without addressing the continuing validity of the "separate but equal" doctrine.

Still, as a result of the LDF's litigation campaign and the decisions of the Court, *Plessy* underwent gradual erosion. In 1950 in *Sweatt v Painter*, the justices held that a newly established black law school, Texas State University for Negroes, was not equal to the law school at the University of Texas. The Court found that the black law school was clearly unequal not only in ways that could be easily measured—the black school had only three part-time faculty, few books in the library, no librarian, and no accreditation—but also in ways that were intangible but that, nevertheless, make for greatness in a law school, such as the position and influence of the alumni and the school's standing in the community. The Court's decision in *Sweatt* signaled that states would be able to maintain segregation only if they provided genuinely equal educational opportunities for black students. Moreover, *Sweatt* made clear that it would be extremely expensive and difficult—perhaps impossible—for the states to do so.

Brown v Board of Education: Separate Is Inherently Unequal

When *Brown v Board of Education* and its four companion cases came before the Court, the LDF lawyers argued that segregation itself was unequal.[77] LDF attorney Robert Carter told the justices, "we abandon any claim of any constitutional inequality which comes from anything other than the act of segregation itself."[78] Moreover, the schools involved in the cases had undergone "equalization" with respect to buildings, curricula, qualifications, salaries of teachers, and other tangible factors. Consequently, the Court could not avoid addressing the issue of whether "separate but equal" was constitutionally acceptable. On May 17, 1954, the Court announced its unanimous decision: "separate educational facilities are inherently unequal." Chief Justice Earl Warren essentially acknowledged that the justices had been unable to determine that the Framers of the Fourteenth Amendment intended to prohibit legally mandated segregated schools. But he maintained that it did not really matter, for "we cannot turn the clock back to 1868 when the Amendment was adopted, or even to 1896 when *Plessy v Ferguson* was written. We must consider public education in the light of its full development and its present place in American life throughout the Nation."[79] In the context of education in the 1950s, Warren held, to separate students from others solely because of their race "generates a feeling of inferiority as to their status in the community that may affect their hearts and minds in a way unlikely ever to be undone."[80]

---

[77]*Brown v Board of Education*, 347 US 483 (1954) (Kansas); *Briggs v Elliott* (South Carolina); *Bolling v Sharpe* (Washington, DC); *Davis v County School Board of Prince Edward County* (Virginia); *Belton v Gebhart* (Delaware).
[78]As quoted in Mark V. Tushnet, *Making Civil Rights Law: Thurgood Marshall and the Supreme Court, 1936–1961* (New York: Oxford University Press, 1994), 173.
[79]*Brown v Board of Education*, 347 US 483 (1954).
[80]*Ibid.*

At the end of his opinion, Warren asked the attorneys to return the next term to present arguments regarding remedies. In 1955 in the case that came to be called *Brown II*, the Court announced that the primary responsibility for implementing the decision would rest with the local school boards. To ensure that the school boards complied, district courts would supervise, using their equity jurisdiction to work out remedies to achieve admission of students "to the public schools on a racially nondiscriminatory basis with all deliberate speed."[81] Although the LDF lawyers urged the Court to announce that desegregation had to occur immediately, the justices, fearing violent resistance in the South, settled on a gradualist approach.

School Desegregation in the South

The Court's remedy met the same massive resistance that some of the justices predicted would result from an order to desegregate immediately. Historian Harvard Sitcoff wrote:

> Defiance of the Court and the Constitution became the touchstone of Southern loyalty, the necessary proof of one's concern for the security of the white race. With the overwhelming support of the South's white press and pulpit, segregationist politicians resurrected John C. Calhoun's notions of "interposition" and "nullification" to rationalize their effort to thwart federal authority. Together they galvanized racist hatred to gain backing for every conceivable diehard tactic of opposition to *Brown*.[82]

Southern schools did not desegregate until confronted with a court order. Consequently, black parents and LDF lawyers had to initiate individual suits against school districts. The southern states enacted more than 450 laws and resolutions to prevent desegregation, including authorizations for the closing of schools that were ordered to desegregate and pupil-placement laws that allowed school boards to assign students to schools based on criteria such as "psychological qualification." Some states provided funds for private-academy tuition so that districts could abolish the public school system.

In 1956, 101 members of Congress from the South signed a "Declaration of Constitutional Principles" asking their states to refuse to obey the Court's desegregation order. "**The Southern Manifesto**" as it was also called, declared that the Supreme Court had no power to demand an end to segregation and that the states would be legally justified in opposing the Court's order. President Dwight D. Eisenhower declined to provide support for the Court's decision. He remarked to one of his aides, "I am convinced that the Supreme Court decision set back progress in the South at least fifteen years. . . . It's all very well to talk about school integration—if you remember you may also be talking about social disintegration. Feelings are deep on this. . . . And the fellow who tries to tell me that you can do these things by force is just plain nuts."[83]

---

[81]*Brown v Board of Education (II)*, 349 US 294 (1955).
[82]Harvard Sitcoff, *The Struggle for Black Equality, 1954–1980* (New York: Hill and Wang, 1981), 26.
[83]*Ibid.*, 26.

With massive resistance in the South and no support from the president or Congress, very little changed in public education for the remainder of the 1950s. In 1957, however, President Eisenhower sent federal troops to Arkansas to stop violence at Central High School in Little Rock. In 1958, the Court declared that threatened or actual violence would not justify the postponement of court orders to desegregate.[84] It was not until Congress provided some support with the Civil Rights Act of 1964 that southern educational systems began to change. The law authorized the Department of Justice to file school desegregation suits. It also provided that any program that was administered in a racially discriminatory manner would be denied federal financial assistance. The United States Office of Education specifically made eligibility for federal aid contingent on compliance with a court-ordered desegregation plan, or in the absence of such a plan, compliance with guidelines for school desegregation issued by the Department of Health, Education and Welfare. Most school districts complied with the guidelines rather than face the possibility of losing financial assistance.

With federal legislation and federal guidelines in place, the Court began to take a less tolerant stance toward dilatory tactics by southern school districts. In 1964, the justices refused to allow local authorities to abandon public education rather than comply with a court order to desegregate.[85] Then in 1968, the Court invalidated a "freedom of choice plan" that operated to preserve the dual school system.[86] In that case, Justice Brennan emphasized that the burden of a school board was to formulate realistically workable plans for a faster and more effective change to a unitary school system. Finally, in 1969 the justices rejected the Nixon Administration's effort to delay the court-ordered desegregation of thirty-three school districts in Mississippi and proclaimed that "all deliberate speed" was no longer constitutionally permissible and that it was the "obligation of every school district . . . to terminate dual school systems at once."[87] Thus, schools in the areas where legal segregation had been the most firmly entrenched finally began to desegregate.

School Desegregation in the North

From 1955 until the end of the 1960s, the Court focused on desegregation in the South where *de jure,* or legally imposed segregation, prevailed. Segregated schools were also common in the North although they stemmed not from legal mandates but from residential and economic patterns—***de facto* segregation.** The Court relied on the *de jure-de facto* distinction to determine whether northern school districts were required to take steps to desegregate. Frequently, the line between the two types of segregation blurred, as it became apparent that northern school officials often intentionally drew district lines and engaged in other tactics to keep the schools segregated. In 1973 in *Keyes v School*

---

[84]*Cooper v Aaron,* 358 US 1 (1958).
[85]*Griffin v Prince Edward County School Board,* 377 US 218 (1964).
[86]*Green v School Board of New Kent County,* 391 US 430 (1968).
[87]*Alexander v Holmes County Board of Education,* 396 US 19 (1969).

District No. 1, Denver, Colorado, the Court declared that a finding of intentional and purposeful segregation in a significant portion of the school system would support a finding that *de jure* segregation characterized the entire system.[88] The Court, nevertheless, attempted to maintain a distinction between school districts in which the racial imbalance was the consequence of a legally segregated system or resulted from the intent to segregate on the one hand and districts where that imbalance could not be linked to any governmental action on the other.[89]

Busing became a national issue when lower court judges began to devise desegregation plans that involved transporting students from their neighborhood school to other areas of their district to achieve a racial balance. A unanimous Court approved busing as a remedy for *de jure* segregation in 1971 in *Swann v Charlotte-Mecklenburg Board of Education.*[90] In that case, the Court upheld a district court plan that included the use of mathematical ratios of black and white students, the pairing and grouping of noncontiguous school zones, as well as bus transportation. Chief Justice Burger's opinion made it clear that the powers of the district courts are remedial. Thus, busing plans and other devices to achieve a racial balance would only be justified where there had been a constitutional violation—where previously officially segregated schools had not produced an acceptable desegregation plan. Moreover, the remedy could reach no further than necessary to correct the violation. Burger's limits had the effect of creating obstacles to desegregation in the North where multidistrict plans were needed to integrate predominantly black schools in urban areas. In fact, the Court declined to approve multidistrict plans in the absence of proof of a constitutional violation.[91]

An End to School Desegregation?

In the second half of the 1980s and throughout 1990s the Rehnquist Court imposed limits on the authority of district judges to implement desegregation plans. For example, in 1989 in *Missouri v Jenkins,* the justices held, by a vote of five to four, that a district judge did not have the authority to alter the property tax rate to raise money for a magnet school program although he could order city authorities to do so. The Court also noted that school boards could not escape their constitutional obligations by arguing that they had insufficient fiscal resources to do so.[92] Five years later, in another round of litigation in the same case, a five-member majority invalidated the district court's order that increased salaries for almost all staff within the Kansas City, Missouri School District as well as the order that required Missouri to continue to fund remedial "quality education" programs because student achievement levels were below national norms. The plan, the Court noted, was designed to attract

---

[88]*Keyes v School District No. 1, Denver, Colorado,* 413 US 189 (1973).
[89]See, for example, *Milliken v Bradley,* 418 US 717 (1973); *Columbus Board of Education v Penick,* 443 US 449 (1979); *Dayton Board of Education v Brinkman,* 433 US 406 (1977); *Dayton Board of Education v Brinkman,* 443 US 406 (1979).
[90]*Swann v Charlotte-Mecklenburg Board of Education,* 402 US 1 (1971).
[91]*Milliken v Bradley,* 418 US 717 (1973).
[92]*Missouri v Jenkins,* 491 US 274 (1989).

nonminority students from outside the district rather than solely to distribute the students within the district to eliminate racially identifiable schools within the district. Thus, the plan was beyond the scope of the district court's powers because the interdistrict remedy went further than providing a remedy for the intradistrict violation. The Court also identified restoration of local control as a primary goal in desegregation cases.[93]

In several cases, the Court has allowed district courts to end judicial supervision of school districts on the grounds that they have achieved unitary status even if they continue to maintain one-race schools as a result of residential patterns. In 1991, the Court held that judicial supervision should end when the effects of state-imposed segregation policies have been eliminated "as far as practicable."[94] The three dissenters—Marshall, Blackmun, and Stevens—objected that the majority had abandoned the goals implied in *Brown v Board of Education*—the elimination of racially segregated schools and prevention of their recurrence. Desegregation plans should not be lifted so long as feasible steps to avoid one-race schools were available. In 1992, the Court held that lower courts could terminate judicial control in incremental stages, withdrawing in certain areas before full compliance with *Brown* was achieved in all areas of school operation. A unitary system had been achieved with regard to transportation, physical facilities, and the assignment of students but remnants of the dual system remained in faculty assignments and the quality of education available to blacks and whites. The federal appeals court held that the district court should retain jurisdiction over all aspects of the school system until it achieved full compliance. The Supreme Court reversed, holding that the district court had the discretion to relinquish control over those areas in which the district had achieved compliance with the principles of *Brown*. Justice Kennedy, who wrote the opinion for the Court, reiterated the limited nature of remedies: "Once the racial imbalance due to the *de jure* violation has been remedied, the school district is under no duty to remedy imbalance that is caused by demographic factors.[95]

The Court's most recent decisions in the area of school desegregation have narrowed remedies for segregation and have established standards that allow district courts to bring an end to judicially devised and supervised desegregation plans. Those are both important developments, but perhaps most crucial is the Court's determination to adhere to the principle that unless the government is responsible for continuing segregation there can be no remedy because there has been no constitutional violation. Consequently, there is no constitutional mandate to eliminate predominantly one-race schools because their existence is not attributable to any specific government action but rather to the persistence of economic disparities and the resulting segregated residential patterns. Some commentators have perceived the Court's decisions in the 1990s as an acknowledgment that court-supervised desegregation, which commonly includes busing to achieve a racial balance, has been a failure and should be abandoned. Others, however, argue that the decisions "reflected the victory of

---

[93]*Missouri v Jenkins*, 515 US 70 (1995).
[94]*Board of Education of Oklahoma City Public Schools v Dowell*, 498 US 237 (1991).
[95]*Freeman v Pitts*, 503 US 467 (1992).

the conservative movement that altered the federal courts and turned the nation from the dream of *Brown* toward accepting a return to segregation."[96]

Standards of Review in Equal Protection Analysis

As we learned in our discussion of the First and Fourteenth Amendments, when a governmental policy infringes on a fundamental right such as freedom of expression, the freedom to exercise one's religious beliefs, or the right to privacy, the policy will be sustained only if the state can show that the policy is necessary to the achievement of a compelling interest. The same type of analysis applies to the Court's decision making in the area of the equal protection clause with only a slight variation. When the Court determines that a challenged policy treats people differently—or classifies—on the basis of some illegitimate criterion or that infringes on a fundamental right it will only sustain the policy if it is tailored to serve a compelling state interest.

Governments classify people all the time in all sorts of different ways. Indeed, distinguishing between people is crucial to legislation. For example, individuals under the age of sixteen cannot obtain a driver's license in most states and people who cannot see well enough to pass an eye examination are not permitted to drive. In those instances, the state classifies people on the basis of age and their ability to see. Such classifications do not present a constitutional problem as long as they are reasonable—that is, so long as they are rationally related to a legitimate state interest. If this sort of classification is challenged, a court will accord it a presumption of rationality—that is, a court will assume that the legislators who made the law had a reason for doing so. The court, in other words, will use the standard known as the **rational basis test.** The case of *Williamson v Lee Optical Company* in 1955 provides a useful illustration. That case involved an equal protection challenge to Oklahoma's scheme for regulating prescriptions for corrective lenses that prohibited opticians from duplicating corrective lenses and fitting them into frames without a prescription from an ophthalmologist or optometrist. That requirement clearly favored ophthalmologists and optometrists by requiring that customers obtain a prescription even if they only wished to have an optician place old lenses into new frames. Justice Douglas sustained the law, however, noting that although it may impose a needless and wasteful requirement, the legislature might have concluded that a written prescription was necessary often enough to require one in every case.[97] Similarly, the Court rejected the claim that state Sunday closing laws violated the equal protection clause by exempting certain businesses. Chief Justice Warren explained that the

> Court has held that the Fourteenth Amendment permits the States a wide scope of discretion in enacting laws which affect some groups of citizens differently than others. The constitutional safeguard is offended only if the classification

---

[96]Gary Orfield, Susan E. Eaton, and the Harvard Project on School Desegregation, *Dismantling Desegregation: The Quiet Reversal of Brown v Board of Education* (New York: The New Press, 1996), 1.
[97]*Williamson v Lee Optical Co.*, 348 US 483 (1955).

rests on grounds wholly irrelevant to the achievement of the State's objective. State legislatures are presumed to have acted within their constitutional power despite the fact that, in practice, their laws result in some inequality. A statutory discrimination will not be set aside if any state of facts reasonably may be conceived to justify it. It would seem that a legislature could reasonably find that the Sunday sale of the exempted commodities was necessary either for the health of the populace or for the enhancement of the recreational atmosphere of the day.[98]

Racial Classifications

When classification schemes involving economic and commercial matters are challenged, the Court applies the deferential, lenient standard of review, the rational basis test, which is also known as minimum scrutiny, and with rare exception upholds the policy.[99] But because racial discrimination was the target of the Fourteenth Amendment, laws that classify on the basis of race trigger a much more rigorous standard of review. Racial classifications, the Court has established, are automatically suspect and require the most exacting scrutiny. Thus, when a classification scheme involves race, the Court subjects it to maximum, or **strict scrutiny**—mere reasonableness will not be sufficient to sustain it. With this standard, the law is presumed to be invalid unless the state can show that the classification is necessary to promote a compelling interest. When the Court elects to apply strict scrutiny, it virtually always invalidates the challenged policy.

There has been one notable exception to that rule, however. In 1944 in *Korematsu v United States*, Justice Black announced that "all legal restrictions which curtail the civil rights of a single racial group are immediately suspect. That is not to say that all such restrictions are unconstitutional. It is to say that courts must subject them to the most rigid scrutiny."[100] In that case the Court sustained the order excluding Japanese Americans from the West Coast after the Japanese attacked Pearl Harbor, reasoning that the exclusion was justified by a "pressing public necessity" as some of the 120,000 Japanese and Japanese Americans living near the West Coast might have engaged in espionage or sabotage.

In subsequent cases, the Court has consistently applied maximum scrutiny to invalidate laws that classify on the basis of race. For example, in *Loving v Virginia* in 1967, the justices held that antimiscegenation statutes—laws prohibiting marriage between two people of different races, which were still on the books in sixteen states—violated the equal protection clause. The state argued that the law did not run afoul of the principle of equal protection because it treated members of both races equally: whites were not allowed to marry blacks and blacks were not allowed to marry whites. Casting that argument aside, the Court announced that antimiscegenation laws were invalid because they were based solely on distinctions according to race and prohibited acceptable conduct on the basis of the race of those who engaged in that conduct.[101]

---

[98]*McGowan v Maryland*, 366 US 420 (1961).
[99]See, for example, *Zobel v Williams*, 457 US 55 (1982) and *Williams v Vermont*, 472 US 14 (1985).
[100]*Korematsu v United States*, 323 US 214 (1944).
[101]*Loving v Virginia*, 388 US 1 (1967).

In 1984, the Court invalidated another racial classification, holding that child custody cannot be granted or denied on the basis of race. In that case, a local judge had granted custody to the white father of a child whose mother—also white—was living with a black man. The judge justified the custody order on the grounds that the mother's living arrangements would cause the child to "suffer from social stigmatization."[102] In 1986, a majority of the Court held that the use of peremptory challenges by the prosecutor in a trial of a black defendant violated the equal protection clause when they were used to exclude all blacks from the jury solely on the basis of race or on the assumption that black jurors would be unable to consider the case impartially.[103]

Laws that discriminate against African Americans constitute the most obvious suspect classification because the central aim of the Fourteenth Amendment was to eliminate the unequal treatment of blacks before the law. The Court, however, has identified additional classifications that are suspect. Much of the Court's equal protection jurisprudence, at least since the Warren era, has been based on the third part of the *Carolene Products* footnote in which Justice Stone suggested that the presumption of constitutionality might not apply when the Court reviews policies "directed at particular religious, or national, or racial minorities; . . . prejudice against discrete and insular minorities may be a special condition, which tends seriously to curtail the operation of those political processes ordinarily to be relied upon to protect minorities, and which may call for a correspondingly more searching judicial inquiry."[104] Thus, the Court has treated all disadvantaging classifications based on national origin or on any race or ethnicity as suspect.[105]

Additionally, in 1971 the Court declared that classifications based on noncitizen status—"alienage"—are suspect.[106] Subsequently, however, the Court fashioned the "political function exception," according to which laws that exclude aliens from positions that are related to the process of democratic self-government are not subject to strict scrutiny. Thus, the Court held that the state may deny a noncitizen a job in law enforcement without violating the equal protection clause.[107] In contrast, the Court invalidated a Texas law that withheld from school districts state funds for the education of children who were not legal residents of the United States and permitted local school districts to deny enrollment to such children. In his opinion for a divided Court, Justice Brennan maintained that the law was unconstitutional even though undocumented aliens cannot be treated as a suspect class.[108] The Court's apparent shifting perspective regarding the proper standard of review for classifications based on noncitizen status prompted Justice Powell to observe, "The decisions of this Court regarding the permissibility of statutory classifications involving aliens has not formed an unwavering line."[109]

---

[102]*Palmore v Sidoti*, 466 US 429 (1984).
[103]*Batson v Kentucky*, 476 US 79 (1986).
[104]*United States v Carolene Products Co.*, 304 US 144 (1938).
[105]See, for example, *Yick Wo v Hopkins*, 118 US 356 (1886), and *Hernandez v Texas*, 347 US 475 (1954).
[106]*Graham v Richardson*, 403 US 365 (1971).
[107]*Foley v Connelie*, 435 US 291 (1978).
[108]*Plyler v Doe*, 457 US 202 (1982).
[109]*Ambach v Norwick*, 441 US 68 (1979).

Classifications Based on Sex

The decision in *Goesart v Cleary* in 1948 illustrates the Court's traditional approach to equal protection challenges to classifications based on sex. A Michigan law provided that no woman could obtain a bartender's license unless she was the wife or daughter of the male owner of a licensed liquor establishment. Justice Felix Frankfurter sustained the law, observing that it was "not without a basis in reason." The legislature, he reasoned, had reasonable grounds to believe that serious moral and social problems could result from women tending bar.[110] Likewise, in 1961 the justices held that the equal protection clause did not prohibit a state from excluding women from jury service. Justice Harlan, who wrote the opinion for the unanimous Court, reasoned that it was constitutionally permissible for the legislature, "acting in pursuit of the general welfare, to conclude that woman should be relieved from the civic duty of jury service unless she herself determines that such service is consistent with her own special responsibilities."[111]

In 1971, the Court for the first time found that a classification based on sex violated the equal protection clause. In *Reed v Reed*, the justices applied the lenient rational basis standard to a provision of the Idaho Probate Code that gave an automatic preference to men over women in the selection of administrators of estates.[112] Chief Justice Burger, who wrote the opinion for a unanimous Court, proclaimed that the interest of administrative convenience that the preference served by eliminating the necessity of reviewing a large number of applications was not a sufficient reason for treating women differently from men in this context. Likewise, the assumption that in most cases a man would be more qualified than a woman was based on a sex-based stereotype that was unacceptable. By striking down a law using the language of that rational basis standard, the Court signaled that it might be moving toward a new position in sex discrimination cases. The decision suggested, at least, that the Court would take a closer look at policies that classified on the basis of sex.

In 1973, the Court came within one vote of declaring sex a suspect classification in a case involving a military service regulation that automatically treated a serviceman's wife as his dependent but required a servicewoman who wished to claim her husband as her dependent to show that her husband was dependent on her for at least one-half of his support.[113] Justice Brennan, who wrote for the plurality, offered several reasons that sex—like race—should be a suspect classification. First, this country has had a long history of sex discrimination. Indeed, he noted that for most of the nineteenth century the position of women was similar to that of blacks under the pre–Civil War slave codes. Second, although much had changed, women still faced pervasive discrimination in education, employment, and the political arena. Third, sex—like race—is an accident of birth and most of the time it bears no relation to an individual's ability to perform or to contribute to society. Finally, Brennan found support for

---

[110]*Goesart v Cleary*, 335 US 464 (1948).
[111]*Hoyt v Florida*, 368 US 57 (1961).
[112]*Reed v Reed*, 404 US 71 (1971).
[113]*Frontiero v Richardson*, 411 US 677 (1973).

establishing sex as a suspect classification in legislation that had been enacted by Congress including the prohibitions on sex discrimination in employment in the Civil Rights Act of 1964 and the Equal Pay Act. Those legislative provisions in conjunction with the Equal Rights Amendment, which Congress passed in 1972, suggested that Congress itself had concluded that classifications based on sex were inherently suspect. Although eight justices agreed that the military regulation was constitutionally impermissible, only four were willing to declare sex to be a suspect classification. Three justices who concurred argued that the Court did not need to decide on a standard of review because ratification of the Equal Rights Amendment would settle the matter.

Only three years later, the Court adopted a new standard of review— **moderate—or heightened scrutiny** for classifications based on sex. The justices invalidated an Oklahoma law that prohibited the sale of beer to women under the age of eighteen and to men under the age of twenty-one and announced that the equal protection clause requires that classifications based on sex serve important governmental objectives and be substantially related to the achievement of those objectives.[114] Subsequently, the Court used the standard of moderate scrutiny to invalidate a variety of policies that disadvantaged women and some that disadvantaged men. Nevertheless, the Court's application of moderate scrutiny has sometimes led it to uphold classifications based on sex in cases in which the policy has compensated for past discrimination against women and where the policy is based on physical differences between men and women. Summaries of some of the decisions in which the Court has sustained sex-based classifications are provided in Table 10-1.

An important issue concerning the reach of the equal protection clause to prohibit sex discrimination is whether single-sex education is permissible. In 1982, the Court held that the exclusion of men from the nursing program at Mississippi University for Women ran afoul of equal protection. Justice O'Connor, who wrote the opinion for the five-member majority, made clear that the standard of review will not be changed when the Court examines policies that discriminate against males rather than females. In either situation, the state must demonstrate that there is an "exceedingly persuasive justification" for the classification. Although the state claimed that the women's college advanced the objective of expanding educational opportunities for women, O'Connor found that the state's objective reflected "archaic and stereotypic notions" and that the policy of excluding men from the School of Nursing "tends to perpetuate the stereotyped view of nursing as an exclusively women's job."[115] The dissenters lamented that the decision signaled an end to single-sex education: "The Court decides today that the Equal Protection Clause makes it unlawful for the State to provide women with a traditionally popular and respected choice of educational environment."[116]

Although the Court's reasoning in *Mississippi University for Women* seemed to make clear that state-operated postsecondary schools may not limit admission to one sex, two state military schools—Virginia Military Institute

---

[114]*Craig v Boren*, 429 US 190 (1976).
[115]*Mississippi University for Women v Hogan*, 458 US 718 (1982).
[116]*Ibid.*

Table 10-1 Sex-Based Classifications Upheld

Case	Policy	Sustained Vote
Kahn v Shevin, 416 US 351 (1974)	$500 property tax exemption for widows but not widowers	7–2. Brennan and Marshall dissented.
Geduldig v Aiello, 417 US 484 (1974)	State disability insurance program that excluded normal pregnancy from coverage for medical disabilities	6–3. Brennan, Douglas, Marshall dissented.
Schlesinger v Ballard, 419 US 498 (1975)	Navy personnel policy that allowed women more time for promotion before mandatory discharge	5–4. Brennan, Douglas, Marshall, White dissented.
Califano v Webster, 430 US 313 (1977)	Old-age Social Security benefits that allowed women not to count some lower earning years	9–0.
Michael M. v Superior Court of Sonoma County, 450 US 464 (1981)	Statutory Rape: males only are criminally liable for sexual intercourse with females under the age of 18	5–4. Brennan, Marshall, Stevens, White dissented.
Roskter v Goldberg, 453 US 57 (1981)	Military Selective Service Act that requires all males to register for the draft but not females	6–3. Brennan, Marshall, White dissented.
Lehr v Robertson, 463 US 248 (1983)	Mothers but not fathers of children born out of wedlock required to be notified prior to adoption proceedings of their children	6–3. Blackmun, Marshall, White dissented.
Nguyen v INS, 533 US 53 (2001)	Different rules for citizenship based on whether mother or father of child born out of wedlock is a citizen	5–4. O'Connor, Souter, Ginsburg, Breyer dissented.

(VMI) and The Citadel—were still refusing to admit women in the 1990s. In 1996, Justice Ruth Bader Ginsburg, who had urged the justices to adopt strict scrutiny when she argued *Reed v Reed* before the Supreme Court as a lawyer for the Women's Rights Project of the American Civil Liberties Union, wrote the opinion for a seven-member majority in *United States v Virginia* holding that VMI could not deny admission to women.[117]

---

[117]*United States v Virginia*, 518 US 515 (1996). Scalia was the sole dissenter. Thomas did not participate.

Virginia argued that the male-only, extremely harsh adversative method of training used at VMI served an important state interest in promoting educational diversity by offering an educational experience that was unavailable elsewhere in the state. The admission of women, the state argued, would require modifications to the program that would destroy its unique character. Although the district court sustained the male-only program, the court of appeals ruled that the state could not offer such a training opportunity to men and deny it to women.

Consequently, the state established a parallel program for women, the Virginia Women's Institute for Leadership (VWIL). Thus, the first question for the Supreme Court was whether there was an **exceedingly persuasive justification** for maintaining a male-only military training program. Could the exclusion of women, in other words, survive the standard of moderate scrutiny? If not, the second question for the Court was whether VWIL provided a remedy for the constitutional violation. Did VWIL provide women with educational opportunities that were sufficiently comparable to those offered by VMI?

Justice Ginsburg found that the state had not supported its policy with an exceedingly persuasive justification. On the contrary, the state's alleged purpose—creating diversity in educational opportunities—was merely a rationalization. She observed that the adversative system is not inherently unsuitable for women as the state had argued and that some women are capable of the activities required of male cadets and will want to participate in the adversative training method. In short, the equal protection clause forbids the exclusion of all women from a program in which some women will want to participate and will be qualified to do so. Ginsburg also found that VWIL failed to provide "substantial equality"—it did not offer the rigorous military training of VMI nor could it provide the benefits that resulted from VMI's prestige and the influence of its alumni. Thus, the women's school did not provide a remedy for the constitutional violation—women must be admitted to VMI.

The Court's development of moderate scrutiny for sex-based classifications has not always resulted in invalidation of challenged policies that treat woman and men differently. In their most recent decisions, however, the justices have found that challenged policies are not substantially related to important governmental interests. Although some of the justices continue to argue that sex discrimination cases should be decided with the rational basis test, a majority has consistently adhered to the moderate standard. Thus, it does not seem likely that the Court will move either to the rational basis test or to maximum scrutiny but that it will continue to hold policies that classify on the basis of sex invalid under the moderate standard of review.

Classifications Based on Sexual Orientation

As discussed, the Court held in 1986 that the right to privacy does not encompass consensual sexual acts between two people of the same sex even in the home.[118] Ten years would pass before the Court agreed to hear another case involving the rights of gays and lesbians. *Romer v Evans* involved a challenge to

---

[118]*Bowers v Hardwick,* 478 US 186 (1986).

Colorado's Amendment 2, a state constitutional amendment adopted by the voters, which repealed existing state and local policies that prohibited discrimination on the basis of sexual orientation. Amendment 2 also prohibited any governmental unit in the state from enacting policies prohibiting discrimination based on sexual orientation unless the state constitution was amended to permit such measures.

Justice Kennedy, who wrote the opinion for the six-member majority, hinted that heightened scrutiny might be justified by the amendment's novelty: "The absence of precedent for Amendment 2 is itself instructive; '[d]iscriminations of an unusual character especially suggest careful consideration to determine whether they are obnoxious to the constitutional provision.'"[119] Still, he declined to use heightened scrutiny and found that the amendment failed even the rational basis test. Amendment 2, he reasoned, had the "peculiar property" of imposing a broad and undifferentiated disability on a single named group. It was unprecedented in the way it disqualified gays and lesbians from seeking protection from the law and "A law declaring that in general it shall be more difficult for one group of citizens than for all others to seek aid from the government is itself a denial of equal protection of the laws in the most literal sense."[120] Moreover, Kennedy could find no relationship between the classification and any legitimate state interests. He concluded therefore that Amendment 2 was based on animus toward gays and lesbians—"to make them unequal to everyone else."[121]

Some commentators have objected to the Court's unwillingness to use heightened scrutiny in *Romer v Evans.* Even though the Court invalidated Amendment 2 its formal adherence to the rational basis test denies the protection to gays and lesbians that women receive. Moreover, some legal scholars have noted that giving approval to the rational basis test in the context of sexual orientation is likely to convey to the lower courts that they have the discretion to uphold discriminatory policies simply by finding them reasonable. In short, "it leaves gays and lesbians at the whim of the judiciary."[122]

In 2003 the Court decided the case of *Lawrence v Texas,* a challenge to a state law that made it a crime for two people of the same sex to engage in "deviate sexual intercourse." As we discussed in the context of the due process clause, the appellants argued that the law was inconsistent with a long-standing right to privacy in matters of intimacy within the home and family. Also central to the challenge was the argument that the law violates the equal protection clause because it treats the "*same* consensual sexual behavior differently depending on *who* the participants are." Like Colorado's Amendment 2, Texas's criminal sodomy law "singles out a certain class of citizens for disfavored legal status," and consequently fails even the rational basis test.[123] Although the majority opinion relied on the right to privacy Justice O'Connor condemned the

---

[119]*Romer v Evans,* 517 US 620 (1996).
[120]*Ibid.*
[121]*Ibid.*
[122]Evan Gerstmann, *The Constitutional Underclass: Gays, Lesbians, and the Failure of Class-Based Equal Protection* (Chicago, IL: University of Chicago Press, 1999), 137.
[123]*Lawrence v Texas,* No. 02-102, Brief for Petitioners. Available: http://supreme.lp.findlaw.com/supreme_court/briefs/02-102/02-102.mer.pet.pdf.

law on equal protection grounds and argued that anti-sodomy laws that criminalize conduct that would otherwise be legal if it takes place between two members of the same sex violate the fundamental values of the Constitution.

Equal Protection and Other Classifications

As noted, the *Carolene Products* footnote provides support for subjecting classifications other than those based on race to heightened scrutiny. Although the Court has declined to hold that "illegitimacy" is a suspect classification subject to strict scrutiny, it has asserted that laws that discriminate against people based on the marital status of their parents at the time of their birth would be held to a higher standard than the rational basis test. Thus, for example, the Court invalidated an Illinois law that allowed children born out of wedlock to inherit by intestate succession only from their mother while children born to parents who were married to each other were allowed to inherit by intestate succession from both parents. The Court noted, "Illegitimacy is analogous in many respects to the personal characteristics that have been held to be suspect when used as the basis of statutory differentiations."[124] A year later, noting that the law was substantially related to legitimate state interests, the justices upheld a legal provision that prohibited children born out of wedlock from inheriting from fathers who died intestate unless paternity had been established while the father was still alive.[125] The Court has continued to assess classifications based on "illegitimacy" that distinguish between the mother and father by the standard that it uses for classifications based on sex—it must serve important governmental objectives and the means employed must be substantially related to the achievement of those objectives.[126]

Even when support for expanding individual rights was at its height during the Warren Court, the justices never held that wealth was a suspect classification. Justices Douglas, Brennan, and Marshall, however, tried to expand the category of suspect classifications beyond race to include the poor as well as women and children born out of wedlock. Their conviction that the judiciary was obligated to protect powerless groups was reflected outside the equal protection area in the Court's rulings that the states must provide counsel and a copy of the trial transcript to poor defendants to allow them an appeal.[127] The Burger Court made it clear, however, that it did not regard classifications based on wealth to be suspect. When a majority sustained state restrictions on public funding for abortions in 1977, Justice Powell noted, "In a sense, every denial of welfare to an indigent creates a wealth classification as compared to nonindigents who are able to pay for the desired goods or services. But the Court has never held that financial need alone identifies a suspect class for purposes of equal protection analysis."[128] Similarly, when the Court upheld the state system

---

[124]Intestate means without a will. *Trimble v Gordon*, 430 US 762 (1977).
[125]*Lalli v Lalli*, 439 US 259 (1978).
[126]*Nguyen v INS*, 533 US 53(2001).
[127]*Griffin v Illinois*, 351 US 12 (1956) and *Douglas v California*, 372 US 353 (1963).
[128]*Maher v Roe*, 432 US 464 (1977).

of funding for public schools based on local property taxes, Justice Powell again outlined the possible consequences of treating wealth as a suspect classification:

> No scheme of taxation, whether the tax is imposed on property, income, or purchases of goods and services, has yet been devised which is free of all discriminatory impact. In such a complex arena in which no perfect alternatives exist, the Court does well not to impose too rigorous a standard of scrutiny lest all local fiscal schemes become subjects of criticism under the Equal Protection Clause.[129]

There is some support for classifications based on wealth to be subjected to heightened scrutiny in the *Carolene Products* footnote as the poor are often unpopular and are likely to lack the resources to work for their rights in the political process. There was also support for expanding suspect classifications to include the poor during the Warren Court. Nevertheless, classifications based on wealth are not likely to be subjected to strict scrutiny during the early years of the twenty-first century.

Equal Protection and Fundamental Rights

The Court will also apply strict scrutiny to policies that classify people in such a way as to infringe on a fundamental right. Rights that the Court has treated as fundamental include the right to vote, to travel between states, and to make reproductive choices. The Warren Court expanded the category of **fundamental rights under the equal protection clause.** In 1966, for example, the justices struck down a state poll tax, emphasizing the special nature of the right to vote[130] and in 1969 invalidated a law limiting eligibility to vote in school board elections to parents or taxpayers.[131] The Court also invalidated one-year residence requirements for welfare assistance in Pennsylvania and Connecticut. In his opinion for the majority in that case, Justice Brennan noted that the classification "touches on the fundamental right of interstate movement" and therefore must be subjected to strict scrutiny.[132] In 1972 in *Eisenstadt v Baird,* the Court invalidated the Massachusetts law that prohibited the sale of contraceptives to unmarried individuals, noting that the law infringed on the rights of single people in violation of the equal protection clause.[133] Commentators termed the Court's extension of equal protection analysis to fundamental rights the "fundamental rights and interests strand" of the new equal protection. The Court even suggested in 1972 that it might replace what was then the two-tiered system—using the rational basis test when economic interests were involved and strict scrutiny for classifications based on race—with a sliding-scale

---

[129]*San Antonio School District v Rodriguez,* 411 US 1 (1973).
[130]*Harper v Virginia State Board of Elections,* 383 US 663 (1966). See also, *Hill v Stone,* 421 US 289 (1975) (limited eligibility to vote in city bond elections to those who had paid property tax unconstitutional).
[131]*Kramer v Union Free School District,* 395 US 621 (1969).
[132]*Shapiro v Thompson,* 394 US 618 (1969).
[133]*Eisenstadt v Baird,* 405 US 438 (1972).

approach in which the level of scrutiny would depend on the right that was at stake. Justice Powell wrote:

> Though the latitude given state social and economic legislation is necessarily broad, when state statutory classifications approach sensitive and fundamental personal rights, this Court exercises a stricter scrutiny. The essential inquiry in all the foregoing cases is, however, inevitably a dual one: What legitimate state interest does the classification promote? What fundamental personal rights might the classification endanger?[134]

One of the opponents of the fundamental rights strand of equal protection, then-Justice Rehnquist, argued in dissent in that case and others that by identifying unenumerated fundamental rights and extending protection to them under the Fourteenth Amendment, the Court was simply reviving the old substantive due process.

In 1973, the Court sharply limited the fundamental rights stand of equal protection when it upheld, by a vote of five to four, systems of funding for public schools based on local property taxes. Although previous cases provided some support for finding education to be a fundamental right, Justice Powell, who wrote the opinion for the majority, held that it was not.[135] The Court in *Brown* stated that "education is perhaps the most important function of state and local government."[136] Powell distinguished *Brown*, however, noting that racial discrimination was the context of that decision, and concluded that the only fundamental rights protected by the equal protection clause are those that are "explicitly or implicitly guaranteed by the Constitution."[137] Education was not one of those rights. Because about 50 percent of funding for public schools comes from the states, the Court's reasoning in that case legitimated the enormous inequities in educational opportunities that result from the arrangement whereby property taxes provide the funding for public schools. A number of state supreme courts, beginning in 1971 with California, have ruled that the inequities that result from the property tax system violate the state constitution and that the state is responsible for ensuring that funding for education is adequate and equitable across the state.[138]

Affirmative Action

One of the most controversial issues during the last thirty years of the twentieth century was whether race may be taken into account when efforts are undertaken to remedy the effects of discrimination. Following the decision in *Brown v Board of Education* in 1954 declaring that legally sanctioned

---

[134]*Weber v Aetna Casualty & Surety Co.*, 406 US 164 (1972).
[135]*San Antonio Independent School District v Rodriguez*, 411 US 1 (1973).
[136]*Brown v Board of Education*, 347 US 483 (1954).
[137]*San Antonio Independent School District v Rodriguez*, 411 US 1 (1973).
[138]The case in California was *Serrano v Priest*, 5 Cal.3d 584 (1971). Other states are Kentucky, Texas, and New Jersey. Public Education, "Facts About School Funding," http://www.pfaw.org/pfaw/general/default.aspx?oid=2454; Foundations of Education, Financing Education, http://admin.vmi.edu/ir/found10.htm

segregated schools violate the Constitution, the Court issued a series of decisions holding segregation unconstitutional in other public facilities ranging from beaches to buses to golf courses and parks.[139] Ten years later in the Civil Rights Act of 1964, Congress prohibited discrimination in public accommodations and employment and forbade public funding for institutions that engaged in discrimination. When President Kennedy proposed a civil rights bill in 1963, opponents attacked it, charging that it would impose racial quotas for employers. To allay such concerns, the Civil Rights Act included a sentence explicitly disavowing quotas. The law established the Equal Employment Opportunity Commission to prevent employment discrimination. The commission lacked enforcement powers, however.

What we now call affirmative action began with executive orders banning discriminatory hiring by federal contractors. Although it was not the first of such orders, President Lyndon Johnson's Executive Order 11246 in 1965 is commonly known as the originating document of affirmative action. Executive Order 11246 gave responsibility for affirmative action to the Labor Department and directed recipients of federal contracts to take steps to recruit qualified minority applicants and to ensure that they were not treated in a discriminatory way in the hiring process. Affirmative action expanded over the years. Not only did the federal government promulgate more regulations but state and local governments also adopted programs. Additionally, a number of traditionally white colleges and universities attempted to increase the enrollment of minorities, and private business began to institute measures to increase the numbers of minorities in areas in which they were seriously underrepresented. The primary **rationale for affirmative action** in the 1960s was that simply prohibiting discrimination would not bring an end to the nation's racial problems, including the large gap between blacks and whites in wealth and education.

No other issue, with the exception of abortion, has prompted so much acrimony between what appear to be irreconcilable opposing positions. Supporters argue that affirmative action is necessary to eliminate the vestiges of our history of slavery, segregation, and discrimination. A conscious effort to include members of previously excluded groups is crucial to the achievement of genuine equality of opportunity. Opponents of affirmative action argue not only that it is unfair to white men but also that it stigmatizes the beneficiaries by creating an impression that they could not succeed without special preferences. Some critics also contend that it does nothing to alleviate the worst problems in black America. In fact, legal scholar Stephen L. Carter has characterized affirmative action as "racial justice on the cheap" because it is the least expensive approach to civil rights and does nothing to help the worst off among African Americans.[140]

The Supreme Court addressed the issue of affirmative action for the first time in 1978 in *Regents of the University of California v Bakke*. Allan Bakke,

---

[139]See, for example, *Mayor of Baltimore v Dawson*, 350 US 877 (1955) (beaches); *Gayle v Browder*, 352 US 903 (1956) (buses); *Holmes v Atlanta*, 350 US 879 (1955) (golf courses); *New Orleans City Park Improvement Association v Detiege*, 358 US 54 (1958) (parks).

[140]Stephen L. Carter, *Reflections of an Affirmative Action Baby* (New York: Basic Books, 1991), 71–72.

a white male engineer in his early thirties applied to the medical school of the University of California–Davis in 1973 and 1974 and each year was denied admission. He brought suit after his second rejection when he discovered that there was a special admissions program under which students who had lower grades and test scores than his were admitted. He claimed that he was denied admission because of his race, contrary to both the Constitution and Title VI of the Civil Rights Act of 1964. The special admissions program reserved sixteen seats in the entering class of one hundred for a separate admissions process, which was designated for members of a minority group or applicants who were economically or educationally disadvantaged.

A divided Court invalidated the Davis plan. A majority, however, did not agree on the constitutionality of affirmative action, as Table 10-2 shows. Justice Powell, who announced the Court's decision, explained that the state's compelling interest in achieving a diverse student body justifies taking race into account in the admissions process. Race may be considered "a plus" as may other factors such as economic background, geographic origin, leadership potential,

Table 10-2   How the Justices Voted in *Regents of University of California v Bakke* (1978)

	Yes	No	Not Relevant in This Case
Should Bakke be admitted?	5 **Powell**, Burger, Stevens, Rehnquist, Stewart	4 Brennan, White, Marshall, Blackmun	—
Was the racial "quota" system at Davis Medical School acceptable in deciding who should be admitted?	4 Brennan, White, Marshall, Blackmun	5 **Powell**,[*] Burger, Stevens, Rehnquist, Stewart	—
Can an applicant's race ever be considered in deciding who should be admitted?	5 **Powell**,[**] Brennan, White, Marshall, Blackmun	—	Burger, Stevens, Rehnquist, Stewart

[*]Powell relied on both constitutional and statutory grounds (Title VI of the Civil Rights Act of 1964). The other four reached only the statutory issue.
[**]Powell said race can be considered if a school is seeking a diverse student body. The other four said race can be considered to redress past discrimination or to increase the number of minority doctors.
Source: "The Landmark *Bakke* Ruling," *Newsweek*, July 10, 1978, 21. Reprinted by permission.

exceptional personal talents, unique work experience, and compassion. No one may be excluded on the basis of race, however. Consequently, Powell reasoned that race may never be considered the decisive factor.

Powell rejected the distinction advanced by the university that racial classifications are not suspect if their purpose is benign rather than invidious—that is, if they are designed to help "discrete and insular minorities" rather than to disadvantage them. He maintained that the Fourteenth Amendment does not permit "the recognition of special wards entitled to a degree of protection greater than that accorded others."[141] The availability of equal protection cannot depend on one's membership in a particular group. Thus, he contended that all racial classifications are subject to strict scrutiny and invalidated the university's program because it was not narrowly tailored to achieve the goal of attaining a diverse student body.

The Court's decisions in several subsequent cases involving affirmative action are summarized in Table 10-3. Considered together, those decisions suggest that the Court found affirmative action programs acceptable if they were a remedy for a specific legal wrong, did not impose too much of a burden on whites, and were flexible—contained goals rather than quotas—and temporary—they would end when the effects of past discrimination had been corrected.

Two years after *Bakke*, the Court addressed the question of the constitutional permissibility of **minority set-aside programs** that attempt to improve the position of minority businesses in competing for government contracts. Such programs reserve a percentage of government contracts for minority-owned businesses. The set-aside program that was challenged and upheld in *Fullilove v Klutznick* was based on a provision in the Public Works Employment Act of 1977 requiring state and local governments that receive grants under the act to expend at least 10 percent of their grants in contracts with minority-owned businesses.[142] Emphasizing that Congress has broad remedial powers to remedy a history of discrimination in government contracting, Chief Justice Burger found that the set-aside program met the standard of strict scrutiny. The Court was as badly divided in *Fullilove* as it had been in *Bakke*. Only Powell and White agreed with Burger, whereas Marshall, Brennan, and Blackmun would not have subjected the program to the toughest level of scrutiny but rather to the moderate standard of review. In dissent, Stewart, Rehnquist, and Stevens argued that the Constitution does not permit any racial classifications.

After the Court's decision in *Fullilove,* a number of state and local governments adopted their own set-aside programs. In 1989 in *City of Richmond v J.A. Croson Co.,* a six-member majority invalidated Richmond's 30 percent set-aside program. Justice O'Connor could find no support for the contention that remedial action was necessary as there had been no showing that anyone in the Richmond construction industry had engaged in illegal discriminatory

---

[141]*Regents of the University of California v Bakke,* 438 US 265 (1978).
[142]*Fullilove v Klutznick,* 448 US 448 (1980).

Table 10-3   Affirmative Action Cases 1978–1990

Case	Ruling	Vote
United Steelworkers of America v Weber, 443 US 193 (1979)	Upheld a collective bargaining agreement that voluntarily aimed at overcoming a company's nearly-all-white craft work force by requiring that at least half of the trainees in an in-plant training program be black until the proportion of blacks in the craft work force matched the proportion of blacks in the local work force. Despite the wording of Title VII of the Civil Rights Act of 1964, the affirmative action program was consistent with the spirit of the Act.	5–2. Burger and Rehnquist dissented. Powell and Stevens did not participate.
Fullilove v Klutznick, 448 US 448 (1980)	Congress's enactment of a 10 percent quota of construction contracts to minority businesses was within its authority under either the Commerce Clause or Section 5 of the Fourteenth Amendment.	6–3. Justices Stewart, Rehnquist, Stevens dissented.
Firefighters Local Union No. 1784 v Stotts, 467 US 561 (1984)	Setting aside least seniority as a basis for laying off workers and substituting race was something not contained in an existing consent decree and was unjustified unless black employees could prove they individually had been victims of discrimination. Mere membership in a disadvantaged class was insufficient reason for departing from a last-hired-is-first-fired policy.	6–3. Brennan, Marshall, Blackmun dissented.

(continued)

Table 10-3   Affirmative Action Cases 1978–1990 *(Continued)*

Case	Ruling	Vote
Wygant v Jackson Board of Education, 476 US 267 (1986)	Preferential protection of minority teachers from layoffs contained in a collective bargaining agreement was unconstitutional. While layoffs were to be conducted on the basis of least seniority, the agreement provided that the percentage of minority personnel released was never to be less than the percentage of minority personnel employed at the time the layoff began.	5–4. Brennan, Marshall, Blackmun, Stevens dissented.
Local 28, Sheet Metal Workers International Association v EEOC, 478 US 421 (1986)	Federal court order imposing a 29 percent nonwhite membership goal (reflective of the proportion of nonwhites in the local work force) on a union and its apprenticeship committee for discrimination against nonwhite workers in selection, training, and admission of members to union was upheld, and the contempt citation and fine for violation of the order were affirmed.	5–4. Burger, White, Rehnquist, O'Connor dissented.
No. 93, International Association of Firefighters v Cleveland, 478 US 501 (1986)	Racial goals and quotas were upheld as a remedy for past discrimination in hiring, assigning, and promoting firefighters by the city.	6–3. Burger, White, Rehnquist dissented.
United States v Paradise, 480 US 149 (1987)	Requirement that 50 percent of promotions throughout the Alabama state troopers were to go to blacks, if qualified blacks were available, was upheld after a showing of forty years of pervasive and systematic discrimination by that state agency.	5–4. Rehnquist, White, O'Connor, Scalia dissented.

Table 10-3   *(Continued)*

Case	Ruling	Vote
Johnson v Transportation Agency, Santa Clara County, 480 US 616 (1987)	Voluntarily adopted affirmative action program for minorities and women that considered sex as one factor in making hiring and promotion decisions until proportions of minorities and women roughly resembled that in local work force, but which did not use quotas, did not violate Title VII of 1964 Civil Rights Act.	6–3. Rehnquist, White, Scalia dissented.
Metro Broadcasting, Inc. v FCC, 497 US 547 (1990)	FCC's policy of giving an enhancement to minority applications for radio and TV licenses and of exempting such applicants from some license transfer procedures was constitutional. Overruled in *Adarand Constructors.*	5–4. Rehnquist, O'Connor, Scalia, Kennedy dissented.

Source: Craig R. Ducat, *Constitutional Interpretation: Rights of the Individual,* Vol. II, 7th ed. (Belmont, CA: West Thomson Learning, 2000), 1246–1247.

conduct. She maintained that numerical disparities in contracts awarded to minority firms and the minority population of Richmond did not establish proof of discrimination. O'Connor concluded that the program was not narrowly tailored to remedy prior discrimination in part because the city had not considered race-neutral alternatives to the 30 percent set-aside and that percentage appeared to be unconnected to any goal "except perhaps outright racial balancing."[143] O'Connor's opinion took the position that underrepresentation of minorities in business may well be due to other factors than discrimination; thus, if the shortage of minority businesses that receive contracts cannot be specifically tied to illegal acts of discrimination, then a race-conscious remedy cannot be justified. Indeed, her opinion seemed to call the validity of most affirmative action plans into question. In dissent, Justice Marshall condemned the majority for sounding "a full-scale retreat from the Court's long-standing solicitude to race-conscious remedial efforts 'directed toward deliverance of the century-old promise of equality of economic opportunity.'"[144]

The emphasis that Justice O'Connor, in her opinion in *Fullilove,* placed on Congress's extensive power under Section 5 of the Fourteenth Amendment to

---

[143]*Richmond v Croson,* 488 US 469 (1989).
[144]*Ibid.*

remedy past discrimination suggested that although a local set-aside program could not survive judicial scrutiny, another federal program might. But in 1995, the Court dispelled the impression that it would treat federal affirmative action programs any more favorably than state or local ones. In *Adarand Constructors, Inc. v Pena*, by a vote of five to four, the Court struck down a federal policy that provided for the prime contractor in a highway project to be paid a bonus if at least 10 percent of the contract amount is subcontracted to minority owned and operated small businesses.[145] Although O'Connor's opinion indicated that an affirmative action plan could survive strict scrutiny if it were narrowly tailored as a remedy for past discrimination, both Justices Scalia and Thomas took the position that no racially conscious plan could be justified under any circumstances. Scalia went so far as to assert that affirmative action is tantamount to racial entitlement that will reinforce and preserve the way of thinking that produced slavery, race privilege, and race hatred and that "In the eyes of government, we are just one race here. It is American."[146]

Two current members of the Court—Scalia and Thomas—have made it clear that they will never support an affirmative action program; three justices—Kennedy, O'Connor, and Rehnquist—might vote to uphold a program that is carefully designed to remedy illegal discrimination; and four—Breyer, Ginsburg, Souter, and Stevens—are likely to uphold some affirmative action programs under the moderate scrutiny approach. Several commentators perceived *Adarand* as a signal that all affirmative action programs are at risk. Moreover, some observers contended that the majority had joined the national debate over affirmative action but rather than engaging in any thoughtful analysis of the issues had taken sides with the anti-affirmative-action sentiment that condemns affirmative action on the grounds that it harms white males. At any rate, the Court's decision in *Adarand* influenced the strategy of supporters of affirmative action to avoid the Supreme Court. In 1996 *Board of Education v Piscataway v Taxman*, for example, after the Court agreed to hear the case, a coalition of civil rights groups obtained a settlement for over $400,000 for a white claimant who charged that she had been fired from her teaching job because of an affirmative action policy.

In the spring of 1996, the Court of Appeals for the Fifth Circuit invalidated the admission program at the University of Texas Law School that gave some help to African American and Hispanic applicants. The judges rejected Powell's reasoning in *Bakke* that race may be considered to advance the state's interest in attaining a diverse student body on the grounds that Powell's argument never represented the view of a majority of the Court. The appeals court instead followed O'Connor's pronouncement in *Adarand* that racial classifications are justified only to remedy the effects of past discrimination and must be narrowly tailored to achieve that end. Texas has a long history of racial discrimination, but the judges held that the university had to show a specific connection between constitutional violations committed by the law school and the current

---

[145]*Adarand Constructors Inc. v Pena*, 515 US 200 (1995).
[146]*Ibid.*

shortage of minorities enrolled there.[147] The Supreme Court declined to hear an appeal from that decision.[148]

In November 1996 and 1998, respectively, voters in California and Washington adopted ballot initiatives ending all affirmative action programs in public employment and education. A federal district court ruled that California's Proposition 209 violated the equal protection clause as well as the supremacy clause of Article VI of the Constitution because it conflicts with the antidiscrimination provisions of the Civil Rights Act of 1964. The Court of Appeals for the Ninth Circuit reversed that decision, however, and the Supreme Court denied certiorari.[149]

In March, 2003 the Court heard oral arguments in the challenge to two affirmative action programs at the University of Michigan.[150] The undergraduate admissions program used a formula in which it gives applicants who are African American, Hispanic, or Native American an extra 20 points toward the 100 points needed to guarantee admission. The University's Law School's admissions process was race conscious but was more flexible and individualized. It nevertheless resulted in the admission of some minority students with lower test scores and grades than white applicants who were denied admission. The Bush Administration joined the case on the side of the students who challenged the program and argued that a "race-neutral alternative" should replace preferential treatment based on race. Texas, Florida, and California use such alternatives, admitting students who graduate in the top specified percent of the high schools in their state[151]

The central issue regarding affirmative action in higher education has remained the same since the 1970s: may race be used as a factor in undergraduate, graduate, and professional school admissions? In June, 2003 a divided Court answered in the affirmative, upholding the University of Michigan Law School's use of race as a factor in admissions. Justice O'Connor, writing for a five-member majority characterized the admission's process as a "highly individualized, holistic review of each applicant's file" in which race is considered but not in a "mechanical way." Thus, she reasoned, it was consistent with Powell's opinion in *Bakke* permitting race to be used as a "plus" in admissions' decisions. The result of the decision was that the position Powell alone adopted in 1978 but which subsequent decisions had undermined and some lower federal courts had repudiated, that there is a compelling state interest in racial diversity in higher education, has now been endorsed by five justices and has stronger support than it did before.[152] O'Connor and Breyer joined the four who dissented from the decision in the law school case to create a six-person majority to invalidate the undergraduate point

---

[147]*Hopwood v Texas*, 78 F 3d 932 (5th Cir. 1996).

[148]*Texas v Hopwood*, cert. Denied 1996.

[149]*Coalition for Economic Equity v Wilson*, 946 F Supp 1480 (ND Cal. 1996), order vacated, 122 F 3d 692 (9th Cir. 1997) cert. Denied 1997.

[150]*Grutter v. Bollinger* (challenge to the Law Schools program), No. 02-241; *Gratz v. Bollinger* (challenge to the program at the College of Literature and the Sciences and the Arts), No. 02-516.

[151]Linda Greenhouse, "On Affirmative Action: High Court Seeks Nuance," *The New York Times*, April 2, 2003.

[152]Linda Greenhouse, "The Supreme Court: Affirmative Action; Justices Back Affirmative Action by 5 to 4, but Wider Vote Bans a Racial Point System, *The New York Times*, June 24, 2003.

Table 10-4   The Justices' Positions on Affirmative Action, 2003

Case	To Uphold	To Invalidate
Grutter v Bollinger, ____ US ____ (2003) University of Michigan, Law school admissions program	O'Connor Breyer Stevens Souter Ginsburg	Rehnquist Scalia Thomas Kennedy
Gratz v Bollinger, ____ US ____ (2003) University of Michigan, Undergraduate Admissions Program (20 points added for minorities)	Ginsburg Stevens Souter	O'Connor Breyer Rehnquist Scalia Thomas Kennedy

system. Rehnquist, who wrote the majority opinion, noted that the program lacked the "individualized consideration" required by the *Bakke* precedent. Table 10-4 shows the division of the Court in both cases. A comparison of Tables 10-2 and 10-4 provides a summary of the evolution of the Court's perspective on the constitutional status of affirmative action.

Equal Protection and Voting

The Fifteenth Amendment prohibits denial of the right to vote on the basis of race, the Nineteenth Amendment provides that the franchise may not be denied on account of sex, and the Twenty-sixth Amendment prohibits denial of the right to vote on the basis of age for those who are eighteen and older. Although there is no provision in the Constitution that grants a general right to vote, the Court has found that the equal protection clause protects equal access to the franchise. Consequently, the justices have invalidated legal provisions making property ownership a requirement for voting[153] and the poll tax—a tax that states required people to pay for the privilege of voting.[154] The Court also struck down Texas's attempt to withhold the franchise from service personnel[155] and Tennessee's requirement that did not allow new residents to vote until they had lived in the state for a year.[156] States have the authority to disenfranchise people who have been convicted of felonies[157] although state laws that prohibit felons from voting for life may be susceptible to a challenge on racial-discrimination grounds because of the disproportionate number of African Americans who have been convicted of felonies.

The Court has held that the Constitution protects voters against electoral schemes that have the effect of diluting their votes. Article I, Section 2, provides

[153]*Kramer v Union Free School District*, 395 US 621 (1969).
[154]*Harper v Virginia State Board of Elections*, 383 US 663 (1966).
[155]*Carrington v Rash*, 380 US 89 (1965).
[156]*Dunn v Blumstein*, 405 US 330 (1972).
[157]*Richardson v Ramirez*, 418 US 24 (1974).

for a census every ten years to determine the number of congressional seats to be allocated to each state. Every ten years when the states find out how many representatives they will have, the state legislature divides the state into congressional districts. Each of those districts elects a member of Congress. Voters can be said to have fair and effective representation only if each congressional district in the state contains approximately the same number of residents. Otherwise, some people's votes—those who live in districts with a higher population—would be diluted. State legislatures also create districts from which state representatives are chosen, and the need to have districts of roughly equal number applies there as well. When the states have either congressional or state legislative districts that have unequal numbers of residents, they are considered to be malapportioned.

Malapportionment became a serious problem by the middle of the twentieth century as a result of major population shifts from rural areas to urban centers and by the refusal of many state legislatures to reapportion their state or congressional districts. By the 1940s, a number of states had not reapportioned their districts since the 1900 census, and they did not want to do so because they knew that seats in rural areas would be lost and incumbents would lose their positions. **Reapportionment** would be likely to result in major shifts in political power within the states from rural to urban and suburban areas with potentially major consequences.

Initially the Court insisted that apportionment was a matter for legislators—Congress determines the number of representatives each state has and the state legislatures devise both congressional and state districts—and that courts "ought not to enter this political thicket."[158] But in 1962 in *Baker v Carr*, the justices held that the courts have jurisdiction to hear challenges to state districting systems brought under the equal protection clause.[159] Two years later in *Wesberry v Sanders*, the Court invalidated Georgia's congressional districting scheme that had been devised by the state legislature in 1931. In 1964, Georgia's ten congressional districts varied in population from 823,680 to 272,154. In that case, the Court did not rely on the equal protection clause but on the requirement in Article I, Section 2, that representatives be elected by the people. Only four months later in *Reynolds v Sims*, the Court held that both houses of a state legislature must be apportioned on a population basis and articulated the one person, one vote principle: "[T]he overriding objective must be substantial equality of population among the various districts, so that the vote of any citizen is approximately equal in weight to that of any other citizen in the State."[160] In the five companion cases to *Reynolds v Sims*, the Court invalidated apportionment schemes in Colorado, New York, Maryland, Virginia, and Delaware. Subsequently, the Court has applied the principle of one person, one vote to county governments, elected special purpose boards that exercise legislative functions, and New York City's Board of Estimate.[161] But it has made

---

[158]*Colegrove v Green*, 328 US 549 (1946).
[159]*Baker v Carr*, 369 US 186 (1962).
[160]*Reynolds v Sims*, 377 US 533 (1964).
[161]*Avery v Midland County*, 390 US 474 (1868) (county government); *Hadley v Junior College District*, 397 US 50 (1970) (special purpose boards); *Board of Estimate of New York v Morris*, 489 US 688 (1989) (New York City's Board of Estimate).

exceptions for certain special purpose units of government, such as water control or irrigation districts, and for governing boards that exercise administrative rather than legislative functions.[162]

The Court has imposed more rigorous standards on state legislatures in devising their congressional districts, which is governed by Article I, Section 2, than for apportionment of state legislatures, which is governed by the equal protection clause. In fact, the justices have allowed deviations from numerical equality in state legislative districts, when they are "based on legitimate considerations incident to the effectuation of a rational state policy." Moreover, as Justice Rehnquist noted in *Mahan v Howell* in 1973, "more flexibility was constitutionally permissible with respect to state legislative reapportionment than in congressional redistricting" because of the interest in the "normal functioning of state and local governments."[163]

When the Court resolved the contested election of 2000 by halting the recount in Florida, the majority relied primarily on the equal protection clause.[164] The Court also relied on Article II, Section 1 (2), which we discussed in Chapter 4. In its brief to the United States Supreme Court, Bush's legal team argued that the Florida Supreme Court's mandate of a manual recount of all possible uncounted legal votes in the state violated the equal protection clause because it "gives the votes of similarly situated voters different effect based on the happenstance of the county or district in which those voters live."[165] Five of the justices—Rehnquist, O'Connor, Scalia, Kennedy, and Thomas—agreed. They reasoned that states may not "by arbitrary and disparate treatment, value one person's vote over that of another" in a way that "dilutes the weight of a citizen's vote." The recount mechanisms, they maintained, failed to satisfy the "minimum requirement for non-arbitrary treatment of voters necessary to secure a fundamental right" because the standard that the Florida high court had chosen for evaluating ballots, "intent of the voter," was too general and allowed for too much variation in the treatment of ballots.[166] The majority was careful to specify that "[o]ur consideration is limited to the present circumstances, for the problem of equal protection in election processes generally presents many complexities." The Court, thereby, avoided the myriad of problems that would have arisen if its reasoning in *Bush v Gore* were to be applied in future cases involving irregularities in voting procedures. The way that the majority limited its decision to the extraordinary circumstances of the dispute over the election was one of the most controversial portions of the decision as it created an impression among that the justices were using the Constitution as a tool to ensure that their political preferences would prevail. Federal Court of Appeals Judge and former Dean of Yale Law School, Guido Calabresi, for example, declared that *Bush v Gore* "was a dangerously bad decision. It was *bad,*

---

[162]*Sayler Land Company v Tulare Lake Basin Water Storage District,* 410 US 743 (1973); *Sailors v Board of Education of Kent County,* 387 US 105 (1967).
[163]*Mahan v Howell,* 410 US 315 (1973).
[164]*Bush v Gore,* 531 US 98 (2000).
[165]As quoted in Howard Gillman, *The Votes that Counted: How the Court Decided the 2000 Election* (Chicago, IL: University of Chicago Press, 2001), 129.
[166]*Ibid.,* 141.

not because its result was necessarily wrong but because it was unprincipled. It was *dangerously* bad because its lack of principle was naked and in a case that had the very highest visibility. And as such, it can all too readily serve to legitimate and make standard unprincipled decisions."[167]

The dissenters in *Bush v Gore* viewed the equal protection problem as a minor issue that could have been remedied without halting the recounts. Justice Souter believed that the Florida courts could have dealt with the issue on their own if the process had not been interrupted. Given the interruption, the United States Supreme Court could have remanded the case back to the Florida courts with instructions to use a standard that would guarantee the equal treatment of the ballots. In Souter's view, the recount should have been allowed to proceed under an improved standard. In his dissent, Justice Breyer conceded that there were legitimate concerns about the differential treatment of identical ballots, but he maintained that there was no justification for halting the recount entirely. Breyer argued that the Florida Supreme Court should have been left to decide whether the recount should proceed. As it was, the majority had crafted a "remedy out of proportion to the asserted harm" and had prevented a more sensible remedy that "would itself redress a problem of unequal treatment of ballots."[168]

The outspoken Harvard law professor Alan M. Dershowitz condemned the majority's reliance on the Fourteenth Amendment as completely inconsistent with the core values of the equal protection clause, which include the elimination of racial discrimination and the protection of fundamental rights. Dershowitz concluded that there was, in fact, an equal protection violation in *Bush v Gore:* "the one produced by the U.S. Supreme Court's decision disenfranchising thousands of voters who cast valid ballots under Florida law, thus enhancing the value of the votes of others who also cast valid ballots."[169]

Minority Representation and Equal Protection

Drawing electoral district lines to the advantage or disadvantage of an individual, party, or group is known as **gerrymandering.** The name originated when Massachusetts Governor Elbridge Gerry devised a salamander-shaped district in 1812 to help his supporters get reelected. When the Alabama legislature changed the city boundaries of Tuskegee in the late 1950s to remove all but four or five of its four hundred black voters but none of its white voters, the Court held that such gerrymandering violated the Fifteenth Amendment.[170] Racial gerrymandering may also violate the equal protection clause of the Fourteenth Amendment.

Under Section 5 of the Voting Rights Act of 1965, reapportionment plans of certain states must be submitted to the United States Attorney General for approval before they go into effect. The law provides that in order to be approved,

---

[167]Guido Calabresi, "In Partial (but not Partisan) Praise of Principle," in Bruce Ackerman, ed., *Bush v Gore: The Question of Legitimacy* (New Haven, CT: Yale University Press, 2002), 67–83, 82.
[168]*Ibid.*, 147.
[169]Alan M. Dershowitz, *Supreme Injustice: How the High Court Hijacked Election 2000* (New York, Oxford University Press, 2001), 81.
[170]*Gomillion v Lightfoot,* 364 US 339 (1960).

plans must have neither a purpose nor effect of "denying or abridging the right to vote on account of race or color." New York State, which was subject to the requirement, enacted congressional and state legislative plans and submitted them to the Attorney General who objected to aspects of the plan for the state legislature: three Senate districts had nonwhite majorities of 91 percent, 61 percent, and 53 percent respectively. The state then devised a new plan that had nonwhite majorities between 70 percent and 75 percent in all three districts. The revised plan also increased black voting power in several other districts. Both the purpose and the effect of the plan were to ensure black representation in those districts. One of the other effects of the revised plan was to split the Hasidic community into two Assembly and two Senate districts. The Court rejected the United Jewish Organizations' claim that the Hasidic Jews had been assigned to electoral districts on the basis of race and that the arrangement diluted their voting power in violation of the Fourteenth and Fifteenth Amendments. By a vote of seven to one, the justices ruled that it was permissible for the state to deliberately increase the nonwhite majorities in certain districts to enhance the opportunity for the election of nonwhite representatives from those districts. The plan "presents no racial slur or stigma with respect to whites or any other race and does not deprive whites, as a group, of 'fair representation.'"[171] Subsequently, the Court affirmed its approval of the practice of designing districts purposely to increase the number of minority elected officials.[172]

The number of African American and Hispanic members of Congress increased in 1992 after a number of new districts with a high percentage of minorities were created. But a number of lawsuits challenged the constitutionality of those new districts. In North Carolina, for example, after two new districts elected African American representatives in 1992, several voters brought suit charging that the race-based redistricting violated the equal protection clause. A three-judge district court dismissed the suit. The Supreme Court by a five-to-four vote in *Shaw v Reno* held that allegations of racial gerrymandering present a Fourteenth Amendment issue that federal courts have jurisdiction to decide. O'Connor, who wrote the opinion for the majority, outlined the proper analysis for the lower court. First, a claim must allege that the state scheme is so irrational "that it can be understood as an effort to segregate votes into separate voting districts because of their race." Second, if the allegation is demonstrated to be true or the state does not answer it, the plan is a violation of the equal protection clause unless the state can demonstrate that it is narrowly tailored to further a compelling governmental interest.[173]

The same five-member majority applied those principles in 1995 to a challenge to one of Georgia's black majority congressional districts and found that the district court had not erred in finding that race was the predominant overriding factor motivating the drawing of the district. Therefore, the redistricting plan could not be upheld unless the state could demonstrate that it was narrowly tailored to achieve a compelling interest.[174] Justice Kennedy, who wrote

[171]*United Jewish Organizations v Carey*, 430 US 144 (1977).
[172]*Thornburg v Gingles*, 478 US 30 (1986).
[173]*Shaw v Reno*, 509 US 630 (1993).
[174]*Miller v Johnson*, 515 US 900 (1995).

the opinion for the majority, noted, moreover, that compliance with the Voting Rights Act would not constitute a compelling interest. The Court's new standard for assessing redistricting plans that create minority districts is, thus, that strict scrutiny is triggered when race is the predominant motivating factor that subordinates traditional race-neutral districting principles, including "compactness, contiguity, respect for political subdivisions or communities defined by actual shared interests."[175] Georgia's redistricting plan went back to the state legislature but the legislators could not agree on a plan so the task of redesigning the congressional districts went to the federal district court. The district court devised a plan with only one majority black district, which civil rights groups challenged. That challenge reached the Court in 1997. The same five-member majority held that one majority black district was sufficient and that the districting plan did not dilute the African American vote.[176]

The Court decided several cases concerning minority districts between 1993 and 2002 and reached similar results by the same voting alignment. Rehnquist, Kennedy, O'Connor, Scalia, and Thomas consider districting to create majority black districts as suspect racial classifications subject to the most exacting judicial scrutiny. In contrast, Breyer, Ginsburg, Souter, and Stevens have consistently objected that strict scrutiny is not necessary—in the context of apportionment racial considerations are legitimate—and that the Court's standard unnecessarily invites litigation.[177] Thus, electoral districts that are created primarily to increase minority-voting power are likely to be struck down but only by the narrowest majority of the current Court. In an important development in 2003 a five-member majority comprised of O'Connor, Rehnquist, Scalia, Kennedy, and Thomas, led the Court to adopt a new approach, which allows consideration of overall minority influence in the political process rather than the actual number of minority voters in a particular district. The dissenters expressed concern that the majority's approach might not be sufficiently protective of black voting power.[178]

Section 2

Representatives shall be apportioned among the several States according to their respective numbers, counting the whole number of persons in each State, excluding Indians not taxed. But when the right to vote at any election for the choice of electors for President and Vice President of the United States, Representatives in Congress, the Executive and Judicial officers of a State, or the members of the Legislature thereof, is denied to any of the male inhabitants of such State, being twenty-one years of age, and citizens of the United States, or in any way abridged, except for participation in rebellion, or other crime, the basis of representation therein shall be reduced in the proportion which the number of such male citizens shall bear to the whole number of male citizens twenty-one years of age in such State.

---

[175]*Ibid.*
[176]*Abrams v Johnson*, 521 US 74 (1997).
[177]See, for example, Ginsburg's dissenting opinion in *Miller v Johnson*, 515 US 900 (1995). Other cases include *Bush v Vera*, 517 US 952 (1996); and *Shaw v Hunt*, 517 US 899 (1996).
[178]*Georgia v Ashcroft*, ____ US ____ (2003). Linda Greenhouse, "In a Momentous Term, Justices Remake the Law, and the Court," *The New York Times*, July 1, 2003.

The first sentence of Section 2 negated the three-fifths clause of Article I, Section 2 (3), of the original Constitution. The second sentence provided for reduction in representation as a punishment for denying the vote to males. For some Republicans the provision was not strong enough—they objected that it implicitly acknowledged that states had the right to limit voting on the basis of race. Section 2, which introduced the word *male* in the Constitution, also reflected Abolitionists' and Republicans' betrayal of the women's rights movement whose leaders had put aside their work for women's suffrage during the war to join the campaign for emancipation and victory for the Union. The betrayal taught women's leaders that woman "must not put her trust in man" and thus helped to galvanize an independent movement for women's suffrage.[179]

Section 3

No person shall be a Senator or Representative in Congress, or elector of President and Vice President, or hold any office, civil or military, under the United States, or under any State, who, having previously taken an oath, as a member of Congress, or as an officer of the United States, or as a member of any State legislature, or as an executive or judicial officer of any State, to support the Constitution of the United States, shall have engaged in insurrection or rebellion against the same, or given aid or comfort to the enemies thereof. But Congress may by a vote of two-thirds of each House, remove such disability.

The original version of Section 3 excluded all those who had voluntarily aided the Confederacy from voting in national elections until 1870. A majority of Republicans, however, believed that disenfranchisement was "vindictive, undemocratic, and likely to arouse opposition in the North."[180] The final version imposed less harsh restrictions and on a smaller group of people by only imposing a bar against holding federal or state office to those who had held office in the United States and then committed treason by aiding the Confederacy. Section 3 made virtually the entire political leadership of the South ineligible for office but allowed unrepentant Confederates who had never held office before the war to run the new state governments. Originally, the disabilities applied to all officials—including postmasters, for example. But in 1872, Congress removed the disabilities from all "except Senators and Representatives of the Thirty-sixth and Thirty-seventh Congresses, officers in the judicial, military and naval service of the United States, heads of departments, and foreign ministers of the United States." In 1898, Congress removed all the restrictions.

Section 4

The validity of the public debt of the United States, authorized by law, including debts incurred for payment of pensions and bounties for services in suppressing insurrection or rebellion, shall not be questioned. But neither the United States nor any State shall assume or pay any debt or obligation incurred in aid of insurrection or rebellion against the United States, or any claim for the loss or emancipation of any slave; but all such debts, obligations and claims shall be held illegal and void.

---

[179]See, for example, Ellen Carol DuBois, *Feminism and Suffrage: The Emergence of an Independent Women's Movement in America*, 1848–1869.
[180]Foner, 254.

Section 4 prohibited payment of the Confederate debt but confirmed that the United States would be responsible for debts it had incurred during the war. This section also made clear that the government would not pay compensation to former slaveholders. Although the idea of compensating slaveholders was thoroughly discredited by the end of the Civil War, it had often been proposed by some opponents of slavery earlier in the nineteenth century. In 1865, President Lincoln raised the idea in a Cabinet meeting but dropped it when it met with unanimous opposition.[181]

Section 5

The Congress shall have power to enforce, by appropriate legislation, the provisions of this article.

After the Fourteenth Amendment went into effect in 1868, Congress, pursuant to its assumed authority under Section 5, enacted several statutes that attacked racial discrimination and violence against blacks by individuals and groups as well as states. For example, the Ku Klux Klan Act of 1871 provided that conspiracies to deprive citizens of the right to vote, hold office, and serve on juries would be federal crimes if the states did not act effectively against them. The law was used to prosecute Klansmen who engaged in a variety of activities to deprive black people of their rights. The Civil Rights Act of 1875 provided in part that "all persons within the jurisdiction of the United States shall be entitled to the full and equal enjoyment of the accommodations, advantages, facilities, and privileges of inns, public conveyances on land or water, theatres, and other places of public amusement."[182]

Between 1875 and 1883, the Supreme Court interpreted Congress's enforcement power narrowly, either invalidating the civil rights legislation or rendering it ineffective. It was also during this period that the Court developed the state action requirement. *United States v Harris* in 1882 involved an indictment of twenty people under the Ku Klux Klan Act of 1871 for conspiring to deprive four black men of equal protection of the law and of their right to be protected from violence while under arrest. The Court held that the conspiracy provision of the law was beyond the power of Congress, noting that when the state has not violated the provisions of the Fourteenth Amendment, the latter confers no power on Congress.[183] A year later in the *Civil Rights Cases* of 1883, the Court invalidated the Civil Rights Act of 1875 on the grounds that it was beyond the power of Congress to regulate private action because the Fourteenth Amendment prohibited only "state action of a particular character."[184] The sole dissenter, Justice John Marshall Harlan, found several grounds on which to uphold the law including Section 5 of the Fourteenth Amendment. He argued that Section 5 gave Congress the responsibility and the power to regulate the

---

[181]*Ibid.*, 74.

[182]Senator Charles Sumner, the author of the bill that became the Civil Rights Act of 1875 believed that the Declaration of Independence and Congress's power to enforce the Thirteenth Amendment provided authority for the law. The Fourteenth Amendment was only a supplement. Alfred Avins, ed., *The Reconstruction Amendments' Debates* (Richmond, VA: Virginia Commission on Constitutional Government, 1967), 597.

[183]*United States v Harris*, 106 US 629 (1882).

[184]*Civil Rights Cases*, 109 US 3 (1883).

behavior of individuals to protect the rights of blacks. Justice Joseph P. Bradley, who wrote the opinion for the majority, maintained that Congress had the authority to enact corrective legislation "such as may be necessary and proper for counteracting such laws as the states may adopt or enforce," but the Fourteenth Amendment did not give Congress the power to interfere in areas that fell within the domain of the states, nor did it empower Congress to "create a code of municipal law for the regulation of private rights."[185]

As a result of those restrictive interpretations of Section 5, it was virtually ignored. Indeed, when Congress enacted the Civil Rights Act of 1964, which included a provision prohibiting discrimination in public accommodations, Congress relied on its power to regulate interstate commerce. In 1966, however, in *Katzenbach v Morgan*, the Court revived Section 5 holding that although it may be used only to remedy constitutional violations, Congress may make the determination that certain actions violate the Constitution even if the Court has previously made a determination to the contrary. In that case the Court upheld a provision of the Voting Rights Act of 1965 that barred states from denying the right to vote to any person who has completed the sixth grade in the United States or Puerto Rico regardless of their language.[186] That provision of the federal law set aside New York's requirement that voters be able to read and write English, which the Court had upheld in 1959.[187] Justice Brennan's opinion for the majority indicated that Section 5 of the Fourteenth Amendment gives Congress the power to interpret the equal protection clause independently of the Court. If Congress may do that, Justice Harlan objected in his dissenting opinion, "then I do not see why Congress should not be able as well to exercise its Section 5 'discretion' by enacting statutes so as in effect to dilute equal protection and due process decisions by this Court."[188]

Brennan answered Harlan's objection in a footnote: Congress has the power to expand rights but "no power to restrict, abrogate, or dilute" the guarantees of the Fourteenth Amendment. **Brennan's "ratchet theory"** as it came to be called was severely criticized by legal scholars who pointed out that there is no support in the Constitution for the principle that Congress may expand but not dilute rights. Additionally, the determination regarding whether Congress had expanded or diluted rights was problematic. For example, if Congress enacted legislation declaring that human life begins at conception, would that be a dilution or an expansion of rights? Congress would argue that it expanded rights, whereas challengers would argue that it diluted constitutionally protected reproductive rights.

At any rate, Congress's expansive powers under Section 5 sustained other provisions of the Voting Rights Act in several cases.[189] The Court's expansive construction of Section 5 also helped give rise to the revival of important civil rights provisions that had not been used since the 1870s. During the civil rights

---

[185]*Ibid.*
[186]*Katzenbach v Morgan*, 384 US 641 (1966).
[187]*Lassiter v Northampton* 360 US 45 (1959).
[188]*Katzenbach v Morgan*, 384 US 641 (1966).
[189]See, for example, *South Carolina v Katzenbach*, 383 US 310 (1966); *Oregon v Mitchell*, 400 US 112 (1970); *City of Rome v United States*, 446 US 156 (1980).

era in the 1960s, the Court sustained the application of Reconstruction-era civil rights statutes forbidding conspiracies to interfere with rights secured by the Constitution and federal law and punishing violations, under color of law, of rights secured by the federal law, giving a broad reading to those statutes and implicitly to Congress's power under Section 5. The Court held that the civil rights laws applied to the Klan-style murder of Lemuel Penn and to the murders of three civil rights workers in Mississippi.[190] In one case, Justice Brennan wrote separately to give an even broader reading to the legislation than the majority and to reiterate his theory of Congress's power under Section 5. The majority found that the law did not reach private conspiracies to interfere with the exercise of the right to equal utilization of state facilities in the absence of discriminatory conduct by state officers because the equal protection clause would not reach such action. But Brennan argued that the legislation reached private conspiracies because the provision was an exercise of congressional authority under Section 5 to prohibit all conspiracies that would interfere with a right secured by the Constitution.

Subsequently, the Court has returned to a narrower construction of Congress's power to enforce the Fourteenth Amendment. For example, in *Aderand Constructors v Pena*, the majority repudiated its earlier position that Congress's power under Section 5 gives it more authority to enact affirmative action plans than the states have when it held that all affirmative action plans—state or federal—are subject to strict scrutiny.[191] Then in 1997, the Court gave its most restrictive interpretation of Congress's power pursuant to Section 5 in *City of Boerne v Flores* when it invalidated the Religious Freedom Restoration Act of 1993 (RFRA), which required a showing of a compelling interest when government action burdens the exercise of religious beliefs.[192]

Brennan's opinion in *Katzenbach v Morgan* would seem to provide authority for RFRA insofar as Congress had made the determination to expand rights under the free exercise clause beyond those that the Court had held to be protected. But in his opinion for the majority, Justice Kennedy distinguished RFRA from the Voting Rights Act, noting that in enacting the Voting Rights Act Congress had a record before it that made it clear that states commonly denied identifiable groups the right to vote whereas there was no evidence that states enacted laws based on religious bigotry. Moreover, the provisions of the Voting Rights Act that were challenged and upheld were confined to certain parts of the country where voting discrimination had been particularly prevalent. The Voting Rights Act also affected only a certain class of state laws—that is, voting laws. Specifically, the provision upheld in *Katzenbach v Morgan* was directed at a particular type of voting qualification—literacy in English—that had a long history as a means of denying the vote on the basis of race. There were no such limits in RFRA. It did not identify and counteract state laws that were likely to be unconstitutional because of their treatment of religion but brought

---

[190]*United States v Guest*, 383 US 745 (1966); *United States v Price*, 383 US 787 (1966).

[191]*Adarand Constructors v Pena*, 515 US 200 (1995). The earlier cases in which the Court seemed to accord more deference to Congress were *Fullilove v Klutznick*, 448 US 448 (1980), and *Richmond v Croson*, 488 US 469 (1989).

[192]*City of Boerne v Flores*, 521 US 507 (1997).

all laws that may incidentally burden the exercise of religion into question. RFRA was not remedial, preventive legislation, Kennedy reasoned, but "it appears, instead, to attempt a substantive change in constitutional protections." In short, RFRA was clearly not remedial but tried to alter the governing law and was therefore not within the scope of Congress's powers under Section 5 of the Fourteenth Amendment.

Following that same line of reasoning, the justices continued to constrain Congress's powers under Section 5 as well as to expand the immunity of the states pursuant to the Eleventh Amendment. In 2000, for example, the Court held that Congress did not have sufficient power to abrogate the states' sovereign immunity because the equal protection clause does not prohibit discrimination on the basis of age. Because Congress cannot create new rights, it does not have the power under Section 5 to enforce the Age Discrimination in Employment Act.[193]

AMENDMENT XV: THE RIGHT TO VOTE: BLACK MEN

Section 1

The right of citizens of the United States to vote shall not be denied or abridged by the United States or by any State on account of race, color, or previous condition of servitude.

Proposed: February 26, 1869   Declared in force by the Secretary of State: March 30, 1870

The Fourteenth Amendment stopped considerably short of guaranteeing suffrage for African Americans. Because Republicans in the Thirty-ninth Congress did not agree that blacks should be enfranchised, Section 2 of the Fourteenth Amendment left voting requirements to the states but promised to penalize states for denying the vote to black males. This arrangement reflected an effort at compromise on the part of Congressional Republicans to ensure passage of the Fourteenth Amendment. In early 1869 both houses of Congress began work on what was to become the Fifteenth Amendment. There were some proposals to include protection not only for the right to vote but also for the right to hold office and to prohibit the states from imposing voting qualifications. A few members of Congress also advocated giving suffrage to women as well as to blacks. But the Fifteenth Amendment, as it turned out, prohibited only denial of the vote on the basis of "race, color, or previous condition of servitude." Despite the Fifteenth Amendment, southern states prevented black citizens from voting by using discriminatory techniques such as racial gerrymandering, literacy tests coupled with grandfather clauses, delegation of authority to "private" all-white associations, and poll taxes. The Supreme Court gradually invalidated all of these devices. One of the first was the grandfather clause, whereby states allowed individuals who had been voters or who were de-

---

[193]*Kimel v Florida Board of Regents*, 528 US 62 (2000). For a discussion of the Eleventh Amendment, see Chapter 9.

scendants of those who had been voters before the Fourteenth or Fifteenth Amendments to register to vote even if they could not meet a literacy requirement. Thus, blacks were often prevented from voting either because they were illiterate or as a result of the discriminatory administration of literacy tests. The Court invalidated Oklahoma's grandfather clause in 1915, observing that it served to perpetuate "the very conditions which the [Fifteenth] Amendment was intended to destroy."[194] Oklahoma then enacted a more complex device providing that all individuals except those who voted in 1914, who were qualified to vote in 1916 but who failed to register between April 30 and May 11, 1916, with some exceptions for sick and absent persons who were given an additional brief period to register, were to be perpetually disenfranchised. That scheme prompted Justice Frankfurter to proclaim that the Fifteenth Amendment prohibited "sophisticated as well as simple-minded modes of discrimination. It hits onerous procedural requirements which effectively handicap exercise of the franchise by the colored race although the abstract right to vote may remain unrestricted as to race."[195] In 1965, the justices invalidated Louisiana's "understanding" tests that required individuals applying to register to vote to pass a test demonstrating sufficient understanding of any section of the United States or Louisiana Constitution. There were no objective standards for the test—the local voting registrar selected the passage and determined whether the applicant had passed. Additionally, the Board of Registration developed the test in cooperation with the state Segregation Committee.[196]

The white southern device of designating political parties private organizations beyond the reach of the Fourteenth or Fifteenth Amendments was a popular method of disenfranchising blacks. In the Democratic South, the important political decisions were made within the party and in the Democratic primary elections. The Court's state action doctrine, which applied to both the Fourteenth and Fifteenth Amendments, allowed states to continue the white primary well into the twentieth century. After the Court invalidated Texas's law excluding blacks from Democratic primaries in 1927 as a violation of the Fourteenth Amendment,[197] Texas gave the power to prescribe membership qualifications to party executive committees. The Court then found that arrangement to be in violation of the Fourteenth Amendment on the grounds that the law made the committee an agent of the state.[198] But when Texas excluded blacks from its state party convention, the Court held that the convention was an organ of a voluntary, private group rather than the state. The state was not involved; thus, there was no constitutional violation.[199]

The Court began to signal a change in its position in 1941 when it held that the federal government had the authority to regulate primary elections where state law made the primary "part of the election machinery."[200] Then in 1944

---

[194]*Guinn v United States*, 238 US 347 (1915).
[195]*Lane v Wilson*, 307 US 268, 275 (1939).
[196]*Louisiana v United States*, 380 US 145 (1965).
[197]*Nixon v Herndon*, 273 US 536 (1927).
[198]*Nixon v Condon*, 286 US 73 (1935).
[199]*Grovey v Townsend*, 295 US 45 (1935).
[200]*United States v Classic*, 313 US 299 (1941).

in *Smith v Allwright*, the Court relied on the Fifteenth Amendment to invalidate the Texas's white primary established by the state convention. Justice Stanley Reed, who wrote the opinion for the majority, found that by virtue of the statutory system that governed the selection of party nominees the party was an agency of the state insofar as it determined who the participants would be in a primary election.[201] Finally, in *Terry v Adams* the justices held that the exclusion of black voters from preprimary elections of a voluntary, "private" club of white Democrats violated the Fifteenth Amendment. The winners of the all-white preprimary usually ran unopposed in the Democratic primary. In his opinion for the majority, Justice Black noted that although the Fifteenth Amendment does not apply to "social or business clubs," it applies to any election in which public officials are chosen.[202]

The activities of civil rights organizations like the Southern Christian Leadership Conference (SCLC) beginning in the late 1950s included voter registration drives and demonstrations protesting the disenfranchisement of African Americans. Both were commonly met with violence. Congress enacted the first civil rights legislation since 1875 in 1957 and 1960. The Civil Rights Act of 1957 created the office of assistant attorney general for civil rights and upgraded the civil rights unit to a division of the Justice Department. The new laws authorized the Justice Department to go into three-judge federal district courts to seek relief for violations of voting rights. Despite such support, litigation proved to be grossly inadequate to the task of bringing an end to voter discrimination. The march that Martin Luther King Jr. and the SCLC organized in Selma, Alabama, in early 1965 was designed to convince the Johnson Administration and Congress of the need for a more effective voting-rights bill. The confrontations between nonviolent demonstrators including children and Selma Sheriff Jim Clark's fire hoses and police dogs appeared on national television. Three Unitarian ministers who had come to Selma to participate in the march were beaten with clubs and one died. Those events generated massive support for federal action to protect voting rights: "Tens of thousands of letters and telegrams poured into Washington petitioning for voting-rights legislation, a plea echoed by most of the nation's press."[203]

On March 15, 1965, President Johnson delivered an address to a joint session of Congress and announced that he would submit a bill to "establish a simple uniform standard which cannot be used, however ingenious the effort, to flout the Constitution." Johnson proclaimed, "Every American citizen must have an equal right to vote. There is no reason which can excuse the denial of that right. There is no duty which weighs more heavily on us than the duty to ensure that right."[204] Congress enacted and the president signed the Voting Rights Act less than five months after the Johnson Administration introduced the bill to Congress.[205] Although Johnson's Attorney General Nicholas Katzenbach drafted a law several months before the Selma protests, the events there

---

[201]*Smith v Allwright*, 321 US 649 (1944).
[202]*Terry v Adams*, 345 US 461 (1953).
[203]Sitcoff, 193.
[204]*Ibid.*, 194.
[205]Howard Ball, "The Voting Rights Act of 1965," in Kermit L. Hall, ed., *The Oxford Companion to the Supreme Court of the United States* (New York: Oxford University Press, 1992), 903.

seemed to have propelled the federal government to action. We discuss the Voting Rights Act at the end of this chapter after considering the Court's early interpretations of Congress's power to enforce the Fifteenth Amendment.

Section 2

The Congress shall have power to enforce this article by appropriate legislation.

After the ratification of the Fifteenth Amendment, Congress promptly passed enforcement legislation beginning with the Enforcement Act of 1870, which dealt primarily with voting rights. The law forbade state officials from discriminating among voters on the basis of race and authorized the president to appoint election supervisors. It also prohibited bribery or intimidation of voters and conspiracies to prevent citizens from exercising their constitutional rights. The Supreme Court's early interpretation of Congress's power to enforce the Fifteenth Amendment paralleled its restrictive interpretation of Section 5 of the Fourteenth Amendment—it focused on the question of whether the law exceeded Congress's power by regulating individual as opposed to state action. For example, in 1876 the Court dismissed an indictment of a Kentucky election official who refused to register a black voter for a state election, holding that the Enforcement Act of 1870 was too broadly drawn. In *United States v Cruikshank,* the Court used the same justification when it dismissed the federal indictments of ninety-six Louisiana whites who were charged with "injur[ing] for having voted at an election."[206] Still, the Court held in 1884 that Congress had the power to protect the right to vote in federal elections against deprivation by private individuals.[207]

In the **Voting Rights Act of 1965,** Congress set about enforcing the Fifteenth Amendment by not only securing the right to vote for African Americans but also ensuring that their votes are not diluted by electoral districting schemes. The Voting Rights Act of 1965 targeted certain sections of the country where the rates of black voting had been the lowest and where a discriminatory test or other device had been in effect in 1964. In 1965, the states covered were Alabama, Alaska, Georgia, Louisiana, Mississippi, South Carolina, and Virginia, plus parts of Arizona, Hawaii, Idaho, and North Carolina. The law authorized the United States Attorney General to appoint federal examiners to supervise registration and voting procedures and, if necessary, to register voters directly. Section 5 of the Voting Rights Act—the "preclearance" section—prohibited the covered states from enacting any changes in their election laws or procedures without approval—preclearance—from the attorney general.[208] The attorney general, moreover, could not give approval unless the state demonstrated that the changes would not have a discriminatory effect. Finally, the Voting Rights Act prohibited literacy tests nationwide.[209] The law has been extended and amended several times—1970, 1975, and 1982. As revised in 1982, Section 2 of the Voting Rights Act—which applies nationwide—allows a voter to challenge a voting practice or

---

[206]*United States v Reese,* 92 214 (1876); *United States v Cruikshank,* 92 US 542 (1876).
[207]*Ex Parte Yarborough,* 110 US 651 (1884).
[208]The law also authorizes a federal district court in Washington, D.C., to give approval but most changes have been precleared by the attorney general.
[209]The prohibition on literacy tests was made nationwide in 1970 and it was made permanent in 1975.

procedure by showing that the results, based on a totality of the evidence presented, are racially discriminatory.[210]

The Voting Rights Act established a system of regulations constituting an unprecedented amount of federal intervention into the states' traditional authority to set qualifications for voting. Nevertheless, the Supreme Court upheld it in 1966 in *South Carolina v Katzenbach*, declaring that "Congress may use any rational means to effectuate the constitutional prohibition of racial discrimination in voting" and that "Congress has full remedial powers to effectuate the constitutional prohibition against racial discrimination in voting."[211] The extent of Congress's powers under Section 2 of the Fifteenth Amendment, Chief Justice Warren noted in his opinion for the majority, is the same as it is for cases concerning the express powers of Congress with relation to the reserved powers of the states. For Warren, the reach of Congress's power was captured by Chief Justice Marshall's opinion in *McCulloch v Maryland* in which he said: "Let the end be legitimate, let it be within the scope of the constitution, and all means which are appropriate, which are plainly adapted to that end, which are not prohibited, but consistent with the letter and spirit of the constitution, are constitutional."[212] In subsequent cases, the justices have upheld all the provisions of the Voting Rights Act except the one lowering the voting age to eighteen in elections for state and local officials.[213]

Litigation regarding the Voting Rights Act in the past several years has not concerned denial of the right to vote but rather the problems of vote dilution and the racial composition of districts as discussed earlier in the context of the equal protection clause of the Fourteenth Amendment.

QUESTIONS

1. How convincing do you find the argument that the Thirteenth Amendment was intended to do more than nullify the laws protecting slavery? Could it have been designed to extend the protection of fundamental rights and equality to the newly freed slaves?[214]

2. The Court's interpretation in the *Slaughterhouse Cases* of the privileges or immunities clause does not appear to be consistent with the understanding of the Framers of the Fourteenth Amendment. How, then, might that interpretation be explained? Can it be justified? Is there any reason that a majority of the Court might have wished to render the clause ineffective as a protection of the rights of individuals against infringement by the states?

3. Did the Court reaffirm the central holding of *Roe v Wade* in *Planned Parenthood v Casey*? Or did the justices, in effect, overrule *Roe*? To what extent does the undue burden standard protect a woman's right to decide to terminate a pregnancy?

---

[210]Ball, 904.
[211]*South Carolina v Katzenbach*, 383 US 301 (1966).
[212]*Ibid.*, quoting *McCulloch v Maryland*, 17 US 316 (1819).
[213]*Oregon v Mitchell*, 400 US 112 (1970). The Twenty-sixth Amendment, proposed and ratified in 1971, set the age at eighteen for all elections.
[214]See, for example, Jacobus tenBroek, *Equal under Law* (New York: Collier, 1969).

4. What weaknesses can you identify in Warren's opinion in *Brown v Board of Education?* Did he adequately resolve the question of the intent of the Framers? Was that an important question? What kind of criticism did he engender by considering the psychological effects on black children of segregation? Why did the Court not rely on the Justice John Marshall Harlan's argument in *Plessy* that the Constitution is color-blind? Is there any way that the Court might have handled *Brown v Board of Education* differently that would have resulted in less resistance and more genuine integration?

5. The Court declared that racial classifications are inherently suspect and subject to strict judicial scrutiny in 1944 in *Korematsu v United States.* Why do you think the Court did not use that rationale or the one from the *Carolene Products* footnote concerning the judiciary's obligation to protect "discrete and insular minorities" to invalidate legally imposed segregation in education in *Brown v Board of Education?*

6. Should sex be a suspect classification? What policies would change if the Court were to move to such an approach?

7. Why do you think the Court declined to apply heightened scrutiny to classifications based on sexual orientation in *Romer v Evans* (1996)? Should sexual orientation be a suspect classification?[215]

8. Compare the Court's interpretation of Congress's authority under Section 5 of the Fourteenth Amendment in *Katzenbach v Morgan* (1966) on the one hand, and *City of Boerne v Flores* (1997) and *Kimel v Florida Board of Regents* (2000), on the other. What differences can you find? Do you agree with Justice Kennedy in *City of Boerne* that in the context of Congress's power to enforce the Fourteenth Amendment the Voting Rights Act is very different from the Religious Freedom Restoration Act? To what would you attribute the differences between *Morgan* and the two more recent cases—the personnel of the Court, the political context, a genuine legal distinction between the two cases?

9. Is Congress's power under Section 2 of the Fifteenth Amendment broader than it is under Section 5 of the Fourteenth? Examine Chief Justice Warren's opinion in *South Carolina v Katzenbach* (1966) and compare it with *City of Boerne* and *Morgan.*

10. In *The Votes that Counted: How the Court Decided the 2000 Presidential Election,* Howard Gillman raises a question about the Supreme Court's reasoning in *Bush v Gore:* "it was not clear why the concern about unequal treatment was a problem with the recount but not, for example, with the original count, which was based on so many different ballot-counting practices throughout the various counties in Florida."[216] Can you find an answer in the Court's *per curiam* opinion?

---

[215]For a useful discussion, see Gerstmann.
[216]Gillman, *The Votes That Counted,* 142.

KEY TERMS

The Emancipation Proclamation
"badges and incidents" of slavery
Black Codes
Joint Committee on Reconstruction
Civil Rights Act of 1866
doctrine of substantive due process
Carolene Products footnote
right to privacy
trimester scheme
undue burden standard
protected liberty interest
"state action" requirement
"separate but equal" doctrine
NAACP Legal Defense and
    Educational Fund Inc.

The Southern Manifesto
de facto segregation
rational basis test
strict scrutiny
moderate—or heightened scrutiny
exceedingly persuasive justification
fundamental rights under the equal
    protection clause
rationale for affirmative action
minority set-aside programs
malapportionment
reapportionment
gerrymandering
Brennan's "ratchet theory"
Voting Rights Act of 1965

SUGGESTIONS FOR FURTHER READING

Please note that the "Suggestions for Further Reading" at the end of Chapter 4 provides a list of books, articles, and Internet sources about the contested election of 2000 and the Supreme Court's role in resolving it.

Ball, Howard. "The Voting Rights Act of 1965." In Kermit L. Hall, ed., *The Oxford Companion to the Supreme Court of the United States.* New York: Oxford University Press, 1992.

Bell, Derrick. *Faces at the Bottom of the Well: The Permanence of Racism.* New York: Basic Books, 1992.

Bergmann, Barbara R. *In Defense of Affirmative Action.* New York: Basic Books, 1996.

Carter, Stephen L. *Reflections of an Affirmative Action Baby.* New York: Basic Books, 1991.

Cortner, Richard C. *The Apportionment Cases.* Knoxville: University of Tennessee Press, 1970.

Davidson, Chandler, and Bernard Grofman, eds. *Quiet Revolution in the South: The Impact of the Voting Rights Act, 1965–1990.* Princeton, NJ: Princeton University Press, 1994.

Epstein, Lee, and Joseph F. Kobylka. *The Supreme Court and Legal Change: Abortion and the Death Penalty.* Chapel Hill, NC: University of North Carolina Press, 1992, Chapters 5 and 6.

Farber, Daniel A., and Suzanna Sherry. *A History of the American Constitution.* St. Paul, MN: West Publishing Co., 1990, Chapters 9–12.

Fiscus, Ronald J. *The Constitutional Logic of Affirmative Action.* Durham, NC: Duke University Press, 1992.

Foner, Eric. *Reconstruction: America's Unfinished Revolution 1863–1877.* New York: Harper and Row, 1988.

Garvey, John H., and T. Alexander Aleinikoff. *Modern Constitutional Theory: A Reader,* 3rd ed. St. Paul, MN: West Publishing Co., 1994.

Gerstmann, Evan. *The Constitutional Underclass: Gays, Lesbians, and the Failure of Class-Based Equal Protection.* Chicago, IL: University of Chicago Press, 1999.

Gillman, Howard. *The Constitution Besieged: The Rise and Demise of Lochner Era Police Powers Jurisprudence.* Durham, NC: Duke University Press, 1993.

Howard, John R. *The Shifting Wind: The Supreme Court and Civil Rights from Reconstruction to Brown.* Albany, NY: State University of New York Press, 1999.

Hyman, Harold M., and William M. Wiecek. *Equal Justice under Law: Constitutional Development 1835–1875.* New York: Harper and Row, 1982.

Kluger, Richard. *Simple Justice: The History of* Brown v Board of Education *and Black America's Struggle for Equality.* New York: Vintage Books, 1977.

Lawrence v Texas, No. 02-102, Brief for Petitioners. Available: http://supreme.lp.findlaw.com/supreme_court/briefs/02-102/02-102.mer.pet.pdf.

Lofgren, Charles A. *The Plessy Case: A Legal-Historical Interpretation.* New York: Oxford University Press, 1987.

McDonagh, Eileen L. *Breaking the Abortion Deadlock: From Choice to Consent.* New York: Oxford University Press, 1996.

Noonan, John T. Jr. *Narrowing the Nation's Power: The Supreme Court Sides with the States.* Berkeley, CA: University of California Press, 2002.

O'Connor, Karen. *No Neutral Ground? Abortion Politics in an Age of Absolutes.* Boulder, CO: Westview Press, 1996.

Orfield, Gary, Susan E. Eaton, and the Harvard Project on School Desegregation. *Dismantling Desegregation: The Quiet Reversal of Brown v Board of Education.* New York: The New Press, 1996.

"Sodomy Laws." Available: http://www.sodomylaws.org/.

Steele, Shelby. *The Content of Our Character: A New Vision of Race in America.* New York: Harper Collins, 1990.

tenBroek, Jacobus. *Equal under Law.* New York: Collier, 1969.

Tushnet, Mark V. *Making Civil Rights Law: Thurgood Marshall and the Supreme Court, 1936–1961.* New York: Oxford University Press, 1994.

11

THE PROGRESSIVE ERA

After ratification of the Fifteenth Amendment in 1870, no amendments were added to the Constitution for the remainder of the nineteenth century. Then, beginning with the Sixteenth Amendment in 1913 four amendments were ratified over a period of seven years. Amendments Sixteen, Seventeen, Eighteen, and Nineteen reflect the goals, which were not entirely consistent, of the **Progressive movement**.[1]

Progressivism was a middle-class urban movement that had begun with demands for reforms such as instituting regulations on utility rates, providing better municipal services, and ridding the cities of corrupt party bosses and machines. Building on the foundations of the earlier Populist movement, Progressivism grew into a nationwide movement in the early years of the twentieth century calling for a wide variety of reforms designed to help America adjust to the dramatic changes brought by industrialization, new technologies, the rise of the corporation, and urban living. The Progressive movement encompassed disparate groups including state and local politicians, settlement house workers, professional administrators, businessmen, intellectuals, journalists, and two presidents of the United States, Theodore Roosevelt and Woodrow Wilson.

Progressivism was distinguished by three basic characteristics. First, Progressives simultaneously accepted large-scale business and industry and were outraged by what they considered to be its worst consequences: the callous pursuit of wealth, the exploitation of workers, and the living conditions of urban slum dwellers. Second, Progressives shared a faith in progress—a belief in human ability to improve the environment and the conditions of life. Third, Progressives were convinced that government intervention in economic and social affairs would be necessary to improve those conditions and they were generally in agreement that reforms would take the form of legislation and other public policies. Historian Richard Hofstadter noted that the Progressives perceived American life to be dominated by corruption and they were firmly convinced that the problem lay in the widespread breaking of the law. Thus, "if the laws are the right laws, and if they can be enforced by the right men, . . . everything would be better." Additionally, Hofstadter noted that the Progressives stressed

---

[1] The following introduction to the amendments of the Progressive era draws heavily from the discussion of Progressivism in Sue Davis, *American Political Thought: Four Hundred Years of Ideas and Ideologies* (Englewood Cliffs, NJ: Prentice Hall, 1996).

universal personal responsibility and personal guilt. In that view, Progressivism conveyed the message that because everyone was responsible for the ugly state of affairs all citizens should participate in the movement for reform. Hofstadter also observed in the Progressive outlook an emphasis on moral rather than material values and a tendency to disparage material achievement.[2]

The overarching theme of Progressivism was a spirit of reform aimed at making corporate industrialism compatible with a democratic society. Its predominant goal was to refashion American government so that it would be capable of containing the private power of business and industry. Many of the reforms, however, were inconsistent and motivated by diverse and contradictory goals. Some Progressives, for example, wanted to expand democracy by increasing the influence that ordinary people had over government. Others wanted to make governments more efficient by concentrating authority in experts. One goal of returning power to the people that was manifested in mechanisms of direct democracy—such as the direct election of Senators provided in the Seventeenth Amendment, the initiative, referendum, recall, the direct primary—clashed with another: making government efficient and centralized. The goal of efficiency envisioned government managed by an elite body of administrators and experts—city commissions and city managers.

There were also sharp differences among Progressives who focused on social reform. Some advocated reforms designed to improve the lives of immigrants from southern and eastern Europe; others advocated legislation to prevent "alien races" from entering the country. One group of reformers, those who founded and worked in the settlement houses, were committed to improving urban life. Other social reformers, such as physicians, social workers, and educators, were motivated by a desire to apply their skills as trained professionals to social problems. Still others used social institutions and the law as instruments of social control. The disfranchisement of African Americans and official segregation was one of the Progressive reforms in the South. The strain of Progressivism that emphasized social control was most evident in the Prohibition movement, which culminated with the Eighteenth Amendment in 1919.

AMENDMENT XVI: INCOME TAXES

> The Congress shall have power to lay and collect taxes on incomes, from whatever source derived, without apportionment among the several States, and without regard to any census or enumeration.
>
> Proposed July 12, 1909   Declared in force by the secretary of state February 25, 1913

The original Constitution in Article I, Section 8, gave Congress the power to "lay and collect Taxes," but Article I, Section 9, forbade imposing direct taxes unless they were apportioned among the states in "Proportion to the Census."

---

[2]Richard Hofstadter, *The Age of Reform: From Bryan to F.D.R.* (New York: Vintage Books, 1955), 203–214.

Thus, if income taxes were **"direct taxes,"** they would be unconstitutional because it would be impossible to apportion them among the states according to their populations.

In 1881, the Supreme Court sustained the 1862 income tax that Congress enacted to help finance the Civil War against the challenge that it was a direct tax. The Court held that direct taxes only included capitation taxes and taxes on land. But in 1895 by a vote of five to four in *Pollock v Farmers Loan & Trust Company,* the justices held that the income tax law of 1894—a flat 2 percent tax on incomes above $4,000—was a direct tax.[3] To the Progressives, the decision in *Pollack* reflected the Court's determination to read the philosophy of laissez-faire into the Constitution. A majority of the Court seemed to have accepted arguments advanced by conservative business interests exemplified by Representative Bourke Cockran. The income tax bill, Cockran argued, was "an assault on Democratic institutions. . . . I oppose it because it is a tax on industry and thrift and is therefore a manifestation of hostility to that desire for success which is the main spring of human activity."[4]

Although the income tax issue was settled constitutionally, politically it remained a source of conflict. The issue helped to create a reform-minded coalition between Progressive Republicans and Democrats. Income tax bills were introduced in Congress despite the Supreme Court's decision. President Theodore Roosevelt endorsed the idea of an income tax in 1907 and in 1908 the Democratic Party platform favored an income tax. An income tax bill was introduced in the Senate in 1909 as an amendment to a tariff bill. Opponents of the measure, convinced that ratification would be impossible, urged its sponsor to drop it in favor of a constitutional amendment. Thus, a constitutional amendment giving Congress the power to tax incomes was introduced in Congress, passed, and ratified by the requisite three-fourths of the states. The northeastern states were the most reluctant to give their approval, prompting legal scholar Alan P. Grimes to comment on the fact that the "champions of equality when the issue was slavery had difficulty accepting this principle when the issue touched upon wealth."[5]

The Sixteenth Amendment overruled *Pollack* and settled the question of the constitutionality of the income tax. It reflected the Progressive impulse to rein in the growing power of private wealth as well as the recognition of the need of a more active role for government to improve the conditions of life, particularly for the poor.

AMENDMENT XVII: DIRECT ELECTION OF SENATORS

> The Senate of the United States shall be composed of two Senators from each State, elected by the people thereof for six years; and each Senator shall have one vote. The electors in each State shall have the qualifications requisite for electors of the most numerous branch of the State legislatures.

---

[3]*Pollock v Farmers Loan & Trust Co.,* 158 US 601 (1895).
[4]As quoted in Alan P. Grimes, *Democracy and the Amendments to the Constitution* (Lexington, MA: Lexington Books, 1978), 70.
[5]*Ibid.,* 74.

When vacancies happen in the representation of any State in the Senate, the executive authority of such State shall issue writs of election to fill such vacancies: *Provided,* that the legislature of any State may empower the executive thereof to make temporary appointments until the people fill the vacancies by election as the legislature may direct.

This amendment shall not be so construed as to affect the election or term of any Senator chosen before it becomes valid as part of the Constitution.

Proposed May 13, 1912 Declared in force by the secretary of state May 31, 1913.

In the last decade of the nineteenth century, reformers condemned the corrupt politics of political bosses in the cities; the bosses often selected candidates for state legislatures and delivered the votes to get them elected. The party bosses and their hand-picked candidates were allied with corporate wealth and stood as an obstacle to reform. The Senate, selected by state legislatures, formed a third level in the system that was controlled by corporate interests. Reformers constantly emphasized the corrupting influence of corporate power and wealth on the political system and pointed to the undemocratically chosen Senate as a major contributor to the problem. From that perspective, democratizing the political system would be a major step in reclaiming power from large corporations and their allies and giving it to the people.

In the 1890s, the House of Representatives several times proposed and passed a constitutional amendment providing for **direct election of senators** by a wide margin. But the Senate refused to let the matter come up for a vote. By 1911, more than half of the states had instituted direct election of senators by directing their state legislatures to vote for the candidate for senator who had received the largest number of votes in a preferential primary. Still, the system was uneven and state legislatures could refuse to vote for the candidates chosen by the people.

In 1911, the House passed a Democratic proposal for an amendment providing for direct election of senators that included a "race rider" giving the state legislatures the authority to regulate elections. The Senate, however, passed an amendment without that provision, and the House eventually deleted theirs over the objection of southern Democrats. The requisite three-fourths of the states ratified within eleven months although the southern states, with the exception of Louisiana, did not act on it.

AMENDMENT XVIII: PROHIBITION

Section 1

After one year from the ratification of this article the manufacture, sale, or transportation of intoxicating liquors within, the importation thereof into, or the exportation thereof from the United States and all territory subject to the jurisdiction thereof for beverage purposes is hereby prohibited.

Section 2

The Congress and the several States shall have concurrent power to enforce this article by appropriate legislation.

Section 3

This article shall be inoperative unless it shall have been ratified as an amendment to the Constitution by the legislatures of the several States as provided in the Constitution, within seven years from the date of the submission hereof to the States by the Congress.

Proposed December 18, 1917   Declared in force by the acting secretary of state January 29, 1919.

Although the Sixteenth and Seventeenth Amendments reflected Progressive goals of bringing corporate power under control and giving more power to the people, the Eighteenth Amendment manifested a different strain of Progressivism—the one that emphasized social control. Sponsored by white Protestant fundamentalists, the **Prohibition movement** flourished in the South. Between 1907 and 1915, eight southern states adopted Prohibition. It primarily had the effect of limiting the sale of alcohol to blacks and poor whites. By 1917, fourteen more states throughout the West had adopted Prohibition. The Prohibition movement was predominantly white, middle-class, rural, and Protestant. The fact of the matter was that the effects of a prohibition amendment would be felt mostly in the urban centers and would serve to keep liquor away from the growing population of new immigrants and other members of the urban underclass.

The Eighteenth Amendment might also be viewed as a continuation of the process that began with the Sixteenth Amendment—a way of purifying politics. From that perspective, one way of ridding politics of corruption was to take power away from wealth and corporate interests and give it to the people. But the view of the advocates of Prohibition was that the people were corruptible as well and alcohol was one of the prime sources of corruption in society. Consumption of alcoholic beverages led to habitual drunkenness, unemployment, beaten and hungry children, abused and abandoned wives, and poverty.

Efforts to limit or ban alcohol consumption began long before the Progressive era. The earliest temperance society was organized in 1808, and in 1833 the United States Temperance Union was created—its affiliated societies totaled more than a million members. In the early 1850s, temperance work resulted in the adoption of various types of legislative prohibition in several states. In the 1840s, large numbers of women joined the temperance movement, and in the 1870s had their own **Woman's Christian Temperance Union.** Women dominated the temperance movement until the turn of the century when the Anti-Saloon League rose to prominence. Many women worked for temperance who were not involved in the woman's rights movement, but most of the leaders of the women's rights movement were also involved in temperance work. The two movements overlapped on some major issues. Even by the end of the nineteenth century, women had only limited legal rights and most had virtually no economic security except that which was provided by husbands or male relatives. The "drunkard" husband as head of the household was likely to drink his wages and leave his wife destitute with no ability to protect her children. Both women's rights and temperance wanted women to be free of the sort of suffering and degradation caused by husbands who drank excessively.

A prohibition amendment was first proposed in 1876 and some forty more times before 1917.[6] It was in that year that both houses of Congress passed the amendment by bipartisan majorities that exceeded the required two-thirds. Most of the opposition came from northern urban centers. Opponents were responsible for the provision delaying Prohibition for a year after ratification and for the seven-year deadline after which the amendment would expire if it had not been ratified. That strategy failed as forty-four state legislatures ratified within thirteen months. By 1922, every state but Rhode Island had ratified it.

In 1919, Congress overrode President Woodrow Wilson's veto and adopted the **Volstead Act** to enforce Prohibition. The law defined as intoxicating any beverage containing more than 0.5 percent alcohol, which meant that beer and wine were banned. The Supreme Court upheld the Volstead Act in the *National Prohibition Cases* in 1920 and declared that the Eighteenth Amendment had been properly enacted.[7] In 1922, the justices upheld the concurrent powers of state and federal enforcement,[8] approved warrantless automobile searches,[9] and wiretaps for telephone surveillance.[10]

The Eighteenth Amendment is the only amendment to the Constitution that has been repealed—the Twenty-first Amendment, ratified in December 1933, repealed Prohibition.

AMENDMENT XIX: THE RIGHT TO VOTE: WOMEN

The right of citizens of the United States to vote shall not be denied or abridged by the United States or by any State on account of sex.

Congress shall have power to enforce this article by appropriate legislation.

Proposed June 4, 1919   Declared in force by the secretary of state August 26, 1920

At the first women's rights convention at Seneca Falls in 1848, which marked the beginning of the organized women's rights movement in America, Elizabeth Cady Stanton presented a series of resolutions in her Declaration of Sentiments. One of the resolutions was a demand for recognition of women's right to vote. The hundred or so people who attended the convention approved all the resolutions unanimously except that one, which a number of participants worried would make the meeting look ridiculous. When Elizabeth Cady Stanton died in 1902, she was still working for suffrage but it was not to become a reality for another eighteen years.

In 1875 in *Minor v Happersatt*, the Supreme Court unanimously held that the right to vote was not one of the privileges or immunities of citizens of the United States protected by the Fourteenth Amendment. Thus, although Virginia

---

[6]Richard B. Bernstein with Jerome Agel, *Amending America: If We Love the Constitution So Much, Why Do We Keep Trying to Change It?* (New York: Times Books, 1993), 173.
[7]*State of Rhode Island v Palmer*, 253 US 350 (1920).
[8]*United States v Lanza*, 260 US 397 (1922).
[9]*Carroll v United States*, 267 US 132 (1925).
[10]*Olmstead v United States*, 277 US 438 (1928).

Minor was a citizen under the Constitution, the state of Missouri had the authority to determine the qualifications of its voters.[11]

Between 1890 when Wyoming was admitted to statehood with women's suffrage and 1919 when Congress proposed the Nineteenth Amendment to the states, thirty states had granted women some form of suffrage either by state constitutional amendment or legislation. Thirteen of those permitted women to vote in presidential elections, seventeen recognized their right to vote in all elections, and eighteen states, including all of the South, did not allow women to vote at all.[12]

Beginning in 1878 at least one proposal for an amendment was proposed in each Congress.[13] But both houses voted on the proposed amendment for the first time in 1915. Alan P. Grimes noted that members of Congress from the West supported the amendment, whereas those from the South opposed it and those from the East were split. The South, which had supported the Prohibition Amendment, did not support women's suffrage at least in part because it had the potential to reopen the issue of racial discrimination in voting. As noted in Chapter 10, white southerners managed to circumvent the Fourteenth and Fifteenth Amendments and deny virtually all black citizens the right to vote. A women's suffrage amendment, in their view, not only raised the prospects of black women exercising the franchise but also the possibility that federal officials would descend on the South to see that the Constitution was observed.

In January 1918, after debating for two months, Congress passed the amendment by exactly a two-thirds majority. The Senate's vote fell short of the necessary two-thirds, however. But the following year, Congress convened in special session and both houses finally passed the amendment by the necessary two-thirds vote. All the southern states rejected it. Nevertheless, the requisite number of states had ratified by August 1920.

The Nineteenth Amendment was consistent with the values and goals of Progressivism because it expanded democracy. But there was another important connection between Progressivism and women's suffrage that may have encouraged Congress to propose and the states to ratify in 1920. Beginning in about 1890, the women's suffrage movement shifted strategies and moved away from its earlier focus on natural rights and equality to support women's demand for the ballot. Movement leaders developed an argument that centered on the positive effect that voting women would have on American politics—the **expediency approach.** The campaign for women's suffrage increasingly emphasized that women's special qualities were needed in politics. Once they had the vote, they would destroy the power of big business and the corrupt political machines and restore power to the people. They would also use government to improve society by promoting child-labor legislation and pure food laws to protect children and consumers.

The Progressive era amendments manifest a discernible pattern. Three of the four reflect the Progressive impulse to take power away from the corrupt

---

[11]*Minor v Happersatt*, 88 US 162 (1875).
[12]Bernstein, 132.
[13]*Ibid.*

politicians who were in league with corporate industrialists and return it to the people. The income tax and prohibition amendments also reflect a willingness to rely on the federal government to improve the conditions of society. The Eighteenth Amendment does not fit the pattern of democratization. Still, Prohibition reflected another strain of Progressivism—social control. Interestingly, the amendment that does not fit the pattern of democratization was repealed after only fourteen years. At least one commentator has noted that the Progressive era amendments lay the groundwork for further democratization of the Constitution.[14]

QUESTIONS

1. Considering the Progressive era amendments as a whole how do they compare to the Reconstruction amendments?

2. What do Amendments Sixteen, Seventeen, Eighteen, and Nineteen have in common?

3. Do you think a majority of the proponents of Prohibition actually considered the elimination of the consumption of alcoholic beverages to be an important goal in itself? If not, what were their goals? What did they hope to achieve with prohibition? Were any of their hopes realized?

4. What might have changed between 1915 when the women's suffrage amendment failed to be passed in Congress and 1919 when Congress approved it? Of the two arguments for women's suffrage—natural rights and expediency—which was likely to be the more effective given the context of the politics of the Progressive era?

KEY TERMS

Progressive movement
direct taxes
direct election of senators
Prohibition movement
Woman's Christian Temperance
   Union

Volstead Act
expediency approach to
   women's suffrage

SUGGESTIONS FOR FURTHER READING

Bernstein, Richard B., with Jerome Agel. *Amending America: If We Love the Constitution So Much, Why Do We Keep Trying to Change It?* New York: Times Books, 1993.

Bordin, Ruth. *Woman and Temperance: The Quest for Power and Liberty, 1873–1900.* New Brunswick, NJ: Rutgers University Press, 1990.

DuBois, Ellen Carol. *Feminism and Suffrage: The Emergence of an Independent Women's Movement in America, 1848–1869.* Ithaca, NY: Cornell University Press, 1978.

---

[14]*Ibid.,* 134.

Goldman, Eric. *Rendezvous with Destiny: A History of Modern American Reform*, Revised ed. New York: Vintage Books, 1956.

Graham, Sara Hunter. *Woman Suffrage and the New Democracy*. New Haven, CT: Yale University Press, 1996.

Grimes, Alan P. *Democracy and the Amendments to the Constitution*. Lexington, MA: Lexington Books, 1978.

Kraditor, Aileen. *The Ideas of the Woman Suffrage Movement, 1890–1920*. New York: Columbia University Press, 1965.

Kyvig, David E. *Alcohol and Order: Perspectives on National Prohibition*. Westport, CT: Greenwood Press, 1985.

Link, Arthur S., and Richard L. McCormick. *Progressivism*. Arlington Heights, IL: Harlan Davidson, 1983.

Noble, David W. *The Paradox of Progressive Thought*. Minneapolis, MN: University of Minnesota Press, 1958.

12

1933 TO 1992

At first glance it may appear that the last seven amendments to the Constitution are simply a collection of miscellaneous provisions. But a more cohesive image of this final group of constitutional amendments begins to emerge if we arrange them according to theme. The Twentieth, Twenty-second, and Twenty-fifth Amendments are all concerned with the president—when terms end, the two-term limit, presidential succession, disability, and vice presidential replacement. All three promote accountability and stability in government. The Twenty-third, Twenty-fourth, and Twenty-sixth Amendments, like the Fifteenth and Nineteenth Amendments earlier, are democratizing provisions that added voters to the electorate and placed additional limits on the ability of states to set voting qualifications. The Twentieth Amendment is also democratizing insofar as it abolished the arrangement whereby members of Congress who had already been voted out of office continued to make laws. The Twenty-seventh Amendment, ratified more than two hundred years after it was proposed as part of the Bill of Rights in the First Congress, is something of a fluke. Nevertheless, it is consistent with the predominant constitutional principle of checking the powers of elected officials to alleviate the potential for abuse, which runs through the structure of the Constitution, the Bill of Rights, and the Progressive era amendments, and is also reflected in the Twenty-second Amendment.

AMENDMENT XX: THE LAME-DUCK AMENDMENT

Section 1

The terms of the President and Vice President shall end at noon on the 20th day of January, and the terms of Senators and Representatives at noon on the 3d day of January, of the years in which such terms would have ended if this article had not been ratified; and the terms of their successors shall then begin.

Section 2

The Congress shall assemble at least once in every year, and such meeting shall begin at noon on the 3d day of January, unless they shall by law appoint a different day.

Section 3

If, at the time fixed for the beginning of the term of the President, the President elect shall have died, the Vice President elect shall become President. If a

President shall not have been chosen before the time fixed for the beginning of his term, or if the President elect shall have failed to qualify, then the Vice President elect shall act as President until a President shall have qualified; and the Congress may by law provide for the case wherein neither a President elect nor a Vice President elect shall have qualified, declaring who shall then act as President, or the manner in which one who is to act shall be selected, and such person shall act accordingly until a President or Vice President shall have qualified.

Section 4

The Congress may by law provide for the case of the death of any of the persons from whom the House of Representatives may choose a President whenever the right of choice shall have devolved upon them, and for the case of the death of any of the persons from whom the Senate may choose a Vice President whenever the right of choice shall have devolved upon them.

Section 5

Sections 1 and 2 shall take effect on the 15th day of October following the ratification of this article.

Section 6

This article shall be inoperative unless it shall have been ratified as an amendment to the Constitution by the legislatures of three-fourths of the several States within seven years from the date of its submission.

Proposed March 3, 1932   Declared in force by the secretary of state February 6, 1933

Although the Twentieth Amendment may seem to represent simply a technical change in the Constitution it was actually one of the final achievements of the Progressive movement insofar as it promoted efficiency and accountability in government. The amendment corrected a problem in the timing of terms of office that arose purely by accident but endured for almost a hundred and fifty years. The delegates to the Philadelphia Convention provided in Article VII that the Constitution would take effect after nine states had ratified it. The ninth state ratified on June 21, 1788; and Congress, still acting under the Articles of Confederation, decided that the new government would convene on the first Wednesday of the following March—March 4, 1789. From then on, presidential and congressional terms began on March 4. Consequently, although they were elected in November, the president and members of Congress did not take office until the following March. Moreover, newly elected members of Congress did not begin their work until thirteen months after they were elected because of the requirement in Article I, Section 4, that Congress begin its annual session on the first Monday in December. Sessions lasted only three months. The arrangement gave newly elected officials enough time to travel to Washington in the eighteenth century but the railroad soon made that time arrangement obsolete. Additionally, before the Seventeenth Amendment instituted direct election of the Senate, state legislatures usually did not select senators until late winter or spring. But senators were elected in November beginning in 1913.

The most serious problem with the timing was that when the second session of one Congress began, the next Congress had already been elected. Thus, members who had been defeated in the election continued to serve from December until the following March. The fact that **"lame ducks"** continued to make legislation seemed to Progressive reformers to be an "affront to democracy."[1] Moreover, the lame-duck sessions came to be marked by obstructionist filibustering.

Senator George W. Norris's resolution, which eventually became the Twentieth Amendment, first passed the Senate in 1923. But House Republicans resisted, and the amendment did not become a possibility until Democrats gained control of the House in 1930. Even then it would be two more years before Congress finally proposed the Norris Lame-Duck Amendment in 1932 and by May 1933 all forty-eight states had ratified it.

AMENDMENT XXI: REPEAL OF PROHIBITION

Section 1

The eighteenth article of amendment to the Constitution of the United States is hereby repealed.

Section 2

The transportation or importation into any State, Territory, or possession of the United States for delivery or use therein of intoxicating liquors, in violation of the laws thereof, is hereby prohibited.

Section 3

This article shall be inoperative unless it shall have been ratified as an amendment to the Constitution by conventions in the several States, as provided in the Constitution, within seven years from the date of submission hereof to the States by the Congress.

Proposed February 20, 1933   Declared in force by the secretary of state December 5, 1933

Although there had been attempts to repeal Prohibition since the Eighteenth Amendment went into effect in 1920, two major factors made its repeal possible in the early 1930s. First, the Congress that proposed the Eighteenth Amendment had a House of Representatives in which the seats were distributed in accordance with an apportionment based on the census of 1910 when a majority of Americans still lived in rural areas. Although the census of 1920 revealed a major shift of the population to urban areas, Congress did not reapportion the seats in the House after that census, waiting instead until 1929. As a result of reapportionment that year, twenty-one states—primarily in the South and West—lost seats in the House to states in the East. Moreover, the seats that those states gained tended to be located in the more metropolitan

[1]Richard B. Bernstein, with Jerome Agel, *Amending America: If We Love the Constitution So Much, Why Do We Keep Trying to Change It?* (New York: Times Books, 1993), 154.

areas. In short, the western and southern rural supporters of Prohibition lost considerable power in Congress to eastern urban opponents.

The Great Depression was a second factor that helped make repeal of Prohibition possible. In urban areas where factories were closing and offices were laying off workers, the prospect of new businesses—breweries and distilleries, for example—that would put people back to work, boost the economy, and produce tax revenues was extremely attractive. Organized antiprohibition groups working for repeal also pointed out that Prohibition encouraged crime and disrespect for the law.

With the amendment to repeal Prohibition, Congress for the first time utilized the option of submitting an amendment to state conventions for ratification. The amendment's supporters—**the "wets"**—found this method of ratification desirable because they feared that the rural-dominated state legislatures would reject the amendment. The "drys" acquiesced because giving the decision to state conventions made it possible for state legislators to evade a divisive issue.[2] The presidential election in 1932 was generally perceived as a contest between the "drys" represented by Herbert Hoover and the "wets" represented by Franklin Delano Roosevelt. The Democratic gain of ninety more seats in the House and twelve in the Senate ensured passage of the repeal amendment in the next Congress. The last lame-duck Congress, however, passed the proposed amendment just two weeks before its members' terms expired. During 1933, thirty-eight states held delegate elections for the state-ratifying conventions and 73 percent of twenty-one million voters cast ballots for delegates who favored repeal of Prohibition.[3] In December 1933, the thirty-sixth state ratified the Twenty-first Amendment and it became the only amendment to repeal another amendment.

The objective of Section 2 of the amendment was evidently to make clear that the states had the authority to ban the "transportation or importation" of alcohol for sale or consumption within the state. Laurence H. Tribe has assigned Section 2 to William N. Eskridge's and Sanford Levinson's catalog of "constitutional stupidities" because by its terms it "directly prohibits . . . the conduct that it was apparently meant to authorize the states to prohibit, freeing them of some (but not all) otherwise applicable limits derived from the rest of the Constitution."[4] Even though it was designed to be a grant of authority to states, as Tribe points out, Section 2 makes it a constitutional violation for an individual to transport liquor into a state in violation of the state's laws. Thus, Section 2 of the Twenty-first Amendment is the only constitutional provision, other than the Thirteenth Amendment, that is directed at the behavior of private individuals. It renders it possible for an individual to violate the Constitution by bringing a glass of wine into a state in violation of its beverage control laws.

The most interesting issues surrounding the Twenty-first Amendment concern the extent to which Section 2 may limit the applicability of other constitu-

[2]Alan P. Grimes, *Democracy and the Amendments to the Constitution* (Lexington, MA: Lexington Books, 1978), 110.
[3]David E. Kyvig, "Twenty-first Amendment," in Kermit L. Hall, ed. *The Oxford Companion to the United States Supreme Court* (New York: Oxford University Press, 1992), 883.
[4]Laurence H. Tribe, "How to Violate the Constitution without Really Trying: Lessons for the Repeal of Prohibition to the Balanced Budget Amendment," in William N. Eskridge, Jr. and Sanford Levinson, eds. *Constitutional Stupidities, Constitutional Tragedies* (New York: New York University Press, 1998), 99–100.

tional provisions. Section 2 limits **Congress's commerce power** where liquor is involved. The Supreme Court has indicated that the amendment creates an exception to the normal operation of the commerce clause.[5] Still, it does not make the commerce clause completely inapplicable but requires consideration of the particular issues involved in each case. The states may not, for example, regulate alcohol that is traveling through the state except as is necessary to prevent illegal diversion of the alcohol in the state.[6] Although the states have extensive power to tax, regulate, and even prohibit the importation of liquor for actual use within the state, the power does not extend to state attempts to accomplish other goals than controlling liquor consumption. Thus, for example, the Court held that Hawaii's 20 percent excise tax on wholesale liquor sales violated the commerce clause because the state was engaging in economic protectionism.[7]

Twenty-first Amendment limits on the commerce power do not extend to congressional spending power. In *South Dakota v Dole*, the Court upheld federal legislation that threatened to withhold federal highway funds in order to induce the states' compliance with a nationwide minimum drinking age.[8] Additionally, the Court has held that the Twenty-first Amendment cannot be used to override the equal protection clause,[9] procedural due process,[10] or the establishment clause.[11] The Court did, however, allow a state's Twenty-first Amendment authority to override the First Amendment in *California v LaRue* in 1972 when a majority held that states and localities could prohibit nude dancing in bars that serve liquor.[12] In 1996, however, the Court explicitly disavowed its reasoning in *LaRue* and announced, "The Twenty-first Amendment does not in any way diminish the force of the Supremacy Clause or . . . the Establishment Clause or the Equal Protection Clause. We see no reason why the First Amendment should not also be included in that list."[13]

AMENDMENT XXII: LIMITS ON PRESIDENTIAL TERMS

Section 1

No person shall be elected to the office of the President more than twice, and no person who has held the office of President, or acted as President, for more than two years of a term to which some other person was elected President shall be elected to the office of the President more than once. But this article shall not apply to any person holding the office of President when this Article was proposed by the Congress, and shall not prevent any person who may be holding the office of President, or acting as President, during the term within which this Article becomes operative from holding the office of President or acting as President during the remainder of such term.

---

[5]*Craig v Boren*, 429 US 190 (1976).
[6]*Carter v Virginia*, 321 US 131 (1944).
[7]*Bacchus Imports, Ltd. v Dias*, 468 US 263 (1984).
[8]*South Dakota v Dole*, 483 US 203 (1987).
[9]*Craig v Boren*, 429 US 190 (1976).
[10]*Wisconsin v Constantineau*, 400 US 433 (1971).
[11]*Larkin v Grendel's Den, Inc.* 459 US 116 (1982).
[12]*California v LaRue*, 409 US 109 (1972); *New York State Liquor Authority v Bellanca*, 452 US 714 (1981);*City of Newport v Iacobucci*, 479 US 92 (1986).
[13]*Liquormart Inc. v Rhode Island*, 517 US 484 (1996).

Section 2

This article shall be inoperative unless it shall have been ratified as an amendment to the Constitution by the legislatures of three-fourths of the several States within seven years from the date of its submission to the States by the Congress.

Proposed March 24, 1947   Certified as adopted by the administrator of general services March 1, 1951

When Franklin Delano Roosevelt decided to run for a third term in 1940, he broke with the practice begun by George Washington that presidents limited themselves to two terms in office. He then ran for and won a fourth term in 1944 but died April 12, 1945. The Congressional elections in 1946 gave Republicans a majority in both the House and the Senate and they wasted no time—in the first week of the first session of the eightieth Congress, seven House Joint Resolutions were introduced calling for a constitutional amendment limiting presidential terms.[14] Opponents of the amendment characterized it as a mean-spirited Republican slap at a great Democratic president. Nevertheless, within two months the Republicans mustered the necessary two-thirds vote with help from a number of southern Democrats. After four years, forty-one state legislatures had ratified the Twenty-second Amendment.

AMENDMENT XXIII: PRESIDENTIAL ELECTORS FOR THE DISTRICT OF COLUMBIA

Section 1

The District constituting the seat of Government of the United States shall appoint in such manner as the Congress may direct: A number of electors of President and Vice President equal to the whole number of Senators and Representatives in Congress to which the District would be entitled if it were a State, but in no event more than the least populous state; they shall be in addition to those appointed by the States, but they shall be considered, for the purposes of the election of President and Vice President, to be electors appointed by a State; and they shall meet in the District and perform such duties as provided by the twelfth article of amendment.

Section 2

The Congress shall have power to enforce this article by appropriate legislation.

Proposed on June 16, 1960   Ratified March 29, 1961.

The proposals that became the Twenty-third and Twenty-fourth Amendments began as something entirely different. During the 1950s at the height of the cold war, some members of Congress worried about how their membership might be replaced in the event that the capital came under nuclear attack. Although the Constitution provided that governors could replace Senators by spe-

---

[14]Bernstein, 158.

cial appointment, there was no such provision for the House. Thus, in 1960 a Senator proposed an amendment to authorize state governors to appoint temporary Representatives until a new election could be arranged. Two senators then put forward amendments to abolish the poll tax and to enfranchise federal officials living in Washington, D.C.

The Senate passed an omnibus package that would have included a prohibition on the poll tax and entitled residents of Washington, D.C., to representation in the House of Representatives. But the House proposed a narrower amendment providing only that residents of the District of Columbia could vote in presidential elections. The Twenty-third Amendment was the result of the compromise between the two chambers. The original proposal for an amendment to allow governors to appoint members of the House was forgotten. The Twenty-third Amendment was ratified in only nine months. Because of the high percentage of African Americans in the District, it raised racial issues and no action was taken on it in the South.

AMENDMENT XXIV: THE PROHIBITION ON THE POLL TAX

Section 1

The right of citizens of the United States to vote in any primary or other election for President or Vice President, for electors for President or Vice President, or for Senator or Representative in Congress, shall not be denied or abridged by the United States or any State by reason of failure to pay any poll tax or other tax.

Section 2

The Congress shall have power to enforce this article by appropriate legislation.

Proposed August 27, 1962   Ratified January 23, 1964

Another democratizing provision that extends the franchise, the Twenty-fourth Amendment prohibits states from requiring payment of a **poll tax** as a condition for voting for president and members of Congress. The poll tax was one of a variety of devices that white southerners developed to deprive African Americans of the right to vote. The amount that states charged as a requirement to vote was small—one dollar in Arkansas, two in Mississippi—but payment had to be made months in advance of the election and the usual requirement was that a voter had to produce proof of payment for two preceding years.

The Senate considered an anti-poll-tax amendment as part of the proposal that became the Twenty-third Amendment. Additionally, the House had passed legislation aimed at eliminating the poll tax on five different occasions during the 1940s.[15] Southern opponents of an anti-poll-tax amendment argued that the poll tax was only used in five states—Alabama, Arkansas, Mississippi, Texas, and Virginia—and that other states had eliminated the poll tax. Therefore, the federal government should simply leave the matter to the states. There

---

[15]Grimes, 133.

was some support in the Senate for outlawing the poll tax through legislation and contentions that an amendment was unnecessary. But ultimately the view prevailed that a constitutional amendment would be a more certain, fast, and efficient way of outlawing the poll tax. The Twenty-fourth Amendment was ratified by the thirty-eighth state in 1964. None of the southern states acted on it.

The Twenty-fourth Amendment prohibited the states from using poll taxes only in presidential and congressional elections. But in 1966 in *Harper v Virginia Board of Electors*, the Supreme Court held that the equal protection clause precludes a state from imposing a poll tax as a requirement to vote in any election.[16]

AMENDMENT XXV: PRESIDENTIAL SUCCESSION AND DISABILITY AND VICE PRESIDENTIAL VACANCIES

Section 1

In the case of the removal of the President from office or of his death or resignation, the Vice President shall become President.

Section 2

Whenever there is a vacancy in the office of the Vice President, the President shall nominate a Vice President who shall take office upon confirmation by a majority vote of both Houses of Congress.

Section 3

Whenever the President transmits to the President pro tempore of the Senate and the Speaker of the House of Representatives his written declaration that he is unable to discharge the powers and duties of his office, and until he transmits to them a written declaration to the contrary, such powers and duties shall be discharged by the Vice President as Acting President.

Section 4

Whenever the Vice President and a majority of either the principal officers of the executive departments or of such other body as Congress may by law provide, transmit to the President pro tempore of the Senate and the Speaker of the House of Representatives their written declaration that the President is unable to discharge the powers and duties of his office, the Vice President shall immediately assume the powers and duties of the office as Acting President.

Thereafter, when the President transmits to the President pro tempore of the Senate and the Speaker of the House of Representatives his written declaration that no inability exists, he shall resume the powers and duties of his office unless the Vice President and a majority of either the principal officers of the executive department or of such other body as Congress may by law provide, transmit within four days to the President pro tempore of the Senate and the Speaker of the House of Representatives their written declaration that the President is unable to discharge the powers and duties of his office. Thereupon

---

[16]*Harper v Virginia Board of Elections*, 383 US 663 (1966).

Congress shall decide the issue, assembling within forty-eight hours for that purpose if not in session. If the Congress, within twenty-one days after receipt of the latter written declaration, or, if Congress is not in session, within twenty-one days after Congress is required to assemble, determines by two-thirds vote of both Houses that the President is unable to discharge the powers and duties of his office, the Vice President shall continue to discharge the same as Acting President; otherwise, the President shall resume the powers and duties of his office.

Proposed July 6, 1965   Ratified February 10, 1967

The Twenty-fifth Amendment responded to questions that were raised by the assassination of President Kennedy and the illnesses of Presidents Eisenhower and Johnson. Section 1 formalized the practice of the eight vice presidents who have acceded to the presidency on the death of the president. It addressed another situation as well: the resignation of a president.

The vice presidency has been vacant eighteen times. Fortunately, during those periods there has been no need to continue down the line of presidential succession that Congress has provided by law: speaker of the House, president pro tempore of the Senate, and then members of the cabinet in order of the creation of their departments.

Section 2 of the Twenty-fifth Amendment provided for a procedure that has some resemblance to the one that is normally followed in the election of a vice president. Once a party selects its presidential candidate by a vote of the delegates to its national convention, that candidate normally chooses a vice presidential running mate, who, after confirmation by the national convention and election along with the president, becomes vice president. Section 2 called on Congress to serve in lieu of the electorate to confirm the president's choice. At the time that the amendment was being considered in Congress and in the states, it was generally assumed that Section 2 would be used after the death of a president had elevated the elected vice president, thereby creating a vacancy in the vice presidency. But Section 2 was used when Vice President Spiro T. Agnew resigned after pleading "no contest" to federal criminal charges in the midst of investigations of President Nixon's involvement in the Watergate affair. Nixon nominated Gerald Ford, Republican from Michigan who was then the minority leader in the House. During the interim between Nixon's nomination of Ford and his confirmation by Congress, there was considerable speculation about what would happen if President Nixon resigned or was removed from office. Very soon after Ford became Vice President, Nixon resigned and Ford became President, leaving the vice president's office vacant. President Ford nominated Nelson Rockefeller, a former four-term governor of New York. After a long examination of Rockefeller's record, Congress confirmed the nomination. For the first time in the history of the United States neither the President nor the Vice President had been chosen by the voters.

Before the Twenty-fifth Amendment became part of the Constitution, Congress had never established procedures for determining how the president's ability to discharge the duties of the office should be assessed. What if, for example, President Kennedy had lingered in a coma following the shooting in

Dallas? Who would be responsible for declaring that he was unable to perform the duties of his office? The issue had come up before. President James Garfield lived for nearly three months after he was shot, and President Woodrow Wilson was incapacitated for several months by a stroke. President Eisenhower had several serious illnesses while he was in office.

The issue arose again after the Twenty-fifth Amendment became part of the Constitution. When President Reagan was shot, he remained out of commission in the emergency room of George Washington University Hospital for about twenty-four hours. His aides did not invoke the Twenty-fifth Amendment, and the cabinet was not asked to consider the matter. In July 1985, when Reagan underwent a several-hour operation, he made a deliberate decision not to invoke Section 3. "I am mindful," he wrote to Vice President George Bush, "of the uncertainties of its application to such brief and temporary periods of incapacity. I do not believe that the drafters of this amendment intended its application to situations such as the instant one." Nevertheless, the president sent a letter to the speaker and to the president pro tempore of the Senate stating that

> consistent with my long-standing arrangement with Vice President George Bush, and not intending to set a precedent binding anyone privileged to hold this Office in the future, I have determined and it is my intention . . . that Vice President George Bush shall discharge those powers and duties in my stead commencing with the administration of anesthesia to me in this instance.

As soon as he was able after his surgery, he sent a second letter affirming his intention to resume his duties.[17]

Section 4 of the Twenty-fifth Amendment addresses the situation in which a president is unable to make a determination about his ability to carry out the duties of the office. The responsibility devolves on the vice president and the Cabinet. The declaration of presidential disability by a majority of the Cabinet is subject to a vice presidential veto. Whenever the Cabinet and the vice president believe the president is unable to discharge the powers and duties of the office, the vice president immediately assumes the powers and duties of the presidency, but is only the acting president. The disabled president remains in office during the time that he is unable to perform his duties.[18]

AMENDMENT XXVI: THE RIGHT TO VOTE: EIGHTEEN-YEAR-OLDS

Section 1

The right of citizens of the United States, who are eighteen years of age or older, to vote shall not be denied or abridged by the United States or by any State on account of age.

---

[17]*Time,* July 22, 1985, 24.
[18]See William Safire, *Full Disclosure* (Garden City, NY: Doubleday & Co., 1977), for a political novel dealing with the ramifications of the Twenty-fifth Amendment.

Section 2

The Congress shall have the power to enforce this article by appropriate legislation.

Proposed March 23, 1971   Ratified June 30, 1971

In the summer of 1970, Congress passed a Voting Rights Act that contained a rider reducing the voting age to eighteen in all elections after January 1, 1971. Proponents argued that Congress had the authority to take such action pursuant to Section 5 of the Fourteenth Amendment. The Supreme Court, after all, had upheld other provisions of the Voting Rights Act of 1965 on those grounds.[19] But the age provision of the Voting Rights Act was challenged and the Supreme Court, by a sharply divided vote, held that Congress had the authority to set the voting age for national but not state elections.[20] The result was that eighteen-year-olds could vote in federal elections but the state could set the voting age for state and local elections. Forty-seven states did not allow eighteen year-olds to vote. Thus, all of those states would have to either lower the voting age or set up new systems with separate registration processes, ballots, and voting machines for state/local and federal elections. The state process of lowering the voting age was extremely cumbersome, as it required amending the state constitutions. Congress could have simply repealed the voting-age provision in the Voting Rights Act but that alternative was never seriously considered.

When Congress convened in January 1971, a resolution was offered for a **constitutional amendment to lower the voting age to eighteen for all elections.** Within two months, the proposed amendment passed by large margins in both houses and was submitted to the states. The requisite three-fourths of the states ratified in less than three-and-a-half months. Eighteen-year-olds were thus qualified to vote in all elections in November 1972, and the states did not have to undertake what would have been an overwhelmingly difficult task of creating the machinery for separate systems for state and federal elections.

AMENDMENT XXVII: THE MADISON AMENDMENT

No Law, varying the compensation for the services of the Senators and Representatives, shall take effect, until, an election of representatives shall be intervened.

Proposed September 26, 1789   Ratified on May 7, 1992

In 1982, Gregory D. Watson, a sophomore at the University of Texas, looking for a paper topic, learned that two of the amendments in the original Bill of Rights had never been ratified. In 1791 when the Bill of Rights became part of the Constitution, only six states had ratified the amendment prohibiting increases in compensation for members of Congress from taking

---

[19]*South Carolina v Katzenbach*, 383 US 301 (1966).
[20]*Oregon v Mitchell*, 400 US 112 (1970).

effect before another election took place. But in 1873, Ohio ratified the amendment. Watson wrote a paper arguing that the amendment was still before the states because it had no time limit attached to it and he urged that it be ratified. He received a C on his paper and his professor told him that the amendment was a dead letter—it would never become part of the Constitution.[21]

Watson embarked on his own ratification campaign, traveling from state to state urging state legislators to introduce it and to work to get it ratified. On May 7, 1992, the thirty-eighth and thirty-ninth states ratified the Twenty-seventh Amendment.

The Archivist of the United States, who since 1982 has had the responsibility for certifying amendments, ruled the Twenty-seventh Amendment ratified. Although a number of congressional leaders expressed reservations, Congress endorsed the amendment with only three "no" votes.

QUESTIONS

1. Do you think Section 2 of the Twenty-first Amendment is a "constitutional stupidity"? Why? Does it give too much power to the states? Alternatively, has the Supreme Court read the states' powers to regulate liquor within their borders too narrowly? What is wrong with making individual behavior the subject of a constitutional provision?

2. What is the importance of the Twenty-second Amendment limiting presidents to two terms in office? How does it comport with the principles of democracy and accountability? What impact might it have on the constitutional structure of checks and balances? Did it promote a balance between the president and Congress?

3. What advantages might there be to allowing presidents to serve more than two terms? Would you favor repeal of the Twenty-second Amendment? There is some support for a constitutional amendment that would limit the president to a single six-year term. Would such an amendment promote accountability in government? Would it be a democratizing amendment? Or would it be another "constitutional stupidity"?

4. Why might there have been opposition in 1970 to granting eighteen-year-olds the vote?

5. Considering the story of the Twenty-seventh Amendment, is it possible that other amendments that have been proposed to the states but never ratified could be ratified? There are four unratified amendments that Congress submitted to the states without stipulating any time limits, including the 1861 Amendment that protected slavery and the 1924 Child Labor Amendment. Some members of Congress expressed concern that the ratification of the Compensation Amendment raised the possibility that these long-forgotten amendments could still be ratified. Is there any basis for such concern?

---

[21]Bernstein, 244.

KEY TERMS

lame ducks

the "wets"

relationship between the
Twenty-First Amendment and
Congress's commerce power

poll tax

reason for constitutional
amendment to lower the voting
age to eighteen for all elections

SUGGESTIONS FOR FURTHER READING

Bernstein, Richard B. "The Sleeper Wakes: The History and Legacy of the Twenty-Seventh Amendment." *Fordham Law Review* 61 (1992), 497–557.

Bernstein, Richard B., with Jerome Agel. *Amending America: If We Love the Constitution So Much, Why Do We Keep Trying to Change It?* New York: Times Books, 1993.

Eskridge, William N., Jr., and Sanford Levinson, eds. *Constitutional Stupidities, Constitutional Tragedies.* New York: New York University Press, 1998.

Feerick, John D. *The Twenty-Fifth Amendment: Its Complete History and Earliest Applications,* 2d ed. New York: Fordham Press, 1992.

Grimes, Alan P. *Democracy and the Amendments to the Constitution.* Lexington, MA: Lexington Books, 1978.

Kyvig, David E. *Repealing National Prohibition.* Chicago: University of Chicago Press, 1979.

PART FOUR

THE DOCUMENTS

THE DECLARATION OF INDEPENDENCE

In Congress, July 4, 1776,

THE UNANIMOUS DECLARATION OF THE THIRTEEN UNITED STATES OF AMERICA

When, in the course of human events, it becomes necessary for one people to dissolve the political bands which have connected them with another, and to assume, among the powers of the earth, the separate and equal station to which the laws of nature and of nature's God entitle them, a decent respect to the opinions of mankind requires that they should declare the causes which impel them to the separation.

We hold these truths to be self-evident, that all men are created equal; that they are endowed by their Creator with certain unalienable rights; that among these, are life, liberty, and the pursuit of happiness. That, to secure these rights, governments are instituted among men, deriving their just powers from the consent of the governed; that, whenever any form of government becomes destructive of these ends, it is the right of the people to alter or to abolish it, and to institute a new government, laying its foundation on such principles, and organizing its powers in such form, as to them shall seem most likely to effect their safety and happiness. Prudence, indeed, will dictate that governments long established, should not be changed for light and transient causes; and, accordingly, all experience hath shown, that mankind are more disposed to suffer, while evils are sufferable, than to right themselves by abolishing the forms to which they are accustomed. But, when a long train of abuses and usurpations, pursuing invariably the same object, evinces a design to reduce them under absolute despotism, it is their right, it is their duty, to throw off such government and to provide new guards for their future security. Such has been the patient sufferance of these colonies, and such is now the necessity which constrains them to alter their former systems of government. The history of the present King of Great Britain is a history of repeated injuries and usurpations, all having, in direct object, the establishment of an absolute tyranny over these States. To prove this, let facts be submitted to a candid world:

He has refused his assent to laws the most wholesome and necessary for the public good.

He has forbidden his governors to pass laws of immediate and pressing importance, unless suspended in their operation till his assent should be obtained; and, when so suspended, he has utterly neglected to attend to them.

He has refused to pass other laws for the accommodation of large districts of people, unless those people would relinquish the right of representation in the legislature; a right inestimable to them, and formidable to tyrants only.

He has called together legislative bodies at places unusual, uncomfortable, and distant from the depository of their public records, for the sole purpose of fatiguing them into compliance with his measures.

He has dissolved representative houses repeatedly for opposing, with manly firmness, his invasions on the rights of the people.

He has refused, for a long time after such dissolutions, to cause others to be elected; whereby the legislative powers, incapable of annihilation, have returned to the people at large for their exercise; the state remaining, in the meantime, exposed to all the danger of invasion from without, and convulsions within.

He has endeavored to prevent the population of these States; for that purpose, obstructing the laws for naturalization of foreigners, refusing to pass others to encourage their migration hither, and raising the conditions of new appropriations of lands.

He has obstructed the administration of justice, by refusing his assent to laws for establishing judiciary powers.

He has made judges dependent on his will alone, for the tenure of their offices, and the amount and payment of their salaries.

He has erected a multitude of new offices, and sent hither swarms of officers to harass our people, and eat out their substance.

He has kept among us, in time of peace, standing armies, without the consent of our legislatures.

He has affected to render the military independent of, and superior to, the civil power.

He has combined, with others, to subject us to a jurisdiction foreign to our Constitution, and unacknowledged by our laws; giving his assent to their acts of pretended legislation:

For quartering large bodies of armed troops among us:

For protecting them by a mock trial, from punishment, for any murders which they should commit on the inhabitants of these States:

For cutting off our trade with all parts of the world:

For imposing taxes on us without our consent:

For depriving us, in many cases, of the benefit of trial by jury:

For transporting us beyond seas to be tried for pretended offences:

For abolishing the free system of English laws in a neighboring province, establishing therein an arbitrary government, and enlarging its boundaries, so as to render it at once an example and fit instrument for introducing the same absolute rule into these colonies:

For taking away our charters, abolishing our most valuable laws, and altering, fundamentally, the powers of our governments:

For suspending our own legislatures, and declaring themselves invested with power to legislate for us in all cases whatsoever.

He has abdicated government here, by declaring us out of his protection, and waging war against us.

He has plundered our seas, ravaged our coasts, burnt our towns, and destroyed the lives of our people.

He is, at this time, transporting large armies of foreign mercenaries to complete the works of death, desolation, and tyranny, already begun, with circumstances of cruelty and perfidy scarcely paralleled in the most barbarous ages, and totally unworthy of the head of a civilized nation.

He has constrained our fellow citizens, taken captive on the high seas, to bear arms against their country, to become the executioners of their friends, and brethren, or to fall themselves by their hands.

He has excited domestic insurrections amongst us, and has endeavored to bring on the inhabitants of our frontiers, the merciless Indian savages, whose known rules of warfare is an undistinguished destruction of all ages, sexes, and conditions.

In every stage of these oppressions, we have petitioned for redress, in the most humble terms; our repeated petitions have been answered only by repeated injury. A prince, whose character is thus marked by every act which may define a tyrant, is unfit to be the ruler of a free people.

Nor have we been wanting in attention to our British brethren. We have warned them, from time to time, of attempts made by their legislature to extend an unwarrantable jurisdiction over us. We have reminded them of the circumstances of our emigration and settlement here. We have appealed to their native justice and magnanimity, and we have conjured them, by the ties of our common kindred, to disavow these usurpations, which would inevitably interrupt our connections and correspondence. They, too, have been deaf to the voice of justice and of consanguinity. We must, therefore, acquiesce in the necessity which denounces our separation, and hold them as we hold the rest of mankind, enemies in war, in peace, friends.

We, therefore, the representatives of the United States of America, in general Congress assembled, appealing to the Supreme Judge of the world for the rectitude of our intentions, do, in the name, and by the authority of the good people of these colonies, solemnly publish and declare, that these united colonies are, and of right ought to be, free and independent states: that they are absolved from all allegiance to the British Crown, and that all political connection between them and the state of Great Britain is, and ought to be, totally dissolved; and that, as free and independent states, they have full power to levy war, conclude peace, contract alliances, establish commerce, and to do all other acts and things which independent states may of right do. And, for the support of this declaration, with a firm reliance on the protection of Divine Providence, we mutually pledge to each other our lives, our fortunes, and our sacred honor.

THE CONSTITUTION OF THE UNITED STATES OF AMERICA[1]

We the People of the United States, in Order to form a more perfect Union, establish Justice, insure domestic Tranquility, provide for the common defence, promote the general Welfare, and secure the Blessings of Liberty to ourselves and our Posterity, do ordain and establish this Constitution for the United States of America.

ARTICLE. I.

Section. 1. All legislative Powers herein granted shall be vested in Congress of the United States, which shall consist of a Senate and House of Representatives.

Section. 2. The House of Representatives shall be composed of Members chosen every second Year by the People of the several States, and the Electors in each State shall have the Qualifications requisite for Electors of the most numerous Branch of the State Legislature.

No Person shall be a Representative who shall not have attained to the Age of twenty five Years, and been seven Years a Citizen of the United States, and who shall not, when elected, be an Inhabitant of that State in which he shall be chosen.

Representatives and direct Taxes[2] shall be apportioned among the several States which may be included within this Union, according to their respective Numbers, which shall be determined by adding to the whole Number of free Persons, including those bound to Service for a Term of Years, and excluding Indians not taxed, three fifths of all other Persons.[3] The actual Enumeration shall be made within three Years after the first Meeting of the Congress of the United States, and within every subsequent Term of ten Years, in such Manner as they shall by Law direct. The Number of Representatives shall not exceed one for every thirty thousand, but each state shall have at Least one Representative; and until such enumeration shall be made, the State of New

---

[1] From the engrossed copy in the National Archives. Original spelling, capitalization, and punctuation have been retained.
[2] Modified by the Sixteenth Amendment.
[3] Replaced by the Fourteenth Amendment.

Hampshire shall be entitled to chuse three; Massachusetts eight; Rhode Island and Providence Plantations one; Connecticut five; New York six; New Jersey four; Pennsylvania eight; Delaware one; Maryland six; Virginia ten; North Carolina five; South Carolina five; and Georgia three.

When vacancies happen in the Representation from any State, the Executive Authority thereof shall issue Writs of Election to fill such Vacancies.

The House of Representatives shall chuse their Speaker and other Officers; and shall have the sole Power of Impeachment.

Section. 3. The Senate of the United States shall be composed of two Senators from each State, chosen by the Legislature thereof, for six Years; and each Senator shall have one vote.[4]

Immediately after they shall be assembled in Consequence of the first Election, they shall be divided as equally as may be into three Classes. The Seats of the Senators of the first Class shall be vacated at the Expiration of the second Year, of the second Class at the Expiration of the fourth Year, and of the third Class at the Expiration of the sixth Year, so that one third may be chosen every second Year; and if Vacancies happen by Resignation, or otherwise, during the Recess of the Legislature of any State, the Executive thereof may make temporary Appointments until the next meeting of the Legislature, which shall then fill such Vacancies.[5]

No Person shall be a Senator who shall not have attained to the Age of thirty Years, and been nine Years a Citizen of the United States, and who shall not, when elected, be an Inhabitant of that State for which he shall be chosen.

The Vice President of the United States shall be President of the Senate, but shall have no Vote, unless they be equally divided.

The Senate shall chuse their other officers, and also a President pro tempore, in the Absence of the Vice President, or when he shall exercise the Office of President of the United States.

The Senate shall have the sole Power to try all Impeachments. When sitting for that Purpose, they shall be on Oath or Affirmation. When the President of the United States is tried, the Chief Justice shall preside: And no Person shall be convicted without the Concurrence of two thirds of the Members present.

Judgment in Cases of Impeachment shall not extend further than to removal from Office, and disqualification to hold and enjoy any Office of honor, Trust or Profit under the United States: but the Party convicted shall nevertheless be liable and subject to Indictment, Trial, Judgment and Punishment, according to Law.

Section. 4. The Times, Places and Manner of holding Elections for Senators and Representatives, shall be prescribed in each State by the Legislature thereof, but the Congress may at any time by Law make or alter such Regulation, except as to the Places of chusing Senators.

---

[4] Superseded by the Seventeenth Amendment.
[5] Modified by the Seventeenth Amendment.

The Congress shall assemble at least once in every Year, and such Meeting shall be on the first Monday in December, unless they shall by Law appoint a different Day.[6]

Section. 5. Each House shall be the Judge of the Elections, Returns and Qualifications of its own Members, and a Majority of each shall constitute a Quorum to do Business; but a smaller Number may adjourn from day to day, and may be authorized to compel the Attendance of absent Members, in such Manner, and under such Penalties as each House may provide.

Each House may determine the Rules of its Proceedings, punish its Members for disorderly Behaviour, and, with the Concurrence of two thirds, expel a Member.

Each House shall keep a Journal of its Proceedings, and from time to time publish the same, excepting such Parts as may in their Judgment require Secrecy; and the Yeas and Nays of the Members of either House on any question shall, at the Desire of one fifth of those Present, be entered on the Journal.

Neither House, during the Session of Congress, shall, without the Consent of the other, adjourn for more than three days, nor to any other Place than that in which the two Houses shall be sitting.

Section. 6. The Senators and Representatives shall receive a Compensation for their Services, to be ascertained by Law, and paid out of the Treasury of the United States. They shall in all Cases, except Treason, Felony and Breach of the Peace, be privileged from Arrest during their Attendance at the Session of their respective Houses, and in going to and returning from the same; and for any Speech or Debate in either House, they shall not be questioned in any other Place.

No Senator or Representative shall, during the Time for which he was elected, be appointed to any civil Office under the Authority of the United States, which shall have been created, or the Emoluments whereof shall have been encreased during such time; and no Person holding any Office under the United States, shall be a Member of either House during his Continuance in Office.

Section. 7. All Bills for raising Revenue shall originate in the House of Representatives; but the Senate may propose or concur with Amendments as on other Bills.

Every Bill which shall have passed the House of Representatives and the Senate shall, before it become a Law, be presented to the President of the United States; If he approve he shall sign it, but if not he shall return it, with his Objections to that House in which it shall have originated, who shall enter the Objections at large on their Journal, and proceed to reconsider it. If after such Reconsideration two third of that House shall agree to pass the Bill, it shall be sent, together with the Objections, to the other House, by which it shall likewise be reconsidered, and if approved by two thirds of that House, it shall become a Law. But in all such Cases the Votes of both Houses shall be determined by yeas

---

[6] Superseded by the Twentieth Amendment.

and Nays, and the Names of the Persons voting for and against the Bill shall be entered on the Journal of each House respectively. If any Bill shall not be returned by the President within ten Days (Sundays excepted) after it shall have been presented to him, the Same shall be a Law, in like Manner as if he had signed it, unless the Congress by their Adjournment prevent its Return, in which Case it shall not be a Law.

Every Order, Resolution, or Vote to which the Concurrence of the Senate and House of Representatives may be necessary (except on a question of Adjournment) shall be presented to the President of the United States; and before the Same shall take Effect, shall be approved by him, or being disapproved by him shall be repassed by two thirds of the Senate and House of Representatives, according to the Rules and Limitations prescribed in the Case of a Bill.

Section. 8. The Congress shall have the Power to lay and collect Taxes, Duties, Imposts and Excises, to pay the Debts and provide for the common Defence and general Welfare of the United States; but all Duties, Imposts and Excises shall be uniform throughout the United States;

To borrow Money on the credit of the United States;

To regulate Commerce with foreign Nations, and among the several States, and with the Indian Tribes;

To establish an uniform Rule of Naturalization, and uniform Laws on the subject of Bankruptcies throughout the United States;

To coin Money, regulate the Value thereof, and of foreign Coin, and fix the Standard of Weights and Measures;

To provide for the Punishment of counterfeiting the Securities and current Coin of the United States;

To establish Post Offices and post Roads;

To promote the Progress of Science and useful Arts, by securing for limited Times to Authors and Inventors the exclusive Right to their respective Writings and Discoveries;

To constitute Tribunals inferior to the supreme Court;

To define and punish Piracies and Felonies committed on the high Seas, and Offences against the Law of Nations;

To declare War, grant Letters of Marque and Reprisal, and make Rules concerning Captures on Land and Water;

To raise and support Armies, but no Appropriation of Money to that Use shall be for a longer Term than two Years;

To provide and maintain a Navy;

To make Rules for the Government and Regulation of the land and naval Forces;

To provide for calling forth the Militia to execute the Laws of the Union, suppress Insurrections and repel Invasions;

To provide for organizing, arming, and disciplining, the Militia, and for governing such Part of them as may be employed in the Service of the United States, reserving to the States respectively, the Appointment of the Officers, and the Authority of training the Militia according to the discipline prescribed by Congress;

To exercise exclusive Legislation in all Cases whatsoever, over such District (not exceeding ten Miles square) as may, by Cession of particular States, and the Acceptance of Congress, become the Seat of the Government of the United States, and to exercise like Authority over all Places purchased by the Consent of the Legislature of the State in which the Same shall be, for the Erection of Forts, Magazines, Arsenals, dock-Yards, and other needful Buildings;—And

To make all Laws which shall be necessary and proper for carrying into Execution the foregoing Powers, and all other Powers vested by this Constitution in the Government of the United States, or in any Department or Officer thereof.

Section. 9. The Migration or Importation of such Persons as any of the States now existing shall think proper to admit, shall not be prohibited by the Congress prior to the Year one thousand eight hundred and eight, but a Tax or duty may be imposed on such Importation, not exceeding ten dollars for each Person.

The Privilege of the Writ of Habeas Corpus shall not be suspended, unless when in Cases of Rebellion or Invasion the public Safety may require it.

No Bill of Attainer or ex post facto Law shall be passed.

No Capitation, or other direct, Tax shall be laid, unless in Proportion to the Census or Enumeration herein before directed to be taken.

No Tax or Duty shall be laid on Articles exported from any State.

No Preference shall be given by any Regulation of Commerce or Revenue to the Ports of one State over those of another: nor shall Vessels bound to, or from, one State, be obliged to enter, clear, or pay Duties in another.

No Money shall be drawn from the Treasury, but in Consequence of Appropriations made by Law, and a regular Statement and Account of the Receipts and Expenditures of all public Money shall be published from time to time.

No Title of Nobility shall be granted by the United States: And no Person holding any Office of Profit or Trust under them, shall, without the Consent of the Congress, accept of any present, Emolument, Office, or Title, of any kind whatever, from any King, Prince, or foreign State.

Section. 10. No State shall enter into any Treaty, Alliance, or Confederation; grant Letters of Marque and Reprisal; coin Money; emit Bills of Credit; make any Thing but gold and silver Coin a Tender in Payment of Debts; pass any Bill of Attainder, ex post facto Law, or Law impairing the Obligation of Contracts, or grant any Title of Nobility.

No State shall, without the Consent of the Congress, lay any Imposts or Duties on Imports or Exports, except what may be absolutely necessary for executing its inspection Laws: and the net Produce of all Duties and Imposts, laid by any State on Imports or Exports, shall be for the Use of the Treasury of the United States; and all such Laws shall be subject to the Revision and Controul of the Congress.

No State shall, without the Consent of Congress, lay any Duty of Tonnage, keep Troops, or Ships of War in time of Peace, enter into any Agreement or Compact with another State, or with a foreign Power, or engage in War, unless actually invaded, or in such imminent Danger as will not admit of delay.

ARTICLE. II.

Section. 1. The executive Powers shall be vested in a President of the United States of America. He shall hold his Office during the Term of four Years, and, together with the Vice President, chosen for the same Term, be elected, as follows:

Each State shall appoint, in such Manner as the Legislature thereof may direct, a Number of Electors, equal to the whole Number of Senators and Representatives to which the State may be entitled in the Congress: but no Senator or Representative, or Person holding an Office of Trust or Profit under the United States, shall be appointed an Elector.

The Electors shall meet in their respective States, and vote by Ballot for two Persons, of whom one at least shall not be an Inhabitant of the same State with themselves. And they shall make a List of all the Persons voted for, and of the Number of Votes for each; which List they shall sign and certify, and transmit sealed to the Seat of the Government of the United States, directed to the President of the Senate. The President of the Senate shall, in the Presence of the Senate and House of Representatives, open all the Certificates, and the Votes shall then be counted. The Person having the greatest Number of Votes shall be the President, if such Number be a Majority of the Whole Number of Electors appointed; and if there be more than one who have such Majority, and have an equal Number of Votes, then the House of Representatives shall immediately chuse by Ballot one of them for President; and if no Person have a Majority, then from the five highest on the List the said House shall in like Manner chuse the President. But in chusing the President, the Votes shall be taken by States, the Representation from each State having one Vote; A quorum for this Purpose shall consist of a Member or Members from two thirds of the States, and a Majority of all the States shall be necessary to a Choice. In every Case, after the Choice of the President, the Person having the greatest Number of Votes of the Electors shall be the Vice President. But if there should remain two or more who have equal Votes, the Senate shall chuse from them by Ballot the Vice President.[7]

The Congress may determine the Time of chusing the Electors, and the Day on which they shall give their Votes; which Day shall be the same throughout the United States.

No Person except a natural born Citizen, or a Citizen of the United States, at the time of the Adoption of this Constitution, shall be eligible to the Office of President, neither shall any Person be eligible to the Office who shall not have attained to the Age of thirty five Years, and been fourteen Years a Resident within the United States.

In Case of the Removal of the President from Office, or of his Death, Resignation, or Inability to discharge the Powers and Duties of the said Office, the Same shall devolve on the Vice President, and the Congress may by Law provide for the Case of Removal, Death, Resignation, or Inability, both of the President and Vice President, declaring what Officer shall then act as Presi-

---

[7] Superseded by the Twelfth Amendment.

dent, and such Officer shall act accordingly, until the Disability be removed, or a President shall be elected.[8]

The President shall, at stated Times, receive for his Services, a Compensation, which shall neither be encreased nor diminished during the Period for which he shall have been elected, and he shall not receive within that Period any other Emolument from the United States, or any of them.

Before he enter on the Execution of his Office, he shall take the following Oath or Affirmation:—"I do solemnly swear (or affirm) that I will faithfully execute the Office of President of the United States, and will to the best of my Ability, preserve, protect and defend the Constitution of the United States."

Section. 2. The President shall be Commander in Chief of the Army and Navy of the United States, and of the Militia of the several States, when called into the actual Service of the United States; he may require the Opinion, in writing, of the principle Officer in each of the executive Departments, upon any Subject relating to the Duties of their respective Offices, and he shall have Power to grant Reprieves and Pardons for Offences against the United States, except in Cases of Impeachment.

He shall have Power, by and with the Advice and Consent of the Senate, to make Treaties, provided two thirds of the Senators present concur; and he shall nominate, and by and with the Advice and Consent of the Senate, shall appoint Ambassadors, other public Ministers and Consuls, Judges of the supreme Court, and all other Officers of the United States, whose Appointments are not herein otherwise provided for, and which shall be established by Law; but the Congress may by Law vest the Appointment of such inferior Officers, as they think proper, in the President alone, in the Courts of Law, or in the Heads of Departments.

The President shall have Power to fill up all Vacancies that may happen during the Recess of the Senate, by granting Commissions which shall expire at the End of their next Session.

Section. 3. He shall from time to time give to the Congress Information of the State of the Union, and recommend to their Consideration such Measures as he shall judge necessary and expedient; he may, on extraordinary Occasions, convene both Houses, or either of them, and in Case of Disagreement between them, with Respect to the Time of Adjournment, he may adjourn them to such Time as he shall think proper; he shall receive Ambassadors and other public Ministers; he shall take Care that the Laws be faithfully executed, and shall Commission all the Officers of the United States.

Section. 4. The President, Vice President and all civil Officers of the United States, shall be removed from Office on Impeachment for, and Conviction of, Treason, Bribery, or other high Crimes and Misdemeanors.

---

[8] Modified by the Twenty-fifth Amendment.

ARTICLE. III.

Section. 1. The judicial Power of the United States, shall be vested in one supreme Court, and in such inferior Courts as the Congress may from time to time ordain and establish. The Judges, both of the supreme and inferior Courts, shall hold their Offices during good Behaviour, and shall, at stated Times, receive for their Services, a Compensation, which shall not be diminished during their Continuance in Office.

Section. 2. The judicial Power shall extend to all Cases, in Law and Equity, arising under this Constitution, the Laws of the United States, and Treaties made, or which shall be made, under their Authority;—to all Cases affecting Ambassadors, other public Ministers and Consuls;—to all Cases of admiralty and maritime Jurisdiction;—to Controversies to which the United States shall be a Party;—to Controversies between two or more States;—between a State and Citizens of another State;[9]—between Citizens of different States,—between Citizens of the same State claiming Lands under Grants of different States, and between a State, or the Citizens thereof, and foreign States, Citizens or Subjects.

In all Cases affecting Ambassadors, other public Ministers and Consuls, and those in which a State shall be Party, the supreme Court shall have original Jurisdiction. In all the other Cases before mentioned, the supreme Court shall have appellate Jurisdiction, both as to Law and Fact, with such Exceptions, and under such Regulations as the Congress shall make.

The Trial of all Crimes, except in Cases of Impeachment, shall be by Jury; and such Trial shall be held in the State where the said Crimes shall have been committed; but when not committed within any State, the trial shall be at such Place or Places as the Congress by Law have directed.

Section. 3. Treason against the United States, shall consist only in levying War against them, or in adhering to their Enemies, giving them Aid and Comfort. No Person shall be convicted of Treason unless on the Testimony of two Witnesses to the same overt Act, or on Confession in open Court.

The Congress shall have Power to declare the Punishment of Treason, but no Attainder of Treason shall work Corruption of Blood, or Forfeiture except during the Life of the Person attainted.

ARTICLE. IV.

Section. 1. Full Faith and Credit shall be given in each State to the public Acts, Records, and judicial Proceedings of every other State. And the Congress may by general Laws prescribe the Manner in which such Acts, Records and Proceedings shall be proved, and the Effect thereof.

Section. 2. The Citizens of each State shall be entitled to all Privileges and Immunities of Citizens in the several States.

---

[9] Modified by the Eleventh Amendment.

A Person charged in any State with Treason, Felony, or other Crime, who shall flee from Justice, and be found in another State, shall on Demand of the executive Authority of the State from which he fled, be delivered up, to be removed to the State having Jurisdiction of the Crime.

No Person held to Service or Labour in one State, under the Laws thereof, escaping into another, shall, in Consequence of any Law or Regulation therein, be discharged from such Service or Labour, but shall be delivered up on Claim of the Party to whom such Service or Labour may be due.

Section. 3. New States may be admitted by the Congress into this Union; but no new State shall be formed or erected within the Jurisdiction of any other State, nor any State be formed by the Junction of two or more States, or Parts of States, without the Consent of the Legislatures of the States concerned as well as of the Congress.

The Congress shall have Power to dispose of and make all needful Rules and Regulations respecting the Territory or other Property belonging to the United States; and nothing in this Constitution shall be so construed as to Prejudice any Claims of the United States, or of any Particular State.

Section. 4. The United States shall guarantee to every State in this Union a Republican Form of Government, and shall protect each of them against Invasion; and on Application of the Legislature, or of the Executive (when the Legislature cannot be convened) against domestic Violence.

ARTICLE. V.

The Congress, whenever two thirds of both Houses shall deem it necessary, shall propose Amendments to this Constitution, or, on the Application of the Legislatures of two thirds of the several States, shall call a Convention for proposing Amendments, which, in either Case, shall be valid to all Intents and Purposes, as Part of this Constitution, when ratified by the Legislatures of three fourths of the several States, or by Conventions in three fourths thereof, as the one or the other Mode of Ratification may be proposed by the Congress; Provided that no Amendment which may be made prior to the Year One thousand eight hundred and eight shall in any Manner affect the first and fourth Clauses in the Ninth Section of the first Article; and that no State, without its Consent, shall be deprived of its equal Suffrage in the Senate.

ARTICLE. VI.

All Debts contracted and Engagements entered into, before the Adoption of this Constitution, shall be as valid against the United States under this Constitution, as under the Confederation.

This Constitution, and the Laws of the United States which shall be made in Pursuance thereof; and all Treaties made, or which shall be made, under the Authority of the United States, shall be the supreme Law of the Land; and the

Judges in every State shall be bound thereby, any Thing in the Constitution or Laws of any State to the Contrary notwithstanding.

The Senators and Representatives before mentioned, and the Members of the several State Legislatures, and all executive and judicial Officers both of the United States and of the several States, shall be bound by Oath or Affirmation, to support this Constitution; but no religious Test shall ever be required as a Qualification to any Office or public Trust under the United States.

ARTICLE. VII.

The Ratification of the Conventions of nine States, shall be sufficient for the Establishment of this Constitution between the States so ratifying the Same.

done in Convention by the Unanimous Consent of the States present the Seventeenth Day of September in the Year of our Lord one thousand seven hundred and Eighty seven and of the Independence of the United States of American the Twelfth. **In witness** whereof We have hereunto subscribed our Names,

Articles in Addition to, and Amendment of, the Constitution of the United States of America, Proposed by Congress, and Ratified by the Legislatures of the Several States, Pursuant to the Fifth Article of the Original Constitution.

AMENDMENT I[10]

Congress shall make no law respecting an establishment of religion, or prohibiting the free exercise thereof; or abridging the freedom of speech, or of the press; or the right of people peaceably to assemble, and to petition the Government for a redress of grievances.

AMENDMENT II

A well regulated Militia, being necessary to the security of a free State, the right of the people to keep and bear Arms shall not be infringed.

AMENDMENT III

No Soldier shall, in time of peace, be quartered in any house, without the consent of the Owner, nor in time of war, but in a manner to be prescribed by law.

---

[10] The first ten amendments were passed by Congress September 25, 1789. They were ratified by three-fourths of the states December 15, 1791.

AMENDMENT IV

The right of the people to be secure in their persons, houses, papers, and effects, against unreasonable searches and seizures, shall not be violated, and no Warrants shall issue, but upon probable cause, supported by Oath or affirmation, and particularly describing the place to be searched, and the persons or things to be seized.

AMENDMENT V

No person shall be held to answer for a capital or otherwise infamous crime, unless on a presentment or indictment of a Grand Jury, except in cases arising in the land or naval forces, or in the Militia, when in actual service in time of War or public danger; nor shall any person be subject for the same offence to be twice put in jeopardy of life or limb; nor shall be compelled in any criminal case to be a witnesses against himself, nor be deprived of life, liberty, or property, without due process of law; nor shall private property be taken for public use, without just compensation.

AMENDMENT VI

In all criminal prosecutions, the accused shall enjoy the right to a speedy and public trial, by an impartial jury of the State and district wherein the crime shall have been committed, which district shall have been previously ascertained by law, and to be informed of the nature and cause of the accusation; to be confronted with the witnesses against him; to have compulsory process for obtaining witnesses in his favor, and to have the Assistance of Counsel for his defence.

AMENDMENT VII

In suits at common law, where the value in controversy shall exceed twenty dollars, the right of trial by jury shall be preserved, and no fact tried by a jury, shall be otherwise reexamined in any Court of the United States, than according to the rules of common law.

AMENDMENT VIII

Excessive bail shall not be required, nor excessive fines imposed, nor cruel and unusual punishments inflicted.

AMENDMENT IX

The enumeration in the Constitution, of certain rights, shall not be construed to deny or disparage others retained by the people.

AMENDMENT X

The powers not delegated to the United States by the Constitution; nor prohibited by it to the States, are reserved to the States respectively, or to the people.

AMENDMENT XI[11]

The Judicial power of the United States shall not be construed to extend to any suit in law or equity, commenced or prosecuted against one of the United States by Citizens of another State, or by Citizens or Subjects of any Foreign State.

AMENDMENT XII[12]

The Electors shall meet in their respective States and vote by ballot for President and Vice-President, one of whom at least, shall not be an inhabitant of the same State with themselves; they shall name in their ballots the person voted for as President, and in distinct ballots the person voted for as Vice-President, and they shall make distinct lists of all persons voted for as President, and of all persons voted for as Vice-President, and of the number of votes for each, which lists they shall sign and certify, and transmit sealed to the seat of the government of the United States, directed to the President of the Senate;—The President of the Senate shall, in the presence of the Senate and House of Representatives, open all the certificates and the votes shall then be counted;—The person having the greatest number of votes for President, shall be the President, if such number be a majority of the whole number of Electors appointed; and if no person have such majority, then from the persons having the highest numbers not exceeding three on the list of those voted for as President, the House of Representatives shall choose immediately, by ballot, the President. But in choosing the President, the votes shall be taken by states, the representation from each state having one vote; a quorum for this purpose shall consist of a member or members from two-thirds of the states, and a majority of all the states shall be necessary to a choice. And if

---

[11] Passed March 4, 1794. Ratified January 23, 1795.
[12] Passed December 9, 1803. Ratified June 15, 1804.

the House of Representatives shall not choose a President whenever the right of choice shall devolve upon them, before the fourth day of March next following, then the Vice-President shall act as President, as in the case of the death or other constitutional disability of the President.—The person having the greatest number of votes as Vice-President, shall be the Vice-President, if such number be a majority of the whole number of Electors appointed, and if no person have a majority, then from the two highest numbers on the list, the Senate shall choose the Vice-President; a quorum for the purpose shall consist of two-thirds of the whole number of Senators, and a majority of the whole number shall be necessary to a choice. But no person constitutionally ineligible to the office of President shall be eligible to that of Vice-President of the United States.

AMENDMENT XIII[13]

Section 1. Neither slavery nor involuntary servitude, except as a punishment for crime whereof the party shall have been duly convicted, shall exist within the United States, or any place subject to their jurisdiction.

Section 2. Congress shall have the power to enforce this article by appropriate legislation.

AMENDMENT XIV[14]

Section 1. All persons born or naturalized in the United States, and subject to the jurisdiction thereof, are citizens of the United States and of the State wherein they reside. No state shall make or enforce any law which shall abridge the privileges or immunities of citizens of the United States; nor shall any State deprive any person of life, liberty, or property, without due process of law; nor deny to any person within its jurisdiction the equal protection of the laws.

Section 2. Representatives shall be apportioned among the several States according to their respective numbers, counting the whole number of persons in each State, excluding Indians not taxed. But when the right to vote at any election for the choice of electors for President and Vice-President of the United States, Representatives in Congress, the Executive and Judicial officers of a State, or the members of the Legislature thereof, is denied to any of the male inhabitants of such State, being twenty-one years of age, and citizens of the United States, or in any way abridged, except for participation in rebellion, or other crime, the basis of representation therein shall be reduced in the proportion which the number of such male citizens shall bear to the whole number of male citizens twenty-one years of age in such State.

---

[13] Passed January 31, 1865. Ratified December 6, 1865.
[14] Passed June 13, 1866. Ratified July 9, 1868.

Section 3. No person shall be a Senator or Representative in Congress, or elector of President and Vice-President, or hold any office, civil or military, under the United States, or under any State, who, having previously taken oath, as a member of Congress, or as an officer of the United States, or as a member of any State legislature, or as an executive or judicial officer of any State, to support the Constitution of the United States, shall have engaged in insurrection or rebellion against the same, or given aid or comfort to the enemies thereof. But Congress may by a vote of two-thirds of each House, remove such disability.

Section 4. The validity of the public debt of the United States, authorized by law, including debts incurred for payment of pensions and bounties for services in suppressing insurrection or rebellion, shall not be questioned. But neither the United States nor any State shall assume or pay any debt or obligation incurred in aid of insurrection or rebellion against the United States, or any claim for the loss or emancipation of any slave; but all such debts, obligations, and claims shall be held illegal and void.

Section 5. The Congress shall have the power to enforce, by appropriate legislation, the provisions of this article.

AMENDMENT XV[15]

Section 1. The right of citizens of the United States to vote shall not be denied or abridged by the United States or by any State on account of race, color, or previous condition of servitude.

Section 2. The Congress shall have power to enforce this article by appropriate legislation.

AMENDMENT XVI[16]

The Congress shall have power to lay and collect taxes on incomes, from whatever source derived, without apportionment among the several States, and without regard to any census or enumeration.

AMENDMENT XVII[17]

The Senate of the United States shall be composed of two Senators from each State, elected by the people thereof, for six years; and each Senator shall have one vote. The electors in each State shall have the qualifications requisite for electors of the most numerous branch of the State legislatures.

---

[15] Passed February 26, 1869. Ratified February 2, 1870.
[16] Passed July 12, 1909. Ratified February 3, 1913.
[17] Passed May 13, 1912. Ratified April 8, 1913.

When vacancies happen in the representation of any State in the Senate, the executive authority of such State shall issue writs of election to fill such vacancies: *Provided*, That the legislature of any State may empower the executive thereof to make temporary appointments until the people fill the vacancies by election as the legislature may direct.

This amendment shall not be so construed as to affect the election or term of any Senator chosen before it becomes valid as part of the Constitution.

AMENDMENT XVIII[18]

Section 1. After one year from the ratification of this article the manufacture, sale, or transportation of intoxicating liquors within, the importation thereof into, or the exportation thereof from the United States and all territory subject to the jurisdiction thereof for beverage purposes is hereby prohibited.

Section 2. The Congress and the several States shall have concurrent power to enforce this article by appropriate legislation.

Section 3. This article shall be inoperative unless it shall have been ratified as an amendment to the Constitution by the legislatures of the several States, as provided in the Constitution, within seven years from the date of the submission hereof to the States by the Congress.

AMENDMENT XIX[19]

The right of citizens of the United States to vote shall not be denied or abridged by the United States or by any State on account of sex.

Congress shall have power to enforce this article by appropriate legislation.

AMENDMENT XX[20]

Section 1. The terms of the President and Vice-President shall end at noon on the 20th day of January, and the terms of Senator and Representatives at noon on the 3d day of January, of the years in which such terms would have ended if this article had not been ratified; and the terms of their successors shall then begin.

Section 2. The Congress shall assemble at least once in every years, and such meeting shall begin at noon on the 3d day of January, unless they shall by law appoint a different day.

Section 3. If, at the time fixed for the beginning of the term of the President, the President elect shall have died, the Vice-President elect shall become

---

[18] Passed December 18, 1917. Ratified January 16, 1919.
[19] Passed June 4, 1919. Ratified August 18, 1920.
[20] Passed March 2, 1932. Ratified January 23, 1933.

President. If a President shall not have been chosen before the time fixed for the beginning of his term, or if the President elect shall have failed to qualify, then the Vice-President elect shall act as President until a President shall have qualified; and the Congress may by law provide for the case wherein neither a President elect nor a Vice-President elect shall have qualified, declaring who shall then act as President, or the manner in which one who is to act shall be selected, and such person shall act accordingly until a President or Vice-President shall have qualified.

Section 4. The Congress may by law provide for the case of the death of any of the persons from whom the House of Representatives may choose a President whenever the right of choice shall have devolved upon them, and for the case of the death of any of the persons from whom the Senate may choose a Vice-President whenever the right of choice shall have devolved upon them.

Section 5. Sections 1 and 2 shall take effect on the 15th day of October following the ratification of this article.

Section 6. This article shall be inoperative unless it shall have been ratfied as an amendment to the Constitution by the legislatures of three-fourths of the several States within seven years from the date of its submission.

AMENDMENT XXI[21]

Section 1. The eighteenth article of amendment to the Constitution of the United States is hereby repealed.

Section 2. The transportation or importation into any State, Territory, or possession of the United States for delivery or use therein of intoxicating liquors, in violation of the laws thereof, is hereby prohibited.

Section 3. This article shall be inoperative unless it shall have been ratified as an amendment to the Constitution by conventions in the several States, as provided in the Constitution, within seven years from the date of the submission hereof to the States by the Congress.

AMENDMENT XXII[22]

No person shall be elected to the office of the President more than twice, and no person who has held the office of President, or acted as President, for more than two years of a term to which some other person was elected President shall be elected to the office of the President more than once.

But this Article shall not apply to any person holding the office of President when this Article was proposed by the Congress, and shall not prevent any person who may be holding the office of President, or acting as President, during the term within which this Article becomes operative from holding the office of President or acting as President during the remainder of such term.

---

[21] Passed February 20, 1933. Ratified December 5, 1933.
[22] Passed March 12, 1947. Ratified March 1, 1951.

AMENDMENT XXIII[23]

Section 1. The District constituting the seat of Government of the United States shall appoint in such manner as the Congress may direct:

A number of electors of President and Vice President equal to the whole number of Senators and Representatives in Congress to which the District would be entitled if it were a State, but in no event more than the least populous State; they shall be in addition to those appointed by the States, but they shall be considered, for the purposes of the election of President and Vice President, to be electors appointed by the State; and they shall meet in the District and perform such duties as provided by the twelfth article of amendment.

Section 2. The Congress shall have power to enforce this article by appropriate legislation.

AMENDMENT XXIV[24]

Section 1. The right of citizens of the United States to vote in any primary or other election for President or Vice President, or for Senator or Representative in Congress, shall not be denied or abridged by the United States or any State by reason of failure to pay any poll tax or other tax.

Section 2. The Congress shall have power to enforce this article by appropriate legislation.

AMENDMENT XXV[25]

Section 1. In case of the removal of the President from office or of his death or resignation, the Vice President shall become President.

Section 2. Whenever there is a vacancy in the office of the Vice President, the President shall nominate a Vice President who shall take office upon confirmation by a majority vote of both Houses of Congress.

Section 3. Whenever the President transmits to the President pro tempore of the Senate and the Speaker of the House of Representatives his written declaration that he is unable to discharge the powers and duties of his office, and until he transmits to them a written declaration to the contrary, such powers and duties shall be discharged by the Vice President as Acting President.

Section 4. Whenever the Vice President and a majority of either the principle officers of the executive department or of such other body as Congress may by law provide, transmit to the President pro tempore of the Senate and the Speaker of the House of Representatives their written declaration that the President is unable to discharge the powers and duties of his office, the

---

[23] Passed June 16, 1960. Ratified April 3, 1961.
[24] Passed August 27, 1962. Ratified January 23, 1964.
[25] Passed July 6, 1965. Ratified February 11, 1967.

Vice President shall immediately assume the powers and duties of the office of Acting President.

Thereafter, when the President transmits to the President pro tempore of the Senate and the Speaker of the House of Representatives his written declaration that no inability exists, he shall resume the powers and duties of his office unless the Vice President and a majority of either the principle officers of the executive department or of such other body as Congress may by law provide, transmit within four days to the President pro tempore of the Senate and the Speaker of the House of Representatives their written declaration that the President is unable to discharge the powers and duties of his office. Thereupon Congress shall decide the issue, assembling within forty-eight hours for that purpose if not in session. If the Congress, within twenty-one days after receipt of the latter written declaration, or, if Congress is not in session, within twenty-one days after Congress is required to assemble, determines by two-thirds vote of both houses that the President is unable to discharge the powers and duties of his office, the Vice President shall continue to discharge the same as Acting President; otherwise, the President shall resume the powers and duties of his office.

AMENDMENT XXVI[26]

Section 1. The right of citizens of the United States, who are eighteen years of age or older, to vote shall not be denied or abridged by the United States or by any State on account of age.

Section 2. The Congress shall have power to enforce this article by appropriate legislation.

AMENDMENT XXVII[27]

No law, varying the compensation for the services of the Senators and Representatives, shall take effect, until, an election of representatives shall be intervened.

---

[26] Passed March 23, 1971. Ratified July 5, 1971.
[27] Passed September 25, 1789. Ratified May 7, 1992.

LEGAL MATERIALS ON THE INTERNET

The Internet provides the fastest way to access judicial decisions as well as a wealth of other legal resources. Listed below are a few websites that I have found particularly useful. Remember that the Internet is constantly changing so it is always a good strategy to use a search engine such as GOOGLE to search for a specific topic. In so doing, one is likely to find a variety of new websites. Additionally, almost all websites listed below have multiple links to other resources. So explore and see what you can find.

Findlaw's Constitution with Annotations serves as a useful supplement to this book.

http://supreme.lp.findlaw.com/constitution/

One of the most useful resources is the Website of the **Law and Courts Section of the American Political Science Association,** which includes a wide variety of links to the major legal websites.

http://www.law.nyu.edu/lawcourts/

Findlaw is an essential legal resource. Findlaw's main webpage is located at:

http://www.findlaw.com/

Findlaw's Supreme Court page contains links that allow one to access a variety of information including biographies of the justices, the Court's calendar for the current term, and the schedule of oral arguments:

http://www.findlaw.com/10fedgov/judicial/supreme_court/index.html

The **Findlaw,** Supreme Court Opinions page is an easy way to access the opinions of the Supreme Court. All cases decided by the nation's highest court since 1893 are included and are easy to find by party name, year, or citation in the United States Reports (e.g. 368 US 248 [1966]) which is the system of citation used throughout this book):

http://www.findlaw.com/10fedgov/judicial/supreme_court/opinions.html

Another convenient way to access the Supreme Court decisions is the **Legal Information Institute's Supreme Court Collection.** Here it is possible to search by topic, author, and party. Additionally, the Supreme Court Collection includes the Supreme Court's calendar.

http://supct.law.cornell.edu/supct/

Findlaw also includes links to the decisions by the United States Courts of Appeals, United States District Courts, and state courts of last resort:

http://www.findlaw.com/casecode/index.html

The legal briefs for a large number of major cases are also available on Findlaw:

http://supreme.lp.findlaw.com/supreme_court/briefs/index.html

An alphabetical list of Historic Supreme Court Decisions that includes a number of decisions before 1893 is available from the Legal Information Institute:

http://supct.law.cornell.edu/supct/cases/name.htm#Case_Name-A

The Historic Supreme Court Decisions are also arranged alphabetically by justice:

http://supct.law.cornell.edu/supct/cases/judges.htm

The United States Supreme Court's Official Website contains the Court's decisions as well as the Court's docket, schedules of oral arguments, the Court rules, and links to related websites:

http://www.supremecourtus.gov/

Oyez, the multimedia website created by Jerry Goldman of Northwestern University offers the opportunity to listen to oral arguments while simultaneously viewing the text of those arguments before the Supreme Court:

http://oyez.nwu.edu/oyez/frontpage

Findlaw also offers Special Coverage of current legal issues. For example, there is a site with documents, laws, cases, and commentary on the War on Terrorism:

http://news.findlaw.com/legalnews/us/terrorism/documents/tribunals.html

Additionally, **Findlaw** has a page with legal commentary in *Writ*:

http://writ.news.findlaw.com/terrorism.html

THE UNITED STATES CODE

There are a number of websites that provide access to the United States Code as well as bills that are pending. These websites allow for searches of the Code by key words, titles, section and a variety of other headings:

Findlaw	http://www.findlaw.com/casecode/uscodes/
United States House of Representatives	http://uscode.house.gov/usc.htm
Legal Information Institute, U.S. Code	http://www4.law.cornell.edu/uscode/
The Library of Congress, Thomas: Legislative Information on the Internet	http://thomas.loc.gov/

LEGAL ISSUES IN THE NEWS

There are a variety of websites that are useful if one is searching for a particular legal issue involved in recent events. Frequently these websites have their own search engines. A few are listed below.

The New York Times	http://www.newyorktimes.com
The Washington Post	http://www.washingtonpost.com/
National Public Radio	http://www.npr.org/news/national/election2000/
The Jurist: Legal Intelligence for an Educated Democracy	http://jurist.law.pitt.edu/index.htm
Legal News from CNN.Com	http://www.cnn.com/LAW/
The National Law Journal	http://www.nlj.com/index.shtml

CREDITS

Table 1.1   Table from "A March of Liberty" by Melvin I. Urofsky. Copyright © 1988 by Melvin I. Urofsky. Reprinted by permission of Alfred A. Knopf, a Division of Random House, Inc.

Table 1.2   Table from "A History of the American Constitution" by Daniel Farber and Susanna Sherry. Copyright © 1990 West Publishing Co. Reprinted by permission.

Table 2.1   Reprinted by permission from "American Constitutional Interpretation," 2/e by Walter F. Murphy et al., © 1995 The Foundation Press.

Table 2.5   Table from *Campaigns and the Court: The U.S. Supreme Court in Presidential Elections*, by Donald Grier Stephenson Jr., © 1999 Columbia University Press. Reprinted with the permission of the publisher.

Table 2.6   Table "Dred Scott v. Sanford" from "The Supreme Court in Periods of Critical Realignment" by William Lasser in *Journal of Politics* 47 (1985): 1174–1187. Copyright © 1985 Journal of Politics. Reprinted by permission.

Table 2.7   "Realigning Elections and the Supreme Court" from "The Supreme Court in Periods of Critical Realignment" by William Lasser in *Journal of Politics* 47 (1985): 1174–1187. Copyright © 1985 Journal of Politics. Reprinted by permission.

Table 3.3   Table adapted from Library of Congress, "Legislation Related to the Attack of September 11, 2001," http://thomas.loc.gov/home/terrorleg.htm.

Figure 4.1   NPR Online, "Election 2000. Available: http://www.npr.org/news/national/election 2000/ .

Table 4.2   Adapted from USATODAY.com. Guide to Government. "The Florida Recount: Chronology of Lawsuits." Available: http://usatoday.findlaw.com/election/election2000timeline.html.

Figure 4.2   Reprinted with permission from the *South Florida Sun-Sentinel*.

Table 4.3   Roger E. Hartley and Lisa M. Holmes, "Increasing Senate Scrutiny of Lower Federal Court Nominees," *Judicature* 80 (May–June 1997): 274–278. Reprinted by permission.

Table 6.2   Table "Six Amendments" from "The Constitution Of The United States: An Unfolding Story," 2/e by Joseph T. Keenan. 1988, Dorsey Press.

Table 7.2   Table "The Division of the Current Court" from "Constitutional Law for a Changing America" by L. Epstein and T.G. Walker, p. 169. Copyright © 1998 CQ Press, Inc. Reprinted by permission.

Table 7.3   Table "Shift from 'The Wall of Separation' " from "Constitutional Law for a Changing America" by L. Epstein and T.G. Walker, pp. 171–172. Copyright © 1998 CQ Press, Inc. Reprinted by permission.

Table 7.6   "Key Provisions" adapted from *Constitutional Interpretation,* 7th edition by C.R. Ducat. © 2000. Reprinted with permission of Wadsworth, a division of Thomson Learning. Fax (800) 730-2215.

Table 8.1   From "The Supreme Court and Legal Change: Abortion and the Death Penalty" by Lee Epstein and Joseph F. Kobylka. Copyright © 1992 by the University of North Carolina Press. Reprinted by permission.

Table 10.2   Table from "The Landmark Bakke Ruling," *Newsweek*, July 10, 1978, p. 21. Copyright © 1978 Newsweek, Inc. All rights reserved. Reprinted by permission.

Table 10.3   "Affirmative Action Cases" adapted from *Constitutional Interpretation,* 7th edition, pp. 1246–1247 by C.R. Ducat. © 2000. Reprinted with permission of Wadsworth, a division of Thomson Learning. Fax (800) 730-2215.

PHOTO CREDITS

Page 1   "Constitutional Convention." Brown Brothers, Sterling, PA. Used with permission.

Page 67   "Capital Building." © Joel Bordon, 1992. Used with permission.

Page 223   "War Protestors—Kids." © AP/Wide World Photos. Used with permission.

Page 467   "U.S. Constitution." © John Feingersh/Stock Boston. Used with permission.

INDEX